BUSINESS DATA COMMUNICATIONS AND NETWORKING

FIFTH EDITION

JERRY FITZGERALD

Jerry FitzGerald & Associates

ALAN DENNIS

The University of Georgia

JOHN WILEY & SONS, INC.
New York • Chichester • Brisbane • Toronto • Singapore

Acquisitions Editor	Beth Lang Golub
Marketing Manager	Leslie Hines
Senior Production Editor	Jeanine Furino
Cover Designer	David Levy
Text Designer	Lynn Rogan
Asst. Manufacturing Manager	Mark Cirillo
Photo Dept. Asst.	Michelle Orlans
Illustration Coordinator	Rosa Bryant
Cover Art	Piet Mondrian, *Victory Boogie-Woogie,* 1943–44. Private Collection

This book was set in 10/12 New Baskerville by University Graphics and printed and bound by Courier Companies. The cover was printed by Lehigh Press.

Library of Congress Cataloging in Publication Data:
FitzGerald, Jerry.
    Business data communications and networking / Jerry FitzGerald,
Alan Dennis. — 5th ed.
      p.   cm.
    Rev. ed. of: Business data communications, 4th ed. c1993.
    Includes index.
    ISBN 0-471-12365-X (cloth : alk. paper)
    1. Data transmission systems. 2. Computer networks. 3. Office
practice—Automation. I. Dennis, Alan. II. FitzGerald, Jerry.
Business data communications. III. Title.
TK5105.F576   1996
004.6—dc20   95-40845
                                                       CIP

Printed in the United States of America

10 9 8 7 6 5

To Eileen and Alec

Dr. Jerry FitzGerald is the principal in Jerry FitzGerald & Associates, a firm he started in 1977. He has extensive experience in risk analysis, computer security, audit and control of computerized systems, data communications, networks, and systems analysis. He has been active in risk assessment studies, computer security, EDP audit reviews, designing controls into applications during the new system development process, data communication networks, bank wire transfer systems, and electronic data interchange (EDI) systems. He conducts training seminars on risk analysis, control and security, and data communication networks.

Dr. FitzGerald holds a Ph.D. in business economics and a master's degree in business economics from the Claremont Graduate School, an MBA from the University of Santa Clara, and a bachelor's degree in industrial engineering from Michigan State University. He is a Certified Information Systems Auditor (CISA) and holds a Certificate in Data Processing (CDP). He belongs to the EDP Auditors Association (EDPAA), the Institute of Internal Auditors (IIA), and the Information Systems Security Association (ISSA). Dr. FitzGerald has been a faculty member at several California universities and a consultant at SRI International.

His publications and software include: *Business Data Communications: Basic Concepts, Security and Design,* 4th edition, 1993; *Designing Controls into Computerized Systems,* 2nd edition, 1990; RANK-IT A Risk Assessment Tool for Microcomputers; CONTROL-IT A Control Spreadsheet Methodology for Microcomputers; *Fundamentals of Systems Analysis: Using Structured Analysis and Design,* 3rd edition, 1987; *Online Auditing Using Microcomputers; Internal Controls for Computerized Systems;* and over 60 articles in various publications.

Dr. Alan Dennis is an Associate Professor of Management Information Systems in the Terry College of Business at The University of Georgia. He has extensive experience in the development and application of software tools to support management decision making, and is well-known for his work with groupware. His groupware research helped in the design of several groupware products now marketed by IBM and Ventana Corporation. Dr. Dennis has served as a consultant to BellSouth, Boeing, IBM, Ventana, the U.S. Department of Defense, and the Australian Army. He is a co-editor (with Dr. Rick Watson and Dr. Bob Bostrom) of Groupware Central, a World Wide Web "journal" on groupware.

Dr. Dennis has a bachelor's degree in computer science from Acadia University in Nova Scotia, Canada and an MBA from Queen's University in Ontario, Canada. His Ph.D. in management information systems is from the University of Arizona. Prior to entering the Arizona doctoral program, he spent three years on the faculty of the Queen's School of Business, and was a principal in BCW Consulting. He was one of the first winners of the AACSB Fellowship in Business and Management.

His current research focuses on the design and use of network-based software to improve group decision making. His theoretical research has examined the fundamental aspects of idea generation, information sharing, and media richness, while his applied research has developed new approaches for strategic planning, business process re-engineering, and information systems requirements definition. Dr. Dennis has published more than 60 business and research articles, including those in *Management Science, MIS Quarterly, Information Systems Research, Academy of Management Journal, Organizational Behavior and Human Decision Making, Journal of Applied Psychology, Communications of the ACM,* and *IEEE Transactions on Systems, Man, and Cybernetics.* His first book, co-authored with his wife, Eileen Dennis, was *Getting Started with Microcomputers,* published in 1986.

PREFACE

Over the past three years, fundamental changes have occurred in data communications and networking that will shape the future for decades to come. Networking applications such as the Internet, World Wide Web, and groupware have exploded into the computing world. We believe that by the turn of the century, these applications will have become as common as word processing is today. Many fundamental technological changes have occurred, or are about to happen. High speed modems providing 200 Kbps data rates over regular telephone lines are entering the market. New backbone network technologies such as ATM, fast ethernet, and switched ethernet will replace today's slower token ring and ethernet LANs. SONET, SMDS, and broadband ISDN that provide 100 Mbps to 10 Gbps will replace current T-1 and T-3 WANs and MANs. Deregulation of the telecommunications industry will also have dramatic effects on how we communicate, obtain information, and access entertainment. Voice, data, and image communication will become integrated, and entrepreneurs will create new applications and entirely new technologies more rapidly than ever before.

Perhaps the most important change has been the recognition of the strategic importance of communications and networking in both the public and private sector. Today, most computers are networked; by the end of the century, *all* will be. We will look back at the 1990s and realize that this was the decade in which the importance of the computer was surpassed by the importance of communications.

Purpose of This Book

Our goal is to combine the fundamental concepts of data communications and networking with practical applications. While technologies and applications change rapidly, the fundamental concepts evolve much more slowly; they provide the foundation from which new technologies and applications can be understood, evaluated, and compared.

This book has two intended audiences. First and foremost, it is a university textbook. Each chapter introduces, describes, and then summarizes fundamental concepts and applications. Management focus boxes highlight key issues and describe how networks are actually being used today. Technical focus boxes highlight key technical issues and provide additional detail. An ongoing case study at the end of the book provides the opportunity to apply these technical and management concepts. Moreover, the text is accompanied by a detailed *Instructor's Manual,* that provides additional background information, teaching tips, and sources of material for student exercises, assignments, and exams.

Second, this book is intended for the professional who works in data communications and networking. The book has many detailed descriptions of the technical aspects of communications, along with illustrations, where appropriate. Moreover, managerial, technical, and sales personnel can use this book to gain a better understanding of fundamental concepts and trade-offs not presented in technical books or product summaries.

What's New in this Edition

Because communications technology and applications have changed dramatically over the past few years, we felt it was time for a major revision. The fifth edition includes numerous new technologies, applications, and examples, as well as chapter objectives, outlines, and summaries, and management and technology focus boxes. We have also increased the management focus of the book by including sections such as selecting network hardware and software, writing RFPs, managing networks, and improving network performance.

The fifth edition is about 25 percent shorter than the fourth edition, despite the added material and two new chapters on network applications and Novell Netware. Much of this reduction was achieved by organizing the book into four major sections.

The first section, *Introduction*, has two chapters. The major change from the fourth edition is the addition of Chapter 2, that discusses network applications. This chapter describes groupware and the Internet and examines their impact on organizations. It provides a brief introduction to Internet services, such as e-mail, gopher, newsgroups, and especially, the World Wide Web. We will use the Web to publish regular updates to this book, teaching tips, and free software. Our goal is to keep users abreast of the very latest developments in technology and applications. (See our home page at http://www.cba.uga.edu/groupware/telecom/home.html.)

As the name suggests, the second section, *Fundamentals of Data Communications and Networking*, presents fundamental concepts. This section (Chapters 3 through 6) covers much of the same issues as Chapters 2 through 5 (and parts of Chapters 9 and 13) in the fourth edition: voice and data communication hardware, data transmission, and the data link layer. There are two major changes in this section. First, two key concepts (client-server versus host-based network architectures; and the use of data communications layers similar to the OSI model) are introduced early and used as organizing themes throughout the rest of the book. By introducing these concepts initially, students can use them as organizing frameworks to integrate the many technical details that follow; without such frameworks, students are left to integrate laundry lists of facts on their own.

Second, new technologies have been added and their implications for management are discussed. New technologies include: client-server computing and middleware; new satellite technologies such as VSAT and DBS; multiplexing, including SLIP, PPP, bonding, inverse multiplexing, and wavelength division multiplexing; modems, such as wireless modems, V.34, and V.34 bis modems; and protocols such as LAP-M and LAP-B. Additions to the management focus include the increasing importance of microcomputers and LANs; the economics of client-server and host-based network architectures and their advantages and disadvantages; advice on media selection; modem pooling; and techniques to reduce transmission errors.

The third section, *Networking,* introduces the network layer and LANs, MANs, WANs, and backbone networks. The chapters in this section, Chapters 7 through 10, correspond to Chapters 6, 7, 9, and 11 in the fourth edition. The major change is the new chapter on backbone networks, the most rapidly changing technology in networking. This chapter summarizes the major components in backbone networks (e.g., bridges, routers, switches), and then focuses on the multitude of new backbone technologies such as fast ethernet (e.g., 100BaseT, 100VG-AnyLAN, full duplex ethernet, and ISO-ENET); FDDI, FDDI-II, and FDDI-C; ATM (ATM25 and ATM51); collapsed backbones; switched ethernet; and dedicated token ring.

The other chapters in this section also have been updated to reflect new technologies, or the increased importance of older ones, such as TCP/IP; SPX/IPX; broadband ISDN; cellular packet networks; frame relay; ATM; and RAID. This section also provides detailed management advice on improving network performance and selecting LAN, WAN/MAN, and BN components.

In the final section on *Network Management,* Chapters 11 through 14 discuss network design, network management, network security, and Novell Netware. They correspond to Chapters 8, 12, and 13 in the fourth edition. The major changes are the addition of a short chapter on Netware's architecture and principal commands, and the elimination of the fourth edition's Chapter 10 on the basics of microcomputers. Once again, new technologies have been added including: intelligent devices, SNMP, RMON, CMIP, NMS, and network agents; firewalls and IP spoofing; call-back modems and pager-based login techniques; and clipper and capstone. Additional management topics include: the shift to LANs and the differences between LAN and WAN managers; the functions of network management; the sources of security threats; and elements of a disaster recovery plan.

Acknowledgments

My thanks to the many people who contributed to the preparation of this fifth edition. I am indebted to the staff at John Wiley & Sons for their support, including: Beth Lang Golub, Information Systems Editor; Jeanine Furino, Senior Production Editor; Madelyn Lesure, Design Director; Linda Muriello, Senior Production Manager; Rosa Bryant, Illustration Coordinator; Mark Cirillo, Manufacturing Manager; and Leslie Hines, Marketing Manager. A special thanks goes to the copy editor, Lorena Akioka of the Selig Center for Economic Growth at The University of Georgia, for her sharp eyes and skillful pen.

Norm Sondak of San Diego State University did an excellent job developing the Next Day Air Service case study. Paul Hays, a Ph.D. candidate at The University of Georgia, developed most of Chapter 14, and provided technical advice on many others. Davis Gleaton, a BBA graduate of The University of Georgia, prepared many of the management focus boxes found throughout the book. My wife, Eileen Dennis, provided many helpful comments and assistance. My colleagues in the Department of Management also provided much needed support, assistance, and advice. I would also like to thank the reviewers for their comments, often under short deadlines:

Dennis Adams, *University of Houston*
John Calvert, *University of Nevada*
Henry D. Crockett, *Portland State University*
Martin Granier, *University College of the Fraser Valley*
Varun Grover, *University of South Carolina*
Jan Guynes, *University of Texas-Arlington*
Gail B. Hamilton, *Maryville University*
Marilyn Littman, *Nova University*
Bruce McLaren, *Indiana State University*
Patricia McQuaid, *Auburn University*
Robert O'Brien, *CUNY-Baruch*
Paul Ross, *Millersville University of Pennsylvania*
Ronald Schwartz, *Wilkes University*
Hanney Shaban, *Northern Virginia Community College*
Glen Shephard, *San Jose State University*
S. Srinivasan, *University of Louisville*

Alan Dennis
Athens, Georgia

BRIEF CONTENTS

CONTENTS

INTRODUCTION TO DATA COMMUNICATIONS

This chapter introduces the concepts of data communications and shows how we have progressed from paper-based systems to modern computer networks. It begins by describing why it is important to study data communications and how the invention of the telephone and the computer has transformed the way we communicate. Next, the basic components of a data communication network are discussed. The chapter concludes with an overview of future trends in communications.

Objectives

- Become familiar with the history of communications and information systems,
- Become familiar with the applications of data communication networks,
- Become familiar with the major components of networks,
- Become familiar with the future trends in communications.

Chapter Outline

Why Study Data Communications?
    A Brief History of Communications in the United States
    A Brief History of Information Systems in the United States
Purpose and Scope of this Book
Definition of Data Communications
    Uses of Data Communications
Components of a Communication Network
    A Wide Area Network Example
    A Local Area Network Example
    Network Model

WHY STUDY DATA COMMUNICATIONS?

It all started around 3300 B.C. with Sumerian clay tablets. They were the ideal way to communicate—as long as you didn't drop them! Next came Greek messengers. Your scroll would always get there—if your runner didn't collapse first. Today you can send and receive vital business information . . . in writing . . . in seconds.

The reasons for studying data communications are embodied in the occupational history of the United States. In the 1800s, America was an agricultural society dominated by farmers. By the 1900s, we had become an industrial society dominated by labor and management. Now, as we approach the twenty-first century, we have moved into an information society dominated by computers, data communications, and highly skilled individuals who use brain power instead of physical power. The industrial society has reached its zenith, and the communication/computer era, dubbed the information society, is advancing rapidly. At no other time in our history, has success (whether individual, corporate, or national) depended so heavily on intelligence and information.

In an industrial society, the strategic resource is *capital.* In an information society, the strategic resource is *information* that must flow on communication networks. This information society started in the mid-1950s.

Knowledge of data communications is even more important when you realize that satellites and fiber optic cable are transforming the earth into a "global village." In other words, the compression of time achieved through electronic communications allows us to be in immediate contact with all other companies or people and to use business information in a timely manner.

In an information society dominated by computers and communications, value is increased by knowledge, and the speed of movement of that knowledge. This new information economy will completely destroy David Ricardo's labor theory of value[1] because in such a society information increases value, not the labor of individuals. Knowledge can be created, it can be destroyed, and it is synergetic because the whole usually is greater than the sum of the parts. In fact, the whole may be many times greater than the sum of the parts if you have the proper communication network to transmit the information. Knowledge that cannot be disseminated (transmitted) may be of zero value.

---

[1]Ricardo said it is a person's labor that adds value to goods and services.

The mainstream of the information age is communications. The value of a high speed data communication network that transmits information is that it brings the message sender and receiver closer together in time. As a result, we have collapsed the *information lag,* which is the time it takes for information to be disseminated worldwide. For example, in the 1800s it might have taken several weeks for a message to reach the United States by ship from England. By the 1900s it could be transmitted within the hour. Today, with modern data communication networks, it can be transmitted within seconds. Collapsing the information lag speeds the incorporation of new information into our daily lives. In fact, today's problem is that we cannot handle the quantities of information we receive.

Finally, the transition from an industrial to an information society means you will have to learn many new technology-based skills. Instead of becoming a specialist in a certain subject and working in that area for a lifetime, you will have to adapt and possibly retrain yourself several times. For that reason, the study of data communications will become a basic tool that can be used during your entire lifetime. You will incorporate your data communication knowledge into several careers, such as circuit designer, programmer, business system application developer, communication specialist, and business manager. Even now, many basic job tasks require technical knowledge in the use of data communications, such as microcomputers in your home connected to national or international communication networks, and personal communication devices like cellular telephones.

In summary, collapsing the information lag may be the single most important reason for you to study communications. This is so because new communication technology is being incorporated into the fabric of the information society as fast as people can learn how to maintain and use this technology. Once you have learned the basics from this textbook, you will need to "keep up with communication technology" for the remainder of your life.

A Brief History of Communications in the United States

Today we take data communications for granted, but it was pioneers like Samuel Morse, Alexander Graham Bell, and Thomas Edison who developed the basic electrical and electronic systems that ultimately evolved into voice and data communication networks. In 1837, Samuel Morse exhibited a working telegraph system; today we might consider it the first electronic data communication system.

In 1841, a Scot by the name of Alexander Bain used electromagnets to synchronize school clocks. Two years later, he patented a printing telegraph—the predecessor of today's facsimile device. Then in 1876, another Scot, Alexander Graham Bell, invented the first telephone capable of practical use that became the basis for our voice communication networks. The telephone was a remarkable improvement, for Morse's telegraph system required the operators at each end to use Morse code. This code, which became an auditory signal at the receiving end, could be interpreted into letters, which then became words, sentences, and paragraphs as the operator wrote them down on paper. Obviously, the telegraph was not going to be the most widely used method of communication.

When the telephone arrived, it was the communication device everyone wanted. In 1879, the first private manual telephone switchboard (PBX—private branch exchange) was installed. By 1880 the first pay telephone was in use, and the telephone became a way of life for Americans because they could call from public telephones. The telephone system grew so rapidly that by the early 1920s there were serious concerns that there would not be enough trained operators to work the manual switchboards. Experts predicted that by 1980, every single woman in America would have to work as a telephone operator (at the time, telephone operators were women) if growth in telephone usage continued at the current rate. The first transcontinental telephone service and the first transatlantic voice connections were both established in 1915. By 1930 the cost of a three-minute telephone call from New York to London was reduced from $45 to $30.

The certificate of incorporation for the American Telephone and Telegraph Company was registered in 1885. By 1889, AT&T had a recognized logo in the shape of the Liberty Bell with the words Long Distance Telephone written on it. By 1910, the Interstate Commerce Commission (ICC) had the authority to regulate interstate telephone business. In 1934, President Franklin Roosevelt approved the Communication Act, which transferred regulation of interstate telephone traffic from the ICC to the Federal Communications Commission (FCC).

Although the transistor would seem to be more related to computers than to communications, it was invented at Bell Laboratories in 1947. The transistor is a major component in today's communication switching systems. In 1951, the first direct long distance customer dialing began. The first international satellite telephone call was sent over the Telstar satellite in 1962, and Touch-Tone telephones were marketed in 1963. Their push buttons were easier to use than rotary dials, and they became quite popular. By 1965, there was widespread introduction of commercial international telephone service by satellite. Picturefone service, which allows users to see as well as talk with one another, began operating in 1969.

The famous Carterfone court decision in 1968 allowed non-Bell equipment to be connected to the Bell System network. This important milestone permitted independent modem manufacturers to connect their equipment to the Bell networks for the first time. Such connections were illegal prior to this decision.

Another key decision in 1970 permitted MCI to provide limited long distance service in competition with AT&T. Throughout the 1970s, there were many arguments and court cases regarding the monopolistic position that AT&T held over other companies wanting to offer communication services. The litigation led to the January 1, 1984 deregulation of AT&T, which is described in Chapter 9.

During 1983 and 1984 traditional radio telephone calls were supplanted by the newer cellular telephone networks. By 1985 Bell Laboratories had invented the ballistic transistor that operates 1000 times faster than the original transistor they invented in 1947. Digital networks, which allow the simultaneous transmission of voice, data, and images, began serving the public in the 1980s.

By 1988 there was considerable competition in both the voice and data communication markets as a number of independent companies began selling communication services in a manner similar to automobile marketing.

In the 1990s, cellular telephones became commonplace, and pocket sized. Demand grew so much that in some cities (e.g., New York and Atlanta), it became difficult to get a dial tone at certain times of the day. The costs of long distance calls decreased to such an extent that it became cheaper to fax a short letter across country than to mail it.

A Brief History of Information Systems in the United States

The natural evolution of business systems, governmental systems, and personal systems has forced the widespread use of data communication networks to interconnect these various systems.

In the 1950s, computer systems used batch processing with discrete files, and users carried their paper documents to the computer for processing. The data communications of that era involved human beings physically carrying paper documents.

During the 1960s, data communication across telephone lines became more common and gave online batch terminals to users who entered their own batches of data for processing. The data communication aspect involved the transmission of signals (messages) from these online batch terminals to the computer and back to the user.

During the late 1960s and into the 1970s, online real-time systems were developed that moved the users from batch processing to single transaction-oriented processing. It was at this point that data communications became a necessity.

As the 1970s progressed, database management systems replaced the older discrete file systems. Integrated systems also were developed, where the entry of an online real-time transaction in one business system might automatically trigger two or three other transactions in other business systems. For example, when an online user from a purchasing department enters data indicating the purchase of 100 executive desks, the system might initiate three related transactions. Transaction 1 might go to the Accounts Payable System. There it sets up the original matching file where the purchase order is matched to the invoice, which in turn is matched to the receiving dock ticket showing receipt of the goods. Transaction 2 might go to the receiving dock to prenotify them to expect 100 executive desks in two months. Transaction 3 might go to the Cash Flow Accounting System so preparations can be made to pay for (cash availability) these executive desks. As you can see, both data communications and data processing are interconnected in online real-time systems.

The 1980s witnessed the widespread adoption of the microcomputer. At first, microcomputers were isolated from the major information systems applications, serving the needs of individual users (e.g., spreadsheets). However, as more people began to rely on microcomputers for essential applications, the need to exchange data among different microcomputers and between microcomputers and central mainframe computers became clear.

By the early 1990s, more than 60 percent of all microcomputers in American corporations were networked—connected to other computers. More importantly, the microcomputer had evolved from a small low-power computer into a very powerful, easy to use system, with a large amount of low-cost software available. Today's microcomputers have more raw computing power than a large mainframe of the 1970s. Perhaps more surprisingly, American corporations have far more total computing power sitting on desktops in the form of the microcomputers than they have in their large central mainframe computers.

As we move closer to the end of this century, the most important area related to computers will be *networking*. This means we will be using more *wide area networks* (WANs) that span the globe, *metropolitan area networks* (MANs) that include a local metropolitan area like a city, *backbone networks* (BNs) that connect an organization's computers together, and especially *local area networks* (LANs) that interconnect the microcomputers located throughout an organization. (See the box on Network Definitions to learn more about networks.) You do not have to be a computer specialist to need some knowledge about the interconnection of mainframe computers, minicomputers, and microcomputers.

We are fast approaching completely distributed systems where information systems applications will be divided among a network of computers, each of which performs some of the overall processing. This form of computing, called client/server computing, will dramatically change the way information systems professionals and regular users interact with computers in the future. The office of the future that interconnects word processors, facsimile devices, copiers, teleconferencing equipment, microcomputers, mainframe host computers, and other equipment will put tremendous demands on data communication networks, and local area networks will have to offer greater reliability and speed.

These networks already have had a dramatic impact on the way business is conducted. Wal-Mart has used wide area networking to become one of the largest forces in the American retail industry and in the process has transformed the industry; at the other end of the spectrum, the lack of a sophisticated wide area network was one of the key factors in the bankruptcy of Macy's.

In retail sales, it is critical to manage inventory. Macy's had a traditional 1970s inventory system. At the start of the season, buyers would order products in large lots to get volume discounts. Some products would be very popular and sell out quickly. When the sales clerks did a weekly inventory and noticed the shortage, they would order more. If the items were not available in the warehouse (and with very popular products it was often the case), it would take six to eight weeks to restock them. Customers would buy from other stores, and Macy's would lose the sales. Other products, also bought in large quantities, would be unpopular and have to be sold at deep discounts.

In contrast, Wal-Mart negotiates volume discounts with suppliers based on total purchases, but does not specify particular products. Buyers place initial orders in small quantities. Each time a product is sold, the sale is recorded and every day or two, the complete list of purchases is transferred over the WAN (usually via a satellite at each store) to the head office, a distribution center, or the supplier. Replacements for the products sold are shipped almost immediately and typically arrive within days. The result is that Wal-Mart seldom has a major problem with overstocking an unwanted product or running out of a popular product (unless, of course, the supplier is unable to produce it fast enough).

The lack of a good WAN can also cost more than money. During Operation Desert Storm, the U.S. Army, Navy, and Air Force lacked one integrated logistics communications network. Each service had its own series of networks, making communication and cooperation difficult. Each day, a Navy F-18 would fly into Saudi Arabia to exchange diskettes full of logistics information with the Army. More than 60 percent of the containers of supplies that arrived in Saudi Arabia from the United States had to

Local Area Network (LAN)   A group of microcomputers or terminals located in the same general area and connected by a common cable (communication circuit) so they can exchange information. LANs are typically used within the same building or a set of buildings situated close together.

Backbone Network (BN)   A large central network that connects all the terminals, microcomputers, mainframes, local area networks, and other communication equipment on a single company or university site. It is sometimes called a Campus Area Network (CAN).

Metropolitan Area Network (MAN)   A network spanning a geographical area that usually encompasses a city or county area. It interconnects various buildings or other facilities within this citywide area.

Wide Area Network (WAN)   A network spanning a large geographical area. Its nodes (microcomputers) can span cities, states, or national boundaries. This network interconnects computers, LANs, BNs, MANs, and other data transmission facilities on a countrywide or worldwide basis.

be unloaded upon arrival to see what was in them before being shipped to combat units; there was no WAN available to provide this information. The logistics information systems and communications networks experienced such problems that some Air Force units were unable to quickly order and receive critical spare parts needed to keep planes flying. The American-based suppliers ended up sending them via Federal Express. Fortunately, the war did not start until the United States and its allies were prepared. Had Iraq attacked, things might have turned out differently.

This decade is bringing forth a new employment specialty, that of the *network administrator*. Previously, a few people administered the organization's wide area or backbone networks. Today, and even more so in the future, the existence of local area networks means many network administrators will be required in organizations. By the year 2000, it will be commonplace for individuals to have networks in their homes. These LANs will interconnect several computing devices (mostly microcomputers), and will be connected by telephone lines, by an optical fiber cable, or by direct satellite transmission to other networks elsewhere in the world.

PURPOSE AND SCOPE OF THIS BOOK

Data communications and networking are very complex subjects, but this is not a complex book. Many books in this field are complex, and rightly so, because they are intended as reference sources for the experienced network designer. This book requires no prior experience in data communications, voice communications, or electronic engineering; rather, it assumes a basic understanding of information systems and a desire to complement this background with a general knowledge of data communications. After completing a course of study based on this book, you should be able to:

- Understand the available alternatives in hardware, software, and transmission facilities,
- Put that understanding to work by making informed decisions among these alternatives,
- Integrate these decisions into a cohesive data communications network design that actually works,
- Understand and remain informed about current technology,
- Perform design activities for networks of increasingly greater scope and complexity as you build experience, judgment, and confidence,
- Market or sell data communication products.

As you read this book, you will encounter many new terms because the world of data communications has its own language. A comprehensive glossary is included at the end of the book because it is not always possible to interrupt the presentation of complex subjects with a thorough definition of a new word. The glossary contains both words and acronyms to ensure that all the jargon of data communications has been included and that the technical details are described thoroughly.

Special Focus boxes in each chapter provide business examples of the concepts discussed and additional discussion of technical details. The summary at the end of each chapter covers the key concepts introduced in that chapter. Rather than being all-inclusive, the summary concentrates on the high-level conceptual detail of the key concepts. The selected references are a sample of current books, serial publications, and computerized literature resources that provide additional information on the topics discussed.

DEFINITION OF DATA COMMUNICATIONS

Data communications is the movement of computer information from one point to another by means of electrical or optical transmission systems. Such systems often are called *data communication networks*. This is in contrast to the broader term *telecommunications*, which includes the transmission of voice video (images and graphics) as well as data. In general, data communication networks are established to collect data from remote points (usually terminals or microcomputers) and transmit that data to a central point equipped with a more powerful microcomputer or a mainframe or minicomputer, or to perform the reverse process, or some combination of the two. Data communication networks facilitate more efficient use of central computers (mainframe, micro, or mini) and improve the day-to-day control of a business by providing faster information flow. They also provide message transfer services to allow computer users to talk to one another via electronic mail. In general, they offer better and more timely interchange of data among their users and bring the power of computers closer to more users. In general, the objectives of most data communication networks are to:

- Reduce the time, effort, and cost required to perform various business tasks,
- Capture business data at its source and rapidly disseminate it,
- Support improved management control of the organization.

Data Communication Usage Modes	Examples of Applications	Typical Characteristics of Transactions
Source data entry and collection	Sales status data Inventory control Payroll data gathering	Transactions collected several times per day or week; direct response message not issued for every transaction
Real-time interactive network	Point-of-sale system Airline reservations Electronic data interchange (EDI)	Transactions arrive frequently (every few seconds) and demand response within a few seconds
Remote job entry (RJE) data collection	Remote high speed reading and printing Local access to distant computer power	Transactions usually bunched and require processing times ranging from minutes to hours. Input and output for each transaction may take seconds or minutes.
Information retrieval	Credit checking Bank account status Insurance policy status Law enforcement Government social services Hospital information systems	Relatively low character volume per input transaction, response required within seconds. Output message lengths usually short but might vary widely with some types of applications.
Conversational timesharing	General problem solving Engineering design calculations Text editing	Conversational response required within a few seconds
Message switching	Company mail delivery and memo distribution	Delivery time requirements range from minutes to hours
Real-time data acquisition and process control	Numerical control of machine tools Remote meter and gauge reading	Remote sensors continuously sampled and monitored at widely varying time intervals
Interprocessor data exchange	Processor, program, and filesharing applications of all types	Infrequent burst arrivals consisting of large data blocks requiring transmission to another CPU, usually within microseconds

Figure 1-1   Data communication usage modes.

Uses of Data Communications

Although data communications can be used in many different situations, business operations that exhibit some of the following characteristics usually benefit the most from a data communication network.

- Widespread use of microcomputers,
- A high volume of mail, messenger service usage, or numerous telephone calls between its various sites (voice communication corridors, that is, telephone calls may be replaced by data corridors),
- Repetitive paperwork operations, such as re-creating or copying information,
- Inefficient and time-consuming retrieval of current business information,
- Slow or untimely handling of the organization's business functions.

Figure 1-1 lists eight types of data communication systems. This figure also summarizes many important characteristics of these typical uses of data communications, giving specific application examples and typical transactions for each application. Consider the information given in the Typical Characteristics of Transactions column, and observe how these characteristics change from one usage to the next.

Also note that today's networks often combine several of the data communication usage modes shown in the left column of Figure 1-1. For example, a local area network interconnecting a firm's departments might be used for source data entry and collection, real-time interactive networking, information retrieval, conversational timesharing, and message switching. As this example demonstrates, networks today are more complex because they are used for multiple tasks.

COMPONENTS OF A COMMUNICATION NETWORK

There are three basic components for a data communication network: a host computer or server (a mainframe, minicomputer, or microcomputer), a client (a terminal or microcomputer), and a circuit over which messages flow.

The *host computer* (or *server*) is the central computer in the network, storing data or software that can be accessed by the clients. In distributed processing or client-server computing, several host computers may be tied together by the data communication network.

The *client* is the input/output hardware device at the other end of a communication circuit. It typically provides users with access to the network and the data and software on the host computer.

The *circuit* is the pathway through which the messages travel. It is typically a copper wire, although fiber optic cable and wireless transmission are becoming more common.

Strictly speaking, a network does not need a host computer. Some networks are designed to connect a set of similar computers which share their data and software with each other. Such networks are called *peer-to-peer* networks because the computers function as equals, rather than relying on a central host computer or server to store the needed data and software.

This next section provides a brief description of two types of networks: a wide area network and a local area network.

A Wide Area Network Example

Figure 1-2 shows one example of a basic data communication network, a wide area network (WAN). The network in this figure is known as a *point-to-point network* because it connects two points, in this case, a single microcomputer to a remote host mainframe computer. This simple network includes terminals, connector cables, modems, local loops, telephone company switching offices, interexchange channel (IXC) facilities, a front end processor, and a host computer.

In this case, the client is a microcomputer or terminal. The *terminals* or *microcomputers* are a human-to-machine interface device where people can enter and receive data or information. This device might have a video screen, printer, and keyboard. In the future, this device may be voice actuated.

The circuit begins with a *connector cable*, which connects the modem to the terminal or microcomputer. The connector cable is called a serial cable or *RS232 interface* because the standard that defines which signal is carried on which wire is the RS232 standard. Depending on their use, these cables have from 9 to 25 wires in them. For example, microcomputer-to-modem cables usually have 9 wires.

The *modem* is a device that converts the direct electrical signals produced by the computer (positive and negative voltages of electricity) to modulated audio signals that can be sent over telephone communication circuits. The electrical pulses produced by the microcomputer or terminal are referred to as *digital* signals. A digital

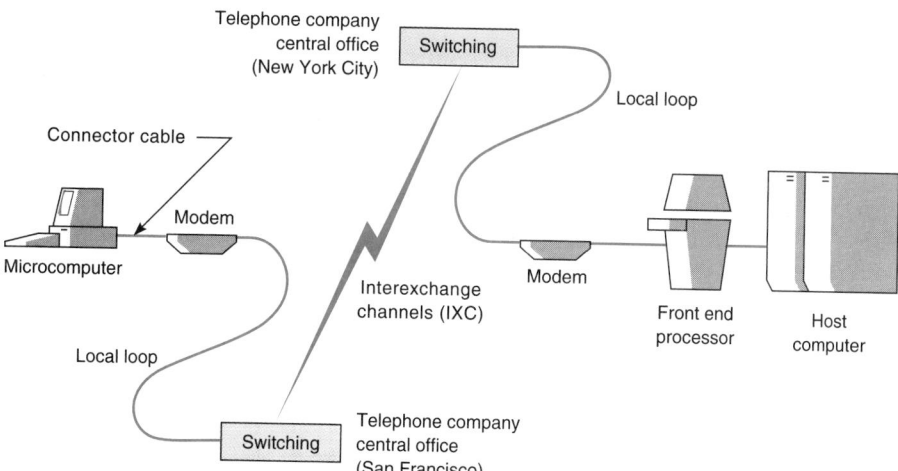

Figure 1-2 Basic data communication network.

signal is discrete because it is either on or off, much like a radio's on/off switch. The audio tones into which these digital pulses are converted are referred to as *analog*. An analog signal can be likened to the human voice because it changes continuously and can assume a wide variety of values. This encoding process puts the transmission into a mode that is compatible with the various transmission media used by the telephone company, such as copper wire, microwave, satellite, and fiber optics.

The *local loops* are the connections or "last mile" that interconnects your home or office to the telephone company central office (switching office), or to the special common carrier network if you are using a common carrier other than the local telephone company.

The *central office* (sometimes called *end office* or *exchange office*) contains the switching and control facilities that are operated by the telephone company or other special common carrier. When you use dial-up communication circuits, your data transmission goes through these switching facilities. When you have a *private leased circuit*, however, the telephone company wires your circuit path around the switching facilities to provide a clear unbroken path from one modem to the other.

The *interexchange channels/circuits* (sometimes called *IXC circuits*) are the circuits that go from one telephone company central office to another central office. These circuits can be microwave circuits, copper wire pairs, coaxial cables, satellite circuits, optical fibers, or some other transmission medium. Usually, the lines are leased from a "common carrier" such as the Bell Operating Companies, AT&T, MCI, or US Sprint, although an organization can install its own lines. A *common carrier* is a company recognized by the FCC or an appropriate state licensing agency as having the right to furnish communication services to individual subscribers or business organizations.

When the message reaches the distant host computer, it first passes through another modem, which converts the signal from analog (frequency tones) back to digital (electrical voltages).

The *front end processor* is a specialized minicomputer with very special software programs. These software programs, along with the front end hardware, control the entire data communication network. For example, a powerful front end processor may have 100 or more modems attached to it through its ports (circuit connect points). By having a front end processor control the communications circuit, the host computer can be used more effectively.

Finally, the *host computer* is the central processing unit (CPU) that processes your request, performs database lookups, and carries out the processing required for the business organization.

A Local Area Network Example

Another example of a data communication network is the local area network shown in Figure 1-3. Where Figure 1-2 showed a network that transmitted between New York City and San Francisco, this figure shows a local area network (LAN) that might be in a single building.

This shows five *microcomputers* (clients) connected by a local area network *cable* (circuit) arranged in a *ring*. In this network, messages move around the ring in one di-

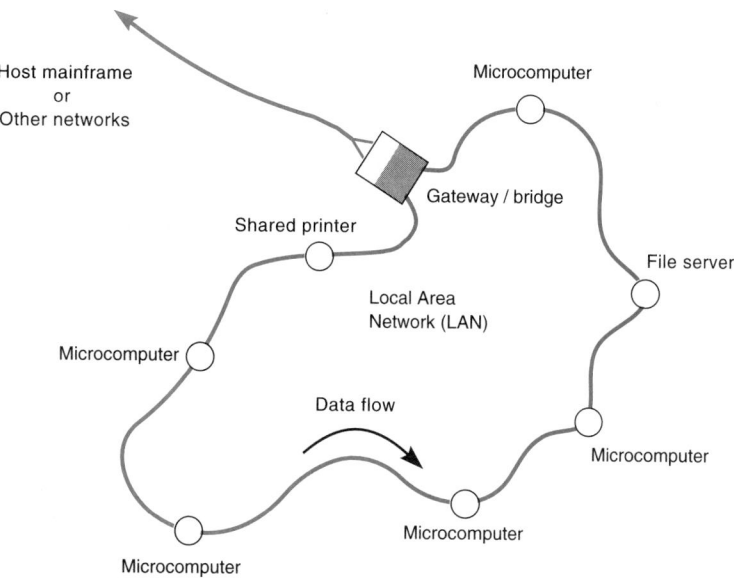

Figure 1-3 Example of a local area network (LAN).

rection only. All computers share the same circuit and must take turns sending messages.

This network also has a *file server* that performs the same functions as the central host computer in the WAN example. The file server is usually a microcomputer (often more powerful than the other microcomputers on the network), but may be a mini-computer or mainframe.

The *bridge* (or a *router* or a *gateway*) is a computer or special device that connects two or more networks. A bridge enables computers on this local area network to communicate with computers on other LANs or WANs.

Network Model

There are many ways to describe and analyze data communication networks. All networks provide the same basic functions to transfer a message from sender to receiver, but each network uses different network hardware and software to provide these functions. All of these hardware and software products have to work together to successfully transfer a message.

One way to accomplish this is to break the entire set of communications functions into a series of layers, each of which can be defined separately. In this way, vendors can develop software and hardware to provide the functions of each layer separately. The software or hardware can work in any manner and can be easily updated and improved, as long as the interface between that layer and the ones around it remain unchanged. Each piece of hardware and software can then work together in the overall network. One of the most commonly referenced network models is the Open Systems

Interconnection (OSI) model. This particular model, which is discussed in Chapter 7, breaks communication networks into seven layers.

In this book, we use a more simple four-layer model to discuss network functions (see Figure 1-4). While these layers are related to the layers in the OSI model, they do not map directly to its layers.

The *application* layer is the application software used by the network user. It is the user's access to the network. By using the application software, the user defines what messages are sent over the network. Chapter 2 discusses two types of network application software: groupware and the information superhighway.

The *network* layer takes the message generated by the application layer and performs three functions before passing the message to the data link layer. First, it translates the destination of the message into an address understood by the network. Second, if there are several possible routes through the network that the message could take to reach its destination, the network layer decides which route to take. Third, it collects message accounting information than can be used to identify how many messages each user has sent (which could be used for billing purposes), and to track errors. Chapters 7 through 14 discuss the network layer.

The *data link* layer takes the message generated by the network layer and performs three functions before passing the message to the physical layer. First, it controls the physical layer by deciding when to transmit messages over the media. Second, it formats the message by indicating where messages start and end, and which part is the address. Depending upon the length of message, it may break it into several smaller messages (called *packets* or *frames*) to make it easier to transmit. Third, it detects and corrects any errors that have occurred in the transmission of the message. Chapter 6 discusses the data link layer.

The *physical* layer, as the name suggests, is the physical connection between the sender and receiver. Its role is to transfer a series of electrical, radio, or light signals through the circuit from sender to receiver. The physical layer includes all the *hardware* devices (e.g., computers, terminals, and modems) and physical *media* (e.g., cables and satellites). The physical layer specifies the type of connection, and the electrical signals, radio waves, or light pulses that pass through it. Chapters 3 and 4 discuss the

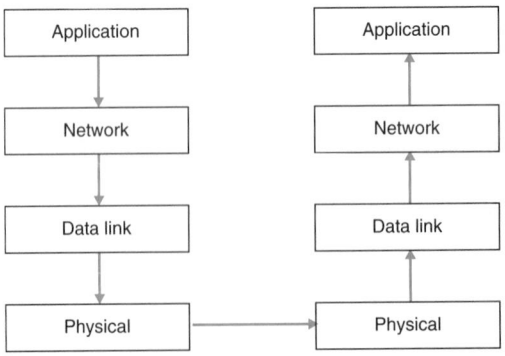

Figure 1-4   4-Layer model

hardware devices present in the physical layer, while Chapter 5 discusses how the physical layer actually transmits data.

All messages sent in a network pass through all layers (see Figure 1-4). The user first creates the message with the application software. This software then passes the message to the network layer. The network layer addresses the messages and selects the next stop on the message's route through the network, then sends the message (complete with address and next stop) to the data link layer. The data link layer formats the message with message start and stop markers (perhaps breaking it into packets), and instructs the physical hardware to transmit it.

When the receiver gets the message, this process is performed in reverse. The physical hardware passes the message to the data link layer, which uses the message start and stop markers to identify the message and its final destination address. The data link layer checks for errors, and if it discovers one, will request the message to be resent. If a message is received without error, the data link layer will then pass the message to the network layer, which will check the address and, if it is destined for this computer, will pass the message to the application layer for processing. If the message is not destined for this computer (but simply had to pass through it on the way to its final destination), the network layer decides which computer to send it to next and passes the message back to the data link layer for retransmission.

It is important to note that for communication to be successful, each layer in one computer must be able to communicate with its matching layer in the other computer. For example, the physical layer connecting the host and client must use the same type of electrical signals to enable each to understand the other (or there must be a device to translate between the two). Likewise, the data link layer in both the host and client must use the same procedures for marking the start and end of messages, or they will not be able understand each other's messages. The same is true for the network layers; if the client network layer cannot understand the address and routing information provided by the host, the message will not be sent to the correct destination. Likewise, the two application layers must be compatible, or the message cannot be processed.

FUTURE TRENDS IN COMMUNICATIONS AND NETWORKING

Between now and the year 2000, data communications will grow faster and become more important than computer processing itself. Both go hand in hand, but we have moved from the computer era to the communication era.

Systems based on communications can be found in virtually every segment of industry. For example:

- Online passenger reservations systems like American Airlines' SABRE and United Airlines' APOLLO have revolutionized the travel industry. They have helped increase these carriers' market shares by as much as 20 percent. Large car rental and hotel chains could not function effectively without their reservations systems.

- Overnight delivery industry leader Federal Express Corporation has the COS-MOS parcel tracking system. COSMOS enables online inquiry of parcel status from remote locations, locates delayed shipments, and sends invoices to customers automatically. The Federal Express delivery vans even carry onboard terminals.

- The Cirrus banking network (now owned by MasterCard) covers 46 states. Its 1425 member banks process some 200 million transactions annually and provide services such as cash withdrawals and balance inquiries from checking, savings, and credit accounts. Other services include direct debit retail point-of-sale transactions and international currency conversions from Cirrus' automated teller machines.

Technological developments are primarily responsible for the enormous increase in the use of communication networks. The two primary technological factors are size and speed. First, the size of electronic components (microprocessor circuits) is decreasing dramatically as circuit density increases. For example, in 1959 one megabyte (1 million bytes) of memory required a space equal to the size of a room 7 feet square by 8 feet high. Today, the same amount of memory requires only about one-quarter cubic inch of space. Moreover, in 1959 one megabyte of memory cost about $25,000. Today, a megabyte costs less than $50.

Second, the speed of microprocessor chips used in data communications has increased by many magnitudes. Advanced 16-megabit chip technology has resulted in dramatic performance enhancements and increased storage capacity. The high speed chip's dynamic random access memory (DRAM) takes only 80 nanoseconds (billionths of a second) to access stored data. At this speed, the single chip can "read" a 2200-page document in only one second.

We are on the threshold of using a totally new type of transistor. This *ballistic transistor* switches 1000 times faster than the transistors used in today's communication switches and microcomputers. The fastest bipolar transistor switches on and off 140 billion times a second.

Superconductors will have a major impact on future data communication circuits. Experiments have shown that superconductors can transmit data at extremely high rates and have the potential to become the building blocks for a new generation of faster communications. Superconductors are materials that conduct electricity without resistance at extremely low temperatures. Based on an assumption that the temperature at which a material becomes a superconductor can continue to be raised, experiments have proven that superconductors will have the ability to transmit data as much as 100 times faster than optical fibers.

It was only about 15 years ago that we were first able to transmit at a speed of 9600 bits per second (bps) on a standard telephone circuit. Using various digital technologies, we now can transmit at 64,000 bits per second on the same telephone circuit, and with the use of fiber optics we can transmit at several hundred million bits per second. In the future, we will transmit at billions of bits per second with fiber optics.

There are three major trends driving the future of communications and networking. All are interrelated and it is difficult to consider one without the others.

Pervasive Networking

In the future, communication networks will be pervasive. This is due to both technological advances, and increasing competition driving down costs. Virtually all computers will be networked in some way to other computers. Computers will be sold with network hardware and software as standard equipment, in much the same way as microcomputers today are sold with Microsoft Windows.

This pervasive networking also means that virtually any computer will be able to communicate with any other computer in the world. The *Internet*, an international group of networks discussed in Chapter 2, has experienced such rapid growth over the past two years that it now connects more than 25 million computers. In this environment, the movement of information and data between people, groups, and organizations will be unprecedented in human history. Some specific issues of interest are discussed next.

Smart Buildings   Older buildings have electrical wiring for 120-volt electric current. Newer buildings, on the other hand, contain wiring for all sorts of uses, such as electricity, data communications, voice communications, image processing, and the many control systems required in large office buildings. A *smart building* consists of many automated systems and their associated electrical and network wiring. Smart building systems that are interconnected by networks include basic controls such as those for heating, ventilation, and air conditioning. Furthermore, they also control lighting, fire safety features, security, electrical power regulation, escalators, elevators, and any other information pathways used by microcomputers or other network computers. Today's smart buildings are already wired for local area networks by using twisted pair, coaxial cable and/or fiber optic cables.

Electronic/Voice Mail   Both electronic mail and voice mail will grow quite rapidly. *Electronic mail* will grow primarily in the business sector and between the homes of individuals owning microcomputers. *Voice mail* will grow as more special common carriers and telephone companies offer voice storing and forwarding systems and as more organizations put voice mail software on their networks.

Teleconferencing   Did you know that every day 20 million meetings are held in the United States and that more than three quarters of these meetings last less than 30 minutes? Over one half of all meetings can be handled by voice communications only, one third of all meetings are for the exchange of information only, and almost 90 percent of American air travel is for business. For these reasons you will see a distinct increase in video *teleconferencing*. With teleconferencing, people from diverse geographic locations can "attend" a business meeting in both voice and picture format. In fact, even documents can be shown and copied at any of the remote locations.

Telecommuting   Another emerging trend is *telecommuting* in which employees perform some or all of their work at home instead of going to the office each day. If you were the telecommuter, some benefits might be less time wasted in driving to work, improved quality of life, optimized scheduling of both your work and personal life,

Management Focus: The Future is Here—in Iowa

A transformation has been taking place in many state schools and hospitals, and within the criminal justice system throughout Iowa with the implementation of the Iowa Communications Network (ICN). Telemedicine, telepathology, teleradiology, distance learning, and telejustice are possible via ICN and its conversion of voice, video and data signals into digital light impulses that are transmitted over hair-thin glass fibers throughout the state.

In the 1970s, Iowa's southeast high schools formed a consortium to construct interactive microwave system providing two-way video and audio links between their school districts. With the 1980s, Iowa began moving into the integration of a telecommunications system that used microwave and cable technology. The ICN was officially created by the passing of a bill in 1989.

As of today, ICN includes 105 schools and colleges, three prisons, an armory, and three hospitals at a total cost of $97.5 million. With schools using distance learning being the most impressive so far, Russian teacher Mark Engle presides over three classes with students as far as 200 miles away with the assistance of ICN and an attending teacher in the other classrooms to ensure students know what is happening.

Iowa is the first to have all of its counties hooked up through a fiber optics communications system that many experts say could be a national model for those states that follow. Other states experimenting with fiber optic networks are North Carolina, Georgia, and Maryland.

Looking into 1995, the ICN plans to bring online hundreds more schools, libraries, and state agencies. However, the biggest problem that Iowa is having comes from its lack of ability to fulfill demand. Other debatable issues are who pays for the network, liability questions, and retaining privacy.

Source: Newsweek, December 19, 1994.

monetary savings on both clothes and travel, less stress, greater time flexibility, and a higher level of concentration at home because of fewer distractions.

One key area in which telecommuting helps is for "at-home" diagnoses of information systems or data communication problems. This is true especially for after-hours work. In an emergency in which a technician has to communicate with the mainframe or network control system, telecommuting is much faster than a long drive by car.

Electronic Data Interchange (EDI) *Electronic data interchange* is the paperless transmission between companies of orders, invoices, and other business documents. It truly is the biggest step toward the paperless office. Companies using EDI have networks interconnecting their microcomputers and computer systems to those at other companies. These connections allow them to initiate transactions electronically and then transmit the transactions to another company where they can be viewed on a microcomputer's video screen or printed if necessary.

EDI improves efficiency and productivity, and reduces the number of times human operators have to handle and process documents. On the other hand, it creates a whole new set of legal problems. The biggest problem is the legal liability of an electronically transmitted document. Historically, a paper document with an official nature has been the primary piece of evidence with regard to the legal authority concerning an order or other business contract. According to historical precedent, the paper document with the proper authorized signature is the "authentication" that an order was placed. Today, business appears to be moving toward public key encryption for authenticating electronic data interchange documents. Public key encryption is discussed in Chapter 13.

The networking technology is available now to implement EDI. The most difficult tasks in making EDI a reality, however, are the agreements among different companies located in different countries as to how they will exchange and format the documents, and the legal questions over the authentication of signatures required on electronically transmitted documents. As with other complicated technologies, there must be standards for them to work effectively. In the United States, the EDI standard is known as ANSI X.12. An international standard called EDI for Administration, Commerce, and Transport (EDIFACT) is being developed.

Transborder Data Flow Many countries currently restrict the flow or movement of data across their national boundaries. The United States is probably the most open with regard to the flow of information into and out of the country. But even it limits *transborder data flow* by restricting the sale or delivery of some technological equipment or information to countries that are viewed as less than friendly.

Canada requires the initial processing of all bank transactions to be done in Canada, and foreign networks can cross the border only at one crossing point. Canada's Banking Act prevents the processing of bank transactions outside Canadian boundaries unless some processing also is performed within the country. Transmitting financial data outside the country, or subsequent manipulation of that data, requires government approval. Germany requires significant local processing of all data transmitted over communication circuits (private or public telephone facilities). Brazil requires corporations to maintain copies of most computer databases inside Brazil, rather than connecting with existing databases outside the country. Most offshore processing of Brazilian data is prohibited. When possible, companies must purchase Brazilian computer equipment and software rather than import it.

France is considering taxing data. Sweden has a data inspection board that must approve the export of data files or the transmission of personal data out of Sweden. In England, secret encryption keys must be shared with the postal and telegraph service. Belgium and France have imposed up to a $400,000 fine for transmitting data defined as sensitive. Spain requires that money be deposited in an escrow account before data files can be transmitted out of the country. Such data protection laws are a type of tariff or duty on the free flow of information.

A preliminary agreement between the United States and the European countries represented by the Organization for Economic Cooperation and Development (OECD) has led to a policy declaration on transborder data flow. This declaration states that it is the intent of the 24 OECD member countries and the United States to "promote access to data and information and related services, avoid the creation of unjustified barriers to the international exchange of data and information, and seek transparency in regulations and policies related to information, computer, and communication services affecting transborder data flow." This policy may help ease the free transfer of information between countries, although there still are political and economic barriers, and the licensed common carriers selling communication services sometimes look out for their own special interests first.

Data Monopoly In addition to transborder data flow, it also is possible to have an intercompany data flow problem within a single country. In this situation, the question is that of a *data monopoly* within a specific country. For example, the U.S. Department of Justice monitors computerized airline reservations systems as a form of data monopoly. The Department has stated that it may seek divestiture of the highly successful airline reservations systems from the airlines that own them. It claims that the United Airlines and American Airlines reservations systems are used to monopolize the sales of airline flights. It contends that these two air carriers tend to get most of the reservations because most travel agencies use one of these two reservations systems. If travel agents have to scroll or page through many different screens to locate competing carrier flights, then they may be more likely to select those flights that are easy to access.

On the international scene, three American airlines filed a complaint with the Department of Transportation charging that the Lufthansa reservations system is biased. The complaint alleges that the flight listings of American carriers are relegated to the third and fourth screens, if they are shown at all. The three U.S. airlines claim to be losing millions of dollars in annual revenues because of the bias built into the Lufthansa system.

These may be the world's first legal issues involving a data monopoly in our information-based society. A monopoly usually involves goods or services, but in this situation it is claimed that basic information is monopolized to enhance one business to the detriment of others. This issue should be watched as a trend for the future. How many other industries or businesses can enhance their own economics through a data monopoly? Do we have the proper laws to address this issue?

As we enter the next century, we are moving from the manufacturing/management era to the information era in which information is the single most valuable resource of an enterprise. Information may become more important than management structure, manufacturing ability, or financial capabilities. Thus, a country that restricts information most likely will slow its economic growth, thereby lowering the standard of living for all its citizens.

The Integration of Voice, Video, and Data

A second key trend is the integration of voice, video, and data communication. In the past, the telecommunications systems used to transmit video signals (e.g., broadcast or cable TV), voice signals (e.g., telephone calls), and data (e.g., computer data or e-

Management Focus: No Longer Just a Phone Company

Once the ugly duckling of American telephone companies, U.S. West is now poised to enter the next era in telecommunications. U.S. West owns 25 percent of Time-Warner's entertainment group, 50 percent of AirTouch Cellular, and 50 percent of Mercury One-2-One, a new wireless company. It also owns the largest cable TV companies in the United Kingdom, as well as cable companies in France and Hong Kong. Its UK cable TV company also offers telephone services in direct competition with British Telecom.

With its purchase of Wometco Cable, the largest cable company in the southern United States, U.S. West is now ready to compete directly with BellSouth, the largest telephone company in the country. U.S. West plans to spend $300 million remaking Wometco to provide 200 TV channels, and two-way services such as in home shopping and video games. Wometco is also planning to introduce a telephone service, pending regulatory approval.

The question, of course, is whether consumers are ready to make telephone calls through their cable TV or order movies and products electronically. "We can't just be the telephone company anymore," says Richard McCormick, U.S. West's chairman. "If we take that attitude, we'll be dinosaurs by 2005."

Bellsouth is not standing still either. It is introducing cable TV service over its telephone lines, pending regulatory approval.

Source: Atlanta Journal-Constitution, February 5, 1995.

mail) were completely separate. One network was used for data, one for voice, and one for cable TV.

This is rapidly changing. The integration of voice and data is largely complete in wide area networks. The interexchange carriers such as AT&T, Sprint, and MCI all provide telecommunication services that support data and voice transmission over the same circuits, even intermixing voice and data on the same physical cable. The integration of voice and data has been much slower in local area networks and local telephone services. Some companies have successfully integrated both on the same network, but most still lay two separate cable networks into offices, one for voice and one for computer access. The biggest problem has been the lack of capacity on the traditional voice networks to support the high volume transmissions generated by local area networks.

The integration of video into wide area networks has been much slower, partly due to legal restrictions; telephone companies are currently prohibited from entering the cable TV industry in the same geographical area in which they provide telephone services. However, this integration is inevitable. Telephone companies have been buying cable TV companies in other regions (e.g., U.S. West purchased a major cable TV company in Georgia), and numerous legal challenges are underway. CNN, in conjunction with Intel, now offers its CNN and Headline News broadcasts digitially. Subscribers to this service receive the regular TV broadcasts in a format that can be transmitted over local area networks. This way, users can receive the same audio and video images as a window on their computer.

Voice/Data Integration   Equipment that combines voice transmission and data transmission over a single communication circuit is already available. Combining these would be very cost effective in most governmental and private business organizations because much higher circuit usage could be achieved at reduced costs. Approximately three quarters of today's communication costs are for voice, and one quarter are for data transmission.

The normal voice telephone systems can have *store and forward* capability for voice information. In other words, if you call someone who is not present, the telephone system accepts your voice message and forwards it to the person when he or she calls in later. The system even can try repeatedly to contact the person until the telephone is answered and your stored message is delivered.

CATV (Cable TV)   The cable television companies will be increasing their role for two-way communications into and out of homes. They are in direct competition with rooftop satellite antennas and the major television networks. These cable TV companies and common carrier data communication businesses may merge into a business cable for the private, commercial, and government markets. This communication pipeline into your home, via both the telephone system and cable TV, is a critical issue because of privacy and security considerations. As an individual consumer, you will need to secure extra privacy for your data and your life. For example, if you use cable TV, someone might build a personality profile of you by determining which television shows you watch. In addition, the TV company could keep track of your purchases, financial transactions, and anything else that is received or transmitted on the cable hooked to your television. Personal privacy may be a concern here.

As the term implies, cable TV traditionally operates over a copper cable. This may change as cable television converts to optical fiber technology. The use of optical fiber will allow cable firms to offer more television channels, interactive television where the user interacts to do such things as play video games supplied by the cable company, and a large selection of movies from which the user chooses.

Satellite   With *home satellite TV,* you will be able to receive TV from many different countries (see Figure 1-5). Such use of satellites by individuals leads to widespread possibilities with regard to the freedom and flow of information and ideas. Because the borders of a country may no longer be closed to the free flow of data, information, and ideas, people around the world may become more politically aware.

The world witnessed the reality of satellite communications during two recent events: Desert Storm and the failed coup in the Commonwealth of Independent States (formerly the USSR) when hard-line Communists tried to overthrow Mikhail Gorbachev. During both events, news reporters used small portable satellite dishes to transmit their news stories from on location and in real time. In the first event, everyone saw a CNN reporter in Baghdad transmitting pictures of the incoming American missiles going by his hotel room window. Later they saw the UN inspection team try to obtain Iraqi nuclear, chemical, and biological weapon information as required by the

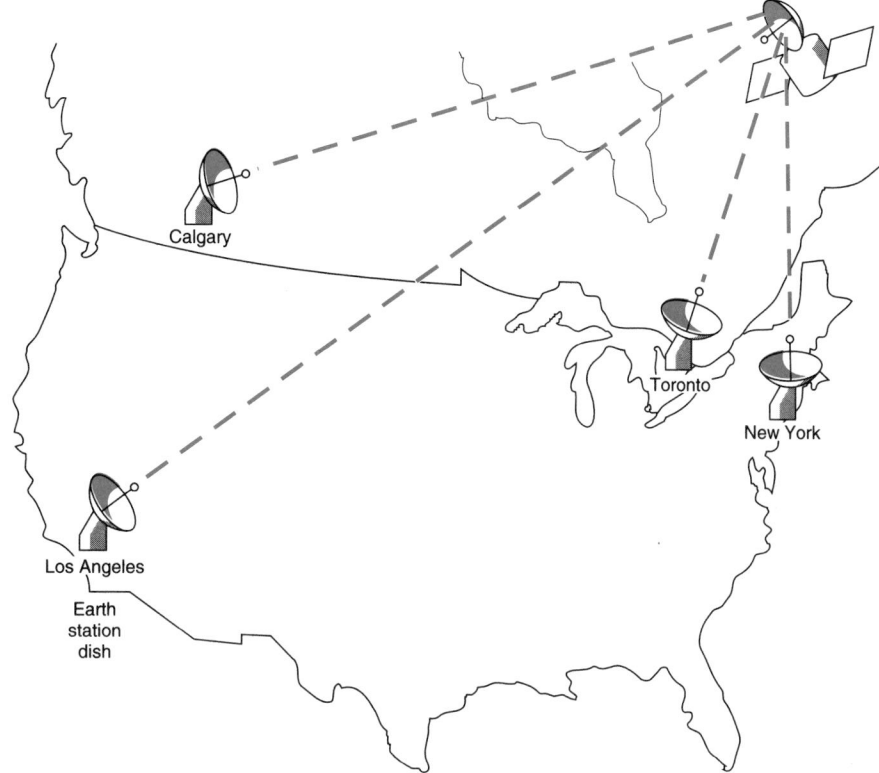

Figure 1-5   International information flow.

cease-fire agreement. The world saw firsthand how this UN team was treated. In the second event, both individual Soviet citizens and other people worldwide were able to witness the fall of the Communist leaders and the rise of democracy. Earlier, the world watched the tearing down of the Berlin Wall and the merging of East and West Germany. These live, real-time news reports have all been possible because of satellite technology.

These satellites also open the future possibility to communicate directly with other people via the satellite dish located on the roof of your house. This satellite dish antenna might lead you to transmit either voice or data directly from your house in the United States to someone else's house in another country.

New Information Services

A third key trend is the provision of new information services on these rapidly expanding networks. In the same way that the construction of the American interstate highway system spawned new businesses, so will the construction of worldwide inte-

Management Focus: Career Opportunities

Numerous career opportunities for telecommunications experts are available in both corporations and government agencies. At a time when doctors, lawyers, dentists, accountants, and MBAs are in good supply, jobs for telecommunication managers abound. The need for qualified analysts and managers in the telecommunication industry is urgent and growing. The demand is acute for two reasons. First, technological innovations have created rapidly changing new products and, second, deregulation has paved the way for new suppliers of communication hardware and software.

Many universities offer telecommunication degrees. For a comprehensive list of telecommunication programs, contact the Manager of Education for the International Communications Association at 1-214-233-3889. Their list describes more than 100 graduate programs, undergraduate programs, and associate certificate and vocational-technical programs.

If you choose a career in telecommunications, remember that this function is a major support service for the way a company conducts its business operations. In other words, communications are changing the way both private companies and government agencies conduct their basic business functions. For this reason, it is desirable to have a basic background in general business subjects, such as finance, marketing, economics, and accounting, to accompany your information systems and communications knowledge. A career in telecommunications will be a very salable item at least through the start of the next century. Today, people with three or four years of experience make annual salaries of $45,000 to $75,000. Telecommunications is a stronger job market than general information systems.

grated communications networks. One of the most important of these is *World Wide Web,* which is discussed in Chapter 2. Other services of interest are discussed next.

Videotex   *Videotex* is the two-way transmission between your home TV set and organizations outside your home. It allows you to talk with a doctor, take courses in your home, provide security services for your house, review information retrieval databases, teleshop from your local store, conduct teleconferences (picture and voice) from your home, play video games, and have access to community meetings. In addition, you can view first-run movies, interconnect with satellite TV programming, use e-mail message networks, connect with your bank, review the most current news stories, or use voice store and forward message systems. Canada already has videotex (called Telidon), as do England and France, but it has not been accepted by the public in the United States.

Audiotex   *Audiotex* is a service in which you dial a telephone number and get connected to a system that provides a voice recording. A simple example is an answering machine. More complex systems consist of interactive audiotex services where, instead of just playing a recorded message, the interactive audiotex allows callers to choose a topic on which they want more information. Current area code 900 telephone numbers allow callers to pick topics such as today's horoscope, the weather, or an update on current sporting events.

Public Networks   *Public networks* will have "standard interfaces" to connect almost any terminal to anything. In other words, any terminal or microcomputer or telephone will be able to communicate with any other terminal or microcomputer or telephone on the public network.

Cellular telephone networks will begin to compete directly with the current wired local loops. With cellular telephone, radio transmission towers are placed in strategic locations throughout a city. The messages from companies or private homes are transmitted over the airways as radio frequency transmissions to these towers. The towers then connect to land-based communication circuits, microwave circuits, or satellite transmission systems for the long haul (interexchange channel or IXC) transmission of voice and data. Cellular telephone local loops could replace the copper wire local loops now in use.

There also will be increasing competition in both the local telephone/data network as well as the long distance market. AT&T, Sprint, MCI, and several other companies have already entered the local telephone market in direct competition against the "baby Bells" that currently provide telephone services to most homes and businesses in America. At present, most of these companies lease telephone access from the local Bell company; that is, rather than installing new telephone lines, they pay the Bell company for the right to use the Bell lines. This is beginning to change, however. In the future, many experts expect that businesses will be able to choose among three to five land-based and cellular companies for local telephone/data services, in much the same way they now have the choice among long distance carriers.

Teleports   One emerging concept is the *teleport*, a large satellite communication dish antenna that uses data transmission frequencies not used in terrestrial communications. This is a promising development because teleports can operate in microwave-congested metropolitan areas. These earth stations are connected with multiple fiber optic cables, coaxial cables, and microwave links to locations throughout the metropolitan area they serve. Teleports usually are constructed by companies that are independent of the telephone companies. The earth station dishes shown in Figure 1-5 are examples of teleports.

A teleport is an urban communication gateway that provides efficient and economical communication services to long distance users. By having these earth stations closer to urban areas, telecommunications, customers receive reliable and economic service. Today's teleport earth station (major hub) ranges in size from 20 to 40 feet in diameter, but each year new technology provides smaller antennas with the same reliability as the older, larger ones. Teleport transmission rates range from 56,000 bits per second to over 2 million bits per second or higher. Furthermore, all-digital bit streams avoid the need for analog-to-digital conversion and, consequently, ensure an almost error-free signal.

About two dozen teleports currently operate in the United States. Operating tele-

Management Focus: Distance Learning in Oklahoma

Need to take a particular class, but don't have the time to drive three hours to the university? Don't give up, because distance learning may be closer than you realize.

Distance learning allows a student to attend classes at another location through interactive networks. Oklahoma State University's (Stillwater) network features real-time video in order to enhance the learning process when students cannot be at the school's main campus.

Their compressed video network is the means through which they offer graduate courses at sites all over the state. The distance learning units making this possible consist of two monitors, two cameras, and a control panel. When a distance-learning class is in session, the instructor stands in front of a set of cameras which he or she manages from the control panel. One of the monitors in the studio displays the image that is being broadcast, and the other shows the students in the classroom located elsewhere.

In 1989, Oklahoma State became the first university in the country to deliver graduate-level courses via a fiber optic network. In 1990, Oklahoma State began adding corporate sites to the network.

The facility offers entire graduate program degrees, including an MBA, an M.S. in electrical engineering, and an M.S. in computer science. Distance learning is here.

Source: LAN Magazine, September 1994.

ports are located in Atlanta, Chicago, Dallas/Ft. Worth, Houston, Washington, D.C., Ocala (Florida), Carteret (New Jersey), Raleigh (North Carolina), Seattle, Los Angeles, San Francisco, and New York City. In larger cities, the distribution area from the teleport is sometimes as far as 250 miles. This means that there are high speed, terrestrial-based communication links from the teleport to customers who may be as far as 250 miles away from the teleport itself. At the New York teleport, businesses are linked to the facility via a fiber optic cable network that has been placed throughout the metropolitan New York area. Communications Satellite Corporation (COMSAT) operates international earth station teleports in New York, Chicago, San Francisco, Houston, and Washington, D.C. These international earth stations offer business customers access to international satellites. Numerous other countries also are setting up international teleport earth stations.

Distance Learning   In an isolated village far above the Arctic Circle, a young Eskimo intently studies a computer screen filled with data, generated as part of a University of Alaska business course delivered entirely by data communications. When she finishes the lesson, the student takes a test that is scored within seconds by a computer 1000 miles away in Anchorage. When she needs to do library research, she turns to an electronic card catalog to find the books she needs.

In the remote Outback of Australia, a student has difficulty tuning out the static during a two-way radio transmission that is used for the Australian "School of the Air." The two Northern Territory schools at Alice Springs and Katherine provide correspondence course radio lessons with weekly problem solving and communications with the teacher. Once a year, the teacher actually visits the students who live in these remote Outback cattle or sheep stations.

. . . .

Summary

Why Study Data Communications?   The information society, where information and intelligence are the key drivers of personal, business, and national success, has arrived. Data communications is principal enabler of the rapid information exchange and will become more important than the use of computers themselves in the future. Successful users of data communications, such as Wal-Mart, can gain significant competitive advantage in the marketplace.

Network Definitions   A Local Area Network (LAN) is a group of microcomputers or terminals located in the same general area. A Backbone Network (BN) is a large central network that connects most everything on a single company site. A Metropolitan Area Network (MAN) encompasses a city or county area. A Wide Area Network (WAN) spans cities, states, or national boundaries.

Network Components   Communication networks are often broken into a series of layers, each of which can be defined separately, to enable vendors to develop software and hardware that can work together in the overall network. In this book, we use a four-layer model. The application layer is the application software used by the network user. The network layer takes the message generated by the application layer and addresses it and determines its route through the network, as well as collecting message accounting information. The data link layer takes the message from the network layer and formats the message to indicate where it starts and ends, decides when to transmit it over the physical media, and detects and corrects any errors that occur in transmission. The physical layer is the physical connection between the sender and receiver, including the hardware devices (e.g., computers, terminals, and modems) and physical media (e.g., cables and satellites).

Future Trends in Communications and Networking   In the future, communication networks will be pervasive. They will be taken for granted in the same way electricity is today. Voice, video, and data communication will be integrated so that any communication network will transmit and deliver any type of data. A multitude of new information services will develop on these new networks in the same way that new services grew in the wake of the American interstate highway system or commercial airline system. These three trends will transform business—and life—as we know it.

Key Terms

Backbone network (BN)	Front end processor (FEP)	Organization-wide network
Cable television (CATV)	Host computer	Point-to-point network
Central office	Interexchange channel	Private leased circuit
Circuit	(IXC)	Satellite
Client	International network	Server
Common carrier	Local area network (LAN)	Single application network
Connector cable	Local loop	Telecommunications
Data communications	Medium	Telecommuting
Data monopoly	Metropolitan area network	Teleconferencing
Digital	(MAN)	Teleport
Distance learning	Microcomputer	Teleprocessing
Electronic data	Modem	Terminal
interchange (EDI)	Multiorganization network	Transborder data flow
Electronic mail (E-mail)	Multiple application	Value added network
Encryption	network	(VAN)
End office	Network Administrator	Voice mail
Exchange office	Networking	Wide area network (WAN)

Selected References

1. Becker, Pat. "LANs Around the World," *LAN Magazine,* vol. 7, no. 4, April 1992, pp. 36–37, 39–40, 42. [Discusses the problems of worldwide networking.]
2. Heller, Martha. "Present and Future Perfect," *LAN Magazine,* vol. 6, no. 10, October 1991, pp. 155, 157, 159–160, 162, 164. [A case study describing the Yale University network.]
3. Herman, Barbara and Tracey Tucker. "Telecomm People of '91," *Teleconnect,* vol. 9, no. 12, December 1991, pp. 58–59, 62–64, 66–68, 71, 74–77. [Gives insight about why some telecommunication managers are successful.]
4. Johnson, Johna Till. "Videoconferencing," *Data Communications,* vol. 20, no. 15, November 1991, pp. 66–68, 70, 72, 80, 82, 84, 86, 88. [Discusses the present and future of videoconferencing.]
5. Kobb, Bennett. "Telecommunications," *IEEE Spectrum,* January 1995.
6. Martin, James. *Telecommunications and the Computer,* 3rd ed. Englewood Cliffs, NJ: Prentice–Hall, 1990.
7. Rowe, Stanford H., II. *Telecommunications,* 2nd ed. New York: Macmillan Publishing Co., 1991.
8. *Scientific American,* vol. 265, no. 3, September 1991. [Special issue devoted to communications, computers, and networks.]
9. Stallings, William and van Slyke, Richard. *Business Data Communications.* New York: Macmillan Publishing Co., 1994.
10. Stamper, David A. *Business Data Communications,* 4th ed. Redwood City, CA: Benjamin/Cummings Publishing Co., 1994.
11. Wright, Benjamin. *Law of Electronic Commerce: EDI, Fax, and E-Mail: Technology, Proof, and Liability.* Boston: Little, Brown & Co., 1991.

Computerized Literature Resources

The use of computers and networks has transformed the way information is stored and can be searched. One important new information resource is the information superhighway (or the Internet). This is discussed in detail in Chapter 2.

Computer also have had a major impact on libraries and methods of locating printed information. One approach to locating printed information is to use subject-oriented indexes, but many feel that using these indexes is too time consuming and tedious. Because of advances in computerized database technology, many of the indexes found in libraries or information centers can be accessed via terminals. In addition, some indexes are available *only* in a computerized format.

The following indexes are available in a number of systems, among them DIALOG (a Knight-Ridder company), ORBIT Information Technologies, and BRS (Bibliographic Retrieval Services). These systems may have just a few indexes, or they may have hundreds of indexes with millions of references. Examples of online databases that may be of interest to data communication educators and professionals are outlined below. Contact your librarian for assistance in using these valuable resources.

Abstracted Business Information. Available only in computerized form. References articles related to the business aspects of data communications such as managing in a data communication environment. Provides bibliographic information and abstracts. 1971–present.

Books in Print. Lists books, symposia, and other monographs sold by American publishers. Excellent for learning what books are available in a particular field. The paper version is indexed by author, title, and subject. The computerized version is useful because terms can be used for which adequate subject indexing is unavailable, as when a subject is either very narrow or an emerging topic. 1948–present.

COMPENDEX (*COMP*uterized *EN*gineering In*DEX*). Emphasizes the engineering aspects of data communications. It is useful for determining how others have applied data communications in an industrial or factory-type situation such as an industrial control application. Includes international journals, technical symposia, reports, government documents, and more. Provides bibliographic citations and abstracts. 1970–present.

INSPEC. The printed counterparts of this computerized index are *Physics Abstracts, Electrical and Electronics Abstracts,* and *Computer and Control Abstracts.* Because computers are an integral part of data communications, the *Computer and Control Abstracts* portion of this database is an excellent resource. Includes the technical aspects of applications, techniques, hardware, software, technological developments, architectures, economics, and the practical aspects of implementing such systems. References are international in scope with abstracts. 1969–present.

PROMT and *Funk and Scott Index.* These complementary indexes share the same database. *PROMT* abstracts marketing-oriented articles that discuss products, processes, and services for sale. Indexing is by product, country or state, and event (for example, sales, new product/process, demand, profits, cost per unit, industry structure/members, regulatory actions). Citations are brief, but abstracts are informative. The *Funk and Scott Index* has no abstracts; it is an index to the same references cited in *PROMT,* plus others that are too short to abstract (for example, a one-line announcement that one firm has contracted with another for a specific product and a specified dollar amount). Items are international in scope and include journals, trade literature, government documents, and more. They focus on data communication equipment, networks, office automation, and telecommunications. 1972–present.

Ulrich's International Periodicals Directory. A guide to journals published in all countries. Provides the name of the journal, publisher information, publication frequency, price, and whether the journal includes such items as advertisements or illustrations. Arranged and indexed by subject. An excellent way to locate journals in a specific field such as computers. The computerized version enhances retrieval because one can obtain the titles of all journals with a specific word in the title. 1932–present.

Questions/Problems

1. What agency of the U.S. government is responsible for regulating interstate telephone business?
2. What type of network allows the simultaneous transmission of voice, data, and video images?
3. What are the electrical pulses that are converted for transmission called?
4. The frequency tones that are transmitted are called _____ .
5. Define superconductor and state its importance.
6. A _____ is an urban communication gateway that provides cost-effective communication services to long distance users.
7. A _____ bypasses the telephone company local loop.
8. Can a microcomputer be both a client and a host?
9. What is the value of information that cannot be transmitted?
10. In an information-based society, the _____ resource is knowledge that creates information.
11. Write your definition of the term *data communications* and compare it with the definition given in the glossary.
12. Define four or five uses of data communications.
13. If the typical characteristics of a transaction are "relatively low character volume per input transaction, response required within seconds, output message lengths usually short but might vary widely with some types of applications," identify some examples of business applications that might use an information retrieval type of network.
14. What is the difference between data communications and telecommunications or teleprocessing?
15. What is a circuit?
16. Compare the definition of local loop in Chapter 1 with that in the glossary. Next, look at Figure 1-2 and be sure you understand the concepts of local loop and central office.
17. Define the progression of systems from the 1950s to the present.
18. Is it possible for a large business organization to have a combination of all seven categories of networks that were described in this chapter?

19. What types of companies can be classified as common carriers?
20. How might transborder data flow restrictions affect a university?
21. Present the issue of data monopoly to an economics instructor and relate his or her comments to your data communication class.
22. Identify the closet college or university offering a degree in telecommunications or data communications.
23. Why would transborder data flow restrictions hamper business?
24. Describe the most recent data communication development you have read about in a newspaper or other periodical.
25. The Uses of Data Communications section in this chapter lists the characteristics of organizations that can benefit from data communication systems. Examine these characteristics and identify who or what function in the organization will benefit and describe how.
26. After completing a course of study based on this textbook, what should you be able to do?
27. Define information lag and discuss its importance.
28. As we approach the year 2000, what will be the most important area related to computers?
29. What is a new employment specialty necessitated by the introduction of LANs?
30. How do LANs differ from MANs, WANs, and BNs?
31. Describe a point-to-point network.
32. Describe electronic data interchange.
33. What makes it so difficult to implement EDI?
34. What is audiotex?
35. What is a smart building?
36. How does videotex differ from audiotex?
37. What are the three fundamental trends driving the future of telecommunications and networking?
38. This chapter discussed several examples of how these three trends might affect the future of networking. Provide some other examples of how these trends may change the way individuals and organizations do business in the future.
39. Describe the four layers that can be used to discuss and analyze networks.

NEXT DAY AIR SERVICE CUMULATIVE CASE STUDY

See appendix at end of book

CHAPTER TWO

NETWORK APPLICATIONS

The widespread availability of data communications and networking has fostered the development and use of several new software applications that have dramatically changed the way we do communicate. Chapter 2 looks at two basic types of these applications. The first, groupware, better enables groups of people to work together, whether they are located in the same office, or halfway around the world; the second is the information superhighway or the Internet. Both have received a good deal of media attention in recent years. Some of this is hype, but some represents the fundamental changes that these applications can bring to today's business world. For example, we will use the Internet regularly to update this textbook with the latest in telecommunications technology. The section on the World Wide Web provides the Internet address that will allow you to access these updates.

Objectives

- Become familiar with several different types of groupware,
- Become familiar with the importance of standards,
- Become familiar with the changes groupware can make in organizations,
- Become familiar with the information superhighway (the Internet),
- Become familiar with several Internet tools for discussion and information retrieval,
- Become familiar with the World Wide Web,
- Become familiar with how you can use the Internet for yourself and your company.

Chapter Outline

Introduction
Groupware

INTRODUCTION

In the early days of information systems, most systems—such as payroll, order entry, and inventory—were designed to improve the productivity of entire departments or organizations. In the 1980s, the introduction of microcomputers enabled the widespread development and use of information systems—such as spreadsheets, and word processors—to support individuals.

By the 1990s, the widespread availability of data communications and networking had begun to change our vision of the computer. We realized that most people in organizations work as members of groups or teams. Along with data communications and networking has come a variety of network application software that allows groups of people to work together more easily. This chapter examines two types of applications software that data communications networks have fostered, which in turn have increased the demand for faster and better networks: groupware, and the information superhighway (or the Internet).

These two applications are the future of information technology. They have the potential to have a greater impact on the way individuals, companies, and even countries function than any computer application has before. The microcomputer revolutionized the way we thought about and used computers; it changed our understanding of computers from big storage and number crunching machines to computers for individual work. Groupware and the Internet will also revolutionize the way we think about and use computers, by making the computer a communications device. Groupware, and the Internet are the initial steps in this transformation.

GROUPWARE

Groupware is software that helps groups of people to work together more productively. This is a very broad definition, but it is difficult to find a more specific one that includes all the different types of groupware applications. Groupware applications are often organized using a two by two grid (see Figure 2-1). Groupware permits people in different places to communicate either at the same time (like a telephone) or at different times. Groupware also can be used to improve communication and decision making among those who work together in the same room, either at the same time or at different times.

Groupware allows people to exchange ideas, debate issues, make decisions, and write reports without actually having to meet face-to-face. Even when groups do meet in the same room at the same time, groupware can improve the meetings. There are many advantages of groupware, but the most important is its ability to help groups make decisions faster, particularly in situations where it is difficult for group members to meet in the same room at the same time.

We now focus our attention on four popular types of groupware: electronic mail, document-based groupware (e.g., Notes), group support systems, and video tele-conferencing.

Electronic Mail

Electronic mail (or *e-mail*) was one of the earliest groupware tools and is also the most heavily used tool today. With e-mail, users create and send messages to one user, several users, or all users on a *distribution list*. Most e-mail software enables users to send text messages and attach documents from word processors or spreadsheets. A few e-mail packages permit users to attach graphics to their messages.

Most e-mail packages allow you to do the same things you do with regular paper mail. You can file messages in electronic file cabinets, forward copies of messages to other users, send "carbon copies" of messages, request automatic confirmation of the delivery of the message, and so on. Many e-mail packages also permit you to filter or

	Same time	Different time
Same place	Group support systems	Group support systems
Different place	Video teleconferencing Desktop video teleconferencing	Electronic mail Document-based groupware

Figure 2-1   Different Types of Groupware

organize messages by priority. For example, all messages from a particular user (e.g., your boss) could be given top priority, so they always appear at the top of your list of messages.

E-mail has several major advantages over regular mail. First, it is fast: delivery of an e-mail message typically takes seconds or minutes, depending upon the distance to the receiver. Even messages sent to other countries usually take only a few minutes, or hours to deliver, compared to days for regular mail or courier services. E-mail users often call regular paper mail *snail-mail* because it moves so slowly by comparison.

A second major benefit is cost. E-mail is cheaper because it costs virtually nothing to transmit the message over the network, compared to the cost of a stamp or a courier charge. E-mail is also cheaper in terms of the time invested in preparing the message. The expectations and culture of sending and receiving e-mail is different from that of sending regular letters. Regular business letters and inter-office memos are expected to be error-free and formatted according to certain standards. A recent analysis of office processes estimated that it costs between $3 to $10 to prepare and send a paper letter, including printing and supply costs, clerical time, and proofreading time. In contrast, most e-mail users accept less well-formatted messages, and slight typographical errors are often overlooked so less time is spent on perfecting the appearance of the message.

E-mail can substitute for the telephone, thus allowing you to avoid *telephone tag* (the process of repeatedly exchanging voice mail messages because neither you nor the person you are trying to call is there when the other calls). A study of telephone tag in large organizations found that it took an average of three calls and messages before the parties actually got to speak to each other. E-mail can often communicate enough of a message so that the entire "conversation" will take less time than a phone call. It is particularly effective for multi-national organizations, which have people working in different time zones around the world.

There are many different types of e-mail software available. Some of the more commonly used packages include: cc:mail, Microsoft Mail, GroupWise, and IBM's Work Group. Choosing one is difficult because each provides a wide range of features and generally good user interfaces. If all e-mail users are on the same network, they probably are using the same e-mail software. However, problems can arise when organizations have many networks or wish to send mail to people in other organizations because not all e-mail software uses the same format for messages. The problem is ensuring that messages from one e-mail package can be understood by another e-mail package.

Several standards have been developed to ensure compatibility between different software packages. Any software package that conforms to a certain standard sends messages that are formatted using its rules. Any other package that understands that particular format can then relay the message to its correct destination; however, if an e-mail package receives a mail message in a different format, it may be unable to process it correctly. Many e-mail packages send using one standard, but can understand messages sent in several different standards. Three commonly used standards are X.400, CMC, and MAPI.

The *X.400* standard was developed by the CCITT standards committee in 1984 (the different standards-making bodies are described in Chapter 7), and was revised in

1988 and 1992. It is the standard generally used by many wide area network and mainframe-based e-mail packages. X.400 is actually a set of seven standards that define in detail how e-mail is to be processed. One part describes how the user's e-mail program (called *user agent*) is to create messages, how to format them for transmission, and how messages are to be processed when they are received. Another part defines how messages created by user agents are to be transmitted through the network by the sender's and receiver's computers (these computers are called *message transfer agents*).

Before you can send an e-mail message using X.400 (or any e-mail package), you must know the receiver's e-mail address (the same way you must know someone's telephone number before you call them). A related set of standards to X.400 is *X.500*, which defines how directories of e-mail addresses (called *phone books*) are to be stored so that users at other computers can access them to find e-mail addresses.

While X.400 is widely used in mainframe networks, vendors of microcomputer packages designed to be used on local area networks have developed their own standards. There is no good reason for this; but most software vendors did not anticipate that computers on local area networks would need to send e-mail messages to computers on other networks and therefore did not adopt the X.400 standard when developing their packages.

In 1994, the same committee that developed X.400, developed a simpler version called Common Messaging Calls 1.0 (*CMC 1.0*). CMC 1.0 defines a minimum set of standard functions that are essentially a scaled down version of X.400. IBM, Lotus, and Microsoft all participated in the development of CMC 1.0, and all have announced that the next versions of their e-mail software will support it. An enhanced standard (called CMC 2.0) that defines many more functions (e.g., distribution lists and directory lists) has also been announced, but vendors have been slow to adopt it.

Microsoft, for example, has developed its own standard (Messaging Application Program Interface or *MAPI*) that is a part of Windows. All Microsoft products support MAPI, and Microsoft has been encouraging other vendors to adopt it. IBM, Lotus, and Novell have all announced that their e-mail programs will support MAPI, simply because of the importance of Windows to the microcomputer and LAN environment.

Document-based Groupware

One of the problems with e-mail is that it lacks a structured way to support an ongoing discussion. Each mail message is a separate item, unrelated to other messages. It is possible to group and file e-mail messages into separate file folders, but there is no overall way to integrate them.

Notes, a document database designed to store and manage large collections of text and graphics, was the first product to provide a solution. Notes was designed by Lotus Corporation but is now owned by IBM. Notes documents can have different sections, and can be organized into hierarchical structures of sections, documents, and folders. Notes can be used as a computer bulletin board to support ongoing discussions. Several topics and sub-topics can be created and everyone in the organization (or selected individuals) can be given access. For example, a topic area about data communications could be created. Users could ask questions about problems they face, contribute

Management Focus: CIA Spies Value in Notes

The Central Intelligence Agency has turned to Notes because of its strong security and flexible data access capabilities. Notes helped redefine the way the agency collects and distributes information, no small feat given that this is the agency's main task.

The goal of the CIA's use of Notes was to replace paper and automate as many processes as possible—in particular the analysis and distribution of reports from overseas offices. Notes also allows the CIA to bring some order to an electronic mail network based on 18 different proprietary systems.

The agency especially liked what it saw in Notes' security technology, including use of public-key encryption and access control lists for limiting who could see what (these are discussed in Chapter 13). It has also taken additional steps to make sure that Notes is secure: an audit trail logs each time a document is accessed, by whom and when it is accessed.

Source: Network World, March 13, 1995.

advice, or post new company policies. These individuals can add messages to the different topics and read those contributed by others. Messages can be easily linked so that it is clear which messages are related to which others.

Notes can also be used to organize a discussion among a certain people, such as a project team working to improve manufacturing quality. Notes might reduce the amount of time the team spends in face-to-face meetings, because many of the issues might be discussed before the meeting actually starts. Notes also could be used to replace standard word processors in preparing the team's reports. Each team member could use Notes to write a portion of the report, which could then be passed to other team members for editing or comments.

In addition, Notes helps automate certain document-based processes (called *work-flow automation*). For example, insurance claims require people from several different parts of an insurance company to work together to process the claim. One person might handle the initial claim, which would then be passed to an insurance adjuster to finish a report. Another person would process the payment. All this paperwork could be replaced if Notes were used to prepare and pass the documents from one person to another.

More than 1.5 million people world-wide now use Notes, a fact that has not escaped the notice of other software vendors. Microsoft recently introduced Microsoft Exchange, a package designed to compete with Notes.

Group Support Systems

Both e-mail and document-based groupware are designed to support individuals and groups working in different places and different times. Neither is very suited to support the needs of groups working together at the same time in the same place. Likewise, both e-mail and document-based groupware provide support for the exchange of text, but neither provides more advanced tools for helping groups make decisions.

Group Support Systems (GSS), also called *electronic meeting systems,* are software tools designed to improve group decision making. Most GSS are used in special purpose meeting rooms that provide each group member with a networked computer, plus large screen video projection systems that act as electronic blackboards (see Figure 2-2). These rooms are equipped with special purpose GSS software that enables participants to communicate, propose ideas, analyze options, evaluate alternatives, and so on. Typically, a meeting facilitator assists the group.

In the GSS meeting, group members can discuss issues verbally as they could in any meeting room; however, they can also use the computers to type ideas and information, which are then shared with all other group members via the network. At first glance, it may seem strange to ask people who are sitting next to each other to type their ideas, because typing is slower than talking. For small groups, typing adds little value.

For large groups, however, typing ideas is faster than talking because only one person can speak at a time. Very few people get a chance to talk, so their ideas and opinions can be overlooked. For example, in a traditional meeting, if 10 people participate equally for one hour, each spends six minutes talking and 54 minutes listening (or at least not contributing). This is a very inefficient use of time. By typing ideas into

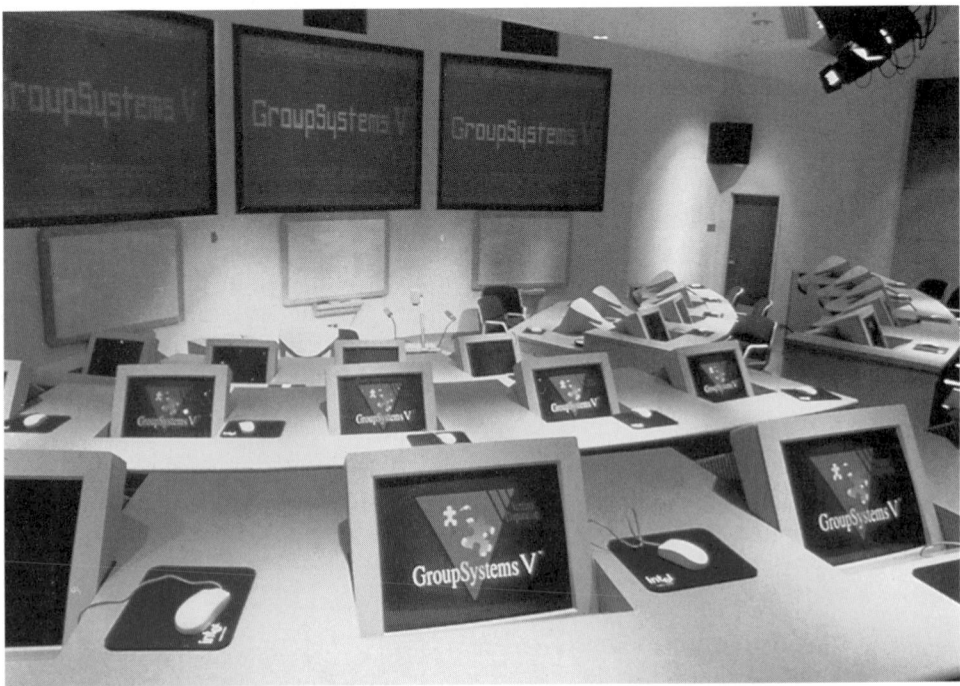

Figure 2-2   A GSS room at the University of Arizona.

Management Focus: The DoD Saves Time and Money with Groupware

The U.S. Department of Defense (DoD) logistics system experienced major problems during the Gulf war. One reason was that the information systems within each of the military services had evolved with little integrated planning; there were a total of 2000 separate logistics information systems in use in the DoD, which made sharing information and supplies very difficult.

The Army and Marine Corps, with support from the Office of the Secretary of Defense, decided to develop one set of standard logistics processes and supporting information systems for all Army and Marine ground units. They began by defining their current processes and systems, which required more than 26 weeks of meetings over a 15-month period at a cost of $3.3 million.

Given the difficulty in defining the current processes and system, the DoD decided to use a group support system to develop the specifications for the new integrated logistics processes and information systems. In 1993, 60 logistics experts from the Army and Marines spent three weeks in the GSS facility at Redstone Arsenal in Huntsville, Alabama, defining the new processes and systems at a total cost of $300,000, a savings of about 90 percent in both time and money.

The project was such a success that in 1994, the DoD conducted a follow-up project to integrate Navy and Air Force systems into the overall system. The results were similar. In three weeks, 80 logistics experts from the Army, Marines, Navy, and Air Force defined the new processes and systems for about $300,000, again a savings of about 90 percent in time and money.

---

a GSS, everyone has the same opportunity to contribute, and ideas can be collected much faster.

In addition, GSS helps to elicit comments made anonymously. Without anonymity, certain participants may withhold ideas because they fear their ideas may not be well received. Participants may also feel a pressure to conform to the majority or more senior participants, whether that pressure is or is not intended.

These systems also provide tools to support voting and ranking of alternatives, so that more structured decision-making processes can be used. Studies of GSS have shown that its use can reduce the amount of time taken to make decisions by 50 to 80 percent. At present, there are no standards for GSS, so products from different vendors are not compatible.

Video Teleconferencing

E-mail, document-based groupware, and GSS all focus on the transmission of text and graphical images. *Video teleconferencing* provides real-time transmission of video and audio signals to enable people in two or more locations to have a meeting. In most cases, video conferences are held in special purpose meeting rooms with one or more cameras and several video display monitors to capture and display the video signals (see Figure 2-3). Special audio microphones and speakers are used to capture and play audio signals. The audio and video signals are combined into one signal that is transmitted through a metropolitan or wide area network to people at the other location. Most video conferences involve people in two meeting rooms, but some systems can support conferences of up to eight separate meeting rooms.

The key benefits of video teleconferencing are the time and cost savings that can result. By using video teleconferencing, meeting participants no longer need to spend time and money in travel. Video teleconferencing was slow to take hold in many organizations because of its high initial installation costs (between $30,000 to $100,000 per meeting room). Today, however, most large organizations with offices in different parts of the country or the world use it.

The transmission of video requires a huge amount of network capacity. To provide adequate video images, most video cameras transmit 20 to 30 images per second. Each image can require 2 to 3 megabits of data, meaning 40 to 90 megabits of data must be transmitted per second. Most video teleconferencing uses data compression to reduce the amount of data transmitted. One simple technique is to transmit only what changes between images. Parts of the image that are the same from one image to the next (e.g., the background) remain unchanged and seldom need to be retransmitted. The amount of network capacity can be significantly reduced by using these and other more complex techniques, or by simply reducing the quality of the video image by

Figure 2-3 A video teleconferencing room at Hewlett-Packard.

not transmitting as frequently. Surprisingly, the most common complaint is not the quality of the video image, but the quality of the voice transmissions. Special care needs to be taken in the design and placement of microphones and speakers to ensure quality sound and minimal feedback.

Like e-mail, most video teleconferencing systems were originally developed by vendors using different formats so that many products were incompatible. The best solution was to ensure that all hardware and software used within your organization was supplied by the same vendor, and to hope that any other organizations with whom you wanted to communicate used the same equipment.

Two video teleconferencing standards developed by CCITT have the promise to reduce many incompatibilities, once they are widely used by vendors. H.261 defines the video image formats, data compression techniques, and transmission rates. H.243 defines communication processes, and provides support for multipoint teleconferencing (where more than two meeting rooms are involved in the same video conference).

One of the fastest growing forms of video teleconferencing is *desktop video conferencing*. Small cameras installed on top of each computer permit meetings to take place from individual offices (see Figure 2-4). Special hardware and software transmit the images across a network to their destination. Setups usually cost from less than $500 per computer for inexpensive systems to more than $4000 each for high quality systems. Some systems have integrated GSS with desktop video conferencing, allowing participants to communicate verbally, and by using the GSS, to attend the same "meeting" while they are sitting at the computers in their offices.

Managing in a Groupware World

Groupware dramatically changes the way people interact. Communication is simpler and faster. Anyone can communicate directly with anyone else, providing that the rules of social behavior permit. Social norms are one of the greatest limiting factors

Figure 2-4 Desktop video conferencing.

in the widespread use of groupware technologies, because the technology changes faster than the people who use it. Changing the way people work takes time.

Improved communication can provide very big paybacks in time and cost savings and increased productivity, especially when you consider that the primary task of most office workers (e.g., consultants, accountants, managers) is the processing and communication of information. A study of 65 Notes users conducted by International Data Corp. found an average three-year return on investment of 179 percent.

Nonetheless, groupware's ability to greatly improve communication can also create problems. Hewlett-Packard's 97,000 employees exchange about 20 million electronic mail messages each month—an average of about 10 messages per person per business day. At Sun Microsystems, the average is 120 messages per person per day. Managing in this glut of information can be difficult. Identifying priorities and not being distracted by less important issues are key to success; otherwise, you can drown in an endless sea of communication.

THE INFORMATION SUPERHIGHWAY

The *information superhighway* or the *Internet* is one of the most important developments in the history of information systems. It is also one of the most overhyped topics in today's business world. In 1994 and 1995, the number of users on the Internet grew by an average of 15 percent per *month*, or more than 400 percent per year. The number of companies with Internet connections grew from about 3000 in 1992 to more than 40,000 by mid-1995. This burgeoning growth also means huge changes.

Strictly speaking, the Internet is not one network, but thousands of networks linked together. It was started by the U.S. Department of Defense in the 1969 as a network of four computers called ARPANET. Its goal was to link a set of computers operated by several universities doing military research. The original network grew as more computers and more computer *networks* were linked to it. By 1974, there were 62 computers attached. In 1983, the Internet split into two parts, one dedicated solely to military installations (called Milnet) and one dedicated to university research centers (called the Internet). In 1988 and 1991, the National Science Foundation built several additional high speed sections of the Internet to connect major research centers.

Originally, commercial traffic was forbidden on the Internet, because the key portions of the network were funded by the U.S. government, and the only users were universities and research institutes. Since the late 1980s, many additional networks have been added to the original Internet. Many new users are businesses, and commercial online services offering connections to anyone willing to pay. The growth in the commercial portion of the Internet has been so rapid that in 1994, the government stopped funding its few remaining circuits. The Internet is now open to commercial traffic.

This increased commercialism and the rapidly increasing number of business users (or at least non-university users) has caused tensions among the old guard in the university/research community, and the "newbies" now joining the net. The cultures and norms of behavior between the two groups are quite different, resulting in many heated discussions. The best advice for new users is to follow the rules of net etiquette (see the focus box later in this chapter).

Because it is a collection of networks, the Internet has no central administration. Each network has it own administrative structure, and most networks have their own *acceptable use policies* that define what behavior is permitted. The Internet was intentionally designed to be very decentralized, and very amenable to new ideas because many of its creators and initial users openly distrusted any central authority. However, this decentralization has led to anarchy in many ways. If you can imagine an interstate highway without speed limits, lane markings, and clearly marked on- and off-ramps, you can visualize the unmanaged nature of the Internet.

Internet provides four basic functions to its users: e-mail, remote login, discussion groups, and information resources. One type of information resource that is growing even faster than Internet itself is the World Wide Web.

E-mail on the Internet

Anyone with access to the Internet can send e-mail to anyone else on the Internet. Internet e-mail addresses have two parts, the individual user's account address and the address of the computer. The computer's address in turn has two parts, the computer name and its domain. The general format is therefore: *user@computer.domain*. Note that the "at" symbol (@) separates the user's account from the computer address, and that a period separates the name of the computer from its domain. Some computer names also have several parts separated by periods, so some addresses may have the format: *user@computer.computer.computer.domain*.

Internet addresses are strictly regulated; otherwise, someone could add a computer to the Internet that had the same address as another computer. Each domain has an addressing board that assigns addresses for its domain. These boards generally do not make value judgments about names; they just ensure there are no duplicates. In one case, a company offering test-preparation courses (e.g., for the SAT, GMAT, MCAT) registered two computer addresses: one was its own name, and the other was the name of its biggest competitor. By doing so, it hoped to prevent its competitor from gaining access to the Internet, and hoped to gain access to customers who thought they were sending e-mail to its competitor. When the competitor discovered this (by attempting to register its address with the board), it sued and a judge ruled that no company could use the name of a competitor as its Internet address.

Obviously, you must know a person's address before you can send an e-mail message. Some e-mail addresses are well known. For example, the e-mail address of the President of the United States is *president@whitehouse.gov* (of course, the President doesn't actually read his e-mail; staff members do). In other cases, finding the e-mail address of someone on the Internet can be difficult because there is no central "phone book."

Most universities and some companies post e-mail directories of their users on their computers in a publicly accessible form (e.g., X.500) that can be accessed via Internet's gopher services (gopher is discussed later in this chapter). There is also an Internet

Technical Focus: Address Domain Names

Since the Internet began in the United States, the American address board was the first to assign domain names to indicate types of organization. Some common U.S. domain names are:

EDU	for an educational institution, usually a university
COM	for a commercial business
GOV	for a government department or agency
MIL	for a military unit
ORG	for a non-profit organization
NET	for an organization with ties to Internet administrative bodies

As networks in other countries were connected to the Internet, they were assigned their own domain names. Some international domain names are:

CA	for Canada
AU	for Australia
UK	for the United Kingdom
DE	for Germany
FR	for France

Many international networks structure their addresses in much the same way as the U.S. does. For example, the UK uses AC to indicate academic institutions and CO to indicate commercial organizations (so an address such as *smith@xyz.ac.uk* would indicate someone at a British university).

directory system sponsored by the National Science Foundation that can be reached using telnet. The use of telnet to find e-mail addresses is discussed in a technical focus box. Some, but not all, computers also can provide addresses using the *whois* command (see the help system on your computer if you wish to see how this command works).

Remote Login

Internet enables users on one computer to login into other computers on the Internet (see Figure 2-5). The command to do this is called *telnet*. Once telnet makes the connection, you can login into the computer as you would if you dialed in with a modem. You must know the account name and password of an authorized user. Telnet

Management Focus: Jokes and Threats Ignite Debate on Anonymity

The use of identity-disguising techniques, such as electronic messages sent anonymously or under a pseudonym, is on the rise on the Internet. There are several anonymous "remailing" sites that accept incoming mail messages, strip off the sender's address, and mail them to their final destination. These remailers have been used to send threats and jokes, and even to support computer crime.

The White House computer network has received threats against the President both under pseudonyms and anonymously. Anonymously sent electronic "mail bombs" temporarily disabled the Pipeline, a popular Internet service in New York City.

An anonymous news release carried a startling announcement that Microsoft had agreed to acquire the Roman Catholic Church in exchange for "an unspecified number of shares of Microsoft common stock." The release, distributed in the guise of an Associated Press news article to thousands of computers around the world, was a prank, its anonymous mastermind untraceable.

A form of electronic money called "digital cash" could become the basic currency for new forms of online shopping and commerce. But it could also lead to virtually untraceable financial transactions that law-enforcement officials fear could usher in entirely new forms of racketeering, money laundering, and other crimes of anonymity.

As a result, the growing use of unsigned messages over computer networks is creating a debate about how best to prevent abuses without stifling the right to speak freely and even anonymously. Complicating matters of government oversight is the fact that the Internet now reaches into 159 countries, and the majority of its users are not subject to any one country's law.

Source: New York Times, December 31, 1994.

can be faster or slower than a modem depending upon the amount of traffic on the Internet. Modems are discussed in Chapter 5. In any event, telnet enables you to connect to a remote computer without incurring long distance telephone charges.

Telnet can be very useful. We authors have used telnet to read and send e-mail extensively when traveling and when on sabbatical in other countries. However, telnet also poses a great security threat, because it means that anyone on Internet can attempt to login to your personal account and use it as they wish. One commonly used security precaution is to prohibit remote logins via telnet unless a user specifically asks for his or her account to be authorized for it. Chapter 13 discusses network security.

Discussion Groups

Discussion groups are Internet users who have joined together to discuss some topic. Discussion groups are formed around just about every topic imaginable, including

Technical Focus: Finding E-mail Addresses Using Telnet

The easiest way to find e-mail addresses is to telephone the person you want to reach and ask them directly. If you don't want to or can't do this, there are two directory services that may prove useful. Both are partially funded by the National Science Foundation and permit anyone to login via telnet.

The first is *ds.internic.net*. The format of the telnet command differs slightly from computer to computer, but the most common way to do this is to type the following at the command prompt: *telnet ds.internic.net*. When connected, this computer will ask you to login. Specify *x500* as the account name; there is no password. The way you perform the search has changed several times since the service was first offered (the software keeps being improved), so we will not describe the details, except for two hints: 1) avoid upper case characters; and 2) format the name as last name, first name. To disconnect, type *quit*.

The second service permits you to use the whois command to locate account names. To connect, type the following at the command prompt: *telnet rs.internic.net*. You do not need to enter an account name or password. After you are connected, type *whois last name, first name*.

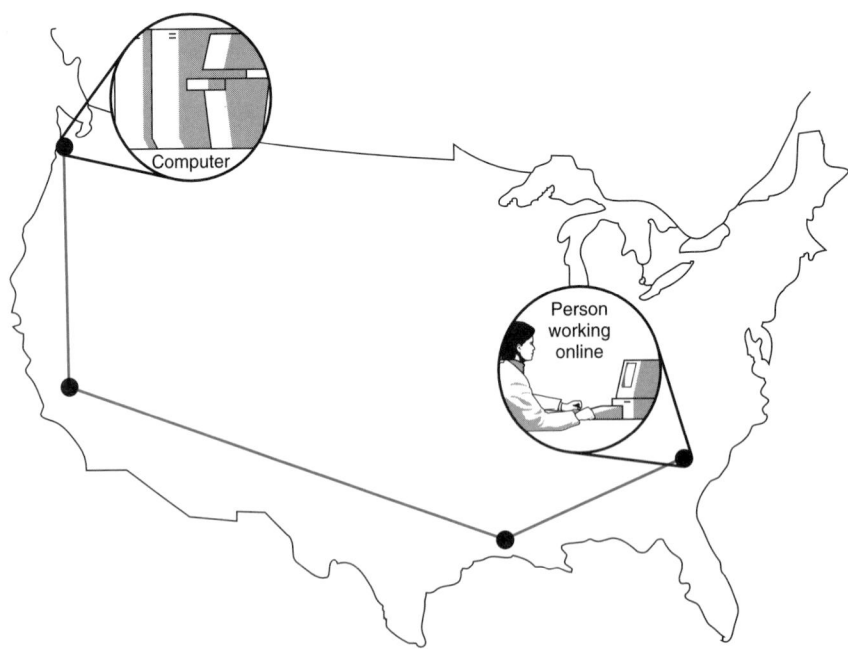

Figure 2-5   Using Telnet to login.

Management Focus: Popular Usenet Newsgroups

The format of newsgroup names is somewhat similar to the format of Internet addresses. There is an overall category, which in turn is divided into more specific topics. The general format for a newsgroup name is: *category.topic.topic.*

The top ten usenet newsgroups in 1994 were:

- news.announce.newusers
- news.answers
- rec.humor.funny
- alt.sex
- rec.humor
- misc.for.sale
- misc.jobs.offered
- comp.unix.questions
- alt.sex.stories
- alt.binaries.pictures.erotica

cooking, skydiving, politics, education, and British comedy. Two are commonly used for business: usenet newsgroups, and listservs.

Usenet Newsgroups   *Usenet newsgroups* are the most formally organized of the discussion groups. Establishing a new one requires a vote of all interested people on Internet. If enough people express interest, the new topic is established.

The newsgroups are just a series of discussions about each topic. The usenet newsgroups are a set of huge bulletin boards on which anyone who wishes can read and post messages. The usenet "newsfeed" of the discussions within each of these groups is available to all computers on the Internet (about 50 megabytes of new messages each *day*). Some network managers choose not to provide access to all topics. For example, some universities do not provide access to the more sexually explicit newsgroups.

The exact commands to gain access to these newsgroups varies from computer to computer. The general process is to subscribe to a specific topic or set of topics. Once you have subscribed, each time you access the newsgroups, you are informed of any new messages added to the topics. You can then read these messages and respond to them by adding your own message.

Listservs   A listserver (or *listserv*) group is similar in concept to the usenet newsgroups, but are generally less formal. Anyone with the right software can establish a listserv, which is simply a mailing list. One part, the *listserv processor,* processes com-

Management Focus: Netiquette

Netiquette is slang for net etiquette. Netiquette covers the rules or generally accepted code of behavior on the Internet. Some netiquette pointers:

- When you first join the net, listen and learn before contributing.
- Read the Frequently Asked Questions (FAQ) information.
- Always double check the address of your message. Even experts sometimes send private messages to public mailing lists by pressing the wrong key.
- Keep your messages brief.
- Don't make private messages public without permission.
- Don't send test messages.
- Don't include complete copies of other messages in your message if the recipients of the message have already seen them; small excerpts of other messages are fine.
- Don't waste others' time by sending "me too" or "I agree" messages.
- In general, spelling doesn't count.
- Don't send unsolicited advertisements. Brief announcements and instructions for interested people to request more information are acceptable.
- Don't flame.
- Don't type in ALL CAPITALS unless you want to SHOUT.
- Always include your name and address in messages; some systems delete them.
- Don't send messages where they don't belong (e.g., don't discuss the Brady Bunch in a Star Trek discussion group).
- Remember that the libel laws apply to the Internet.
- Copyright laws also apply. Don't send copyrighted material over the Internet without written permission from the copyright owner.
- You can use symbols to indicate the feelings you would normally communicate with your vocal tone. For example, to indicate you're joking, you could type :)
- Don't believe everything you read. Not everyone knows what they are talking about, and people can put on fake personas (some celebrities do send messages, but most messages from famous people are fake).

mands such as requests to subscribe, unsubscribe, or to provide more information about the listserv. The second part is the *listserv mailer*. Any message sent to the listserv mailer is re-sent to everyone on the mailing list. To use a listserv, you need to know the addresses of both the processor and the mailer.

To subscribe to a listserv, you send an e-mail message to the listserv *processor*, which adds your name to the list (see the technical focus box for the message format). It is important that you send this message to the processor, not the mailer, otherwise your

There are many different commands that can be sent to the listserv processor to perform a variety of functions. These commands are included as lines of text in the e-mail message sent to the processor. Each command must be placed on a separate line. Some useful commands include:

- SUBSCRIBE mailer-name your-name
  Subscribes you to a mailing list (e.g., *subscribe maps-l robin jones*).
- UNSUBSCRIBE mailer-name your-name
  Unsubscribes you from the mailing list (e.g., *unsubscribe maps-l robin jones*).
- HELP
  Requests the listserv to e-mail you a list of its commands.
- LIST
  Requests the listserv to e-mail you a list of all listserv groups that are available on this listserv processor.
- LIST DETAILED
  Requests the listserv to e-mail you a detailed description of all listserv groups that are available on this listserv processor.
- LIST GLOBAL
  Requests e-mail list of all listserv groups known to this listserv processor (both locally and anywhere on the Internet).

subscription message will be sent to everyone on the mailing list, and you may feel embarrassed.

For example, you can join the listserv on cruising the Internet. The processor address is *listerv@unlvm.bitnet,* and the mailer address is *cruise-l@unlvm.bitnet.* To subscribe, you send an e-mail message to *listerv@unlvm.bitnet* containing the text: *subscribe cruise-l your name.* To send a message to everyone on this listserv, you would e-mail your message to *cruise-l@unlvm.bitnet.* Listservs generally are more focused than the usenet news groups and have fewer members. They are harder to find than the usenet newsgroups because literally anyone can create one. There is no centrally managed list of listservs; one listserv tries to keep up with new listservs. To get a list of listservs, send an e-mail message to *listserv@bitnic.educom.edu* with the message *list global.*

Information Resources

One of the biggest uses of Internet is to find information. There is so much free information available on the Internet that there is something for just about everyone. The problem is finding it. In this section, we discuss four major ways of finding and

Once you have logged into an FTP site, you must use a series of commands to send and receive files. Most FTP sites have files organized in a series of directories, similar to the directories on DOS microcomputers. Each directory can have a set of files, and additional directories (so you can have a hierarchy or tree of directories). Before you can get or send files, you must first select the right directory. Some useful commands include:

HELP	Display a list of commands.
DIR	Display a list of files in the current directory.
CD name	Change the directory to the directory called "name."
CDUP	Change directory to the one above the current directory.
GET name	Get the file called "name"; that is, transfer the file from the FTP site to your computer.
PUT name	Put the file called "name"; that is, transfer the file from your computer to the FTP site.
ASCII	Files at FTP sites can be either text files or binary files (e.g., programs, compressed files). The ASCII command specifies that the files will be text files.
BIN	The BIN command specifies the files will be binary files. If you are getting or putting a binary file, you *must* enter the BIN command *before* you enter the GET or PUT command. If you forget, FTP will transfer the file, but it will be unreadable.
QUIT	Logoff of the FTP site (you can also use BYE or EXIT).

getting information: FTP, archie, gopher, and veronica. Of all of these, gopher is probably the most useful. One other major information resource that is growing faster than any other is the World Wide Web. It is discussed in the next section.

File Transfer Protocol (FTP)   *File Transfer Protocol* (FTP) enables you to send and receive files over the Internet. Almost anyone can establish an FTP site, which permits anyone on Internet to login and send and receive files. There are two types of FTP sites: closed and anonymous. A closed site requires users to have permission before they can connect and gain access to the files. Access is granted by providing an account name with a secret password.

The most common type is an *anonymous FTP* site, which permits any Internet user to login using the account name of *anonymous*. The password is anything you want to type, but most anonymous FTP sites request that you type your Internet account name (e.g., smith@allstate.edu) as the password. This allows them to track who is accessing

Technical Focus: Public Access Archie Sites

If your computer does not have archie, you can telnet to any of the following public access archie sites to search for files:

archie.internic.net	(United States)
archie.ans.net	(United States.)
archie.rutgers.edu	(United States)
archie.au	(Australia)
archie.doc.ic.ac.uk	(United Kingdom)

their files. The process for getting and sending files via FTP is shown in the technical focus box.

Many files available via FTP are programs that do various things (e.g., data compression, file utilities). Each program is written for a specific type of computer and won't work on any other (e.g., DOS, Macintosh, UNIX). Many files are compressed to reduce the amount of disk space they require. Since there are many types of data compression programs, it is possible that a file you want has been compressed by a program you lack, so you won't be able to use the file even if you do receive it. That's one of the ''advantages'' of the decentralized, no-rules structure of the Internet.

Archie   The problem with FTP is finding the files you want. *Archie* is a tool that allows you to search virtually all the public available anonymous FTP sites worldwide for specific files of interest. Most (but not all) computers on the Internet have archie, but there are many different types of archie programs. Some versions of archie are menu driven. You simply select the options you want from the menu and type the key word on which to begin a search. Other versions of archie are command driven and require you to use commands to search for files. The command-driven versions of archie are so different that our only suggestion is to use the help command or ask your network manager for help.

Gopher   *Gopher* is a menu-based tool that allows you to search for publicly available information posted on the Internet. Originally developed at the University of Minnesota, it was called gopher because the university's mascot is a gopher and because the tool ''goes for'' things.

Most (but not all) computers on the Internet provide a gopher. Because each is menu-driven, different sites put different information on their gophers. You can use the menus on your gopher to search for information. The type of information available is as big as anyone's imagination: e-mail address directories, weather reports, foreign exchange information, books, and games are some of the more general examples.

Each gopher will only let you search the information it knows. Some gophers are

---

Technical Focus: Public Access Gopher Sites

If your computer does not have gopher, you can telnet to any of the following public access gopher sites:

gopher-gw.micro.umn.edu	(University of Minnesota; login as *gopher*)
consultant.micro.umn.edu	(University of Minnesota; login as *gopher*)
gopher.uiuc.edu	(login as *gopher*)
uxl.cso.uiuc.edu	(login as *gopher*)
panda.uiowa.edu	(login as *panda*)
info.anu.edu.au	(login as *info*)

---

better because they are updated with new information daily. Many contain links to other gophers so you can use one gopher to connect to another and then search using the information it has. The "mother of all gophers" is the one at the University of Minnesota, so it is a good site to use to search for information. Other good gophers include those run by NYSERnet (nysernet.org), the Library of Congress (marvel.loc.gov), Washington and Lee University in Virginia (liberty.uc.wlu.edu), and the University of Michigan (una.hh.lib.umich.edu).

Veronica   Finding information can still be difficult because not all gophers may know about the information you are seeking, and because it takes time to work through the gopher menus. *Veronica* is an alternative; veronica is to gopher what archie is to FTP. Veronica enables you to search all publicly available gopher sites by specifying key words (including *and* and *or* to form complex searches) to find information on a specific topic. Veronica will search all the gophers it knows to look for a menu item containing those key words. A scaled down version, called *Jughead* is also available on some computers. Jughead only searches the top levels of menus in the gophers it knows, instead of all the levels.

Many gophers also provide veronica. If your gopher does not, telnet to the gopher sites listed in the focus box.

World Wide Web

One of the fastest growing information resources is *World Wide Web*. The Web is to the Internet what Windows is to DOS. Most of the information on Internet is text-based; useful, but not very pretty. The Web provides a graphical user interface and enables the display of rich graphical images, pictures, full motion video, and sound clips (provided you have a sound board and speakers in your computer). As Figure 2-6 shows, the Web is the most common way for businesses to establish a presence on the Internet.

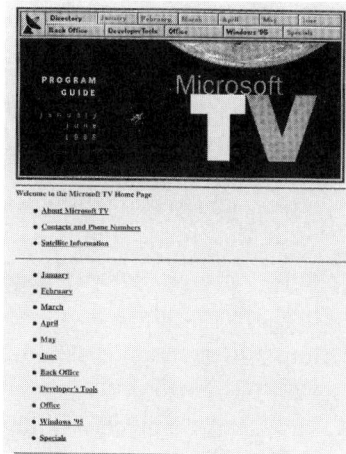
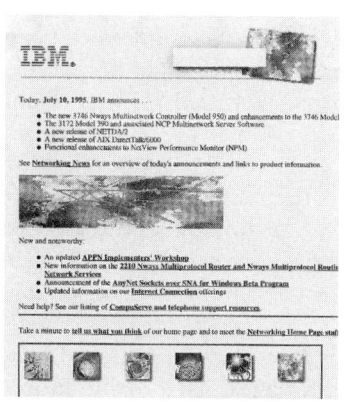
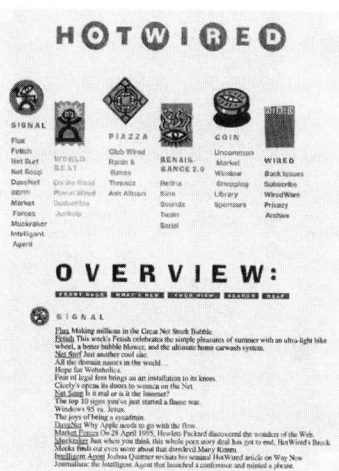

Figure 2-6 Some typical Web sites.

The Web was first developed by Tim Berners-Lee at the European Laboratory for Particle Physics (CERN) in Geneva in 1990. His original idea was to develop a database of information on physics research, but he found it difficult to fit the information into a traditional database. Instead, he decided to use a *hypertext* network of information. With hypertext, any document can contain a link to another document.

The Web has two major components, a Web *browser* and a Web *server*. A browser is a software package that enables a user to access a Web server. There are many Web browsers available, including Mosaic, Netscape, Cello, and WinWeb. Some of these are available commercially through computer stores; others are available free via FTP on the Internet.

To use a browser to access a Web server, you must enter the server's addresses or

Technical Focus: Useful Web Addresses

Many Web browsers provide pointers to the more well-known and useful pages on the Web, so check your browser for more interesting pages. Some other useful Web addresses are:

http://tcbworks.mgmt.uga.edu:8080/~adennis/home.htm	Updates to this book.
http://www.cern.ch	CERN's home page.
http://www.yahoo.com	Yahoo, a web directory.
http://www.cs.colorado.edu/home/mcbryan/wwww.html	A web crawler.
http://www.biotech.washington.edu/webcrawler/webquery.html	A web crawler.

URL (Universal Resource Locator). All Web addresses begin with seven characters: *http://*. A Web server stores information in a series of text files called *pages*. These text files or pages use a structured language called *HTML* (Hypertext Markup Language) to store their information. HTML enables the author of a page to define different typestyles and sizes for the text, titles, and headings, and a variety of other formatting information. HTML also permits the author to define links to other pages that may be stored on the same Web server, or on any Web server anywhere on the Internet. Most browsers show these links by highlighting text in a different color, usually blue. To use a link to go to a new page, you simply click on the text, and the browser takes you to the new page.

The idea behind these links is that you can access an initial page that provides a menu of topics with links to other pages that provide more detail or more in-depth menus. Because you can link to any Web server on the Internet, you can decentralize the storage of information. For example, while the Web at CERN may provide an overall *home page* (i.e., main starting point) about particle physics, research teams at other centers and universities elsewhere may maintain pages that provide more detailed information about different sub-areas of particle physics.

HTML is fairly easy to learn, so you could develop your own Web page. Several Web servers provide pages that have good tutorials on HTML (see the Web focus box). The easiest way to develop a page is to start with a page developed by someone else. Since most browsers allow you to save the HTML file of any page you access, you only have to modify what they have done, rather than starting from scratch.

The Web also provides support for FTP and gopher. You can use a Web browser to get files and information via FTP and gopher (simply provide the gopher's Internet address and start the URL with gopher:// rather than http://). We believe that the Web will gradually replace the separate programs used today (i.e., FTP, gopher, archie,

Management Focus: The Good, the Bad, and the Ugly of the Web

The Good

- It is easy to create pages and publish information.
- It is relatively inexpensive to start and maintain a page.
- Navigating from page to page is simple.
- There is a browser for almost every type of computer and operating system.

The Bad

- Because of immature technology, some browser and server software have bugs.
- Graphics take a long, long time to transfer over the Internet, particularly when there is a lot of traffic.
- Addresses change regularly, so you never really know what is out there.
- Largely untested software and unknown network capacity requirements so the impact on individual Web servers and the Internet as a whole is unknown.
- Weak or non-existent server security means anyone can visit your site.
- Weak or non-existent browser security permits some Web servers to track and build mailing lists from user ids of everyone who visits.

The Ugly

- Not all browsers display HTML the same way, so what looks good with one browser may not with another.
- Not all browsers support all types of graphic files, so some graphics may not display.
- Graphics require a large amount of network capacity, so some users cannot view any graphics.

Source: "Internet Boomtown," *Datamation,* January 15, 1995.

and veronica) because it is so much simpler to use and because it makes more sense to have one program that does everything.

As with other information resources on the Internet, the key problem with the Web is finding the information you need. There is no central directory of all the pages because almost anyone can develop and post a page on a Web server. There are three ways to discover interesting and useful Web pages. First, someone could tell you about a page, or you could read an advertisement listing the Web address. Second, you could find a link to the page from another page, either from one on a related topic or from one of the directories that several organizations maintain. Third, you could use a *web crawler,* which searches through all the Web servers it knows to find information about a particular topic.

ACCESSING AND USING THE INTERNET

Most universities and many companies have access to the Internet from their internal networks. Accessing the Internet is simple, because there is already a network connection, but you will need the basic tools that allow you to access the Internet (e.g., telnet, gopher). In some cases, special network software may be needed in order for some tools (particularly Web browsers) to operate over your network.

If your organization does not have Internet access, you may need to use a commercial service. Many new companies (called *access providers*) now offer connections to the Internet. You must have a modem that will enable your computer to telephone the computer operated by your access provider (modems are discussed in Chapter 5). You also must have some special communications software which usually is supplied by the access provider. Some access providers charge a flat monthly fee for unlimited access (much like the telephone company), while others charge per hour of use (much like a long distance telephone call). Your usage patterns will help you determine which is best.

In addition to Internet access providers, there are several commercial *online services* that provide a variety of information resources and discussion groups in addition to Internet access. Most charge a fixed monthly fee, plus a certain amount per hour of use.

In 1995, the most popular online services were America Online (about a 35 percent market share), CompuServe (about a 30 percent market share), and Prodigy (about a 25 percent market share). All other online services together account for about 10 percent of the market. Of these services, CompuServe is often rated as having the best business-related information with the greatest range and depth of information on stocks and financial data, computer and software support, and travel. America Online is often rated as the easiest to use and being the best suited to personal use. Prodigy has excellent health information, sports information, and online shopping. In late 1995, amid much controversy, Microsoft started its own online service, Microsoft Network, which will compete vigorously with the big three services.

The online services change almost monthly, adding new services, providing better interfaces, and revising cost structures. New services constantly arrive, offering new ideas and healthy competition. Any detailed discussion of these services included in this book would be obsolete by the time you read it. The best advice is to study the services before you choose one, and to read articles in *PC Magazine, PC Computing,* and *Byte.*

Finding Information

Finding information on the Internet is an art, not a science. One of the best places to start is by finding a good gopher server or Web directory. If you can find a good server that is regularly updated with the type of material in which you are interested, you can start your search there.

Many of the good gopher or Web sites get busy very quickly during prime searching hours, but it is possible to use sites in other time zones. For example, American servers are often very busy during the day and early evening hours, but are quite available in the middle of the night when most potential users are asleep. The same is true of sites in Europe, Asia, and Australia—except that they are asleep during the hours when we are awake and vice versa. If the American servers are busy, use one on another continent.

Formatting keyword searches for archie, veronica, jughead, and Web crawlers is also an art. Remember that any letter you type must be matched exactly. If you are looking for cooking information and search on ''cooking,'' you will miss anything that has the word ''cookbook.'' The best idea is to use the shortest possible form of the key word. Some searches are case-sensitive (i.e., an *A* is different from an *a*), so learn the commands to ignore upper and lower cases. Likewise, some versions of tools enable you to request the list of information in chronological order, so you can find the most recent information first. Most tools have help information or online manuals. Read them to learn the search commands before—not after—you search.

Many versions of gopher and Web browsers let you use ''bookmarks'' to mark interesting sites, making it easy for you to return to a specific menu item or page. Bookmarks help you to personalize your search tools to make it easier to find pertinent information.

Sometimes the best Internet resource is people. Many sites post e-mail addresses of people whom you can contact for assistance in finding information. In other cases, there are listservs or usenet newsgroups where you can post questions asking for help. But don't e-mail just anyone for answers to your questions, unless you know they are there to help.

Doing Business on the Internet

Almost 90 percent of companies with sales over $350 million have access to the Internet. Many are actively using it to do business. Making money by doing business on the Internet is still a risky proposition (see the next focus box). While some businesses are making a profit, others have quickly failed. This is also true for businesses in the ''real'' world; only about 20 percent of new businesses are still operating five years later.

Many companies are very interested in getting on the Internet, but lack the expertise to do so; therefore, one of the most profitable niches today is providing consulting, training, and services for how to do business via the Internet, rather than actually doing it. This may change as more people gain expertise and as more potential customers become familiar with using the Internet.

For this reason, much business use of the Internet is not for making money per se, rather it is to find information, improve communications, and provide information—most of the same reasons that individuals use the Internet. Uses of the Internet in business can be grouped into three broad categories: using Internet tools for business purposes, providing information, and making business transactions.

Using Internet Tools   Many of the Internet tools previously discussed can be applied to business use as well as personal use. The Internet is a convenient way to provide e-

Management Focus: The Internet? Bah!

The Internet is being oversold. Consider its key benefits.

Usenet newsgroups allow anyone to post messages. Every voice can be heard cheaply and easily. The resulting noise is like citizens band radio, complete with handles, harassment, and anonymous threats. When everyone shouts, few listen.

Consider electronic publishing. Ever try reading a book on disk? It's rather unpleasant. And you can't take a laptop to the beach.

Won't the Internet be useful in governing? Many Internet addicts clamor for government reports. But when documents were posted during an election campaign in New York, fewer than 30 people accessed them.

Then there's business on the Internet. Instant catalog shopping. So how come my local mall does more business in an afternoon than the Internet does in a month? The Internet is missing the key ingredient of capitalism: salespeople.

What the Internet hucksters won't tell you is that the Internet is an ocean of unedited data, without any validation. I tried to find the date of the Battle of Trafalgar by searching the Web. Hundreds of pages turned up. One was a story written by an eighth grader, another was a computer game that didn't work, and a third was an image of the London monument. On the Internet, you don't know what to ignore and what is worth reading.

Source: Newsweek, February 27, 1995.

mail between geographically separated company offices. Some groupware tools are also moving onto the Internet. A low-cost desktop video conferencing tool called CU-See-Me enables users to hold video conferences with up to eight people. While the video images are not of the highest quality, it is far cheaper than traditional video conferencing services. Even telephone services (of similarly low quality) are available virtually free of charge over the Internet, bypassing the traditional long distance telephone companies.

The tools for accessing information resources can be used to gain business intelligence. Stock reports, market information, demographic data, reports on the activities of other companies, information on market niches, and many other useful pieces of competitive information are available online, often before they are widely available in other media.

The Internet can also be used to make business contacts. The presence of company employees in usenet discussion groups and on listservs that cover issues relevant to the company's business can be used to demonstrate the company's expertise in the subject area. It is also a useful way to identify business contacts, either business partners, consultants, or potential clients.

Providing Information Many companies use Internet to attract and keep customers. Many companies have pages on the Web that describe their products. For example, a network of car dealers has posted information about the latest models on the Web, complete with technical details and photographs. Customers can view these pages and obtain information without going to the dealer. One dealer estimates that he sells two or three cars per month (that he would not otherwise have sold), based on the Web page. The *Economist* estimates that it receives a dozen subscription requests via Internet each month. Neither has a great deal of impact on total profit, but certainly enough to justify the cost of the Web.

Other companies provide newsletters with information of latest products and tips on how to use them. IBM and Microsoft, for example, use the Web to provide information on the latest versions of their software, and on products that have been announced but not yet released. Hewlett-Packard provides technical support information on the Web. Links to these companies (and the car dealer network already described) above are provided by Yahoo (see the technical focus box earlier in the chapter).

One big problem is helping customers find your Web page. Your Web address can be published in product information brochures and regular newsletters for use by existing customers, but this does not help potential customers who don't know about your company. There are several commercial services that provide directories with links to companies doing business on the Web, similar to the way that the yellow pages in your telephone book provides telephone numbers for businesses. These services charge each company for providing a link to their page. They in turn advertise their directories widely, so that many potential customers can find them. Some of these directory services focus on specific types of products; for example, one service may list businesses offering professional services to other businesses, while another may provide a Web "mall" full of retail products.

Making Business Transactions   At present, only a few businesses actually make sales over the Internet. Due to the lack of security, most simply advertise their products and provide a telephone number to call to make a purchase. Information flowing over the Internet, such as credit card numbers, can be copied by any computer through which the message flows, making it easy to "steal" information.

Another problem is verifying the transaction. Suppose your broker receives an e-mail message from your account asking for the purchase of 100 shares. The broker has no way of guaranteeing that the message actually came from your account (there are ways to mask a true address) and that you actually sent it (a hacker could have stolen your password).

Until security is improved, few businesses will use the Internet to conduct business transactions. Several companies are now developing ways to improve security (which is discussed in detail in Chapter 13). Once security has been improved, the Internet may transform the way we do business. It may replace traditional catalog selling. It may provide another advertising medium for retailers and consumer products companies. It may replace the telephone for credit card approvals. It may revolutionize check clearing and provide an easy way for electronic banking and bill payment. Companies may use the Internet for electronic funds transfer or electronic data interchange to automate ordering at the wholesale level.

The catch, of course, is improving security. It may take some time before security on the information superhighway is adequate. Until then, many businesses and consumers may hesitate to use it for business.

Management Focus: Internet Losses—Where's the Money?

Business big and small flock to the Internet as if there were a gold rush, and many are finding that they have something in common with the '49ers of old. They are pioneers hoping to strike it rich on a lucky hunch, but often are left mining for profits in barren places.

With 5 percent of American households subscribing to America Online, Prodigy, CompuServe or another private online service, and an estimated 20 million people using Internet to visit computers around the world, corporate America is rushing into cyberspace.

Retailers are creating ''electronic storefronts'' to sell everything imaginable. For example, Roderick Braithwaite of Victoria, British Columbia built an electronic store-front to sell backpacks. He put the catalog of a mail order backpack company on the Web, and posted the address widely. He sold only two backpacks.

Mark Radcliffe of Palo Alto, California had a similar experience. He placed a $30 abridged version of a popular multi-media law handbook for sale in an online book-store. About 1000 people looked at the book, but so far, he hasn't sold any.

On the other hand, Wes Kussmaul's venture was an online encyclopedia. Users began talking with each other and Delphi Internet Services Corp., a commercial online service based in Cambridge, was the result. Here, keeping subscribers interested in-volved giving users what they want.

There are two problems with using the Internet for commercial use. First, businesses must invent new business practices in an industry that is not yet really an industry. Second, business lack the tools that are standard in the broadcast and publishing industries, such as those to measure the size of the user base, to help choose the advertising medium, and syndicators who can deliver groups of news articles, opinion pieces, and cartoons.

In the early days of the gold rush, it wasn't the prospectors who got rich; it was the folks selling the steamship tickets, blue jeans, and pick axes. Likewise, the fastest way to make money off the Internet may be to sell products and services to those trying to strike it rich.

Source: The Boston Globe, November 22, 1994; and *Forbes,* January 30, 1995.

Summary

Electronic Mail   Electronic mail was one of the earliest groupware tools and is also the most heavily used tool today. With e-mail, users create and send messages to one user, several users, or all users on a distribution list. E-mail is faster and cheaper than regular mail, and can substitute for telephone conversations in some cases. Several standards have been developed to ensure compatibility between different software packages, including X.400/X.500, CMC, and MAPI.

Document-based Groupware   Notes was the first document-based groupware product. It is a document database designed to store and manage large collections of text and graphics to support ongoing discussions. Discussions can be organized into a hierarchical structure of sections, documents, and folders. Notes can also be used to automate certain document-based processes (called workflow automation).

Group Support Systems   Group Support Systems are software tools designed to improve group decision making in special purpose meeting rooms that provide networked computers and large screen video projection systems. These rooms are equipped with special-purpose GSS software that enables participants to communicate, propose ideas, analyze options, evaluate alternatives, and so on.

Video Teleconferencing   Video teleconferencing provides real-time transmission of video and audio signals to help people in different locations to have a meeting. In most cases, video teleconferencing is done in special purpose meeting rooms that have one or more cameras and several video display monitors to capture and display the video signals. The key benefits of video teleconferencing are the time and cost savings that can result. With desktop video conferencing—the fastest growing form—small cameras are installed on top of each user's computer so that participants can hold meetings from their offices. Some systems have integrated GSS with desktop video conferencing.

The Information Superhighway   The information superhighway or the Internet is one of the most important developments in the history of information systems. It is growing by an average of 15 percent per month. Strictly speaking, the Internet is not one network, but thousands of networks linked together. There is no overall central administration of the Internet which is its greatest strength and its greatest weakness. The Internet enables e-mail to be sent to any user on literally any of the seven continents. It also enables remote logins via telnet.

Discussion Groups   Discussion groups are Internet users who have joined together to discuss some topic. There are discussion groups on just about every topic imaginable, from cooking, skydiving, and politics, to education and British comedy. Usenet newsgroups are the most formally organized; they are a set of huge bulletin boards on which anyone on the Internet can read and post messages. A listserver (or listserv) is simply a mailing list. The listserv processor processes listserv commands such as requests to subscribe and unsubscribe, while the listserv mailer mails any message it receives to everyone on the mailing list.

Information Resources   One of the major uses of the Internet is to find information. There are five ways to find and get information: FTP, archie, gopher, veronica, and the Web. File Transfer Protocol (FTP) enables you to send and receive files over the Internet. An anonymous FTP site permits any Internet user to login using anonymous as the account name. Archie is a tool that allows you to search virtually all the publicly available anonymous FTP sites worldwide for specific files of interest. Gopher is a menu-based tool that enables you to search for publicly available information posted on the Internet. It is probably the most heavily used tool. Veronica is to gopher what archie is to FTP; it enables you to search all publicly available gopher sites by specifying key words.

World Wide Web   One of the fastest growing information resources is the World Wide Web. The Web is to the Internet what Windows is to DOS. The Web provides a graphical user interface and enables the display of rich graphical images, pictures, full motion video, and sound clips (provided you have a sound board and speakers in your computer). The Web is the most common way for businesses to establish a presence on the Internet. The Web has two major components, a Web browser and a Web server. A browser is a software package for accessing a Web server that stores files using HTML.

Accessing and Using the Internet   Most universities and many companies have access to the Internet from their internal networks. If your organization does not have access, you may need to use a commercial service, either an access provider or online information service. Finding information on the Internet is an art not a science. One of the best places to start is by finding a good gopher server or Web directory that is regularly updated with the type of material in which you are interested. Almost 90 percent of companies with sales over $350 million have access to the Internet. Many are actively using it to do business, although making money by doing business on the Internet is still risky. Uses of the Internet in business can be grouped into three broad categories: using Internet tools for business purposes, providing information, and making business transactions (although because of security concerns, very few companies make business transactions this way).

Key Terms

America Online	Home page	Prodigy
Anonymous FTP	Hypertext Markup	Snail mail
Archie	Language (HTML)	Telephone tag
Common Messaging Calls	H.261	Telnet
(CMC)	H.243	Universal Resource
CompuServe	Information Superhighway	Locator (URL)
Desktop video	Internet	Usenet newsgroups
teleconferencing	Internet access providers	Veronica
Discussion groups	Jughead	Video teleconferencing
Distribution list	Listserv	Web browser
E-mail	Messaging Application	Web crawler
File Transfer Protocol	Program Interface	Web server
(FTP)	(MAPI)	Workflow automation
Gopher	Netiquette	World Wide Web
Group support systems	Notes	X.400
Groupware	Online services	X.500

Selected References

1. Ayre, Rick and Robin Raskin. "The Changing Face of Online," *PC Magazine*, February 21, 1995, 108–175.
2. Braun, Eric. *The Internet Directory*. Greenwich, CT: Fawcett Columbine, 1994.
3. Churbuck, David, "Where's the Money?" *Forbes*, January 30, 1995, 100–108.
4. *Internet World*, published six times a year.
5. Jessup, Len and Joe Valacich. *Group Support Systems*, New York: Macmillian, 1993.
6. Kehoe, Brendan. *Zen and the Art of the Internet*, Englewood Cliffs, NJ: Prentice Hall, 1994. The text of the book is also available via FTP at emoryul.cc.emory.edu in the /computing/reference/networking/Internet directory.
7. Krol, Ed. *The Whole Internet*, O'Reily & Associates, 1994. Also available through the Web at http://nearnet.gnn.com/gnn/wic/index.html.
8. *NetGuide*, published six time a year
9. *The Internet Unleashed*, Indianapolis: Sams, 1994.
10. *Wired*, published monthly.

Questions/Problems

1. What is groupware?
2. Describe four types of groupware. What are the benefits and limitations of each?
3. How can you find an e-mail address?
4. What do the X.400 and X.500 standards do and why are they important?
5. What is CMC?
6. What is MAPI?
7. What is Notes and how can it be used to improve productivity?
8. How can group support systems improve productivity?
9. Describe two types of videoconferencing. Which do you think will be more common in five years? Why?
10. How does groupware change the way you manage in an organization?
11. What is the information superhighway? What can you use it to do?
12. What do the following tools enable you to do: telnet, FTP, gopher, archie, veronica, and jughead?
13. What are usenet newsgroups? How might they help you as a student?
14. What is a listserv and how could you use it to get information?
15. What is the worldwide web? How is it different from the other Internet tools?
16. Use the Internet to see what the weather is in Hilo, Hawaii; Nome, Alaska; New York City; and Miami. Which city would you prefer?
17. Use your Web browser to connect to the page for this textbook. What interesting information did you find?
18. Use your Web browser to connect to the page for this textbook. Do the Internet scavenger hunt.
19. What are the principal differences between the major online services? Which would you recommend for business use? for personal use?

20. How can you find information on the Internet?
21. How can the Internet be used for business?
22. Will the Internet become an essential business tool like the telephone or will it go the way of the dinosaurs? Discuss.

NEXT DAY AIR SERVICE CUMULATIVE CASE STUDY

See appendix at end of book

CHAPTER THREE

TELEPHONE COMMUNICATION HARDWARE

This chapter introduces the hardware components that comprise the telephone communication network that originally was developed for voice telephone calls. It is this network that is used for much of the wide area network data communication traffic, especially when the transmission speed is 28,800 bits per second or less. Virtually all dial-up calls (direct distance dial or DDD) that transmit data use this network. A "voice grade" leased line, such as one from a corporate headquarters to a remote sales branch, also uses this network. This chapter focuses on the hardware used in today's voice communications network including switches, PBXs, cellular telephones, and fax machines, and also discusses several newer telephone services. The voice communications network and the effects of the break up of AT&T, and several wide area networking services provided by AT&T and its competitors are discussed in Chapter 9.

Objectives

- Become familiar with the telephone,
- Become familiar with the telephone network, and some of its hardware devices such as echo suppressors, TASI equipment, and voice call multiplexing,
- Understand the need for switching and several types of switches,
- Understand private branch exchanges (PBX) and their applications,
- Become familiar with cellular technology (cellular telephones, pagers, and personal digital assistants) and their applications,
- Become familiar with fax machines,
- Become familiar with several special purpose devices (interactive voice response, automatic number identification, and voice mail) and their applications.

Chapter Outline

THE TELEPHONE

A telephone network establishes a voice communication path between any two telephones within the network. In order to accomplish this communication successfully, the network needs a device to convert the sound waves produced by the human voice at the sending end into electrical signals for the telephone. Then it must have another device to reconvert these electrical signals into sound waves so they can be heard by the person at the receiving telephone. All this must be accomplished in a way that allows the receiver of the call to hear the original voice sounds of the sender with a minimum of distortion.

Telephone instruments contain devices for converting the audible sound signals humans produce into electromagnetic signals that can be sent through the telephone. These *converters* permit the passage of signals from one medium to another. Although it is possible to have only one device for converting sounds to electromagnetic impulses

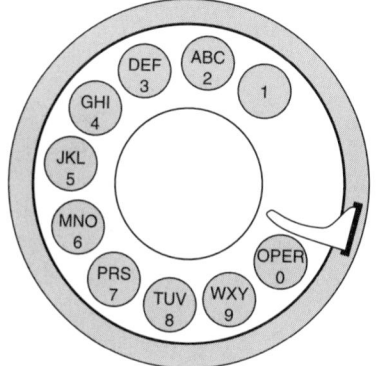 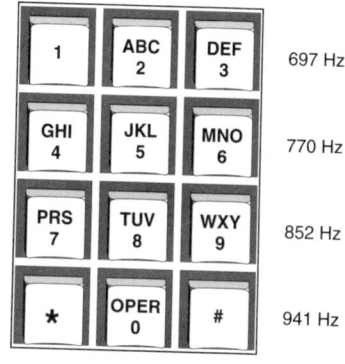

Figure 3-1 Rotary dial and Touch-Tone keypad on a telephone. The rotary dial telephone produces a specific number of electrical pulses for each digit dialed. The tone dialing on a keypad produces frequencies, which are in hertz or cycles per second; therefore, Hz = Hertz = Cycles per second.

and back again, telephones usually have two separate converters. The *microphone* converts mechanical vibrations in the air (the sound waves) into electrical signals for transmission in an electrical circuit. At the other end, the telephone *speaker* changes the electrical voice signals back into an audible sound by magnetically vibrating a diaphragm that is synchronized with the incoming electric voice signals.

There are two ways to dial a telephone. The left half of Figure 3-1 shows the older rotary dialing mechanism, and the right half shows the newer Touch-Tone. The rotary dial generates electrical pulses on the telephone line by opening and closing an electrical relay when the dial is turned and released. When you dial a 7, the telephone instrument generates seven electrical pulses, each approximately 1/20 of a second long. Rotary dial, *dial-pulsing* telephones are the dinosaur of the telephone industry.

The right half of Figure 3-1 shows the layout of a Touch-Tone telephone keypad, which is typical of the newer, more sophisticated technique called *dual tone multifrequency* (DTMF) Touch-Tone dialing. The keypad on a *tone-dialing* telephone has two sets of frequencies, as shown on the right and bottom borders of the figure. When you dial the number 7, the tone that is transmitted to the central office is a combination of 852 hertz and 1209 hertz.

VOICE COMMUNICATION NETWORK

The basic voice communication telephone network is not only the largest, but also one of the oldest of our twentieth-century data communication networks. This network includes the telephone in your home. In today's business communication cost structure, voice calls represent more than half of the amount spent for communications;

Management Focus: Five Famous Firsts of Telephone Communication

1. The first telephone directory, a single sheet listing of 50 names, was published in February 1878 in New Haven, Connecticut. There were no telephone numbers or addresses. You had to ring the operator with a hand crank and ask for the person or business by name.

2. The first telephone numbers and names appeared in the Lowell, Massachusetts telephone book in 1880 during a measles epidemic. The purpose was to help inexperienced operators make connections when they did not know all the subscribers.

3. The first yellow pages directory appeared in 1883 in Cheyenne, Wyoming. It was not a business directory, but merely the result of a printer running out of white paper.

4. The first yellow pages directory with business listings and advertisements was printed in Detroit, Michigan in 1906.

5. Herbert Hoover was the first President to have a telephone on his desk. Prior to 1929, the President had to use a telephone booth outside his office.

less than half the cost is spent on true data transfer. This network is the one that connects your telephone to the telephone company *end office* (also called *central office* or *exchange office*) where switching is performed.

Switching includes identifying and connecting independent transmission circuits to form a continuous path from your telephone to the telephone you are calling. The end office uses the telephone number you dialed as an ''address'' and searches out the other telephone so the two can be connected. Figure 3-2 shows the interconnection of telephones through the end office in our basic voice network. Note that the local loop on this figure is simply a set of two twisted pair wires (i.e., four wires) that

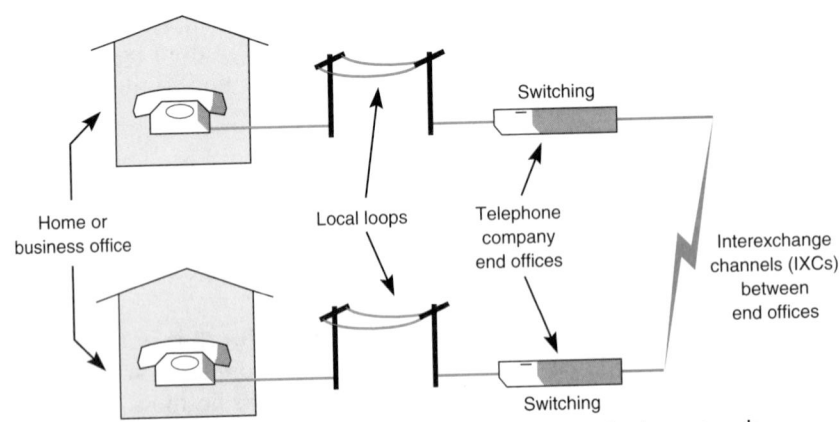

Figure 3-2   Telephone interconnection in the voice communication network.

go from your home to the telephone company end office where the electronic switching system equipment is located. In most cases, telephones only use one set of twisted pair wires. Thus it is easy to add a second telephone number to most homes or offices by using this second, spare set of twisted pair wires. Some businesses use this second pair to provide data transmission, although transmission of data over traditional twisted pair voice grade lines does have some limitations, as we shall discuss in Chapter 5.

Calls made within the same end office or interoffice trunks are known as *local calls* (see Figure 3-3). Calls that use the tandem trunks and the tandem office are known as *unit calls,* for which there may be an extra charge for each minute of time. The calls that use toll trunks are known as *long distance calls.*

The worldwide telephone network is so complicated that it would be difficult to present a single drawing showing its configuration. Department of Defense officials have indicated that the network in the United States is so integrated that it offers a unique emergency backup capability, for it would be almost impossible to destroy all communications in the United States. It should be noted that even though Figure 3-3 shows telephones at the end of the local loops, terminals or other data transmission equipment also might be attached to the dial-up telephone network.

Voice grade leased circuits are normal telephone circuits that have been taken out of

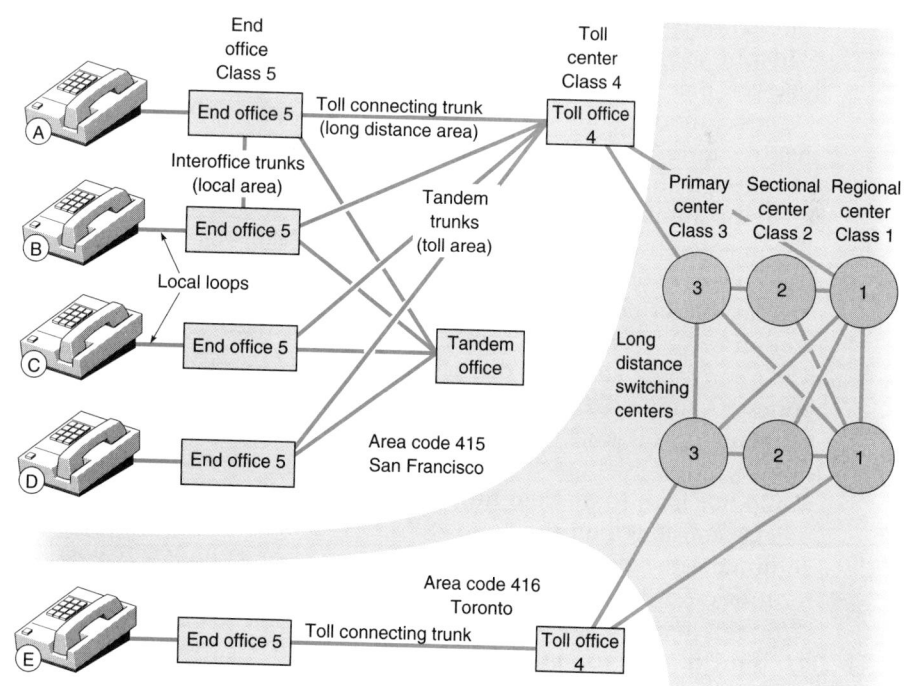

Figure 3-3   End office hierarchy. The end office (class 5), tandem office, and toll office (class 4) route calls throughout a city. Calls going outside a city use the class 3, 2, and 1 switching centers. Depending on the distance of the call and the traffic on the circuits, a call from Telephone A to Telephone E could be routed either by its most efficient route (5–4–3–3–4–5) or by its least efficient route (5–4–3–2–1–1–2–3–4–5).

dial-up telephone service by the common carrier (telephone company) and dedicated to one organization. These leased communication facilities sometimes are called *private circuits, private lines, leased circuits,* or *dedicated circuits.* The leasing organization makes them available for use on a 24-hour basis, seven days a week. It might be helpful to understand the distinction between a leased circuit and a dial-up circuit. If you have a leased circuit from New York to Atlanta, it is one unbroken circuit path between the two cities. This circuit is "wired around" any telephone switching equipment at the telephone company central offices; therefore, switching equipment cannot cause errors or distortion of messages. When not leased, the same dial-up circuit is wired through all the switching equipment required to locate the telephone numbers that are dialed. Dial-up circuits do not have one continuous, unbroken circuit path between these cities. Voice grade circuits are the most common form of leased communication channel or facility. Leased circuits used for voice calls often are called *trunk lines* by the people who manage the voice telephone systems.

Area Codes

Until 1995, the middle digit of every area code in the United States was either a 1 or a 0. The telephone company set them up this way because the telephone company's central office switches were programmed to use the 1 or 0 in the area code as a signal to identify a long distance call. The demand for telephone service has grown so rapidly, however, that about five area codes per year become "full."

The solution is to add new area codes. But so many new area codes have been added that in late 1994, the United States was running out of area codes. There simply were not enough three-digit numbers with 1's and 0's as the middle digit; therefore, in 1995, the numbers 2 through 9 began to be used as middle digits in new area codes. The first non-traditional area code was 335 in Alabama. Today there are 792 available area codes in the United States, up from 152 before the new middle digits were added.

Did you ever notice that area codes appear to be placed around the country rather randomly? One explanation of this anomaly is the fact that area codes were set up when everyone had rotary dial telephones. The lower numbers were assigned to the busiest locations, like 212 for New York City and 213 for Los Angeles. The same policy could not be followed as the telephone system continued to grow because all the lower numbers were used quickly. In reality, what once was a good plan designed so people would not have to dial the higher digits (such as 7, 8, or 9) stopped working as we quickly consumed all the area codes having lower digits. This meant we could not continue with the philosophy of giving the lower numbers to the busiest telephone locations. Furthermore, with today's push-button telephones, it no longer makes a difference because it takes the same amount of time to dial either a 1 or a 9. In contrast, a 0 is the most time-consuming digit to dial with rotary dial telephones.

Area codes are used for dialing to other areas within a single country. For that reason, the 415 area code for San Francisco also might be used in another country. Consequently, a *country code* precedes the area code when you are calling another country. You can obtain a complete set of these country codes from the telephone company by calling 1-800-874-4000 and asking for extension 101. As an example of various country codes, the country code for Russia (formerly the USSR) is 7, the country code for Australia is 61, and the country code for the United Kingdom is 44. People who call the United States or Canada from other countries must dial 1 for our joint country code.

When dialing an international call from the United States, you first must dial 011, which provides direct access to an international telephone line. This is required because callers in a country like the United States can dial all the telephone numbers in their own area codes without dialing any other special numbers. To dial outside your area code, you must first dial a 1 before the area code to tell the system you want to dial a number in another area code. Furthermore, you must dial 011 to dial outside your country.

Putting all this together, if you wanted to call the U.S. embassy in Moscow in Russia, you would dial 011-7-095-252-2451. The 011 in this number directs the call to an international telephone line. The 7 tells the telephone switching equipment that you are calling Russia. The 095 is the city code (area code) for Moscow and its suburbs. The telephone number 252-2451 represents the telephone for the embassy. It is dismaying for Americans to learn that there are only 91 simultaneous telephone circuits between the United States and Russia, and only about 57 of these 91 circuits terminate in Moscow. To send a facsimile to Moscow may require dialing many times over several days before you can make a connection. Incidentally, whereas the United States has seven-digit telephone numbers throughout the country, this is not true in all other countries. In fact, some countries have a mixture—for example, seven-digit telephone numbers in metropolitan areas but only six-digit numbers in rural areas. These six-digit numbers usually indicate old switching equipment that is incompatible with the international dialing system. They can be used only for in-country calls, not international calls.

The best way for you to see the area codes for the area in which you live is to look in the front of your local telephone directory. Somewhere in the first 20 to 40 pages is a full-page map showing the United States with its time zones and all the area codes. In addition, the directory contains a list of the major cities, as well as other municipalities near you, so you can see their specific area codes. Finally, many telephone directories also list the international country codes and major foreign city codes within each country.

Echo Suppression/Cancellation

Dial-up circuits often have a problem with echoes. *Echoes* arise in telephone circuits for the same reason that acoustic echoes occur: there is a reflection of the electrical wave from the far end of the circuit.

Telephone companies install *echo suppressors* on two-wire circuits to prevent this echo. The echo suppressor permits transmission in one direction only. When you talk, your voice closes the echo suppressor. When the other person starts talking, his or her voice closes the echo suppressor in that direction; because you have stopped talking, your echo suppressor opens. Obviously, if you are both talking, the power of your voices so overwhelms the echoes that you do not hear them. This is because the echo

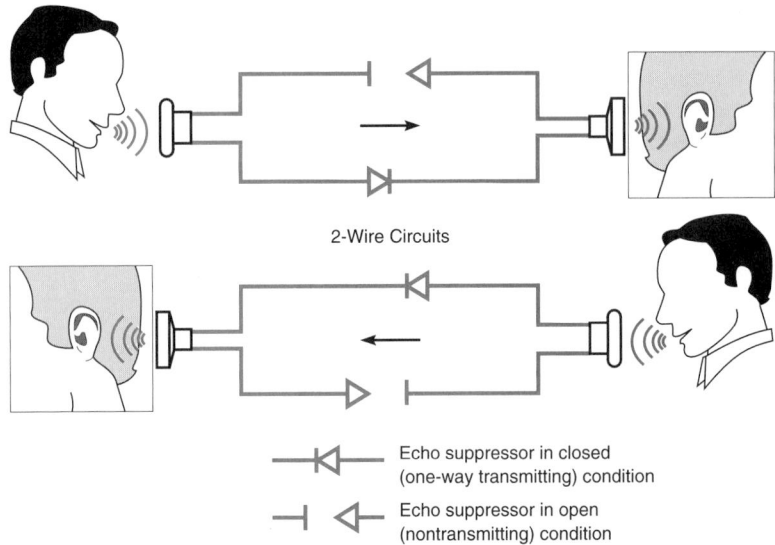

2-Wire Circuits

Echo suppressor in closed (one-way transmitting) condition

Echo suppressor in open (nontransmitting) condition

Figure 3-4 Echo suppressors.

suppressors close in both directions when you both talk. Figure 3-4 depicts the operation of echo suppressors. Lease data circuits (private dedicated lines) do not have echo suppressors; they are present only in dial-up circuits.

One approach to controlling echo is to reduce the *propagation time*—the time it takes a signal to travel from one end of a pair of wires to the other end. If two speakers are 1000 miles apart, the propagation delay is about 10 milliseconds so the round-trip echo delay is 20 milliseconds. When the echo delay is 20 milliseconds or less, anything the speaker hears is simultaneous with his or her own speech, and it is not interpreted as an echo; therefore, no problem exists. As the echo delay approaches 45 milliseconds, however, the echo sounds like an echo and it interferes with the conversation. Longer echo delays may make conversation almost impossible because the returning echo is a mimic of the original spoken words.

When a computer is dialed using a modem (see Chapter 5), there is a loud ringing tone as the computer answers. The purpose of this tone is to disable the echo suppressors. The tone is held on the line for approximately 200 to 400 milliseconds in order to disable or close the echo suppressors in both directions. Immediately after the tone ceases, the carrier wave signal comes up, perhaps a 1700 hertz tone, and it is this carrier wave signal that keeps the echo suppressors closed in both directions. If the carrier wave is lost (perhaps because of an electrical failure) for approximately 150 to 300 milliseconds, the echo suppressors reopen. This reopening causes the dial-up data transmission to have many garbled or destroyed characters. The only choice at this point may be to redial the call and start over in order to close the echo suppressors in both directions.

To meet today's high speed data communication needs, a different type of echo control equipment is used on many circuits at PBX connections, public switched network gateways, and in private networks. These devices, called *echo cancellers,* do not just suppress the echo; they subtract it. An echo canceller contains an internal model of the echo delay for the circuit on which it is being used. The echo canceller subtracts the amount of propagation time from the original signal on the circuit. This internal model of the echo delay adjusts automatically, thereby allowing the canceller to handle a wide variety of different circuit conditions to minimize echoes. The basic difference between the two devices is that an echo suppressor suppresses the return of the echo, whereas the echo canceller subtracts the echo from the original signal.

TASI (Voice Calls)

The *Time Assignment Speech Interpolation* (TASI) technique is used on some of today's long distance voice lines. It allows for the packing of extra voice conversations into a fixed number of circuits.

Usually when two people conduct a telephone conversation, both parties do not speak at the very same moment, and for a small portion of the time neither speaks. Most long distance voice circuits are four-wire circuits. When each person speaks, only one pair of the four wires is used. Thus, two of the four wires always are empty, unless both people speak simultaneously, which does not last very long.

TASI electronic switching equipment detects a user's first word, and within a few milliseconds, the equipment assigns a communication circuit to that speaker. Actually, an almost undetectable portion of the first syllable may be lost, but it is seldom noticed in voice communications. When a person ceases talking, the circuit is switched away and given to someone else. When the person speaks again, the TASI equipment assigns a new circuit path. Occasionally, if the circuits are overloaded, the TASI equipment may be unable to find a free path. Even though it is for a very brief period, several words might be lost when this occurs (see Figure 3-5).

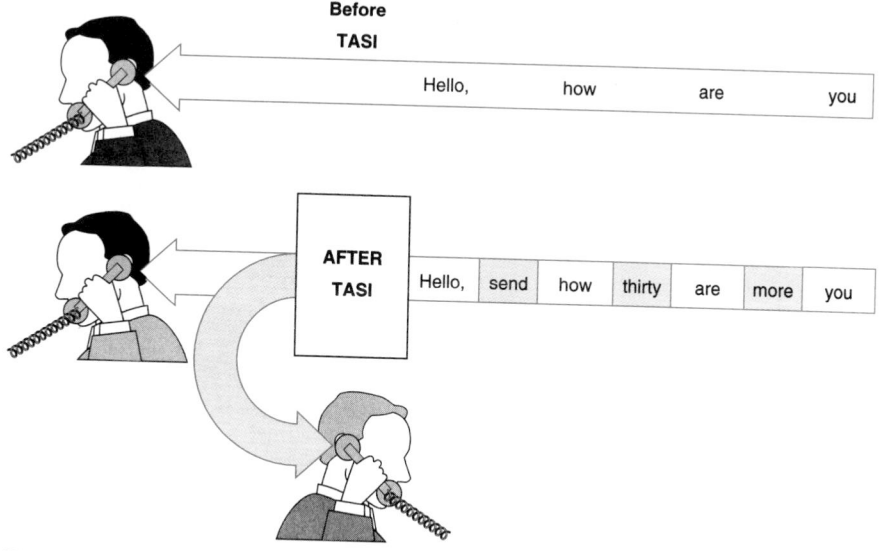

Figure 3-5   Before and after TASI.

Name	Number of Voice Grade Circuits
Group	12
Supergroup	60
Master Group	600
Jumbo Group	3,600
Jumbo Group Multiplex	10,800

Figure 3-6   Group multiplexing.

The benefit of TASI equipment is that more voice calls can be handled simultaneously than there are circuits.

Voice Call Multiplexing

Multiplexing means to combine more than one telephone call on a high speed circuit. In this case, the telephone company takes groups of calls that are destined for the same area and multiplexes them together. This permits groups of calls to travel on a single coaxial cable, microwave system, satellite transmission, or optical fiber transmission media. Figure 3-6 shows the names given to these groupings and the number of voice grade circuits in each group.

For example, assume your company already has multiplexed 16 conversations onto one outgoing circuit. The telephone company may further multiplex this one circuit into a "group" for transmission to its destination. This means your 16 conversations are transmitted as only one of the 12 calls in the group (see Figure 3-6). In addition, the telephone company may again multiplex it into a jumbo group of circuits. Data multiplexing is discussed in Chapter 4.

SWITCHES (VOICE AND DATA)

In the very early days of telephone communication, telephones were connected to each other with point-to-point or multipoint dedicated circuits (i.e., party lines) similar to the telegraph. This system was able to easily connect very small numbers of telephones, but quickly fell apart when larger numbers of telephones had to be connected to each other. Figure 3-7 depicts this situation; it shows six telephones with every telephone individually connected to every other telephone. Fifteen lines are needed in this case. The number of lines needed for this type of network is calculated as:

$$\text{Number of lines} = \frac{N\,(N-1)}{2}$$

where $N =$ the number of telephones (or terminals or microcomputers)

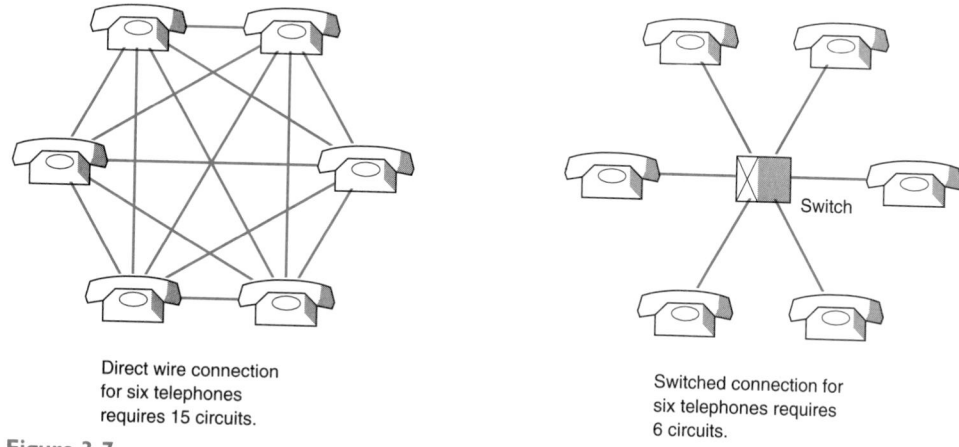

Direct wire connection
for six telephones
requires 15 circuits.

Switched connection for
six telephones requires
6 circuits.

Figure 3-7

A more economical and flexible interconnection arrangement is to allow for tempo-rary connections between any two telephones that wish to communicate with each other. This process is called *switching,* a methodology that eliminates the need for direct wire connection between all station pairs in a network. In this case, all tele-phones are connected to a central switch, which has the ability to temporarily connect any telephone to any other telephone. In this case, the 15-line configuration can be reduced to a 6-line configuration, consisting of one line from each telephone to the central switch. This same technique is used in data communication networks to con-nect computers or entire computer networks together.

Circuit Switching

Circuit switching is the most common type of switched network. Your home telephone uses circuit switched connections. In *circuit switching,* the central switch site (usually the telephone company's central office) establishes a connection between two devices (telephones or computer devices), and messages go directly from one to the other. Picture this as a voice message going from one telephone to another telephone after the two communication circuits are switched together at the telephone company cen-tral office. Messages can only flow if both devices are available and able to be directly connected. If two telephones cannot be switched together (connected), you get a busy signal and have to redial later. The major disadvantage of circuit switching is that you cannot get a message through the network if the two circuits cannot be connected. For this reason, store and forward networks are more popular for data commu-nications.

Store and Forward Switching

With *store and forward* switching, if one of the devices is busy, the central switching site stores the incoming message from the sending device (e.g., by copying it to disk), and retransmits that message to the destination when the device becomes available. With modern high speed computers, many data communication networks are able to combine store and forward switching with circuit switching. These networks first attempt circuit switching, but if the destination device is busy, store and forwarding is used. This combination offers data communication network users the highest level of throughput.

Store and forward switching is commonly used for data communications, and has only recently become available for voice communications. AT&T, MCI, and several other companies now provide a calling service that enables you to leave a message if the phone you are calling is busy. The service continuously tests the destination telephone so whenever it becomes free, the service rings the telephone and delivers your stored message.

End Office Switches

There are many very large, high speed switches within telephone company end or central offices. Figure 3-3 showed the five classes of these switches. They are used to search out telephone numbers and switch circuits so two telephones can be connected together, even though one of the telephones may be in San Francisco and the other in London. One of the more popular *end office switches* is the AT&T 5ESS switch. This is an extremely reliable high speed switch used for circuit switching and even store and forward in some cases. In addition to the high speed switching of calls, it can automatically route calls to alternate circuits when the original circuit is overloaded or temporarily out of service, queue calls with an automatic call-back option for better utilization of facilities, connect multiple location switching systems together, and the like.

Newer switching schemes (software and hardware) are being implemented throughout the United States. In the past, your telephone call went to a switch in a local end office that telephoned ahead to the next end office so your call could be routed. Although this whole process was automatic, it used not only some of the voice grade circuit capacity between cities for routing calls but also some of the capacity for turning one of the circuits over to you when the call was routed and the person at the other end picked up the telephone.

A new switching scheme is called *Common Channel Signaling System 7* or simply SS7. This method uses an entirely separate computer network for the purpose of setting up and routing calls. It does not use the regular voice telephone network for the mechanics of routing calls. SS7 uses a second network for call routing because the switching computers of the regular voice telephone network are nearly overloaded with data relating to traffic and other signaling required to handle millions of voice and data calls.

Digital Switches

There are several types of *digital switches. Digital data switches* (also called *digital cross-connect switches*) provide users with a way of switching between different host mainframe computers (as shown in Figure 3-8). A digital data switch can manage traffic and set

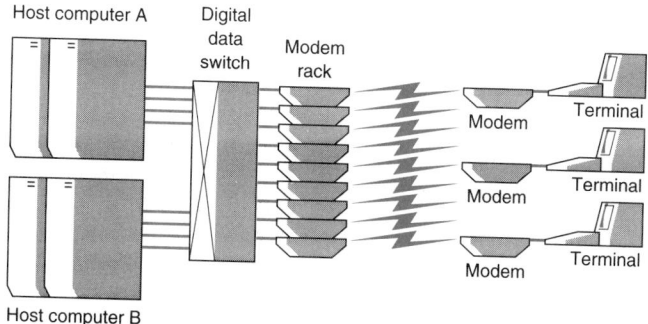

Figure 3-8   Digital data switch. A modem rack is a cabinet at the central site that holds many modems. Sometimes only the modem circuit cards are in the rack, and sometimes the entire modem box is in the rack. The digital data switch can connect any modem in the modem rack to any of the four ports in either host computer A or host computer B.

up inbound and outbound queues of messages during periods of peak usage in order to maximize available resources. Digital data switches offer port contention, which is a sharing of the ports on a front end processor. This sharing can be done on a first-come, first-served basis, or some incoming messages can be given priority over others. Some digital data switches provide security restriction through the use of passwords.

A *digital matrix switch* combines technologies found in T-1 multiplexers, PBXs (switchboards), and circuit switches. Digital matrix switches are used to change connections between ports, such as on a front end processor. When a front end fails, the network control center operator can type a command on the switch's console to change the terminal and modem port connections. This effectively moves each modem and circuit combination to the spare front end processor.

Network Switches

Even though switching can be built into the front end processor, statistical multiplexer/concentrator, PBX, or host computer, there are many stand-alone network switches. A typical stand-alone switch might have 12 or more communication circuits that operate at different speeds. The system should be able to support various types of networks and be expandable to handle more communication circuits.

A stand-alone switch should be able to dial and receive calls automatically, as well as switch messages between any of its circuits. Another feature should be a delivery/verification/confirmation response, with the message sender getting a positive delivery acknowledgment that shows when the message was received. Finally, a good switch should provide for storage of an adequate number of in-transit messages (at least 500). It should have the ability to retrieve messages that were sent during the day, possibly during previous days, and message logging for transaction trails or historical purposes. Some switches also provide alarms in case of circuitry failure and self-diagnostics to locate the failure.

PBX (SWITCHBOARDS)

A *private branch exchange* (PBX) is a switch (more commonly called a switchboard) operated for one organization into which all telephone lines connect. The term *PABX (private automatic branch exchange)* was popular for many years, but today the term PBX is more common. Usually, several circuits go from this switchboard to the telephone company's end office. These circuits generally are referred to as trunk lines when they are devoted primarily to voice transmissions from a switchboard. In data transmission, we refer to these same circuits as leased circuits, private circuits, or dedicated circuits.

Figure 3-9 illustrates the differences between using and not using a PBX. Without a PBX, all telephones must be connected directly to the telephone company's trunk line. Each telephone has a separate telephone number, and forwarding a call from one telephone to another is difficult. For each of these telephone connections, the company must pay a monthly connection fee.

With a PBX, all telephones are connected to the one PBX, which is connected to the trunk line. This PBX performs much the same functions as a switch. All calls made to any of the company's telephones are connected to the PBX, which switches them to the correct telephone. It is also simple to have one central telephone number, from which an internal company operator or computerized system can forward (i.e., switch) calls to a specific telephone. Each telephone has its own number, the last four or five digits of which are an internal organization telephone extension number. In this way, incoming telephone calls can go directly to the telephone being called. People within the organization can dial inside extensions (four or five digits) or outside telephone calls to other organizations, also bypassing the telephone company and the switchboard operator. Any central telephone numbers still can be routed to a switchboard operator if the organization wishes.

PBX Benefits

PBXs provide many other benefits, the most important of which is cost saving. All telephones in a company are seldom in use simultaneously. Most companies do not

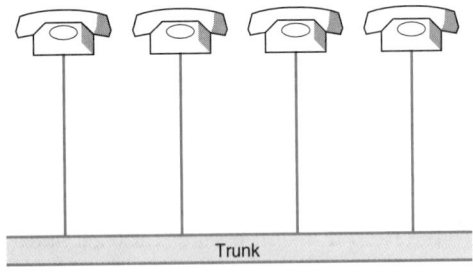

Without PBX

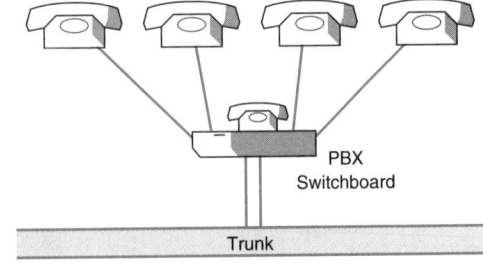

With PBX

Figure 3-9

Management Focus: PBX Fraud

Estimates of telephone fraud losses in the United States range from $500 million to $4 billion per year. One type of fraud involves thieves obtaining access codes to the user's PBX account. Once they have this access, the hackers break the password required for access to long distance services. Upon obtaining access to the system, hackers can make personal use of the services to further other criminal enterprises, or to sell the access code for a profit.

While the sale and use of remote access dialing codes appears less frequently, this particular crime is on the rise. The loss to one corporation exceeded $220,000 within the first 13 hours after the fraudulent activation of a remote-access dialing code.

Instead of fighting over losses and who is responsible for paying the bill, carriers are working aggressively to eliminate the fraud. They now use software that quickly spots unusual calling patterns much like stock trading software searches for a trend. They can then alert the owner of the PBX to verify the unusual charges.

AT&T Global Business Communications Systems formed an investigative team which will "track the theft of business long distance service to the hacker's hideout." The sole purpose of the team is to monitor, track, and catch phone-system bandits in the act of committing toll fraud.

Sources: Datamation, September 15, 1994; *Business Week,* July 13, 1992; *The FBI Law Enforcement Bulletin,* July 1994.

need one trunk line connection for every telephone they have. With a PBX, you can connect as many telephones as you like to the PBX, and have a different number of connections from the PBX to the telephone company's trunk line. For example, a company with 100 telephones that expected no more than 25 percent of its telephones to be in use at one time might pay for only 25 trunk line connections. This results in considerable savings, although if more than 25 users attempted to make or receive a call, they would get a busy signal.

To control voice calls, business organizations install *call management systems.* These systems monitor telephone call traffic, point out peak periods, identify the number of operators needed to handle different call volumes, and keep track of telephone operator efficiency and other factors relevant to voice telephone communications. Call accounting software is a specialized database application which records every call that is completed or other specific actions. This output usually is called the *station message detail recording* (SMDR), but some vendors use their own terminology.

Recording the SMDR records is the first task in call accounting, followed by processing the records, assessing the cost of calls made, and reporting and administration. Before widespread use of microcomputers, many companies connected a serial printer to the PBX's serial port to record the information on each call.

Today's systems send this output to a call recorder, which holds the SMDR data until it is transferred to a microcomputer for analysis. The software, called a *call accounting package,* can "price" the calls and prepare a bill for each telephone extension.

Most call accounting packages come with a standard repertoire of call accounting reports. At the minimum, you can expect a report detailing the calls made from each extension, including the time, length, total cost, cost per minute, average call length, the number called, and so forth. Some packages can group the telephone extensions according to an organization's departments and divisions. The best programs produce ad hoc reports on demand.

Call monitoring systems monitor the levels of call activity by showing the current status of various trunk lines, the number of calls in progress, the number of calls waiting in queues, the wait time before incoming calls are answered, the length of calls, the number of calls lost because the caller hangs up, and the status of different operators. Such information helps manage telephone operator performance by measuring the number of calls handled, the length of each call, the percentage of time spent on the telephone, the average time on hold, and the time spent waiting to be connected.

Some of these systems actively control outgoing telephone circuits by not allowing certain area codes or the first three digits of certain telephone exchanges to be dialed, thereby restricting outgoing calls. *Least cost routing* means that the PBX can decide the least expensive route to place a long distance call. For example, the PBX could choose between a telephone trunk line the organization already leases, different common carriers, or dial-up. In this case, the lease line would have the lowest cost, with varying common carriers next, and dial-up the highest cost. But these functions need to be programmed into the PBX by specifying the area codes and the carriers. As a result, the addition of new area codes sometimes cause problems; every PBX needs to be reprogrammed to add the new area code and the interexchange carrier's charges into the list of valid area codes.

Other features include the ability to make outgoing long distance calls from outside the office served by the PBX. With this feature, the user calls into the PBX (from home, for example), dials an authorization code and gets a dial tone that can be used to make long distance calls. In this way, the call is paid for by the company (using whatever volume discounts apply), rather than by the individual caller.

Most local telephone companies now offer extra cost services that provide many of the same benefits of a PBX. The CENTREX service, for example, offers call forwarding, call holding, automatic call backs, conference calling, paging, and more. For those companies that do not want to pay the initial purchase cost for a PBX, these services can be valuable.

Digital PBX

The newest PBXs, called fourth generation, are all-digital and therefore sometimes referred to as a *digital PBX*. Digital PBXs are popular because the switching is so fast and so error free that it allows high speed data transmissions to go through the same switchboard as the one used for voice communications. In fact, if you are using a digital switchboard, your voice transmissions must be digitized prior to going through the switchboard. With digital switchboards, therefore, everything is transmitted in a digital format. These PBXs have three main characteristics: distributed architecture, nonblocking operation, and integrated voice and data.

Digital PBXs use a *distributed architecture* that is either hierarchical or fully distributed. *Hierarchical systems* distribute routine functions to the switching module, but real control resides in the central processor. In *fully distributed systems,* the switch module processes its calls independent of any other system component. Fully distributed systems are said to be inherently more reliable because failure of a single control module, no matter how catastrophic, cannot produce overall system outages. Proponents of the hierarchical system counter that fully distributed PBXs cannot perform under high load conditions because of internode control and synchronization problems.

In a *nonblocking operation,* intraoffice calls *always* can be placed between any two telephones within an organization. For example, if the switchboard carries lines for 2000 telephones within the organization, then 1000 people always can be talking with people at the other 1000 extensions. *Integrated voice and data* means both voice and data can be transmitted over the same communication circuit and through the same PBX.

These newer digital PBXs can use digital transmission and switching techniques because they are designed with 32-bit microprocessor chips that act as the central controller/central intelligence. A typical digital PBX permits individual telephones or microcomputers to be connected directly to the central digital switchboard (see Figure 3-10). A local area network can be controlled from within the switchboard. Microcomputer workstations on the local area network connect to the switchboard in a star configuration, and the PBX digital switch redirects messages among microcomputers connected to the local area network.

Now there are even wireless PBXs. One wireless PBX is capable of supporting 2000 lines and 400 simultaneous telephone calls. This system does not have a nonblocking switch. A *wireless PBX* uses spread spectrum radio technology in frequencies just above 900 megahertz. The obvious major benefit of a wireless PBX is that twisted pair telephone wires do not have to be installed throughout the building for connecting the telephones to the PBX. Once a telephone message leaves the PBX, it is on regular telephone cabling for the trunk lines to the local loop between the business and the

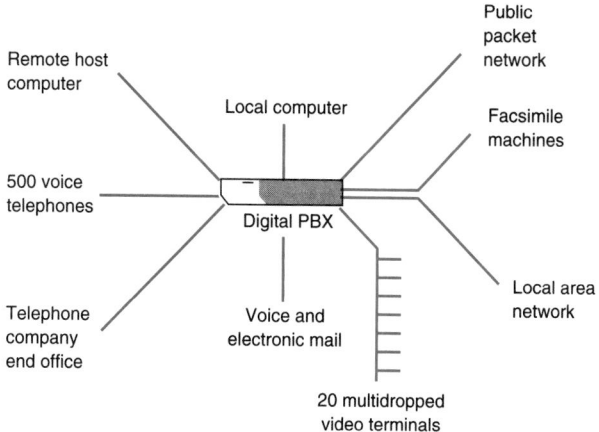

Figure 3-10 Digital PBX.

Management Focus: Buying a PBX

Here are some features to look for when buying a PBX:

- Call forwarding
- Call holding/transfer
- Conference calling
- Voice mail
- Ability to connect to dictation equipment
- Least cost routing to ensure that long distance calls are routed over the least cost communication service
- Paging people throughout a facility
- Speed calling in which often-used numbers are stored in the system
- Station message detail recording (SMDR) to provide cost accounting information
- Nonblocking switching
- Ability to change a telephone number through software rather than rewiring to a new telephone instrument
- Automatic call-back where a calling party encountering a busy station can be called back automatically when the called station becomes available
- Simultaneous transmission of voice and data
- Format and protocol conversion that allows the interconnection of different vendors' word processors, host mainframes, microcomputers, and terminals
- Authorization codes to restrict access for security purposes
- Connection to high speed outgoing circuits, such as T-1.

telephone company. The wireless part of the PBX is within the building, not between the building and the telephone company's central office.

CELLULAR TECHNOLOGY

Cellular technology is becoming increasingly popular. Its most common use is to provide *cellular telephone* services, but the cellular network is also being used more and more often by data communication devices such as pagers and personal digital assistants (PDAs).

Cellular technology is a form of high frequency radio in which antennas are spaced strategically throughout a metropolitan area (see Figure 3-11). A service area or city is divided into many cells, each with its own antenna. This arrangement generally

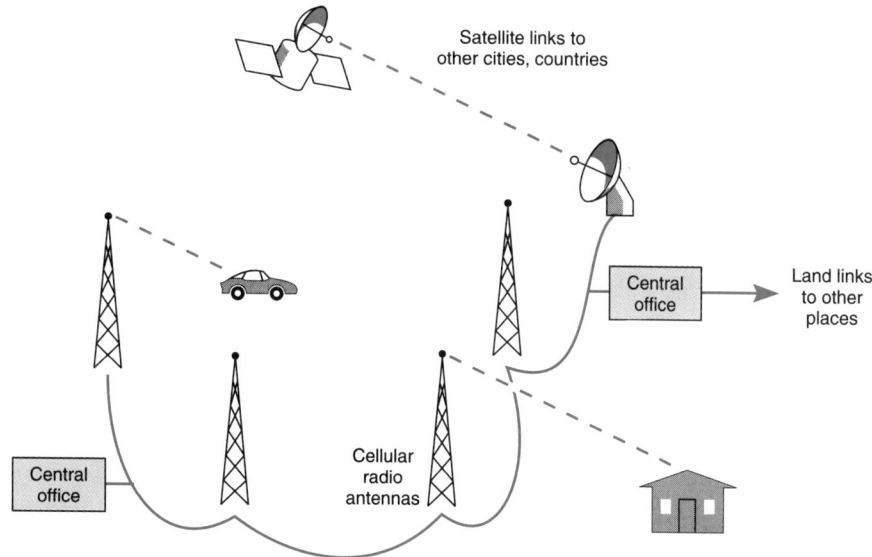

Satellite links to
other cities, countries

Central
office

Land links
to other
places

Central
office

Cellular
radio
antennas

Figure 3-11   Cellular radio system.

provides subscribers with reliable mobile telephone service of a quality almost that of a hardwired telephone system. Users (voice or data transmission) dial or log into the system, and their voices or data are transmitted directly from their automobile, home, or place of business to one of these antennas. In this way, the cellular system replaces the hardwired local loop.

This system is intelligent. For example, as you drive your automobile across the service area or city, you move away from one antenna and closer to another. As the signal weakens at the first antenna, the system automatically begins picking up your signal at the second antenna. Transmission is switched automatically to the closest antenna without communication being lost.

When you speak on a cellular telephone, anyone might be listening to your conversation. Cellular telephone calls are transmitted over the 870 to 890 megahertz frequency bands, which are easily accessible by today's scanners. These devices can scan the frequencies and stop and listen in on the specific frequency your call is using. Even though federal law says it is illegal to manufacture scanners for this frequency range or to use them to listen in on a cellular telephone call, it is virtually impossible to enforce this law because thousands of people own scanners.

Cellular telephone fraud is also becoming a problem. Unscrupulous people purchase a cellular telephone and remove its security EPROM (erasable programmable read only memory) and replace it with "thumbwheel" EPROM substitutes. They do this by turning the wheels at random until they discover some other person's cellular telephone security code, at which point they can begin making calls on that code—at least until that person receives the next telephone bill. Some of the more sophisticated fraud perpetrators use scanners and laptop microcomputers to find large numbers of cellular telephone codes automatically. As yet, this type of fraud is not very common,

Management Focus: Airwaves Auction

The federal government set out to sell the sky and the enormous sale brought in a total collection of $833 million for the U.S. Treasury. The FCC raised $617 million from the sale of ten licenses for nationwide advanced paging networks. In addition to this, it took in $216 million from the sale of some 300 licenses that may be used for interactive television services in the future.

The biggest winners of the licenses were already prominent in wireless communications, with Paging Network Inc. and McCaw Cellular Communications in the front runnings. Another company backed by the Microsoft Corporation and its billionaire founders, William H. Gates and Paul Allen, also purchased a license.

Most companies that won paging licenses plan to offer a new service called "acknowledgement paging" in which a pager automatically responds to a message with a signal indicating that the message got through. Holders of the most valuable licenses plan more elaborate networks that would allow users to enter messages on their computers or personal ditigial assistants (PDAs) and transmit them anywhere in the country.

The results of the auction vividly demonstrate how precious the nation's airwaves are at a time when wireless communications business is seeing explosive growth.

Source: The New York Times, July 30, 1994.

but owners of cellular telephones should check their bills immediately. Also, remember that you pay for both incoming and outgoing cellular airtime. Thus, you pay not only for calls you make, but also for calls other people make to you.

A pager may be better for incoming calls than a cellular telephone if you want to save money and also have more security. For security reasons, you should not provide cellular telephone numbers to strangers. Instead, you should provide a beeper number for others to call you, and then you call them back on the cellular telephone. This procedure is more secure and eliminates the cost of incoming cellular calls.

The real future of cellular technology is based on the philosophy of dividing the entire United States, or even the world, into cells so a person can call from anywhere to anywhere. It would be easy to interconnect the cells of the entire United States with the cells of, say, France by using either satellite communications or fiber optic undersea cables. Most of us think of a telephone as a fixed-location device (located in our home, school, business, or pay telephone booth), but cellular pay telephones will appear in taxicabs, buses, and trains. (They already are in airplanes and as emergency phones on interstate highways.) Burglar alarm system will use cellular radio because when burglars defeat alarm systems, 90 percent of the time they do it by cutting the telephone wires. Paramedic rescue units already use cellular radio.

The telephone is also rapidly becoming a personal item. You will carry it with you, just as you might carry a calculator or a microcomputer. Thirty years ago, no one anticipated that we all would have electronic calculators small enough to carry with us. In the future, you will have small portable cellular telephones, with the number assigned to you, and the telephone unit will be carried rather than connected to the wall of your home. AT&T already is offering personal telephone numbers with the 700 area code, that a person can use for life.

FACSIMILE (FAX) MACHINES

Transmission of an exact picture of a hard copy document, including legal signatures, is one of the most important features in today's business office. This is especially true for legal contracts, medical records and authorizations, and for the control of business records.

Facsimile machines have evolved through four generations (Groups 1, 2, 3, and 4). Groups 1 and 2 are older analog machines, whereas Group 3 is a newer analog machine. Group 4 machines transmit digitally. Most of today's fax machines are Group 3. The older analog machine can take six minutes to transmit one 8 ½ by 11 page. The Group 3 machines take less than one minute per page. Group 4 machines are just entering the marketplace. They will improve copy quality dramatically and reduce the actual transmission time for a standard Group 3 business letter from its current 20-second average to only 3 seconds. The Group 3 machines can transmit a page in 20 seconds, but by the time the fax handles the call setup, transmits the page for 20 seconds, and disconnects the call, the total time to transmit the one page is about one minute. The top speed for Group 3 is 9600 bits per second, but it is 64,000 bits per second for Group 4 fax machines.

Facsimile transmission can be threatening to post office authorities because you can fax a letter from one area to another for anywhere from 10 cents to 90 cents, depending on the volume of traffic per month and the cost of communication circuits. For this reason, facsimile transmission is in direct competition with both electronic mail and regular mail.

Once a facsimile device is connected to a communication circuit, the following basic steps take place during transmission.

- You establish the call either by manually dialing your telephone or by having an automatic call placed (physical circuit connection).
- The fax machine handles the pre-message procedure, or *handshaking*, which consists of identifying the called station (facsimile machine) and any other procedures that might be required to set up the session.
- The fax machine transmits the message (the *session*), which involves synchronization between the two devices, any error detection and correction methodologies, and movement of the message from one facsimile device to the other.
- The fax machine completes the post-message procedure, which includes END OF MESSAGE signaling at the conclusion of the page, any signaling that signifies

Technology Focus: Fax/Voice Switches

Did you ever wonder how a *Fax/Voice switch* works? These switches allow you to connect both a facsimile machine and a voice telephone to the same telephone circuit. The reason, of course, is to save the monthly cost of a second telephone circuit. When a call comes in, the switch automatically connects to the facsimile machine or rings the voice telephone, depending on which is the correct action. If the incoming call is a facsimile, most Group 3 fax machines transmit an 1100 hertz tone every three seconds. This is called the CNG (*Calli*NG) tone. When the switch hears the tone, it automatically switches to the facsimile machine. If the switch does not hear the tone, it allows the voice telephone to ring. In fact, the telephone can become an answering machine in addition to a "plain vanilla" telephone.

more than one page, end of transmission, and anything else required to end the session (physical circuit disconnected).

A technological breakthrough for FAX is in the use of microcomputers. A fax card or fax modem can be added to transform a microcomputer into a transmitting or receiving facsimile machine. Microcomputer users can create a file on their microcomputer and send it directly to a remote fax machine without having to print it, physically carry it to a facsimile machine that scans it, and then transmit it. Users also can receive a fax file, display it, manipulate it on a microcomputer screen, and then print it or send it to another fax terminal.

The international Group 3 facsimile standard provides for transmission of any text or graphics image over ordinary telephone circuits. A scanner in the facsimile device breaks the original document into pixels (dots) at 203 per inch horizontally and 98 dots per inch vertically. Then it converts the pixels into a bit stream to feed into a modem. The receiving device takes the bit stream and prints the image. The most sophisticated devices use laser printers.

Because facsimile images always are pictures, a page can occupy a considerable amount of storage. Typically, it is 30 to 60 kilobytes for a page of text or 120 kilobytes in fine mode. This is true even when using Group 3's data compression scheme. A 20-megabyte hard disk devoted to facsimile images can store only 170 fine-mode pages. As a standard ASCII computer file, a page takes up only 2 to 4 kilobytes; thus, an ASCII page transmitted at 1200 bits per second is faster than a facsimile page transmitted at 9600 bits per second.

The Group 4 standard resolution is 400 by 400 dots per inch and requires an improved compression scheme. It also is designed for all-digital telephone circuits instead of analog dial-up telephone circuits; therefore, Group 4 facsimiles are not yet able to operate on standard dial-up voice grade telephone circuits. Finally, fax machines have been so reduced in size that they now can be used in your automobile or carried in your briefcase.

Management Focus: Buying a Fax Machine

The following are some features to consider when you are purchasing a fax machine:

- The fax type or group
- Type of paper (thermal paper is cheapest, but fades within 6 to 12 months; plain paper is preferred)
- Automatic protocol conversion so a Group 3 machine can communicate with a Group 1 or 2 machine
- Automatic speed selection at 2400, 4800, or 9600 bits per second
- Memory to hold incoming documents when the fax is out of paper
- Sender's name and fax telephone number, which are printed automatically at the top margin
- Time, date, and page number stamp
- Broadcasting so the same document can be sent to a list of phone numbers
- Selectable contrast and resolution
- Delayed calling to enable unattended transmission during evening hours to reduce long distance charges
- Ability to serve as a backup copier
- Copy reduction to reduce oversize documents
- Detailed activity reporting to record usage
- Encryption and secret identification codes
- Automatic re-try to keep trying to reach busy numbers without being manually redialed
- Acknowledgment of all sent and received documents
- Fine and superfine switches. Group 3 fax machines transmit in pixels (dots). The standard fax is 203 by 98 pixels. By pressing the fine button, you improve resolution to 203 by 196. Superfine improves resolution still more to 203 by 391.

SPECIAL PURPOSE DEVICES

Interactive Voice Response (IVR)

Interactive voice response is a voice processing application that gives callers specific information based on *unique* information the callers provide to the IVR system. IVR is interactive communications, and it is different from auto-attendant operation.

An *auto-attendant operation* simply *routes* callers based on information the callers provide by Touch-Tone; it does not return information to the caller. Notice that the caller does not have to supply any unique information; the caller just presses the proper key on a Touch-Tone telephone in order to be routed to another function or person.

Another voice application is *audiotex,* which gives every caller the *same* information. If a system allows the caller to press certain keys on the Touch-Tone telephone so it can determine what the caller wants to receive, that is auto-attendant. The part of the process that gives the caller the latest news, the current weather, or the lottery numbers is audiotex because it gives every caller the same information. *Fax-on-demand* is similar to audiotex, except that instead of listening to a recorded message, callers enter a fax number, and the requested information is automatically faxed to them.

It is possible for a system to combine all three features. For example, assume Jane Smith wonders if the bank received her last bank-by-mail check and decides to call the bank to find out her current checking account balance. Upon receiving the call, the auto-attendant feature allows her to press the proper keys to determine whether she wants to talk with an operator, receive information on banking hours, go directly to someone's extension telephone, or receive unique information on her bank account. If Ms. Smith presses the key to learn about banking hours, the information she hears is the audiotex portion of the system because every caller who presses that key hears the same message. On the other hand, once Ms. Smith presses the proper key to receive unique financial information related to her bank account, then that is the interactive voice response part of the system. That part might instruct her to use the Touch-Tone keypad to enter her checking account number. If the checking account number she provides is valid, the IVR then might instruct her to enter the last four digits of her Social Security number. If that number matches the one stored with her checking account number, the system looks up the balance in Ms. Smith's checking account and, using a voice response system, supplies the current balance. Notice that the auto-attendant feature routes calls to wherever they should go, whether it is a human operator, an audiotex system, or an interactive voice response system. The audiotex part provides each caller with the same message, in this example, the bank's operating hours. By contrast, the interactive voice response part extracts unique information from the system and delivers it to a specific customer. As you deal with voice telephone systems, it may be important to understand the subtle differences between auto-attendant, audiotex, and interactive voice response systems. See the box on IVR for Car Dealers for an example of how such a system works.

Automatic Number Identification (ANI)

Automatic number identification (ANI) is a service that provides customers with the telephone number of the incoming caller. There are various uses for ANI service. For example, the calling telephone number can be displayed in a little window on your telephone. This allows the option of not answering the call, assuming you know it is from a telephone number you do not want to answer. Some companies use ANI to record the number for future use, to route the call to a specialized telephone sales agent, or to send it to an IVR unit. This routing can be quite sophisticated. For example, if the call came in on a certain set of 800 numbers, it will route it to the IVR;

Management Focus: Interactive Voice Response for Car Dealers

Car dealers can use IVR to great advantage. For example, a dealer can check the stock and order parts over the telephone without the benefit of a human telephone operator. To do this, the dealer calls an 800 number and uses a Touch-Tone telephone to enter the appropriate dealer number and password. Then there are four choices: Check the price and availability of a part, enter an order, check the status of an order that already has been placed, or exit the system. When checking on prices and availability of a part, the dealer enters the 14-digit part number. The system responds in a digitized human voice whether the part is in stock, the current dealer price for the part, and the suggested retail price.

To place the order, the dealer enters the part number and the quantity required. The system reads the order back to the dealer in a digitized voice. Because the dealer places the order directly into a computer, order fulfillment begins immediately. If the order is placed before noon, it will be delivered the next day. If the dealer orders the entire stock of a part, the database is updated immediately so the next caller who asks for information on that part will hear that no stock is available. Should the dealer have difficulty using the IVR system, the appropriate Touch-Tone codes can be touched for connection to a real person who can provide assistance. A system such as this, when combined with electronic data interchange (EDI), will someday be the ultimate in reducing paperwork and increasing the productivity and efficiency of parts ordering and billing. EDI would be used for invoicing the dealer and for handling payments, thereby automating the entire process.

but if it shows that the call came in from a normal area code like 305 or 415, it will route the call to a telephone sales agent. The caller's telephone number can also be passed to a microcomputer which uses it to retrieve the caller's records from a database so the telephone operator can have immediate access to all needed information.

ANI has become tangled in the privacy debate because it is easily confused with its consumer-oriented counterpart, Caller ID. The end results of ANI and Caller ID are the same; that is, numbers for calls originating in an equal access central office are delivered to the person being called. The difference is that *Caller ID* operates within the service area of a particular group of central offices such as within a city, whereas ANI applies to long distance calls. Caller ID also incorporates the capability for calls to be transmitted with a *privacy blocking designator* in which the caller enters a code that blocks transmission of his or her telephone number. This prevents the person being called from seeing the telephone number of the person placing the call.

Intelligent Port Selector

Intelligent port selectors (also called *rotary switches*) are nothing more than devices that answer incoming telephone calls and connect to the first available telephone line or

Management Focus: Facts by Fax

Several companies combine IVR and fax technologies to provide information services via telephone. *Consumer Reports* is a national consumer magazine that provides ratings of a variety of products. Consumers can order reprints of these ratings by calling *Consumer Reports* facts by fax number. The caller enters the code of the desired product (listed in back of every magazine), a credit card number, and the telephone number of his/her fax machine. Within minutes, the desired information is sent.

data port. If there were ten ports, it would try port 1, then port 2, port 3, and so on. If any one was available, you would be connected. If all ten were busy, you would get a busy signal and would have to redial later. For example, suppose we have four telephone numbers ranging from 555-1200 to 555-1203 and they are hooked onto a rotary switch. Our organization would advertise only the 555-1200 number on the firm's stationery. If someone were to call the 555-1200 number and two calls were already in progress, the rotary switch would switch over the calls in progress (that is, it would skip over the numbers 555-1200 and 555-1201) and ring the 555-1202 number.

Now let us assume further that our firm does a lot of work using both voice telephones and fax machines. In this assumption, we also might have four fax machines connected with the voice telephones on our four incoming telephone circuits. Now when someone calls, the rotary switch "rings down" or skips over the circuits that are busy. On reaching the first free circuit, it determines whether the incoming call is a voice telephone call or an incoming facsimile message and routes the incoming call to the appropriate device.

Voice Mail

The public telephone network that handles voice messages has been around for over 100 years. Because this network is primarily a circuit switching system, it has one tremendous disadvantage. When the remote telephone is already in use or no one is present to answer calls, the telephone call (the message) cannot be completed. Both voice mail and e-mail overcome this disadvantage.

With regard to voice mail, great technical advances have occurred to make the telephone more accessible, easier to use, more attractive, and a true message switching system. In other words, *voice mail* is a store and forward switching system as opposed to a circuit switching system. Voice mail is a flexible means of sending a spoken message to someone, even when the person is not at the telephone. The sender speaks into the telephone, and the message is stored for later forwarding to its recipient. In effect, this turns the telephone system into a message switching system.

Actually, voice mail is the transmission of a voice message to a recipient's voice mailbox. Using a Touch-Tone telephone with its standard 12-key dialing pad, the caller can record a message, listen to the message before transmitting it, and even change

Management Focus: Voice Mail Fraud

Business are reporting a rash of voice mail break-ins by hackers who commandeer unused voice mailboxes and use or sell them for illicit purposes. Such voice mail thefts mean that transactions can be conducted without people meeting each other or revealing telephone numbers that can be traced back to them.

Stealing information from competitors is also on the rise. Thousands of voice mail systems are penetrated weekly by competitors, disgruntled present and former employees, and freelance hackers looking for information that might have street value.

One of the reasons for this chaos is that many systems are set so that until an owner changes it, the password for a voice mailbox is its extension number. This makes access easy for an experienced hacker.

Standard Duplicating Machines Corp. distributes duplicating and collating equipment. Its main competitor, Duplo Manufacturing Corp., hired a former Standard salesman. The salesman quickly went to work fishing through his former employer's voice mailboxes until he tipped a competitor off to his illegal activities. It took months before the espionage was discovered. More than 230 calls to Standard's 800 number were traced back to the ex-employee's home or Duplo offices.

A Dallas-based oil service company also observed the dangers of voice mail when bidding on a major drilling contract. After the first day of negotiations, an executive left a voice-mail message for a colleague, indicating terms of the company's bid. Their competitor won the bid the next day, but after bringing in a detective, the company found the message had in fact been intercepted by their competitor.

Sources: Forbes, January 17, 1994; *The Economist,* August 13, 1994.

---

it if necessary. The message then can be sent to one or more recipients or even to a predefined group, such as a department within a corporation or government agency. When it is convenient, the recipients check their voice mailboxes, scan to see who sent incoming messages, and choose to listen to some now while saving others for later. Recipients can listen to the message, stop playing it if they are interrupted, skip ahead or back, or replay the message at will. After hearing the message, the recipient can generate a voice reply immediately and send it to the person who sent the original message. Other options might be to forward the message to a third party and, of course, to discard the original message.

Voice mail has five major advantages over the traditional telephone. With voice mail, it is no longer necessary to

- Place several calls to a person to find that person near the telephone,
- Move meeting schedules to match time zone differences around the world,
- Place a number of calls to send a similar message to many different people,
- Type your messages,
- Wait at your telephone to receive an important message.

Management Focus: Buying a Voice Mail System

When you purchase a voice mail system, some important features to consider are:

- Various security levels that restrict access to the system by requiring an access password and a follow-up security code.
- Type of hardware to be used, such as 12-key Touch-Tone telephones.
- Training aids such as booklets, audio prompting, or, if you have a video display telephone, a help key that provides pictorial representations.
- Keypad templates to help users remember how to use the 12 keys.
- Other message addressing schemes such as to individuals, to a unique telephone, to groups of individuals, to preorganized numeric codes, to system directories, or custom methods used by an individual organization.
- Type of system data that might accompany the message, such as date of call and time, address of sender and receiver, time of message, or other system data.
- Provision for priorities or different message categories.
- Ability of users to give answers to requests or to request information via IVR.
- Depending on size and cost considerations, systems starting with one port and going up to 256 ports for incoming telephone circuits (trunk lines).
- Capability of interfacing with PBX and microcomputers.
- Activity reporting, including accounting functions and various other business reports that a system administrator can use for maintenance, billing, and security.
- Message desk option, with which an operator can transfer a voice mail message from a non-user, or an outside user can enter a voice mail message.
- Outdialing, or the ability to dial an outside call (local or long distance or pager) automatically in order to deliver a user's voice mail message to another user or non-user of the system. This is helpful for contacting someone during nonbusiness hours when people are less likely to check their voice mail.
- Edit functions, including stop, start, skip forward, skip backward, delete, reply, add, and subtract are important for users who want to replay and edit messages.
- Broadcast abilities, allowing one message to be directed to multiple users.
- Automatic time and date stamping of messages.
- Message forwarding, whereby a user who has received a message can send it to another system user and also can add dialogue to the first message. This is similar to memo passing.
- Speed control, so the user can slow down or speed up the received message.
- Variable message lengths, depending on disk storage capabilities.

The sender can place a call without interrupting the recipient, without having to know whether the recipient is in the office, and without regard to the time of day or night.

In general, public telephone users more readily accept voice mail than e-mail. This is because e-mail requires, first, the ability to type and, second, access to a keyboard in order to type the text of a message. Psychologically, human beings were built to accept and transmit voice messages, whereas the ability to enter text messages must be learned as a special skill. More people can speak than can write a complete sentence correctly, let alone type a message.

Finally, the prime advantage for voice mail is that everyone who currently has a Touch-Tone telephone already has the terminal required to use this system and basically understands how this terminal (the telephone) works. To see how one of the voice mail systems works, use your telephone and dial 1-800-6WATSON.

Summary

Voice Communication Network   Voice communications cost most organizations far more than data communications. Most calls are made by switching them through the network, although it is possible to lease circuits that are then dedicated to the use of one organization. Most voice calls today are multiplexed or combined using TASI in order to use telephone circuits more efficiently.

Switches

Switches are used to connect telephones and data communication devices (e.g., terminals and computers). With circuit switching, a physical connection is established between the two devices. Circuit switching only works if both devices are available simultaneously. With store and forward switching, messages are stored until the destination device is available and then transmitted. Store and forward switching is primarily used for data communications.

PBX (Private Branch Exchange)

PBXs are switches used by one organization to manage their voice (and sometimes data) communications. PBXs reduce costs by reducing the number of connections to the telephone company's trunk lines, by automatically selecting the least expensive long distance carrier, and by providing call management software to help identify how communications services are being utilized by each user. Most PBXs provide call forwarding and holding, voice mail, and long distance calling.

Cellular Technology

The most common use of cellular technology is for cellular telephones, although this same network is also used for pagers and personal digital assistants. Several new networks are being introduced that will enable more simple transfer of data over the cellular network.

Fax Machines

Fax machines enable the rapid transfer of documents from one location to another, sometimes for less cost than the U.S. mail. Fax boards for microcomputers are now commonly available so that it is easy to send and receive faxes via computers.

Special Purpose Devices

Interactive voice response enables organizations to have callers route their calls, select information, or request faxed information by using their telephone to select items from verbal menus. Automatic number identification displays the caller's number on the telephone or can be passed to microcomputer systems to automatically retrieve customer information so that the telephone operator has immediate access to all of the caller's records. Intelligent port selectors can route calls to any available telephone line is a bank of lines. Voice mail allows callers to leave messages and people to check messages at any time.

Key Terms

Area code	Country code	Fax
Audiotex	Dedicated circuit	Fax/Voice switch
Auto-attendant operation	Dial-up call	Intelligent port selector
Automatic number	Dial-up circuit	Interactive voice response
identification (ANI)	Digital cross-connect switch	(IVR)
Call accounting package	Digital data switch	Key system
Call management system	Digital matrix switch	Leased circuit
Call monitoring system	Digital PBX	Line
Caller ID	Digital transmission	Local call
Camp-on	Dual tone multifrequency	Long distance call
Cellular telephone	(DTMF)	Node
Central office	Echo	Nonblocking operation
Circuit	Echo canceller	Privacy blocking designator
Circuit switching	Echo suppressor	Private automatic branch
Common Channel	End office	exchange (PABX)
Signaling System 7	End office switch	Private branch exchange
Conference call	Exchange office	(PBX)
Control signaling	Facsimile	Propagation time

Session
Station message detail recording (SMDR)
Store and forward switch
Switching

Time Assignment Speech Interpolation (TASI)
Transmission speed
Trunk line

Unit call
Voice grade leased circuit
Voice mail
Wireless PBX

Selected References

1. Fermazin, Tom. "How to Prevent the Misuse and Abuse of Your Voice Mail System," *Voice Processing Magazine,* vol. 4, no. 2, February 1992, pp. 34–37.
2. Gilder, George. "What Spectrum Shortage?" *Forbes,* vol. 147, no. 11, May 27, 1991, pp. 324–325, 328, 330, 332.
3. Leibowitz, Ed. "ANI Phenomenon," *Teleconnect,* vol. 9, no. 11, November 1991, pp. 136, 138–141.
4. ———. "PBX Technology Advances," *Teleconnect,* vol. 9, no. 7, July 1991, pp. 98, 100.
5. Newton, Harry. *Newton's Telecom Dictionary: The Official Glossary of Telecommunications and Computer Acronyms, Terms and Jargon,* 4th ed. New York: Telecom Library, Inc., 1991.
6. Oppedahl, Carl, et al. *The Phone Book: How to Get the Telephone Equipment and Service You Want—and Pay Less for It.* Mt. Vernon, NY: Consumer Reports Books, 1991.
7. Padgett, Kim Wilson, ed. "Accounting for Your Company's Calls," *Voice Processing Magazine,* vol. 3, no. 11, November 1991, pp. 30–31, 33.
8. Tedesco, Eleanor H. *Telecommunications for Business.* Boston: PWS-Kent Division of Wadsworth Publishing Co., 1990.

Questions/Problems

1. The basic voice telephone system commands _____ of the amount spent for data transfer.
2. Name the three basic types of telephone calls.
3. Why are leased circuits more error-free than other dial-up circuits?
4. What are the functions of a call management system?
5. What is the significance of the 1 or 0 in an area code?
6. There are two factors in all telephone calls, whether voice or data messages. What are they?
7. How do echo suppressors differ from echo cancellers?
8. TASI is a means of packing more conversations into a fixed number of circuits. How does it do this?
9. Why are switches needed?
10. What is the important feature that makes store and forward systems attractive?
11. What is it called when intraoffice calls always can be placed between two telephones in an organization (e.g., no busy signals)?
12. What makes digital transmission and switching possible in the newer digital switchboards?
13. When are data PBX switches used?

14. With _____ , incoming or outgoing calls are routed directly to the person being called without intervention by the operator. (This hardware is located at the telephone company central office.)
15. How is data-over-voice accomplished?
16. In a data-over-voice system, what does the separator box do and what may it do in the future?
17. Can circuit switching and store and forward switching be combined in the same system? If so, describe how it would work.
18. If you have 11 microcomputers to interconnect without switching, how many lines (circuits) are required?
19. What is the difference between a private circuit, a leased circuit, and a dedicated circuit?
20. When you dial a call, sometimes you get a 60 pulses per minute busy signal and sometimes a 120 pulses per minute busy signal. What is the difference?
21. Define the difference between circuit switching and message switching.
22. What is a PBX? Define it.
23. How does voice mail differ from electronic mail (e-mail)?
24. What is the purpose of a telephone system?
25. How do dial-pulsing telephones differ from tone-dialing telephones?
26. What is a voice-grade leased circuit called?
27. How do you dial from the United States to another country?
28. How does interactive voice response differ from auto-attendant operation?
29. Describe audiotex.
30. What are the various types of fax machines?
31. What are the advantages and disadvantages of fax cards in microcomputers?
32. Discuss the legal issues surrounding cellular phones.
33. How does the cellular network avoid losing calls as telephones move?

NEXT DAY AIR SERVICE CUMULATIVE CASE STUDY

See appendix at end of book

CHAPTER FOUR

DATA COMMUNICATION HARDWARE

This chapter introduces three fundamental network architectures: host-based, client-based, and client–server. It then discuss characteristics of the basic hardware used in data communications networks: hosts, clients, circuits, and special purpose communication devices. One commonly used data communication device is the modem, which is discussed in detail in Chapter 5.

Objectives

- Understand the differences between host-based, client-based, and client-server networks,
- Understand the principal hardware components in data communication networks,
- Become familiar with different types of network hosts and clients,
- Understand the different types of physical channels provided in networks,
- Become familiar with the major communication media,
- Become familiar with various communications devices.

Chapter Outline

Network Architectures
    Host-Based Architectures
    Client-Based Architectures
    Client–Server Architectures
Hosts
    Mainframe
    Minicomputer
    Microcomputer

NETWORK ARCHITECTURES

As mentioned in Chapter 1, there are three fundamental components in a data communication network: the host computer or server, the client computers, and the network circuits that connect them. The host and clients must work together (communicating over the circuits) to do what the application programs require.

There are three fundamental network architectures. In *host-based networks,* the host computer performs virtually all of the work. In *client-based networks,* the client computers perform most of the work. In *client-server networks,* the work is shared between the hosts and clients.

The work done by any application program can be divided into three general areas. The first is the storage of data; most application programs require data to be stored and retrieved, whether it is a small file such as a memo produced by a word processor, or a large database such as an organization's accounting records. The second function is the processing of the data, which also can be simple or complex depending upon the application. The third function is the presentation of information to the user and the acceptance of the user's commands. These three functions, *data storage, processing,* and *presentation,* are the basic building blocks of any application program.

In this section, we discuss these three architectures, and contrast the benefits and limitations of each. The rest of this chapter will delve into the specific characteristics of hosts, clients, circuits, and other network devices in greater detail. Figure 4-1 summarizes the three architectures.

Host-based networks

Clients (terminals)

Hosts (mainframes)
Presentation
Processing
Data storage

Client-based networks

Clients (microcomputers)
Presentation
Processing

Hosts (microcomputers)
Data storage

Client-server networks

Clients (microcomputers)
Presentation
Processing

Hosts (microcomputers, minicomputers, mainframes)
Processing
Data storage

Figure 4-1 Network Architectures

Host-Based Architectures

The very first data communications networks were host-based, with the host computer (usually a central mainframe computer) performing all three functions. The clients (usually terminals) simply enabled users to send and receive messages to and from the host computer. The clients merely captured key strokes and sent them to the host for processing, and accepted instructions from the host on what to display.

This very simple architecture often works very well. Application software is developed and stored on one computer and all data are on the same computer. There is one point of control, because all messages flow through the one central host. In theory, there are economies of scale, because all computer resources are centralized (but more on cost later).

The fundamental problem with host-based networks is that the host must process all messages. As the demands for more and more network applications grow, many host computers become overloaded and unable to quickly process all the users' demands. User access becomes difficult. Response time becomes slower, and network managers are required to spend increasingly more money to upgrade the host computer. Unfortunately, upgrades to host computers are "lumpy." That is, upgrades come in large increments and are expensive (e.g., $1 million); it is difficult to upgrade "a little."

In the late 1970s and early 1980s, intelligent terminals were developed that could perform some of the presentation function (intelligent terminals are discussed in more detail in the next section). This relieved only a little of the bottleneck, however, because the host still performed all of the processing and data storage. Hosts became somewhat less overloaded, but the network became more complex: developing applications was more difficult, and there were more points of failure.

Client-Based Architectures

In the late 1980s, there was an explosion in the use of microcomputers and micro-computer-based local area networks. Today, more than 60 percent of most organizations' total computer processing power (called MIPS: million instructions per second) now resides on microcomputer-based LANs, not in centralized mainframe-based host computers. As this trend continues, many experts predict that by the end of the century, the host mainframe computer will contain 20 percent or less of an organization's total computing power.

Part of this expansion was fueled by a number of low-cost, highly popular applications such as word processors, spreadsheets, and presentation graphics programs. It was also fueled in part by managers' frustrations with application software on host mainframe computers. Most mainframe software is not as easy to use as microcomputer software, is far more expensive, and can take years to develop. In the late 1980s, many large organizations had application development backlogs of two to three years; that is, getting any new mainframe application program written would take years. New York City, for example, had a six-year backlog. In contrast, managers could buy microcomputer packages or develop applications in a few months.

With client-based architectures, the clients are microcomputers on a local area network, and the host computer is a server on the same network. The client computers do all the presentation and processing; the server simply stores the data. (See Figure 4-1.)

This simple architecture often works very well. However, as the demands for more and more network applications grow, the network circuits can become overloaded. The fundamental problem in client-based networks is that all data on the server must travel to the client for processing. For example, suppose the user wishes to display a list of all employees with company life insurance. All the data in the database (or all the indices) must travel from the server where the database is stored over the network circuit to the client, which then examines each record to see if it matches the data requested by the user. This can overload the network circuits, because far more data are transmitted from the server to the client than the client actually needs.

Client–Server Architectures

Client–server architectures attempt to balance the processing between the client and the server by having both do some of the processing. In these networks, the client performs all presentation functions, the host performs all data storage functions, and both handle parts of the processing. (See Figure 4-1.) Typically, the client accepts user requests, and processes them into database requests that are transmitted to the server. The server accepts the requests, processes them against the database, and transmits the results to the client. The client accepts the results and presents them to the user.

For example, if the user requests a list of all employees with company life insurance, the client would accept the request, format it so that it could be understood by the server, and transmit it to the server. Upon receiving the request, the server searches the database for all matching records and then transmits only the pertinent records to the client, which would then present them to the user. The same would be true for database updates; the client accepts the request and sends it to the server. The server processes the update and responds (either accepting the update or explaining why not) to the client, which displays it to the user.

Most large organizations today are developing client–server networks. This architecture has been the focus of many articles in computer magazines, and many vendors have developed products. In fact, the interest in these products has been so intense that some experts have joked that labeling coffee makers as client–server devices would double their sales.

Client–server networks have some important benefits compared to host-based networks. First and foremost, they are scaleable. That means it is easy to increase or decrease the storage and processing capabilities of the servers. If one server becomes overloaded, you simply add another server and move some of the applications or data storage to it. The cost to upgrade is much more gradual and you can upgrade in smaller steps (e.g., $10,000).

Client–server networks also support many different types of clients and servers. You are not locked into one vendor as is often the case in host-based networks. Likewise, it is possible to connect computers that use different operating systems so that users can choose which type of computer they prefer (e.g., combining both IBM microcomputers and Apple Macintoshes on the same network). Some types of computers and operating systems are better suited to different tasks (e.g., transaction processing, real time video, mathematical processing). Client–server networks allow you to match the needs of individual applications to different types of computers to maximize performance.

Finally, because no single host computer supports all the applications, the network is generally more reliable. There is no central point of failure that will halt the entire network if it fails, as there is in a host-based network. If any one server fails in a client–server network, the network can continue to function using all the other servers (but, of course, any applications that require the failed server will not function).

Client–server networks also have some critical limitations, the most important of which is their complexity. All applications in a client–server network have two parts, the software on the client, and the software on the server. Writing this software is more complicated than writing the traditional all-in-one software used in host-based networks. Programmers often need to learn new programming languages and new programming techniques, which requires retraining.

Even updating the network with a new version of the software is more complicated, too. In a host-based network, there is one place in which application software is stored; to update the software, you simply replace it there. With client–server networks, you must update all clients and all servers. For example, suppose you want to add a new server and move some existing applications from the old server to the new one. All application software on all clients that send messages to the application on the old server must now be changed to send to the new server. While this is not conceptually difficult, it can be an administrative nightmare.

One of the strengths of client-server networks is that they enable software and hardware from different vendors to be used together. But this is also one of their disadvantages. There are currently few standards for client-server networks, so not all

Management Focus: Power Company Juices Up Its Customer Service

The Washington Water Power Company (WWP) wanted to write new applications and modify its old ones to better reflect its business processes and to improve its efficiency. However, the organization relied on a host-based mainframe environment which made the goals either impossible or so difficult that the IS department was years behind on implementing changes requested by managers.

WWP decided to scrap its old Cobol-based, mainframe-bound customer service application in favor of client–server software that runs partly on the mainframe and partly on a new Novell Netware LAN. The new system cost $16.5 million, but offers numerous benefits including saving $500,000 per year in operating costs. The system is also portable, so WWP will be able to use it should the utility decide to scrap the mainframe altogether or move to different client hardware. It is also easy to program, so new applications can be written quickly or old ones easily modified.

The mainframe was kept because it better suited WWP's nightly large batch process than PC-based servers. Also, storing more than 20 gigabytes of data was impractical on anything other than the mainframe. Without a compelling reason to switch, WWP was eager to recoup its investment in mainframe storage arrays.

The new system solves many problems and inconveniences. When WWP and Electronic Data Systems Corp. (EDS) designed it, they made sure that all the applications fit together. The new system looks like one application to the user, and accesses one database.

Source: InfoWorld, February 6, 1995.

software and hardware is compatible. For this reason, client–server networks are sometimes called "bleeding edge" technology.

One solution to these problems is *middleware,* software that sits between the application software on the client and the application software on the server. Middleware does two things. First, it manages the message transfer from clients to servers (and vice versa) so that clients need not know the specific server that contains the application's data. The application software on the client sends all messages to the middleware, which addresses things to the correct server. The application software on the client is therefore protected from any changes in the physical network. If the network layout changes (e.g., a new server is added), only the middleware has to be updated.

The second function of middleware is to translate between incompatible software. Not all tools used to developed client software are compatible with all the tools used to develop server software. Developers of client and server software tools could write interfaces that would enable them to communicate with all other tools on the market, but this would be very time-consuming.

Many middleware tools began as translation utilities that enabled messages sent from a specific client tool to be translated into a form understood by a specific server tool. Today, there are two emerging standards for middleware: Distributed Computing Environment (DCE) and Object Request Broker (ORB). Any software tool that uses

Management Focus: Shutting Down a Mainframe

I turned off my first mainframe at 1:11 P.M. on March 2, 1995. The mainframe I was turning off was a small one: an IBM 4381 Model 13. It had 16 megabytes of RAM and 7.5 gigabytes of disk space. Because it cost more than $250,000 per year to operate, it had reached the end of its cost-effective life. It was replaced by two microcomputers, one of which had more RAM and disk space than the 4381 had. It cost about as much to pay someone to haul the 4381 away as it did to buy one of the replacement microcomputers.

What made the moment of shutdown so sad was that I was surrounded by people who had spent most of their careers caring for it—people who now needed to learn an entirely new set of computer and network systems and an entirely new approach to application development, people late in their careers for whom the transition might prove as difficult as it had for the 4381.

Source: InfoWorld, April 17, 1995.

these standards can communicate with any middleware product that uses them. The middleware tool can then translate from this format into the specific format used by any other client–server tool for which it is programmed.

The Economics of Client–Server Networks

Much of the debate between host-based and client–server networks has centered on cost. One of the great claims of host-based networks in the 1980s was that they provided economies of scale. Manufacturers of big mainframes claimed it was cheaper to provide computer services on one big mainframe than on a set of smaller computers.

The microcomputer revolution changed this. The standard measure of computing power is the MIPS: million instructions per second. In 1992, the average cost for mainframe hardware was $80,000 per MIPS. By 1995, this had dropped to about $35,000 per MIPS, as the prices for mainframes dropped sharply in the face of rapidly declining sales. The cost per MIPS for microcomputer hardware in 1995 was $25. Microcomputer hardware is more than 1000 times cheaper than mainframe hardware for the same amount of computing power.

With cost differences like these, it is easy to see why there has been a sudden rush to microcomputer-based client–server networks. The problem with these cost comparisons is that they overlook the increased complexity associated with developing application software for client–server networks. Several surveys have attempted to discover the cost for software development and maintenance in client–server networks. The truth is, no one really knows, because we do not have enough long-term experience with them. Most experts believe that it costs four to five times more to develop and maintain application software for client–server networks than it does for host-based networks. As more companies gain experience with client–server applications, as new products are developed and refined, and as standards mature, these costs probably will decrease. The architecture of the future is client–server, although there will always be a place for host-based networks.

HOSTS

A computer's suitability to serve as the host for an online, real-time data communication network depends on both its own capabilities and the capabilities of other attached hardware. Many computers today can be used this purpose, provided the ancillary hardware can handle the tasks for which the host computer is inefficient. In other words, the characteristics that make a computer suitable for data communications do not necessarily make it good for "number crunching." In particular, data communication work involves many short periods of activity to service a single arriving or departing character or message. A computer whose hardware or software makes this kind of operation too clumsy does not perform well in the data communication environment. There are three typical types of hosts: mainframe computers, minicomputers, and microcomputers.

Mainframe

This host is a general purpose mainframe computer with a wide area network (WAN) encompassing a large geographical area. It is used for both data communications and application processing, but its emphasis is on the online, real-time data communication portion of the system. In this configuration, there is a distinct division of labor between the front end processor and the general purpose computer (see Figure 4-2).

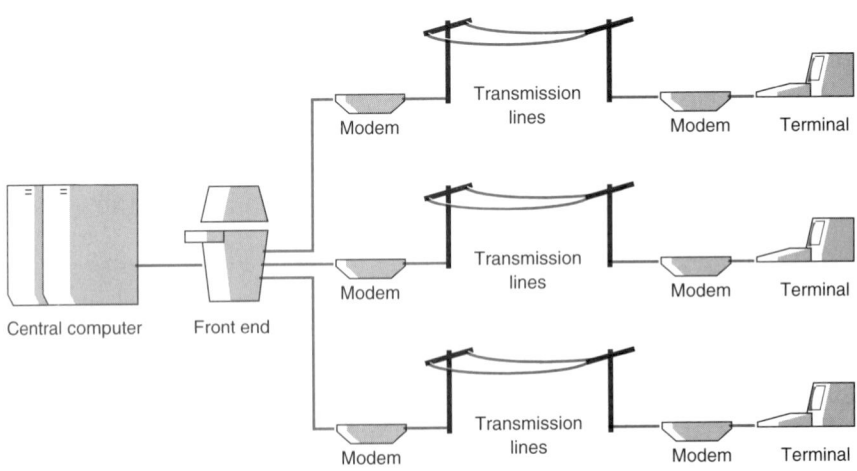

Figure 4-2   Front end/central computer configuration.

As our networks have grown, so too have their demands on the host mainframe. These demands have outpaced the mainframe's ability to handle both its own processing tasks and those required to control network communications. As a result, the front end processor has assumed many of the mainframe's communication control tasks. Front end processors are discussed in more detail later in this chapter.

Minicomputer

A second type of host is a *minicomputer*, which handles a specific set of communication facilities and terminals. Figure 4-3 shows a stand-alone communication configuration in which the minicomputer is able to handle all communication tasks. Manufacturers often use it for process control, and in areas where the user queries a database on the status of a certain product, inventory level, or the like (e.g., a database server in a client–server configuration). This field is dominated by minicomputers that were developed and programmed for special purpose processing and communication functions, but these computers are being replaced by local area networks.

Microcomputer

The final category is a network that uses microcomputers, micro-to-mainframe connections, and local area networks. Although some people may think of this configuration as just a small network, many are large local area networks handling several hundred microcomputers. Usually, this type of network is totally within the corporate/ government business office or facility/campus area. It does not require long-distance communication circuits, and, when users want to transmit outside of this local network, they must address messages so that these can be transferred to other networks through the gateway. Because these networks are so important in today's business and scientific

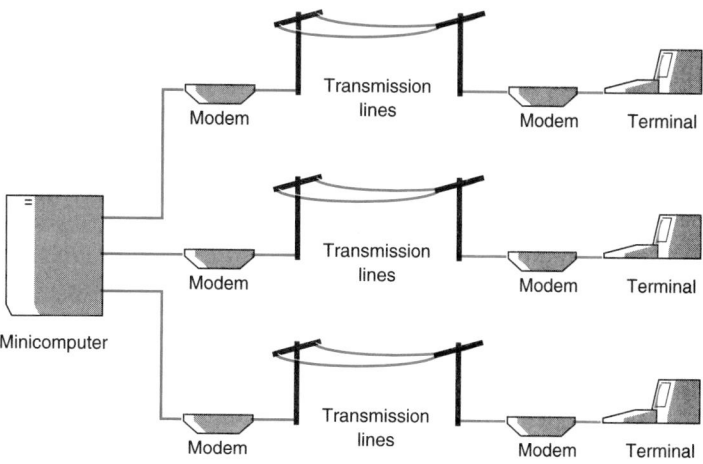

Figure 4-3   Stand-alone communication configuration.

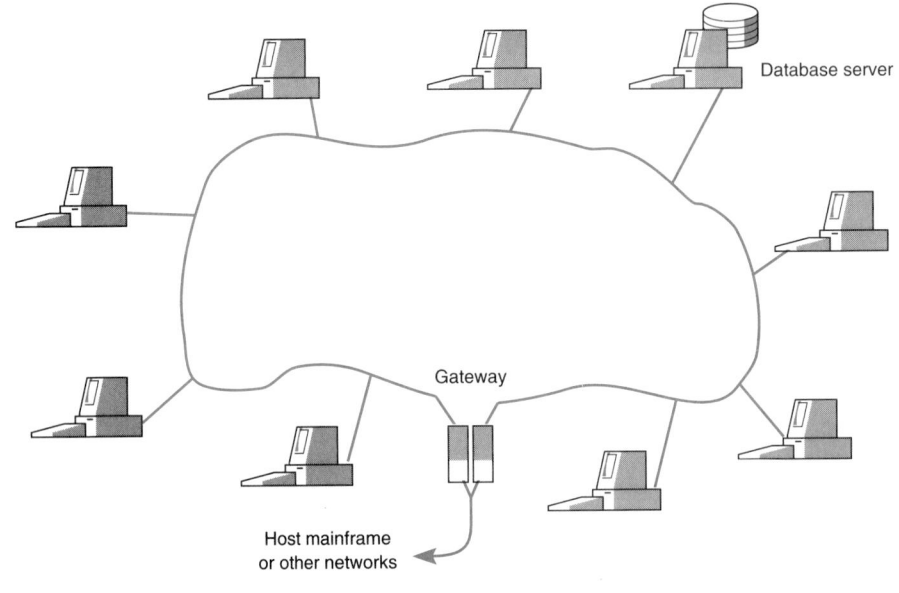

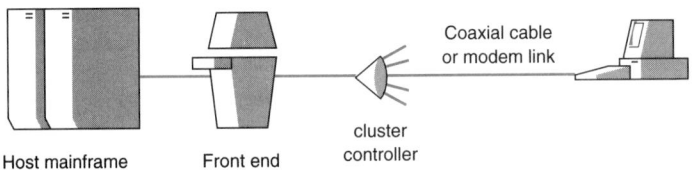

Figure 4-4 Local area network (top) and a micro-to-mainframe connection (bottom).

environment, Chapter 8 is dedicated to local area networks (LANs). Figure 4-4 shows both a LAN and a micro-to-mainframe configuration.

CLIENTS

The client, which is the input/output hardware device at the user's end of a communication circuit, probably is the one piece of equipment with which you are most familiar. There are three major categories of clients: terminals, microcomputers/workstations, and special purpose terminals.

Terminals

General purpose video terminals typically have a television screen and a typewriter keyboard. These *video display units* (VDU) sometimes are referred to as video display terminals (VDT) or cathode ray tubes (CRT). Alphanumeric video terminals are used in the business office, whereas graphic video terminals are used by graphic designers.

When online transaction processing systems became common in the 1970s, so did the use of terminals. The very first terminals were known as *dumb terminals,* so named because they do not participate in the processing of the data they display. These terminals do not have any internal storage for memory or any microprocessor chips. They have the bare minimum required to operate as input and output devices, simply translating messages from the user to the communications circuit, but doing nothing more.

Most dumb terminals use *asynchronous* transmission; that is, when a character is typed, the terminal immediately transmits the character through the data communications circuit to the host. Host computers must have memory buffers for each terminal to assemble the entire message before acting on it. Every keystroke pressed on a dumb terminal has to be processed by the host computer, so simple activities such as pressing the up arrow key or tab key to move the cursor around the screen requires processing time on the host computer. Obviously, the primary problem with dumb terminals is that they place an immense burden on the host computer. But, they are relatively cheap.

Intelligent terminals were developed to reduce these processing demands. An intelligent terminal has an internal memory and a built-in, programmable microprocessor chip. Many simple processing functions such as moving the cursor or displaying certain words in different colors are done by the terminal, thus saving processing time on the host. Intelligent terminals also typically send messages as entire blocks (called *synchronous* transmission) rather than one letter at a time, further saving processing time at the host. The downside, however, is that intelligent terminals are more expensive than dumb ones.

The market for intelligent terminals has been superseded by microcomputers. It makes little sense to buy an expensive intelligent terminal, when for only 20 to 30 percent more, you can buy a microcomputer that is far more capable.

Microcomputers and Workstations

These devices are either general purpose microcomputers or specially designed input/ output workstations that have custom-designed microprocessor chips. Many vendors have developed customized workstations for use in graphics design, manufacturing, banking, and other special situations. The basic input/output device is a microcomputer. Its functions include editing and storing data, performing mathematical calculations, and prompting for information using forms; all can be handled locally without assistance from the host mainframe computer.

Technically, there is a difference between a workstation and a microcomputer. A *workstation* usually provides all the tools professionals need for their daily work. Among these tools are specialized applications like mathematical modeling, computer-assisted design (CAD), intensive programming, and networking. Today's workstation has much more computing power than the average microcomputer. Workstations must offer true multi-tasking capability so the user does not have to wait for the computer to finish one job or program before starting the next. On the other hand, a *microcomputer* may not have the ability to handle all the specialized applications, and its multi-tasking ability may be significantly less. Most microcomputer users may be satisfied with printer sharing and telecommunications as a replacement for true multi-tasking capability. The primary use of a microcomputer is for such functions as word processing, accounting, and spreadsheet modeling. As microcomputers acquire more powerful microprocessor chips (Pentium, Power PC, and beyond), they may become as powerful as contemporary workstations. Therefore, today you may be able to see the difference between a workstation and a microcomputer, but tomorrow they may be the same.

Special Purpose Terminals

Some terminals are designed for special purposes. One of the most common is a *transaction terminal*, designed to support certain business transactions. A familiar example is the automated teller machine (ATM) used by banking institutions for cash dispensing and related functions. Your telephone is another type of transaction terminal that accepts voice or data transactions for transmission by using the Touch-Tone keypad.

Other transaction terminals are point-of-sale terminals in a supermarket; these enter charges directly from the supermarket to your bank account, or they can be used for verifying credit or verifying checks. These terminals can be built into electronic cash registers. For an example of how transaction terminals are used, see the focus box on communications in the rental car industry.

Remote job entry terminals are another type of special purpose terminal. Usually, they are terminal stations where several types of devices are connected. Data often are transmitted from a host computer to a remote job entry terminal that might have a video terminal, a high speed printing terminal, several data entry devices (such as disk or tape), and perhaps a microcomputer. These terminals operate at higher speeds because large quantities of data are transmitted from them to the central host computer.

Attributes of Terminals and Microcomputers

Shopping for terminals or microcomputers can be difficult because there are many attributes to be considered. The selected terminal, microcomputer, or workstation must be compatible with the communication protocols used by the network and the host, and its general characteristics and uses must meet the user's specific day-to-day business requirements. For example, a bargain terminal may have the wrong code format or an incompatible protocol, which requires the additional purchase of a protocol converter. When selecting a terminal or microcomputer, you should consider the following features, which often affect productivity.

Ergonomics and Flexibility   To prevent muscular aches and fatigue, terminals and microcomputers should have movable keyboards, document holders, and screens that tilt to a comfortable viewing angle. The height of the video screen and its ability to tilt might be crucial to the terminal operator who wears bifocals. Computer furniture often requires that video screens be placed above eye level. This should be considered when purchasing such furniture because users (especially those who wear bifocals) should be able to look *down* onto the screen to prevent neck strain.

Screen Quality   Always obtain the highest possible video monitor resolution. For example, some monitors have resolution of 1280 (horizontal) by 1024 (vertical) pixels, although 640 by 480 is more common. The higher the resolution (a greater number of pixels), the clearer the picture and the less eyestrain. (*Pixels* are "picture elements"; each one is a small dot on a video tube.) Also, the smallest dots (pixels) produce better resolution (0.28 dot size is good).

Larger screens (e.g., 17-inch rather than 14-inch) have larger characters, which make for easy viewing. Cursors should be visible from eight feet away, and they should be seen easily at three feet. Sometimes it is advantageous to have the option of either a blinking cursor, an extra large cursor, or one that remains lighted constantly.

Adjustments for image size, brightness, focus, and contrast are desirable to accommodate the various operators who might use a video terminal. An anti-glare screen should be used because glare is a major complaint of video terminal or microcomputer users.

Screen color is controversial. Generally speaking, displays with black characters on white screens are the most legible. Many users, however, feel that yellow on green is the easiest to see and tends to reduce eyestrain. Color monitors are often preferred because color tends to reduce eyestrain and enhance productivity because color makes it easier to understand an application.

The characters on the video monitor tube should not jitter or flicker because this movement causes eyestrain. By using a magnifying glass to look at the characters, you should be able to determine whether they jitter or flicker. The best choice is a non-interlaced monitor.

Data Entry Technology   The most popular method of entering data is through use of a keyboard and mouse or trackball, but there are other methods. For example:

Light pens are used to touch the screen. The light activates what you touch.

A *touch screen* works the same way as light pens, except you touch a portion of the screen with your finger to make a selection.

Direct voice entry is becoming feasible, but it still is in the early stages of technological development. Many systems can recognize pre-trained words if spoken distinctly with pauses between words. Systems that can recognize continuous speech are still very expensive.

Management Focus: Communications in the Rental Car Industry

One major application for large national and international communication networks is the rental of automobiles. Avis Rent-A-Car was the first major company to develop an online real-time rental car network. This network interconnects the major locations where automobiles are rented, picked up, and returned.

A rental car network is quite similar to an airline network because it records rental agreements with people who rent the cars, calculates the cost and mileage used, keeps track of dates when cars must be returned, and performs other general accounting functions.

Both Hertz and Avis, in their latest round of technological one-upsmanship, introduced handheld computer terminals that allow service representatives to completely check in returning cars almost before customers can unbuckle their seat belts. The Avis service, called Roving Rapid Return, allows customers to get a receipt immediately without having to enter the rental agency building, stand in line, and wait while someone processes the rental contract.

When a car enters the Avis lot, for example, a service representative enters the Avis registration number on the car's rear window into one of the handheld terminals. The terminal, which is linked locally to the Avis worldwide "Wizard" network by FM radio, retrieves the driver's name and rental information from a central mainframe database. It displays the customer's name so the service representative can use it while obtaining the car's odometer reading and gas tank level. Once that information has been entered, the mainframe totals the customer's bill and instructs the terminal's printer to produce a final receipt if the credit card number was given earlier. The customer can leave as soon as the receipt is printed. The Hertz express check-in service operates in a similar manner.

Page scanners automatically read a printed page and enter it into the computer. Some scanner software only has the ability to scan graphics, some can scan only text, and some can do both.

Small cameras are available for the *direct digital entry* of graphics or full motion video in to the computer system.

CIRCUITS

Network Configuration

Network configuration is the basic physical layout of the network. There are two fundamental network configurations: point-to-point and multipoint. In practice, most complex computer networks have many circuits, some of which are point-to-point, and some of which are multipoint.

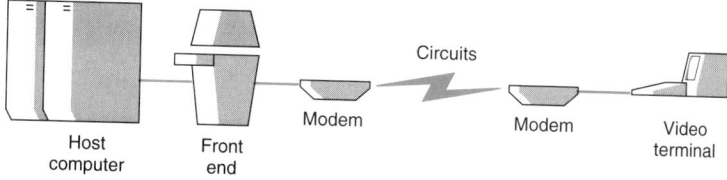

Figure 4-5   Point-to-point configuration.

Figure 4-5 illustrates a *point-to-point configuration,* which is so named because it goes from one point to another. Because it connects one client to one host, these circuits sometimes are called *two-point circuits.* This type of configuration is quite advantageous when the remote terminal transmits enough data to fill the entire capacity of the communication circuit. When an organization builds a network using point-to-point circuits, each client has its own circuit running from itself to the host; many point-to-point circuits may emanate from the host to the various clients wherever they are located. This can get very expensive, particularly if there is some distance between the clients and the host. When you use the dial-up telephone network to make a telephone call, that is a point-to-point connection.

Figure 4-6 shows a *multipoint configuration* (also called *multidrop*). In this configuration, many terminals or microcomputers are connected on the same circuit. This means that each device must share the circuit with the other devices, much like a party line in telephone communications. The disadvantage is that only one device can use the circuit at a time. When one device is sending or receiving data, all others must wait. This multipoint configurations typically are used when each terminal or micro-

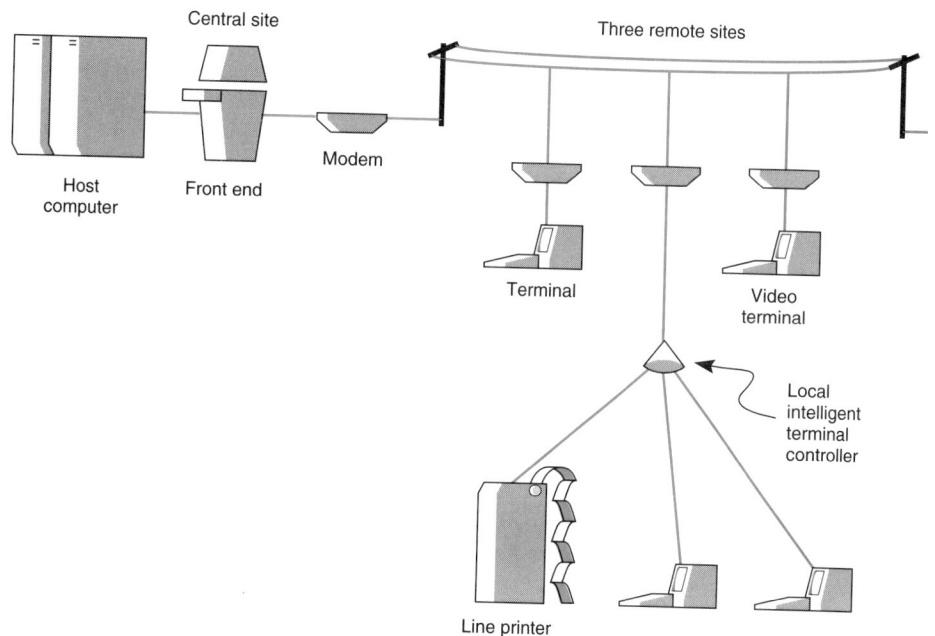

Figure 4-6   Multipoint configuration with three drops.

computer does not need to continuously utilize the entire capacity of the circuit, and thus users perceive few delays.

The advantage of multipoint circuits is that they reduce the amount of cable required and typically use the available communication circuit more efficiently. Imagine the amount of cable required if the network in Figure 4-6 was designed with separate point-to-point circuits. Multipoint configurations are often cheaper than point-to-point configurations. When there are various branch offices or government agencies throughout a building, a city or state, multipoint configurations can be a very efficient method of interconnection.

Data Flow

Circuits can be designed to permit data to flow in one direction or in both directions. Actually, there are three ways to transmit: simplex, half duplex, and full duplex (see Figure 4-7).

Simplex is one-way transmission, such as that in radio or TV transmission.

Half duplex is two-way transmission, but you can transmit in only one direction at a time. A half duplex communication link is similar to a walkie-talkie link; only one "system" can talk at a time and the other must listen. Instead of using talk and listen buttons, computers use *control signals* to negotiate which system will send and which will receive data. The amount of time half duplex communication takes to switch between sending and receiving is called *turnaround time* (also called *retrain time* or *reclocking time*). The turnaround time for a specific circuit can be obtained from its technical specifications (often between 20 to 50 milliseconds). Europeans use the term *simplex circuit* to mean a half duplex circuit.

With *full duplex* transmission, you can transmit in both directions simultaneously, with no turnaround time. This is the opposite of simplex, which transmits messages unidirectionally.

How do you choose which data flow method to use? Obviously one factor is the application. If data only ever need to flow in one direction (e.g., from a remote sensor to a host computer), then simplex is probably the best choice. In most cases, however, data must flow in both directions.

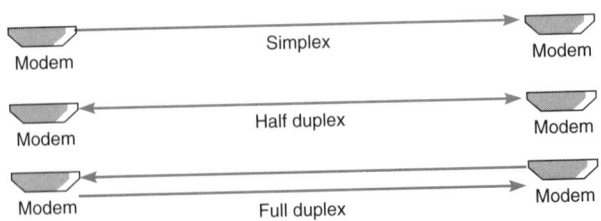

Figure 4-7 This shows simplex, half duplex, and full duplex transmission.

Technical Focus: Transmission Circuit Terminology

Medium   The medium is the matter or substance that carries a message from one point to another. The medium might be copper wires, a thin strand of glass, or air in a satellite transmission because the electromagnetic signal travels through the air from a ground station to a satellite in space.

Circuit   A circuit is simply the path over which data move. It can be a copper wire, a through-the-air satellite link, or a combination of the two. Note the contrast between circuit, which is a path, and medium, which is the material over which the message travels.

Line   This term frequently is used interchangeably with circuit; however, this usage is not completely accurate. Line implies a physical connection between two points, such as a copper wire. By contrast, circuit is more accurate when referring to satellite or microwave transmissions because there is no physical connection. Line, the older of the two terms, was used by those who worked with voice telephone systems that existed long before data communications.

Link   A link is an unbroken circuit path between two points.

Channel   This term can be confusing because common usage allows for two definitions. In the first, channel is used interchangeably with circuit, such as when there is a communication channel or a communication circuit between two points. In the second, channel means the subdivision of a circuit. For example, a company that has a communication circuit between Los Angeles and New York subdivides it into four channels or subchannels so four different messages can be transmitted simultaneously over a single circuit.

The initial temptation is to presume that a full duplex channel is best; however, each circuit only has so much capacity to carry data. Creating a full duplex circuit means that the available capacity is divided—half in one direction and half in the other. In some cases, it makes more sense to build a set of simplex circuits in the same way a set of one-way streets can speed traffic. In other cases, a half duplex circuit may work best. For example, terminals connected to mainframes often transmit data to the host, wait for a reply, transmit more data, and so on in a turn-taking process; seldom does traffic need to flow in both directions simultaneously. Such a traffic pattern is ideally suited to half duplex circuits.

Communication Media (Circuits/Channels)

The *medium* (or media if there is more than one) is the matter or substance that carries the voice or data transmission. Many different types of transmission media are currently in use, such as copper (wire), glass or plastic (fiber optic cable), or air (microwave or satellite). There are two basic types of media. *Guided media* are those in which the message flows through a physical media such as a twisted pair wire, coaxial cable, or fiber optic cable; the media "guides" the signal. *Radiated media* are those in which the message is broadcast through the air, such as infrared, microwave, or satellite.

In many cases, the circuits used in wide area networks are provided by the various common carriers who sell usage of them to the public. We call the circuits sold by the common carriers *communication services.* Chapter 9 describes specific services available in the United States. The following sections describe the medium and the basic characteristics of each circuit type, in the event you were establishing your own physical network, while Chapter 9 describes how the circuits are packaged and marketed for purchase or lease from a common carrier. If your organization has leased a circuit from a common carrier, you are probably less interested in the media used, and more interested in whether the speed, cost, and reliability of the circuit meets your needs.

Twisted Pair Wire   *Wire cables* are insulated pairs of wires that can be packed quite closely together (see Figure 4-8). Bundles of several thousand wire pairs are placed under city streets and in large buildings. Wire cables usually are twisted (*twisted pair wires*) to minimize the electromagnetic interference between one pair and any other pair in the bundle. Your house or apartment probably has a set of two twisted pair wires (i.e., four wires) from it to the telephone company central switching office. One pair is used to connect your telephone; the other pair is spare. Wire cables also are being replaced by more efficient transmission media, such as coaxial cable, microwave, satellite, or optical fibers. The wire pair that connects your telephone to the wall plug is a wire cable. It is not twisted because it is so short and, if twisted, it would not look nice. Twisted pairs used in LANs are discussed in Chapter 8.

Coaxial Cable   Figure 4-9 shows a single coaxial cable and a bundle of coaxial cables. Each *coaxial cable* has a copper core (the inner conductor) with an outer cylindrical

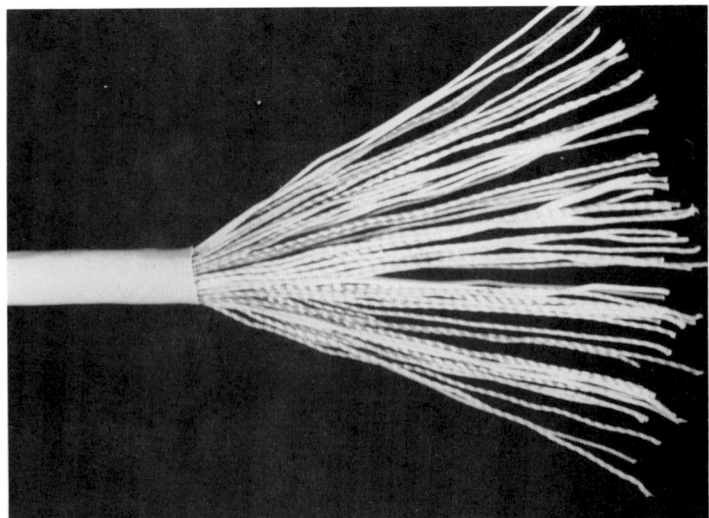

Figure 4-8   Twisted wire pair cables.

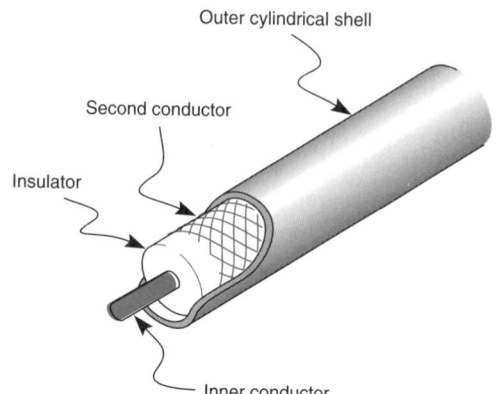

Outer cylindrical shell

Second conductor

Insulator

Inner conductor

Figure 4-9 Coaxial cables. Cut-away view (bottom) of a single coaxial cable and a cross-sectional view (top) of a bundle of 20 coaxial cables.

shell for insulation. The outer shield, just under the shell, is the second conductor. Coaxial cable has substantially more transmission capacity than a twisted pair cable, and is therefore more efficient. A 2-inch diameter bundle of coaxial cables like those shown in Figure 4-9 can handle approximately 20,000 voice or data telephone calls simultaneously. Because coaxial cables have very little distortion and are less prone to interference, they tend to have low error rates. Coaxial cables also are discussed in the context of local area networks in Chapter 8.

Fiber Optic Cable   Twisted pair and coaxial cable are the most common types of guided media, however, a relatively new medium, *fiber optics,* is becoming much more widely used. Instead of carrying telecommunication signals in the traditional electrical form, this technology utilizes high speed streams of light pulses from lasers or LEDs (light emitting diodes) that carry information inside hair-thin strands of glass or plastic called optical fibers. Plastic is being used less, however, because glass can be made into a purer product, enabling the signal to be transmitted over a greater distance. A new, extremely pure *halide glass* will increase the distance that fiber optic cables can travel. Figure 4-10 shows a fiber optic cable and depicts the optical core, the cladding, and how light rays travel in optical fibers.

An average cable bundle contains about 72 fibers, and a large cable contains about 144 fibers. A cable bundle for use within a building contains from 24 to 36 fibers. The earliest fiber optic cable systems were multimode, meaning they carried several light waves down the fiber simultaneously. But multimode cables were plagued by excessive signal weakening (attenuation) and dispersion (spreading of the optical pulse). Single mode optical fiber cables transmit a single direct beam of light. It achieves higher performance, in part because the core diameter has been reduced from 50 microns to about 8 to 10 microns. This smaller diameter core allows the fiber to send a concentrated light beam farther than multimode because the light strikes the core/cladding boundary at a much smaller angle, causing less attenuation and dispersion.

Fiber optic technology is a revolutionary departure from the traditional message-carrying systems of copper wires, or microwave and satellite radio signals discussed next. One of the main advantages of fiber optics is that it can carry huge amounts of information at extremely fast data rates. This capacity makes it ideal for the simultaneous transmission of voice, data, and image signals. In most cases, fiber optic cable is less restricted under harsh environmental conditions than its metallic counterparts. It is not as fragile or brittle as might be expected, and it is more resistant to corrosion than copper. The only chemical that affects optical fiber is hydrofluoric acid. Also, in case of fire, an optical fiber can withstand higher temperatures than copper wire. Even when the outside jacket surrounding the optical fiber has melted, a fiber optic system still can be operational in an emergency signaling system.

Infrared Transmission   *Infrared* transmission uses low frequency light waves (below the visible spectrum) to carry the data through the air on a direct line-of-sight path between two points. This technology is similar to the technology used in infrared TV remote controls. It is prone to interference, particularly from heavy rain, smoke, and fog that obscure the light transmission.

Unlike satellite and microwave systems, infrared is not bound by many government regulations. Transmitters are also quite small, so it can be easier to install and use. Infrared is not very common, but it is sometimes used to transmit data between adjacent buildings. A version of infrared has also been adopted by some portable microcomputer manufacturers to transfer data between the portable and a desktop microcomputer at distances of less than three feet.

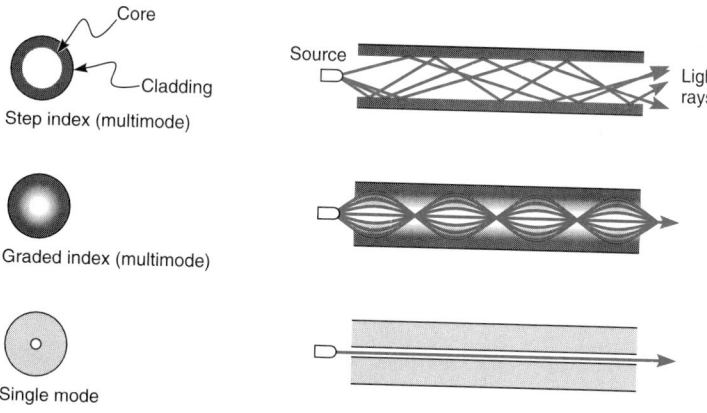

Figure 4-10 Fiber optic cable compared to twisted pair.

Microwave Transmission A *microwave* is an extremely high frequency radio communication beam that is transmitted over a direct line-of-sight path between any two points. As its name implies, a microwave signal is an extremely short wavelength, thus the word *MICRO*wave. Microwave radio transmissions perform the same functions as cables. For example, Point A communicates with Point B via a through-the-air microwave transmission path, instead of a copper wire cable. Because microwave signals approach the frequency of visible light waves, they exhibit the same characteristics as light waves, such as reflection, focusing, or refraction. As with visible light waves, microwave signals can be focused into narrow, powerful beams that can be projected over long distances. Just as a parabolic reflector focuses a searchlight into a beam, a parabolic reflector also focuses a high frequency microwave into a narrow beam. As the distance between communication points increases, towers are used to elevate the radio antennas to account for the Earth's curvature and maintain a clear line-of-sight path between the two parabolic reflectors (see Figure 4-11). A microwave acts as a carrier for hundreds of different simultaneous messages, whether standard voice telephone calls or data transmissions.

This transmission medium is the one most used for long distance data or voice transmission. It does not require the laying of any cable because long distance horn antennas with microwave repeater stations are placed approximately 25 to 30 miles apart. A typical long distance horn antenna might be 10 feet wide, although over shorter distances in the inner cities, the dish antennas might be less than two feet in diameter. Larger cities are becoming microwave congested; so many microwave dish antennas have been installed that they interfere with each other, and the air waves are saturated. This problem will force future users to seek alternative transmission media,

Figure 4-11   A typical microwave tower.

Figure 4-12 Short haul intracity microwave dish antenna.

such as satellite or optical fiber links. Figure 4-12 shows a short haul intracity micro-wave dish antenna, which can connect two buildings or two local area networks several miles apart.

Satellite Transmission   Transmission via *satellite* is similar to transmission via micro-wave except, instead of transmitting to another nearby microwave dish antenna, it transmits to a satellite 22,300 miles in space. Figure 4-13 depicts a geosynchronous satellite—geosynchronous means that the satellite remains stationary over one point on the Earth. Figure 4-14 shows the satellite in operation.

One disadvantage of satellite transmission is the delay that occurs because the signal has to travel out into space and back to Earth *(propagation delay)*. For half duplex transmission, the typical signal propagation time is approximately 0.5 second for the round-trip delay. This is because the message has to travel from Point A on the ground to the satellite, and then from the satellite to Point B on the ground (see Figure 4-14). In addition, the acknowledgment that the message was received without errors must do the reverse, going from Point B to the satellite and from the satellite to Point A. This covers four links of 22,300 miles each, and 4 times 22,300 divided by 186,000

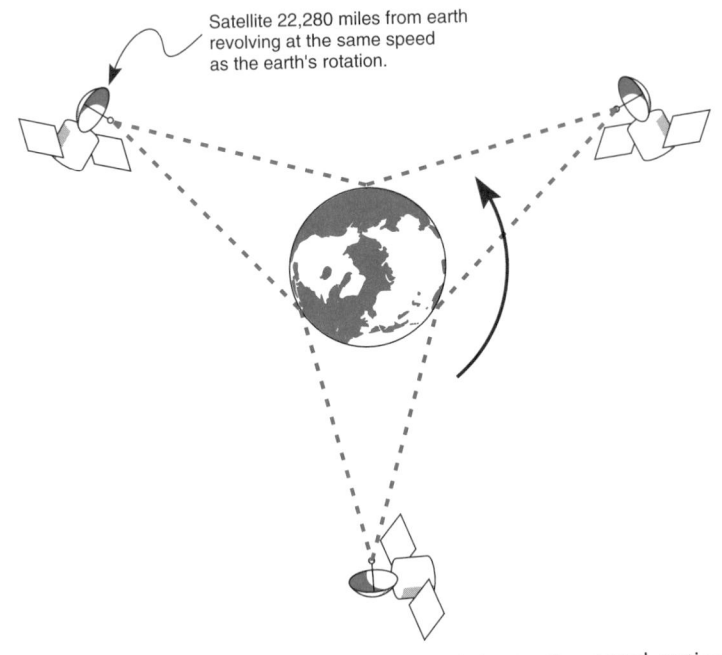

Satellite 22,280 miles from earth
revolving at the same speed
as the earth's rotation.

Figure 4-13 Satellite in operation transmitting to its ground station antennas.

Figure 4-14 Satellite in operation transmitting to its ground station antennas.

equals 0.48 second. (Microwaves travel at 186,000 miles per second.) Moreover, there may be a further delay as the circuits from the ground station to your business office go through ground-based switching equipment. The delay is controlled by the common carriers to avoid disrupting voice telephone conversation. In data communications, however, this delay can prove difficult.

One of the problems associated with some types of satellite transmission is *raindrop attenuation*. This problem occurs because some satellite transmissions waves at the high end of the spectrum are so short they can be absorbed by raindrops. It is not a major problem, but engineers need to work around it.

Security poses a serious problem for satellite communications because it is easy to intercept the transmission as it travels through the air. Laser communication systems, which have begun to revolutionize long distance data transmission on Earth through the use of fiber optics, now are moving into the satellite arena. Where terrestrial-based fiber optic networks now send pulses of laser light down hair-thin fibers of glass, future satellites will exchange information by transmitting laser beams across thousands of miles of space. Such laser *intersatellite link* (ISL) systems currently are under development in Germany, France, and the United States. One major American laser ISL application is to cross-link military satellites in geostationary orbits 22,300 miles high so they can communicate between themselves without having to rely on a vulnerable ground station on Earth.

New *Ku-band* satellites use waves that are so short they can be caught and concentrated in much smaller dish antennas, called very small aperture terminals (VSAT), that can be installed on virtually any building (or vehicle). A typical Ku-band satellite network provides either one-way or full duplex communications among VSATs installed at a large number of remote branch offices and a larger Earth dish or "hub" installed at a central site.

These large Earth dish hubs can cost as much as several hundred thousand dollars. Companies such as Tymnet and AT&T Communications offer shared services to customers. This means users only have to buy inexpensive VSATs instead of a significantly more expensive central hub dish. To put this cost in perspective, you can lease one-tenth of a satellite transponder for less than $10,000 per month. This portion of a transponder can support a 120-node full duplex network. (*Transponders* in the satellite receive the incoming signals and retransmit them back to Earth.)

In late 1994, RCA introduced a direct broadcast satellite (DBS) system that enables homeowners or businesses to install 18-inch KU-band VSATs to receive satellite broadcasts for about $700. DBS lets owners receive more than 150 TV channels of higher quality video and audio than traditional cable TV. The real potential for DBS lies not only in the replacement of cable TV, but with the coming integration of video, voice, and data, as another high speed circuit into the home and office.

One problem, however, is satellite crowding in space. There is now both orbit and frequency congestion among the various satellites. Figure 4-15 depicts a band of satellites around the Earth, first as if you were looking at it from space, and then from Earth. You can place only so many synchronous satellites around the band. Notice that this figure shows a four-degree separation between each satellite. If you brought them too close together, they would touch. Because of frequency congestion—most of the available frequencies are in use today—we will have to expand the available frequencies to meet future needs for satellite data, voice, and image transmission.

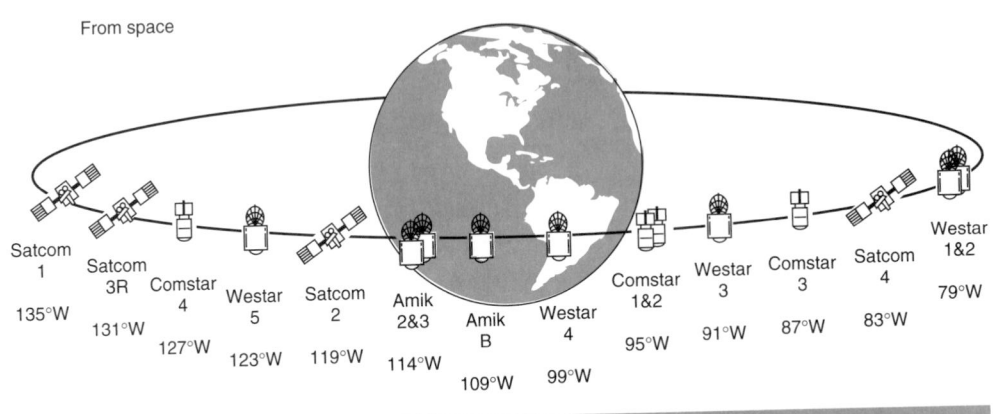

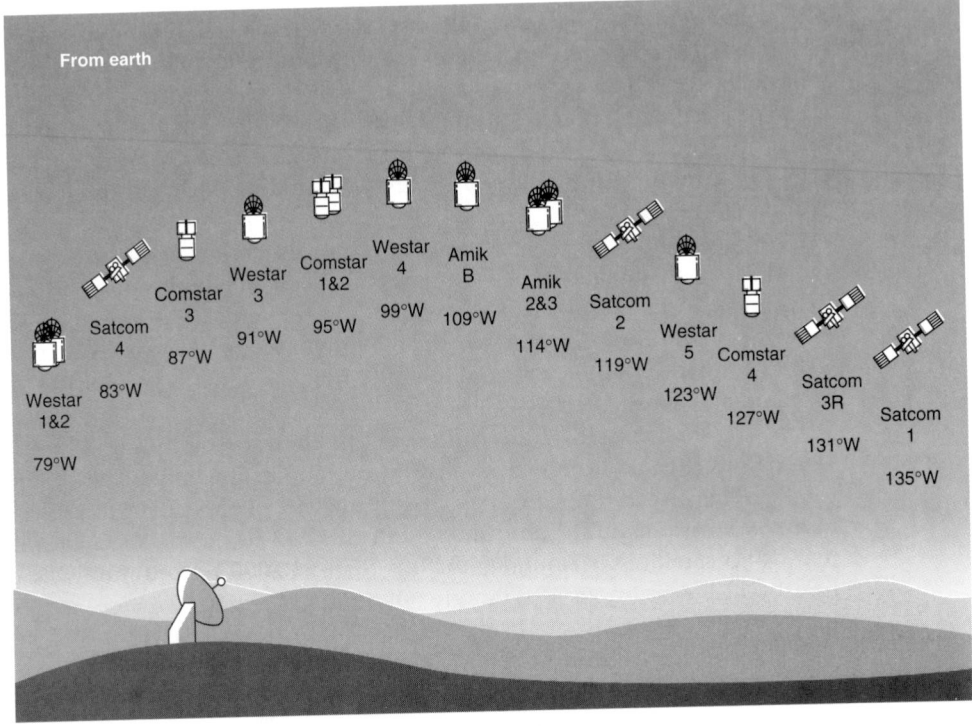

Figure 4-15 Geosynchronous satellite band around the equator.

Look at the top half of Figure 4-15 and find your location on the globe. Then chart an imaginary line from where you are to one of the satellites. Notice how this line tends to go directly south, or possibly a little southeast or southwest, if you are in the United States. For this reason, satellite dishes in the United States usually face south and possibly southeast or southwest, depending on which satellite is being used for signal reception. Daniel Boone and Kit Carson may have looked for moss on the north side of a tree for compass direction, but today's high-tech adventurer looks for the southerly direction of a satellite dish.

Media Selection

Which media are best? It is hard to say, particularly when manufacturers continue to improve various media products. Several factors are important in selecting media, as Figure 4-16 summarizes.

- The *type of network* is one major consideration. Some media are only used for wide area networks (microwaves and satellite), while others typically are not (twisted pair, coaxial cable, and infrared)—although we should note that some old WAN networks still use twisted pair. Fiber optic cable is unique in that it can be used for virtually any type of network.

- *Cost* is always a factor in any business decision. Costs are always changing as new technologies are developed and as competition among vendors drives prices down. Among the guided media, twisted pair wire is generally the cheapest, coaxial cable is somewhat more expensive, and fiber optic cable is the most expensive. The costs of the radiated media are generally driven more by distance than any other factor: for short distances (several hundred meters), infrared is cheapest; for moderate distances (several hundred miles), microwave is cheapest; and for long distances, satellite is cheapest.

- *Transmission distance* is a related factor. Twisted pair wire and coaxial cable can only transmit data a short distance: twisted pair typically from 100 to 300 meters, and coaxial cable typically from 200 to 500 meters. Fiber optics cable can transmit up to 30 miles. To transmit data over longer distances, a device that receives the data and retransmits it on a new segment of cable must be used. This increases cost, and adds more devices in the network that can fail.

	Twisted Pair	Coaxial Cable	Fiber Optics
Network Type	LAN	LAN	any
Cost	Low	Moderate	High
Transmission Distance	Short	Short	Moderate
Security	Good	Good	Very Good
Error rates	Low	Low	Very Low
Transmission Speed	Low-High	Low-High	High-Very High
	Infrared	**Microwave**	**Satellite**
Network Type	LAN	WAN	WAN
Cost	Low	Moderate	Moderate
Transmission Distance	Moderate	Long	Long
Security	Poor	Poor	Poor
Error rates	Moderate	Low-Moderate	Low-Moderate
Transmission Speed	Low	Moderate	Moderate

Figure 4-16   Media Summary

Management Focus: Satellite Communications Improves Performance

Boyle Transportation hauls hazardous materials nationwide for both commercial customers and the government, particularly the Department of Defense. The Department of Defense recently mandated that hazardous materials contractors use mobile communications systems with up-to-the-minute monitoring when hauling the Department's hazardous cargoes.

After looking at the alternatives, Boyle realized that it would have to build its own system. It needed a relational database at its operations center that contained information about customers, pickups, deliveries, truck location, and truck operating status. Data are distributed from this database via satellite to an antenna on each truck. Now, at any time, Boyle can notify the designated truck to make a new pick up via the bi-directional satellite link, and record the truck's acknowledgement.

Each truck contains a Qualcomm Inc. mobile data terminal connected to the Qualcomm satellite network. Each driver uses a keyboard to enter information, which transmits the location of the truck. This satellite data is received by the main offices via a leased line from the satellite Earth station.

This system increased productivity by an astounding 80 percent over two years, while administration costs only increased by 20 percent.

- *Security* is primarily determined by whether the media is guided or radiated. Radiated media (infrared, microwave, and satellite) are the least secure because their signals are easily intercepted. Guided media (twisted pair, coaxial, and fiber optics) are more secure, with fiber optics being the most secure.

- *Error rates* are also important. Radiated media are most susceptible to interference and thus have the highest error rates. Among the guided media, fiber optics provides the lowest error rates, coaxial cable the next best, and twisted pair the worst—although twisted pair is generally better than the radiated media.

- *Transmission speeds* vary greatly among the different media. It is difficult to quote specific speeds for different media because transmission speeds are constantly improving, and because they vary within the same type of media depending upon the specific type of cable and the vendor. In general, both twisted pair and coaxial cable can provide data rates from 1 to 100 Mbps (one million bits per second), while fiber optic cable ranges from 100 Mbps to 2 Gbps (2 billion bits per second). Infrared generally provides 1 to 4 Mbps, while microwave and satellite range from 20 to 50 Mbps.

SPECIAL PURPOSE COMMUNICATION DEVICES

In this section, we discuss five categories of communication devices that do specific things as part of the communication network. *Front end processors* perform certain network functions for a host computer so that the host need not spend as much time managing the network. *Multiplexers* break one high speed communication circuit into several lower speed circuits so that many different devices can simultaneously use it. Multiplexers can also combine several low speed circuits into one high speed circuit. *Protocol converters* connect networks that use different protocols. As we will discuss in Chapter 7, *protocols* are the formal rules that define how data are transmitted in a communication (e.g., the rules of English grammar and syntax). *Line adapters* allow more terminals to be connected to one circuit, or more than one circuit to a terminal.

Front End Processors (FEP)

In general, most large mainframe computers that act as host computers for large wide area networks are loaded with heavy processing demands; they have very little spare processing capacity to perform data communications functions. Where these data communications functions place a heavy demand on the host computer, there is considerable pressure to move them onto special purpose devices. This increases the efficiency of the network because each of these devices can be designed specifically to meet assigned tasks. Often it is cheaper to buy several special purpose devices than to upgrade the host computer. Figure 4-17 is an example of this.

One key device in this movement is the *front end processor* (FEP), which can take two forms. The first is a nonprogrammable, hardwired, communication control unit designed by the computer manufacturer to adapt specific line and terminal characteristics to the computer. The second form is a minicomputer or microcomputer that can handle some or all the communication input/output activity as well as perform some processing.

The primary application of the FEP is to serve as the interface between the host

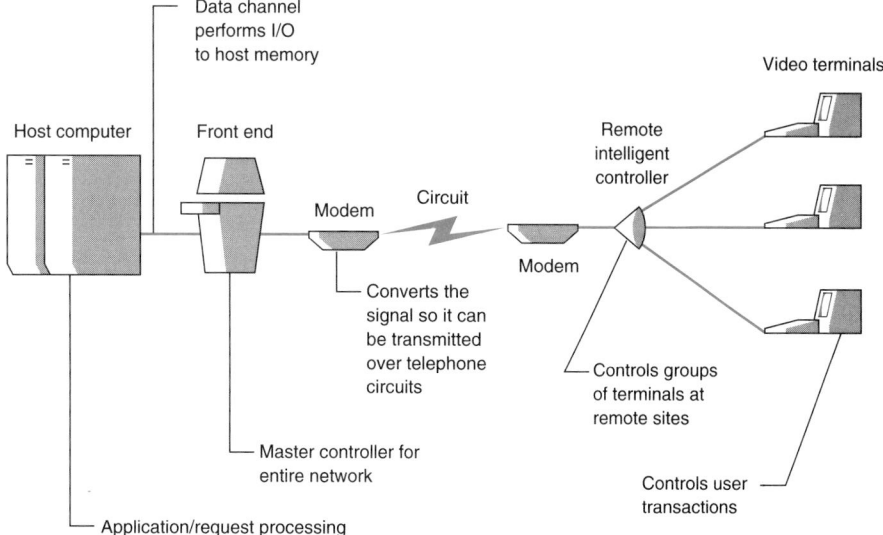

Figure 4-17   Downline network control.

computer and the data communication network with its hundreds or even thousands of terminals or microcomputers. It performs all the functions associated with the data link layer described in Chapter 6 (controlling access to the circuit, formatting messages to mark their beginning and end, and controlling errors). The FEP also performs the same functions as protocol converters (translating between different communication formats used by different devices). Another function is *message switching*, which reroutes a message destined for some other terminal or computer in the network without going through the host computer.

Many of the newer and more powerful front end processors can do *message processing*. For example, the processor might receive inquiry messages from remote terminals, process the messages to determine the specific information required, retrieve the information from an attached disk, and send it back to the inquiring terminals without involving the host computer. In networks of this type, application-oriented processing is as important as message receipt and transmission.

Channel Extenders   A *channel extender* is a scaled-down, less expensive front end processor (see Figure 4-18) that links remote host computers or minicomputers to the central host facilities. Channel extenders attach directly to the host mainframe at the same place where a front end processor connects. In addition to this interconnection they support disk drives, high speed printers, and microcomputers. Although channel extenders may be slower and less powerful than front end processors, they provide a less expensive way to improve response time for users at remote locations, offload some of the front end data communication traffic from local area networks or micro-to-mainframe connections within a building, or handle data processing requirements if the central site has problems. As their software becomes more powerful, the gen-

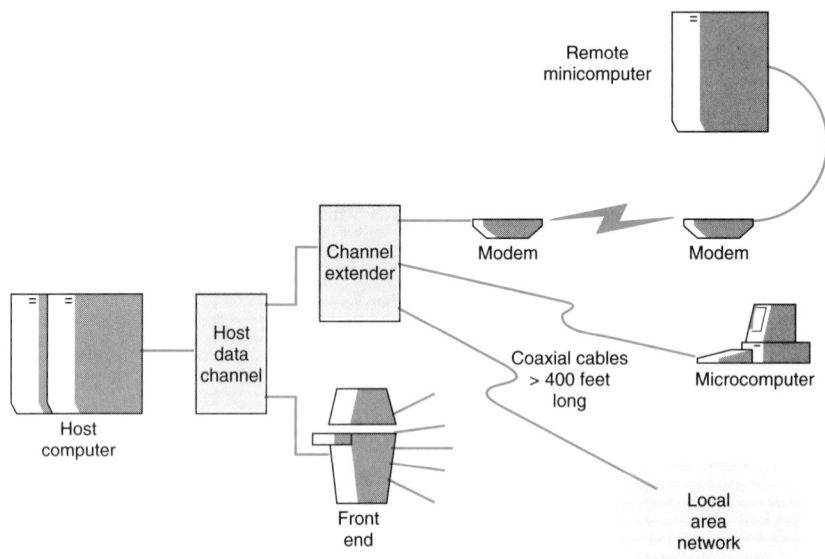

Figure 4-18   Channel extender.

eration of channel extenders now in use will begin to compete directly with front end processors.

Intelligent Controllers   Intelligent controllers are scaled-down FEPs. *Remote intelligent controllers,* sometimes called *intelligent terminal controllers,* reside at the distant or far end of a communication circuit and control 4 to 32 terminals. They are used because they reduce the transmission costs between the terminals and the host computer, and because they reduce the processing on the host.

A *central site intelligent controller* is connected directly to a single port on the front end processor, and can handle up to 32 outgoing lines. It reduces the processing on the FEP, and increases the number of lines available.

The use of microcomputers as terminals is causing a problem with intelligent controllers because they are being overwhelmed with data transmissions from microcomputers. Transmissions on circuits connecting terminals and hosts used to be short messages and data transfers. Now we are transmitting entire files of data (thousands of characters) by using microcomputers that can overload controllers originally built to handle many short transactions of 100 characters or less. If many microcomputers start transmitting files simultaneously, it can bring down (crash) the controller, which delays everyone's processing.

Multiplexers

To *multiplex* is to place two or more simultaneous transmissions on a single communication circuit. Multiplexing a voice telephone call means that two or more separate conversations are sent simultaneously over one communication circuit between two different cities. Multiplexing a data communication network means that two or more messages are sent simultaneously over one communication circuit.

Multiplexing usually is done in multiples of 4, 8, 16, and 32 simultaneous transmissions over a single communication circuit. Figure 4-19 shows a typical four-level multiplexed circuit. Note that two multiplexers are needed for each circuit; one to combine the four original circuits into the one multiplexed circuit and one to separate them back into the four separate circuits.

An important aspect of multiplexing is *transparency,* which means the multiplexer does not interrupt the flow of data. No device is aware of the multiplexer regardless of the type of circuit. When the circuit is multiplexed at one end and demultiplexed at the other, each user's terminal or microcomputer thinks it has its own separate connection to the host computer.

Generally speaking, the multiplexed circuit must have the same capacity as the sum of the circuits it combines. For example, if each of the four terminals in Figure 4-19 transmits at 9600 bits per second, then the multiplexed circuit must transmit at 38,400 bits per second.

Why Multiplex?   The primary benefit of multiplexing is to save money. Figure 4-20 shows how several levels of multiplexing can save on communication costs. The first

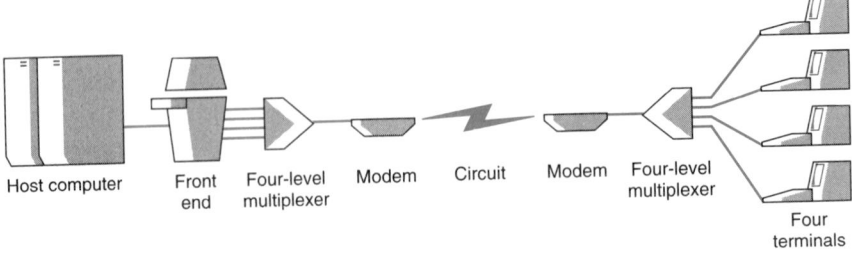

Figure 4-19   Multiplexed circuit (TDM).

level of multiplexing occurs where four terminals are multiplexed onto a single IXC (interexchange channel) for transmission to a distant site (e.g., San Diego to Phoenix, Los Angeles to Phoenix, and San Francisco to Denver). The second level multiplexes the resulting signals over a signal IXC circuit (e.g., Phoenix to Chicago, and Denver to Chicago). Finally, the third level multiplexes these signals over a single IXC circuit from Chicago to New York.

As you examine this illustration, think about how much more circuit mileage would be involved if you had a point-to-point circuit going from the front end processor to each of the 24 terminal locations. Also, consider how an alternative multipoint configuration (see Figure 4-21), might be used to connect the various terminal device locations, in contrast to one that uses multiplexing.

Multiplexers can be separated into three major categories: frequency division multiplexers (FDM), time division multiplexers (TDM), and statistical time division multiplexers (STDM). In general, TDM is preferred to FDM, because it provides higher data transmission speeds and because TDM multiplexers are simpler. STDM is also fairly common because of its more efficient use of the available circuit capacity. Wave-

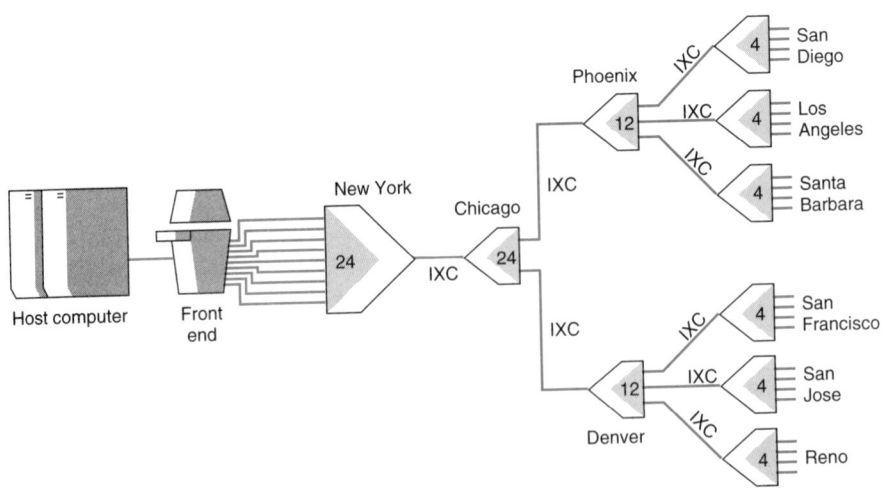

Figure 4-20   Multiplexing and concentrating.

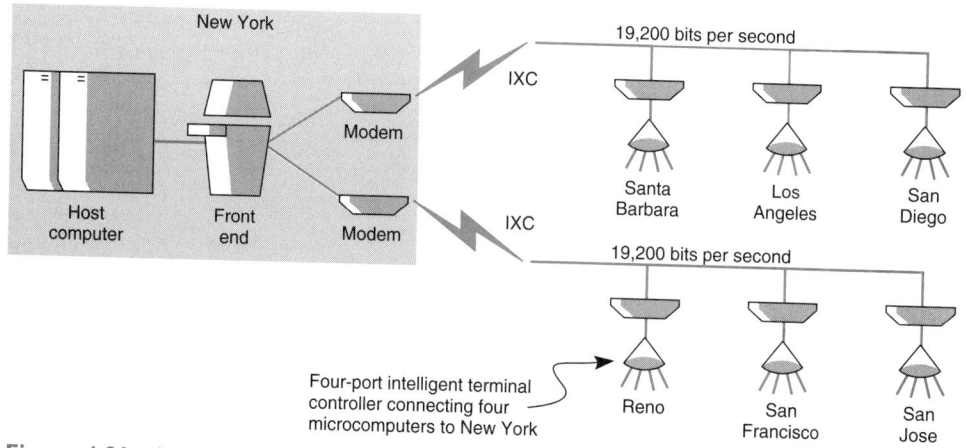

Figure 4-21 A multipoint configuration in which two multipoint circuits replace a multiplexed configuration.

length division multiplexing (WDM) is a newer version of FDM for fiber optic cable that may increase network capacity dramatically.

Frequency Division Multiplexing (FDM)   *Frequency division multiplexing* can be described as dividing the circuit "horizontally" so that many signals can travel a single communication circuit simultaneously. The circuit is divided into a series of separate channels, each transmitting on a different frequency, much like series of different radio or TV stations. All signals exist in the media at the same time, but because they are on different frequencies, they do not interfere with each other.

Figure 4-22 illustrates the use of FDM to divide one circuit into four *subchannels*. Similar to the way radio stations must be assigned separate frequencies to prevent interference, so must the signals in a FDM circuit. The *guardbands* in Figure 4-22 are the unused portions of the circuit that separate these frequencies from each other.

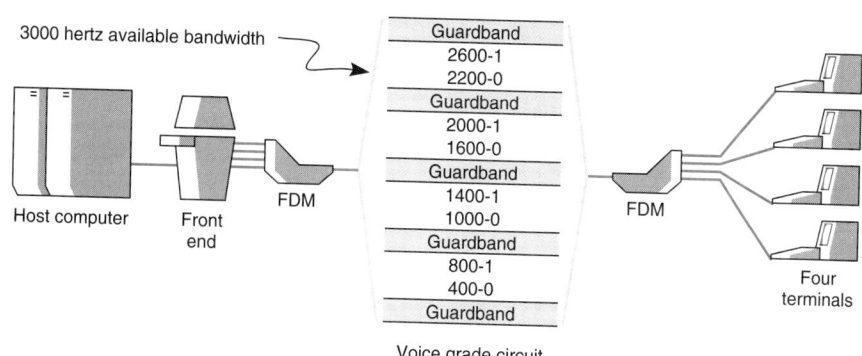

Figure 4-22 Frequency division multiplexed circuit (FDM).

Another characteristic of FDM is that all subchannels need not end at the same location. They can be at separate locations, such as on different floors in a building or even at different locations within a city. Therefore, FDM can be used in a multipoint network where each terminal operates at a different frequency and each terminal is in a different physical location.

Frequency division multiplexers are somewhat inflexible because once you determine how many subchannels are required, it may be difficult to add more without purchasing an entirely new multiplexer capable of handling additional subchannels. In addition, maintenance costs more for frequency division multiplexing equipment than for time division multiplexing equipment.

Time Division Multiplexing (TDM) *Time division multiplexing* shares a communication circuit among two or more terminals by having them take turns, dividing the circuit "vertically." In Figure 4-23 a character is taken from each terminal, transmitted down the circuit, and delivered to the appropriate device at the far end. Time on the circuit is allocated even when data are not being transmitted, so that some capacity is wasted when some terminals are idle.

Time division multiplexing generally is more efficient than frequency division multiplexing, because it does not need guardbands. Guardbands use "space" on the circuit that otherwise could be used to transmit data. It is not uncommon to have time division multiplexers that share a line among 32 different low speed terminals. It is easy to change the number of subchannels in a time division multiplexer. All TDM channels usually originate at one location and all terminate at another location. Time division multiplexers generally are less costly to maintain.

Statistical Time Division Multiplexing (STDM) *Statistical time division multiplexing* is the exception to the rule that the capacity of the multiplexed circuit must equal the sum of the circuits it combines. STDM allows more terminals or computers to be

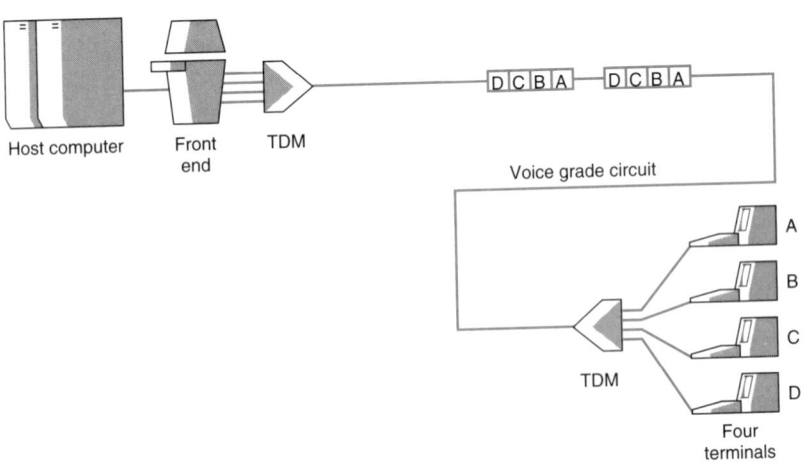

Figure 4-23   Time division multiplexed circuit (TDM).

connected to a circuit than FDM or TDM. If you have 12 terminals or microcomputers connected to a multiplexer and each can transmit at 9600 bits per second, then you should have a circuit capable of transmitting 112,000 bps (12 times 9600). However, not all terminals will be transmitting continuously at their maximum transmission speed. Users typically pause to read their screens or spend time typing at lower speeds. Therefore, you do not need to provide a speed of 112,000 bps on the multiplexed circuit. If only six terminals are transmitting at the same time, 56,000 bps might be enough, depending upon how quickly the specific terminals or microcomputers and their users generate or request data. STDM is called *statistical* because selecting the transmission speed for the multiplexed circuit is based on a statistical analysis of the usage requirements of the circuits to be multiplexed.

The key benefit of STDM is that it provides more efficient use of the circuit and saves money. You can buy a lower speed, less expensive circuit than you could using FDM or TDM.

STDM introduces two additional complexities. First, because data from different devices are intermixed on the multiplexed circuit, all data must be identified by an address that specifies the device to which it belongs. For example, assume an STDM multiplexes individual characters from 12 terminals. In this case, a terminal address is added to the character and is inserted into the data stream. In Figure 4-24, notice that, in addition to the eight bits for each individual character, we have added five

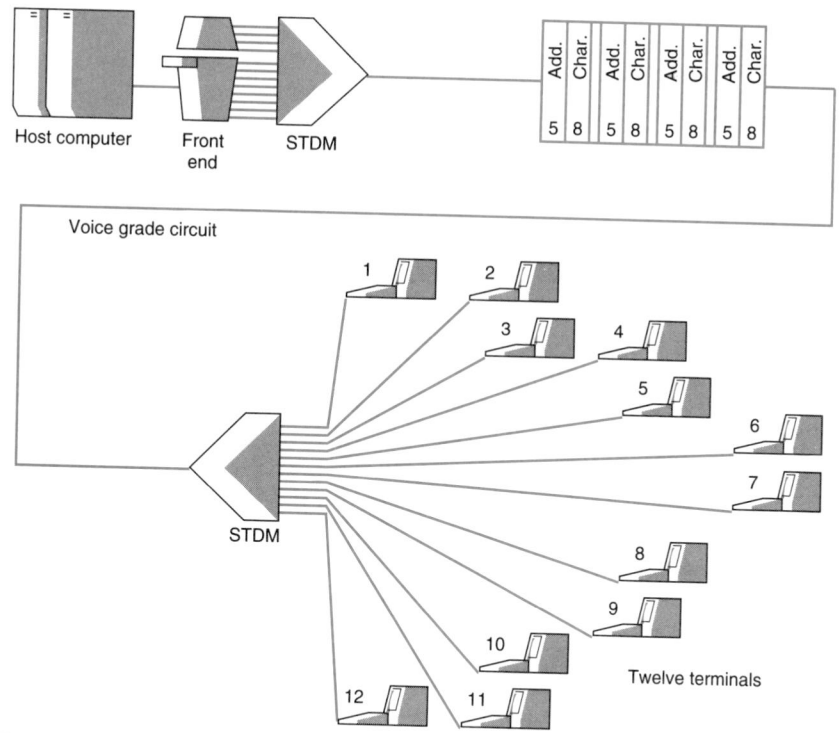

Figure 4-24 Statistical time division multiplexing (STDM).

Management Focus: Communications for the Airlines

Almost everyone is familiar with data communications in the airline industry. American Airlines' SABRE system was the first automated airline reservations system. Today, there are several other major systems, including those developed by United Airlines and Lufthansa. An interconnecting network maintained by Aeronautical Radio Incorporated (ARINC) is used by all the airlines to transfer messages among these various systems.

All major air carriers have individual communication networks for reservations, flight planning, inventory, control, flight scheduling, and all the other applications required to run a major airline. Airline networks use circuits leased from the telephone companies and other common carriers and combine front end processors and terminals for an efficient network layout.

American Airlines and United Airlines have the largest base of terminals installed in travel agents' offices as well as for their own use. There is a correlation between the number of airline booking terminals in travel agents' offices and the number of flights booked on that airline. For example, the American Airlines' SABRE system books an average of 470,000 airline reservations a day. They are handled by over 8000 reservation operators located at five regional sites and through 68,000 terminals located in 14,000 travel agencies.

Several years ago, this network was spread inefficiently over 1100 separate voice and data lines. In a major overhaul, the network was consolidated onto 45 high capacity digital lines carrying both voice and data. Multiplexers channel the messages to 14 connection sites and split them out to their destinations. Traffic on the SABRE network has doubled, while operating costs have increased by only 30 percent.

bits of address space *(Add)*. These five bits allow you to address 32 different terminals using binary counting ($32 = 2^5$). Now the multiplexer takes a character from each terminal only when the terminal has a character to send. The technique used is to scan through the 12 terminals and take characters from, say, terminals 1, 4, 5, and 12. These are sent immediately. Then all 12 are scanned again to determine which terminals need servicing. The process is repeated indefinitely. At the other end of the communication circuit, the character is given to the proper device because the 5-bit address included with each 8-bit character identifies the terminal device. Remember, with regular time division multiplexing, there is no terminal addressing; each time position in the circuit is dedicated to a specific device. If only three terminals were transmitting, then one position would contain a blank (nothing) when transmitted.

The second problem is that STDM can cause time delays. If *all* devices start transmitting or receiving at the same time, the multiplexed circuit cannot transmit all the data it receives because it does not have sufficient capacity. Therefore, STDM must have internal memory to store the incoming data that it cannot immediately transmit. When traffic is particularly heavy, you may have a 1 to 30-second delay.

Another type of STDM involves multiplexing entire messages from terminals. With this type of multiplexer you *interleave* entire messages rather than characters. For example, when terminal 1 has a message to send, the multiplexer picks up the entire message (all of its characters) and puts it in a frame, after which the multiplexer immediately scans for the next terminal that has an entire message to send, and continues this process until the frame is full. The primary difference is that the first statistical scheme is for character-by-character transmission, whereas the second scheme is for block transmission. This reduces the amount of overhead addresses transferred, but can increase delays.

Fast Packet Multiplexing (FPM)   A *fast packet multiplexer* is an advanced form of STDM that combines voice, video, and data transmissions. As the name suggests, it typically supports high data transmission rates (1 to 2 Mbps). The major difference is that fast packet multiplexers can determine which transmissions are more important, such as voice transmissions (voice transmissions often exhibit *talk spurts*). It has the ability to send the more important voice transmissions first and fast, which is vital because voice transmission is not very tolerant of delays. Delays can cause gaps in words that are very distracting to the people having conversations.

To achieve greater packet transmission speed, fast packet multiplexers remove repetitive characters from data transmissions and gaps (when no one is speaking) from digitized voice transmissions. This multiplexing allows both the data and voice to be sent with less capacity on the multiplexed circuit. The remaining capacity can be used for more data or voice transmissions.

Inverse Multiplexing   Multiplexing was developed to combine several low speed circuits for transmission across one high speed circuit. It can also be used to do the inverse—combine several low speed circuits to make them appear as one high speed circuit. (See Figure 4-25.)

One of the most common uses of inverse multiplexing is to provide *T-1* circuits for wide area networks. T-1 circuits provide data transmission rates of 1.544 Mbps (1,544,000 bits per second) by combining 24 slower speed circuits (64,000 bps). As far as the users are concerned, they have access to one high speed circuit, even through their data actually travel across a set of slower circuits. T-1 and other circuits are discussed in Chapter 9.

Multiplexing and inverse multiplexing used to be done primarily by proprietary hardware. Each vendor's technology was incompatible with others. This wasn't a major

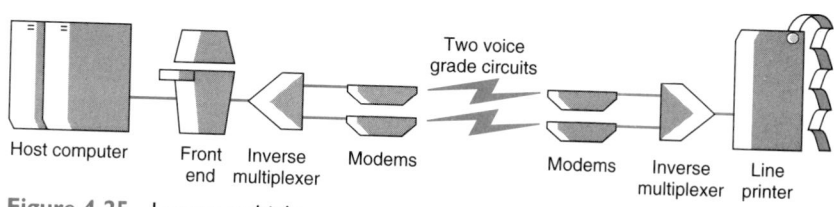

Figure 4-25   Inverse multiplexer.

problem when each company owned its own networks and communicated only with itself. You simply made sure that you bought multiplexers in pairs from the same vendor.

This changed as networks became more integrated and widespread. Equipment from different vendors need to communicate with each other because the computer on one end of a multiplexed circuit is apt to be talking with a computer owned by someone else at the other. Now several groups of vendors have drafted proposed standards for inverse multiplexing. Any company that produces multiplexing hardware or software to these standards can talk with equipment made by other vendors who also support those standards.

Two important proposed standards for inverse multiplexing are BONDING (Bandwidth ON Demand Interoperatibility Networking Group) and multilink Point-to-Point Protocol (PPP); PPP is a successor to Serial Line Internet Protocol (SLIP). Neither standard is official, but both have been adopted by numerous vendors. Both operate in software and hardware by splitting outgoing messages from one client or host across several low speed circuits and combining incoming messages from several circuits into one circuit so that the client or host thinks it has a faster circuit.

Bonding combines several 56 Kbps or 64 Kbps circuits into one higher speed circuit. PPP can combine circuits of different speeds (e.g., a 64,000 bps circuit with a 14,400 bps circuit), with data allocated to each circuit is based on speed and need. PPP enables the user to change the circuits allocated to the PPP multiplexed circuit in mid-transmission so that the PPP circuit can increase or decrease the capacity. Bonding does not permit the circuit capacity to change dynamically, and takes longer to initialize before data transmission can begin. Most experts predict PPP will become more popular.

Wavelength Division Multiplexing (WDM) Fiber optic cable has traditionally carried only one circuit at a time. A new multiplexing technique called wavelength division multiplexing (WDM) now permits up to 10 simultaneous circuits (each up to 622 Mbps over short distances or 200 Mbps over long distances) to be transmitted on fiber optic cables. WDM is a variant of frequency division multiplexing, sending each circuit on a separate wavelength of light. In the future, WDM can be expected to support 20 to 50 circuits in one fiber optic cable, providing total data rates of up to 31 Gbps (31 billion bps).

Concentrators In today's terminology, *concentrators* are special forms of statistical multiplexers. In fact, they originally were intelligent multiplexers (statistical time division multiplexers). Multiplexers generally have end user terminals or microcomputers attached to them, whereas concentrators do not. For example, in Figure 4-20, the hardware devices located in San Diego, Los Angeles, Santa Barbara, San Francisco, San Jose, and Reno probably are true multiplexers because they are attached to end user terminals. On the other hand, the hardware devices in Phoenix, Denver, Chicago, and New York probably are concentrators because they do not have end user terminals attached. The data communication hardware industry is very changeable, and because vendors change terms to suit marketing purposes this definition won't always work.

Protocol Converters

Protocols are the rules that allow two machines to communicate. When you use English to communicate, there are various rules (or protocols) you must observe, such as grammar and punctuation.

Protocol converters are hardware or software that interconnect two dissimilar computer systems or terminals so they can communicate with each other. As an analogy, if someone who speaks only English wants to talk to a person who speaks only French, they would need an interpreter. This language interpreter serves the same purpose as a protocol converter.

Protocol conversion is one of today's hottest topics, particularly when you consider its application to the problem of micro-to-mainframe communications. In general, the basic approaches to protocol conversion are divided into four categories: hardware protocol converter boxes, add-on circuit boards for microcomputers, software in host computers, and local area network gateways.

Hardware Protocol Converter Boxes *Hardware protocol converter boxes* convert the communication protocol used by one computer vendor to that required for another computer vendor's equipment. For example, some protocol converters allow an asynchronous terminal to communicate with IBM host computers that use Synchronous Data Link Control (SDLC) or Binary Synchronous Communications (BSC) protocols. Other protocol converters allow asynchronous terminals to interconnect with public packet switching protocols, such as X.25. These three protocols (SDLC, BSC, and X.25) are discussed in Chapter 6. In today's networks, protocol converters might be located at either the host or terminal end of the circuit.

Add-On Circuit Boards *Add-on circuit boards* convert microcomputers' protocols to the protocol of the host computer to which they are transmitting. For example, there are two distinct types of add-on protocol conversion boards for IBM microcomputers. The first converts the microcomputer into a 3278 terminal that plugs directly into a 3270 terminal controller via a coaxial cable. The second makes the IBM microcomputer function as a 3278 terminal, one with an already built-in terminal controller. These add-on circuit boards are used for protocol conversion, which offers the user a direct micro-to-mainframe link with IBM host mainframe computers.

Software Protocol Conversion Packages In addition to these approaches, host mainframe *software protocol conversion packages* can support almost any terminal or microcomputer. If an organization has a very large number of terminals or microcomputers to connect to its host mainframe computer, software protocol conversion may be the most cost-effective method because the software package at the host mainframe can support hundreds of remotely located terminals or microcomputers. The user, however, must remember that the host mainframe computer software uses some of the computer cycles, which may slow processing or overload the host mainframe central computer. A hardware protocol converter or conversion software for the front end processor does not use or interfere with host mainframe computer cycles.

Management Focus: Communications in Banking

One of the major users of data communications is the banking industry. The increased pace and mobility of society have placed a tremendous demand on financial institutions. Customers require around-the-clock service, multiple banking locations, and virtually instantaneous response to their transactions. To meet these demands, financial institutions have implemented massive data communication networks, automated teller machines (ATMs), and automated funds management systems not only for individuals, but also for business organizations and government agencies.

The three main applications in banking are checking accounts, savings accounts, and loans. One customer may have several checking, savings, and loan accounts scattered across several bank branches. All activities of this customer are cross-referenced and transmitted through the data communication network. This cross referencing provides standardization of procedures and customer service across all branches, as well as the ability to extend banking services for easier customer access at any time. Such networks also increase marketing opportunities for the bank to sell additional services to customers, such as stock sales, and to provide more timely and comprehensive customer information for management analysis.

Once a bank or group of banks develops a data communication network and interconnects it with one or more host computer processing locations, then any or all of these services can be offered. Some of these financial services include:

- Automated teller machines where users can deposit or withdraw money, make transfers between different bank accounts, and pay bills.
- At-home banking and telephone-based bill paying services, which are being tested for use with the public telephone system and cable television.

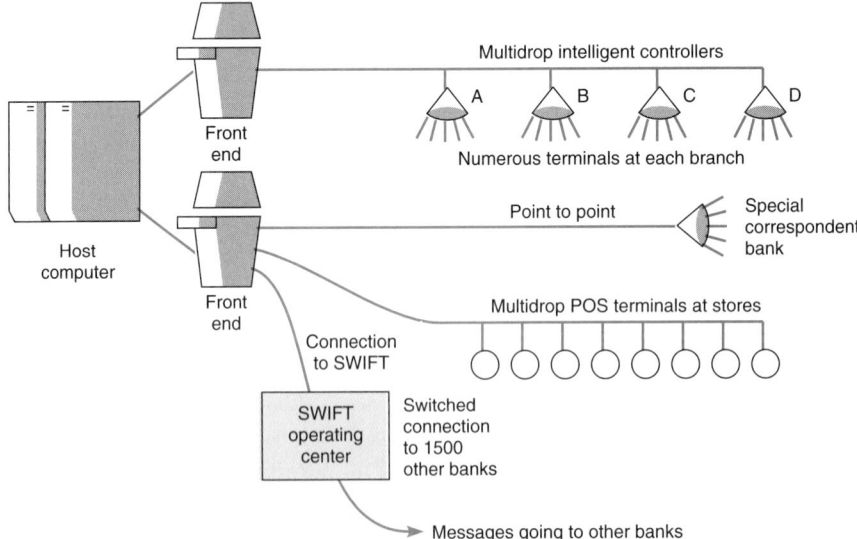

Figure 4-26   Bank networks. The terminals at bank branches A through D may be video terminals for tellers, ATMs for customers, or microcomputers.

- Point-of-sale (POS) terminals tied directly to a customer's bank account from the retail store in which the POS terminal is located.
- Automated clearing houses (ACHs) that facilitate the paperless dispensing and collection of thousands of financial transactions on a real-time basis.
- National and international electronic funds transfer networks, check verification, check guarantees, credit authorizations, and the like.

Many of the networks developed by banks are private networks that combine point-to-point leased circuits, dial-up circuits, multidrop, multiplex, and packet switching. Figure 4-26 shows a typical bank's retail network. As we move into home banking, they also will include any of the combinations of private home networks. It should be noted that banking networks that once were located within a city are now operated across state and country borders. Many banks now participate in shared networks where a bank network system in one area of the country interconnects to another bank network elsewhere.

LAN Gateways as Protocol Converters   *Gateways* are hardware devices that connect local area networks to other dissimilar networks. They do this by translating one network protocol into another, thereby overcoming both hardware and software incompatibilities. For example, if an organization were to connect a 40-microcomputer local area network to its IBM mainframe, the connection probably would be made through a gateway if the protocols were dissimilar. In this case, local area network users would address their messages to the mainframe. Each message would contain the gateway address, the mainframe address (assuming there were several mainframes), and some sort of final destination address in the mainframe, such as a database, an e-mail system, or another terminal connected to the mainframe. Gateways are covered in more detail in Chapter 10.

Line Adapters

Rather than being one specific piece of hardware, *line adapters* are a class of communication hardware. The line adapter performs a specific task or allows interconnection of terminals or microcomputers to host mainframe computers in many types of configurations.

Line Interface Module   *Line interface modules* enable terminal users to connect to more than one network and switch between them, without plugging or unplugging any connector cables. For example, this device allows a terminal user to connect to both a central host computer and a local minicomputer, alternately accessing screens from either one by using simple keyboard instructions. An extremely simple line interface module used with microcomputer printers is the two-position switch box that allows users to connect two printers to one microcomputer. In this case, users manually switch to whichever printer they need.

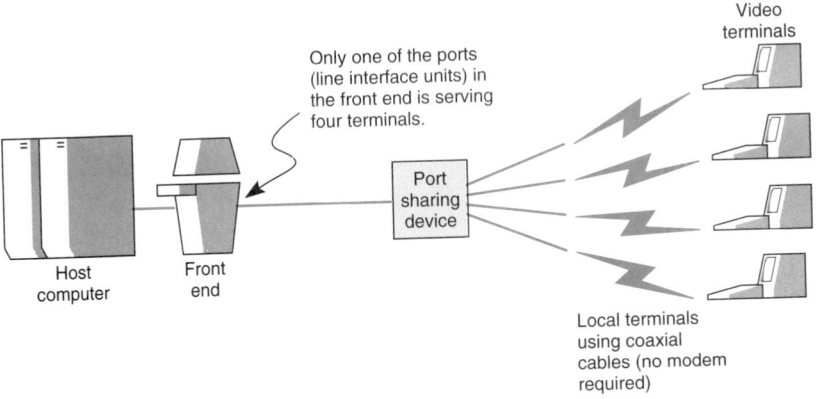

Figure 4-27 Port sharing device.

Port Sharing Device A *port sharing device* allows several incoming communication circuits to use a single port on a front end processor. All front end processors have a fixed capacity of ports. For example, if such a processor is designed to handle 50 ports, up to 50 incoming circuits can be connected to it. A port sharing device may be used when users want to exceed this design capacity. Look at Figure 4-27, where you will observe that four incoming communication circuits employ only one port on the front end processor because a port sharing device is used. A channel extender is a more sophisticated port sharing device. Although use of a port sharing device may not be a long-term solution, it can be a short-term holding action until a new network can be configured or new hardware purchased.

Line Splitter Line splitters are similar to port sharing devices except in the matter of location. Line splitters are located at the remote end of the communication circuit, whereas port sharing devices are at the central site close to the host mainframe computer. A *line splitter* is a "switch" that allows several terminals to be connected to a single modem and ensures that only one terminal at a time uses the circuit. With a line splitter, costs are reduced to that for a single communication circuit.

Summary

Network Architectures There are three fundamental network architectures. In host-based networks, the host computer performs virtually all of the work. This simple architecture works very well, except that the host mainframe can become overloaded. In client-based networks, the client computer does most of the work; the host or server is used only for data storage. In client–server networks, the work is shared between the hosts and clients. The client performs all presentation functions, the host handles all data storage, and both perform parts of the processing. Client–server networks can be cheaper to install and often better balance the network loads, but are far more complex and costly to develop and manage.

Basic Hardware The basic hardware for any data communication network is a host computer (mainframe, minicomputer, or microcomputer), a client (dumb terminal, smart terminal, special purpose terminal, or microcomputer), and the circuit through which the data flow. Microcomputers are becoming the most common client because, unlike dumb terminals, they can do some of the processing, thus reducing the load placed on the host computer. Smart terminals can also perform some processing, but microcomputers do so much more for only a little additional cost.

Network Configuration Networks can be configured so that there is a separate circuit from each client to the host (called a point-to-point confirmation) or so that several clients share the same circuit (a multipoint configuration). Point-to-point configurations are simpler to operate, but they can be very expensive because of the amount of cable required to connect each client to the host, particularly if there is considerable distance between them. Multipoint connections are cheaper and more common, but require the clients to take turns sharing the circuit with all others on it.

Data Flow Data can flow through the circuit in one direction only (simplex), in both directions simultaneously (full duplex), or by taking turns so that data sometimes flow in one direction and then in the other (half duplex). Half duplex is commonly used because many applications do not need data to flow in both directions simultaneously; for example, some applications require the client to send a message to the host and wait for a reply, before transmitting new data. Simplex is also becoming common for the same reasons that cities sometimes use one-way streets to help traffic flows.

Media Media are either guided, in that they travel through a physical cable (e.g., twisted pair wires, coaxial cable, or fiber optic cable), or radiated, in that they are broadcast through the air (e.g., infrared, microwave, or satellite). The choice is important if you are building your own network; it is less important if you are leasing a circuit from a carrier who guarantees the circuit's performance. Among the guided media, fiber optic cable can transmit data the fastest with the fewest errors and offers greater security, but costs the most; twisted pair is the cheapest and most commonly used. The choice of radiated media depends more on distance than any other factor; infrared is the cheapest for short distances, microwave for moderate distances, and satellite for long distances.

Front End Processor A front end processor is a special purpose device typically found in wide area networks that performs many network control functions so the host computer is free to do other tasks. The goal is to reduce the processing time the host spends to manage the network.

Multiplexer A multiplexer is a device that combines several simultaneous low speed circuits on one higher speed circuit so that each low speed circuit believes it has a separate connection to the host. In general, the transmission capacity of the high speed circuit must equal or exceed the sum of the low speed circuits (e.g., one 57,600 bps circuit could multiplex a maximum of four 14,400 bps circuits). With frequency division multiplexing, each low speed circuit is allocated a separate frequency on the high speed circuit. With time division multiplexing, the most commonly used type of multiplexing, each low speed circuit is allocated a separate time slice on the high speed circuit. Relying on the fact that few terminals or microcomputers transmit continuously, statistical time division multiplexing combines more low speed circuits than the high speed circuit can support (e.g., six 14,000 bps circuits on one 56,000 bps circuit), although problems can occur if all low speed circuits actually transmit at once. Inverse multiplexing, which enables several low speed circuits to be treated as one high speed circuit, will become very important as PPP and bonding become more popular.

Protocol Converter   Different networks use different protocols (transmission rules or formats). Protocol converters translate the protocol used in one network to that used in another network just the way an interpreter translates between people speaking English and French.

Key Terms

Bonding
Central site intelligent
  controller
Channel
Channel extender
Client-based network
Client–server network
Concentrator
Data storage
Dumb terminal
Fast packet multiplexing
  (FPM)
File transfer time
Frequency division
  multiplexing (FDM)
Front end processor
Host-based network
Host computer
Intelligent controller

Intelligent terminal
Interleave
Inverse multiplexing
Line adapter
Line control
Line interface module
Line splitter
Multidrop circuit
Multiplex
Point-to-point protocol
  (PPP)
Port
Port sharing device
Presentation
Processing
Protocol
Protocol converter
Remote intelligent
  controller

Remote job entry terminal
Retrain time
Serial line internet
  protocol (SLIP)
Statistical time division
  multiplexing (STDM)
T-1 circuit
Terminal
Time division multiplexing
  (TDM)
Transaction terminal
Transparent multiplexing
Turnaround time
Video display unit (VDU)
Wavelength division
  multiplexing (WDM)
Workstation

Selected References

1. *Auerbach Data Communications Reports.* Published monthly by Auerbach Publishers, 6560 N. Park Drive, Pennsauken, NJ 08109.
2. *Black Box Catalog of Data Communications and Computer Devices.* Published monthly by the Black Box Corp., P.O. Box 12800, Pittsburgh, PA 15241 (412-746-5530).
3. *Communications Products & Systems.* Published bimonthly by Gordon Publications, 13 Emory Avenue, Randolph, NJ 07869-1380.
4. *Data Communications Catalog.* Published by Misco, One Misco Plaza, Holmdel, NJ 07733 (800-333-5640).

5. *Data Communications Product Catalog.* Published by South Hills Datacomm/Cord Cable Co., 760 Beechnut Drive, Pittsburgh, PA 15205 (800-245-6215).

6. *Datacomm Catalog.* Published by Glasgal Communications, 151 Veterans Drive, Northvale, NJ 07647.

7. *Datapro Reports on Data Communications.* Published monthly by Datapro Research Corp., 1805 Underwood Boulevard, Delran, NJ 08075.

8. Minoli, Dan. "Channel Extension: Stretching the Corporate Network," *Network Computing,* vol. 2, no. 11 (November 1991) 102–103, 106–107.

9. *Network Products Directory.* Published annually by Glasgal Communications, Inc., 151 Veterans Drive, Northvale, NJ 07647 (201-768-8082).

10. *Telecom Gear: The Market Place to Buy and Sell Telecommunications Equipment.* Published monthly by Telecom Gear/Telecom Jobs, 12 West 21st Street, New York, NY 10010.

Questions/Problems

1. What are the different types of network architectures?
2. Describe the three basic functions of an application software package.
3. What are the advantages and disadvantages of host-based networks versus client–server networks?
4. What is middleware and what does it do?
5. Suppose your organization was contemplating switching from a host-based architecture to client–server. What problems would you foresee?
6. Which is less expensive: host-based networks or client–server networks? Explain.
7. Is the host computer a part of the communication network? Explain why or why not.
8. How do workstations differ from microcomputers?
9. What is the function of a front end processor?
10. State the two forms a front end processor can take.
11. What are the two most common complaints of video terminal operators?
12. What single factor distinguishes transaction terminals from other types of terminals?
13. What distinguishes a dumb terminal from other types of terminals?
14. Name at least three ways data can be entered into a terminal.
15. Review the list of functions of a front end processor. Identify what you consider to be its most important functions.
16. Can you identify the major categories of terminals discussed in this chapter?
17. What is the purpose of multiplexing?
18. Multiplexing usually is done in multiples of _____ ?
19. Of the different types of multiplexing, what distinguishes
    a. Frequency division multiplexing (FDM)?
    b. Time division multiplexing (TDM)?
    c. Statistical time division multiplexing (STDM)?
    d. Wavelength division multiplexing (WDM)?
20. What function do remote intelligent controllers serve?
21. What function do central site intelligent controllers serve?
22. Discuss the role of controllers in file transfer.
23. What is a protocol?

24. What is the purpose of a protocol converter?
25. What is the primary disadvantage of software protocol converters?
26. How does a channel extender differ from a front end processor?
27. What is the function of a line interface module?
28. In what situation are port sharing devices used?
29. What is a multipoint circuit?
30. What is the term used to describe the placing of two or more signals on a single circuit?
31. If you were buying a multiplexer, why would you choose either TDM or FDM?
32. Three terminals (T_1, T_2, T_3) are to be connected to three computers (C_1, C_2, C_3) so that T_1 is connected to C_1, T_2, to C_2, and T_3 to C_3. All are in different cities. T_1 and C_1 are 1500 miles apart, as are T_2, C_2 and T_3 and C_3. The points T_1, T_2, and T_3 are 25 miles apart, and the points C_1, C_2, and C_3 also are 25 miles apart. If telephone lines cost $1 per mile, what is the line cost for three independent lines? If a multiplexer pair costs $2000, can you save money by another arrangement of the lines? If so, how much?
33. What is the function of inverse multiplexing?
34. What are SLIP, PPP, and bonding?
35. How does a local area network gateway function as a protocol converter?

NEXT DAY AIR SERVICE CUMULATIVE CASE STUDY

See appendix at end of book

CHAPTER FIVE

DATA TRANSMISSION

The basic technical concepts of data transmission are approached from the nonmathematical viewpoint of what happens as a message moves from a terminal or microcomputer over the communication circuit to the host. Three different types of transmission are described: digital transmission of digital data; analog transmission of digital data; and digital transmission of analog voice data. You do not need an engineering-level understanding of the topics in order to be an effective manager of data communication applications. It is important, however, that you understand the basic concepts.

Objectives

- Understand digital transmission of digital data,
- Understand analog transmission of digital data,
- Be familiar with modems and several standard types of modems,
- Understand digital transmission of analog data.

Chapter Outline

Introduction
Digital Transmission of Digital Data
    Coding
    Transmission Modes
    Baseband Transmission
Analog Transmission of Digital Data
    Bandwidth on a Voice Circuit
    Modulation
    Capacity of a Voice Circuit

INTRODUCTION

There are two fundamentally different types of data: *digital* and *analog*. Computers produce digital signals that are binary, either on or off. In contrast, telephones produce analog signals whose electrical signals are shaped like the sound waves they transfer.

In general, networks designed to transmit primarily computer data are likely to be digital, and networks designed to transmit voice data are likely to be analog. This is not always case, however. Digital computer data can be transmitted over a telephone network by using a special device called a modem. A modem at the sender's computer translates the computer's digital signals into analog signals that can flow through the voice communication network, and a second modem at the receiver's end translates the analog signals back into digital signals.

Likewise, it is possible to translate analog voice data into digital data for transmission over computer networks using a device called a codec. Once again there are two codecs, one at the sender's end and one at the receiver's end. Why bother to translate voice into digital? The answer is that digital transmission is "better" than analog transmission. Specifically, digital transmission offers five key benefits over analog transmission:

- Digital transmission produces fewer errors than analog transmission. Because the transmitted data is binary (only two distinct values), it is easier to detect and correct errors.

- Digital transmission is more efficient. In Chapter 4, we mentioned that time division multiplexing (TDM) is more efficient than frequency division multiplexing (FDM) because TDM requires no guardbands. TDM is used for digital transmission, while FDM is used for analog transmission.

- Digital transmission permits higher maximum transmission rates. Fiber optic cable, for example, is designed for digital transmission.

- Digital transmission is more secure because it is easier to encrypt.

- Finally, and most importantly, integrating voice, video, and data on the same circuit is far simpler with digital transmission.

Technology Focus: Digital Versus Analog Signals

An analog signal is simply a signal that varies continuously within a range of values. The signals from telephones, radios, and television generally are analog in nature. These transmission systems traditionally have been analog because digital circuit technology has only become practical within the last 20 years or so. It is interesting to note that Samuel Morse's digital telegraph (1837), which preceded Bell's analog telephone system (1876) by almost 40 years, was the inspiration for Bell's invention. Analog is also called *broadband*.

In an analog system, data are represented by measurements on a continuous scale, so the accuracy of the machine is determined by the accuracy of the scale. An analog signal usually is represented as amplitude, phase, or frequency, the magnitude of which gives the value of some physical quantity like temperature or time. In our case, the quantities are the binary 0 or the binary 1. In other words, a high-pitched frequency might be a binary 0, and a low-pitched frequency might be a binary 1. Try this on a Touch-Tone telephone by pressing the number 1 and then the number 2. You will hear two distinct tones. The frequency received by pressing 1 could be a binary 0, and the frequency received by pressing 2 could be a binary 1.

By contrast, digital communication is the transmission of discrete signals over a transmission channel. Normally it involves two discrete voltages for binary 0's and 1's. A digital receiver must be capable of correlating a received signal with a finite set of digital values or symbols. A digital signal is either on or off like a light switch, whereas an analog signal varies like a dimmer switch, which allows you to vary the intensity of a light rather than just turn it on or off. Digital is also called *baseband*.

For these reasons, most newer long distance telephone circuits built by the common carriers over the past decade use digital transmission. In the future, most transmissions (voice, data, and video) will be sent digitally.

DIGITAL TRANSMISSION OF DIGITAL DATA

All computer systems in our discussion transmit binary data, or data forms that are intrinsically binary (i.e., ones or zeros). For these data to be understood by both the sender and receiver, both must agree on a standard methodology for representing the letters, numbers, and symbols that compose messages. A very precise set of terminology has come to be associated with such transmission.

Coding

A *character* is a symbol that has a common, constant meaning for some group of people. A character might be the letter A or B, or it might be a number such as 1 or 2.

Characters also may be special symbols such as ? or &. Characters in data communications, as in computer systems, are represented by groups of *bits* that are binary zeros (0) and ones (1). The groups of bits representing the set of characters that are the "alphabet" of any given system are called a *coding scheme*, or simply a *code*.

A *byte* is a group of consecutive bits that is treated as a unit or character. One byte normally is comprised of 8 bits and usually represents one character; however, in data communications some codes use 5, 6, 7, 8, or 9 bits to represent a character. These differences in the number of bits per character arise because the codes have different numbers of characters to represent and different provisions for error checking.

Coding is the representation of one set of symbols by another set of symbols. For example, representation of the character A by a group of 7 bits (say, 1000001) is an example of coding. Codes for representing the information vary both in the number of bits used to define a single character and in the assignment of bit patterns to each particular character. For example, the bit group 1000001 may represent the character A in one coding scheme, but the bit group 11000 may represent the character A in some other coding scheme.

There are two predominant coding schemes in use today. *United States of America Standard Code for Information Interchange* (USASCII), or more commonly *ASCII*, is the most popular code for data communications and is the standard code on most terminals and microcomputers. There are two types of ASCII; one is a 7-bit code that has 128 valid character combinations, and the other is an 8-bit code that has 256 combinations. The number of combinations can be determined by taking the number 2 and raising it to the power equal to the number of bits in the code. In this case $2^7 = 128$ characters or $2^8 = 256$ characters. *Extended Binary Coded Decimal Interchange Code (EBCDIC)* is IBM's standard information code. This code has 8 bits, giving 256 valid character combinations.

Transmission Modes

Parallel Mode   *Parallel mode* is the way the internal transfer of binary data takes place inside a computer. If the internal structure of the computer is 8-bit, then all eight bits of the data element are transferred between main memory and the central processing unit simultaneously on 8 separate connections. The same is true of computers that use a 32-bit structure; all 32 bits are transferred simultaneously on 32 connections.

Figure 5-1 shows how all eight bits of one character could travel down a parallel

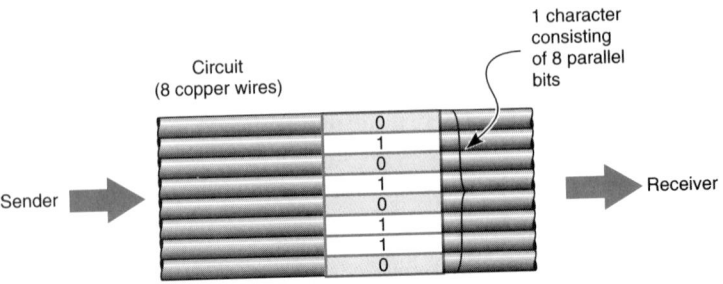

Figure 5-1   Parallel transmission of an 8-bit code.

Technology Focus: Basic Electricity

There are two general categories of electrical current: direct current and alternating current. *Current* is the movement or flow of electrons. The conventional flow of current is from + to −. Voltage is a measure of the potential difference between the plus and minus ends of an electrical circuit or battery. *Direct current* (DC) travels in only one direction in a circuit, whereas *alternating current* (AC) travels first in one direction (+) and then in the other direction (−).

Picture AC as the continuous flow of electrical current, first as a positive voltage (+) and then as a negative voltage (−). If it were a battery (it is not), the polarity of the battery terminals would reverse itself; the plus would become minus and then change back again. Because of these constant reversals in alternating current, first the electrical current flows in one direction and then it flows in the other direction. The plus (+) or minus (−) measurements are known as *polarity*. The number of times the polarity reverses itself every second is called the *frequency, hertz,* or *cycles per second.*

Picture DC as a circuit in which you have a battery (batteries are DC), so the electrical current always flows from the positive (+) terminal post to the negative (−) terminal post under the force of voltage. The electrical current flows in one direction only; positive is always positive, and negative is always negative with direct current.

A copper wire transmitting electricity acts rather like a hose transferring water. We use three common terms when discussing electricity. *Voltage* is defined as electrical pressure—the amount of electrical force pushing electrons through a circuit. In principle, it is the same as pounds per square inch in a water pipe. *Amperes* (amps) are units of electrical flow, or volume. This measure is analogous to gallons per minute for water. *Watt* is the fundamental unit of electrical power. It is a rate unit, not a quantity. You obtain the watt by multiplying the volts by the amperes.

---

communication circuit. Parallel transfer is used rarely in data communications, but most printers use parallel communication. This is possible only when the printer is very close to the computer because parallel cables require many wires (one for each bit) and may not work reliably in lengths over 25 feet.

Serial Mode   *Serial mode* is the predominant method of transferring information in data communications. Serial transmission means that a stream of data is sent over a communication circuit sequentially in a bit-by-bit fashion as shown in Figure 5-2.

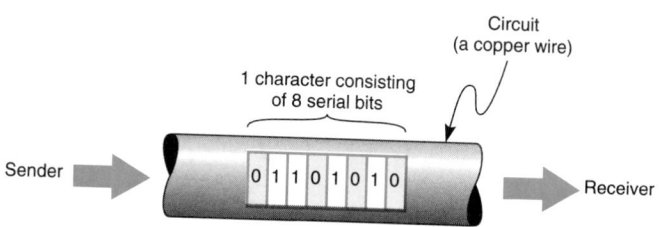

Figure 5-2   Serial transmission of an 8-bit code.

Serial transmission is distinguished from parallel because the transmitting device sends a single bit, then a second bit, and so on, until all the bits are transmitted. It takes n iterations or cycles to transmit n bits. Thus serial transmission is considerably slower than parallel transmission—seven times slower in the case of ASCII (because there are seven bits).

Baseband Transmission

Digital transmission is the transmission of electrical pulses. This digital information is binary in nature in that it only has two possible states, a 1 or a 0 (sometimes called *mark* and *space*). The most commonly encountered voltage levels range from a low of $+3/-3$ to a high of $+24/-24$ volts. Digital signals are usually sent over wire of no more than a few thousand feet in length. Digital signals are commonly referred to as *baseband signals.*

Figure 5-3 shows three types of digital signaling techniques. With *unipolar* signaling, the voltage is always positive or negative (like a DC current). Figure 5-3 illustrates a unipolar technique in which a signal of 0 volts (no current) is used to transmit a zero, and a signal of $+5$ volts is used to transmit a 1.

An obvious question at this point is if 0 volts means a zero, how do you send no data? This is discussed in detail in Chapter 6. For the moment, we will just say that there are ways to indicate when a message starts and stops, and when there are no messages to send, the sender and receiver agree to ignore any electrical signal on the line.

In *bipolar* signaling, the 1's and 0's vary from a plus voltage to a minus voltage (like an AC current). The first bipolar technique illustrated in Figure 5-3 is called non-return-to-zero because the voltage alternates from $+5$ volts (indicating a 1) and -5

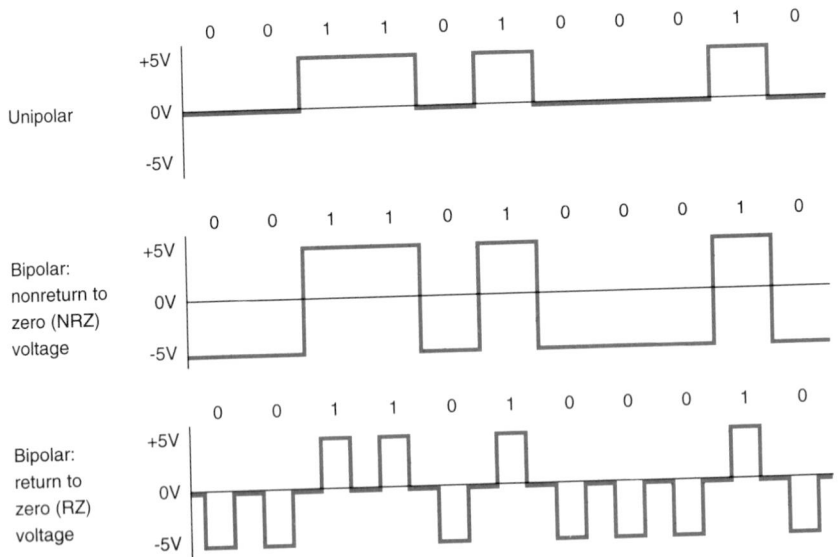

Figure 5-3 Unipolar and bipolar signals (digital).

volts (indicating a zero), without ever returning to zero volts. The second bipolar technique in this figure is called return-to-zero because it always returns to zero volts after each bit before going to +5 volts (for a 1) or −5 volts (for a zero). In Europe, bipolar signaling sometimes is called *double current* signaling because you are moving between a positive and negative voltage potential.

In general, bipolar signaling experiences fewer errors than unipolar signaling because the signals are more distinct. Noise or interference on the transmission circuit is less likely to cause the bipolar's +5v to be misread as a −5v than it is to cause the unipolar's 0v as a +5v. This is because changing the polarity of a current (from positive to negative, or vice versa) is more difficult than changing its magnitude.

ANALOG TRANSMISSION OF DIGITAL DATA

There are many occasions when data need to be transmitted over a voice communications network. Many people work at home and use a microcomputer to dial-up a host computer at their office to transmit data or check their e-mail. Telephone networks were originally built for human speech rather than for data. They are designed to transmit the electrical representation of sound waves, rather than the binary data used by computers.

This type of transmission, called *analog transmission,* takes place when the signal sent over the transmission media continuously varies from one state to another in a wavelike pattern. This is analogous to having a dimmer switch on a lamp that allows the light to vary from very bright to very dim, but it is a continuous varying light as contrasted with a light that just turns on and off. (The on/off switch is digital.) Analog transmission is also called broadband transmission, particularly when it also uses frequency division multiplexing.

Modems translate the digital binary data produced by computers into the analog signals required by voice transmission circuits (see Figure 5-4). One modem is used by the transmitter to produce the analog signals and a second by the receiver to translate the analog signals back into digital signals.

Bandwidth on a Voice Circuit

Figure 5-5 shows a typical sound wave. Every sound wave has two parts, half above the zero point (i.e., positive) and half below (i.e., negative). Both halves are the same distance away from zero. This distance or height is called *amplitude.* Our ears detect amplitude as the loudness or volume of sound. The length of the sound wave is often expressed as the number of waves per second or *frequency.* Frequency is expressed in hertz (Hz).[1] Our ears detect frequency as the pitch of the sound. Human hearing

---

[1]Hertz is the same as "cycles per second," therefore, 20,000 hertz is equal to 20,000 cycles per second. One hertz (Hz) is the same as 1 cycle per second. One kilohertz (kHz) is 1000 cycles per second (kilocycles); 1 megahertz (MHz) is 1 million cycles per second (megacycles); and 1 gigahertz (GHz) is 1 billion cycles per second.

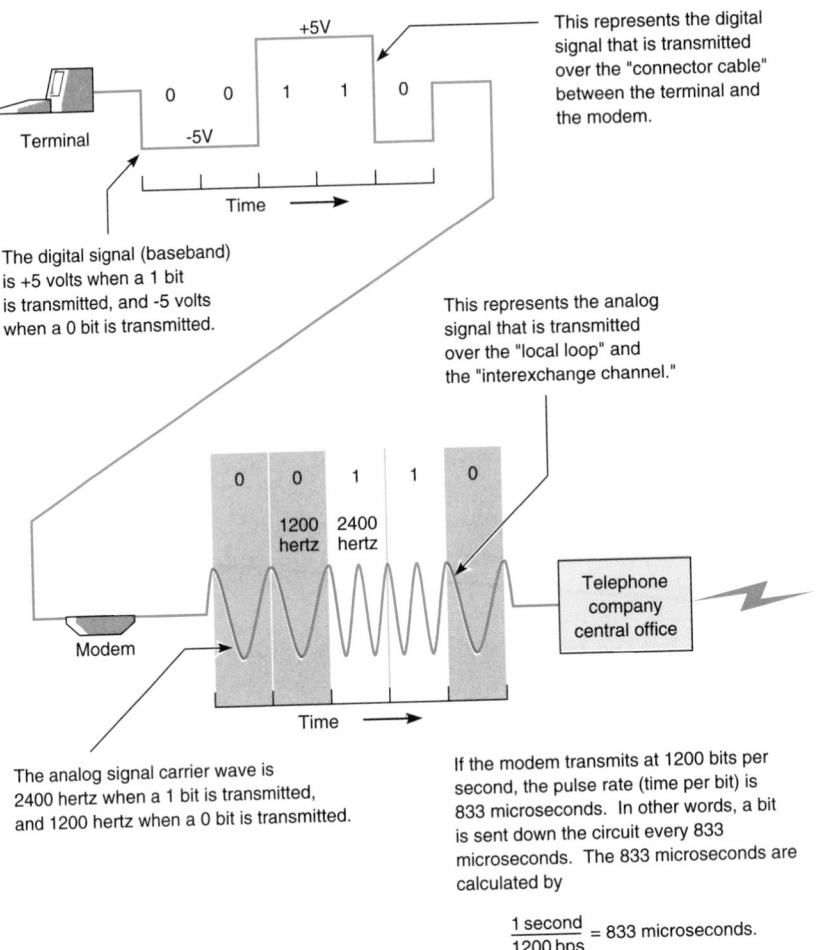

This represents the digital signal that is transmitted over the "connector cable" between the terminal and the modem.

The digital signal (baseband) is +5 volts when a 1 bit is transmitted, and -5 volts when a 0 bit is transmitted.

This represents the analog signal that is transmitted over the "local loop" and the "interexchange channel."

The analog signal carrier wave is 2400 hertz when a 1 bit is transmitted, and 1200 hertz when a 0 bit is transmitted.

If the modem transmits at 1200 bits per second, the pulse rate (time per bit) is 833 microseconds. In other words, a bit is sent down the circuit every 833 microseconds. The 833 microseconds are calculated by

$$\frac{1 \text{ second}}{1200 \text{ bps}} = 833 \text{ microseconds.}$$

Figure 5-4 Operation of a modem.

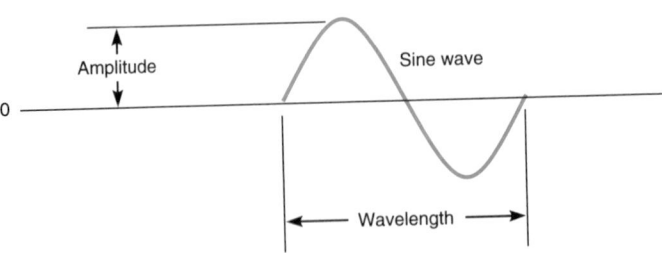

Figure 5-5 Sound wave.

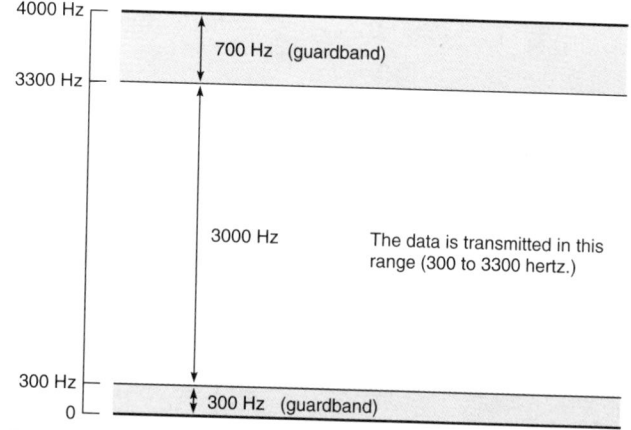

Figure 5-6   Voice grade circuit bandwidth (0 to 4000 hertz).

ranges from about 20 hertz to about 14,000 hertz, although some people can hear up to 20,000 hertz. *Bandwidth* refers to a range of frequencies. It is the difference between the highest and the lowest frequencies in a band; thus the bandwidth of human voice is from 20 Hz to 14,000 Hz or 13,880 Hz.

The bandwidth of a voice grade telephone circuit is from 0 to 4000 Hz, or 4000 Hz; however, not all of this is available for use by telephone or data communications equipment. Figure 5-6 shows how this 4000 hertz bandwidth is allocated. To start, there is a 300 hertz *guardband* at the bottom of the bandwidth and a 700 hertz guardband at the top. These prevent data transmissions from interfering with other transmissions when these circuits are multiplexed using frequency division multiplexing. Figure 5-7 demonstrates how the guardbands provide 1000 hertz of empty space between adjacent communication circuits. This leaves the bandwidth from 300 to 3300 hertz or a total of 3000 Hz for your voice or data transmission. This is adequate for most speech, although it cannot convey the high notes in music.

There are many bandwidths wider than a voice grade communication circuit. Figure 5-7 shows the bandwidth for the satellite transmission as being from 12 gigahertz to 14 gigahertz, which is a bandwidth of 2 billion hertz. If you divide 2 billion hertz by the 4000 hertz of a voice circuit, you can see that it is theoretically possible to have 500,000 voice circuits on that one satellite transmission circuit. In real life, this is not possible because of various supervisory signals and other interfering electronic functions, although many thousands of telephone circuits can fit on one satellite link.

Modulation

Basic Modulation   *Modulation* is the technique that modifies the form of a digital electrical signal so the signal can carry information on a communication medium. The modulated signal often is referred to as an *analog signal*. The signal that does the

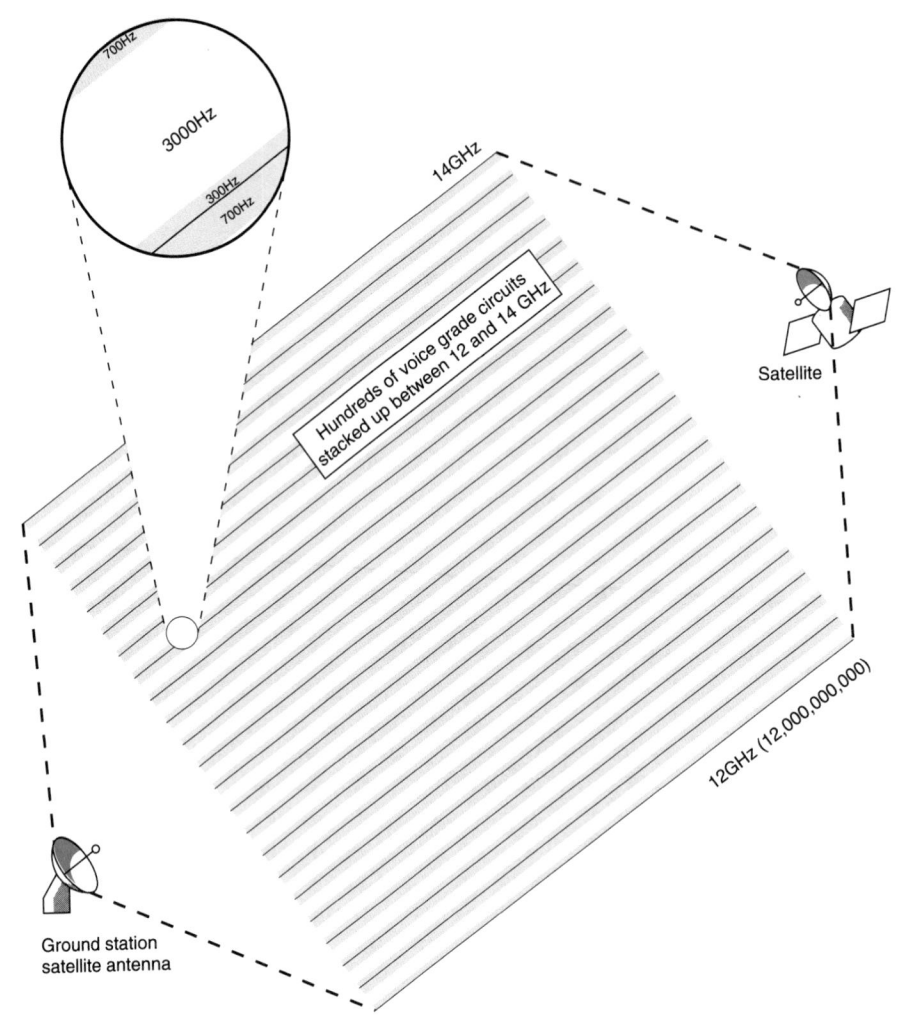

Figure 5-7 Guardbands.

carrying is the carrier wave, and modulation changes the shape of the carrier wave to transmit 0's and 1's. There are three fundamental methods of *analog modulation:* amplitude modulation, frequency modulation, and phase modulation.

With *amplitude modulation* (AM), the amplitude or height of the wave is changed. One amplitude is defined to be zero, and another amplitude is defined to be a one. The amplitude modulation shown in Figure 5-8 depicts a case where the highest amplitude (tallest wave) represents binary 1's and lowest amplitude represents binary 0's. Amplitude modulation is suitable for data transmission, and it allows efficient use of the available bandwidth of a voice grade line; however, it is more susceptible to noise (more errors) during transmission.

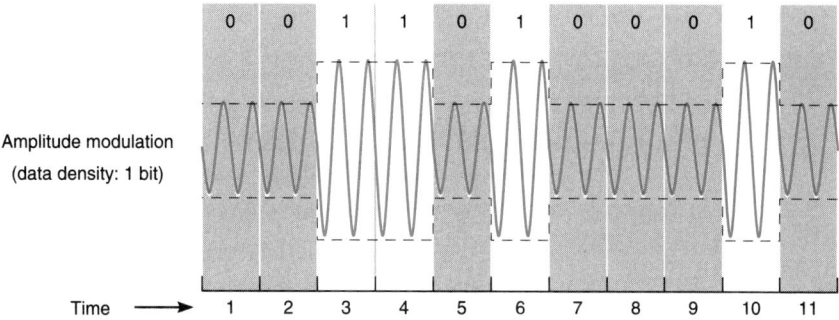

Figure 5-8 Amplitude modulation.

Frequency modulation (FM) (also called *frequency shift keying* (FSK)), is a modulation technique whereby each 0 or 1 is represented by a number of waves per second (i.e., a different frequency). In this case, the amplitude does not vary. One frequency (i.e., a certain number of waves per second) is defined to be a one, and a different frequency (a different number of waves per second) is defined to be a zero. In Figure 5-9, the higher frequency wave (more waves per time period) equals a binary 1, and the lower frequency wave equals a binary 0.

Phase modulation (PM) is the most difficult to understand. Phase refers to the direction in which the wave begins. Until now, the waves we have shown start by moving up and to the right (this is called a 0° phase wave). Waves can also start down and to the right. This is called a phase of 180°. With phase modulation, one phase is defined to be a zero and the other phase is defined to be a one. Figure 5-10 shows the case

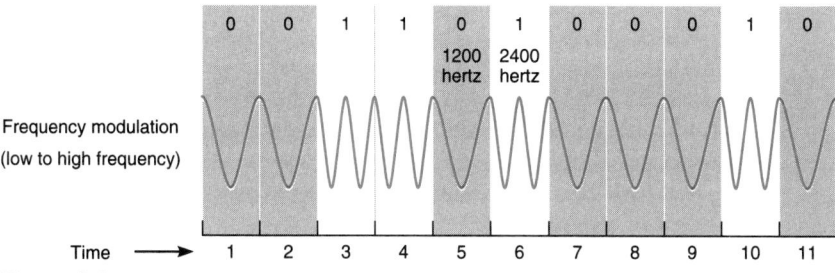

Figure 5-9   Frequency modulation.

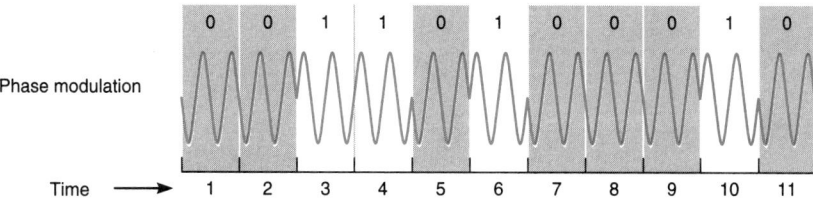

Figure 5-10   Phase modulation.

where a phase of 0° is defined to be a binary 1 and a phase of 180° is defined to be a binary 0.

Phase modulation has two related techniques. Figure 5-11 shows *phase shift keying* (PSK) for a stream of 0 and 1 bits. Notice that every time there is a *change* in the binary value (0 or 1), there is a 180° change in the phase. In a 180° phase change, the wave immediately goes in the other direction. A 180° phase change can be seen easily. The other common type of phase modulation is *differential phase shift keying* (DPSK). In DPSK there is a 180° phase change every time a 1 bit is transmitted; otherwise the phase remains the same (see Figure 5-12).

Sending Multiple Bits Simultaneously   Each of the three basic modulation techniques (AM, FM, and PM) can be refined to send more than one bit at one time. For example, basic amplitude modulation sends one bit per wave (or "signal") by defining two different amplitudes, one for a 1 and one for a 0. It is possible to send two bits on one wave or signal by defining four different amplitudes. Figure 5-13 shows the case where the highest amplitude wave is defined to be two bits, both 1's. The next highest amplitude is defined to mean first a 1 and then a 0, and so on.

This technique could be further refined to send three bits at the same time by defining eight different amplitude levels or four bits by defining 16 amplitude levels, and so on. At some point, however, it becomes very difficult to differentiate between the different amplitudes. The differences are so small that even a small amount of noise could destroy the signal.

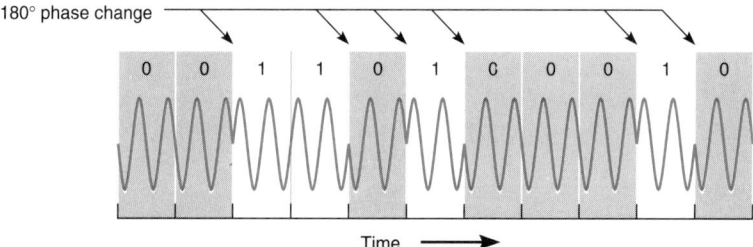

Figure 5-11   Phase shift keying (PSK). The sine wave changes 180° every time there is a change from 1 to 0 or from 0 to 1.

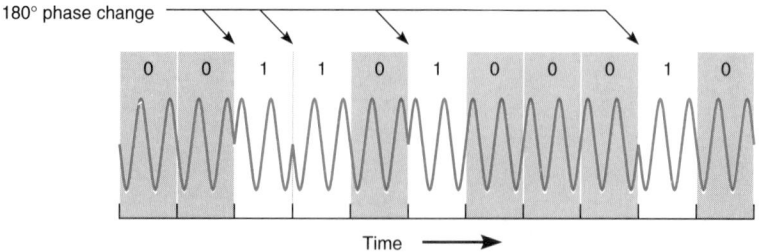

Figure 5-12   Differential phase shift keying (DPSK). The sine wave changes 180° every time a 1 is transmitted.

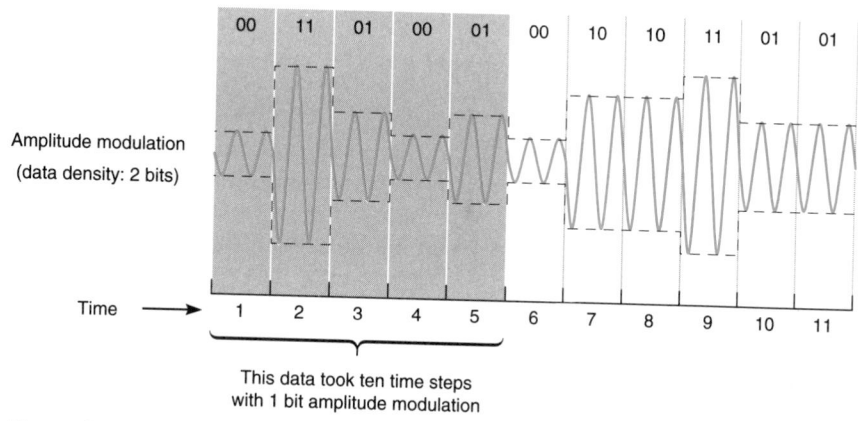

Figure 5-13

This same approach can be used for frequency modulation and phase modulation. Two bits could be sent on the same signal by defining four different frequencies, one for 11, one for 10, and so on, or by defining four phases (0°, 90°, 180°, and 270°). Three bits could be sent by defining eight frequencies and or eight phases (0°, 45°, 90°, 135°, 180°, 225°, 270°, and 315°). These techniques are also subject to the same limitations as amplitude modulation; as the number of different frequencies or phases becomes larger, it becomes difficult to differentiate among them.

In practice, the maximum number of bits that can be sent with any *one* of these techniques is about three bits. When there are more than eight different amplitudes, frequencies, or phases, it becomes extremely difficult to tell them apart.

The solution is to combine modulation techniques. It is possible to use amplitude modulation, frequency modulation, and phase modulation techniques on the same circuit. For example, we could combine amplitude modulation with four defined amplitudes (capable of sending two bits) with frequency modulation with four defined frequencies (capable of sending two bits) to enable us to send four bits on the same signal.

One popular technique is *quadrature amplitude modulation* (QAM). QAM involves splitting the signal into eight different phases (three bits) and two different amplitudes (one bit), for a total of 16 different possible values. Thus, one signal in QAM can represent four bits. The problem with all high speed modulation techniques is that they are more sensitive to imperfections in the communication circuit.

Trellis coded modulation (TCM) is a modulation technique related to QAM that combines phase modulation and amplitude modulation. There are several different forms of TCM that transmit five, six, seven, or eight bits per signal, respectively.

Bits per Second versus Baud   Bits per second and baud are terms used incorrectly much of the time. They often are used interchangeably, but they are not the same. In reality, the network designer or network user is interested in bits per second because it is the bits that are assembled into characters, characters into words and, thus, business information.

A *bit* is a unit of information whereas a *baud* is a unit of signaling speed, the number of times per second the signal on the communication circuit changes. The *bit rate* and the *baud rate* coincide only when one bit is sent on each signal. For example, if we use amplitude modulation with two defined amplitudes, we send one bit on one signal. Here the bit rate equals the baud rate; however, if we use QAM, we can send four bits on every signal. The bit rate would be four times the baud rate. If we used an 8-bit TCM, the bit rate would be eight times the baud rate. Virtually all of today's modems send multiple bits per signal.

Capacity of a Voice Circuit

Bandwidth is what you examine when determining the capacity of a voice grade circuit. By capacity, we mean the maximum data rate at which signals can be transmitted. Having a wider bandwidth provides faster *transmission speeds*. This means more data can be transmitted in the same amount of time, that is, we have greater *throughput*. On voice grade lines, the modem controls the speed at which data bits can be transmitted, but the 3000 hertz bandwidth limits the maximum speed. In practice, it is possible to use faster modems, but without expanding the limited bandwidth capacity on the voice telephone network, it makes little sense to do so.

As an analogy, think of bandwidth as a water pipe. A 1-inch diameter water pipe allows only a certain amount of water to pass through it. You can raise the water pressure and get a somewhat greater quantity of water through the pipe, but there is a physical limitation as to how many gallons per minute can pass through a 1-inch diameter pipe. If you need more gallons per minute, your only option is to install a larger 2-inch diameter pipe. When people say, "I need more bandwidth," they actually are saying they need to increase their bits per second transmission speed.

Now, let us examine the relationship between bandwidth, baud, and bits per second. The maximum signaling rate (i.e., baud rate) in any circuit depends upon the bandwidth available and the signal to noise ratio (the strength of the signal compared to the amount of noise in the circuit). You will recall that bandwidth is measured in hertz. Hertz is the number of cycles or *waves* per second, and it is the maximum number of waves per second that determines the maximum baud rate. Simply put, the maximum baud rate is usually the same as the bandwidth.[2] If the circuit is very noisy, the maximum baud rate may fall as low as 50 percent of the bandwidth. If the circuit has very little noise, it is possible to transmit at slightly over the bandwidth. The number of bits per second depends upon the modulation technique as discussed above.

For example, assume a situation that uses a dial-up voice circuit, with 3000 hertz available. Under normal circumstances, the maximum baud rate is therefore 3000

---

[2]In theory, it is possible to send signals at twice the bandwidth. Each wave has two parts (half above zero, half below). It is therefore possible to use only half of a wave for each signal, thus using one wave or cycle to send two signals; however, this is not yet practical.

baud. If we were to use basic amplitude modulation (one bit per baud), the maximum data rate would be 3000 bits per second (bps). If we were to use QAM (four bits per baud) the maximum data rate would be 4×3000 baud = 12,000 bps. Using TCM (with six bits per baud), the maximum data rate would be 6×3000 baud = 18,000 bps.

MODEMS

Modem is an acronym for *MO*dulator/*DEM*odulator. A modem takes the digital electrical pulses received from a terminal or computer and converts them into a continuous analog signal that is needed for transmission over an analog voice grade circuit. Modems can either be external to the computer or terminal and connected by cable, or can be internal. Most modems today are both data and fax modems in that they can transfer computer data as well as acting as fax machines.

Modems are classified by the speed at which they operate. The less expensive modems used with microcomputers usually operate at 2400, 9600, 14,400, or 28,800 bits per second. With larger and more centralized networks, modems traditionally operate at speeds of 14,400, 19,200, 38,400, 50,000, 56,000, 1,544,000 bits per second, and higher. Even with progress toward all-digital networks, we still need modems to pass data over the thousands of currently installed analog circuits, most of which will not be able to operate digitally for many years.

Types of Modems

Standard Modems   Most standard modems today accept commands entered from a microcomputer keyboard. This command language controls their functions, such as changing speed and dialing calls. For example, if you use a Hayes modem or a Hayes-compatible modem that uses the same language, then you type the letters AT to enter a command. These letters instruct the modem to pay attention to the next set of letters because they constitute a command or parameter change. Therefore, typing the sequence ATD tells the modem to pay attention, and the D tells it to dial a number. The complete command might be ATD555-1212, which tells the modem to pay attention, and to dial 555-1212.

Intelligent Modems   Beyond standard modems is a classification that might be called *intelligent* or *advanced modems*. These more expensive modems contain microprocessor chips and internal read only memory (ROM) coding to provide sophisticated communication protocols and diagnostic checking within the modem itself.

Some of the newer, more sophisticated modems cross over the boundaries that define other pieces of hardware. For example, some modems not only perform digital-to-analog conversion but also operate as multiplexers, security restrictor devices, encryption devices, error detection and retransmission devices, and so forth. The

Technology Focus: Modem Lights

Did you ever wonder what all those modem lights mean? While their significance might vary from modem to modem, here is an explanation of the lights on a typical modem.

MR—Modem Ready. Indicates when the power is turned on.

TR—Terminal Ready. Shows that the modem has received a signal from the microcomputer or terminal to which it is connected, telling it that the microcomputer or terminal is now ready to do something, such as send data.

SD—Send Data. Shows when data are being sent from the RS232 serial port (usually COM1) of your microcomputer to the modem.

RD—Receive Data. Shows when the modem is receiving data from the distant computer and the modem in turn is sending it to the RS232 serial port (usually COM1) of your microcomputer.

OH—Off-Hook. Indicates when the modem is off-hook with regard to the telephone line (i.e., the modem's equivalent of picking up the phone). If the light is on, you are connected to the telephone company and using the circuit.

CD—Carrier Detect. Indicates when the modem detects a carrier wave tone from a distant modem.

AA—Auto Answer. Tells that the modem is set to answer incoming calls automatically.

V.22—Indicates when the modem is set to work using the V.22 Standard.

V.32bis—Indicates when the modem is set to work using the V.32bis Standard.

problem is that there are many types of hybrid equipment on the market. As a result, it is no longer possible to say that a device is solely a modem because it might be a combination modem, multiplexer, and encryption device.

Short Haul Modems Another type of modem is a *short haul modem* in which you use your own wire pair cable to transmit direct electrical signals. Sometimes this is called a 20-milliamp circuit (also called *current loop* signaling). Inexpensive (costing as little as $40) devices can serve as the interface for any COM1 port on a microcomputer (RS232 port) from a modem to a standard 20-milliamp loop system. Typically, these systems transmit at 19,200 bits per second over a distance of up to several miles. This type of modem also is called a *line driver*. Such short haul modems are used within buildings, a plant, college campus, or university facility. An example of a line driver is one that operates asynchronously over full duplex, four-wire circuits at speeds up to 19,200 bits per second for a distance of more than one mile. In general, when modems transmit over longer distances they need to send data slower to prevent errors. When this same line driver is used at lower speeds, transmission distance increases to 18 miles at 110 bits per second.

Microcomputer users sometimes need short haul modems. For example, if you want to directly connect two microcomputers together using a point-to-point circuit (not a

Technology Focus: Modem Commands

Each modem may use a different command language to control its functions. The most popular language was developed by Hayes for use in their modems. Many other modem manufacturers use this same language and therefore are "Hayes compatible."

All commands begin with the letters AT. The letters that follow determine the command. Some useful commands include:

A	Answer the call without waiting for the telephone to ring
A/	Repeat last command
B	Put the modem in V.22 mode
C	Switch between the transmit carrier being off or on
D#	Dial a telephone number (#)
DS	Dial stored telephone number
D$	Display a list of ATD commands
E	Switch between echoing or not echoing characters
F	Switch between half duplex and full duplex
H	Switch between the modem being on or off the hook
I5	Display settings and stored telephone numbers
L	Set the speaker volume
M0	Turn off the speaker
M1	Turn off the speaker after a connection is made
M2	Turn on the speaker
O	Use for digital loopback testing
X4	Display the progress of the call (e.g., busy signal)
Z	Reset to default settings
$	Display a list of AT commands
&F	Reset to the factory settings
&Z = #	Store a phone number (#) for dialing using the ATDS command
&$	Display a list of AT& commands

local area network), and they are several thousands of feet apart, a short haul modem may be the answer. One such device consists of a box approximately the size of a cigarette pack. Because short haul modems do not require an external power source (they get their power through the serial port), they sometimes are referred to as *modem eliminators*. These tiny modems are able to send data down the cable for distances of approximately 3000 feet at 9600 bits per second, or up to 6 miles at 1200 bits per

Management Focus: Modem Pooling Saves Money

Most modems are not in use at all times. In fact, even "heavily used" modems are often idle 50 percent of the time. Traditionally, companies have purchased one modem for every user who needs access to voice communication circuits. With *modem pooling,* several users share the same modem or set of modems. This is similar in concept to the use of a PBX to share a smaller set of telephone lines among a group of users.

Modem pooling saves money by reducing the number of modems that need to be purchased. It also reduces the number of connections to the common carrier's trunk lines. These costs can be significant, when you realize that annual cost of a business telephone connection can be three to five times the cost of a modem.

Pooling is typically done by a combination of hardware and software. For a local area network implementation, a special modem/communication server is used to manage the pool of modems. The users connect to the modems and dial out via the LAN. For a PBX implementation, the users connect to the PBX, which manages the modems.

Modem pooling is usually transparent; users do not notice that they do not have their own modem connected to their computer. If modems are heavily used, however, some users may have to wait for an available one modem. Such delays and the wasted management time and frustration that accompany it may outweigh savings. Modem pooling can be a wise decision, provided that you buy enough modems to prevent delays.

second. This type of short haul modem is analogous to increasing your RS232 cable beyond its 50-foot maximum length.

Wireless Modems   Wireless communication is emerging as one of the most innovative and rapidly growing markets in data transfer. Technology enables companies to transfer data quickly and efficiently worldwide. *Wireless modems* transmit the data signals through the air instead of by using a cable. They sometimes are called a *radio frequency modem.* This type of modem is designed to work with cellular technology, and wireless local area networks. One primary user of wireless modems are personal digital assistants (PDAs). Wireless modems are not yet perfected, but the technology is rapidly improving.

One problem is that wireless modems are denied half of their functionality; it is cost-prohibitive to send the large data files that fax machines generate over the narrow bandwidth of a radio channel. If a fax is sent via cellular telephone, it will cost about $6 to $13 per page. The high cost is primarily due to the slowness of transmission and the sheer size of the fax files—from 25K to 80K per page of text. In the future, increased transmission speeds and data compression will reduce these costs (while there are several standards for data compression for computer data transmission as discussed below, there are no widely accepted standards for data compression in faxes).

Modem Standards

There are many different types of modems available today. Before data can be transmitted between two computers (or a terminal and a computer) using modems, both need to use the same type of modem. Fortunately, several standards exist for modems. Any modem that conforms to a standard can communicate with any other modem that conforms to the same standard. But before you buy a very high speed modem (e.g., V.34 with V.42bis), remember that before you can use it, the computer at the other end of the telephone line also has to support the same standard.

Many new modems support several standards (some high speed, some low speed) so that they can communicate with a variety of different modems. When these modems connect to another modem, they attempt to use the highest speed standard available and, if unsuccessful, keep trying lower speeds until they find one that works. These modems can change data rates during transmission, so if a circuit is noisy, they can slow down to reduce the effects of errors. This changing of data rates during transmission is called *fast retrain*. In the following section, we summarize some important modem standards.

V.22 Modems   *V.22* modems have been the standard modem used for many years, but they are fast becoming obsolete. They can transmit at either 1200 baud or 2400 baud. Remember that the maximum baud in a normal voice grade line is 3000 baud. Rather than transmit at this rate, V.22 uses a lower baud rate so that it is less affected by noise. V.22 uses frequency modulation (FSK) to send one bit per baud, resulting in a data rate of 1200 bps or 2400 bps.

V.32 and V.32bis Modems   *V.32* modems provide full duplex transmission at 9600 bits per second over dial-up telephone circuits. V.32 modems transmit at 2400 baud using QAM (4 bits per baud) to achieve the 9600 bps data rate. In addition to offering this fast transmission over dial-up circuits, V.32 modems often are used for backing up leased telephone circuits. *V.32bis* modems provide data rates of 14,400 bits per second by transmitting at 2400 baud using a form of TCM that provides 6 data bits per baud.

One problem you may encounter when using V.32 or faster modems is that some telephone companies use TASI to interleave many different calls onto one high speed communication circuit. TASI's constant switching between circuits causes breaks large enough that the V.32 modem cannot maintain the 9600 bits per second speed. When this happens, it has to drop to a lower speed.

Some telephone companies design their TASI dial-up circuits to disengage automatically when a data call is detected. One way in which TASI circuits detect data calls is by the inband signaling tone sent to disable the echo suppressers.

V.34 and V.34bis Modems   *V.34* modems are the first of a new breed which was developed based on the assumption that the telephone network uses digital—not analog—transmission beyond the local loop. In other words, the analog signals produced by telephones are converted to digital signals at the telephone company's central office and transmitted digitally through the network to the last central office, where they are

Management Focus: Move to Digital Means Money in the Bank

Dennis Breen, vice president of Branch Banking and Trust Company of Wilson, NC, is in charge of his company's data communications network serving approximately 230 banks in North and South Carolina. Their traditional computer network used telephone-based analog technology.

Although the North Carolina telephone company was encouraging large scale computer users to make a significant transition to digital, Breen had vowed never to move to digital unless the economics of such a move made sense, or they needed higher bandwidth that would force them to add digital circuits. Both happened.

Breen had an analog network using a multiplexor as the backbone connection, which had 4800 bps analog circuits. These were converted to 56 Kbps digital circuits at almost no additional cost. Circuit costs did climb a little but maintenance and leasing costs of analog equipment dropped. Also, they were able to eliminate some older multiplexors and some other network equipment associated with the analog network. This meant that Branch could do more things and provide customers with more services and have the network operate more quickly.

The bank's new digital network uses the backbone multiplexor to connect a pure digital network to each branch location, providing transmission speeds up to 56 Kbps. The centralization of equipment for the network in one site saves money by reducing the need for trained network staff at remote sites, while increasing the bank's control of the network. Flexibility of the data network is also imperative, given the growing number of acquisitions that banks are making today.

Source: Communication News, September 1993.

translated back into analog signals over the local loop to be received at the opposite end's telephone.

Such digital circuits are much more error free than older analog circuits. Building on this assumption, V.34 uses baud rates above the 2400 baud used by V.32 and V.32bis modems. The actual baud rates depend upon the quality of the circuit (e.g., 2700, 3000, 3300, and 3600). When V.34 modems first connect, they go through a "handshaking" sequence that tests the circuit and determines the optimum combination of baud rate, modulation technique, and error control mechanisms that will produce the highest throughput. The V.34 standard defines more than 50 valid combinations of baud rate and modulation technique (the maximum is 28,800 bps at 3600 baud using 8-bit TCM). During the transmission, this optimal combination can be changed if the modems encounter more or fewer errors than expected.

The maximum data rate is 28,800 bps, but even a short, poor quality local loop can have sufficient noise to cause the V.34 to drop its baud rate or use a modulation technique with fewer bits per baud, resulting in a much lower data rate. Nonetheless, tests of V.34 modems have shown that even in high noise circuits, they produce higher data rates than V.32bis modems.

V.34bis modems are an extension to the V.34 standard. *V.34bis* modems provide a better handshaking routine and can accommodate voice transmissions, but the real interest lies in their higher data transmission rates: 33.6 Kbps. This is accomplished by increasing the baud rate to 4200 baud while still using 8-bit TCM. There is some concern that many of today's lower quality telephone lines will be unable to support such high baud rates, even with the substantially higher signal to noise ratio than is used in other modems (i.e., higher signal strength to overpower noise).

V.42bis Modems (Data Compression) A modem's transmission rate is the primary factor that determines the throughput rate of data, but it is not the only factor. *Data compression* can increase throughput of data over a communication link literally by compressing the data.

One simple way to compress data is to examine it and send an instruction that provides a count of any characters that repeat themselves in sequence. This basic technique is called *run length encoding*, and it normally is used in combination with other techniques. Another technique, called *code book compression*, uses specific codes to indicate a pattern of characters and phrases stored in each data compressor's memory. Thus, one character can be sent over a link to indicate many other characters.

A more complex method of encoding actually replaces standard ASCII and EBCDIC code. This technique, called *Huffman encoding*, employs coding tables that use a different number of bits to represent characters based on how often that character is used. Frequently used characters (e.g., the letter E) may be defined using only four bits, while seldom used characters (e.g., X), may be defined using 11 bits. Different Huffman tables optimize this technique for different applications or languages. A more flexible method, *adaptive Huffman encoding*, uses a mathematical algorithm to update the tables in real time to optimize the compression capability.

MNP 5, a data compression standard common in the United States, uses both run length encoding and Huffman encoding. It typically provides a compression ratio ranging between 1.3:1 and 2:1. A 2:1 compression ratio means that for every two characters in the original signal, only one is needed in the compressed signal (e.g., if the original signal contained 1000 bytes, only 500 would be needed in the compressed signal).

V.42bis is the Consultative Committee on International Telegraph and Telephone (CCITT) standard for data compression. It uses a dictionary of commonly used 4-byte character combinations. Rather than sending the actual data, it instead sends an index to the dictionary entry. The actual gain provided by V.42bis compression depends upon the actual data sent, but usually ranges from 3.5:1 to 4:1 (i.e., almost four times as much data can be sent per second using V.42bis than without it). Although MNP 5 is more established, and manufacturers of modems using it lobbied hard against the formalization of V.42bis, the benefits of V.42 bis are obvious: it provides twice the data compression capability of MNP 5.

V.42bis compression can be added to almost any modem standard; thus a V.32 modem providing a data rate of 14,400 bps, could provide a data rate of 57,600 bps when upgraded to use V.42bis. A V.34 modem providing a 28,800 bps data rate could provide 115,200 bps with V.42bis. V.34bis modems could provide 133.4 Kbps with V.42bis. Early tests of V34/42bis modems have found actual data rates of around 110

Management Focus: Buying a Modem

Here is a list of the many features to consider when buying a modem:

- The most important consideration is speed; most users will want V.32bis or V.34 with V.42bis data compression.
- Many modems provide fax capabilities.
- Some modems can be turned on or off from a remote station. These contain automatic answering and calling capabilities, so a remote terminal can be started from thousands of miles away.
- Some modems allow the simultaneous transmission of both voice and data. One model allows a voice conversation to go over the circuit while simultaneously transmitting a data stream of 19,200 bits per second.
- Many modems today have built-in diagnostic routines for self-checking of their own circuits to determine where a fault might lie.
- *Loopback* functions for diagnostic purposes are an important feature for businesses that have many modems. Automatic loopback allows the user to set a remote modem on loopback and send a message to that modem. The message is retransmitted (or "looped back") to the original sender, where it can be checked for accuracy to help diagnose where a fault might occur in the network. Loopback switches help diagnose whether the problem is in the connector cable between the terminal and modem, in the modem, or in the local loop communication circuit.
- Microprocessor circuits are built into some modems for automatic *equalization* to compensate for electronic instabilities on the transmission line. This equalization compensates for delay distortion that causes errors, requiring retransmission of messages.
- Some modems have *split streaming* by which the modem transmits four message streams at different speeds. This also is referred to as a *multiport modem*.
- Some modems can perform network analysis, monitoring such features as the RS232 interface and circuit characteristics, although this is usually performed by other test equipment. Tests are conducted during normal data transmission using out-of-band signaling (unused portions of the bandwidth in the guardbands).

Kbps over a variety of U.S. telephone networks. Tests in Europe, where digital transmission is less common, have been less promising.

Remember, these data rates are provided using the standard voice grade circuit that until recently was traditionally limited to 2400 bps. Once V.34 modems using V.42bis data compression methods are more common, the use of the voice telephone network to transmit computer data will grow exponentially. Some manufacturers are even predicting that 8:1 data compression ratios will be available in the near future, theoretically boosting transmission rates on standard voice grade telephone lines over 230 Kbps.

There are two drawbacks. First, compressing already compressed data provides little gain. Many data files transferred over modems are compressed to begin with; bulletin boards and Internet FTP sites routinely compress files before they are posted for use. Therefore, 28,800 bps may be the effective data rate, not 115.2 Kbps.

The second problem is that data rates over 100 Kbps place considerable pressure on the traditional microcomputer serial port controller that controls the communication between the serial port and the modem (the UART chip ([Universal Asynchronous Receiver/Transmitter]). Put simply, most UARTs rely on the microcomputer's CPU to transfer data. At these high data transmission rates, when the CPU gets overloaded (as is common in Windows-based multi-tasking environments), data get lost. The solution is to replace the UART chip with a newer version or to use a special board provided by the V.34 modem manufacturer.

DIGITAL TRANSMISSION OF ANALOG DATA

In the same way that digital computer data can be sent over analog telephone networks using analog transmission, analog voice data can be sent over digital networks using digital transmission. This process is somewhat similar to the analog transmission of digital data. A pair of special devices called codecs (*CO*de/*DECo*de) are used in the same way that a pair modems is used to translate the data to send across the circuit. One codec is attached to the sending device (e.g., a telephone) and translates the incoming analog voice signal into a digital signal for transmission across the digital circuit. A second codec at the receiver's end translates the digital data back into analog data for processing.

Pulse Amplitude Modulation

Analog voice data must be translated into a series of binary digits before they can be transmitted. One means of doing this is called *Pulse Amplitude Modulation* (PAM). With PAM-based methods, the amplitude of the sound wave is sampled at regular intervals, and translated into a binary number. Figure 5-14 shows an example where eight different amplitude levels are used (i.e., each amplitude level is represented by three bits). The top diagram shows the original signal and the bottom diagram the PAM signal.

A quick glance will show that the PAM signal is only a rough approximation of the original signal. The original signal had a smooth flow, but the PAM signal has jagged "steps." The difference between them is called *quantizing error*. Voice transmissions using PAM-based methods that have a great deal of quantizing error sound metallic or machine-like to the ear.

There are two ways to reduce quantizing error and improve the quality of the PAM signal, but neither is without cost. The first method is to increase the number of amplitude levels. This minimizes the difference between the levels (the "height" of

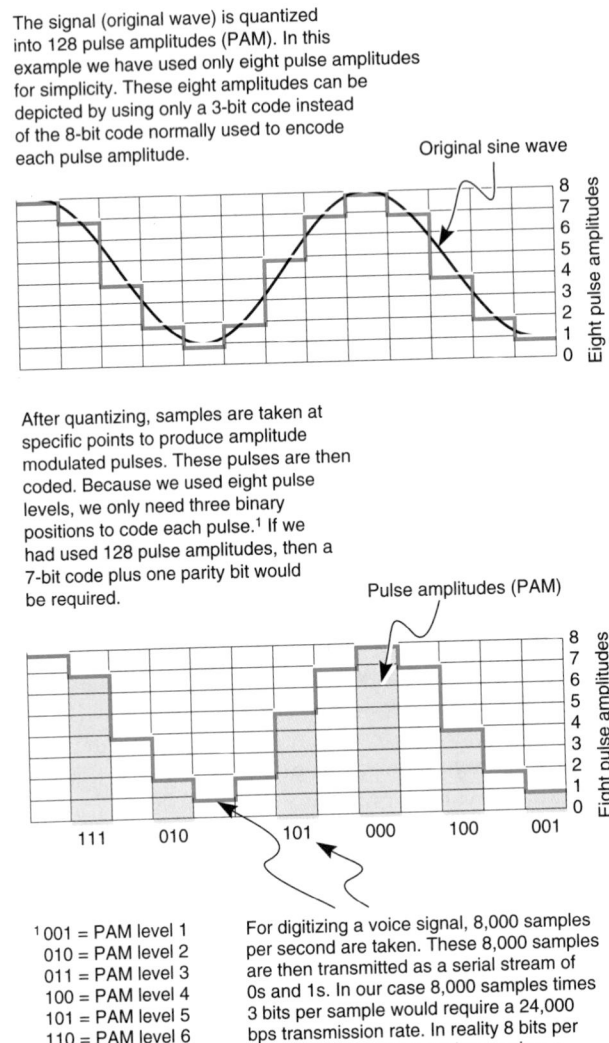

The signal (original wave) is quantized into 128 pulse amplitudes (PAM). In this example we have used only eight pulse amplitudes for simplicity. These eight amplitudes can be depicted by using only a 3-bit code instead of the 8-bit code normally used to encode each pulse amplitude.

After quantizing, samples are taken at specific points to produce amplitude modulated pulses. These pulses are then coded. Because we used eight pulse levels, we only need three binary positions to code each pulse.[1] If we had used 128 pulse amplitudes, then a 7-bit code plus one parity bit would be required.

[1] 001 = PAM level 1
010 = PAM level 2
011 = PAM level 3
100 = PAM level 4
101 = PAM level 5
110 = PAM level 6
111 = PAM level 7
000 = PAM level 8

For digitizing a voice signal, 8,000 samples per second are taken. These 8,000 samples are then transmitted as a serial stream of 0s and 1s. In our case 8,000 samples times 3 bits per sample would require a 24,000 bps transmission rate. In reality 8 bits per sample times 8,000 samples requires a 64,000 bps transmission rate.

Figure 5-14 Pulse amplitude modulation (PAM).

the "steps") and results in a smoother signal. In Figure 5-14, we could define 16 amplitude levels instead of 8 levels. This would require four bits (rather than the current three bits) to represent the amplitude, thus increasing the amount of data needed to transmit the PAM signal.

No amount of levels or bits will ever result in perfect quality sound reproduction, but in general, seven bits ($2^7 = 128$ levels) reproduces human speech adequately. Music, on the other hand, usually requires 16 bits ($2^{16} = 65,536$ levels).

The second method is to sample more frequently. This will reduce the "length" of each "step," also resulting in a smoother signal. To obtain a reasonable quality voice

Management Focus: High Speed Modems Save Time and Money

High speed modems save on line charges. Before transmitting data, you may want to calculate how long the process will take. *File transfer time* can be estimated easily by using the following formula:

$$\text{File transfer time} = \frac{\text{Number of bytes} \times \text{Number of bits per byte}}{\text{Bits per second transmission speed}}$$

This formula will provide a close estimation, but it will not be accurate to the second, because it does not take into account control characters that may be transmitted to control the transmission flow, nor the need to retransmit data due to errors.

For example, a 50-page document or a good-sized spreadsheet might be a 150,000-byte file. With a 2400 bps modem (and 8 bits per byte), the transfer time would be:

$$(150,000 \text{ bytes} \times 8 \text{ bits per byte})/2400 \text{ bits per second} = 500 \text{ seconds.}$$

As you see, the formula shows an approximate time of 8 1/3 minutes. As a rule of thumb, you might add 10 percent to this figure to account for transmission errors and the required control characters. When you do this, the time required to transmit this file is approximately 9 minutes.

Using a V.32bis modem (14,400 bps) cuts this time to about one and a half minutes. A V.34 modem (28,800 bps) would require 45 seconds. After adding V.42bis data compression to the V.34 modem, this time drops to about 12 seconds.

While a few minutes of long distance telephone time is not too costly, it can add up over the course of a year. Most high speed modems cost about $100 more than low speed modems, but can save many times that amount each year in reduced communication costs and staff time savings. A general guideline is to buy the fastest modem your communication lines can support.

----

signal, one must sample at least twice the highest possible frequency in the analog signal. You will recall that the highest frequency transmitted in telephone circuits is 3300 hertz. Thus PAM-based methods used to digitize telephone voice transmissions must sample the input voice signal at a minimum of 6600 times per second. Sampling more frequently than this (called *oversampling*) will improve signal quality. For quality reproduction of music, for example, 16 or 32 times oversampling is common.

Pulse Code Modulation

PAM is a family of techniques that includes many different specific formats. For example, one type of PAM could sample 6600 times per second using 128 amplitude levels (i.e., seven bits), while another type of PAM could sample at 13,200 times per second using 256 levels (i.e., eight bits). The most commonly used type of PAM is

Pulse Code Modulation (PCM). With PCM, the input voice signal is sampled 8000 times per second (slightly above the minimum of 6600 times per second discussed above). Each time the input voice signal is sampled, eight bits are generated; therefore, the transmission speed on the digital circuit must be 64,000 bits per second (8 bits per sample $\times$ 8,000 samples per second).

Summary

Digital Transmission of Digital Data   Digital transmission (also called baseband transmission) is done by sending a series of electrical (or light) pulses through the media. Digital transmission is preferred to analog transmission because it produces fewer errors, is more efficient, permits higher maximum transmission rates, is more secure, and simplifies the integration of voice, video, and data on the same circuit. With unipolar digital transmission, the voltage changes between zero volts to represent a binary 0 and some positive value (e.g., +15v) to represent a binary 1. With bipolar digital transmission, the voltage changes polarity (i.e., positive or negative) to represent a 1 or a 0. Bipolar is less susceptible to errors.

Analog Transmission of Digital Data   Modems are used to translate the digital data produced by computers into the analog signals for transmission in today's voice communication circuits. Both the sender and receiver need to have a modem. Data are transmitted by changing (or modulating) a carrier sound wave's amplitude (height), frequency (length), or phase (shape) to indicate a binary 1 or 0. For example, in amplitude modulation, one amplitude is defined to be a 1 and another amplitude is defined to be a 0.

Bits per Second Versus Baud   Baud is the number of signals sent per second. Baud is often used interchangeably with bits per second, but they are not the same. It is possible to send more than one bit on every signal (or wave). For example, with amplitude modulation, you could send two bits on each wave by defining four amplitude levels. You can combine techniques to send even more bits. Two popular techniques are QAM, which sends four bits per signal, and TCM which sends anywhere from five to eight bits per signal; both use a combination of amplitude and phase modulation.

Bandwidth and the Capacity of a Voice Circuit   The range of frequencies available in a circuit is called bandwidth. Voice telephone lines can transmit sound waves with frequencies from 300 hertz to 3300 hertz, so their bandwidth is 3000 hertz (3300-300). The capacity or maximum data rate that a circuit can provide is determined by multiplying the baud rate (signals per second) by the number of bits per signal. Generally (but not always), the baud rate is the same as the bandwidth, so bandwidth is often used as a measure of capacity. The maximum data rate of a voice telephone circuit is the baud rate times the number of bits per signal. At 2400 baud with QAM (four bits per signal), the maximum data rate would be 2400 × 4 = 9600 bits per second. Using 6-bit TCM at 2400 baud would produce a data rate of 14,400 bps.

Modems   Many categories of modems are currently available, including:

- V.22 which sends at 2400 bits per second using 2400 baud (one bit per baud using frequency modulation),
- V.32 which sends at 9600 bits per second using 2400 baud (four bits per baud using QAM),
- V.32bis which sends at 14,400 bits per second using 2400 baud (six bits per baud using TCM),
- V.34 which sends at 28,800 bits per second.

V.42bis is a data compression standard that can be combined with any of the foregoing types of modems to reduce the amount of data in the transmitted signal by a factor of four. Thus a V.34 modem using V.42bis could provide an effective data rate of 28,800 × 4 = 115,200 bps.

Digital Transmission of Analog Data   Because digital transmission is better, analog voice data are sometimes converted to digital transmission. Pulse code modulation (PCM) is the most commonly used technique. PCM samples the amplitude of the incoming voice signal 8000 times per second and uses 8 bits to represent the signal. PCM produces a reasonable approximation of the human voice, but more sophisticated techniques are needed to adequately reproduce more complex sounds such as music.

Key Terms

Amplitude
Amplitude modulation (AM)
Analog modem
Analog signal
ASCII
Bandwidth
Baseband
Baud
Bipolar
Bits per second (bps)
Broadband
Carrier wave
Codec
Coding
Connector cable
Cycles per second
Differential phase shift keying (DPSK)
EBCDIC

External modem
File transfer time
Frequency
Frequency modulation (FM)
Frequency shift keying (FSK)
Hertz (Hz)
Intelligent modem
Internal modem
Mark
Modem
Modem eliminator
Modem pooling
Multiport modem
Parallel
Phase
Phase modulation (PM)
Phase shift keying (PSK)
Polarity

Pulse Amplitude Modulation (PAM)
Pulse Code Modulation (PCM)
Quadrature amplitude modulation (QAM)
Quantizing error
Retrain time
Serial
Short haul modem
Space
Trellis coded modulation (TCM)
Unipolar
V.22
V.32
V.32bis
V.34
V.42bis
Wireless modem

Selected References

1.   *Auerbach Data Communications Reports.* Published monthly by Auerbach Publishers, 6560 N. Park Drive, Pennsauken, NJ 08109, 1965–present.
2.   *Black Box Catalog of Data Communications and Computer Devices.* Published monthly by the Black Box Corp., P.O. Box 12800, Pittsburgh, PA 15241.
3.   *Communications Products & Systems.* Published bimonthly by Gordon Publications, 13 Emory Avenue, Randolph, NJ 07869-1380.
4.   *Datacomm Catalog.* Published by Glasgal Communications, 151 Veterans Drive, Northvale, NJ 07647.
5.   *Datapro Reports on Data Communications.* Published monthly by Datapro Research Corp., 1805 Underwood Boulevard, Delran, NJ 08075.
6.   Gofton, Peter W. *Mastering Serial Communications.* Berkeley, CA: Sybex, Inc., 1986.
7.   Lewallen, Dale. "High Speed Modem," *PC/Computing,* vol. 5, no. 1, January 1992, pp. 206–208.
8.   *Telecom Gear: The Market Place to Buy and Sell Telecommunications Equipment.* Published monthly by Telecom Gear/Telecom Jobs, 12 West 21st Street, New York, NY 10010.

Questions/Problems

1.   How are data transmitted in parallel?
2.   What feature distinguishes serial mode from parallel mode?
3.   What is coding?
4.   Briefly describe the two most important coding schemes.
5.   What is the most commonly used connector cable?
6.   Can amplitude modulation be used for data communications?
7.   In what one way does frequency modulation differ from amplitude modulation?
8.   To what does bipolar apply?
9.   Why is bipolar signaling used?
10. How does baseband differ from broadband?
11. Are bits per second and baud the same thing? Explain.
12. What is a modem?
13. What governs transmission speed?
14. How are modems classified?
15. What is the purpose of loopback?
16. Define retrain time.
17. One of the modem lights is OH. What does that mean?
18. If you had to transmit a 10-page term paper of 20,000 bytes to your professor, approximately how long would it take (file transfer time) if your modem speed was 2400 bits per second?
19. Suppose you want to transmit a file of information to your corporate headquarters. How long will it take if there are 10,500 records of 95 bytes each, with 8 bits per byte? Assume you have a modem that transmits at 9600 bits per second.

20. If your modem transmits at 2400 *baud* using QAM, what is your data transmission rate in bits per second? If the modem includes V.42bis with a 4 to 1 data compression ratio, what is the data rate in bits per second you actually see?
21. Describe the importance of Trellis Coded Modulation.
22. Describe four common modem standards.
23. Why is V.42bis data compression so useful?

Appendix: Connector Cables

When a message leaves the microcomputer or terminal and begins to move onto the network, the first component it encounters is the *connector cable* between the microcomputer (or terminal) and the circuit. When people discuss connector cables, the focus is on the standards (such as RS232 or RS449).

RS232 (DB-25)/RS449 (DB-9)   When people talk about connector cables, they frequently refer to them as a RS232, DB-25, RS449, or DB-9. This is because each connector cable is based on a specified standard. Calling the connector by its standard designation allows everyone to know precisely which connector is being discussed.

The RS232 standard is the most frequently mentioned. It was first issued in 1962, and its third revision, RS232C, was issued in 1969. The RS232D standard was issued in 1987 to expand on RS232C. The RS232D standard also is known as the EIA-232-D.

The *RS232* connector cable that is the standard interface for connecting data terminal equipment (DTE) to data circuit terminating equipment (DCE). The newer RS232D is specified as having 25 wires and using the DB-25 connector plug like the one used on microcomputers. If this connector cable is attached to a microcomputer, people may refer to it simply as DB-25; if it is not attached to a microcomputer, they may refer to it as the RS232 interface.

Data terminal equipment (DTE) comprises the data source, the data sink, or both. In reality, it is any piece of equipment at which a data communication path begins or ends, such as a terminal. *Data circuit terminating equipment (DCE)* provides all the functions required to establish, maintain, and terminate a connection. This includes signal conversion and coding between the DTE and the common carrier's circuit, including the modem. A modem is DCE.

Figure 5-15 shows a picture of the RS232D interface plug and describes each of its 25 protruding pins. It is the standard connector cable (25 wires/pins) that passes control signals and data between the terminal (DTE) and the modem (DCE). This standard has been supplied by the Electronic Industries Association (EIA). Outside the United States, this RS232D connector cable is known as the V.24 and V.28. The V.24 and V.28 standards have been accepted by the international standards group known as the Consultative Committee on International Telegraph and Telephone (CCITT). These standards provide a common description of what the signal coming out of, and going into, the serial port of a computer or terminal looks like electrically. Specifically, RS232 provides for a signal changing from a nominal +12 volts to a

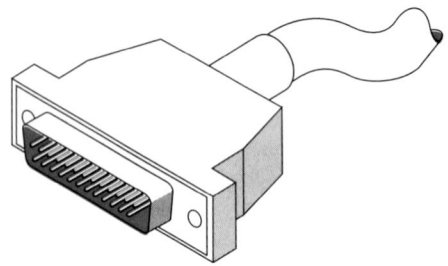

Pin	Circuit Name
1	Shield
2	Transmitted Data
3	Received Data
4	Request to Send
5	Clear to Send
6	DCE Ready
7	Signal Ground
8	Received Line Signal Detector
9	(Reserved for testing)
10	(Reserved for testing)
11	(Unassigned)
12	Secondary Received Line Signal Detector/Data Signal Rate Select (DCE source)
13	Secondary Clear to Send
14	Secondary Transmitted Data
15	Transmitter Signal Element Timing (DCE source)
16	Secondary Received Data
17	Receiver Signal Element Timing (DCE source)
18	Local Loopback
19	Secondary Request to Send
20	DTE Ready
21	Remote Loopback/Signal Quality Detector
22	Ring Indicator
23	Data Signal Rate Select (DTE/DCE source)
24	Transmitter Signal Element Timing (DTE source)
25	Test Mode

Figure 5-15 RS232D and V.24 interface (DB-25). The terminal connection to the modem is defined by the Electronic Industries Association (EIA) specification, which specifies the use of a 25-pin connector and the pin on which each signal is placed.

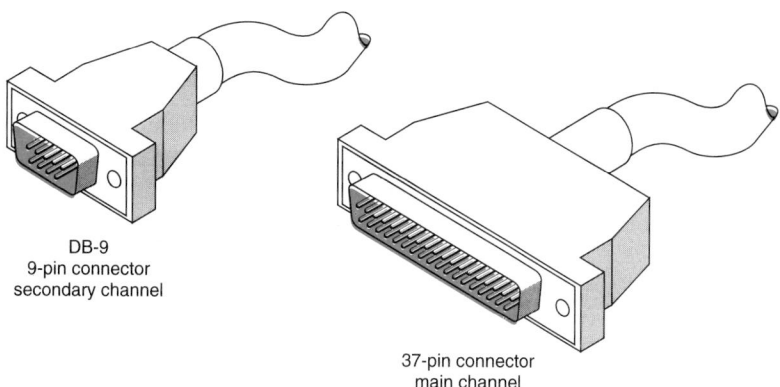

DB-9
9-pin connector
secondary channel

37-pin connector
main channel

37-Pin Connector				9-Pin Connector	
First Segment Assignment		**Second Segment Assignment**			
Pin	**Function**	**Pin**	**Function**	**Pin**	**Function**
1	Shield	20	Receive Common	1	Shield
2	Signaling Rate	21	Unassigned	2	Sec. Receiver Ready
	Indicator	22	Send Data	3	Sec. Send Data
3	Unassigned	23	Send Timing	4	Sec. Receive Data
4	Send Data	24	Receive Data	5	Signal Ground
5	Send Timing	25	Request to Send	6	Receive Common
6	Receive Data	26	Receive Timing	7	Sec. Request to
7	Request to Send	27	Clear to Send		Send
8	Receive Timing	28	Terminal in Service	8	Sec. Clear to Send
9	Clear to Send	29	Data Mode	9	Send Common
10	Local Loopback	30	Terminal Ready		
11	Data Mode	31	Receiver Ready		
12	Terminal Ready	32	Select Standby		
13	Receiver Ready	33	Signal Quality		
14	Remote Loopback	34	New Signal		
15	Incoming Call	35	Terminal Timing		
16	Select Frequency/ Signaling Rate Selector	36	Standby Indicator		
17	Terminal Timing	37	Send Common		
18	Test Mode				
19	Signal Ground				

Figure 5-16 RS449 interface and DB-9 connector. RS449 is a new EIA specification augmenting RS232C. This specification calls for use of a 37-pin connector. For those devices using a side, forward, reverse, or secondary channel, a second 9-pin connector is specified. RS449 provides for additional control and signaling.

nominal −12 volts. The standard also defines the cables and connectors used to link data communication devices. This is the cable that connects the modem to your microcomputer.

The RS232 has a maximum 50-foot cable length, but it can be increased to 100 feet or more by means of a special low capacitance, extended distance cable. This is not advised, however, because some vendors may not honor maintenance agreements if the cable is lengthened beyond the 50-foot standard.

As an illustration, let us present the cable distances for Texas Instruments' products. The cable length of the RS232 varies according to the speed at which you transmit. For Texas Instruments, the connector cable length can be up to 914 meters (1 meter = 1.1 yards) when transmitting at 1200 bits per second, 549 meters when transmitting at 2400 bits per second, 244 meters when transmitting at 4800 bits per second, and 122 meters when transmitting at 9600 bits per second. When end users operate at maximum distances, it is important to remember that they must meet the restrictions on all types of equipment used, including the electrical environment, cable construction, and cable wiring. This means that when you want to operate at a maximum cable distance, you must contact the terminal and/or modem vendors to obtain their maximum cable distance before you proceed.

The *RS449* standard has been adopted as U.S. Federal Standard 1031. The RS449 is shown in Figure 5-16. A 4000-foot cable length can be used, there are 37 pins instead of 25 (useful for digital transmission), and various other circuit functions have been added, such as diagnostic circuits and digital circuits. In addition, secondary channel circuits (reverse channel) have been put into a separate 9-pin connector known as a *DB-9.* The serial port on your microcomputer may be either a DB-9 or a *DB-25.*

For some of the new features, look at pin 32 (SELECT STANDBY). With this pin, the terminal can instruct the modem to use an alternate standby network such as changing from a private leased line to a public packet network, either for backup or simply to access another database not normally used. In other words, a terminal can be connected to two different networks, and the operator can enter a keyboard command to switch the connection from one network to another. With regard to LOOP-BACK (pins 10 and 14), the terminal can allow basic tests without special test equipment or the manual exchanging of equipment or cables.

With microcomputers, the RS232 and RS449 also are referred to as D-type connectors. The RS232 may be called a DB-25, and the 9-pin RS449 may be called a DB-9. Look at Figure 5-17 to see the microcomputer pin configurations for these two connectors.

There are also X.20 and X.21 interface cables. The *X.20* interface is for asynchronous communications, and the *X.21* is for synchronous communications. Each is based on only 15 pins (wires) connecting the DTE and the DCE, and fewer pins requires an increased intelligence in both the DTE and the DCE. X.20 and X.21 are international standards intended to provide an interface with the X.25 packet switching networks discussed later in this book.

Another option that may become available in the near future is a fiber optic cable in place of the standard RS232 electrical cables. Currently, by using fiber optic cable, we can locate a terminal 1000 meters (3280 feet) from a host mainframe computer. With a 1000-meter fiber optic cable, these products can communicate at speeds rang-

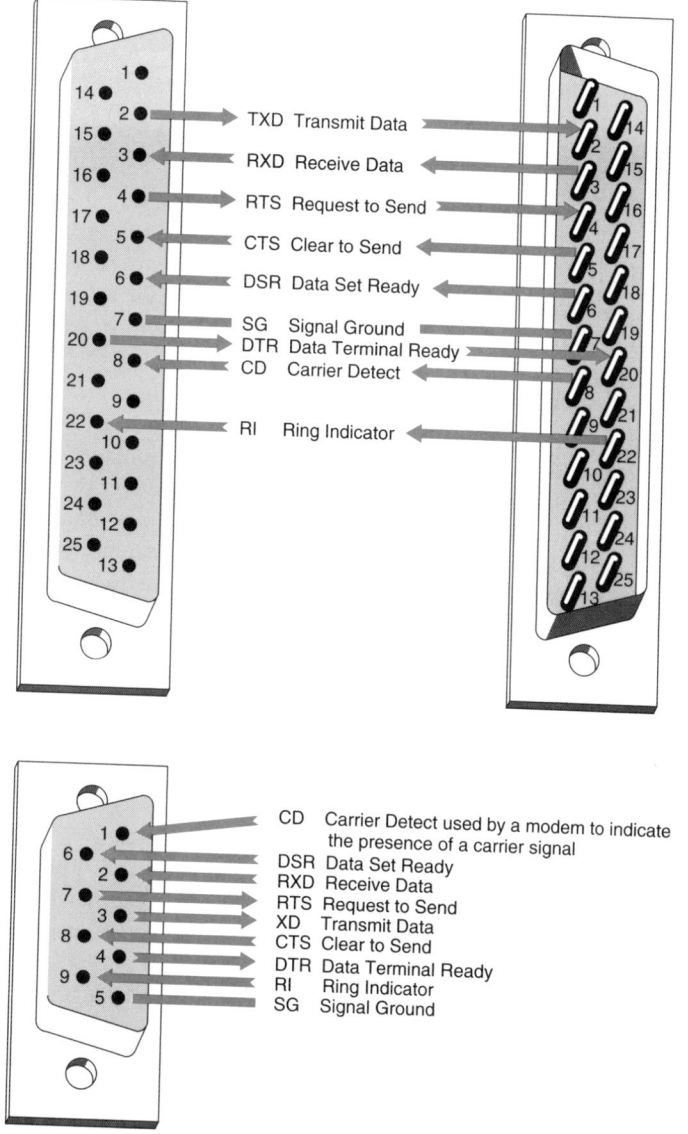

Figure 5-17   Typical 25-pin (RS232) and 9-pin IBM (PC/AT) modem connector for microcomputers.

ing from 19,200 bits per second up to twice that speed. Therefore, you get not only greater distance (1000 meters) but also greater speed. This may be another example in which fiber optics eventually will replace electronics.

The *high speed serial interface* (HSSI) is beginning to appear in new products. HSSI defines the physical and electrical interface between the DTE and the DCE equipment. It was developed by Cisco Systems of Menlo Park, California, and T3plus of Santa

Clara, California. They have submitted it to the American National Standards Institute, which also formalized the EIA-232 and V.35 standards. HSSI allows data transfers over the connector cable at 52 million bits per second, whereas RS-449 cannot handle more than 10 million bits per second. HSSI is a 50-pin connector using shielded twisted pair cabling.

Null Modem Cable Connections   *Null modem cables* allow transmission between two microcomputers that are next to each other (six to eight feet apart) without using a modem. If you discover that the diskette from your microcomputer will not fit into another one, that transmitting over telephone lines is impossible, or that you cannot transmit data easily from one microcomputer to another for any reason, then it is time to get a null modem cable.

First, bring the two microcomputers close together. Next, obtain a null modem cable (more on the pin connections shortly). The cable runs from the serial communication port on the first microcomputer to the serial communication port on the second one. The cable is called a "null" modem cable because it eliminates the need for a modem. You can either build a null modem cable or buy one from any microcomputer store. Null modem connector blocks are available to connect between two cables you already own. Basically, a null modem cable switches pins 2 and 3 (TRANSMIT and RECEIVE) of the RS232 connector plug.

To transfer data between two microcomputers, just hook the null modem cable between them and call up one of the computers by using the communication software you normally use. To do so, put one microcomputer in answer mode and use the other one to call it, but skip the step of dialing the telephone number. After the receiving computer has answered that it is ready, the data can be sent, just as you would on a normal long distance dial-up connection.

Data Signaling/Synchronization   Let us look at *data signaling* or *synchronization* as it occurs on a RS232 connector cable. Figure 5-18 shows the 13 most frequently used pins of the 25-pin RS232 connector cable. A microcomputer is on the left side of the figure and a modem is on the right.

Do you ever wonder what happens when you press the "send" key to transmit synchronous data? When a synchronous block of data is sent, the microcomputer and the modem raise and lower electrical signals (plus and minus voltages of electricity) between themselves over the RS232 connector cable. This usually is a nominal $+12$ or -12 volts. For example, a modem with a RS232 interface might indicate that it is on and ready to operate by raising the signal on pin 6, DATA SET READY. (Data set is an older term for a modem.) When a call comes in, the modem shows the microcomputer that the telephone line is ringing by raising a signal on pin 22, the RING INDICATOR. Raising a signal means putting $+12$ volts on the wire or pin. The microcomputer may then tell the modem to answer the call by raising a signal on pin 20, DATA TERMINAL READY. After the modems connect, the modem may indicate the connection status to the microcomputer by raising a signal on pin 8, CARRIER DETECT. At the end of the session, the microcomputer may tell the modem to drop the telephone call (release the circuit) by lowering the signal on pin 20, DATA TER-

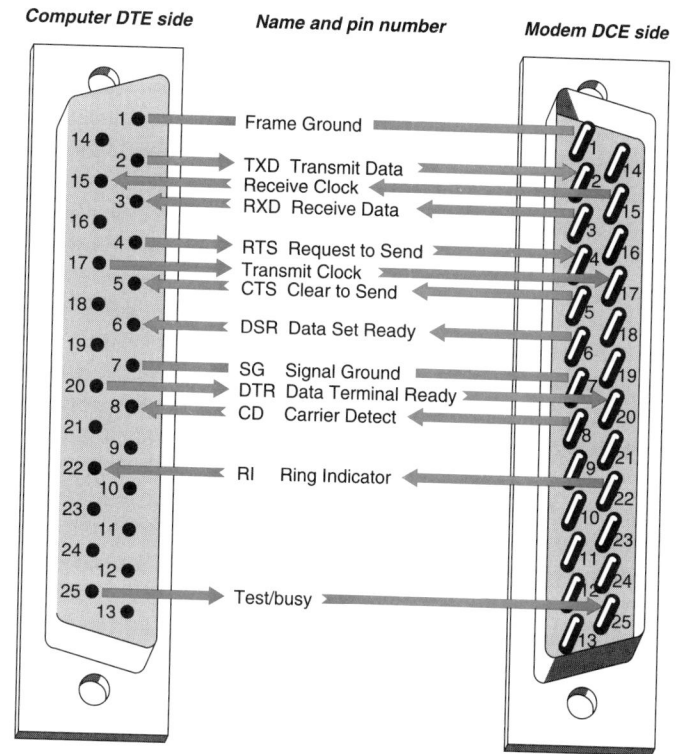

Figure 5-18   RS232 modem control (13 most used pins).

MINAL READY. The REQUEST TO SEND and CLEAR TO SEND signals go over pins 4 and 5, which are used in half duplex modems to manage control of the communication channel. Incidentally, some of these basic procedures may vary slightly from one manufacturer to another.

Follow the pins and signal direction arrows in Figure 5-18 as we discuss an example that handles the flow of a block of synchronous data. When the microcomputer operator presses the "send" key to transmit a block of data, pin 4, REQUEST TO SEND, transmits the signal from the microcomputer to the modem. This informs the modem that a block of data is ready to be sent. The modem then sends a CLEAR TO SEND signal back to the microcomputer by using pin 5, thus telling the microcomputer that it can send a synchronous block of data.

The microcomputer now out-pulses a serial stream of bits that contain two 8-bit SYN (synchronization) characters in front of the message block. A SYN character is 0110100 (decimal 22 in ASCII code). This bit stream passes over the connector cable to the modem using pin 2, TRANSMIT DATA. The modem then modulates this data block to convert it from the digital signal (plus and minus voltages of electricity) to an analog signal. From the modem, the data go out onto the local loop circuit between your business premises and the telephone company central office. From there, they go to the long distance interexchange channels (IXC) and the receiving end's telephone company central office. Then they move to the local loop, into the modem, across the connector cable, and into the host mainframe computer at the other end of the circuit.

This process is repeated for each synchronous message block in half duplex transmission. The data signaling that takes place between the microcomputer and the modem involves the REQUEST TO SEND, CLEAR TO SEND, and TRANSMIT DATA pins. Accurate timing between blocks of data is critical in data signaling and synchronization. If this timing is lost, the entire block of data is destroyed and must be retransmitted.

NEXT DAY AIR SERVICE CUMULATIVE CASE STUDY

See appendix at end of book

CHAPTER SIX

DATA LINK LAYER

The data link layer controls the way messages are sent on the physical media. Both the sender and receiver have to agree on the rules or *protocols* that govern how they will communicate with each other. A *data link protocol* determines who can transmit at what time, where a message begins and ends, and how a receiver recognizes and corrects a transmission error. In this chapter we discuss these processes, as well as several important sources of noise that cause errors.

Objectives

- Understand the reasons for having layers in data communications systems,
- Understand the role of the data link layer,
- Become familiar with two basic approaches to controlling access to the media,
- Become familiar with common sources of error and their prevention,
- Understand three common error detection and correction methods,
- Become familiar with several commonly used data link protocols.

Chapter Outline

Introduction
　　The Importance of Layers
　　The Open Systems Interconnection (OSI) Model
Media Access Control
　　Controlled Access
　　Contention
　　Relative Performance

INTRODUCTION

In Chapter 1, we introduced the concept of layers in data communications. Chapters 3 through 5 discussed the hardware, media, and transmission characteristics of physical layer. The physical layer accepts and transmits a stream of bits without understanding their meaning or structure. It is the data link layer that creates meaning to these bits. The data link layer determines:

- Who is able to transmit at a given time (*media access control*).
- How a receiver detects when a transmission error has occurred and corrects it (*error control*).
- How a receiver knows where a character or entire message begins and ends (*message delineation*).

Before we discuss the data link layer in more detail, it is important to understand the reason for using layers, and one of the most commonly used models for defining the layers in a data communications network: the OSI model.

The Importance of Layers

We defined communication networks in terms of four layers—physical, data link, network, and application—and how each must work together in order for messages to be sent from sender to receiver. One way to understand the concept of layers is to view it as a set of four different software programs, each of which performs some function in transmitting a message from one computer or terminal to another.

For example, the user defines what messages are sent over the network by using the application layer software. The application layer then passes the user's message to the network layer. The network layer addresses the message (translates the destination of the message into an address understood by the network), routes it (decides which route through the network the message should take), and passes the message (plus addressing and routing information) to the data link layer. The data link layer formats the message for transmission by indicating where the message begins and ends, decides when to transmit the message, and detects and corrects any errors that occur. The data link layer then passes the message (plus its message delineation and error control information, and the network layer's addressing and routing information) to the physical layer. The physical layer translates the series of bits given to it by the data link layer into electrical, radio, microwave, or light signals and physically transmits them to their destination where this process is reversed and the message is received by the application layer.

For communication to be successful, each layer in the sending computer must be compatible with the corresponding layer in the receiving computer. For example, the physical layer connecting the sender and receiver must use the same type of electrical signals so each can understand the other. Likewise, the data link layer in both sender and receiver must use the same protocols for marking the start and end of messages, or they will not be able understand each other's messages. The same is true for the network layers; if the receiver's network layer cannot understand the address and routing information provided by the sender, the message cannot be understood and sent to the correct destination. All computers must use the same set of physical, data link, and network *protocols*, or have devices between them to translate from one protocol to another.

To better understand the use of layers, imagine the data being sent across the network as a document that has so many pages that they must be separated into several stacks and placed in a series of separate interoffice envelopes. Each envelope is identified by a sequence number so the recipient knows the correct order in which to read the pages. Each of these interoffice envelopes then is inserted into a large mailing envelope with the destination office address added for mailing purposes. In this example, the typed pages represent application data, the interoffice envelopes represent network layer packets, and the large mailing envelopes represent data link layer packets. The application data are surrounded by a network packet, which in turn is surrounded by a data link packet.

In this book, we use a simple four-layer model to organize the functions performed in the network. Networks used in the real world often further break the network layer into several separate layers, each of which perform different functions. Thus in practice, there may be many other types of packets, so that the application data is contained inside as many as four or five separate packets inside each other—much like those famous Russian dolls!

The Open Systems Interconnection (OSI) Model

The most commonly used model for defining network layers is the OSI model. During the late 1970s, the International Standards Organization created the Open System

Layer	Sending building	Receiving building
Application layer — 7	Employees on the seventh floor convert input from a terminal or application program into a "message block," which includes the data (message contents) along with the sender's and receiver's addresses. When the block is complete, they pass it to the sixth floor. Application programs or terminals access the network only at this floor.	Workers here identify the receiving terminal or application program and display the message on the screen of the network user's microcomputer or pass it to the application program.
Presentation layer — 6	Workers on the sixth floor convert code (EBCDIC to ASCII or vice versa), define the format of the data, and (when requested) encrypt the data and compress it before passing the message block to the fifth floor.	On the sixth floor employees convert code (ASCII to EBDIC) and, if required, decompress and decrypt the message.
Session layer — 5	Those on the fifth floor mark the beginning and ending of message blocks, set up a session connecting two terminals (log-in, passwords, user ID, etc.), end sessions, and determine whether the transmission will be half duplex or full duplex before passing the message blocks to the fourth floor.	Fifth floor workers hold all message blocks until they have received the entire message, which they pass to those on the sixth floor.
Transport layer — 4	Fourth floor employees divide very long message blocks into shorter message blocks for transmission, add a sequence number to each block, add a checksum for error detection, check for duplicate blocks, retransmit the blocks after an error or a timeout, add security to message blocks, and pass the message blocks to the third floor.	Those on the fourth floor recalculate checksums to confirm receipt of all message blocks and request retransmission of a block that appears damaged or is missing.
Network layer — 3	Third floor employees resize the message blocks into packets (usually 128 characters) to meet specific network requirements, attach the addresses and sequence numbers to each packet, identify routes for packets through the network, and then pass the packets to the second floor.	The third floor workers recount incoming packets for error, security, and billing purposes, and reconvert the packets to message blocks.
Data link layer — 2	Workers here supervise the transmission. They insert the packet into a frame that becomes the envelope for carrying the packet during transmission, add a frame sequence number, confirm checksums for error detection, keep a copy of the frame to use for retransmission in case of error, and then pass the completed frame to the first floor for transmission.	On the second floor they recalculate the checksum, request frame retransmission if there is an error, confirm arrival, and log-in the frame.
Physical layer — 1	The first floor is concerned with hardware, whereas the upper floors are concerned with software. The hardware on the first floor includes the RS-232 connector cables, modems, and circuits. What began on the seventh floor as a long message block is now sent over the circuits as a frame containing a packet in the form of a serial stream of bits.	First floor employees reconvert the bits into frames.

Notice that the people on the fourth floor confirm the receipt of all packets that belong to the same message block, whereas the second floor only confirms the correct receipt of a single frame (containing one packet).

Packet/Frame ....1001010.......

Figure 6-1 This figure depicts the OSI model as a seven-floor office building in which people handle messages instead of software programs doing the work. A message to be sent across the network enters the OSI software at the seventh floor, travels down to the first floor, goes out the front door, travels across the network, and reaches the other building, where it travels through the front door and up to the receiving terminal on the seventh floor of that building.

Interconnection (OSI) subcommittee whose task was to develop a framework of standards for computer-to-computer communications. In 1984, this effort produced the *Open Systems Interconnection Reference Model*, which is commonly referred to as the OSI Model.

The OSI model has seven layers (see Figure 6-1). It was originally developed for mainframe-oriented networks, so some of the layers do not apply to local area networks. The first two layers of the OSI model (physical, data link) and the last (application) correspond to the same layers used in this book. The middle four layers in the OSI model have been condensed into one (the network layer) for presentation in this book.

Layer 1: Physical Layer   The *physical layer* is concerned primarily with transmitting data bits (0's or 1's) over a communication circuit. This layer defines the rules by which ones and zeros are transmitted, such as voltages of electricity, timing factors, full duplex or half duplex transmission, and connector cable standards, such as RS232 and RS449.

Layer 2: Data Link Layer   The *data link layer* manages the basic transmission circuit established in layer 1 and transforms it into a circuit that is free of transmission errors as far as layers above are concerned. A major task of layer 2 is to solve the problems caused by damaged, lost, or duplicate message frames so the succeeding layers are shielded from transmission errors and can therefore presume that no errors occur.

Because layer 1 accepts and transmits only a serial stream of bits without understanding their meaning or structure, the data link layer must create and recognize message boundaries and check for errors. Layer 2 performs error detection, correction, and retransmission, definition of the beginning and end of the message, resolution of competing requests for the same communication link, and flow control, which keeps a rapidly transmitting device from ''drowning'' a slower receiver.

The data link layer is sometimes further divided into two sublayers: the *media access control* (MAC) sublayer and the *logical link control* (LLC) sublayer. The MAC sublayer performs most of the data link layer functions. The LLC sublayer is just an interface between the MAC sublayer and software in layer 3 (the network layer) that enables the software and hardware in the MAC sublayer to be separated from the logical functions in the LLC sublayer. In this way, the LLC sublayer performs a similar role to that performed by middleware in client-server networks. By separating the LLC sublayer from the MAC sublayer, it is simpler to change the MAC hardware and software without affecting the software in layer 3. The most commonly used LLC protocol is IEEE 802.2.

Layer 3: Network Layer   The *network layer* performs addressing and routing. It actually controls the operation of the combined layers, 1, 2, and 3, which are sometimes called the *sub-network*. Software at this layer accepts messages from layer 4, and ensures that the packets are directed to their proper destination. After its routing has been established, the packet is passed down to the data link layer.

Layer 4: Transport Layer   The *transport layer* often is called the *host-to-host layer* or *end-to-end layer* because it establishes, maintains, and terminates logical connections for the transfer of data between end users. It is responsible for generating the address of the end user, breaking a large data transmission into smaller packets if needed, ensuring that all the packets have been received, and eliminating duplicate packets. The transport layer deals with end-to-end issues, such as procedures for entering and departing from the network.

The transport layer can multiplex several streams of messages onto one physical circuit, or use inverse multiplexing to create one fast circuit from several slower ones. It also performs flow control by controlling the movement of messages, whereas layers 1 and 2 control the physical flow of packets or frames.

Layer 5: Session Layer   The *session layer* is responsible for initiating, maintaining, and terminating each logical session between end users. To understand the session layer, think of your telephone. When you lift the receiver, listen for a dial tone, and dial a number, you begin to create a physical connection that goes through layer 1 as a person-to-network protocol. When you start speaking with the person at the other end of the telephone circuit, you are engaged in a person-to-person session; the session is the dialogue between the two of you.

This layer is responsible for managing and structuring all sessions. Session initiation must arrange for all the desired and required services between session participants, such as logging onto circuit equipment, transferring files, using various terminal types, and performing security checks. Session termination provides an orderly way to end the session, as well as a means to abort a session prematurely. It may have some redundancy built in to recover from a broken transport (layer 4) connection in case of failure. The session layer also handles session accounting so the correct party receives the bill. In many networks, the functions defined at this layer are actually performed by the data link layer (layer 2) or the transport layer (layer 4), so no software is actually present at layer 5.

Layer 6: Presentation Layer   The *presentation layer* formats the data for presentation to the user. Its job is to accommodate the totally different interfaces on different terminals or computers so the application program need not worry about them. It is concerned with displaying, formatting, and editing user inputs and outputs. For example, layer 6 might perform data compression, translation between different data formats, and screen formatting. Any function (except those in layers 1 to 5) that is requested sufficiently often to warrant finding a general solution is placed in the presentation layer, although some of these functions can be performed by separate hardware and software (e.g., encryption).

Layer 7: Application Layer   The *application layer* is the end user's access to the network. Its primary purpose is to provide a set of utilities for application programs. Each user program determines the set of messages and any action it might take upon receipt of a message. Other considerations at this layer include network management statistics, remote system initiation and termination, network monitoring, application diagnostics, making the network transparent to users, simple processor sharing between host computers, use of distributed databases, and industry-specific protocols (such as those in banking).

MEDIA ACCESS CONTROL

Media access control refers to the need to control when devices transmit. With point-to-point full duplex configurations, media access control is unnecessary because there are only two devices on the circuit and full duplex permits either device to transmit at any time. Asynchronous transmission, for example, permits devices to transmit whenever a key is pressed. There is no media access control.

Media access control becomes important when several devices share the same communication circuit, such as a point-to-point configuration with a half duplex line that requires devices to take turns, or a multipoint configuration in which several devices share the same circuit. Here, it is critical to ensure that no two devices attempt to transmit data at the same time—or if they do, there must be a way to recover from the problem. Media access control is critical in local area networks and will be discussed in more detail in Chapter 8. There are two fundamental approaches to media access control: controlled access, and contention.

Controlled Access

Most computer networks managed by a host mainframe computer use controlled access. In this case, the mainframe or its front end processor controls the circuit and determines which devices can access the media at what time. Controlled access is also common in local area networks.

X-ON/X-OFF   *X-ON/X-OFF* is one of the oldest media access control protocols, dating back to the days of the teletype. It was not really designed for computer networks, but is still used today. X-ON/X-OFF is only used for the transmission of text messages (not binary files such as .EXE files), often on half duplex circuits between two computers, or between a computer and a printer.

The basic concept is simple. Computer A sends something to computer B, and computer B acknowledges that it is ready to receive it by sending an X-ON signal, which tells A to begin transmitting. Computer A periodically pauses its transmission to let computer B send a message. If B is receiving without problems, it does nothing, and A continues to transmit. If B becomes busy, it sends the X-OFF signal and A stops transmitting until B sends an X-ON signal.

Because the X-ON and X-OFF signals can be easily lost during transmission, this simple scheme can lead to confusion. More sophisticated approaches have been developed, so its use is rapidly fading.

Polling   *Polling* is the process of sending a signal to a terminal, giving it permission to transmit or asking it to receive. With polling, the client terminals and microcomputers store all messages to be transmitted. Periodically, the host or FEP *polls* the client to see if they have data to send. If the client has data to send, it does so. If the client has no data to send, it responds negatively, and the host or FEP asks another client if it has data to send.

In other words, polling is analogous to a classroom situation in which the instructor calls on the students who raise their hands. The instructor acts like the FEP or host. To gain access to the media, students raise their hands and the instructor recognizes them so they can contribute. When they have finished, the instructor again takes charge, and allows someone else to comment.

There are several types of polling. With *roll call polling,* the front end processor works consecutively through a list of clients, first polling terminal 1, then terminal 2, and so on, until all are polled (see Figure 6-2). Roll call polling can be modified to select clients in priority so that some get polled more often than others. For example, one could increase the priority of terminal 1 by using a polling sequence such as 1, 2, 3, 1, 4, 5, 1, 6, 7, 1, 8, 9.

Typically, roll call polling involves some waiting time because the front end processor has to poll a terminal and then wait for a response. The response might be an incoming message that was waiting to be sent, a negative response indicating nothing is to be sent, or the full "time-out period" may expire because the terminal is tem-

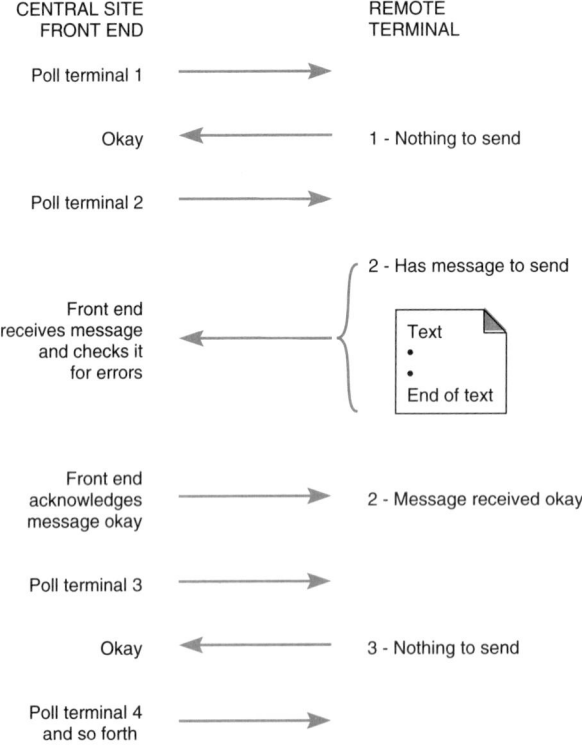

Figure 6-2   Roll call polling for half duplex transmission.

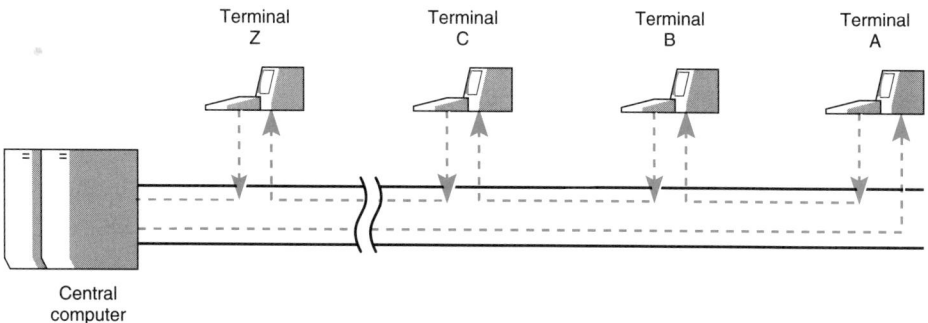

Figure 6-3 Hub go-ahead polling on a multipoint circuit.

porarily out of service (e.g., the terminal is malfuctioning or the user has turned it off). Usually, a timer "times out" the terminal after waiting several seconds without getting a response. If some sort of fail-safe time-out is not used, the system poll might lock up indefinitely on an out-of-service terminal.

Hub go-ahead polling is often used in multipoint configurations (see Figure 6-3). The front end processor passes the poll to the most remote device on the multipoint circuit, which sends its message and passes the poll to the next device. That device then passes the poll to the next device, and so on, until it reaches the front end processor, which restarts the process by passing the poll to the farthest device. This technique relieves the front end processor of many polling tasks because the terminals manage the process. Hub go-ahead polling requires more intelligence in each of the terminals so dumb terminals cannot be used.

Contention

Contention is the opposite of controlled access. Devices wait until the circuit is free (i.e., no other devices are transmitting), and then transmit whenever they have data to send.

As an analogy, suppose that you are talking with some friends at a restaurant. Each person tries to "get the floor" when the previous speaker finishes. Usually, the others yield to the first person who jumps in at the precise moment the previous speaker stops. Sometimes two people attempt to talk at the same time, so there must be some technique to continue the conversation after this verbal "collision."

Relative Performance

Which media access control approach is best: controlled access or contention? There is no simple answer. The key consideration is throughput—which approach will permit the most amount of user data to be transmitted through the network.

In general, contention approaches work better than controlled approaches for small networks that have low usage. In this case, each device can transmit when necessary without waiting for permission. In high volume networks, many devices want to transmit at the same time, and a well-controlled circuit prevents collisions. We will discuss this issue in the context of local area networks in more detail in Chapter 8.

ERROR CONTROL IN NETWORKS

Before describing the control mechanisms that can be implemented to protect a network from errors, you should realize that there are *human errors* and *network errors*. Human errors, such as a mistake in typing a number, usually are controlled through the application program. Network errors, such as those that occur during transmission, are controlled by the network hardware and software.

There are two categories of network errors: *corrupted data* (data that have been changed) and *lost data*. The factors to consider when selecting an error control system are the maximum error rate that can be tolerated, the cost of increased accuracy compared with the cost of correcting errors, and the future cost of errors remaining in the received data or information.

What Are Network Errors?

Network errors are a fact of life in today's data communication networks. Depending on the type of circuit, they may occur every few hours, minutes, or seconds because of noise on the lines. No network can eliminate all errors, but most errors can be prevented, detected, and corrected by proper design. Interexchange carriers that lease data transmission circuits provide statistical measures specifying typical error rates and the pattern of errors that can be expected on the circuits they lease.

Normally, errors appear in bursts. In a *burst error,* more than one data bit is changed by the error-causing condition. In other words, errors are not uniformly distributed in time, even though common carriers usually list their *error rates* as the number of bits in error divided by the number of bits transmitted, without reference to their nonuniform distribution. For example, the error rate might be given as 1 in 500,000, meaning there is 1 bit in error for every 500,000 bits transmitted.

The fact that errors tend to be clustered in bursts rather than evenly dispersed is both good and bad. If the errors were not clustered, an error rate of 1 bit in 500,000 would make it rare for two erroneous bits to occur in the same character. Consequently, simple character checking schemes would be effective at detecting errors. When errors are #ore or less evenly distrib#ted, it is not hard to det#rmine the meaning, even when the error rate is high, as it is in this #entence (1 charac#er in 20). But bursts errors are the rule rather than the exception, often obliterating a hundred or more bits at a time. This makes it more difficult to recover the meaning, so more reliance must be placed on knowledge of the message #######[1] or on special logical or numerical error detection and correction methods. The positive side is that there are long periods of error-free transmission, meaning that only a very few messages encounter errors.

The error rate in transmissions sent over the dial-up network (i.e., telephone company circuits) varies from one circuit to another. Dial-up lines are more prone to errors than private dedicated lines because they have less stable transmission parameters. In some cases, users must transmit the data at a slower speed because higher transmission speeds are more error prone. Because different calls use different circuits, they usually experience different transmission conditions. A bad line is not necessarily a serious problem because a new call may use a better line.

What Causes Errors?

Line noise and *distortion* can cause data communication errors. The focus in this section is on electrical media such as twisted pair and coaxial cable, as they are more likely to suffer from noise than optical media such as fiber optical cable. In this case, noise is undesirable electrical signals (for fiber optic cable, it is undesirable light). Noise is introduced by equipment or natural disturbances, and it degrades the performance of a communication line. Noise manifests itself as extra bits, missing bits, or bits whose states have been "flipped," (i.e., changed from 1 to 0 or vice versa) and the result is an error in the message. Line noise and distortion can be classified into roughly eleven categories: white noise, impulse noise, cross-talk, intermodulation noise, echoes, attenuation, attenuation distortion, delay distortion, jitter, harmonic distortion, and line outages.

White noise or gaussian noise (the familiar background hiss or static on radios and telephones) is caused by the thermal agitation of electrons and therefore is inescapable. Even if the equipment were perfect and the wires were perfectly insulated from any and all external interference, there still would be some white noise. White noise usually is not a problem unless it becomes so strong that it obliterates the transmission. In this case, the strength of the electrical signal is increased so it overpowers the white noise; in technical terms, we increase the signal to noise ratio.

Impulse noise (sometimes called *spikes*) is the primary source of errors in data communications. Impulse noise is heard as a click or a crackling noise and can last as long as 1/100 of a second. Such a click does not really affect voice communications, but it can obliterate a group of data, causing a burst error. At 300 bits per second, three bits would be changed by a spike of 1/100 of a second, whereas at 14,400 bits per second, 144 bits would be changed. Some of the sources of impulse noise are voltage changes in adjacent lines or circuitry surrounding the data communication line, telephone switching equipment at the exchange branch offices, arcing of the relays at older telephone exchange offices, tones used by network signaling, maintenance equipment used for line testing, lightning flashes during thunderstorms, fluorescent lights, and poor electrical connections in the data communication equipment.

[1]In case you could not guess, the word is "context."

Cross-talk occurs when one circuit picks up signals in another. You experience cross-talk during telephone calls when you hear other conversations in the background. It occurs between line pairs that are carrying separate signals, in multiplexed links carrying many discrete signals, in microwave links in which one antenna picks up a minute reflection from another antenna, and in any telephone circuits that are too close to each other or are not electrically balanced. Cross-talk between lines increases with increased communication distance, increase proximity of the two wires, increased signal strength, and higher frequency signals. Wet or damp weather can also increase cross-talk. Like white noise, cross-talk has such a low signal strength that it normally is not bothersome.

Intermodulation noise is a special type of cross-talk. The signals from two circuits intermodulate and form a new signal that falls into a frequency band different from both that is reserved for another signal. This type of noise is similar to harmonics in music. On a multiplexed line, many different signals are amplified together, and slight variations in the adjustment of the equipment can cause intermodulation noise. A maladjusted modem may transmit a strong frequency tone when not transmitting data, thus producing this type of noise.

Echoes and echo suppression can cause errors. (Echo suppressors were discussed in Chapter 3.) An echo suppressor causes a change in the electrical balance of a circuit, which may reflect signals back down the circuit. When the echo suppressors are disabled, as in data transmission, this echo returns to the transmitting equipment. If the strength of the echo is strong enough to be detected, it causes errors. Echoes, like cross-talk and white noise, have such a low signal strength that they normally are not bothersome. Echoes can also occur in fiber optic cables when connections between cables are not properly aligned.

Attenuation is the loss of power a signal suffers as it travels from the transmitting device to the receiving device. Some power is absorbed by the medium or is lost before it reaches the receiver. As the medium absorbs power, the signal becomes weaker, and the receiving equipment has less and less chance of correctly interpreting the data. This power loss is a function of the transmission method and circuit medium. Attenuation increases as frequency increases or as the diameter of the wire decreases.

Attenuation distortion refers to the fact that high frequencies lose power more rapidly than low frequencies during transmission. The received signal can thus be distorted by unequal loss of its component frequencies, so that lower frequency waves are received properly, but high frequency waves are lost.

Delay distortion refers to the distortion of the signal that occurs because different frequencies travel at slightly different speeds through the media. If data are transmitted at two different frequencies, then the bits transmitted at one frequency may travel slightly faster than the bits transmitted at the second frequency.

Jitter may affect the accuracy of the data being transmitted because minute variations in amplitude, phase, and frequency always occur. The generation of a pure carrier signal in an analog circuit is impossible. The signal may be impaired by continuous and rapid gain and/or phase changes. This jitter may be random or periodic. Phase jitter during a telephone call causes the voice to fluctuate in volume.

Harmonic distortion usually is caused by an amplifier on a circuit that does not correctly represent its output with what was delivered to it on the input side. *Phase hits* are short-term shifts "out of phase," with the possibility of a shift back into phase.

Line outages are a catastrophic cause of errors and incomplete transmission. Occasionally, a communication circuit fails for a brief period. This type of failure may be caused by faulty telephone-end office equipment, storms, loss of the carrier signal, and any other failure that causes a short circuit.

Error Prevention

There are many techniques to prevent errors (or at least reduce them) depending upon the situation.

Shielding   Shielding (protecting wires by covering them with an insulating coating) is one of the best ways to prevent impulse noise and cross-talk. Many different types of wires and cables are available with different amounts of shielding. In general, the greater the shielding, the more expensive the cable, and the more difficult it is to install.

Moving Cables   Relocating cables away from sources of noise (especially power sources) can also reduce impulse noise and cross-talk. For impulse noise, this means avoiding lights and heavy machinery. Locating communication cables away from power cables is always a good idea. For cross-talk, this means physically separating the cables from other communication cables.

Changing Multiplexing Techniques   Cross-talk and intermodulation noise is often caused by improper multiplexing. Changing techniques (e.g., from FDM to TDM), or changing the frequencies or size of the guardbands in frequency division multiplexing can help.

Improving Connection Quality   Many types of noise (e.g., echoes, white noise, jitter, harmonic distortion) can be caused by poorly maintained equipment or poor connections and splices among cables. This is particularly true for echo in fiber optic cables, which is almost always caused by poor connections. The solution here is obvious: retune the transmission equipment and redo the connections.

Amplifiers and Repeaters   To avoid attenuation, telephone lines have *repeaters* or *amplifiers* spaced throughout their length. The distance between them depends on the amount of power lost per unit length of the transmission line. An amplifier takes the incoming signal, increases its strength, and retransmits it on the next section of the circuit. They are typically used on analog circuits such as the telephone company's voice circuits. The distance between the amplifiers depends on the amount of attenuation, although one- to ten-mile intervals are common. On analog circuits, it is important to recognize that the noise and distortion present are *also* amplified, along with the signal. This means some noise from a previous circuit is regenerated and amplified each time the signal is amplified.

Repeaters are commonly used on digital circuits. A repeater receives the incoming signal, translates it into a digital message, and retransmits the message. Because the message is re-created at each repeater, noise and distortion from the previous circuit are not amplified. This provides a much cleaner signal and results in a lower error rate for digital circuits.

Equalization   An *equalizer* is a piece of equipment that compensates for both attenuation distortion and delay distortion. Equalizers are built into some modems. The telephone company can perform equalization on private leased circuits and dial-up calls.

Conditioning   If the circuit is provided by a common carrier such as the telephone company, you can lease a more expensive *conditioned* circuit. A conditioned circuit is one that has been certified by the carrier to experience fewer errors. There are several levels of conditioning that provide increasingly fewer error at increasingly higher cost. Conditioned circuits employ a variety of the techniques described previously (e.g., equalization, shielding) to provide less noise.

Error Detection

It is possible to develop data transmission methodologies that give very high *error detection and correction* performance. The only way to do error detection and correction is to send extra data with each message. These error detection data are added to each message by the data link layer of the sender based on some mathematical calculations performed on the message (in some cases, error detection methods are built into the hardware itself). The receiver performs the same mathematical calculations on the message it receives and matches its results against the error detection data that were transmitted with the message. If the two match, the message is assumed to be correct. If they don't match, an error has occurred.

In general, the larger the amount of error detection data sent, the greater the error protection achieved. However, as this protection is increased, the throughput of useful data is reduced, because more of the available capacity is used to transmit these error detection data and less is used to transmit the actual message itself. Therefore, the efficiency of data throughput varies inversely as the desired amount of error detection and correction is increased.

Three common *error detection methods* are parity checking, longitudinal redundancy checking, and polynomial checking (particularly checksum and cyclic redundancy checking).

Parity Checking   One of the oldest and simplest error detection methods is *parity*. With this technique, one additional bit is added to each byte in the message. The value of this additional *parity bit* is based on the number of 1's in each byte transmitted. This parity bit is set to make the total number of ones in the byte (including the parity bit) either an even number or an odd number. For example, for *even parity* using 7-bit ASCII:

- The letter *V* is encoded 0110101. Because there is an even number of 1's (four) a 0 is added in the parity (eighth) position, yielding V = 01101010.
- The letter *W* is encoded 0001101, which has three 1's (an odd number of 1's). Therefore, a 1 is added in the parity position to make the number of 1's even, yielding W = 00011011.

A little thought will convince you that any single error (a switch of a 1 to a 0 or vice versa) will be detected by a parity check, but nothing can be deduced about which bit was in error. You will know an error occurred, but not what the error was. Moreover, if *two* bits are switched, the parity check will not detect any error. Of course, it may be possible to sense an error because the resulting code—although correct in parity—is "forbidden" (undefined or inappropriate in its context), but such detection requires more circuitry or software. It is easy to see that parity can detect errors only when an odd number of bits have been switched; any even number of errors cancel each other out. Therefore, the probability of detecting an error, given that one has occurred, is only about 50 percent. Many networks today do not use parity because of its low error detection rate. When parity is used, protocols are described as having *odd parity* or *even parity*.

Longitudinal Redundancy Checking (LRC)   The longitudinal redundancy checking (LRC) method was developed to overcome the problems with parity's low probability of detection. LRC adds one additional character, called the block check character (BCC), to the end of the entire message or packet of data. The value of the BCC is determined in the same manner as the parity bit, but by counting longitudinally through the message, rather than by counting vertically through each character. The first bit of the LRC is determined by counting the number of 1's in the first bits of all characters in the message, and setting the first bit of the LRC to a 1 or a 0 depending upon whether the sum is odd or even. The second bit of the BCC is determined by counting the number of 1's in the second bits of characters in the message, and so on for all bits in the BCC. LRC is usually used in conjunction with parity, producing an error detection rate above 98 percent.

For example, suppose we were to send the message "DATA" using odd parity and LRC with 7-bit ASCII:

	Letter	Parity bit
D	1000100	1
A	1000001	1
T	1010100	0
A	1000001	1
BCC	1101111	1

(Note that the parity bit in the BCC is determined by parity, not LRC.)

Polynomial Checking   A 98 percent error detection rate is reasonably good, but it is still not perfect. Like LRC, *polynomial checking* adds a character or series of characters to the end of the message based on a *mathematical algorithm.*

With the *checksum* technique, a checksum (typically, one byte) is added to the end of the message. The checksum is calculated by adding the decimal value of each character in the message, dividing the sum by 255, and using the remainder as the checksum that is transmitted to the other end of the communication circuit. The receiver calculates its own checksum in the same way and compares it with the transmitted checksum. If the two values are equal, the message is presumed to contain no errors. The checksum detects close to 95 percent of the errors.

One of the most popular of the polynomial error checking schemes is *cyclical redundancy check* (CRC). It adds 8, 16, 24, or 32 bits to the message. A communication protocol using a 16-bit CRC calculates a 16-bit number that is a function of all the data in the message. This 16-bit number is added to the end of the message block. The receiver recalculates its own 16-bit CRC as the block is received. If the numbers are the same, everything is acceptable. If they are different, an error has occurred.

With CRC, a message is treated as one long binary polynomial, P. Before transmission, the data link layer (or hardware device) divides P by a fixed binary polynomial, G, resulting in a whole polynomial, Q, and a remainder, R/G. So, $P/G = Q + R/G$.

The remainder, R, is appended to the message before transmission, as a check sequence k bits long. The receiving hardware divides the received message by the same G, which generates an R. The receiving hardware checks to ascertain whether the received R agrees with the locally generated R. If it does not, the message is assumed to be in error.

CRC performs quite well. An 8-bit CRC (CRC-8) detects 99.969 percent of the errors; CRC-16 (16 bits) detects at least 99.99 percent of them. CRC-24 (24 bits) allows only three bits in 100 million to go undetected, and the error rate of 3×10^{-8}. Today, 32-bit CRC codes are popular because they have an even higher error detection rate.

Error Correction via Retransmission

Once error has been detected, it must be corrected. The simplest, most effective, least expensive, and most commonly used method for error correction is retransmission. With retransmission, a receiver that detects an error simply asks the sender to retransmit the message until it is received without error. This is often called Automatic Repeat reQuest (ARQ). ARQ networks are of two types: stop and wait or continuous.

Stop and Wait ARQ   With *stop and wait ARQ,* the sender stops and waits for a response from the receiver after each message or packet of data. After receiving a message or packet, the receiver sends either an acknowledgment *(ACK)* if the message was received without error, or a negative acknowledgment *(NAK)* if the message contained an error. If it is an NAK, the sender resends the previous message. If it is an ACK, the sender continues with the next message. Stop and wait ARQ is, by definition, a half duplex transmission technique (see Figure 6-4).

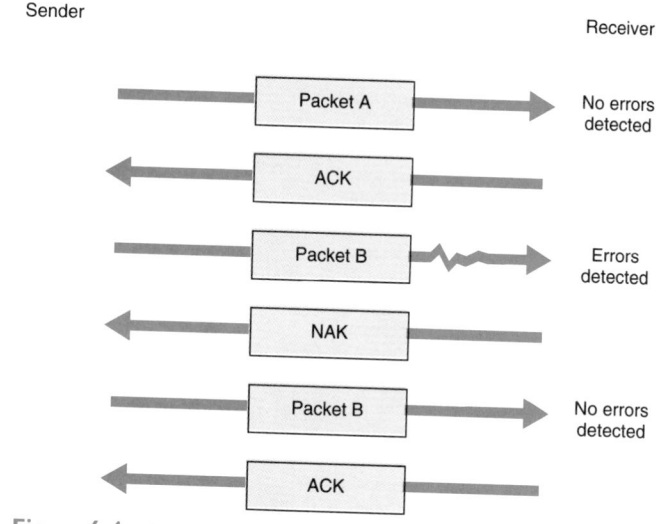

Figure 6-4 Stop and wait ARQ.

Continuous ARQ   With *continuous ARQ,* the sender does not wait for an acknowledgment after sending a message; it immediately sends the next one. While the messages are being transmitted, the sender examines the stream of returning acknowledgments. If it receives an NAK, the sender retransmits the needed messages. The packets that are retransmitted may be only those containing an error (called Link Access Protocol for Modems [LAP-M], or may be the first packet with an error and all those that followed it (called Go-Back-N ARQ). LAP-M is better because it is more efficient.

Continuous ARQ is by definition a full duplex transmission technique, because both the sender and the receiver are transmitting simultaneously (the sender is sending messages, and the receiver is sending ACKs and NAKs). Continuous ARQ is sometimes called *sliding window.* Figure 6-5 illustrates the flow of messages on a communication circuit using continuous ARQ.

Forward Error Correction

Forward error correction uses codes containing sufficient redundancy to prevent errors by detecting and correcting them at the receiving end *without* retransmission of the original message. The redundancy, or extra bits required, varies with different schemes. It ranges from a small percentage of extra bits to 100 percent redundancy, with the number of error detecting bits roughly equaling the number of data bits. One of the characteristics of many error correcting codes is that there must be a minimum number of error-free bits between bursts of errors. For example, one such code, called a *Hagelbarger code,* corrects up to six consecutive bit errors provided that

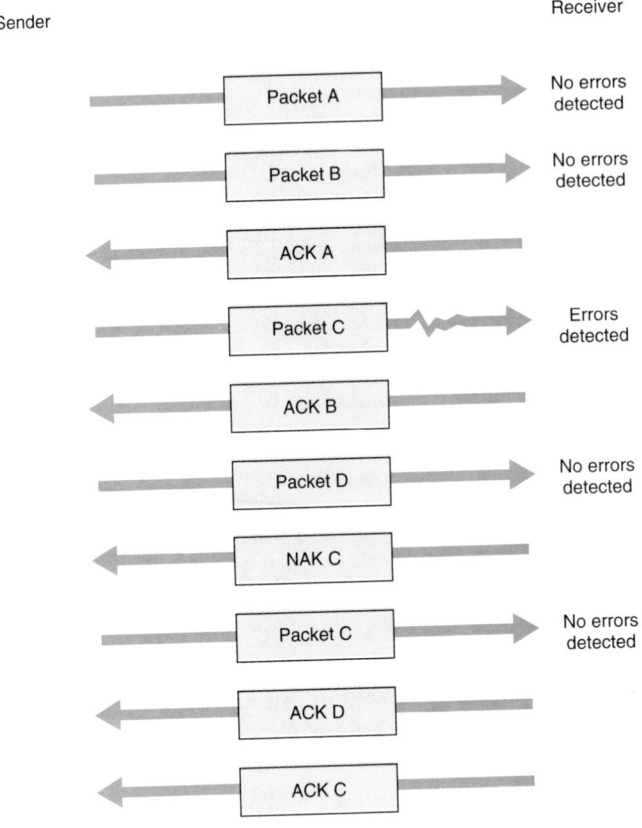

Figure 6-5   Continuous ARQ.

the 6-bit error group is followed by at least 19 valid bits before more error bits are encountered. Bell engineers have developed an error correcting code that uses 12 check bits for each 48 data bits, or 25 percent redundancy. Still another code is the *Bose-Chaudhuri code,* which, in one of its forms, is capable of correcting double errors and can detect up to four errors.

To show how such a code works, consider this example of a forward error checking code, called a *Hamming code,* after its inventor, R. W. Hamming. This code associates even parity bits with unique combinations of data bits. Using a 4-data-bit code as an example, a character might be represented by the data bit configuration 1010. Three parity bits P_1, P_2, and P_4 are added, resulting in a 7-bit code, shown in the upper half of Figure 6-6. Notice that the data bits (D_3, D_5, D_6, D_7) are 1010, and the parity bits (P_1, P_2, P_4) are 101.

As depicted in the upper half of Figure 6-6, parity bit P_1 applies to data bits D_3, D_5, and D_7. Parity bit P_2 applies to data bits D_3, D_6, and D_7. Parity bit P_4 applies to data bits D_5, D_6, and D_7. For the example, in which D_3, D_5, D_6, $D_7 = 1010$, P_1 must equal 1 because there is only a single 1 among D_3, D_5, and D_7 and parity must be even. Similarly, P_2 must be 0 because D_3 and D_6 are 1's. P_4 is 1 because D_6 is the only 1 among D_5, D_6, and D_7.

Now, assume that during the transmission, data bit D_7 is changed from a 0 to a 1 by line noise. Because this data bit is being checked by P_1, P_2, and P_4, all three parity bits now show odd parity instead of the correct even parity. (D_7 is the only data bit that is monitored by all three parity bits; therefore, when D_7 is in error, all three parity bits show an incorrect parity). In this way, the receiving equipment can determine which bit was in error and reverse its state, thus correcting the error without retransmission.

The lower half of Figure 6-6 is a table that determines the location of the bit in error. A 1 in the table means that the corresponding parity bit indicates a parity error. Conversely, a 0 means the parity check is correct. These 0's and 1's form a binary number that indicates the numerical location of the erroneous bit. In the previous example, P_1, P_2, and P_4 checks all failed, yielding 111, or a decimal 7, the subscript of the erroneous bit.

Forward error corection is commonly used in satellite transmission. A round trip

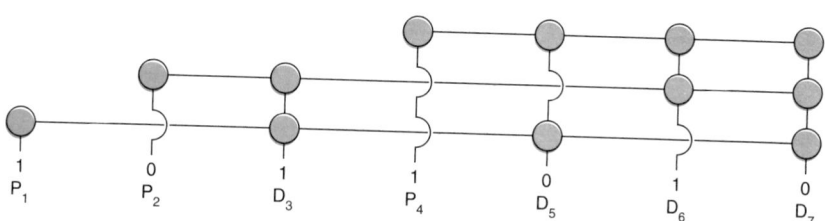

Checking Relations Between Parity Bits (P) and Data Bits (D)

0 = Corresponding parity check is correct 1 = Corresponding parity check fails			Determines in which bit the error occured
P_4	P_2	P_1	
0	0	0	no error
0	0	1	P_1
0	1	0	P_2
0	1	1	D_3
1	0	0	P_4
1	0	1	D_5
1	1	0	D_6
1	1	1	D_7

Interpreting Parity Bit Patterns

Figure 6-6 Hamming code for forward error correction.

from the Earth station to the satellite and back includes a significant delay. Error rates can fluctuate depending on the condition of equipment, sun spots, or the weather. Indeed, some weather conditions make it impossible to transmit without some errors, making forward error correction essential. Compared to satellite equipment costs, the additional cost of forward error correction is insignificant.

The use of forward error correction in broader markets such as modem-based communications is limited today but is becoming more common as chip implementations of forward error correction are coming on the market. The V.32 modem standard, for example, includes forward error checking.

DATA LINK PROTOCOLS

In this section, we outline several commonly used data link layer protocols, which are summaried in Figure 6-7. Here we focus on message delineation, which indicates where a message starts and stops, and the various parts or *fields* within the message. For example, you must clearly indicate which part of a message or packet of data is

Protocol	Size	Error Detection	Retransmission	Media Access
File Transfer Protocols				
XMODEM	132	8-bit Checksum	Stop-and-wait ARQ	Controlled Access
XMODEM-CRC	132	8-bit CRC	Stop-and-wait ARQ	Controlled Access
XMODEM-1K	1028	8-bit CRC	Stop-and-wait ARQ	Controlled Access
YMODEM	1029	16-bit CRC	Stop-and-wait ARQ	Controlled Access
ZMODEM	*	32-bit CRC	Continuous ARQ	Controlled Access
KERMIT	*	24-bit CRC	Continuous ARQ	Controlled Access
Synchronous Protocols				
BSC	*	8-bit LRC	Stop-and-wait ARQ	Controlled Access
SDLC	*	16-bit CRC	Continuous ARQ	Controlled Access
HDLC	*	16-bit CRC	Continuous ARQ	Controlled Access
Token Ring	*	32-bit CRC	Stop-and-wait ARQ	Controlled Access
Ethernet	*	32-bit CRC	Stop-and-wait ARQ	Contention

*Varies depending upon the message length.

Figure 6-7   Protocol summary.

the error control portion, otherwise the receiver cannot use it properly to determine if an error has occurred.

Asynchronous Transmission

Asynchronous transmission often is referred to as start–stop transmission because the transmitting device can transmit a character whenever it is convenient, and the receiving device will accept that character. It is typically used on point-to-point full duplex circuits (i.e., circuits that have only two devices on them), so media access control is not a concern.

With *asynchronous transmission,* each character is transmitted independently of all other characters. In order to separate the characters and synchronize transmission, a *start bit* and a *stop bit* are put on each end of *each* individual character. For example, if we are using 7-bit ASCII with even parity, the total transmission is 10 bits for each character (1 start bit, 7 bits for the letter, 1 parity bit, 1 stop bit).

The start bit and stop bit are the opposite of each other. Typically, the start bit is a 0 and the stop bit is a 1. There is no fixed distance between characters because the terminal transmits the character as soon as it is typed, which varies with the speed of the typist. The recognition of the start and stop of each message (called *synchronization*) takes place for an individual character because the *start bit* is a signal that tells the receiver to start sampling the incoming bits of a character at a fixed rate so the data bits can be interpreted into their proper character structure. A *stop bit* informs the receiver that the character has been received and resets it for recognition of the next start bit.

When the sender is waiting for the user to type the next character, no data is sent; the communication circuit is idle. This idle time really is artificial—some signal must be sent down the circuit. For example, suppose we are using a unipolar digital signaling technique where +3 volts indicates a 1 and 0 volts indicates a 0 (see Chapter 5). Even if we send 0 volts, we are still sending a signal, a 0 in this case. Asynchronous transmission defines the *idle signal* (the signal that is sent down the circuit when no data are being transmitted) as the same as the stop bit. When the sender finishes transmitting a letter and is waiting for more data to send, it sends a continuous series of stop bits. Figure 6-8 shows an example of asynchronous transmission.

Some older protocols have two stop bits instead of the traditional single stop bit. The use of both a start bit and a stop bit is changing; some protocols have eliminated the stop bit altogether.

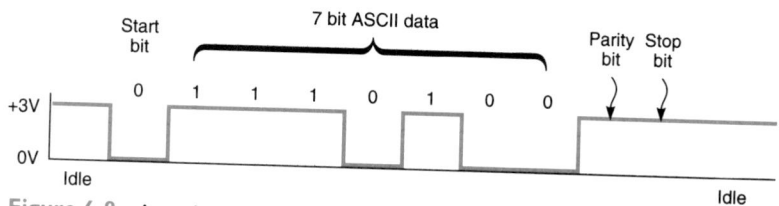

Figure 6-8 Asynchronous transmission.

Asynchronous Microcomputer File Transfer Protocols

Today, data transmission by microcomputers often means the transfer of data files. In general, microcomputer file transfer protocols are used on asynchronous point-to-point circuits, typically across telephone lines via a modem. All file transfer protocols have two characteristics in common. First, these protocols are designed to transmit error-free data from one computer to another. Second, since there is a large amount of data to be transmitted, it makes more sense to group the data together into blocks of data that are transmitted at the same time, rather than sending each character individually via standard asynchronous transmission. This section discusses the structure of the data blocks (also called packets) used by several common protocols.

XMODEM   The *XMODEM* protocol takes the data being transmitted and divides it into blocks (see Figure 6-9). Each block has a start of text character (STX), a 1-byte block number, 128 bytes of data, and a 1-byte checksum for error checking. Even though this protocol was developed for micro-to-micro communications, it often is used for micro-to-mainframe communications where the host mainframe can support the XMODEM protocol. XMODEM is one of the protocols that uses a stop and wait ARQ half duplex mode of transmission.

    XMODEM-CRC improves error detection accuracy of the XMODEM protocol. It replaces the checksum with a more rigorous one-byte *cyclical redundancy check* (CRC-8).

    XMODEM-1K increases the efficiency of XMODEM-CRC by using data blocks of 1024 bytes instead of the 128-character blocks of the original XMODEM. Efficiency and throughput is discussed in more detail later.

YMODEM   The primary benefit of the *YMODEM* protocol is CRC-16 error checking. YMODEM is the XMODEM-1K protocol with CRC-16 error checking and multiple file transfer capability, although there are several other minor differences as well.

ZMODEM   *ZMODEM* is a newer protocol written to overcome some of the problems in packet switching networks like SprintNet or Tymnet. It is not a subset of XMODEM but instead incorporates features of several protocols. It uses a more powerful error detection method (CRC-32) with continuous ARQ. ZMODEM also dynamically adjusts its packet size according to communication circuit conditions to increase efficiency. It is the preferred protocol of most bulletin board systems.

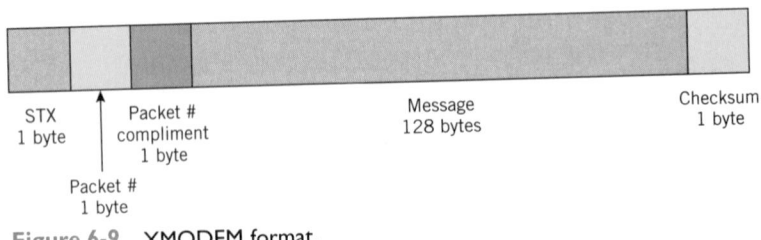

STX
1 byte

Packet #
compliment
1 byte

Packet #
1 byte

Message
128 bytes

Checksum
1 byte

Figure 6-9   XMODEM format.

KERMIT   *KERMIT* is a very popular protocol (and yes, it is named after Kermit the Frog of Sesame Street fame). The KERMIT protocol was developed by Columbia University, which released it as a free software communication package. The KERMIT sofware is distributed by Columbia University's Center for Computing Activities in New York City for a minimal charge. Various versions of KERMIT can be found on public bulletin board systems and downloaded to your microcomputer.

KERMIT is an extremely flexible protocol that can be adjusted to support a variety of different packet sizes and error detection methods. Kermit typically uses 1000-byte packets with CRC-24, but these are adjusted during transmission to optimize performance. It uses either stop-and-wait ARQ or continuous ARQ. It is suited especially to micro-to-mainframe connections, but it works equally well with microcomputer-to-microcomputer or mainframe-to-mainframe connections. KERMIT communication-based programs provide error-checked transfer of text and binary files using both 7- and 8-bit codes.

Synchronous Transmission

With *synchronous transmission,* all the letters or data in one group of data is transmitted at one time as a block of data. This block of data is called a *frame* or *packet,* depending upon the protocol, but the meaning is the same. For example, a terminal or microcomputer will save all the keystrokes typed by the user and only transmit them when the user presses a special "transmit" key. In this case, the start and end of the entire packet must be marked, not the start and end of each letter. Synchronous transmission is often used on both point-to-point and multipoint circuits that have many computers and terminals attached. Use on multipoint circuits means that each packet must include a destination address and a source address, and that media access control is important.

The start and end of each packet (synchronization) is established by appending a predetermined group of characters at the beginning and end of each packet. The characters are called synchronization characters (SYN). Depending upon the protocol, there may be anywhere from one to eight SYN characters. After the SYN characters, the transmitting device sends a long stream of data bits that may contain thousands of bits. Knowing what code is being used, the receiving device counts off the appropriate number of bits for the first character, assumes this is the first character, and passes it to the computer. It then counts off the bits for the second character, and so on.

In summary, asynchronous data transmission means each character is transmitted as a totally independent entity with its own start and stop bits to inform the receiving device that the character is beginning and ending. Synchronous transmission means whole blocks of data are transmitted as packets after the sender and the receiver have been synchronized.

There are many protocols for synchronous transmission. These protocols fall into three broad categories: byte-oriented protocols, bit-oriented protocols, and byte-count protocols. In this next section, we discuss five common synchronous data link protocols.

Binary Synchronous Communication (BSC)   The *Binary Synchronous Communication* protocol is primarily a mainframe protocol. BSC was developed by IBM in 1967, but is still in use because many organizations have not had the need or the money to upgrade to newer protocols like SDLC and HDLC described below. BSC is called a *byte-oriented protocol* because it uses special one-byte characters (i.e., eight bits) to mark the start and end of the message, and all characters in the message must also be 8 bits in length. BSC transmission takes place in a half duplex transmission mode, using a stop and wait ARQ. It uses a controlled access media access protocol.

Figure 6-10 shows a BSC message format. The message begins with one or two SYN (sync characters) that are fixed 8-bit characters (00001110). The SOH (start of heading) is an 8-bit character (00000001) that indicates the start of the message or data packet. It is followed by other header control characters that address the message to a specific device or for other control purposes such as an ACK or NAK. The header ranges from one to seven bytes. The STX (start of text) is another special 8-bit character (00000010) that marks the actual start of the message to be processed by the sender, while the ETX (end of text, 00000011) marks the end of the message. These two characters (STX and ETX) sandwich the message text characters so they can be identified easily. Finally, there is a block check character (BCC), which is a 1-byte LRC used for error detection.

One of the problems with BSC lies in the use of a special character to mark the end of the message (ETX). The ETX is simply a pattern of bits, like any other pattern of bits. ETX is a *reserved* character, one that it is impossible to type on a terminal because no key can generate that bit pattern. BSC was originally designed to transmit only text characters, but today it is also used to transmit non-text binary data files. It is possible that one of the bytes in the data file has the same bit pattern as the ETX. In this case, the data byte would be wrongly interpreted as an ETX, and the receiver would presume that the packet had ended, losing all the data that followed.

This is called a *transparency problem,* because the protocol is not "transparent"—it cannot automatically send all types of data with any bit pattern. BSC has a way around this problem, but it is cumbersome. First, for the transmission of packets containing binary data, all control characters (e.g., STX, ETX) are preceded by a second control character called Data Link Escape (DLE, 00000100). Second, any data byte in the binary file that has the same bit pattern as the DLE has a second DLE character "stuffed" in front of it. If the receiver sees two DLE bytes in a row, it automatically deletes one of them and treats the second DLE as data. Any other character that follows a DLE is treated as a control character.

Synchronous Data Link Control (SDLC)   SDLC is another mainframe protocol developed by IBM in 1972. SDLC is a *bit-oriented protocol,* because the control fields and

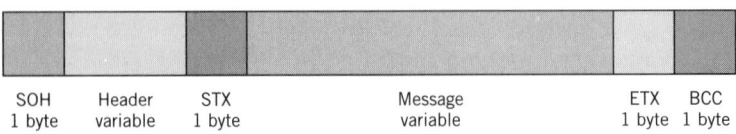

| SOH | Header | STX | Message | ETX | BCC |
| 1 byte | variable | 1 byte | variable | 1 byte | 1 byte |

Figure 6-10   BSC format.

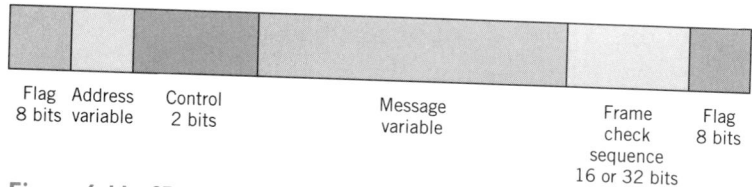

Figure 6-11   SDLC format.

the data do not have to be in 8-bit bytes. SDLC is therefore more flexible than byte-oriented protocols such as BSC. It uses a controlled access media access protocol.

Figure 6-11 shows a typical SDLC packet (or "frame" as it is called). Each SDLC frame begins and ends with a special bit pattern (01111110), known as the flag. The *beginning flag* indicates the position of the address and control frame elements and initiates error checking procedures. The *ending flag* terminates the error checking procedures. The *address field* identifies the destination. The *control field* identifies the kind of frame that is being transmitted, either information or supervisory. The *information frame* is used for the transfer and reception of messages, frame numbering of contiguous frames, and the like. The *supervisory frame* is used to transmit acknowledgments (ACKs and NAKs). The *message field* is of variable length and is the user's message. The *frame check sequence field* is a 16-bit or 32-bit cyclical redundancy checking (CRC) code.

SDLC and other bit-oriented protocols suffer from the same transparency problems as byte-oriented protocols. The binary data to be transmitted can also contain the same bit pattern as the flag (01111110), which, if not corrected, will cause the premature end of the frame and loss of data in the same way as an uncorrected ETX causes problems for BSC. The solution here is similar to that of stuffing an extra DLE into the message. Any time the sender encounters five 1's in a row in the data to be transmitted, the sender "stuffs" one extra bit, a 0, into the message and continues to transmit. Anytime the receiver encounters five 1's and a 0 (i.e., 111110), the receiver automatically deletes the 0 and continues to process the data stream. This technique, called *bit stuffing,* is a little more efficient than the character stuffing used by BSC, but is still cumbersome.

High-level Data Link Control (HDLC)   HDLC is a formal standard developed by the International Organization for Standardization (ISO). HDLC is essentially the same as SDLC, except that the address and control fields can be longer. HDLC also has several additional benefits that are beyond the scope of this book, such as a larger sliding window. It uses a controlled access media access protocol. One variant—Link Access Procedure-Balanced (LAP-B)—uses the same frame structure as HDLC, but is a scaled down version of HDLC (i.e., provides fewer of those benefits mentioned that are "beyond the scope of this book").

Token Ring (IEEE 802.5)   One very popular local area network protocol is token ring. Token ring was developed by IBM in the early 1980s, and later became a formal

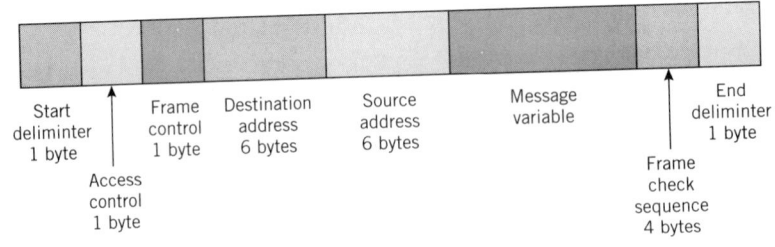

Figure 6-12   Token ring format.

standard of the Institute of Electrical and Electronics Engineers (IEEE) called IEEE 802.5. It uses a controlled access media access protocol.

Figure 6-12 shows a typical token ring frame. Token ring is a byte-oriented frame like BSC, but does not suffer the same transparency problems. Each token ring frame starts and ends with a special delimiter. This delimiter is a special electrical signal that is produced in a manner different from any other pattern of bits,[2] and thus cannot be confused with data bits. The next two fields, *access control* and *frame control*, are control fields used by the media access protocol described at the end of this chapter. The *destination address* specifies the receiver, while the *source address* specifies the sender. The *frame check sequence* is a 32-bit CRC code.

Ethernet (IEEE 802.3)   Ethernet is another very popular LAN protocol developed jointly by Digital, Intel, and Xerox in the 1970s. Since then, ethernet has become a formal standard called IEEE 802.3.[3] Ethernet is a *byte-count protocol* because instead of using special characters or bit patterns to mark the end of a frame, it includes a field that specifies the length of the message portion of the frame. It uses a contention media access protocol.

Figure 6-13 shows a typical ethernet frame. Unlike BSC, SDLC and HDLC, ethernet does not use a character to mark the start of the frame, but relies instead on a special pattern of SYN characters to mark the start. The *destination address* specifies the receiver, while the *source address* specifies the sender. The *length* indicates the length in 8-bit bytes of the message portion of the frame. The maximum length of the message

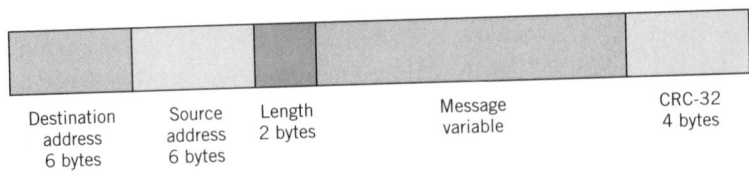

Figure 6-13   Ethernet format.

[2]Token ring uses differential manchester encoding, which is a special form of bipolar signaling. The delimiter violates the rules of this signaling technique, so that the data link layer can distinguish it from data.
[3]A competing version of ethernet called Ethernet II is also available. Ethernet II and IEEE 802.3 ethernet are similar, but differ enough to be incompatible. In this book, we discuss only IEEE 802.3 ethernet.

is 1500 bytes. The frame ends with a CRC-32 *frame check sequence* used for error detection. Unlike BSC, SDLC, and HDLC, ethernet has no transparency problems. Any bit pattern can be transmitted because ethernet uses the number of bytes, not control characters, to delineate the message.

Isochronous Transmission

A third technique, *isochronous transmission,* combines the elements of both synchronous and asynchronous data transmission. Each character is required to have both a start bit and a stop bit, however, as in synchronous data transmission, the sender and receiver are synchronized. The synchronization time interval between successive bits is specified to be an even multiple of the length of one code bit. That is, all periods of no transmission consist of one or more 1-character time intervals. This common timing provides greater precision between the transmitting and receiving equipment than can be achieved with asynchronous techniques only. As a result, data can be transmitted at higher speeds.

Figure 6-14 illustrates the relationships and differences between asynchronous, synchronous, and isochronous transmission. In asynchronous transmission, there is no determination of the spacing between individual characters (indefinite time). Thus, both the sending and receiving equipment must have clocks to determine the time length of a bit, and the receiver must have special recognition circuitry to determine the beginning and end of a character. With synchronous transmission, the clocking

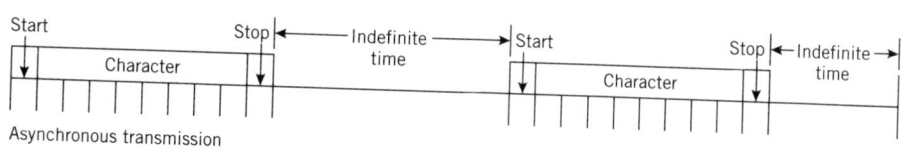

Asynchronous transmission

Synchronous transmission

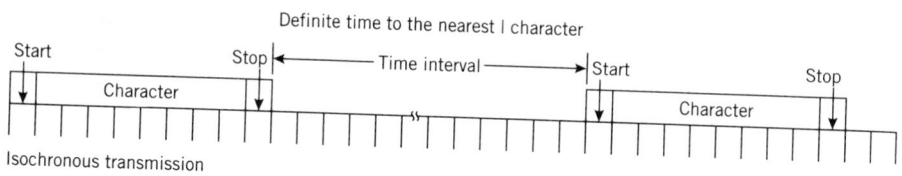

Isochronous transmission

Figure 6-14 Comparison of serial transmission methods (asynchronous, synchronous, isochronous).

signal synchronizes the receiver to the sender before a long block of data is transmitted. In isochronous transmission, the clocking is supplied by the sending modem, and the receiving modem synchronizes to it for short periods. Each character begins on some multiple of the length of the bit element.

TRANSMISSION EFFICIENCY

One objective of a data communication network is to move the highest possible volume of accurate information through the network. The higher the volume, the greater the resulting efficiency and the lower the cost. Network efficiency is affected by characteristics of the circuits such as error rates and transmission speed, as well as by the speed of transmitting and receiving equipment, the error detection and control methodology, and the protocol used by the data link layer.

Each protocol we discussed uses some bits or bytes to delineate the start and end of each message. These bits and bytes are necessary for the transmission to occur, but they are not part of the message. They add no value to the user, but they count against the total number of bits that can be transmitted.

Each communication protocol has both information bits and overhead bits. *Information bits* are those used to convey the user's meaning. *Overhead bits* are used for purposes such as error checking, and marking the start and end of characters and packets. A parity bit used for error checking is an overhead bit because it is not used to send the user's data; if you did not care about errors, the overhead error checking bit could be omitted and the users could still understand the message.

Transmission efficiency is defined as the total number of information bits (i.e., bits in the message sent by the user) divided by the total bits in transmission (i.e., information bits plus overhead bits). For example, let's calculate the transmission efficiency of asynchronous transmission. Assume we are using 7-bit ASCII. We have 1 bit for parity, plus 1 start bit and 1 stop bit. Therefore, there are 7 bits of information in each letter, but the total bits per letter is 10 (7 + 3). The efficiency of the asynchronous transmission system is 7 bits of information divided by 10 total bits for an efficiency of 70 percent.

In other words, with asynchronous transmission, only 70 percent of the data rate is available for the user; 30 percent is used by the transmission protocol. If we have a communication circuit capable of transmitting 9600 bits per seconed (bps), the user sees an effective data rate of 6720 bps. This is very inefficient.

It should be noted that if any other control characters are needed, such as message character counts or other control characters sent at the end of your transmission, the efficiency drops below 70 percent. On the other hand, if no stop bit is used, the efficiency increases to {7/9} or 77.8 percent.

The same basic formula can be used to calculate the efficiency of synchronous transmission. Suppose we are using SDLC. In this case, the bits of information are calculated by determining how many "information" characters are in the message block. If the message portion of the frame contains 100 information characters, using an 8-bit code, there are 8 bits times 100 characters, or 800 bits of information. Next, the total number of bits is the 800 bits of information, plus all the overhead bits that are inserted for delineation and error control. Figure 6-11 shows that SDLC has a beginning flag (8 bits), an address (8 bits), a control field (8 bits), a frame check sequence (assume we use a CRC-32 with 32 bits), and an ending flag (8 bits). This is a total of 8+8+8+32+8=64 overhead bits; thus efficiency is 800 / (800 + 64) = 92.6 percent. If the circuit provides a data rate of 9600 bps, the effective data rate available to the user is about 8890 bps.

This example shows that synchronous networks usually are more efficient than asynchronous networks and some protocols are more efficient than others; the longer the message (1000 characters as opposed to 100), the more efficient the protocol. For example, suppose the message in the SDLC example was 1000 bytes. The efficiency here is 99.2 percent (8000 / (8000 + 64)), giving an effective data rate of about 9524 bps.

This example should also show why YMODEM (with a message length of 1024 bytes) is more efficient than XMODEM (with a message length of 128 bytes). The general rule is that the larger the message field, the more efficient the protocol.

So why not have 10K or even 100K packets to really increase efficiency? The answer is that anytime a packet is received containing an error, the entire packet must be retransmitted. Thus, if an entire file were sent as one large packet (e.g., 100K), and one bit was received in error, the entire 100K packet has to be sent again. Clearly this is a waste of capacity. Furthermore, the probability that a packet contains an error increases with the size of the packet; larger packets are more likely to contain errors than smaller ones, simply due to the laws of probability.

Thus in designing a protocol, there is a trade-off between large and small packets. Small packets are less efficient, but are less likely to contain errors and "cost" less (in terms of circuit capacity) to retransmit if there is an error. (See Figure 6-15.)

Throughput is the total number of information bits received per second, after taking into account the overhead bits and the need to retransmit packets containing errors. Generally speaking, small packets provide better throughput for circuits with more

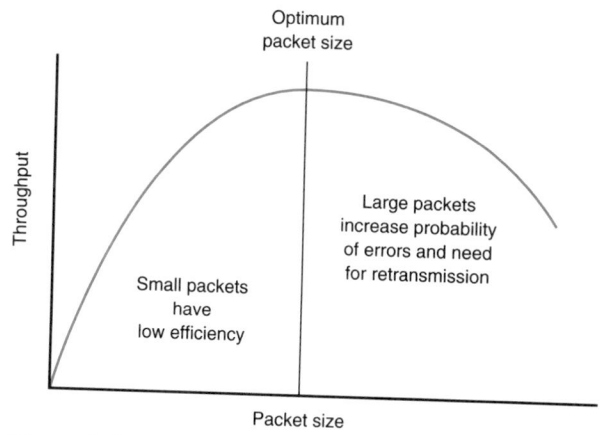

Figure 6-15

Management Focus: Sleuthing for the Right Packet Size

Optimizing performance in a network, particularly a client server network, can be difficult because few network managers realize the importance of the packet size. Selecting the right—or the wrong—packet size can have greater effects on performance than anything you might do to the server.

Standard Commercial, a multinational tobacco and agricultural company, noticed a decrease in network performance when they upgraded to a new server. They tested the effects of using packet sizes from 500 bytes to 32,000 bytes. In their tests, a packet size of 512 bytes required a total of 455K bytes transmitted over their network to transfer the test messages. In contrast, the 32K packet sizes were far more efficient, cutting the total data by 44 percent to 257K bytes.

However, the problem with 32K byte packets was a noticeable response time delay because messages were saved until the 32K byte packets were full before transmitting.

The ideal packet size depends upon the specific application and the pattern of messages it generates. For Standard Commercial, the ideal packet size appeared to be between 4K and 8K. Unfortunately, not all software vendors enable network managers to fine-tune packet sizes in this way.

Source: Infoworld, January 16, 1995.

errors, while larger packets provide better throughput in less error-prone networks. Packet sizes vary greatly among different networks, but most packet sizes tend to be from 50 bytes to 10,000 bytes in length.

Throughput (TRIB)

Calculating the actual *throughput* of a data communication network is complex. Many factors other than the packet size affect throughput; the most important are the transmission rate and the communication circuit capacity because capacity determines the absolute upper limit of speed. Terminals using a multipoint configuration are a factor because the circuit must be shared. Terminals that are multiplexed become a factor because each terminal uses a reduced capacity (a subset of the total capacity on the circuit). Another factor is the capability of the front end processor to handle multiple incoming and outgoing communication circuits. If the front end cannot handle circuits or messages simultaneously, the capacity of the network is degraded. Software design is another factor because it determines which protocol is used and whether transmission is in full or half duplex. Propagation time, especially on satellite circuits, affects throughput as does the time required for the host computer to process a request, perform a lookup, or update a database. Error rates in hardware, in software, and on the communication circuit affect throughput because of possible retransmissions of the same message. The polling scheme (central control) or whether the system operates on a contention basis affects throughput, too.

FORMULA FOR CALCULATING TRIB

$$\text{TRIB} = \frac{\text{Number of information bits accepted}}{\text{Total time required to get the bits accepted}}$$

$$\text{TRIB} = \frac{K(M - C)(1 - P)}{M/R + T}$$

where K = information bits per character
M = block length in characters
R = modem transmission rate in characters per second
C = average number of noninformation characters per block (control characters)
P = probability that a block will require retransmission because of error
T = time between blocks in seconds, such as modem delay/turnaround time on half duplex, echo suppressor delay on dial-up, and propagation delay on satellite transmission. This is the time required to reverse the direction of transmission from send to receive or receive to send on a half duplex (HDX) circuit. It can be obtained from the modem specification book and may be referred to as *reclocking time.*

The following TRIB example shows the calculation of throughput assuming a 4800 bits per second half duplex circuit.

$$\text{TRIB} = \frac{7(400 - 10)(1 - 0.01)}{(400/600) + 0.025} = 3908 \text{ bits per second}$$

where K = 7 bits per character (information)
M = 400 characters per block
R = 600 characters per second (derived from 4800 bits per second divided by 8 bits/character)
C = 10 control characters per block
P = 0.01 (10^{-2}) or one retransmission out of 100 blocks transmitted—1%
T = 25 milliseconds (0.025) turnaround time.

If all factors in the calculation remain constant except for the circuit, which is changed to full duplex (no turnaround time delays, $T = 0$), then the TRIB increases to 4054 bits per second.

Look at the equation where the turnaround value (T) is 0.025. If there is a further propagation delay time of 475 milliseconds (0.475), this figure changes to 0.500. For demonstrating how a satellite channel affects TRIB, the total delay time is now 500 milliseconds. Still using the figures above (except for the new 0.500 delay time), we reduce the TRIB for our half duplex, satellite link to 2317 bits per second, which is almost one half of the full duplex (no turnaround time) 4054 bits per second.

Figure 6-16 Calculating TRIB.

The term *transmission rate of information bits* (TRIB) describes the effective rate of data transfer. It is a measure of the effective quantity of information that is transmitted over a communication circuit per unit of time. The American National Standards Institute (ANSI) provides definitions for calculating the transfer rate of information bits. TRIB calculations may vary with the type of protocol used because of different numbers of control characters required and different time between blocks. The basic TRIB equation is shown in Figure 6-16, along with an example. If you want to computerize the TRIB calculation, the book by Gilbert Held listed at the end of this chapter contains a 32-line Microsoft Quick Basic Program to do so.

Summary

OSI Model   The OSI model is one of the most widely used overall network architectures by which much communication software is designed. It has seven layers. The physical layer is concerned primarily with transmitting data bits (0's and 1's) over a communication circuit. The data link layer manages the basic transmission circuit established in the physical layer and transforms it into a circuit that is free of transmission errors. The network layer provides for the functions of internal network operations such as addressing and routing. The transport layer establishes, maintains, and terminates "logical" connections for the transfer of data between end users. The session layer is responsible for initiating, maintaining, and terminating each logical session between end users. The presentation layer carries out a selectable set of message transformations and formatting to present data to the end users. The application layer is the end user's access to the network.

Media Access Control   Media access control refers to controlling when devices transmit. There are three basic approaches. With central control, a host mainframe or front end processor polls client devices to see if they have data to send; devices can transmit only when they have been polled. With decentralized control, there is no host, but the devices themselves manage when they can transmit by passing a token to each other; no device can transmit unless it has the token. With contention, devices listen and transmit only when no other devices are transmitting. In general, contention approaches work better for small networks that have low levels of usage, while central or decentralized control approaches work better for networks with high usage.

Sources and Prevention of Error   Errors occur in all networks. Errors tend to occur in groups (or bursts) rather than one bit at a time. The primary sources of errors are impulse noises (e.g., lightning), cross-talk, echo, and attenuation. Errors can be prevented (or at least reduced) by shielding the cables, moving cables away from sources of noise and power sources, using repeaters (and to a lesser extent amplifiers), and improving the quality of the equipment, media, and their connections.

Error Detection and Correction   All error detection schemes attach additional error detection data to the user's message based on a mathematical calculation. The receiver performs the same calculation on incoming messages, and if the results of this calculation do not match the error detection data on the incoming message, an error has occurred. The most common error correction technique is simply to ask the sender to retransmit the message until it is received without error. A different approach, forward error correction, includes sufficient information to allow the receiver to correct the error in most cases without asking for a retransmission.

Message Delineation   Message delineation means to indicate the start and end of message. Asynchronous transmission uses start and stop bits on each letter to mark where they begin and end. Synchronous techniques (e.g., BSC, SDLC, HDLC, token ring, ethernet) or microcomputer files transfer protocols (e.g., XMODEM, YMODEM, ZMODEM, Kermit) group blocks of data together into ''packets'' or ''frames'' that use special characters or bit patterns to mark the start and end of entire messages.

Transmission Efficiency and Throughput   Every protocol adds additional bits to the user's message before sending it (e.g., for error detection). These bits are called overhead bits because they add no value to the user; they simply ensure correct data transfer. The efficiency of a transmission protocol is the number of information bits sent by the user divided by the total number of bits transferred (information bits plus overhead bits). Synchronous transmission provides greater efficiency than asynchronous transmission. In general, protocols with larger packet sizes provide greater efficiency than those with small packet sizes. The drawback to large packet sizes is that they are more likely to be affected by errors and thus require more retransmission. Small packet sizes are therefore better suited to noisy circuits and large packets to ''clean'' circuits.

Key Terms

ACK
Amplifier
Application layer
Asynchronous transmission
Attenuation
Attenuation distortion
Automatic Repeat reQuest
   (ARQ)
Binary synchronous
   communications (BSC)
Burst error
Central access control
Checksum
Contention
Continuous ARQ
Cross-talk
Data link layer
Decentralized access
   control
Delay distortion
Echo
Efficiency
Error detection and
   correction
Error detection with
   retransmission

Error prevention
Error rate
Ethernet (IEEE 802.3)
Even parity
Forward error correction
Frame
Gaussian noise
Go-Back-N
Hamming code
Harmonic distortion
High-level data link
   control (HDLC)
Hub go-ahead polling
Human error
Impulse noise
Intermodulation noise
Isochronous transmission
Jitter
KERMIT
Layer
Link access procedure-
   balanced (LAP-B)
Link access procedure for
   modems (LAP-M)
Line noise
Line outage

Logical link control (LLC)
   sublayer
Media access control
Media access control
   (MAC) sublayer
NAK
Network layer
Odd parity
Open systems intercon-
   nection (OSI) model
Packet
Parity bit
Physical layer
Polling
Polynomial checking
Presentation layer
Repeater
Roll call polling
Selecting
Session layer
Start bit
Stop and wait ARQ
Stop bit
Synchronization
Synchronous data link
   control (SDLC)

Synchronous transmission
Throughput
Token
Token ring (IEEE 802.5)

Transmission efficiency
Transmission rate of
   information bits (TRIB)
Transport layer

White noise
XMODEM
YMODEM
ZMODEM

Selected References

1. Held, Gilbert. *Practical Network Design Techniques.* New York: John Wiley & Sons, Inc., 1991.
2. *Byte: The Small Systems Journal.* Published monthly by McGraw–Hill, 1 Phoenix Hill Lane, Peterborough, NH 03458.
3. Dvorak, John C., and Nick Anis. *Dvorak's Guide to PC Telecommunications.* Berkeley, CA: Osborne/McGraw–Hill, 1990.
4. *PC Tech Journal for the IBM Systems Professional.* Published monthly by Ziff–Davis Publishing Co., 1 Park Avenue, New York, NY 10016.

Questions/Problems

1. Why are layers important? What does the layered approach provide to data communication software development?
2. What are the most important points to remember about *each* of the OSI model's seven layers?
3. What does the data link layer do?
4. Define two fundamental types of errors.
5. Errors normally appear in _____ , which is when more than one data bit is changed by the error-causing condition.
6. If a network has a very high error detection and correction performance, what is sacrificed to have this error-free environment?
7. What time of day normally has more errors on dial-up lines?
8. Is there any difference in the error rates of lower speed lines and of higher speed lines?
9. Is there any difference in the error rates of dial-up lines and of private leased lines?
10. Briefly define noise.
11. How is line noise manifested?
12. Compare three of the eleven categories of noise and distortion.
13. Two of the eleven categories of noise and distortion discussed in this chapter are related to attenuation. How do they differ?
14. There are many approaches to error control. Describe three approaches, including how they work, the probability of detecting an error, and any other benefits or limitations.
15. Describe three ways in which error detection with retransmission can be handled.
16. What is the simplest and least expensive method of reducing data transmission errors?

17. Name three common methods of detecting errors.
18. Briefly describe how even parity, odd parity, and no parity work.
19. Briefly describe how polynomial checking works.
20. How does cyclical redundancy checking work?
21. How does forward error correction work? What distinguishes it from other error checking methods?
22. A number of error detecting and correcting methods are discussed in this chapter. What distinguishes each one from the others?
23. Under what circumstances is forward error correction desirable?
24. Discuss five approaches to preventing or reducing errors.
25. What are the two steps required to ensure that the software provides proper integrity of the messages being transmitted?
26. What is the biggest drawback of the binary synchronous communications (BSC) protocol?
27. Which is the simplest (least sophisticated) protocol described in this chapter?
28. How do transmission errors affect messages in asynchronous and synchronous transmission?
29. What are SYN characters and what do they do?
30. What purpose does the parity bit serve?
31. What is transmission efficiency?
32. How do information bits differ from overhead bits?
33. What is the function of a repeater?
34. What causes attenuation?
35. How do analog amplifiers differ from digital repeaters?
36. How do polling and selecting differ?
37. How efficient would a 6-bit code be in asynchronous transmission if it had one parity bit, one start bit, and two stop bits? (Some very old equipment uses two stop bits.)
38. Are stop bits necessary?
39. What is the transmission rate of information bits if you use EBCDIC (eight bits with one parity bit), a 400-character block, 9600 bits per second modem transmission speed, 20 control characters per block, an error rate of 1 percent, and a 30-millisecond turnaround time?
40. What is the TRIB in question 39 if you add a half-second delay to the turnaround time because of satellite delay?
41. How is Automatic Repeat reQuest used?
42. What are two types of ARQ?

NEXT DAY AIR SERVICE CUMULATIVE CASE STUDY

See appendix at end of book

CHAPTER SEVEN

NETWORK LAYER

In this chapter, we discuss two fundamental elements of the network layer. The first is *network topology*, the basic geometric layout of the network. The second is *routing*, the process of determining the route or path that a message will travel through the network from the sending computer to the receiving computer. Network *standards* are important to ensure that hardware and software from different vendors operated by different companies can communicate, so we also discuss several commonly used standard network protocols.

Objectives

- Understand the concept of layers in network design,
- Understand four common network topologies,
- Become familiar with different types of routing,
- Become familiar with the role of standards and how standards are developed,
- Understand four common standard network protocols,
- Become familiar with IBM's SNA architecture.

Chapter Outline

INTRODUCTION

Before we discuss the functions performed by the network layer and several standard network protocols, we should review the four basic types of networks we have defined.

A *local area network* (LAN) is a group of microcomputers or other workstation devices located in the same general area and connected by a common circuit. A LAN covers a clearly defined small area, such as one floor or work area, a single building, or a group of buildings. In general, LANs use multipoint circuits, where all computers must take turns using the same shared circuit. The upper left diagram in Figure 7-1 shows a small LAN located in the records building at McClellan Air Force Base in Sacramento. LANs support high speed data transmission compared standard telephone circuits, commonly operating at 2 to 20 million bits per second (Mbps). LANs are discussed in Chapter 8.

Most LANs are connected to a *backbone network* (BN), a larger, central network connecting several LANs, other BNs, metropolitan area networks, and wide area networks. Backbone networks typically span up to several miles, and provide very high speed data transmission, commonly to 10 to 150 Mbps. The second diagram in Figure 7-1 shows a backbone network that connects the LANs located in several buildings at

McClellan AFB. BNs have characteristics of both LANs and MANs/WANs, so they are discussed in Chapter 10.

A *metropolitan area network* (MAN) connects LANs and BNs located in different areas to each other and to wide area networks. MANs typically span from 3 to 30 miles. The third diagram in Figure 7-1 shows a MAN connecting the backbone networks at several military and government complexes in Sacramento. Some organizations develop their own MANs using similar technologies as BNs. These networks provide very fast transmission rates, but can prove costly to install and operate over long distances. Unless an organization has a continuing need to transfer large amounts of data, this type of MAN is too expensive. More commonly, organizations use public data networks provided by local carriers (e.g., the telephone company) as their MANs. With these MANs, data transmission rates typically range from 64 Kbps to 5 Mbps, although newer technologies promise data rates of over 600 Mbps. MANs are discussed in Chapter 9.

Wide area networks (WANs) connect BNs and MANs (see Figure 7-1). Most organizations do not build their own WANs by laying cable, building microwave towers, or sending up satellites (unless they have unusually heavy data transmission needs or highly specialized requirements such as the Department of Defense). Instead, most organizations lease circuits from inter-exchange carriers (e.g., AT&T, MCI, Sprint), and use those to transmit their data. WAN circuits provided by inter-exchange carriers come in all types and sizes, but typically span hundreds or thousands of miles and provide data transmission rates from 64 Kbps to 2 Gbps. WANs and MANs are discussed in Chapter 9.

The distinctions between these different types of networks are becoming blurry. Some network technologies now used in local area networks were originally developed for wide area networks, while some LAN technologies have influenced the development of MAN products. Any rigid classification of technologies is certain to have exceptions.

NETWORK TOPOLOGY

Networks can be classified by their *topology*, which is the basic geometric arrangement of the network. The basic topologies used to lay out networks are ring, bus, star, and mesh. Ring, bus, and star topologies are commonly used in LANs and BNs. Star and mesh topologies are commonly used in MANs and WANs. In many cases, the networks are built using a combination of topologies.

Ring Topology

A *ring topology* connects all computers in a closed loop, with each computer linked to the next. Messages pass around the ring in one direction only to each computer in turn. The time required for the data to travel around the ring between the interconnected computers is called the *walk time*. Figure 7-2 shows a basic ring topology.

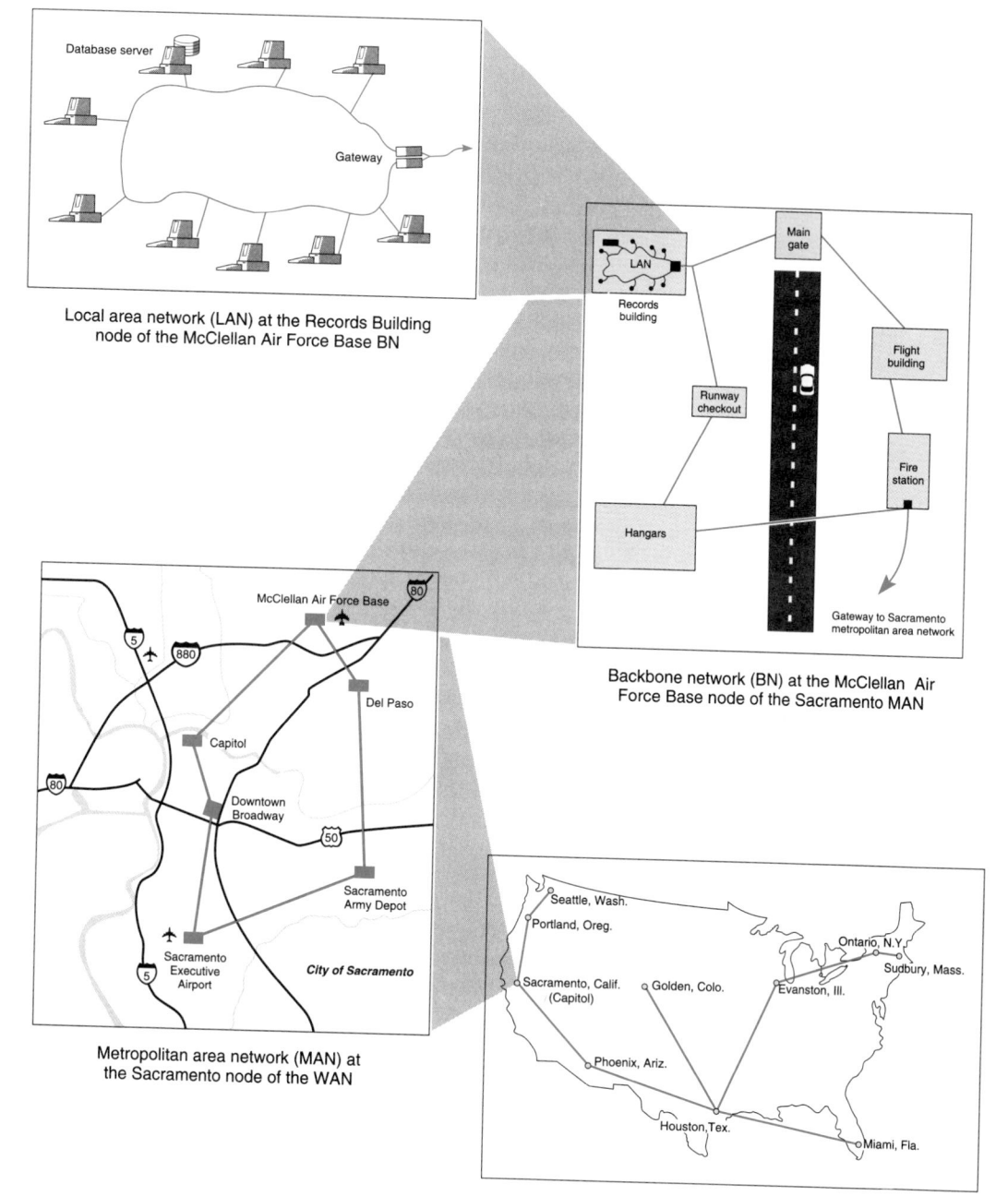

Local area network (LAN) at the Records Building
node of the McClellan Air Force Base BN

Backbone network (BN) at the McClellan Air
Force Base node of the Sacramento MAN

Metropolitan area network (MAN) at
the Sacramento node of the WAN

Wide area network (WAN) showing Sacramento
connected to nine other cities throughout the U.S.

Figure 7-1 Shows the hierarchical relationship of a local area network (LAN) to a backbone network (BN) to a metropolitan area network (MAN) to a wide area network (WAN).

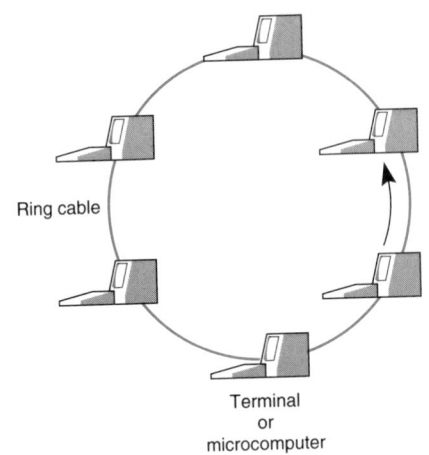

Figure 7-2 Ring topology.

Each computer on the ring has a unique address. As the messages travel around the ring, the computers check the address of the incoming signal. It the message is not addressed to it, the message is retransmitted to the next computer on the ring. If the message is addressed to that computer, it generates an acknowledgment (or negative acknowledgment) to the message sender, and transmits it to the next computer on the ring. The loss of a single computer normally does not hinder the operation of the network, but a break in the cable is catastrophic and will stop the network altogether.

Bus Topology

A *bus topology* connects all stations to one circuit running through the entire network. Data *may* pass directly from one computer to another, or it may be routed through a head end controller, which sends it back down the cable in the opposite direction (see Figure 7-3). With some bus networks, the message always must go to the head

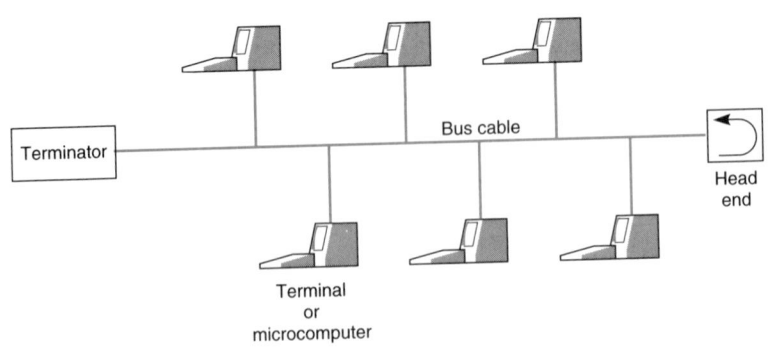

Figure 7-3 Bus topology.

end and then back down the cable to the computer to which it is addressed. Other bus networks allow the message to go directly to the destination computer.

As with the ring topology, the loss of a single computer on a bus does not hinder the operation of the network, but a break in the central cable will stop the network from functioning. Bus topologies are popular because hundreds of computers can be connected to a single bus.

Star Topology

A *star topology* connects all computers to one central computer or network device that routes messages to the appropriate computer (see Figure 7-4). Each computer is linked by a separate point-to-point circuit through the central connection point. Because the central computer receives all messages in the network, it must have sufficient capacity to handle traffic peaks; otherwise it may become overloaded. Any breaks in the cable affect only the one computer on that circuit; however, all the computers are connected to a central point, so if the central point fails, the entire network fails.

Mesh Topology

In a true *mesh topology,* every computer is connected to every other computer by its own point-to-point communication circuit, but this is seldom done because of the extremely high cost. Instead, usually one or more computers become switching centers, interconnecting computers with others. Figure 7-5 shows a mesh network, of which the public telephone system is an example.

The effects of the loss of computers or cables in a mesh network depend entirely upon the circuits available in the network. If there are many possible routes through

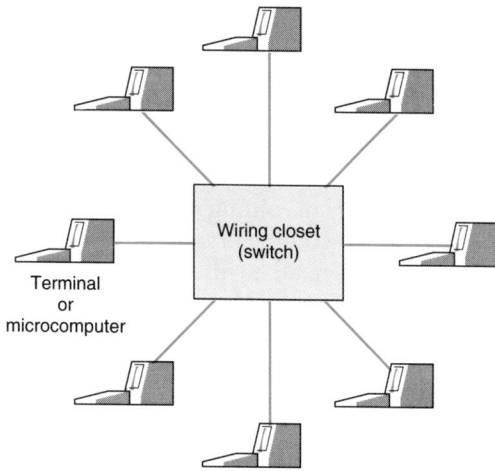

Figure 7-4 Star topology.

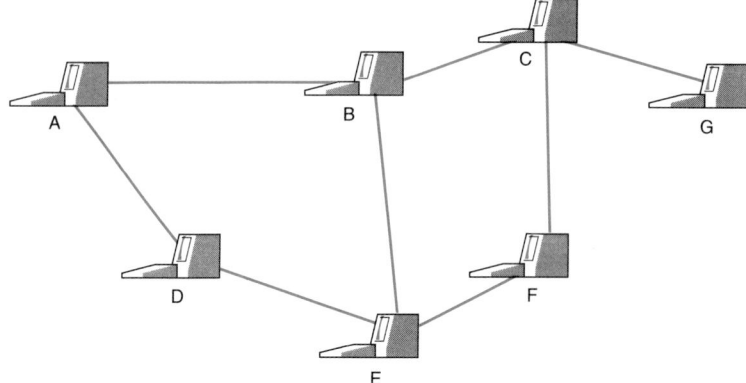

Figure 7-5   Mesh topology.

the network, the loss of one or even several circuits or computers may have few effects beyond the specific computers involved. However, if there are only few circuits in the network, the loss of even one circuit or computer may seriously impair the network.

NETWORK ROUTING

In many networks, especially mesh networks, there are many possible routes or paths a message can take to get from one computer to another. For example, in Figure 7-5, a message sent from computer A to computer F could travel first to computer B then to computer C to get to computer F—or it could go to computer D first and then to computer E to get to computer F.

Routing is the process of determining the route or path through the network that a message will travel from the sending computer to the receiving computer. There are two fundamental approaches to routing: centralized and decentralized.

Centralized Routing

With centralized routing, all routing decisions are made by one central computer. Star networks use centralized routing, and in this case, routing decisions are rather simple. All computers are connected to the central computer by individual point-to-point circuits, so any message received is simply retransmitted on the point-to-point circuit connected to the destination.

Centralized routing can also be used in mesh networks. In this case, one computer in the network is designated as the network routing manager. This computer (or the person managing this computer) develops a *routing table* that specifies how messages will travel through the network. The routing table is transmitted to each computer, which uses it until it is replaced by a new table. Each computer or device has its own version of the routing table that tells it where to send messages.

Destination	Route
A	A
C	C
D	A
E	E
F	E
G	C

Figure 7-6   Routing table.

In its simplest form, the routing table is a two-column table. The first column lists every computer and device in the network, while the second column lists the computer or device to which this computer should send messages if they are destined for the computer in the first column. Figure 7-6 shows a routing table that might be used by computer B in Figure 7-5.

The primary advantage of centralized routing is its simplicity. Only one computer (or computer manager) has to develop the routing table (or more properly, the set of routing tables). All other computers simply use the routing tables. They "waste" no resources on developing their own routing table.

There are three key disadvantages to centralized routing. First, if anything happens to the one computer developing the routing tables, they cannot be changed until that computer is fixed, or until a new computer is selected to build routing tables. Second, the routing table usually does not reflect changing network conditions, such as computers that are overloaded by many messages (at least not as rapidly as decentralized routing). Third, when routing tables are changed, network capacity is "wasted" to transmit the new routing tables to all computers.

Decentralized Routing

Decentralized routing allows all computers in the network to make their own routing decisions following a formal routing protocol. In MANs and WANs, the routing table for each computer is developed by its individual network manager (although network managers often share information). In local area networks or backbone networks, the routing tables used by all computers on the network are usually developed by one individual or a committee. Most decentralized routing protocols are self-adjusting, meaning that they can automatically adapt to changes in the network configuration (e.g., adding and deleting computers and circuits). There are three types of decentralized routing.

Static Routing   With *static routing*, the routing table is developed by the network manager, and changes only when computers are added to or removed from the network. For example, if the computer recognizes that a circuit is broken or unusable (e.g., after the data link layer retry limit has been exceeded without receiving an acknowledgment), the computer will update the routing table to indicate the failed circuit. If an alternate route is available, it will be used for all subsequent messages. Otherwise, messages will be stored until the circuit is repaired. When new computers are added to the network, they announce their presence to the other computers, who automatically add them into their routing tables. Static routing is commonly used in ring networks and occasionally in mesh networks.

Routing Information Protocol (RIP) is a commonly used static routing protocol. The network manager uses RIP to develop the routing table. When new computers are added, RIP simply counts the number of computers in the possible routes to the destination and selects the route with the least number. *Distributed Update Algorithm* (DUAL), a more sophisticated version of RIP, considers the costs associated with each route to choose the cheapest route.

Dynamic Routing *Dynamic routing* is one of the most common types used in mesh networks. Its goal is to improve network performance by routing messages over the fastest possible route, away from traffic on busy circuits and busy computers. An initial routing table is developed by the network manager, but is continuously updated by the computers themselves to reflect changing network conditions, such as network traffic. This updating can be done by monitoring outgoing messages to see how long they take to transmit and how long it takes for the receiving computer to acknowledge them. A more common approach is to have each computer periodically report how busy it is so that all the computers connected to it can assess the traffic on each route and update their tables to avoid trouble spots.

Open Shortest Path First (OSPF) is a commonly used dynamic routing protocol that uses the number of computers in a route as well as network traffic and error rates to select the best route. *Service Advertisement Protocol* (SAP) is another example of a dynamic routing protocol.

There are two drawbacks dynamic routing. First, it requires more processing by each computer in the network than centralized routing or static routing. Computing resources are devoted to adjusting routing tables rather than sending messages, which can slow down the network. Second, the transmission of status information (e.g., how busy each computer is) ''wastes'' network capacity. Some dynamic routing protocols transmit status information every minute, which can significantly reduce performance.

Broadcast Routing *Broadcast routing* sends the message to all computers, but it is only processed by the computer to which it is addressed. This routing is typically used only in bus networks.

Connectionless versus Connection-Oriented Routing

Some messages or blocks of application data are small enough that they can be transmitted in one packet or frame at the data link layer. However, in other cases (e.g., file transfer), the application data in one ''message'' is too large and must be broken into several packets. As far as the application layer is concerned, the message should be transmitted and received as one large block of data. It is therefore up to the sender's network layer to break the data into several smaller packets that can be sent by the data link layer across the circuit. At the other end, the receiver's network layer must receive all these separate packets from its data link layer and recombine them into one large block of data that is passed to the receiver's application layer as though it were received intact. There are two fundamental ways that these sets of packets can be routed through a network.

Connectionless Routing   Connectionless routing means each packet is treated separately and makes its own way through the network. It is possible that different packets will take different routes through the network depending upon the type of routing used and the amount of traffic. Because packets following different routes may travel at different speeds, they may arrive out of sequence at their destination. The sender's network layer therefore puts a sequence number on each packet, in addition to information about the message stream to which the packet belongs. The network layer must reassemble them in the correct order before passing the message to the application layer.

Connection-Oriented Routing   Connection-oriented routing sets up a *virtual circuit* between the sender and receiver. A virtual circuit is one that *appears* to the application software to use point-to-point circuit-switching, even though it actually uses store and forward switching. In this case, a temporary virtual circuit is defined between the sender and receiver. The network layer makes one routing decision when the connection is established, and all packets follow the same route. All packets in the same message arrive at the destination in the same order in which they were sent. In this case, packets only need to contain information about the stream to which they belong; sequence numbers are not needed, although many connection-oriented protocols include a sequence number to ensure that all packets are actually received.

Connection-oriented routing has greater overhead than connectionless routing, because the sender must first "open" the circuit by sending a control packet that instructs all the intervening devices to establish the circuit routing. Likewise, when the transmission is complete, the sender must "close" the circuit. Connection-oriented protocols tend to have more overhead bits in each packet, as you will see in the Network Protocols section.

NETWORK STANDARDS

The Importance of Standards

Standards are necessary in almost every business and public service entity. For example, before 1904, fire hose couplings in the United States were not standard, which meant a fire department in one community could not help in another community. The transmission of electric current was not standardized until the end of the nineteenth century so customers had to choose between Thomas Edison's direct current (DC) and George Westinghouse's alternating current (AC).

The primary reason for standards is to ensure that hardware and software produced by different vendors can work together. Without networking standards, it would be difficult—if not impossible—to develop networks that easily share information. Standards also mean that customers are not locked into one vendor. They can buy hardware and software from any vendor whose equipment meets the standard. In this way, standards help to promote more competition and hold down prices.

The use of standards makes it much easier to develop software and hardware that link different networks because software and hardware can be developed one layer at a time. The software or hardware defined by the standard at one network layer can be easily updated, as long as the interface between that layer and the ones around it remains unchanged.

The Standards Making Process

There are two types of standards: *formal* and *de facto.* A formal standard is developed by an official industry or government body. For example, the modem standards discussed earlier (e.g., V.32, V.34) are formal standards. Unfortunately, formal standards typically take many years to develop, during which a new technology may have emerged, making them less appealing.

De facto standards are those that emerge in the marketplace and are supported by several vendors, but have no official standing; Microsoft Windows is an example. In the telecommunications industry, de facto standards often become formal standards once they have been widely accepted.

The formal *standardization process* has three stages: specification, identification of choices, and acceptance. The *specification* stage consists of developing a nomenclature and identifying the problems to be addressed. In the *identification of choices* stage, those working on the standard identify the various solutions and choose the optimum solution from among the alternatives. *Acceptance,* which is the most difficult stage, consists of defining the solution and getting recognized industry leaders to agree on a single, uniform solution. As with many other organizational processes that have the potential to influence the sales of hardware and software, standards making processes are not immune to corporate politics and the influence of national governments.

International Organization for Standardization (ISO)   One of the most important standards-making bodies is the *International Organization for Standardization* (ISO), which makes technical recommendations about data communication interfaces. (The abbreviation ISO comes from its French name.) ISO is based in Geneva, Switzerland. The membership is comprised of the national standards organizations of each ISO member country. In turn, ISO is a member of the International Telecommunications Union (ITU), whose task is to make technical recommendations about telephone, telegraph, and data communication interfaces on a worldwide basis. ISO and ITU usually cooperate on issues of telecommunication standards, but they are mutually independent standards-making bodies and they are not required to agree on the same standards.

Management Focus: A Call for Term Limits in Standards Development

It takes anywhere from five to ten years to finalize a major formal standard. With new generations of products entering the market every two years, formal standards development may become irrelevant. Unless the standards process is streamlined and professionalized, vendors and users may turn their backs on slow in coming, formal standards.

Consider recent networking developments. The past five years has seen the introduction of fast ethernet, switched ethernet, FDDI, FDDI-II, and numerous other products (see Chapter 10). This means that by the time it is finalized, a standard that was five years in development has now been supplanted by several new generations.

Part of the problem behind the slow standards process may lie in human nature. Standards committees are made of individuals from many companies and organizations. For some, there may be strong disincentives to finalize a standard. Corporate interests and the desire for monthly all-expense-paid trips to international cities for committee meetings may dampen the enthusiasm for a quick process. Even worse, some individuals are members of several standards committees working on the same technologies that develop slightly different standards—requiring more meetings to harmonize the different standards.

The sad fact is that users and vendors must pay for this slow, unprofessional process, since vendors must load the costs of the standardization process into their products. The standards process should mimic normal business practices, complete with production cycles and strict deadlines. In this light, term limits could be placed on standards groups to ensure that they disband once their work is done.

Source: Network World, February 16, 1995.

International Telecommunications Union–Telecommunications Standardization Sector (ITU–TSS) The Telecommunications Standardization Sector (ITU–TSS) is the technical standards-setting organization of the United Nations International Telecommunications Union (ITU). It was formerly called the *Consultative Committee on International Telegraph and Telephone* (CCITT). It too is based in Geneva, Switzerland, and is comprised of representatives from over 150 national Postal Telephone and Telegraphs (PTTs), private telecommunication agencies, as well as industrial and scientific organizations. ISO is a member of ITU–TSS. The PTTs are telephone companies outside of the United States. In the United States, we call them the regional Bell operating companies (RBOCs), American Telephone & Telegraph (AT&T), or common carriers. ITU–TSS establishes recommendations for use by PTTs, other common carriers, and hardware and software vendors.

American National Standards Institute (ANSI) The *American National Standards Institute* is the coordinating organization for the United States' national system of standards and is comprised of about 900 companies. ANSI is a standardization organization, not a standards-making body. ANSI accepts standards developed by other organizations and publishes them as American standards. Its role is to coordinate the development of voluntary national standards and to interact with ISO in order to develop national standards that comply with ISO's international recommendations. ANSI is the United States' voting participant in ISO and ITU–TSS.

Institute of Electrical and Electronics Engineers (IEEE)   The *Institute of Electrical and Electronics Engineers* is a professional society in the United States whose standards committees focus on local area network standards. Other countries have their own similar groups; for example, the British counterpart of IEEE is the Institution of Electrical Engineers (IEE).

Electronic Industries Association (EIA)   The *Electronic Industries Association* is an ANSI-accredited standards organization that develops a variety of standards, including equipment standards. Possibly its most prominent standard is the RS232 connector cable. Membership is drawn from manufacturers of telecommunication equipment and other electronics components.

National Institute of Standards and Technology (NIST)   Formerly known as the National Bureau of Standards in Washington, D.C., the *National Institute of Standards and Technology* is an agency of the U.S. Department of Commerce that develops federal information processing standards for the federal government. Among its many test facilities is the Network Protocol Testing and Evaluation Facility which has eight laboratories for research in the design, implementation, and testing of computer network protocols. This facility develops prototype implementations of protocols and then tests them in a variety of communication environments.

National Exchange Carriers Association (NECA)   The *National Exchange Carriers Association*'s T-1 Committee (accredited by ANSI) is comprised of representatives from domestic telecommunication manufacturers, carriers, users, and other interested parties. The T-1 Technical Subcommittee develops North American wide area network telecommunication standards.

Corporation for Open Systems (COS)   The *Corporation for Open Systems* is a nonprofit corporation established in 1986. Formed under the auspices of the Computer and Communication Industry Association, the organization has members from computer and communication equipment vendors and users. Although COS is not a standards-setting body, it was established to accelerate the introduction of products based on international standards, principally those based on the OSI model discussed later in this chapter. COS is very powerful because its members are important leaders in the world of communications. The COS goal is to stimulate the development of interoperable communication products from different vendors. In addition to promoting standards, COS operates a center to test compatible hardware and software.

COS members contribute funds to the COS Strategy Forum, the primary decision-making body at the technical level. The Forum's numerous subcommittees deal with specific technical issues and are responsible for submitting recommendations to the

Strategy Forum for approval. While the standards developed by the international standards-making bodies generally concentrate on a particular layer of the OSI model, COS users assemble a number of standards to produce a profile that supports a particular application or hardware.

Electronic Data Interchange (EDI) EDI is the working name for Electronic Data Interchange for Administration, Commerce, and Transport *(EDIFACT)*. EDI allows the electronic interchange of business documents like purchase orders or invoices. These documents can have graphics as well as ASCII characters. It is the only standard ever specified for international EDI networks, and it has been embraced by the ISO as the premier standard for international EDI. The *Electronic Data Interchange* standard was formulated in 1985 by European and North American network users who were concerned that diverging sets of standards on the two continents would greatly inhibit international EDI.

EDI defines major components of the ANSI EDI standard. Although EDIFACT is supported by users in Europe and the Far East, Canadian and American users are reluctant to embrace it because they already have invested in networks based on the EDI standard developed by the ANSI committee. Unfortunately, EDIFACT is not totally compatible with the ANSI standard.

Legally Enforceable Standards

Legally enforceable standards are defined and enacted into law by the governments of various countries. In the United States, we have criminal punishment for three types of computer criminals: those who gain access to federal computers, those who gain unauthorized access to computers at financial institutions that are covered by federal laws, and those who gain access to computers that hold national security data. The U.S. Department of Justice has a computer crime unit that is responsible for prosecuting crimes and encouraging stiffer penalties for convicted computer criminals. The FBI, U.S. Secret Service, and the military are all adding staff to combat computer crimes. Moreover, many states now have their own laws on computer and communication security. Security is such an important topic that Chapter 13 is devoted to it.

Federal Wiretap Statute The *Federal Wiretap Statute,* enacted in 1968, protected only voice communications from interception. The primary thrust of this law was to prevent the illegal ''tapping'' of a telephone line or the illegal recording of voice telephone conversations. It was not until 1986 that an electronic privacy law was passed relating directly to data communications.

Electronic Communications Privacy Act of 1986 This act makes it a federal crime to intercept electronic communications, such as data communications or electronic mail, or to tamper with the computers in a data network. The 1986 law prohibits the interception of data and image communications on private networks and the unauthorized access of network computers if stored messages are obtained or altered. Under this law, individuals are subject to penalties of up to $100,000 and ten years in prison if the crime is committed for commercial gain or malicious reasons. Fines for organizations can be up to $250,000. The privacy of network users also is protected under this law. Law enforcement officials need a court order to obtain electronic messages, and electronic mail services cannot disclose the content of messages transmitted over their services without the sender's authorization.

This act has been amended to define "access" to include the intentional transmission or distribution of unauthorized software that damages computer data, software, or hardware. This amendment relates directly to viruses. Felony penalties can run as high as five years in prison and a $250,000 fine. The act further specifies that anyone who unknowingly, but recklessly, transmits destructive software can face a misdemeanor penalty of up to one year in jail and a fine of $5,000. Under this amendment, a person is subject to a misdemeanor and a fine if that person accidentally, but recklessly, transmits a virus to someone else's computer. The amended law also extends the reach of the original law beyond just federal computers. It now includes any computer used in interstate commerce or communications. Finally, it allows civil actions that can result in the payment of damages to those who suffer losses due to computer abuse.

Computer Fraud and Abuse Act of 1986   In 1986, Congress also passed the *Computer Fraud and Abuse Act*, which expands federal jurisdiction of interstate computer crimes involving private sector computers. It also hits the so-called pirate bulletin board systems that exchange computer passwords. Specifically, the law makes it a federal offense to access a computer in a fraudulent scheme to steal, and it makes it a felony to alter or destroy data, hardware, or software without authorization. The law also makes it a federal misdemeanor for an individual to traffic in computer passwords belonging to others, if there is a clear intent to defraud. Fines of up to $100,000 and ten years in prison are imposed on those who intentionally gain unauthorized access to computer systems to damage records or to steal records or money.

Computer Security Act of 1987   The *Computer Security Act* became law at the end of 1987. This act shifts power away from the National Security Agency (NSA) and transfers it to the National Institute of Standards and Technology (NIST) by requiring NIST to establish security standards and training programs for federal agencies using unclassified information systems. (NSA is an intelligence unit of the U.S. Department of Defense, and NIST is an agency of the U.S. Department of Commerce.) The security of classified systems is still NSA's responsibility. The major impact of this law is to give total control of the data encryption standard (DES), which is used widely by both federal government agencies and private industry, to the National Institute of Standards and Technology.

Computer Virus Eradication Act of 1988   Signed into law in 1988, the *Computer Virus Eradication Act* is meant to fight the spread of computer viruses. It provides for up to ten years in prison, a fine, or both, for anyone who "knowingly inserts into a program for a computer, or a computer itself, information or commands, knowing or having reason to believe that such information or commands may cause loss, expense, or risk to health or welfare.'' This law also prohibits giving such programs to others and allows for civil action against perpetrators.

NETWORK PROTOCOLS

There are many different network layer protocols. This section discusses three of the most commonly used ones, as well as the American government's standard. It is important to note that these protocols perform most of the same functions; however, they are different enough to be incompatible. Figure 7-7 summarizes these standards and compares them to the OSI model and the four-layer model used in this book.

Several venders have recently announced software with *multiprotocol stacks*, which means that the software supports several different network protocols. The software recognizes which protocol an incoming message uses and automatically uses that protocol to process the message.

This Book	OSI Model	TCP/IP	IPX/SPX	X.25	GOSIP	SNA	SNA APPN
Application layer	Application layer	Process	Application	Application	Application	Transaction services	Application
Network layer	Presentation layer		Transport SPX			Presentation	Presentation services
	Session layer				Session	Data flow control	
	Transport layer	Transport TCP		Transport X.3	Transport	Transmission control	Multiprotocol transport SNA APPC TCP/IP IPX
	Network layer	Internet IP	Network IPX	Network PLP	Network IP PLP	Path control	
Data link layer	Data link layer	Network Access 802.3 802.4 802.5	Data link 802.3 802.4 802.5	Data link LAP-B	Data link 802.3 LAPB 802.4 HDLC 802.5 FDDI	Data link control SDLC	Network 802.3 802.5 802.4 HDLC
Physical layer	Physical layer	LAP-B	Physical	Physical	Physical	Physical	Media

Figure 7-7   Network architectures.

Source ID	Destination ID	Sequence number	ACK number	Header legnth	Unused	Flags	Flow control	CRC 16	Urgent pointer	Options	User data
16 bits	16 bits	32 bits	32 bits	4 bits	6 bits	6 bits	16 bits	16 bits	16 bits	Varies	Varies

Figure 7-8 TCP packet.

TRANSMISSION CONTROL PROTOCOL/INTERNET PROTOCOL (TCP/IP)

The *Transmission Control Protocol/Internet Protocol* (TCP/IP) probably is the oldest networking standard, developed for the U.S. Department of Defense's Advanced Research Project Agency NETwork (ARPANET) in the 1970s. It is also the most popular network protocol, used by almost 50 percent of all installed backbone, metropolitan, and wide area networks. TCP/IP is the network protocol used on the Internet. TCP/IP allows reasonably efficient and error-free transmission between different systems. Because it is a file transfer protocol, it can send large files of information across sometimes unreliable networks with great assurance that the data will arrive uncorrupted. TCP/IP is compatible with a variety of data link protocols (see Figure 7-7), which is one reason for its popularity. In a 1995 survey of mainframe network managers, 79 percent said that TCP/IP was critical to their future plans (another 18 percent said it was important).

As the name implies, TCP/IP has two parts. TCP performs the functions of the transport layer in the OSI model (e.g., breaking the data into smaller packets, numbering them, ensuring each packet is reliably delivered, and putting them in the proper order). IP performs the role of the network layer in the OSI model (e.g., routing and addressing). IP software is used at each of the intervening computers through which the message passes; it is IP that routes the message to the final destination. IP can use either static routing (RIP) or dynamic routing (OSPF) to make routing decisions. The TCP software only needs to be active at the sender and the receiver, because TCP is only involved when data comes from or goes to the process layer (i.e., the application layer in OSI terminology).

TCP/IP can operate either as connection-oriented or connectionless. TCP is inherently connection-oriented while IP is inherently connectionless. When connection-oriented routing is desired, both TCP and IP are used; when connectionless routing is desired, only IP is used and TCP is bypassed. However, since TCP is bypassed, the application layer must perform these functions of TCP (e.g., ensuring that all packets

Version number	Header legnth	Type of service	Total legnth	Identifiers	Flags	Packet offset	Hop limit	Protocol	CRC 16	Source address	Destination Address	Options	User data
4 bits	4 bits	8 bits	16 bits	16 bits	3 bits	13 bits	8 bits	8 bits	16 bits	32 bits	32 bits	Varies	Varies

Figure 7-9 IP packet (version 4).

Version number	Flow name	Total legnth	Next header	Hop limit	Source address	Destination address	User data
4 bits	24 bits	16 bits	8 bits	8 bits	128 bits	128 bits	Varies

Figure 7-10 IP packet (version 6).

are received and putting them in the correct order). Connectionless routing is commonly used when the application data or message can fit into one packet.

A typical TCP packet has 192-*bit* header of control information (see Figure 7-8). Among other fields, it contains the source and destination, packet sequence number, and error checking information. Two forms of IP are currently in use. The older form is IP version 4 (IP4), which also has a 192-*bit* header (see Figure 7-9). This header contains source and destination addresses, packet length, and packet number. IP4 is being replaced by IP6, which has a 320-*bit* header (see Figure 7-10). The primary reason for the increase in the packet size is an increase in the address size from 32 bits to 128 bits. Simply put, the dramatic growth in the usage of the Internet meant that unless the addressing format was changed, we would have run out of addresses by the turn of the century. IP6's simpler packet structure makes it easier to perform routing, supports a variety of new approaches to addressing, and enables TCP/IP to support connection-oriented routing even better. The changes included in IP6 also suggest ways to improve TCP, so a new version of TCP is currently under development.

TCP/IP will support a variety of data link protocols, but is typically combined with ethernet. The maximum amount of application data that can be sent in one packet depends upon the data link protocol used. With ethernet, the maximum size is 1498 bytes if IP4 is used; 1470 if both TCP and IP4 are used. Figure 7-11 illustrates how data might be transmitted using TCP/IP and ethernet.

Internetwork Packet Exchange/Sequenced Packet Exchange (IPX/SPX)

Internetwork Packet Exchange/Sequenced Packet Exchange (IPX/SPX), based on a routing protocol developed by Xerox in the 1970s, is the primary network protocol used by Novell Netware. About 40 percent of all installed local area networks use it.

As the name implies, IPX/SPX has two parts, and is similar to TCP/IP in concept, but different in structure. SPX performs the functions of the transport layer in the OSI model (e.g., breaking the data into smaller packets, numbering them, ensuring each packet is reliably delivered, and putting them in the proper order). IPX performs the role of the network layer in the OSI model (e.g., routing and addressing). The

Ethernet packet header	IP packet	TCP packet	User data	Ethernet packet trailer

Figure 7-11 Data transmission using TCP/IP and ethernet.

Management Focus: The IP Address Mess

Sparked by the rising popularity of Internet, an acute shortage of official IP addresses is making it extremely difficult for companies installing TCP/IP networks to get the addresses they need.

The Internet address structure offers three types of addresses: Classes A, B, and C. Class A is utilized for up to 250 computers, while Class B allows up to 64,000 computers, and Class C for up 16 million. Nearly 60 percent of Class B addresses have been allocated, leaving 7000 more to assign. Only about 20 percent of the Class C has been allocated, but the problem with Class C addresses is that they make internal routing much more difficult.

The Internet Network Information Center (InterNIC), the organization funded by the government's National Science Foundation to hand out assigned addresses to the public, is now forcing companies to submit detailed engineering plans to qualify for addresses. However, the review of these plans can take a very long time, which slows implementation. Even worse, the plans can be rejected. As a result, some users are opting to set up TCP/IP networks without assigning InterNIC addresses to their computers. While this system works for internal purposes, it prohibits links to the Internet.

Source: Network World, December 19, 1994.

IPX software is used at each of the intervening computers through which the message passes; it is IPX that routes the message to the final destination. IPX can be configured to use either static routing with RIP or dynamic routing with SAP.

IPX/SPX can operate either as connection-oriented or connectionless. SPX is inherently connection-oriented while IPX is inherently connectionless. Both are used when connection-oriented routing is desired. When connectionless routing is desired, only IPX is used; SPX is bypassed. However, since SPX is bypassed, the application layer must ensure that all packets are received. Connectionless routing is usually used when the application data or message can fit into one packet.

A typical SPX packet has 12-*byte* header of control information (see Figure 7-12). It contains among other fields, the source and destination, and packet sequence number. A typical IPX packet has a 30-*byte* header, as Figure 7-13 shows. This header contains source and destination addresses, and packet length.

IPX/SPX can be combined with a variety of data link protocols (see Figure 7-7). The maximum amount of data that can be sent in one packet depends upon the data

Control	Type	Source ID	Destination ID	Sequence number	ACK number	Allocation number	User data
1 byte	1 byte	2 bytes	2 bytes	2 bytes	2 bytes	2 bytes	Varies

Figure 7-12 SPX packet.

Management Focus: TCP/IP for Windows

Just as Microsoft Windows is the most popular PC-based operating environment, Novell Netware is the most popular LAN environment. Unfortunately, getting them to work together can be tricky. As each has evolved, network managers have managed to keep the problem under control, enabling both to coexist in a stable, if not always happy, relationship.

But, just as that problem is being solved, users are demanding access to the Internet. The most common network protocol on the Internet is TCP/IP, something not commonly combined either with LANs or Windows.

Windows 95 theoretically provides support for both TCP/IP and IPX/SPX with the WinSock DLL, but this has proven problematic. Numerous third party vendors also provide software that claims to integrate Windows, TCP/IP, and IPX/SPX, but they too have problems, ranging from difficult installation procedures to incompatibilities among the three.

The integration of Windows, TCP/IP, and IPX/SPX clearly will happen, and will provide a big value for network managers and network users. Unfortunately, like many new products (and the Windows/Netware integration before it), it may take a few years.

Source: LAN Times, December 19, 1994.

link protocol used. With ethernet, the maximum size is usually 1488 bytes if IPX is used; 1476 if both SPX and IPX are used.

X.25

X.25 is a standard developed by ITU–TSS for wide area networks. It is a mature, global standard used by many international organizations. It also has two parts (see Figure 7-7). Packet layer protocol (PLP) is the routing protocol that performs the network layer functions (e.g., routing and addressing). X.3 performs the transport layer functions (e.g., creating and reassembling packets). As with TCP/IP and IPX/SPX, X.25 can operate either connectionless or connection-oriented modes.

There are several types of PLP packets. A typical PLP packet to transmit data (as opposed to network control information) has a 3-*byte* header. PLP is typically combined

Checksum	Lensill	Control	Type	Destination address	Destination network address	Destination socket	Source address	Source network address	Source socket	User data
2 bytes	2 bytes	1 byte	1 byte	6 bytes	4 bytes	2 bytes	6 bytes	4 bytes	2 bytes	Varies

Figure 7-13   IPX packet.

with LAP-B at the data link layer. ITU–TSS recommends that packets contain 128 of application data, but can support packets containing up to 1024 bytes.

Government Open Systems Interconnection Protocol (GOSIP)

When procuring new communication equipment, agencies in the U.S. government are required to specify communication products that support the *Government Open Systems Interconnection Protocol* (GOSIP). GOSIP defines a subset of the OSI-compliant protocols the government says it will use. In other words, GOSIP is not a network protocol or a network architecture, it defines the standard protocols that vendors must support if they want to sell their products to the U.S. government. Figure 7-7 lists the protocols specified by GOSIP.

SYSTEMS NETWORK ARCHITECTURE (SNA)

IBM developed its own architecture and protocols for networking, called *Systems Network Architecture* (SNA). SNA describes an integrated structure that provides for all modes of data communications and upon which new data communication networks can be planned and implemented. SNA is similar to the OSI model in concept, but is different in implementation (see Figure 7-7); SNA is not OSI compliant.

The major problem with SNA is that it uses proprietary non-standard protocols at the network layer and above. This means that it is difficult to integrate SNA networks with other networks that use industry standard network layer protocols. Routing messages between SNA networks and other networks, and even between IBM SNA networks and IBM LANs (which use industry standard protocols) requires special equipment. In many cases, network managers using both IBM SNA and IBM LANs have built two separate networks into the same offices, laying two sets of cable to each location, one for SNA, one for the LAN. For this reason, use of SNA is prohibited under GOSIP, although some exempt agencies have been permitted to purchase SNA-based networks for their IBM mainframes. IBM has announced a new form of SNA (APPN) that uses industry standard protocols, as discussed next. In a 1995 survey of mainframe network managers, 68 percent said that SNA and APPN was not important to their future plans (9 percent said it was critical and 23 percent said it was important).

SNA is built around four basic principles. *First*, SNA encompasses distributed functions in which many network responsibilities can be moved from the central computer to other network components, such as remote concentrators. *Second*, it describes paths between the end users (programs, devices, or operators) of the data communication network separately from the users themselves, thus allowing network configuration modifications or extensions without affecting the end users. *Third*, it uses the principle of device independence, which permits an application program to communicate with an input/output device without regard to any unique device requirements. This also

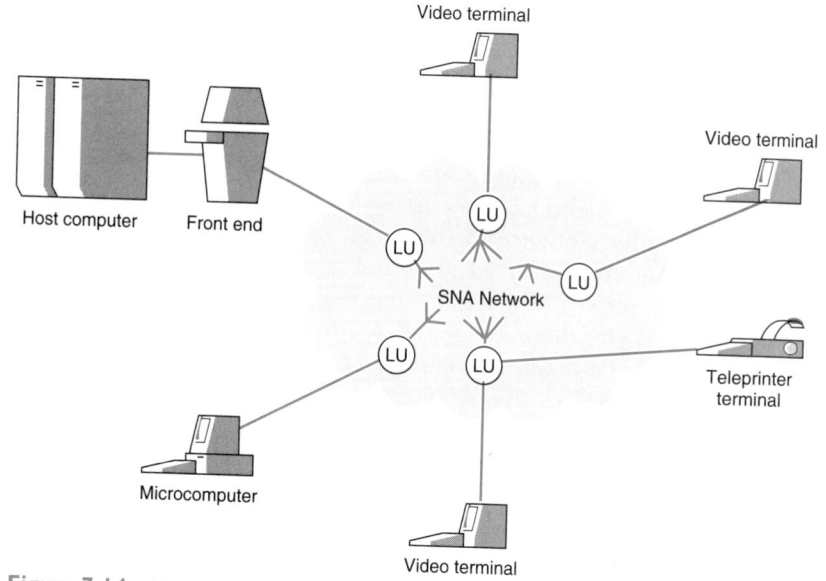

Figure 7-14   SNA session.

allows application programs and communication equipment to be added or changed without affecting other elements of the communication network. *Fourth,* SNA uses both logical and physical standardized functions and protocols for the communication of information between any two points. This means there can be *one* architecture for general purpose and industry terminals of many varieties, and *one* network protocol.

The appropriate place to begin understanding the SNA concept is to look at it from the viewpoint of the end user (see Figure 7-14). The end user (terminal operator) talks to the network through what is called a *logical unit* (LU). These logical units are implemented as program code or microcode (firmware), and they provide the end user with a point of access to the network. The program code or microcode can be built into the terminal or implemented into an intelligent terminal controller, concentrator, or remote front end.

Before one end user of an SNA network can communicate with any other end user, each of their respective logical units must be connected in a mutual relationship called a *session.* Because a session joins two logical units, it is called a *LU-LU session.* Figure 7-14 depicts the interconnection of logical units when one end user wants to talk to another. The terminal user enters the request to talk to another terminal, and the network's software connects the two LUs.

The exchange of data by end users is subject to a number of procedural rules that the logical units specify before beginning the exchange of information. These procedural rules specify how the session is to be conducted, the frame size, the amount of data to be sent by one end user before the other end user replies, actions to be taken if errors occur, the transmission speed, sequencing, what route the frame will take, what to do if the circuit fails, and the like.

Each logical unit (LU) in a network is assigned a network name. Before a session begins, the SNA network determines the network address that corresponds to each LU network name. This scheme allows one end user (for example, a terminal operator) to establish communication with another end user (for example, an application program) without having to specify where that end user is located in the network. These network names and addresses are used for addressing messages.

The flow of data between users moves between two logical units in a session. This flow moves as a bit sequence carried in an Synchronous Data Link Control (SDLC) frame and generally is referred to as a *message unit*. The message unit also contains the network addresses of the logical unit that originated the message and the logical unit that is to receive the message. These are the basic protocols at work.

A session between a pair of logical units is initiated when one of them (the end user) issues a REQUEST TO SEND message. Once a session has been activated between a pair of logical units, they can begin to exchange data. This is where the SDLC protocol handles the movement of data to have an orderly data flow. A session between a pair of logical units is deactivated when one of them sends a deactivation request or when some other outside event—intervention by a network operator or failure at some other part of the network—interrupts the session.

The logical organization of an SNA network, regardless of its physical configuration, is divided into two broad categories of components: network addressable units and path control network.

Network Addressable Units

Network addressable units (NAUs) are sets of SNA components that provide services enabling end users to send data through the network and helping network operators perform network control and management functions. Physically, network addressable units are hardware and programming components within terminals, intelligent controllers, and front end processors. Network addressable units communicate with one another through the path control network (discussed in the next section).

There are three kinds of network addressable units in SNA (see Figure 7-15). The first one, the logical unit (LU), has already been introduced. The second is the *physical unit* (PU), which is a set of SNA components that provides services to control communication links, terminals, intelligent controllers, front end processors, and host computers. Each terminal, intelligent controller, front end processor, and the like contains a physical unit that represents that particular device to the SNA network. The third kind of network addressable unit is the *system services control point* (SSCP). This also is a set of SNA components, but its duties are broader than those of the physical units and logical units. Physical units and logical units represent machine resources and end users, whereas the SSCP manages the entire SNA network or a significant part of it called a *domain*. An SSCP controls many other devices.

Just as sessions exist between logical units, sessions can exist between other kinds of network addressable units, such as a *SSCP-LU, SSCP-PU,* or *SSCP-SSCP session.* Figure 7-15 shows the location of LUs, PUs, and SSCPs in a network. In a family, the mother, father, and children are all PUs. You conduct an LU session when speaking with your

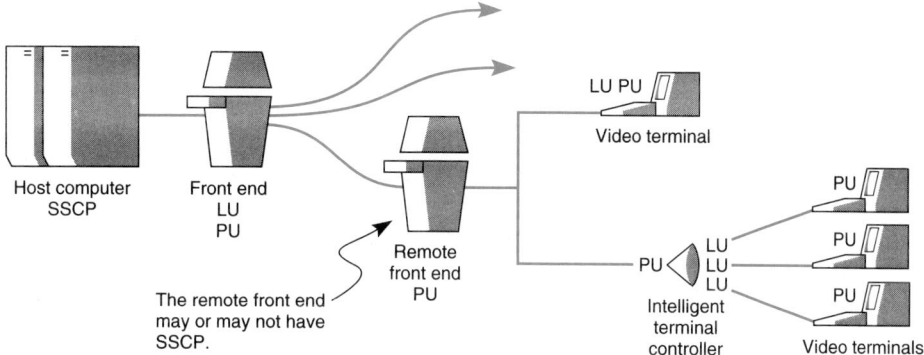

Figure 7-15   SNA SSCPs/LUs/PUs.

father, mother, sister, or brother, but your mother or father is the SSCP controlling the children's LUs.

Systems Network Architecture defines a *node* as a point within the SNA network that contains SNA components. For example, each terminal, intelligent controller, and front end processor that is designed into the SNA specifications can be a node.

An expanded definition of a node is any microcomputer, minicomputer, mainframe computer, or database that constitutes a point on the network at which data might be stored, forwarded, input into the network, or removed from the network as output. Depending on which vendor's literature you read, they might refer to a node as a *station,* an *intelligent microprocessor-based device,* a *terminal,* or a *workstation.*

Each SNA node contains a physical unit that represents that node and its resources to the system services control point. When the SSCP activates a session with a physical unit (SSCP-PU session), it makes the node (terminal, intelligent controller, or front end processor) containing that physical unit an active part of the SNA network. It is convenient to think of an SNA node as being a terminal, intelligent controller, or front end processor within the network. Certain more powerful nodes also can be an SSCP.

Path Control Network

Remember that the logical organization of SNA is divided into two broad categories of components: network addressable units and the path control network. The *path control network* provides for routing and flow control. Logical units must establish a path before an LU-LU session can begin. Each SSCP, PU, and LU has a different network address, which identifies it to other network addressable units as well as to the path control network. Path control provides for the following:

- Virtual routing so all sessions can send their messages by different routes,
- Transmission priorities,
- Multiple links to maximize throughput,

- Message pacing (flow control) to keep a fast transmitter from drowning a slow receiver,
- Ability to detect and recover from errors as they occur,
- Facilities to handle disruption because of a circuit failure,
- Facilities to inform network operators when there is a disruption in the network.

The path control network has two layers: the *path control layer* and the *data link control layer* (similar to layers 2 and 3 in the OSI model). Routing and flow control are provided by the path control layer, whereas transmitting data over individual links is provided by the data link control layer, which uses SDLC.

Telecommunication Access Programs

Access to SNA networks is controlled by a series of telecommunications access programs, including TCAM, VTAM, NCP, and CICS. Each provides certain functions, although there is some overlap among the four. All are not used at the same time.

Telecommunications Access Method (TCAM) The *telecommunications access method* provides the basic functions needed for controlling data communication circuits. It provides facilities for polling terminals, transmitting and receiving messages, detecting errors, automatically retransmitting erroneous messages, translating code, dialing and answering calls, logging transmission errors, allocating blocks of buffer storage, and performing online diagnostics to facilitate the testing of terminal equipment. It supports asynchronous terminals, synchronous communications, and audio response units. Residing in the host computer, TCAM's most significant features are those for network control and system recovery. An operator control facility also provides network supervision and modification.

TCAM handles the data communications in a network that uses a high degree of multiprogramming. Unlike the prior basic data communication software, TCAM has its own control program that commands and schedules traffic-handling operations. In some cases, it can handle an incoming message by itself without passing it to an application program—for example, routing a message to another terminal in a message switching system. TCAM also provides status reporting on terminals, lines, and queues. It has significant recovery and serviceability features to increase the security and availability of the data communication network. The checkpoint and restart facilities are very good. TCAM has prewritten routines for checkpointing, logging, date and time stamping, sequence numbering and checking, message interception and rerouting, and error message transmission, and it supports a separate master terminal for the data communication network operator.

Virtual Telecommunications Access Method (VTAM) The *virtual telecommunications access method* is the data communication software package that complements IBM's advanced hardware and software. It resides in the host computer. VTAM manages a network structured on SNA principles. It directs the transmission of data between the application programs in the host computer and the components of the data communication network. It operates with front end processors. The basic services performed by VTAM include establishing, controlling, and terminating access between the application programs and the terminals. It moves data between application programs and terminals and permits application programs to share communication circuits, communication controllers, and terminals. In addition, VTAM controls the configuration of the entire network, creates virtual connections, and permits the network to be monitored and altered.

When VTAM establishes sessions, one end of the session is understood to be the host and the other the terminal. VTAM makes the mainframe the primary end of the session and the remote terminal the secondary end. In technical terms, the host program is said to be the *primary logical unit* (PLU), and the terminal or microcomputer is considered to be the *secondary logical unit* (SLU). Only the primary logical unit can start a session, end the session, and perform key aspects of error recovery. When personal computers are linked to SNA hosts, they are considered to be secondary logical units just like terminals.

VTAM can be the sole telecommunication access method in the host, or it can operate in conjunction with the Network Control Program (described next), which allows some of the network control functions to be offloaded to the front end processor.

Network Control Program (NCP)   The *network control program* is a telecommunication access method located in the front end processors that control IBM's Synchronous Data Link Control (SDLC) communications between host computers and remote terminals. (SDLC is the protocol developed for SNA by IBM.) It also works with host resident VTAM software to route information through networks. NCP routes data and controls its flow between the front end processor and any other network resources. These other network resources can be the host mainframe computer or an intelligent control unit located either locally or at the remote end of the communication link. IBM's primary network control program is the Advanced Communication Function/ Network Control Program (ACF/NCP). Network control programs reside in the front end processor, primarily in IBM's 3704, 3705, 3725, and 3745. NCP is *not* a replacement for TCAM or VTAM; it provides an interface with TCAM and VTAM by taking over some of their functions and moving them to the front end.

NCP can handle polling, error detection, error recovery, and intermediate routing. It provides some flow control (such as various types of message pacing), prevents network congestion, provides Internetwork communication, and insulates VTAM from being overburdened by having to speak to an excessive number of other protocols. NCP version 5 supports dial-up lines and improves support for multipoint lines. It also supports SDLC's PU 2.1 functionality, enabling the front end processor to initiate sessions with remote terminals. With NCP version 5, one front end processor can communicate with other front end processors via an IBM token ring network. It includes load balancing across network bridges and backbone rings, port swapping, backup capabilities, and remote controller support. NCP is IBM's effort to move the telecommunication access method software out from the host mainframe to the front end processor. NCP is the only one of these five telecommunication access programs that actually resides in a front end processor; all the others reside in the host mainframe.

Customer Information Control System (CICS)   Some functions overlap between the telecommunication access programs such as TCAM and Customer Information Control System (CICS) (a teleprocessing monitor), both of which reside in the host computer. IBM's front end has its own program called the Network Control Program or NCP (this also is a telecommunication access program). TCAM and NCP overlap; therefore, functions such as polling/selecting can be performed from either the host computer or the front end processor.

Teleprocessing monitors such as CICS are software programs that directly relieve the host computer's operating system of many tasks involved in handling message traffic between the host and the front end or the host and other internal central processing unit (CPU) software packages (such as the host database management system). Generally speaking, teleprocessing monitors perform such functions as message handling, access methods, task scheduling, and system recovery. The teleprocessing monitor acts as the interface with the telecommunication access programs on one side and with all of the host computer's software on the other side. Teleprocessing monitors must be the interface with various operating systems, computer architectures, database management systems, security software packages, and application programs.

Customer Information Control System (CICS) is the world's most widely used mainframe teleprocessing monitor. It may not be perfect, but even IBM's direct competitors implicitly acknowledge that CICS has few alternatives. Whatever supplants it will be an evolving CICS rather than a totally new replacement. CICS is a table-driven teleprocessing program that offers 64 layers or systems it can service. Like any other teleprocessing monitor, CICS runs in conjunction with the host computer's operating system. CICS takes over the communication-related tasks that previously were handled by the operating system, thus allowing the operating system to concentrate on other control tasks or application programs.

CICS also offers an additional level of security. It can accommodate a unique password and identification for each terminal operator and allow access only to the specific functions assigned to that operator password and/or terminal identifier. It can assign highly sensitive functions to a specific terminal or a group of terminals. Some security features might be security sign-on fields, darkened password fields, and a complete log of terminal sign-ons, including any security violations.

Other tasks conducted by teleprocessing monitors such as CICS are logging of all messages (both input and output), accounting procedures for cost control, restart and recovery procedures in case of failure, utility features that perform special maintenance tasks, and queue management of both inbound and outbound message queues, as well as the ability to place priorities on messages and/or queues. A teleprocessing monitor should be able to interact with multiple front end processors, terminals, microcomputers, and various data communication transmission speeds. The monitor provides input/output job task queue management, various methods of instituting priorities for certain transactions or jobs, file and database management, application program management, task and resource control, restart and recovery procedures in case of failure, and special utilities that carry out tasks often enough to warrant establishing them as a utility feature (OSI model layer 6). It keeps track of accounting features and operating statistics and isolates various programs or parts of the system from other programs or parts of the system. In other words, a teleprocessing monitor can be considered a "mini" operating system with data communication interfaces.

Advanced Peer-to-Peer Networking and the "New" SNA

A newer part of IBM's systems network architecture is *Advanced Peer-to-Peer Networking* (APPN). This approach supports peer-to-peer communication between two or more network devices in which either side can initiate sessions. No *primary–secondary* relationship exists, and either side is able to poll or answer to polls. Before the introduction of peer-to-peer communications, a primary–secondary relationship always existed where only one of the two nodes could initiate or start a communication session.

IBM has announced, but not yet implemented, a new form of SNA that provides two important advantages over the current SNA. First, the "new" SNA will support a variety of industry standard network and data link protocols. This will solve many of the problems that now exist in integrating SNA networks with other networks. Second, the host computer does not have to mediate the connection between the two end user terminals or computers. This allows microcomputers to speak as equals to the host mainframe computer, and eliminates the bonds of IBM micro-to-mainframe emulation that confine the microcomputer to terminal status in its communications with host mainframes.

SUMMARY

Topology   There are four common network topologies (the basic geometric arrangement of the network): ring, bus, star, and mesh. Ring, bus, and star topologies are commonly used in LANs and BNs. Star and mesh topologies are commonly used in MANs and WANs. A ring topology connects all workstations in a closed loop, and messages pass to each workstation in turn. A bus topology connects all stations to one circuit running through the entire network. A star topology connects all computers to one central computer or network device that routes messages to the appropriate computer. In a mesh topology, computers are connected to each other by point-to-point circuits.

Routing   Routing is the process of selecting the route or path through the network that a message will travel from the sending computer to the receiving computer. With centralized routing, all routing decisions are made by one central computer. Star networks use centralized routing. With decentralized routing, all computers in the network make their own routing decisions. There are three major types of decentralized routing. With static routing, the routing table is developed by the network manager, and remains unchanged until the network manager updates it. With dynamic routing, the goal is to improve network performance by routing messages over the fastest possible route; an initial routing table is developed by the network manager, but is continuously updated to reflect changing network conditions, such as message traffic. With broadcast routing, the message is sent to all computers, but it is only processed by the computer to which it is addressed.

Connectionless versus Connection-Oriented Routing   Some messages or blocks of application data are small enough that they can be transmitted in one packet or frame at the data link layer. However, in other cases (e.g., file transfer), the application data in one "message" is too large and must be broken into several packets. Connectionless routing means that each packet is treated separately and makes its own way through the network. With connection-oriented routing, the network layer makes one routing decision for all the packets and all packets for that message take the same route.

Standards   Standards ensure that hardware and software produced by different vendors can work together. A formal standard is developed by an official industry or government body. De facto standards are those that emerge in the marketplace and are supported by several vendors, but have no official standing. Many different industry and government standards-making organizations exist.

Network Protocols   Many different standard network protocols exist to perform addressing, routing, and packetizing. All provide formal definitions for how addressing and routing is to be executed, and specify packet structures to transfer this information between computers. TCP/IP, IPX/SPX, and X.25 are commonly used routing protocols.

SNA   SNA is IBM's proprietary non-standard network architecture. It is difficult to integrate SNA networks with other networks that use industry standard network layer protocols. Routing messages between SNA networks and other networks, and even between IBM SNA networks and IBM LANs (which use industry standard protocols) requires special equipment. IBM has announced a new form of SNA that uses industry standard protocols.

Key Terms

Advanced peer-to-peer networking (APPN)
American National Standards Institute (ANSI)
Backbone network (BN)
Broadcast routing
Bus topology
Centralized routing
Computer Fraud and Abuse Act

Computer Security Act
Computer Virus Eradication Act
Connectionless routing
Connection-oriented routing
Consultative Committee on International Telegraph and Telephone (CCITT)
Corporation for Open Systems (COS)

Customer information control system (CICS)
Decentralized routing
Dynamic routing
Electronic Communications Privacy Act
Electronic data interchange (EDI)
Electronic Industries Association (EIA)
Federal Wiretap Statute

Government open systems
  interconnection
  protocol (GOSIP)
Institute of Electrical and
  Electronics Engineers
  (IEEE)
International Organization
  for Standardization
  (ISO)
International
  Telecommunications
  Union–Telecommunica-
  tions Standardization
  Sector (ITU–TSS)
Internetwork packet
  exchange/Sequenced
  packet exchange (IPX/
  SPX)
Local area network (LAN)
Logical unit (LU)
Mesh topology

Metropolitan area network
  (MAN)
National Exchange
  Carriers Association
  (NECA)
National Institute of
  Standards and
  Technology (NIST)
Network addressable unit
  (NAU)
Network control program
  (NCP)
Network layer
Node
Packet layer protocol
  (PLP)
Path control network
Physical unit (PU)
Presentation layer
Ring topology
Routing

Routing table
Standards
Star topology
Static routing
Systems network
  architecture (SNA)
System services control
  point (SSCP)
Telecommunications
  access method (TCAM)
Topology
Transmission control
  protocol/Internet
  protocol (TCP/IP)
Virtual circuit
Virtual telecommunica-
  tions access method
  (VTAM)
Wide area network (WAN)
X.25
X.3

Selected References

1. Chappel, Laura. *Netware Guide to LAN Analysis.* San Jose, CA: Novell Press, 1993.
2. Guruge, Anura. "IBM Radically Reformulates SNA," *Data Communications,* vol. 20, no. 5, April 1991, 72+. [First article of two called "The New SNA."]
3. *International Standards Index.* Denver: Information Handling Services. Annual index with bimonthly updates. (Call 1-800-241-7824 for information about the index and its corollary publications.)
4. "Just When You THOUGHT IP was Safe," *Datamation,* November 1, 1994, 71–72.
5. Knight, Ivor. "Telecommunications Standards Development," *Telecommunications,* vol. 25, no. 1, January 1991, 38–42.
6. Layland, Robin. "The End for IBM's FEP?" *Data Communications,* vol. 20, no. 5, April 1991, 73+. [Second article of two called "The New SNA."]
7. "The Future of IP," *LAN Times,* December 19, 1994, 43.
8. Randesi, Steve, and Don Czubek. "SNA Goes for a Ride," *LAN Magazine,* vol. 7, no. 4, April 1992, 109+.

Questions/Problems

1. Compare and contrast the four basic types of networks.
2. Compare and contrast the four basic network topologies.
3. What type of network(s) (LAN, BN, MAN, and/or WAN) are most likely to use a ring, a bus, a star, and a mesh topology?

4. Describe three types of decentralized routing. What are the advantages and disadvantages of each?
5. What are the differences between connectionless and connection-oriented routing?
6. Describe the three stages of standardization.
7. What is the purpose of a data communication standard?
8. What are the two most important standards-making bodies with regard to data communications and how do they differ?
9. Name three other communication standards-setting organizations.
10. Outline four U.S. statutes related to communication security.
11. What is the difference between ISO and OSI?
12. Describe three "legally enforceable standards."
13. How does TCP/IP work?
14. Who is the primary user of TCP/IP?
15. How does IPX/SPX work?
16. Who is the primary user of IPX/SPX?
17. What is X.25?
18. Who is the primary user of X.25?
19. Describe the networking protocol used by the U.S. government as a standard for its agencies.
20. What are the four basic principles of Systems Network Architecture (SNA) and why are they important?
21. In SNA, how does the end user communicate with the network?
22. How does synchronous data link control (SDLC) relate to systems network architecture (SNA)?
23. What is the primary problem with SNA?
24. How does TCAM differ from VTAM?
25. What is CICS and what does it do?

NEXT DAY AIR SERVICE CUMULATIVE CASE STUDY

See appendix at end of book

CHAPTER EIGHT

LOCAL AREA NETWORKS

The preceding chapters provided the fundamental understanding of the four layers in a typical network. This chapter draws together these fundamental concepts to describe local area networks (LANs). We first summarize the three major components of a LAN, and then describe the two most commonly used LANs (token ring and ethernet), plus several other LANs. The chapter ends with a discussion of how to improve LAN performance and how to select a LAN.

Objectives

- Understand the role of a LAN in organizations,
- Understand the three major components of LANs,
- Understand how Ethernet LANs operate,
- Understand how Token Ring LANs operate,
- Become familiar with three other types of LANs,
- Understand how to improve LAN performance,
- Become familiar with the issues involved in selecting a LAN.

Chapter Outline

Introduction
    Why Use a LAN?
    Types of LANs
LAN Components
    Network Interface Cards
    Network Cables and Hubs
    Network Operating Systems

INTRODUCTION

Today's "hot button" is local area networking, linking computers into a network that provides the standard office functions of word processing, electronic mail, file sharing, file transfer, printer sharing, and Internet access. Most large organizations have numerous local area networks (LANs) connected by backbone networks. In many cases, these LANs also provide access to organization's host mainframe computer. In this chapter, we discuss the fundamental components of a LAN, and summarize several commonly used LANs—ethernet and token ring. Both standards are supported by many vendors and together account for almost 85 percent of all LANs installed today.

Why Use a LAN?

There are two basic reasons for developing a LAN: information sharing and resource sharing. *Information sharing* refers to having users who access the same data files, exchange information via electronic mail, or search the Internet for information. For example, a single purchase order database might be maintained so all users can access its contents over the LAN. (Many information sharing applications were described in Chapter 2.) The main benefit of information sharing is improved decision making, which makes it generally more important than resource sharing.

Resource sharing refers to one computer sharing a hardware device (e.g., printer) or software package with other computers on the network in order to save costs. For example, suppose we have 30 computers on a LAN, each of which needs access to a word processing package. One option is to purchase 30 copies and install one on each computer. This would use disk space on each computer and require a significant amount of staff time to perform the installation and maintain the software, particularly if the package were updated regularly.

An alternative is to install the software on the network for all to use. This would eliminate the need to keep a copy on every computer and free up disk space. It would also simplify software maintenance because any software upgrades would be installed once on the network server; staff would no longer have to upgrade all computers.

In most cases, not all users would need to access the word processing package simultaneously. Therefore, rather than purchasing a copy for each computer in the network, you could instead purchase ten copies, presuming that only ten users would simultaneously use the software. Of course, the temptation is to purchase only one copy of the software, and permit everyone to use it simultaneously. The cost savings would be significant, but this is illegal. Virtually all software licenses require one copy to be purchased for each simultaneous user. Most companies and all government agencies have policies forbidding the violation of software licenses, and many now terminate employees who knowingly violate them.

One approach to controlling the number of copies of a particular software package is to use *LAN metering software* that prohibits using more copies of a package than there are installed licenses. Many software packages now sell LAN versions that do this automatically, and a number of third-party packages are also available.

Nonetheless, the Software Publishers Association (SPA) in Washington, D.C., estimates that 50 percent of the software in the United States is used illegally. SPA has recently undertaken an aggressive *software audit* program to check the number of illegal software copies on LANs. Whistle-blowers receive rewards from SPA, while the violating organizations and employees are quickly brought to court. SPA will work with companies that voluntarily submit to an audit, and offers an audit kit that scrutinizes networks in search of software sold by SPA members. (Call 1-202-452-1600 for a copy.)

Types of LANs

There are many different ways to classify LANs. One common way is to group them by categories: dedicated server LANs, peer-to-peer LANs, and zero-slot LANs. This chapter focuses primarily on dedicated server LANs because they account for more than 70 percent of all installed LANs, although many of the issues are also common in peer-to-peer networks.

Dedicated Server Networks A *dedicated server LAN* can connect with almost any other network, can handle very large databases, has a dedicated network server, and uses sophisticated LAN software. Moreover, high-end dedicated server LANs can be easily interconnected to form enterprise-wide networks or, in some cases, replace the host mainframe central computer. Generally speaking, the dedicated server is a powerful microcomputer or minicomputer.

With dedicated server LANs, the network has one or more computers that only support the network by providing access to files and other network resources. The server's usual operating system (e.g., DOS) is replaced by a network operating system. Special purpose network communication software is also loaded on each client or user computer, and is the link between the client computer's operating system and the network operating system on the server. This set of communication software provides the protocols that allow data transmissions to take place. Three software components must work together and in conjunction with the network hardware to enable communications: the network operating system in the dedicated server, the network communication software that interconnects the server to the user computers, and the application software that runs on the server and client computers.

There are many different types of dedicated server LANs. Four common types are file servers, database servers, print servers, and communication servers (see Figure 8-1).

File servers allow many users to share the same set of files on a common, shared disk drive. The size of hard disk volume can be of any size, limited only by the size of the disk storage itself. Files on the shared disk drive can be made freely available to all network users, shared only among authorized users, or restricted to only one user.

A *database server* is more powerful than a file server. It not only provides shared access to the files on the server, but also can perform database processing on those files associated with client-server computing. For example, database servers can receive requests for information contained in a database (e.g., find all customers in New York) and search through the database to find the requested information, which is then sent back to the client requesting the information. In contrast, file servers can only send entire files, requiring any processing to be done by the client. The key benefit of database servers is that they reduce the amount of data moved between the server and the client workstation. They can also minimize data loss and prevent widespread data inconsistencies if the system fails.

Print servers handle print requests on the LAN. By offloading the management of printing from the main LAN file server or database server, print servers help reduce the load on them and increase network efficiency in much the same way that front end processors improve the efficiency of host computers. Print servers have traditionally been separate computers, but many vendors now sell "black boxes" that perform all the functions of a print server at a quarter of the cost of a stand-alone computer.

Communications servers are dedicated to performing communication processing. There are three fundamental types: fax servers, modem servers, and access servers. As the name suggests, *fax servers* manage a pool of fax-boards that enable LAN users to send or receive faxes. One problem with fax servers is that someone usually has to read the incoming faxes and send them to the intended recipient. While some systems attempt to scan the incoming fax to recognize the receiver's name, the success of this depends upon how the sender created the fax.

Access servers and *modem servers* allow users to dial into and out of the LAN by telephone. Dialing into the LAN is accomplished with an access server, whereas dialing

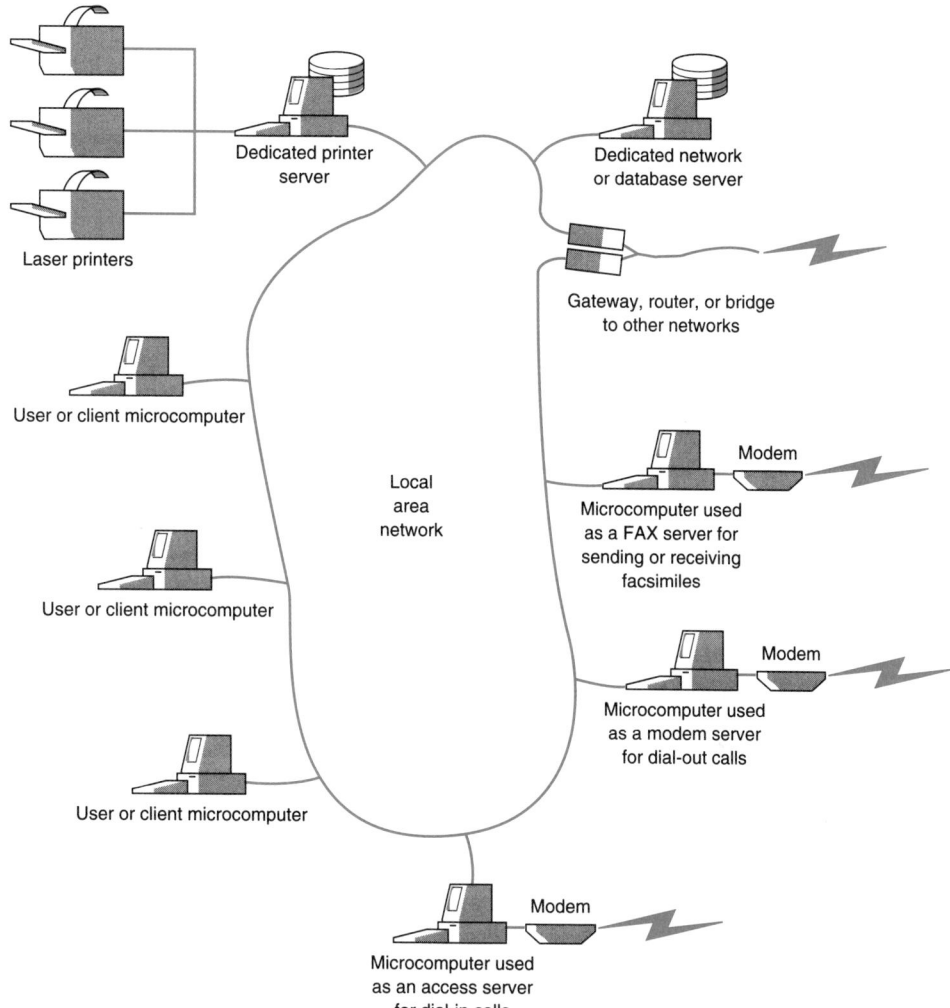

Figure 8-1   A typical LAN.

out is accomplished with a modem server. An access server connects to the LAN and retrieves applications from the network server's hard disk to run on its own CPU or to transfer files to the computer that dialed into the LAN. Callers dialing into an access server can check their e-mail, transfer files, print files, run application programs, or send faxes via the fax server. Access servers are ideal for database applications in which the amount of information moved is small and does not require high speed beyond the limited capabilities of regular voice grade telephone lines. (Remember that LANs typically provide data transmission rates of 1 to 20 Mbps, while telephone lines typically provide only 14.4 Kbps to 115.2 Kbps).

Peer-to-Peer Networks Because *peer-to-peer networks* do not require a dedicated server, any computer can function as both a user and a server, sharing its hard disk and printer with any other computer on the network. All computers run special network software that enables them to function both as a client and as a server. Authorized users can connect to any computer in the LAN that permits access and use their hard drives and printer as though they were physically attached to their own computers. Peer-to-peer networks are often slower than dedicated server networks because if you access a computer that is also being used by its owner, it slows down both the owner and the network.

In general, peer-to-peer LANs have less capability, support a more limited number of computers, provide less sophisticated software, and can prove more difficult to manage than dedicated server LANs. However, they are cheaper both in hardware and software. Peer-to-peer LANs are most appropriate for sharing resources in small LANs. Examples of peer-to-peer LANs include Artisoft's LANtastic, Novell's Netware Lite, and Windows for Workgroups.

Zero-Slot LANs The lowest level of capability for a LAN is the inexpensive *zero-slot LAN,* so called because they do not require a network interface circuit card; the zero-slot LAN adapter plug can be plugged into a serial or parallel port instead of taking up one of the computer's expansion slots. Zero-slot LANs cost from one-tenth to one-half the amount of more powerful dedicated server LANs.

Zero-slot LANs operate like peer-to-peer networks and provide limited capabilities such as file transfer, file sharing, printer sharing, and e-mail. The zero-slot LAN op-

Management Focus: LANs at Hallmark

Hallmark has turned the need to greet others into a $3 billion empire with operations in 100 countries. But while the company's cards make it easier for others to keep in touch, Hallmark's financial managers had less luck communicating. Management was struggling under time-consuming and unwieldy financial reporting process, because since 1992, Hallmark acquired 22 international subsidiaries, each with different financial information systems. Integrating their information with the rest of Hallmark was challenging.

To unify and streamline financial reporting, the greeting card giant undertook a massive re-engineering of its standard operating practices. In conjunction with its new information system, Hallmark implemented a client-server solution to bridge the gulf between the mainframe-based American corporate offices and the PC-based international offices.

Client-server LANs were installed at both the American corporate headquarters and the international headquarters. The LANs use Compaq computer servers running Microsoft LAN Manager, and connect a total of 120 Compaq PC clients. Comshare Commander consolidates data from multiple general ledgers, enables simpler financial analysis, and serves as a front end to Hallmark's old mainframe-based financial system.

The re-engineering has paid off in numerous ways: Hallmark has redesigned its financial statement, reduced the monthly book-closing time by 40 percent, and cleared the way for more timely and relevant information to be delivered to senior management worldwide.

Source: InfoWorld, December 19, 1994.

erating system works in conjunction with the computer's operating system. Installing a zero-slot LAN usually takes only a short time because it does not require a circuit card. They are typically able to handle up to 30 computers, which can be increased by connecting several zero-slot LANs together.

LAN COMPONENTS

There are five basic components to a LAN (see Figure 8-2). The first two are the client computer and the server (but see the section on peer-to-peer networks). These have been discussed in Chapter 4 and earlier in this chapter, and will not be discussed further. The other three components are: network interface cards, network cables and hubs, and network operating system.

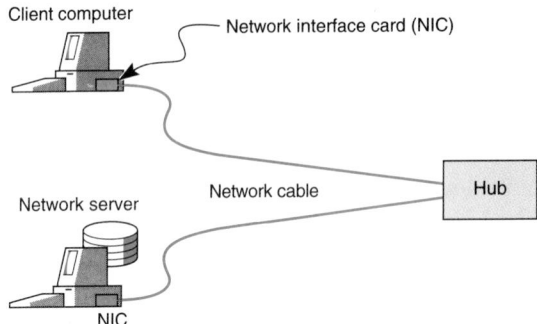

Figure 8-2   LAN Components.

Network Interface Cards

Most computers are not yet delivered with a built-in network interface. (The exception are Macintosh computers, which have a built-in network capability called AppleTalk.) As a result, one of the first steps when installing a LAN is to install a special *network interface card* (NIC). The NIC allows the computer to be physically connected to the network cable, which provides the physical layer connection among the computers in the network.

Most NICs are installed inside the computer. The computer must be physically opened and the NIC inserted into a slot on the computer's bus. A few computers, particularly laptops, have an NIC already installed, or a special port that enables networking cards to be installed without physically opening them (i.e., PCMCIA slots). Both trends reflect the growing importance of networking.

One type of NIC is designed to be installed externally on a computer's parallel or serial port, rather than internally in a slot. These NICs, called *pocket adapters* because they can fit in a shirt pocket, are primarily used for laptop computers that do not have built-in NICs or PCMCIA slots. They provide network connections that otherwise would be impossible. They are usually quite slow, however, due to the limitations in the way most computers manage their parallel and serial ports. In general, they provide a data transmission rate of less than 130 Kbps. A few computers with redesigned parallel ports and newer pocket adapters can provide data rates of up to 1 Mbps, which is still far less than traditional networks with internal NICs.

Network Cables and Hubs

Each computer must be physically connected by network cable to the other computers in the network. The selection of a LAN topology can be influenced greatly by the type of cable that already exists in the building where the LAN is to be installed. Just as

Technology Focus: Commonly Used Network Cable Standards

Name	Type	Data Rate (Mbps)	Distance (Meters)	Often Used by	Cost ($/foot)
Category 1*	UTP	1	90	Modem	.10
Category 2	UTP	4	90	Token Ring-4	.05
Category 3	UTP/STP	10	100	10BaseT Ethernet	.13
Category 4	UTP/STP	16	100	Token Ring-16	.18
Category 5	UTP/STP	100	200	100BaseT Ethernet**	.25
RG-58	Coax	10	185	10Base2 Ethernet	.30
RG-8	Coax	10	500	10Base5 Ethernet	.85
X3T9.5	Fiber	100	2000	FDDI**	1.00

*Category 1 is standard voice grade twisted pair, but can also be used to support low speed analog data transmission.
**100BaseT and FDDI are discussed in Chapter 10.

highways carry all kinds of traffic, the perfect cabling system also should be able to carry all kinds of electronic transmissions to all corners of the building.

Network Cable   Most LANs are formed with a blend of *unshielded twisted pair* (UTP) wires, *shielded twisted pair* (STP), coaxial cable, and fiber optic cable (although fiber optic cable is far more commonly used in backbone networks discussed in Chapter 10). You even can obtain wireless LANs that run on infrared or radio frequencies, eliminating the installation of cables. (Common cable standards are discussed in the technology focus box. We should add that these cable standards specify the minimum quality cable required; it is possible, for example, to use category 4 UTP for a 10BaseT ethernet.)

Many LANs use a combination of shielded and unshielded twisted pair. Although initially it appeared that twisted pair would not be able to meet long-term capacity and distance requirements, today this is one of the leading LAN cabling methodologies. Its low cost, the availability of shielded wiring that can handle higher transmission speeds, and the high data rates attainable through the use of new transmission methodologies make it very useful.

Coaxial cable is also commonly used. By definition, coaxial cable is shielded because its outer conductor is also a shield. Coax is physically larger than twisted pair, weighing anywhere from 20 to 90 pounds per 1000 feet, which can be detrimental in an overhead ceiling, especially if it collapses because of the cable's weight! Coax is also not very flexible, so it cannot be bent around sharp corners easily.

Fiber optic cable is even thinner than unshielded twisted pair and therefore takes far less space when cabled throughout a building. It also is much lighter, weighing less than 10 pounds per 1000 feet. Because of its high capacity, fiber optic cabling is perfect for backbone networks, although it is beginning to be used in LANs.

While most LANs use only one type of cable, it is possible to buy devices that permit different types of cable to be connected together. A *BALUN* (*BAL*anced *UN*balanced) is a small device about one-half inch in diameter and 3 inches long, which connects balanced twisted pair cabling with unbalanced coaxial cable. One end has a standard twisted pair connection and the other has a standard screw-in coaxial connector lead. Similar devices are available to connect fiber optic cable to twisted pair and coax, but are significantly larger and more expensive, because they must convert between electricity and light.

Network Hubs   Network hubs go by many names depending upon the type of network and the specific vendor, such as *concentrator, multistation access unit, transceiver,* or *repeater*. Network hubs serve two purposes. First, they provide an easy way to connect network cables. In general, network cables can be directly connected by splicing two cables together. For example, T-connectors are often used to connect coaxial cable but they leave little room for expansion; a technician must cut the cable and install a new connector to add a new connection (see Figure 8-3).

A better approach is to use a hub in any area in which the network might expand. A hub can be thought as a junction box, permitting new computers to be connected to the network as easily as plugging a power cord into an electrical socket (see Figure 8-4). Hubs are commonly available in 4-, 8-, and 16-port sizes, meaning that they pro-

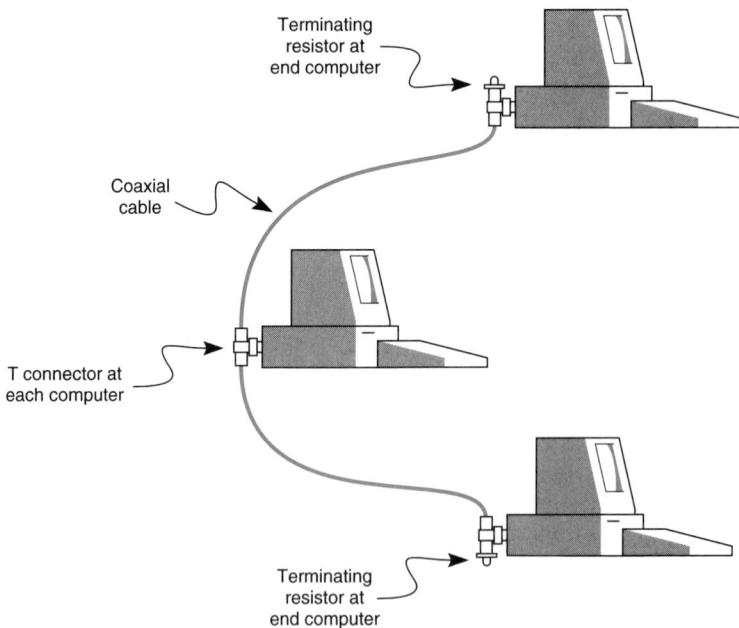

Figure 8-3   A three-station Ethernet LAN using coaxial cable and T-connectors.

Figure 8-4

vide anywhere from 4 to 16 ports into which network cables can be plugged. When no cables are plugged in, the signal bypasses the unused port. When a cable is plugged into a port, the signal travels down the cable as though it was directly connected to the cables attached to the hub. Some hubs also enable different types of cables to be connected and perform the necessary conversions (e.g., twisted pair to coaxial cable, coaxial cable to fiber optic).

Second, hubs act as repeaters or amplifiers. Signals can travel only so far in a network cable before they attenuate and can no longer be recognized (attenuation was discussed in Chapter 6). All LAN cables are rated for the maximum distance they can be used (see the technology focus box). Any LAN that spans more than these distances—and most LANs do—must use hubs with repeaters or amplifiers.

Some hubs are "smart" because they can detect and respond to network problems. For example, a "smart" hub could detect faulty transmissions from a failing network card, and disable the incoming port so that the card could not send any more messages that would disrupt the network. Many "smart" hubs go one step farther and alert the network manager about the problem and the action taken. With "smart" hubs, finding and fixing faults is much easier.

Network Cable Plans   In the early days of LANs, it was common practice to install network cable wherever it was convenient. Little long-term planning was done. Hubs were placed at random intervals to meet the needs of the few users and cable laid

Management Focus: Cable Problems at The University of Georgia

Like many organizations, the Terry College of Business at The University of Georgia is headquartered in a building built before the computer age. When LAN cabling was first installed in the early 1980s, no one foresaw the rapid expansion that was to come. Cables and hubs were installed piecemeal to support the needs of the handful of early users.

The network eventually grew far beyond the number of users it was designed to support. The network cable plan gradually became a complex, confusing, and inefficient mess of cables. There was no logical pattern for the cables, and there was no network cable plan. Worse still, no one knew where all the cables and hubs were physically located. Before a new user was added, a network technician had to open up a ceiling and crawl around to find a hub. Hopefully, the hub had a spare port to connect the new user, or else the technician would have to find another hub with an empty port.

To complicate matters even more, asbestos was discovered. Now network technicians could not open the ceiling and work on the cable unless asbestos precautions were taken. This meant calling in the University's asbestos team, and sealing off nearby offices. Installing a new user to the network (or fixing a network cable problem) now took two days and cost $2000.

The solution was obvious. In 1994, the University spent $400,000 to install new twisted pair cable to every office, and to install a new high speed fiber optic backbone network between network segments.

where it was convenient. The exact placement of the cables and hubs was often not documented, making future expansion more difficult—you had to find the cable and a hub before you could add a new user.

With today's explosion in LAN use, it is critical to plan for the effective installation and use of LAN cabling. The cheapest time to install network cable is during the construction of the building; adding cable to an existing building can cost significantly more. Indeed, the costs to install cable (i.e., paying those doing the installation and additional construction) are often as much as the cost of the cable itself, making it expensive to re-install the cable if the cable plan does not meet the organization's needs.

Most buildings under construction today have a separate LAN cable plan as they do for telephone cables and electrical cables. The same is true for older buildings in which new LAN cabling is being installed. Most cable plans are similar in style to electrical and telephone plans. Each floor has a telecommunications wiring closet that contains one or more network hubs. Cables are run from each room on the floor to this wiring closet. It is common to install 20 to 50 percent more cables than you actually need to make future expansion simple. Any reconfiguration or expansion can be done easily by adding a network hub and connecting the unused cables in the wiring closet.

Management Focus: Managing Network Cabling

You must consider a number of items when installing cables or when performing cable maintenance. You should:

- Perform a physical inventory of any existing cabling systems and document those findings in the network cable plan.

- Properly maintain the network cable plan. Always update cable documentation immediately upon installing or removing cable or hubs. Insist that any cabling contractor provide "as-built" plans that document where the cabling was actually placed, in case of minor differences from the construction plan.

- Establish a long-term plan for the evolution of the current cabling system to whatever cabling system will be in place in the future.

- Obtain a copy of the local city fire codes and follow them. For example, cables used in airways without conduit need to be plenum-certified (i.e., covered with a fire retardant jacket).

- Conceal all cable as much as possible to protect them from damage and for security reasons.

- Properly number and mark both ends of all cable installations as you install them. If a contractor installs cabling, always make a complete inspection to ensure that all cables are labeled.

This saves the difficulty and expense of attempting to locate network hubs and installing new cables.

Wireless LANs   *Wireless LANs* are an alternative method of "cabling" a local area network. They use the same protocols (ethernet, for example) as other LANs, but they transmit data through the air rather than through coaxial cable, twisted pair, or fiber optic cable. Most wireless LANs have a NIC that is installed in the computer which, in turn, is connected to an external infrared or radio transmitter. Some wireless LANs are wireless only between the hubs; the NICs are connected via traditional cabling to a network hub which contains the transmitter.

The primary advantage of a wireless LAN is the lack of wiring. In an old building where wiring is difficult and costs are extremely high, wireless LANs offer a low cost alternative. Wireless LANs are also being used increasingly with laptop computers, permitting new capabilities for mobile computing. When configured with a wireless network, a set of laptops becomes an effective way to provide a portable groupware configuration. The focus box describes another application.

Wireless LANs have two disadvantages. The first is the increased opportunity for noise to disrupt transmissions. The result is usually much slower data transmission rates than "wired" networks. Wireless networks usually provide data rates of only 1 to

Management Focus: AT&T Lets Wireless Users Roam

AT&T's WaveLAN is the most popular wireless LAN with more than a 50 percent market share. A WaveLAN NIC connects to a PCMCIA slot on laptop computers and provides a wireless radio connection up to 75 meters to a network hub.

WaveLAN also permits users to ''roam,'' move from one hub to another, while still maintaining a continuous network connection. This dramatically improves the potential applications for wireless networks.

Grandview Hospital in Dayton, Ohio, for example, has created a wireless network where medical workers carry laptop computers with WaveLAN. The hospital is totally covered by a series of WaveLAN hubs, so workers can be anywhere in the hospital and have access to medical information.

Source: LAN Times, October 17, 1994.

Management Focus: The Birth of Wireless Standards

The Portable Computer and Communications Association (PCCA) is a non-profit association whose mission is to establish common hardware, software, and network standards for portable computers. Since PCCA was established in 1992, membership has grown to more than 60 corporations, including AMD, RDIS, Compaq, Erricsson, Hewlett–Packard, IBM, Intel, McCaw Cellular, Microsoft, Motorola, PCSI, RAM, RIM, and Rockwell.

Today, we take the compatibility of wired modems for granted, since they all use the Hayes modem command set and work with all of the software on the market. However, this was a direct result of the PCCA Modem Standards Committee's first attempt for a de facto standard protocol for wired modems.

PCCA is now working to broaden the standards to include wireless transmission. It also plans to work with the FCC, the FAA, and the airlines to develop wireless standards for use in aircraft.

Open standards will guarantee that any product built to the PCCA modem standards will function properly. If hardware, software, and network vendors build to the PCCA standards, the results should yield transparent connectivity to the end user.

Source: Mobile Office, March 1995.

3 Mbps (although newer microwave-based wireless networks under development promise 100 Mbps data rates). A second disadvantage is the lack of security. Anyone near a wireless network can easily eavesdrop and potentially steal corporate secrets. The solution is to encrypt data before transmission, but this is not yet built into most wireless networks.

Network Operating System

The *network operating system* (NOS) is the software that controls the network. The NOS provides the software that performs the functions associated with the data link and the network layers, and must interact with the application software and the computer's own operating system. Every NOS provides two sets of software: one that runs on the network server(s), and one that runs on the network client(s). Most provide different versions of their client software that run on different types of computers, so that PC-DOS/Windows computers, for example, can function on the same network as Apple Macintoshes.

NOS Server Software   The NOS server software enables the file server, print server, or database server to operate. In addition to handling all the required network functions, it acts as the application software by executing the requests sent to it by the clients (e.g., copying a file from its hard disk and transferring it to the client, printing a file on the printer, executing a database request and sending the result to the client).

NOS server software typically replaces the normal operating system on the server (although some NOS server software runs in conjunction with the host operating system [e.g., IBM LAN sever]). In general, NOS that replace the existing operating system provide better performance and faster response time because they are optimized for their limited range of operations. The upcoming focus box introduces several common NOS.

NOS Client Software   The NOS software running at the client computers provides the data link layer and network layer. To work effectively with the application software, the NOS must also work together with the client's own operating system. Many operating systems were designed with networking in mind (e.g., UNIX). In this case, the integration of the NOS into the client operating system is simple.

Unfortunately, the most popular operating system for computers, DOS, was not designed to support networking. The solution to this is shown in Figure 8-5. Appli-

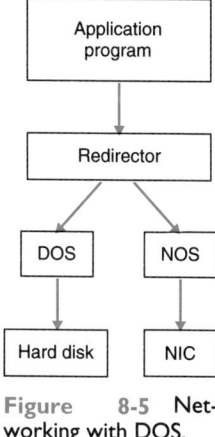

Figure   8-5   Networking with DOS.

Management Focus: Popular Network Operating Systems

The most popular network operating system in the world is the **Novell Netware** family of NOS, holding almost a 70 percent market share worldwide. Novell supports a wide variety of topologies, protocols, types of computers, and languages (e.g., English, French, and Japanese). It was one of the first NOS, and has consistently been the market leader in performance, but over the past few years, new Netware versions have not been as innovative as earlier ones. Novell supports 802.3, 802.4, and 802.5 protocols (described later in this chapter) and a host of others. Chapter 14 provides a brief introduction to Novell Netware.

The second most popular NOS is **Microsoft's LAN Manager** and its successors, **Windows for Workgroups** and **Windows NT**. This group of NOS holds a 10 percent worldwide market share and is rapidly growing; about one-third of network managers surveyed in 1995 said they were planning to buy NT (just under 40 percent said they were planning to buy Netware). NT is a 32-bit NOS, which mean it is inherently faster than 16-bit NOS like Novell. Ultimate performance, of course, depends on hard disk management, an area where Novell still appears to have the edge. Given Microsoft's past track record and strength in application software, some analysts expect sales of Windows NT to overtake those of Novell by 1997. Windows NT supports 802.3, and 802.5 protocols, among others.

The third most popular NOS is **Artisoft's LANtastic** (a peer-to-peer NOS) with just under a 10 percent market share. LANtastic has long been the market leader in peer-to-peer NOS, providing many features commonly found in server-based NOS at a much lower cost. Several newer companies now offer competing peer-to-peer NOS, but LANtastic continues to prosper. LANtastic supports ethernet, and its own proprietary protocol.

The fourth most popular NOS is **IBM's LAN Server** with a 7 percent market share. IBM was slow to develop a competent NOS, but the current version of LAN server, which runs under OS/2, supports a variety of industry standard protocols (e.g., 802.5), as well as IBM's proprietary SNA network protocols.

There are many other NOS available, however, these four together account for more than 90 percent of all NOS sold in the world. If you're in a large organization (or even a small one), chances are you'll be using one them.

---

cation programs use DOS to perform many functions, such as reading or writing to files. DOS can only access files that exist on the local computer's disk drives; it cannot access any files on the network server. Any requests to access files on the network server must be processed by the NOS client software.

NETBIOS (NETwork Basic Input/Output System) is an extension to DOS that enables it to communicate over a network. NETBIOS provides a program called Redirector that sits on top of DOS. All requests to read or write files or any other function that could be network related (e.g., printing) are examined by the redirector. Requests that access the computer's local hard disks or printers are passed to DOS for processing. Any requests that access the network hard disks or printers are passed to the NOS for processing.

One problem is that these requests must be in a format that the NOS can understand. Each NOS is produced by a different vendor, and therefore may use different formats. One approach would be to write the application software to generate requests in the format required by one particular NOS (but of course, the application software could not work with a different NOS). A better solution should be obvious at this point.

The solution is to define a set of standards—called *application program interfaces* (API)—for use at the application layer in the network. Any application software that uses a particular API format to issue requests can communicate with any NOS that uses the same API. NETBIOS is one of the more popular APIs for DOS. Other operating systems also use APIs to format requests from application software to the NOS.

Network Profiles   A *network profile* specifies what resources on each server are available for network use by other computers and which devices or people are allowed what access to the network. The network profile normally is configured when the network is established, and remains in place until someone makes a change. In a LAN, the server hard disk may have various attributes that can or cannot be accessed by a specific network user. Furthermore, a specific password may be required to grant network access to the resources.

If a device such as a hard disk on one of the network's computers is not included on the network profile, it cannot be used by another computer on the network. For example, if you have a hard disk (C) on your computer and your computer is connected to this LAN but the hard disk is not included on the network profile assignment list, then no other computer can access it.

In addition to profiling disks and printers, you must build a *user profile* for each person who uses the LAN in order to add some security. Each device and each user is assigned various access codes and only those users who login with the correct code can use a specific device. Most LANs keep audit files to track who uses which resource. Security is discussed in Chapter 13.

ETHERNET (IEEE 802.3)

Almost 50 percent of all LANs in the world use ethernet. The Ethernet LAN standard was originally developed by DEC, Xerox, and Intel. It has since become a standard formalized by the Institute of Electrical and Electronics Engineers (IEEE) as IEEE 802.3.

Topology

Ethernet uses a bus topology. All computers are connected to one circuit running the length of the network (see Figure 8-6). The top part of this figure shows the *logical topology*. All messages from any computer flow onto the central cable and to all com-

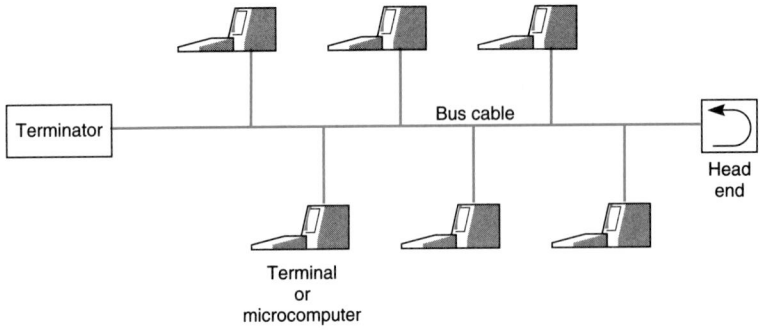

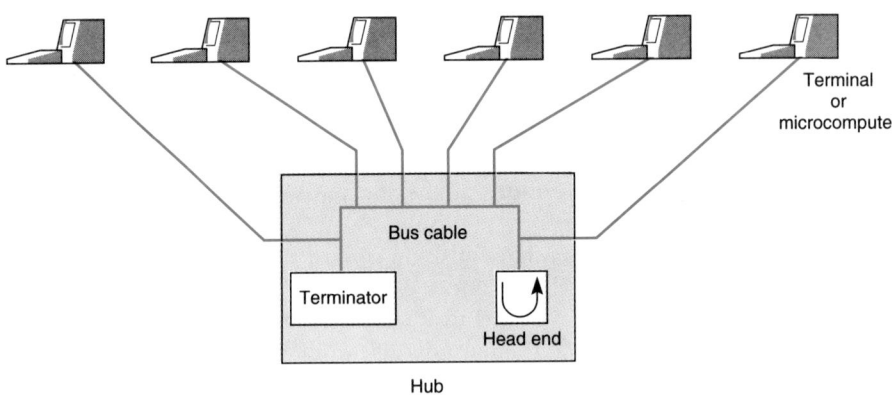

Figure 8-6 Ethernet topology.

puters on the bus. Computers receive messages intended for all computers, but only process those addressed to themselves.

The term *bus* implies a high speed circuit and a limited distance between the computers, such as within one building. These distances can be increased by using a hub, which is a repeater. The bottom part of Figure 8-6 shows the *physical topology* of an ethernet LAN when a hub is used. From the outside, an ethernet LAN *appears* to be a star, because all cables flow into the central hub. Nonetheless, it is really a bus.

Most ethernet LANs span sufficient distance to require several hubs. In this case, the hubs are connected via cable in the same manner as any other connection in the network (see Figure 8-7).

Media Access Control

When several computers share the same communication circuit, it is important to control their access to the media. If two computers on the same circuit transmit at the

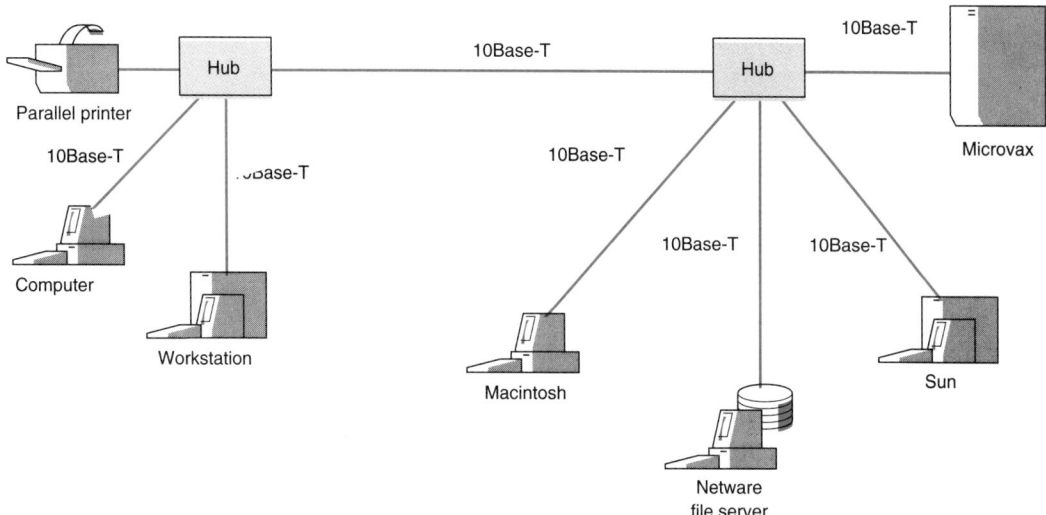

Figure 8-7   An example of an ethernet LAN with two hubs.

same time, their transmissions will become garbled. These "collisions" must be prevented, or if they are permitted to occur, there must be a way to recover from them. This is called media access control.

Ethernet uses a contention-based media access control technique called Carrier Sense Multiple Access with Collision Detection (CSMA/CD). CSMA/CD, like all contention-based techniques, is very simple in concept: wait until the bus is free and then transmit. Computers wait until no other devices are transmitting, and then transmit their data. As an analogy, suppose you are talking with a small group of friends (four or five people). As the discussion progresses, each person tries to "grab the floor" when the previous speaker finishes. Usually, the other members of the group yield to the first person who jumps in right after the previous speaker.

Ethernet's CSMA/CD protocol can be termed "ordered chaos." As long as no other computer attempts to transmit at the same time, everything is fine. However, it is possible that two computers located some distance from one another can both listen to the circuit, find it empty, and begin to transmit simultaneously. This simultaneous transmission is called a *collision*. The two messages collide and destroy each other.

The solution to this is to listen while transmitting, better known as *collision detection* (CD). If the NIC detects any signal other than its own, it presumes that a collision has occurred, and sends a jamming signal. All computers stop transmitting and wait for the circuit to become free before trying to retransmit. The problem is that the computers which caused the collision could attempt to retransmit at the same time. To prevent this, each computer waits a random amount of time after the colliding message disappears before attempting to retransmit. Chances are both computers will choose a different random amount of time and one will begin to transmit before the other,

---

Technical Focus: Installing a LAN

Buying a LAN usually is easier than getting it to work. Before you buy, recognize that the LAN implementation includes cabling the building, installing hardware and software, testing the LAN, training the users, establishing network security, managing the system, supervising the ongoing maintenance of the LAN, and planning future enhancements.

During the LAN's implementation, you must either install the cabling yourself or contract for someone to pull the wires through the building to each computer location. Do not be surprised if the installation of the cabling costs far more than the purchase of the cable itself.

Hardware installation means setting up each computer or workstation, along with any centralized items such as the server. Software installation means installing the NOS onto the server (if you have one) and onto all user computers.

By the end of software installation, you should have the cabling in place, the user computers connected, and the software up and running. Testing can begin. Testing is the process that verifies all the LAN features and equipment are working properly.

At this point, you must establish general operating policies, and the levels of security to be provided. This includes what files and directories are public (accessible to everyone), who is authorized to put files on the server, and how to prevent the spread of viruses.

Training begins simultaneously with testing. Users must be trained in how to use the new LAN software commands so they can send files to a shared printer and transfer or modify files on a file server.

---

thus preventing a second collision. However, if another collision occurs, the computers wait a random amount of time before trying again. This does not eliminate collisions completely, but it reduces them to manageable proportions.

Types of Ethernet

There are many different types of ethernet, but all are classified as either baseband or broadband. *Baseband* uses digital signaling. It treats the cable as one single channel, so it can carry only a single transmission at any one moment. *Broadband* uses analog signaling and splits the cable into many different channels (using frequency division multiplexing) so more than one transmission can occupy the LAN cable at the same time; thus we can intermix voice, data, and image signals on the same network. Baseband is less complex, and usually is less expensive because it does not need modulation devices (i.e., modems) built in the NICs.

The original ethernet specification was a 10 Mbps data rate using baseband signaling on thick coaxial cable, called *10Base5* or "Thick Ethernet." Today, thin coaxial cable (*10Base2*) is rapidly replacing the original thick coax because it is considerably cheaper and easier to work with, although it is limited to 185 meters between hubs. The 10Base2 standard is often called "Thin Ethernet" or "Cheapnet."

Another standard type of ethernet is *1Base5* (1 Mbps to a maximum distance of 500 meters, using a star topology). The 1Base5 standard, called "Starlan" after the AT&T product that introduced it, is rarely used because of its low data transmission rate.

10BaseT is the most commonly used type of ethernet. The name means 10 million bits per second, baseband, and the "T" means it uses *twisted pair wiring* (actually unshielded twisted pair). It was the 10BaseT standard that revolutionized ethernet, and made it the most popular type of LAN in the world. The extremely low cost of 10BaseT made it very inexpensive compared to its foremost competitor, IEEE 802.5 token ring, which is discussed next.

Broadband ethernet also is available as a *10Broad36* network. Again, 10Broad36 means 10 Mbps, broadband, with a maximum distance of 3600 meters. The 10Broad36 standard is most commonly used in backbone networks (discussed in Chapter 10). Several new types of ethernet that transmit at 100 Mbps have been developed. These are also discussed in detail in Chapter 10.

TOKEN RING (IEEE 802.5)

The second most popular type of LAN is token ring. Almost 40 percent of all LANs worldwide are token ring LANs. Token ring was originally developed by IBM, and has since been standardized by IEEE as IEEE 802.5.

Topology

As the name suggests, token ring uses a *ring topology*. A ring topology connects all computers on the LAN in one closed loop circuit. The top half of Figure 8-8 shows a the logical topology. All messages pass to each computer in turn. Computers receive messages intended for all computers, but only process those addressed to themselves; they transmit other messages to the next computer in the ring.

The bottom part of Figure 8-8 shows the *physical topology* of a token ring LAN when a hub is used. From the outside, a token ring LAN *appears* to be a star—because all cables flow into the central hub—but it is truly a ring, with messages passing from one computer to the next. Most token ring LANs span sufficient distance to require several hubs. In this case, the hubs are connected via two cables like any other connection in the network.

Now compare the bottom of Figure 8-6 with the bottom of Figure 8-8. From the outside, token ring and ethernet LANs look almost identical. They have the same physical topology (a star), but really use a very different topology internally.

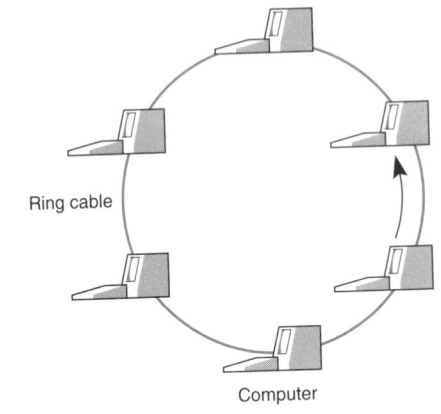

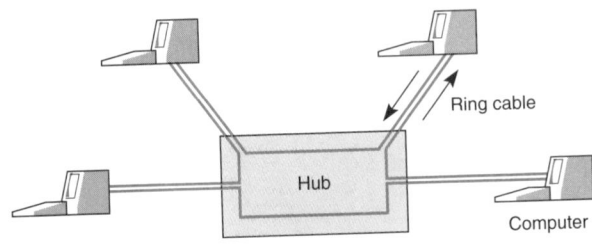

Figure 8-8   Token ring topology.

Media Access Control

All computers in a token ring LAN share the same common circuit, so it is essential that access to the media be controlled by the data link layer. Token ring uses a controlled-access technique called token passing.

The *token passing* access method can be compared to a relay race in which the track belongs to you as long as you have the baton. When your run is finished, you hand the baton to the next runner. In a token-passing network, the baton is the *token,* a short electronic message that is generated when the network is started.

The token moves between the computers on the network in a predetermined sequence (much like roll call polling). A computer with a message to transmit waits until it receives what is called a *free token;* that is, a token available for use. The computer then changes the free token into a *busy token,* attaches its message to it, and retransmits it on the circuit to the next computer in the sequence. Should that computer want to transmit a message, it must wait, because the token is busy. It simply forwards the message with the busy token to the next computer in sequence. When the token and message arrives at the destination computer, it copies the data in the message, sets the acknowledgment (ACK) bit (or NAK if there was an error in transmission), and the message continues around the ring, making a complete round trip back to the transmitting computer. The transmitting computer then removes the message and inserts a new free token on the ring (see Figure 8-9). Most token passing methods restrict the maximum number of messages that a computer can transmit before issuing a free token and permit other computers to send messages so that one computer cannot monopolize the circuit.

One problem with token-passing protocols is dealing with "lost" tokens. Suppose the computer that has the token crashes before it can retransmit it, or suppose a computer that has just transmitted a message (and marked the token as busy) crashes

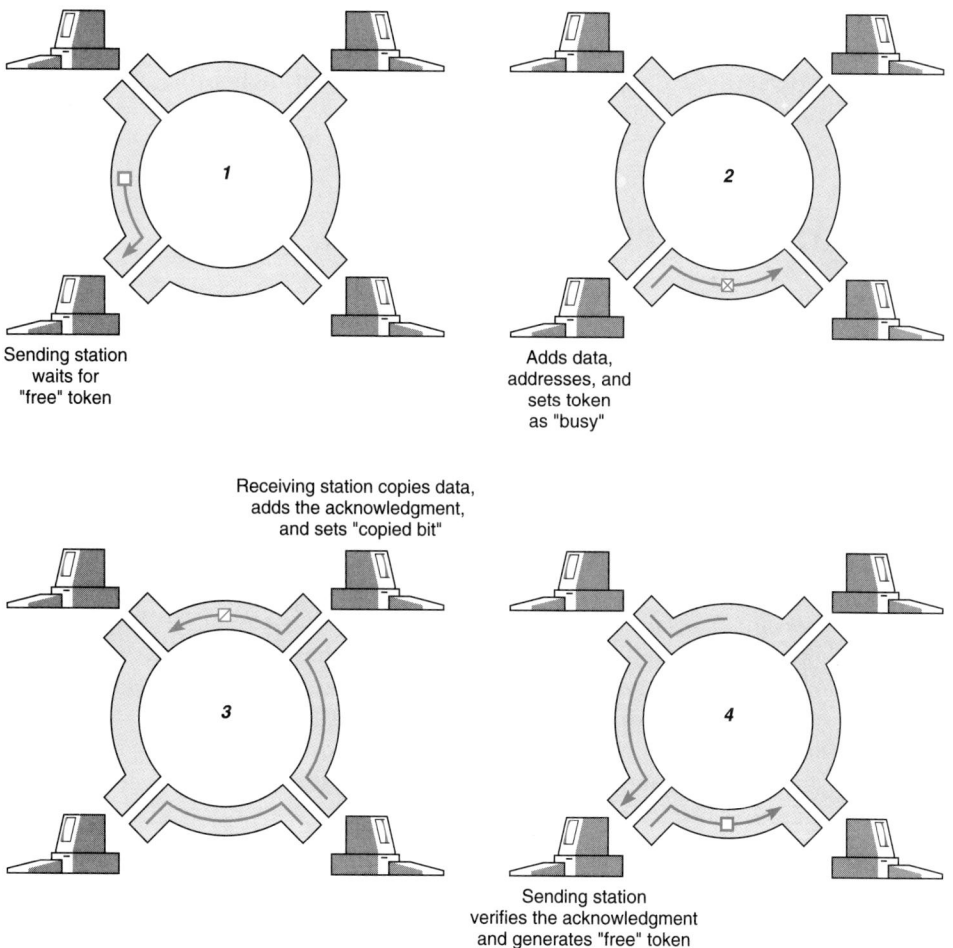

Figure 8-9   Message transfer with token ring.

before it can receive an acknowledgment and create a free token. In this case, the token is "lost" because no other computer on the network can use the token. Unless some action is taken, the entire network will cease to function.

The solution is to designate one computer in the network to be the *token monitor*. If no token circulates through the network for a certain length of time or if a busy token circulates too often, the token monitor will create a new free token (and destroy the busy token if necessary). Unfortunately, the problem is not that simple, because the computer that crashed (causing the lost token) could be the token monitor itself. Therefore, there is a backup token monitor to ensure the first token monitor is operating; it steps in if the primary token monitor malfunctions.

Types of Token Ring

There are two common types of token ring. The original token ring was Token-ring-4, operating at 4 Mbps over unshielded twisted pair (UTP) . The newer token ring is Token-ring-16, which operates at 16 Mbps over higher quality UTP cable.

OTHER TYPES OF LANS

Manufacturing Automated Protocol (IEEE 802.4)

An IEEE 802.4 *token-bus network* is a token passing network that uses a bus topology. While all computers on the bus receive each message, they only process messages addressed to themselves. Media access control is done by token passing. The network maintains a table of addresses for each computer. The address bears no resemblance to where a computer is located physically on the bus network, but is simply the order in which a computer receives the token. A computer requiring the token frequently is listed several times in the table so it can receive the token more often.

When a transmission is complete, the token passes from the computer that just finished its transmission to the computer having the next address in the table. When the last addressed computer in the network has completed its work, it sends the token back to repeat the process. In a token bus, each computer receives the token, inserts the information it wishes to send, and sends the token to its destination. At its destination, that computer copies the information, acknowledges it, and sends it back to the sending computer, which then passes the token on to the next computer for transmission.

The Manufacturing Automated Protocol (MAP) developed by General Motors in the early 1980s uses IEEE 802.4. It was developed before hardware and software using the OSI model were common. The goal was to provide an open, non-proprietary network architecture that could be used by many different companies buying from many different vendors (at the time, this was in sharp contrast to IBM's SNA architecture). There are several types of MAP that provide data transmission rates of 1 Mbps,

Management Focus: The Hidden Costs of LANs

Over the last few years, the costs of LANs have steadily decreased. Today ethernet NICs can be purchased for between $50 and $150, and low-cost NOS are available for about $75 to $150 per computer. Network cable is less than 20 cents a foot and hubs cost less than $250. On the surface, building a LAN appears cheap, about $250 to $350 per computer.

This is misleading, because there are many hidden costs that surface only after you begin installing and operating the LAN. Experienced LAN managers plan on at least $1000 per computer for a LAN installation. The cost of installing cabling alone in a large multi-floor building, for example, can cost from $200 to $2000 per computer. Often overlooked or underestimated LAN installation costs include:

- LAN software: network operating system software.
- Application software: multiple copies of application software.
- Servers: computers, plus upgraded memory, and fast large hard disks.
- LAN hardware: hubs, cables, NICs, and uninterruptible power supplies.
- Printers: printers, cables, and print servers.

An even greater hidden cost is that for network management (which is discussed in Chapter 12). A recent survey found the average *annual* network management cost was $1270 per computer—*more than the initial installation cost!* On average, it costs more to manage a LAN each year than to initially install one.

The amount of energy and money devoted to LAN operations depends on the complexity of the LAN. A part-time network supervisor probably can manage a small network used primarily for word processing. A large network with 100 users dispersed throughout a multi-story building requires a full-time LAN manager with top-notch technical and programming skills. As a rule of thumb, it requires one half of a full-time equivalent (FTE) person for administering a LAN with 15 computers, one and a half FTEs for 50 stations, and two FTEs for 100 stations. Other operating costs include:

- Network administration: cost of the network administrator and staff who add and delete users, answer questions, set priorities, and so on.
- Maintenance: installation of upgrades, fixing cables or hardware "glitches," and correcting incompatibilities between network software and application programs.
- Training: specialized training for the network administrator and all network users.
- Security: costs related to network security such as changing passwords regularly, or installing specialized security hardware and software.
- Backup: backing up the network server daily. Also may include purchase of specialized backup hardware and software.
- Future growth: planning for and purchasing additional LAN resources.

5 Mbps, 10 Mbps, and 20 Mbps. MAP is still used in the automotive sector, but its popularity is declining now that vendor-independent standard protocols such as ethernet and token ring have become common.

Arcnet

Arcnet (Attached Resource Computing Network) is another popular peer-to-peer LAN. Arcnet was developed by Datapoint Corporation in 1977 in response to the need for a low-cost PC LAN. Arcnet is a baseband token-passing bus or star architecture, but does not conform to IEEE 802.4. Its low cost has made Arcnet very popular—so much so that ANSI is expected to designate Arcnet as ANSI standard 878.1. The Arcnet Trade Association (ATA), which is accredited by ANSI to set standards, plans to seek approval of the International Organization for Standardization to make Arcnet a worldwide standard after ANSI approves it.

Arcnet originally transmitted over a coaxial cable at 2.5 Mbps. Transmission over twisted wire pairs or fiber optic cable was added later. The newer Arcnet Plus transmits at 20 Mbps over coaxial cable. When Arcnet has a bus configuration, the maximum distance between computers is 1000 feet.

AppleTalk

All Macintosh computers have a built-in network feature called *AppleTalk* to interconnect its computers. This is a nonstandard set of protocols that perform most of the functions in the seven-layer OSI model. It works with the Apple cabling system known as *LocalTalk*. LocalTalk transmits at 230 Kbps, it has a 1000-foot cable length, and it supports up to 32 computers. AppleTalk was a major innovation when it was first introduced because it automatically provided networking, and did so very simply.

Like ethernet, LocalTalk uses a carrier sense multiple access (CSMA) scheme to put packets on the network. It does not rely on collision detection, but instead reserves space on the media as a collision avoidance procedure (CSMA/CA). *LocalTalk link access protocol* (LLAP) sends out a small 3-byte packet to signal its intent to put data on the network. This packet tells the other Macintoshes to wait until the data from the first Mac have been sent before attempting to send their data. If collisions occur, they happen between these preliminary 3-byte packets instead of between the data packets.

The major problems with AppleTalk are its very slow data transmission rate and its use of non-standard protocols. Now most networked Apple computers use ethernet.

IMPROVING LAN PERFORMANCE

When LANs had only a few users, performance was usually very good. Today, however, when most computers in an organization are on LANs, performance can be a problem. Performance is usually expressed in terms of throughput: how can we permit the largest amount of user data to be transmitted through the network at the least cost? In this section, we discuss how to improve throughput. We focus on dedicated server networks, because they are the most commonly used type of LANs, but many of these concepts also apply to peer-to-peer networks.

A LAN is only as fast as its slowest component. Every LAN has a *bottleneck*, a narrow point in the network that limits the number of messages that can be processed. The only way to improve performance is to find the bottleneck, and eliminate it by upgrading whichever component was causing the limitation; upgrading any other part of the LAN will have no impact on performance. Once you do this, of course, some other part of the network will become the new bottleneck, so the game of improving performance is one of moving the bottleneck.

Generally speaking, the bottleneck will lie in one of two places. The first is the computers attached to the network. In this case, the client computers have no difficulty sending requests to the network server, but the server lacks sufficient capacity to process all the requests it receives in a timely manner. The second location is the network circuit. The network server can easily process all the client requests it receives, but the physical network circuit lacks enough capacity to transmit all the requests to server.

So, to improve performance, you must locate the bottleneck. To do so, you simply watch the utilization of the server during periods of poor performance. If the server utilization is high (e.g., 60 to 100 percent), then the bottleneck is the server; it cannot process all the requests it receives in a timely manner. If the server utilization is low during periods of poor performance (e.g., 10 to 40 percent), then the problem lies with the network circuit; the circuit cannot transmit requests to the server as quickly as necessary. Things become more difficult if utilization is in the mid-range (e.g., 40 to 60 percent). This suggests that the bottleneck may shift between the server and the circuit depending upon the type of request, and suggests that both should be upgraded to provide the best performance.

Now, we will focus attention on ways to improve the server and the circuit to remove bottlenecks. These actions address only the supply side of the equation; that is, increasing the capacity of the LAN as a whole. The other way to reduce performance problems is to attack the demand side: reduce the amount of network use by the clients, which we also discuss.

Improving Server Performance

Improving server performance can be approached from two directions simultaneously: software and hardware.

Software   The NOS is the primary software-based approach to improving network performance. Some NOS are faster than others, so replacing the NOS with a faster one will improve performance.

Because a network server primarily reads and writes information to and from disk, the best NOS are highly tuned to improve the disk access speed on the server. Two commonly used techniques are disk caching and disk elevatoring. *Disk caching* stores commonly used data in memory. Because memory is much faster than disk, performance is greatly improved. The problem, of course, is that there is never enough memory to store all the data on the disk. But even if only 20 to 30 percent of the data needed are present in memory, disk caching can improve performance significantly.

Disk elevatoring refers to the order in which data are accessed on the hard disk. Hard disks are designed with a read/write head that must physically move to sections of the disk. Requests from clients to read or write information can be processed in the order they are received, but this is very inefficient. A hard disk is much like an office building with the read/write head like an elevator that moves between floors (i.e., sections on the disk). Processing read/write requests in the order received may mean the read/ write head goes to floor 30 (i.e., section 30) then floor 55, then floor 40, then floor 60, and so on. Elevators never move to floors in the order in which the buttons are pressed because they would have to travel past floors and go back to them. Instead they arrange a group of requests to minimize the distance they must travel. Disk elevatoring works the same way. Requests are constantly grouped and processed so that the read/write head travels the minimum distance, thus significantly improving server speed.

Each NOS provides a number of software settings to fine tune network performance. Depending upon the number, size, and type of messages and requests in your LAN, different settings can have a significant effect on performance. The specific settings differ by NOS, but often include things such as the amount of memory used for disk caches, the number of simultaneously open files, the amount of buffer space, and so on.

Hardware   One obvious solution if your network server is overloaded is to buy a second server (or more). Each server is then dedicated to supporting one set of application software (e.g., one handles e-mail, another handles the financial database, and another processes customer records). The bottleneck can be broken by carefully identifying the demands each major application software package places on the server, and allocating them to different servers.

Sometimes, however, most of the demand on the server is produced by one application that cannot be split across several servers. In this case, the server itself must be upgraded. The first place to start is with the server's CPU. Faster CPUs mean better performance. If you are still using an old 486-based computer, this may be the answer; you probably need at least a pentium-based computer to function well as a LAN server. Clock speed also matters; the faster the better. Most computers today also come with CPU-cache (a very fast memory module directly connected to the CPU). Increasing the cache will increase CPU performance.

A second bottleneck is the amount of memory in the server. Increasing the amount of memory increases the probability that disk caching will work, thus increasing performance.

A third bottleneck is the number and speed of the hard disks in the server. The primary function of the LAN server is to process requests for information on its disks. Slow hard disk(s) give slow network performance. The obvious solution is to buy the fastest disk drive possible. Even more important, however, is the number of hard disks. Each computer hard disk has only one read/write head, meaning that all requests must go through this one device. By using several smaller disks rather than one larger disk (e.g., four 550 megabyte disks rather than one 2 gigabyte disk), you now have four read/write heads, each of which can be used simultaneously, dramatically improving throughput. A special type of disk drive called *RAID*(Redundant Array of Inexpensive Disks) builds on this concept, and is typically used in applications requiring very fast processing of large volumes of data, such as multi-media. Of course, RAID is more expensive than traditional disk drives, but costs have been shrinking. RAID can also provide fault tolerance, which is discussed in Chapter 13.

A fourth bottleneck is the network interface card itself. Simply put, some network interface cards (NICs) are faster than others. Some NICs provide built-in CPUs to perform some of the network functions usually handled by the server (much like front end processors in mainframe networks). Others provide memory and cache to improve the access time to and from the network.

Several vendors sell special purpose network servers that are optimized to provide extremely fast performance. Many of these provide RAID and use *Symetric Multi-Processing* (SMP) that enables one server to use up to 16 CPUs. Each of these CPUs may be an Intel chip such as 486 or Pentium, or may be RISC-based. Such servers provide excellent performance, but cost more than a standard microcomputer (often $20,000 to $50,000).

Improving Circuit Capacity

Improving the capacity of the circuit means increasing the volume of simultaneous messages the circuit can transmit from network clients to the server(s). One obvious approach is simply to buy a bigger circuit. For example, if you are now using 4 Mbps token ring, upgrading to 16 Mbps will improve capacity. Two other basic approaches are to re-examine the LAN protocol used (i.e., ethernet versus token ring), and to segment the network.

Ethernet versus Token Ring   Token ring performance should be about 60 percent better than ethernet, because token ring provides a 16 Mbps data transmission rate compared to ethernet's 10 Mbps. Unfortunately, it is more complicated than this. The question of whether token ring or ethernet provides the best performance really comes down to how the two manage the available transmission rates; in other words, the media access control approaches they use: token passing versus CSMA/CD.

In general, contention approaches such as CSMA/CD work better than controlled approaches such as token passing for small networks that have low usage. In this case, each computer can transmit when necessary without waiting for permission. Since usage is low, there is little chance of a collision.

The opposite is true for large networks with high usage: token passing works better. In high volume networks, many computers want to transmit and the probability of a collision using CSMA/CD is high. Collisions are very costly in terms of throughput because they waste circuit capacity during the collision and require both computers to retransmit later. Controlled access prevents collisions and makes more efficient use of the circuit. Tests of various ethernet LANs show that when they are heavily used, the actual data throughput drops by almost 50 percent to about 5 Mbps, due to collisions. In contrast, tests of token ring networks show that even when they are heavily used, the actual throughput is almost the entire 16 Mbps. So, when throughput performance matters, token ring is about three times as fast as ethernet.

A second performance consideration is response time. Generally speaking, response time in token ring networks is more consistent than that in ethernet networks. As already noted, response time for token passing may be worse when the circuit is little used (because the token is passed to all computers in turn). However, response time generally does not increase as rapidly in token ring networks as traffic increases (see Figure 8-10). The key to selecting the fastest protocol is to find the cross-over point between token ring and ethernet.

There are limits on how long a computer can transmit in token ring networks, so that no one monopolizes the network. In ethernet networks, there is a greater chance that one computer could monopolize the network. Response time in token ring networks is therefore more consistent and predictable.

So why is ethernet so popular? Cost is always a factor. In general, 10BaseT ethernet cables, NICs, and hubs cost about 20 to 40 percent less than their token ring counterparts.

Network Segmentation If there is more traffic on a LAN than the network circuit and media access protocol can handle, the solution is divide the LAN into several smaller segments. Breaking a network into smaller parts is called *network segmentation*. By carefully identifying how much each computer contributes to the demand on the server, and carefully spreading those computers to different network segments, the network bottleneck can often be broken.

Most servers can support up to as many as 16 separate networks or network segments, simply by adding one NIC into the server for each network. As the number of NICs in the server increase, however, the server spends more of its processing capacity monitoring and managing the NICs, and has less capacity left to process client requests. Most experts recommend no more than three or four NICs per server. There are two ways to create more network segments: one is to use more servers, each dedicated to one or more segments; and the other is to use a backbone network to connect different segments. Backbone networks are discussed in Chapter 10.

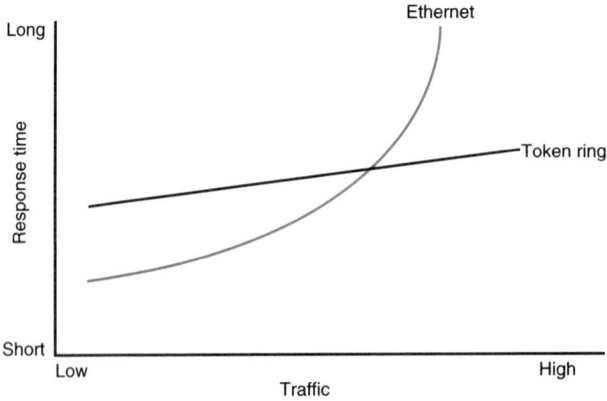

Figure 8-10 Response times in ethernet versus token ring.

Reducing Network Demand

Upgrading the server hardware and software, choosing a different LAN protocol, or segmenting the LAN are all strategies to increase network capacity. Performance also can be improved by attempting to reduce the demand on the network.

One way to reduce network demand is to move files to client computers. Heavily used software packages that continually access and load modules from the network can place unusually heavy demands on the network. While user data and messages are often only a few kilobytes in size, today's software packages can be many megabytes in size. Placing even one or two such applications on client computers can greatly improve network performance (although this can create other problems, such as increasing the difficulty in upgrading to new versions of the software).

Another way is to increase the use of disk caching software on the client machines in order to reduce the client's need to access disk files stored on the server. SMARTDRV is a common disk caching software for PCs.

Because the demand on most LANs is uneven, network performance can be improved by attempting to move user demands from peak times to off-peak times. For example, early morning and after lunch are often busy times when people check their e-mail. Telling network users about the peak times, and encouraging them to change their habits may help; however, in practice, it is often difficult to get users to change. Nonetheless, finding one application that places a large demand on the network and moving it can have a significant impact (e.g., printing several thousand customer records after midnight).

SELECTING A LAN

Selecting a LAN for your organization is not easy. The marketplace is crowded with vendors, all claiming their products are the best. To complicate matters, the small, simple LAN you start with today may turn into a large multi-floor, multi-building, or enterprise-wide network in the future. You should start by asking some basic questions: how many users are expected, how much data will be stored and transmitted, how easy it will be to add workstations, what cabling is needed, whose software should be selected, and how much security is needed. The design steps in Chapter 11 will help in LAN selection, as will the key issues for selecting LANs that are examined in the following discussion. These issues are summarized in Figure 8-11. One cautionary note before we proceed. Many high speed network technologies developed for backbone networks are finding their way into LANs, replacing traditional ethernet and token rings. In selecting a LAN, you should also consider these new technologies.

One of the first issues that must be addressed is the protocol—ethernet or token ring—and whether the system will be *baseband* (one message at a time) or *broadband* (multiple messages paths). These considerations are critical in determining the LAN's growth potential. Token ring offers some benefits, but new backbone technologies discussed in the next chapter suggest that ethernet may have some additional benefits.

Protocol	LAN management software
Baseband/Broadband	Future growth
Configuration/topology	Internetworking
Cabling	Security features
Wireless	Printer features
Network operating system	Electronic mail/voice mail
Vendor service and support	Backup and recovery
Reliability	Electrical power protection
Ease of use	Vendor contracts
Performance	On-site spares
Vendor application support	Documentation
Application systems	Training
Number of computers	Outside consultant
Number of users	Legal issues
Servers	Employee use policies
Distance between computers	Network manager
Client computer hardware	
Network interface cards	

Figure 8-11   Factors in selecting a LAN.

Network *topology* is another key decision. Is it best to have a star, bus, or ring? The choice is influenced by what cable scheme, protocol, and vendor is picked. Both bus and ring topologies physically look the same. One option is to use a bus topology between floors and a ring or bus on each floor.

Then you must decide which *cabling* to use: unshielded twisted pair, shielded twisted pair, coaxial cable, or fiber optics. Remember, the cost of installing the cables through the building may be greater than the cost of the cable itself, so many companies choose high speed twisted pair cable. While it is more expensive than the lower speed cable they need now, it provides an easy upgrade path when they decide to use higher speed LANs. Conversely, a *wireless LAN* may be more cost-effective.

The *network operating system* is another critical consideration because it must work together with the various computer operating systems, computers, and other LAN hardware, as well as interfacing with application programs and host mainframe. Perhaps the most important aspect of the NOS is how easy it is to manage (network management is discussed in Chapter 12). Novell Netware has a 70 percent market share, so there is a good chance that it will be one of the NOS considered.

At this point, you also must take into account the *reliability* of the vendor, NOS, and the hardware. You should evaluate the level of *vendor service and support.* Other details pertaining to software evaluation include its *ease of use,* its *performance,* and the availability and kind of *vendor application support.* A review of the *application systems* is vital to be sure they can run on the proposed LAN. In general, it is safer to purchase all network components from one vendor—because, this way, blame cannot be shifted to someone else if something goes wrong.

Management Focus: What You Should Expect from a NOS

There are seven fundamental network functions that a NOS can provide:

- Network directory: an integrated database that provides access to all users, information, and resources located anywhere in the network.
- Messaging: automatic transfer of data and messages using a variety of industry standard applications and APIs (e.g., e-mail).
- Network management: a single point of control for all network resources that provides easy to use graphical tools.
- Security: a variety of network security features including auditing and encryption.
- Routing support: the ability to use of a variety of network layer routing protocols such as TCP/IP and SPX/IPX to simplify internetworking.
- File services: data compression and the ability to store files from many different types of computers (e.g., DOS, Macintosh, UNIX).
- Print services: ability for users to simply direct their print requests to any authorized printer anywhere in the network.

Source: Novell, *Guide to Networking,* 1995.

The maximum *number of computers* probably will be an issue in the future, and it is one you must plan for now. Today, you may develop a LAN with only a dozen computers, but will the LAN be able to grow to meet the demand five years from now? Many companies install more cable and hubs with more ports then they need to simplify future growth.

In addition, the *number of users* must be considered. How many people might use this LAN? Remember, you may have several users at a single computer. Even though the number of computers may not increase, the added number of users may prompt server overload. This might mean that the LAN operating system software is unable to handle user requirements and specific business needs such as database retrievals, processing application programs, e-mail, and file transfer.

Another critical decision is the *server.* You must decide whether you are going to use dedicated file server(s) and, if so, how many. The server(s) may be standard computers, or ones designed specifically as network servers. You must also decide whether to have print servers, access/modem servers, fax servers, network servers, or database servers.

The *distance between computers* is important. In general, LAN segments are limited to 100 to 1000 feet between each computer, 3000 feet from the network server to the computer, and up to 7000 feet in end-to-end length. (This is not absolute because you always can add repeaters or amplifiers to extend the medium for several thousands more feet; however, there are often limits on the number of repeaters or amplifiers in one LAN circuit.)

The *client computer hardware* is another factor. You already may have many of the computers to be connected to the LAN. In this case, you must determine whether each will function properly with the LAN. Remember that one vendor's LAN software or hardware (network server) may not handle another vendor's hardware or software protocols. Still another hardware consideration is whether the required *network interface cards* can plug into the equipment you already own. Are there enough slots? Do you need full- or half-length slots?

Determine whether it is possible to actively manage the LAN and all of the related network elements with *LAN management software*. For example, you must decide if third-party software, such as menu support, memory management, word processing, and spreadsheets, work with the LAN's operating system. Chapter 12 discusses network management.

Future growth should be a major point. You must determine whether the LAN can grow to meet the changing needs of the organization's application systems, geographic locations, interconnectivity, users, and hardware requirements. Is there enough built-in flexibility and modularity for the LAN to survive if or when *LAN standards* change?

You must determine whether the LAN is going to *internetwork* with another corporate LAN or backbone network, the organization's host mainframe, or some of the public dial-up networks outside of the organization. The question to ask is, what devices are needed to connect our network with the corporate host mainframe or other LANs within the organization? These are discussed in more detail in the next two chapters.

Security features must be installed to protect each user's data. Remember, each user may have data that differ in sensitivity or risk. Another security consideration is whether users should have computers without any disk storage devices attached. Consider virus protection, passwords, and file security controls, all of which are discussed in Chapter 13.

Various *print features* must be made available at the shared printer. Will some users need special purpose printers? Both *e-mail* and *voice mail* are big features on LANs, although you may opt not to put voice transmission on the LAN.

Proper *backup and recovery* procedures must be provided. The server disk certainly must be backed up, and recovery features for each user's disk files must be provided. *Backup electrical power* or surge/sag protection may be required on both the electric utility power lines and any connecting telephone lines. What is being done to protect against static electricity? *Vendor contracts* should require quick vendor response when service support is needed. *On-site spares* for critical hardware should be procured.

Proper written *documentation* should be provided for all the hardware, software, users, and so forth. *Training* must be considered. You must examine both the cost of the training and the time required for each user to attend these training sessions. Another consideration is who will do the training; perhaps an *outside consultant* may be required.

Legal issues, such as purchasing the proper software licenses and formulating policies on employee copying of software, must be addressed. *Employee use policies* should prohibit the use of personal diskettes and software on the organization's LANs. Such policies help prevent the spread of computer viruses and the theft of privileged information. These policies also should address the connection of employee-owned hardware to the organization's LANs. A decision should be made about whether there will be a *network manager* to run and administer the LAN.

· ·

Summary

Why Use a LAN?   The two basic reasons for developing a LAN are information sharing and resource sharing. Information sharing refers to business needs that require users to access the same data files, exchange information via e-mail, or search the Internet for information, as discussed in Chapter 2. Resource sharing refers to one computer sharing a hardware device (e.g., printer) or software package with other computers on the network. The main benefit of resource sharing is cost savings, while the main benefit of information sharing is improved decision making.

Types of LANs   A dedicated server LAN can connect with almost any other network, handle very large databases, has a dedicated network server, and use sophisticated LAN software. Moreover, high-end dedicated server LANs can be interconnected easily to form enterprise-wide networks or, in some cases, replace the host mainframe central computer. Four common types of dedicated server LANS are file servers, database servers, print servers, and communication servers. All computers on a peer-to-peer LAN run special network software that enable them to function both as a client and as a server. Zero-slot LANs operate like peer-to-peer networks and provide limited capabilities such as file transfer, file sharing, printer sharing, and e-mail.

LAN Components   The Network Interface Card (NIC) enables the computer to be physically connected to the network cable, which provides the physical layer connection among the computers in the network. Most LANs are formed with a combination of unshielded twisted pair (UTP) wires, shielded twisted pair (STP), coaxial cable, and fiber optic cable. Network hubs provide an easy way to connect network cables and act as repeaters or amplifiers. Most new buildings built today have a separate LAN cable plan as they do for telephone cables and electrical cables. Wireless LANs use the same protocols (ethernet, for example) as other LANs, but they transmit data through the air rather than by cable. The network operating system (NOS) is the software that performs the functions associated with the data link and the network layers, and interacts with the application software and the computer's own operating system. Every NOS provides two sets of software: one that runs on the network server(s), and one that runs on the network client(s). A network profile specifies what resources on each server are available for network use by other computers and which devices or people are allowed what access to the network.

Ethernet (IEEE 802.3)   Ethernet is the most commonly used LAN in the world, accounting for almost 50 percent of all LANs. Ethernet uses a bus topology and a contention-based technique media access technique called Carrier Sense Multiple Access with Collision Detection (CSMA/CD). There are many different types of ethernet that use different network cabling (e.g., 10Base2, 10Base5, 10BaseT, and 10Broad36).

Token Ring (IEEE 802.5)   Token ring is the second most popular type of LAN, with almost 40 percent of the worldwide market. Token ring uses a ring topology with a controlled-access technique called token passing.

Other Common LANs   The manufacturing automated protocol (MAP) uses IEEE 802.4, a token passing network that uses a bus topology. MAP, found primarily in the automotive sector, is declining is use. Arcnet (Attached Resource Computing Network) is a popular peer-to-peer LANs. Arcnet is a baseband token passing bus or star architecture, but does not conform to the IEEE 802.4. Macintosh computers have a built-in network feature called AppleTalk, which is very slow and uses non-standard protocols, so its use is rapidly declining.

Improving LAN Performance   Every LAN has a bottleneck, a narrow point in the network that limits the number of messages that can be processed. Generally speaking, the bottleneck will lie either in the network server or the network circuit. Server performance can be improved with a faster NOS that provides better disk caching and disk elevatoring, by buying more servers and spreading applications among them, or by upgrading the server's CPU, memory, NIC, and the speed and number of its hard disks. Circuit capacity can be improved by using token ring rather than ethernet, and by segmenting the network into several separate LANs. Overall LAN performance also can be improved by reducing the demand for the LAN by moving files off the LAN, using disk caching on the client computers, and by shifting the user's routines.

Selecting a LAN   There are many issues to be considered in selecting a LAN including: protocol (ethernet vs. token ring), configuration/topology, network operating system, vendor service and support, application systems, number and type of servers, client computers and users, and network interface cards.

Key Terms

Access server	Cabling	Dedicated server
AppleTalk	Cable plan	Disk caching
Application program interface (API)	Cheapnet	Disk elevatoring
	Client computer	Distance between computers
Arcnet	Coaxial cable	
Backbone network (BN)	Collision	Electrical power protection
Backup and recovery	Collision avoidance (CA)	Ethernet
BALUN	Collision detection (CD)	Facsimile server
Baseband	Communications server	Fiber optic cable
Bottleneck	Concentrator	File server
Broadband	CSMA/CA	Free token
Bus topology	CSMA/CD	Hub
Busy token	Database server	IEEE 802 standards

Information sharing
Internetworking
LAN management software
LAN metering software
Legal issues
LocalTalk link access
  protocol (LLAP)
Logical topology
Manufacturing automated
  protocol (MAP)
Media-access control
  (MAC) protocol
Modem server
Multistation access unit
  (MAU)
NETBIOS
Network interface card
  (NIC)
Network operating system
  (NOS)
Network profile

Network segmentation
Network server
PCMCIA slot
Peer-to-peer networks
Physical topology
Print server
Pocket adapter
Redundant array of
  inexpensive disks
  (RAID)
Repeater
Resource sharing
Ring topology
Shielded twisted pair
  (STP)
Software audit
Software Publishers
  Association (SPA)
Thick ethernet
Thin ethernet

Token
Token-bus network
Token monitor
Token passing
Token priority
Token-ring network
Topology
Transceiver
Twisted pair wiring
Unshielded twisted pair
  (UTP)
User computer
User profile
Zero-slot LAN
Wireless LAN
1Base5
10BaseT
10Base2
10Base5
10Broad36

Selected References

1. Berline, Gary, and Ed Perratore. "Portable, Affordable, Secure: Wireless LANs," *PC Magazine,* vol. 11, no. 3, February 11, 1992, 291+.
2. Chappell, Laura, *Netware LAN Analysis.* San Jose, CA: Novell Press, 1993.
3. Derfler, Frank J., Jr. "Connectivity Simplified: An Introduction to the Ways of Networking," *PC Magazine,* vol. 11, no. 6, March 31, 1992, 251+.
4. Derfler, Frank J., Jr., et al. "LAN Fundamentals Part 2: Low-Cost LANs Grow in Features and Performance," *PC Magazine,* vol. 11, no. 7, April 14, 1992, 299+.
5. Herron, D. Keith, and Joanne T. Witt. "LAN Software Licensing Poses Problems," *LAN Times,* vol. 9, no. 6, April 6, 1992, 45–46. (Part 1 of two-part article.)
6. Herron, D. Keith, and Joanne T. Witt. "LAN Software Licensing Poses Problems," *LAN Times,* vol. 9, no. 7, April 20, 1992, 45–46. (Part 2 of two-part article.)
7. *LAN Magazine.* Published monthly by Miller Freeman, Inc., 600 Harrison Street, San Francisco, CA 94107, 1976 to present.
8. Lowe, Doug, *Networking for Dummies.* San Mateo, CA: IDG Books, 1994.
9. Mathias, Craig J. "Wireless LANs: The Next Wave," *Data Communications,* vol. 21, no. 5, March 21, 1992, 83–87.
10. *Network World,* "Server Searching," January 30, 1995, 33–38.
11. Sloan, John P., and Ann Drinan, eds. *Handbook of Local Area Networks.* Boston: Auerbach Publishers, 1991.
12. Stephenson, Peter. "The Peer Connection," *LAN Magazine,* vol. 6, no. 6, June 1991, 121+.
13. *Smart LAN Performance Test.* A software package available for $50 from Innovative Software, Attn: LAN Test, 9875 Widmer Road, Lenexa, KS 66215 (1-800-331-1763).

Questions/Problems

1. Define local area network.
2. What are the distinguishing features of a LAN?
3. What are two reasons for developing LANs?
4. Describe the distinctions made between the different types of LANs.
5. In some LANs, most of the computers can talk only with the server computer, but others use no server. What are these two approaches called?
6. What is required to make DOS work on a network?
7. Some inexpensive local area networks are not "true" LANs. How do these differ from true LANs?
8. Discuss the legal issue of using single-computer license software on networks.
9. What is the difference between using a word processor on a single computer and using one on a LAN?
10. What are the commonly used topologies of a local area network?
11. How does baseband differ from broadband?
12. Briefly describe CSMA, CD, and CA.
13. Why should CSMA/CD networks be built so that no more than 50 percent of their capacity is dedicated to actual network traffic?
14. Define the terms 1Base5, 10Base2, 10Base5, 10Broad36, and 10BaseT.
15. What two methods of LAN access are supported by the IEEE 802 committee?
16. How does a token passing network operate?
17. Should you select a network because of its protocol or its performance characteristics? Explain.
18. What factors limit or promote network availability and capability more than any other?
19. It is said that hooking some computers together with a cable does not make a network. Why?
20. Assume you want to install a local area network using IBM-compatible equipment. What must you know about the computers' operating systems?
21. What factors influence the selection of LAN topology?
22. It is possible to have a radio-based LAN. Why would you want or not want it?
23. What cable media do LANs normally use?
24. What is the purpose of a BALUN? (See Balanced and Unbalanced in the Glossary.)
25. Assume you want to install a LAN but are concerned about its cost. Realizing there are both inexpensive and expensive LANs, what features should you compare to help in making a decision?
26. Discuss what makes LAN selection so difficult.
27. This chapter discusses a number of key issues that must be considered when selecting a LAN. Explain six of them.
28. What is ethernet? How does it work?
29. What is token ring? How does it work?
30. How many transmission channels are on a broadband LAN? On a baseband LAN?
31. Name two popular LAN protocols.
32. What is data grade twisted pair wiring?

33. Discuss which of the key issues for selecting a LAN would be the most important at your college, university, or company.
34. Describe four important concerns when installing a LAN.
35. What is the function of LAN metering software?
36. Why is it important to control illegal copies of software on a LAN?
37. What is the difference between thick ethernet and cheapnet?
38. What are the two types of token passing networks and how are they different?
39. Describe Arcnet.
40. Describe MAP.
41. Describe Appletalk.
42. What are the three levels of capability into which LANs typically fall?
43. What types of LANs use servers?
44. What is the most important characteristic of a server?
45. Name at least three types of servers.
46. Discuss the primary advantages and disadvantage of wireless LANs.
47. Discuss why it is important for organizations to enforce policies restricting use of employee-owned hardware and software and unauthorized copies of software.
48. What is a bottleneck and how can you locate one?
49. How can you improve network performance?
50. What are disk caching and disk elevatoring and why are they useful?
51. Why does network segmentation improve LAN performance?

NEXT DAY AIR SERVICE CUMULATIVE CASE STUDY

See appendix at end of book

CHAPTER NINE

METROPOLITAN AND WIDE AREA NETWORKS

Most organizations do not build their own medium or long distance communication circuits, preferring instead to rent or lease them from common carriers. Therefore, this chapter focuses on the telecommunications *services* offered by common carriers for use in MANs and WANs, not the underlying technology that the carriers use to provide them, because network managers purchase services, not technologies. We begin by discussing the common carriers, tariffs, and deregulation in the United States. We analyze the types of MAN and WAN services—dialed circuits, dedicated circuits, switched circuits, and packet switched networks—that are available from these carriers. We conclude by discussing how to improve MAN and WAN performance, and how to select services.

Objectives

- Understand the role of common carriers in organizational MANs and WANs,
- Become familiar with the common carriers and the nature of competition in the United States,
- Understand the four basic categories of MAN and WAN circuits,
- Become familiar with dialed circuit services,
- Become familiar with dedicated circuit services,
- Become familiar with switched circuit services,
- Become familiar with packet network services,
- Understand how to improve MAN and WAN performance,
- Become familiar with several factors in selecting MAN and WAN services.

Chapter Outline

Introduction
    Types of Communication Services
Telephone Network
    Common Carriers, Tariffs, and Deregulation
    Communications in the United States
Dialed Circuit Services
    Direct Distance Dialing (DD)
    AT&T Megacom Wide Area Telephone Service (WATS)
    AT&T MEGACOM
    DIAL-IT 900
Dedicated Circuit Services
    Voice Grade Channels
    Wideband Analog Services
    Digital Services
    T Carrier Circuits
    Synchronous Optical Network (SONET)
    Satellite Services
Switched Circuit Services
    Integrated Services Digital Network (ISDN)
    Switched Multimegabit Data Service (SMDS)
Packet Switched Networks
    Packetizing
    Packet Transmission
    Public Packet Switched Networks
    Cellular Digital Packet Networks
    Frame Relay
    Asynchronous Transfer Mode (ATM)
    Public Data Networks
    Software Defined Networks (Virtual Networks)
Improving MAN/WAN Performance
    Improving Computer Performance
    Improving Circuit Capacity
    Reducing Network Demand
Selecting MAN/WAN Services
Summary

INTRODUCTION

Metropolitan area networks (MANs) typically span from 3 to 30 miles and connect backbone networks (BNs) and LANs. MANs also provide dial-in and dial-out capability to LANs, BNs, and mainframes. Wide area networks (WANs) connect BNs and MANs across longer distances, often hundreds or thousands of miles.

The communication media used in MANs and WANs were described in Chapter 4 (e.g., twisted pair, coaxial cable, fiber optics, microwave, satellite, cellular, infrared). Some organizations build their own metropolitan and wide are networks using these media, but most do not. Most organizations cannot afford to lay long stretches of cable, build microwave towers, or lease satellites. Instead, most rent or lease circuits from common carriers such as AT&T, MCI, BellSouth, PACTEL, or NYNEX. As a customer, you do not actually lease cables per se; you simply lease circuits that provide certain transmission characteristics. The carrier decides whether it will use twisted pair, coaxial, fiber optics, etc. for your circuits.

A *communication facility* is the medium that carries voice, data, or image transmissions from one point to another. Even though there are separate data and voice communication facilities, technology is evolving toward a single facility that can handle voice, data, and image communications. The most prominent examples of this are Integrated Services Digital Network (ISDN) and T carriers, both of which will be described later in this chapter.

Types of Communication Services

Once the various media are assembled to form communication facilities, the common carriers offer them to the public as packages of *communication services.* An organization that wants to develop a voice or data communication network will select from a variety of these services supplied by AT&T, MCI, US Sprint, GTE, one of the seven regional Bell operating companies, or one of the other common carriers. Each of the following sections describes selected services from the viewpoint of the network user or designer, but we will skip the detailed technical specifications because the organizations that use them have little need to know, and little ability to specify which will be used.

Communication services are categorized by the way organizations pay for and control them. *Private circuit services* (also called *dedicated circuits* or *leased lines*) are dedicated point-to-point circuits leased for a fixed monthly fee based on the distance between the two nodes. Private circuits are available for the exclusive use by the organization twenty-four hours a day, seven days a week. They are so much at the lessee's disposal that one might think the circuits were owned by the organization, even though the organization generally cannot choose whether they are wire pairs, microwave, coaxial cable, or optical fiber.

Charges for *measured use services* are based on how much the system is used. For example, charges for direct dialed services, such as a call from your home telephone, are based on the duration of the conversation (minutes), distance (miles) of the call, and the carrier's rate structures (tariff). Charges for packet switched services are calculated on a per minute or per packet basis. Wide Area Telephone Service (WATS) has a fixed monthly fee for a fixed number of hours of circuit usage. If the allotted time is exceeded, another per hour rate is charged.

It is helpful to understand the distinction between a *leased circuit* and a *measured use circuit.* If you lease a circuit from San Francisco to Los Angeles, it is one unbroken path. In other words, this leased circuit is wired around any switching equipment at telephone company central offices. By contrast, a measured use dial-up circuit goes through all the switching equipment in the telephone company central office; every time a call is placed this way, a new circuit path is established.

Communication services are categorized into four basic groups based on the types of service they offer. A *dialed circuit* is exactly that; a person simply uses a modem to make a regular dialed telephone call from one point to another through the telephone network. Dialed services are typically only used for low speed, low volume data transmission.

A *dedicated circuit* is a point-to-point circuit that connects two offices; the circuit is made available for the exclusive use of the leasing organization, which pays a monthly lease fee and has these circuits dedicated for its sole use.

A *switched circuit* is one in which the organization establishes network connection points at a variety of locations and uses the carrier's network to make temporary (switched) connections between the locations as needed. Usage charges are typically based either on the *time* the network is utilized or on the *volume* of data transmitted.

A *packet network* works very much like a switched circuit, except that it is dedicated to the transmission of data. The user breaks data transmission into pre-defined packets that conform to the protocols of the packet networks. The organization is charged only on its usage of the network. Billings are based on the *volume* of data packets transmitted. Using switched circuits or packet switched networks relieves the user of network design problems, most network operations tasks, maintenance and troubleshooting, and other technical operations that are required when private dedicated circuits are chosen.

THE TELEPHONE NETWORK

Common Carriers, Tariffs, and Deregulation

A *common carrier* is a government-regulated private company that sells or leases communication services and facilities to the public. Common carriers are profit-oriented, and their primary products are communication circuits and related services for voice, data, and image transmissions. Because this marketplace has been deregulated in the United States, common carriers now supply a much broader range of computer-based services, such as the manufacturing and marketing of microcomputers, specialized communication hardware, software, and computer operations offered from the telephone company's switching centers. Remember, *deregulation* simply means that these common carriers can enter into other types of businesses instead of offering only communication circuits. They still are regulated on the prices they can charge for their communication circuit services, but not on their other businesses.

The biggest of the more than 1200 common carriers in the United States and Canada are AT&T, the seven regional Bell operating companies (RBOCs), Bell Canada, MCI Communications, US Sprint, and General Telephone and Electronics (GTE). Most other carriers are small and offer communication facilities to a very small segment of the population.

Tariffs   A *tariff* is the schedule of rates (prices) and description of services to be received when a particular type of communication service is purchased or leased. The circuits are leased, but hardware may be either leased or purchased. The best example is the price structure for home telephones and the description of what is provided for the basic monthly fee. A monthly fee allows you to be connected to the dial-up telephone network; you must either buy the phone or rent one at an additional price.

Tariffs are filed with the appropriate federal and state regulatory agency. The best known regulatory agency is the *Federal Communications Commission* (FCC), a federal government agency that regulates interstate and international communications to and from the United States. Every common carrier engaging in interstate or international communications is under its jurisdiction and subject to its regulations.

Each state has its own *public utilities commission* (PUC) to regulate intrastate communications. Although the federal government is continuing its deregulation of common carriers, not all PUCs are following the same course.

A common carrier wanting to sell communication services must have its services approved. To do so, it must file basic information with either the FCC or the state PUC and provide details about its offered services, the proposed charges, and so on. These documents, or tariffs, are the basis of the contract between the common carrier and the user of that common carrier's communication service (see the box on sources of tariff information).

We also use *tariff* in another way. The FCC publishes many numbered tariffs, or rulings, that the common carriers must follow. Two of the more controversial are Tariff 12 and Tariff 15. *Tariff 12* relates specifically to custom-designed networks. For the first time, common carriers are permitted to offer special pricing to an individual organization by filing a "custom" Tariff 12, dealing only with that one organization. This tariff allows large users of data communication services to bid for customized packages of voice and data services at large discounts. The contracts generally last for three to five years. In effect, this is similar to the discounting a merchandiser receives if it goes to a manufacturer and obtains a special discount if it buys in large quantities. Tariff 12 also allows common carriers to enter into a facilities management operation so they can implement and manage an organization's entire communication requirements.

Tariff 15 permits AT&T to single out certain customers to offer them discounted service prices in response to another competitor's offer. Tariff 15 allows AT&T to match, but not beat, competitors' prices for communication services (circuits). Not surprisingly, the various common carriers and the FCC are constantly in disputes over these tariffs.

Management Focus: Sources of Tariff Information

Teleresource Service

Bell Communications Research
Bellcore Customer Service
60 New England Ave.
Piscataway, NJ 08854
201-669-2000
A service of the Bellcore Federal
Regulatory Resource Center. Compiles
and reviews FCC filings, rulings, and
other sources of information. Provides
daily updates to clients.

International Transcript Services, Inc.

2100 M St., N.W.
Washington, D.C. 20037
202-857-3800
Provides FCC document retrieval and
copying services.

Fair Press Services

Division of Washington Information
Group, Ltd.
P.O. Box 19352
20th Street Station
Washington, D.C. 20036
202-463-7323
Offers daily delivery of 43 categories of
FCC documents.

Lynx Technologies, Inc.

P.O. Box 268
Little Falls, NJ 07424
201-256-7200
Provides a range of in-depth tariff
information, including tariffs between
the United States and other countries,
within foreign countries, and from
country to country overseas.

**Center for Communications
Management Information**

11300 Rockville Pike
Rockville, MD 20852
301-816-8950
Provides access to CCMI tariff analysts
and other staff who interpret tariffs and
explain their intricacies to users.

**Telecommunications Information
Services, Inc.**

9 La Crue St.
Concordville, PA 19331
215-558-1770
Provides tariff information, as well as
custom research and analysis of tariffs.

Tele-Tech Services

Division of Telecommunication Systems
Technology, Inc.
P.O. Box 757
McAfee, NJ 07428
201-827-4421
Provides virtually all intrastate and
interstate tariffs.

Valucom, Inc.

501 Church St., N.E., Suite 303
Vienna, VA 22180
703-255-0700
Provides tariff information, custom
research and analysis, and online
database and tariff services.

Deregulation   Although there are many similarities in the way data communication activities have evolved in the United States and in Europe, there also are many differences. One of the primary differences is that the data communication industry in the United States operates as a series of private companies that are regulated by the government, whereas in Europe and many other countries of the world, the PTTs (postal telephone and telegraph services) are government monopolies that own, control, and sell all voice and data communication services.

If the industry were deregulated as in the United States, it may be more innovative, cost effective, and able to develop new services faster. On the other hand, if the industry were a regulated monopoly, as in many countries, it may be overburdened because it supports other government agencies (such as postal services) that drain its resources. Such a situation generally fosters an agency that is uneconomical and not very innovative. Other differences might stem from the fact that government-owned monopolies may be based on pressures created by unemployment, protection of industrial and technical markets, political considerations, national defense considerations, and cultural or social traits within a specific country. Europe's many geographical, political, and economic differences probably account for the reason that the European PTTs are more sensitive than the United States to the need for international standards.

All countries have either a government regulatory agency to control privately run communication services and prices (a *regulation situation*), or are themselves the sole supplier of communication services (a *monopoly situation*). For example, Germany's Deutschen Bundepost and France's Postes Telephonique et Telegraphique are the monopoly suppliers of communication services in those countries. In South America, the federal governments are the sole suppliers of communication services, regardless of whether the service is voice or data, but this is changing.

Like the United States, Canada has deregulated the communication environment and regulates only communication services and prices through its Canadian Radio-Television and Telecommunications Commission (CRTC). The Canadian CRTC is similar to the FCC in the United States. Mexico has deregulated Telefonos de Mexico, attracting billions of dollars of investment capital for new fiber optic networks—yet many Mexican towns still lack reliable telephone service. In the United Kingdom, the Post Office Commission formerly provided voice and data communication services. Until recently, the British Post Office was a government monopoly that handled both mail and telecommunication services. Then it became a private company, and now the British government regulates communications rather than being the monopoly supplier. Japan and Australia also now only regulate communications. After massive deregulation of Telecom Australia's monopoly, Australia only regulates communications rather than being the sole supplier. Netherlands' monopoly powers have been severely restricted, but it remains halfway between being a monopoly and a deregulated communication environment.

In a monopoly, private businesses cannot use communication circuits and telecommunication equipment unless they have been either manufactured, sold, or approved by the monopoly government agency. This severely limits the growth of the country's businesses and reduces the country's economic growth.

Management Focus: South America Has Promise for the Diligent

Privatization of telephone services in Latin America offers big opportunities for investors and a rapid path to modernization for countries struggling with low telecommunications quality, low penetration, and a lack of resources and technical skill to make any substantial improvements. Latin America is the only place left in the world where you can earn a 50 to 100 percent return on your investment.

The trend towards privatization has brought two shifts in government thinking. First, they have begun to recognize that a modern telecommunications infrastructure is necessary for the economic development of their countries, and are thinking about the most efficient way to upgrade it. Second, they are moving away from centralized government control to private enterprise solutions, which is not easy because most government telephone companies are social institutions first and businesses second.

The question of how to use investment funds also may be a problem. In many cities, the basic telephone infrastructure is collapsing; new local loops need to be added immediately. At the same time, some businesses are demanding enhanced services such as ISDN and videoconferencing.

Privatization and investment is merely the first step in building a quality telecommunications infrastructure. It does not address accelerating growth in the infrastructure, but it is necessary for a country to compete in the global marketplace.

Source: Telephony, November 23, 1992.

In a regulated situation, businesses can use communication circuits from competing common carriers and communication hardware from many different vendors. Regulation occurs by controlling the prices common carriers charge for their services. In addition, the common carriers restrict the communication industry by requiring communication equipment manufacturers to meet various technical standards or specifications on the type of signals allowed to be sent over the country's communication circuits. For example, modem manufacturers must transmit signals that are within certain specified limits if they are to be approved for use in the United States. In reality, this is a protective measure to ensure that one manufacturer's equipment does not harm another's or, especially, the communication circuits offered by various common carriers.

Communications in the United States

In the United States, 90 percent of the telephone system used to be run by AT&T. During the last few years of deregulation, the 22 telephone companies owned by AT&T, and AT&T itself, were essentially divided in two parts. The individual phone companies continued to supply local telephone services to your home or business, and AT&T handled long distance telephone services.

Regional Bell Operating Companies (RBOCs)   The 22 individual telephone companies originally owned by AT&T were consolidated into seven *regional Bell operating companies* (RBOCs). Figure 9-1 shows how the country was divided, gives the name of each of the seven companies, and lists the original telephone companies that were grouped together to form each new RBOC.

Because of deregulation, the RBOCs now offer services as well as the communication circuits. Each of the seven companies has marketing agreements with manufacturers of office automation equipment, multiplexers, switchboards (PBXs), modems, cellular mobile telephone equipment, and so forth. The next stage in deregulation will allow these companies to manufacture their own equipment and computers. Of course, this will place them in direct competition with other computer manufacturers such as IBM and Digital Equipment Corporation.

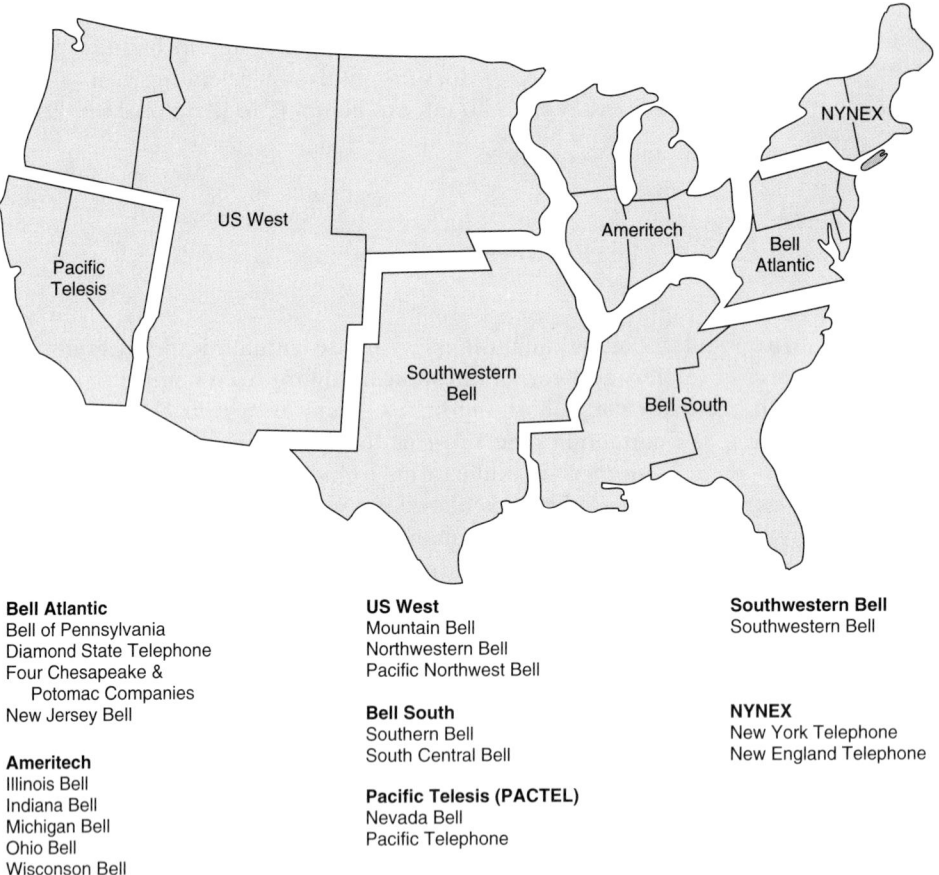

Bell Atlantic
Bell of Pennsylvania
Diamond State Telephone
Four Chesapeake &
   Potomac Companies
New Jersey Bell

Ameritech
Illinois Bell
Indiana Bell
Michigan Bell
Ohio Bell
Wisconson Bell

US West
Mountain Bell
Northwestern Bell
Pacific Northwest Bell

Bell South
Southern Bell
South Central Bell

Pacific Telesis (PACTEL)
Nevada Bell
Pacific Telephone

Southwestern Bell
Southwestern Bell

NYNEX
New York Telephone
New England Telephone

Figure 9-1   Seven Bell Operating Companies (BOCs), also called local exchange companies or Regional Bell Operating Companies (RBOCs).

American Telephone & Telegraph (AT&T)   At divestiture, AT&T retained its long distance communication services, now called *AT&T Communications.* AT&T also retained the Bell Laboratories (research division) and its manufacturing divisions, primarily Western Electric. As a result, AT&T's primary business is long distance communication services. Integrated with the long distance and networking operations is the manufacturing unit for information systems equipment. Another major division is AT&T International, which markets communication products abroad.

With the AT&T divestiture came numerous other common carriers that now compete directly for the long distance communication services market; the largest of these are MCI Communications and US Sprint. Moreover, telephone instruments are no longer a monopoly item; you decide whether to purchase your own telephone and local telephone service from another vendor or lease it from the telephone company.

Local Access Transport Areas (LATAs)   The service area of each of the seven regional Bell operating companies is broken into *local access transport areas* (LATAs). These areas outline the geographic area *within* which the individual RBOC can offer service (*intraLATA*) and where it must turn service over to another supplier (*interLATA*), primarily AT&T, MCI, or US Sprint. These LATAs define the areas in which the *local exchange companies* can provide local exchange and exchange access services.

Local exchange service is provided when the telephone company supplies a local loop. *Exchange access service* is provided when the local telephone company interconnects through the end office so your local loop can be connected to a long distance telephone company. Service *between* LATAs is provided by interexchange carriers like AT&T, MCI, or US Sprint.

Equal access is a vital issue brought about by deregulation. According to the terms of the deregulation agreements, local exchange companies must provide all carriers of long distance services with access to local end office switches that are equal in type, quality, and price to that which they sell to AT&T affiliates. Exchange access may be equal, but this does not necessarily mean that all interexchange services are equal because the investment in maintenance, servicing, and equipment is the deciding factor in determining which carrier has the highest quality of service. What equal access means in practice is that all the long distance carriers have equal use of the switches in an end office. If you want to place a pay telephone call with a specific carrier, for example, you first dial that specific carrier's access code before dialing the telephone number. The three major carrier access codes are 10288 for AT&T, 10222 for MCI, and 10333 for US Sprint.

LATAs are modeled on the concept of standard metropolitan statistical areas (SMSAs). Where possible, LATAs are based on communities of interest and conform to state boundaries. Most states are comprised of several LATAs, but some of the sparsely populated states are a single LATA. There are approximately 200 LATAs in the continental United States. A number of them span state lines because they are based on SMSAs rather than political boundaries.

The Pacific Telesis (PACTEL) RBOC has ten LATAs for California (Figure 9-2). As you can see from the figure, some of these LATAs are quite large. For example, a call from San Francisco north to the city of Eureka stays within one LATA service area, and so PACTEL collects the full long distance charge for it. By contrast, a call from

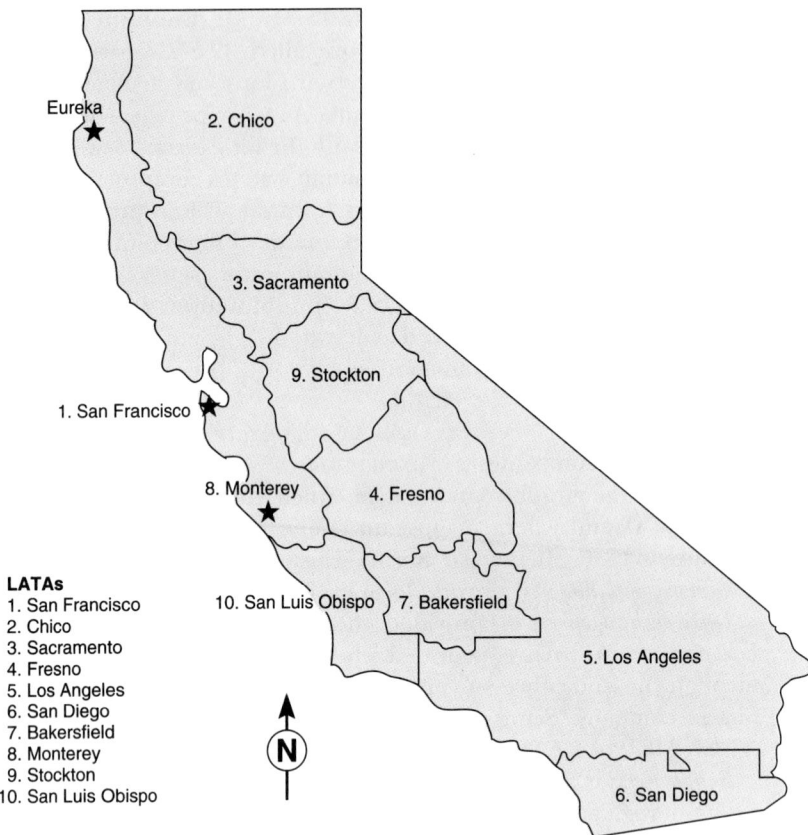

Figure 9-2   Local access transport areas (LATAs) for California.

San Francisco south to Monterey crosses the LATA boundary, and so the charges for the call are collected by a long distance interexchange carrier.

Long Distance Common Carriers *AT&T* used to be the only long distance carrier in the United States. Since deregulation, it has expanded its services to include high speed data transmission, international toll-free dialing (like 800 numbers in the United States), and network management. AT&T is part of a consortium that is spending $3 billion to lay undersea high speed fiber optic cables to improve transmission. In the area of telecommunication equipment, AT&T is well established in Europe and the Far East. Its overseas market is very big, employing 22,000 people and generating about 15 percent of its $37 billion in annual revenues. Moreover, this market will grow even more because AT&T is acquiring NCR Corporation. This acquisition is expected to add another 27,000 employees outside the United States and more than $3 billion to AT&T's international revenues.

MCI Communications Corporation (MCI) started in the United States as a small common carrier providing discount communication services, and was the primary player in the events precipitating AT&T's breakup. Today it is an international common carrier, providing direct dialing from the United States to 180 countries and international toll-free service to 25 countries. MCI began its international operations in 1983 when it bought Western Union International, Inc., from the Xerox Corporation. It continued expanding internationally when it bought RCA Global Communications in 1988 from General Electric. The latter acquisition secured its ties to many foreign telephone authorities. MCI has teamed with British Telecommunications PLC to provide a transatlantic high-capacity fiber optic cable that will be able to handle its increased international traffic. In addition, MCI offers what it calls Global Communication Service, which negotiates transmission links with foreign telecommunication authorities, manages international voice and data networks, and provides billing in any currency.

US Sprint Communications Company (US Sprint) is the third largest long distance common carrier in the United States. It, too, has increased international traffic. Moreover, US Sprint is marketing multinational private networks and what are called carrier-select markets. Similar to equal access in the United States, carrier select simply means travelers can select the long distance carrier of their choice when dialing from another country. US Sprint has aligned itself with France Telecom and Germany's Deutsche Telekom to enhance its international markets. Because recent FCC rulings will make it more difficult for foreign companies to invest in the United States, these alliances could pose problems for Sprint. US Sprint also owns an international public data network called SprintNet, which has links to 108 countries. It also is developing another private data network that will use switching hubs in 20 countries to link financial centers in Europe and the Pacific Rim.

Competition among the RBOCs and Interexchange Carriers   Regulations in the telecommunications industries were dramatically changed in 1995. As we write this, the impact is just beginning to be felt. Long distance interexchange carriers have begun to offer local exchange services within LATAs in direct competition with RBOCs. These services bypass the RBOCs, lowering costs to organizations using these services—and deprive the RBOCs of a major source of revenue (estimates of this revenue loss range as high as 20 percent). In response, the RBOCs are beginning to compete in the long distance interexchange market and to manufacture their own communication equipment. Likewise, competition is heating up as cable TV companies scramble to offer telephone services, and the RBOCs and interexchange carriers try to develop cable TV services.

AT&T is also seeking permission to offer a personal communication network (PCN) service. *Personal communication networks* use a wireless digital technology that can support both voice and data communications, as well as advanced network switches that are located in the RBOC end offices. Unlike traditional cellular telephone service, PCN is a complete network architecture. It can be used instead of the local loop between homes or businesses and the regional RBOC end office. In this case, it bypasses the local loop, thereby reducing basic revenues for the RBOCs that are bypassed. Instead of paying the regional RBOC a monthly fee for the telephone service, you pay that same fee to the operator of the PCN. If a long distance carrier like AT&T offers PCN service, it can be tied into that common carrier's long distance network. This tie-in can provide end-to-end digital connectivity for users in all the cities served

---

Management Focus: MCI Local Loop Fiber Optic Networks

MCI Communications could save customers big bucks on their communications bills with the implementation of MCI's local synchronous optical network (SONET). This installation will reduce access fees that the long distance carrier pays to local carriers to reach many of its big customers. MCI now pays 45 cents of every revenue dollar in these local access fees.

MCI Metro has already completed several local loop installations in Atlanta with plans to build similar networks in another to 19 American markets. The projected cost of this is about $2 billion, part of a $20 billion overall network upgrade.

Source: Computerworld, January 10, 1994.

---

by the PCN, in effect, connecting your home telephone to the worldwide telephone network.

Complicating matters has been the explosive growth in the cellular telephone market, which has grown by 30 to 40 percent over the past few years. In contrast, the long distance market has grown by 20 percent, and the local market by 5 percent. Both the interexchange carriers and the RBOCs have been bidding against each other to acquire cellular companies.

Likewise, the international communication market has become very competitive for interexchange carriers and the RBOCs. It is a direct effect of the deregulation of the telephone industry, not only in the United States but also in other countries, and as a result, the general public and businesses worldwide are benefiting.

DIALED CIRCUIT SERVICES

Direct Distance Dialing (DDD)

Direct distance dialing (also called *dial-up*) facilitates data transmission via a normal voice telephone network. A person dials the host computer telephone number using a modem, receives appropriate control signaling, enters password or authorizations, and connects to the host computer system.

Direct distance dialing uses an entirely different circuit path between the two telephone company central offices each time a number is dialed. Charges are based on the distance between the two telephones (in miles) and the time the connection is held open (the data transmission). The data communication user pays the same rate as the individual who uses the telephone for voice communication.

Dial-up voice grade circuits have more noise and distortion than a private leased voice grade circuit because the signals go through the telephone company's central office switching equipment, although the new digital switches bring DDD very close to the quality of a private leased circuit.

The telephone company does not make special conditioning available for DDD circuits because each dialed call gets a different circuit path or routing. Equalization, however, can be obtained by using a more expensive high speed modem that performs this automatically. The DDD rate of transmission (bits per second) may be a little less than can be achieved on a private leased circuit because there is more noise and distortion.

AT&T Megacom Wide Area Telephone Services (WATS)

The *AT&T Megacom WATS* is a special bulk rate service that allows direct dial telephone calls, although it may be replaced by a different service in the future. It can be used for both voice communications and data transmission. *Wide area telephone services* (WATS) uses the 800 and 888 area code series in the United States. An international megacom WATS is available to 175 international locations, and it, too, uses the 800 and 888 area codes.

The 48 contiguous states are divided into about 60 different WATS service areas. (Some states have more than one service area.) The geographical coverage of WATS from any one of these areas is determined by the *band of service* to which the customer subscribes. For example, interstate service from *California* uses six bands:

- **Band 1**: Arizona, Idaho, Nevada, Oregon, Utah, and Washington
- **Band 2**: Colorado, Montana, Nebraska, New Mexico, and Wyoming
- **Band 3**: Iowa, Kansas, Minnesota, Missouri, North Dakota, Oklahoma, South Dakota, and Texas
- **Band 4**: Alabama, Arkansas, Illinois, Indiana, Kentucky, Louisiana, Michigan, Mississippi, Tennessee, and Wisconsin
- **Band 5**: Connecticut, Delaware, Florida, Georgia, Maine, Maryland, Massachusetts, New Hampshire, New Jersey, New York, North Carolina, Ohio, Pennsylvania, Rhode Island, South Carolina, Vermont, Virginia, Washington, D.C., West Virginia, Hawaii, Puerto Rico, and the U.S. Virgin Islands.
- **Band 6**: Alaska

The state of California has two service areas, Northern California and Southern California, each of which is a different WATS band. The list of states served in bands 1 to 5 differs, depending on the state. For example, band 1 from Missouri includes Arkansas, Illinois, Iowa, Kansas, Kentucky, Nebraska, Oklahoma, and Tennessee. As might be guessed, the first five bands out of New York are almost the direct opposite of bands 1 to 5 out of California. Band 5 out of California is similar to band 1 out of New York. When a customer subscribes to a band, such as band 4, service is automatic to all lower bands (in this case, 1 to 3).

Interstate WATS service has no relationship to *intrastate WATS service*. California, for example, has a northern and a southern service area; therefore, WATS intrastate service can be for northern California only, southern California only, or statewide. In-

Management Focus: 800 and 888 Numbers

The traditional "toll-free" number in the United States and Canada has been the "800" number. There are approximately 7.64 million possible numbers in the 800 area code.

By early 1995, about 210,000 toll-free numbers were being assigned each month, with that amount growing by about 10,000 per month. Based on this growth, there would be no 800 numbers left by early 1996. Therefore, in March 1995, the industry telephone numbering committee announced the adoption of a new toll-free area code—888.

terstate WATS service does not include your home state; therefore, it is necessary to lease both interstate and intrastate WATS if access is needed to your home state.

Interstate WATS service is available on the basis of the first 25 hours of usage, the next 75 hours, and over 100 hours of usage per month. Flat fees for a specified number of usage hours are charged for either intrastate or interstate WATS.

If WATS service is used for data communications and the call lasts less than 60 seconds, billing is for one minute of usage (one minute average call holding time). WATS service also is limited to one direction only; it is either *outward dialing* or *inward dialing*. Inward (In-WATS) and outward (Out-WATS) capability cannot be combined onto a single WATS circuit, so the user must subscribe to both.

AT&T has combined all of its WATS and WATS-like services into a single family that includes Pro WATS I, Pro WATS II, Pro WATS III, Megacom WATS, All Pro WATS, the Pro WATS state plan, Multi-Location WATS, and the old WATS. AT&T's intent is to replace its usage-sensitive banded WATS scheme with a new one based on distance. This new distance-sensitive pricing structure is expected to benefit AT&T's WATS users by lowering their costs and simplifying network optimization.

AT&T Megacom

As previously mentioned, AT&T is replacing its banded pricing WATS service with a scheme based on distance. This new service, called AT&T Megacom, has two variations, the AT&T Megacom Service and the AT&T Megacom 800 Service.

The *AT&T Megacom service*, which is outbound, replaces outward dialing WATS It gives users a simplified pricing structure that allows them to save on calls to anywhere in the United States, Puerto Rico, and the U.S. Virgin Islands. This new pricing is based on the mileage and duration of each call rather than on the geographic areas associated with the old WATS rates. Megacom eliminates the banded geographic pricing structure under WATS, and users are billed at the same rates for calls within the same area code, regardless of distance.

Technology Focus: How 800 and 888 Area Code Numbers Work

To see how a toll-free 800 call is handled, let us follow a call as it moves through the network. Assume that the number is 1-800-999-5676 and that you have New York Telephone as your local telephone company.

When you begin dialing, New York Telephone sees this call as a 1+ number, a long distance call that should be assigned to AT&T, MCI, US Sprint, or the like. The local telephone switching equipment then checks the first six digits of the number, which is 800-999. The local telephone company immediately knows it is an 800 call and one that should be switched to MCI because the 999 identifies it as an MCI call. If the first six digits were 800-542, the call would be switched to AT&T because 542 designates AT&T.

The local telephone company now routes the call to the MCI point of presence (POP) switching office. The *point of presence* is the switching office to which the local telephone terminates subscribers' circuits for long distance dial-up or leased line communications. At this point, whether the call is destined for MCI, US Sprint, or AT&T, it enters a large network database switch. The MCI switch receives all the information about the call, including the 800 number dialed and the telephone number from which the call originated. The MCI network database switch knows it has a call coming from, let's say, 212-591-6500 and going to 800-999-5676. The database switching computer might look at the time of day, the day of the week, or even a specific day of the year. After looking at these parameters, it then sends a message through the network to indicate a call coming from New York City, and the call starts moving through the network to the destination number in less than a second.

In actuality, the destination number may not be the 800 number. Depending on the time of day, day of week, or specific day of the year, the switch knows from its database to translate the 800 number to another number. For example, if the call is made before noon on any day, it might convert the number dialed (800-999-5676) to 415-291-0616. After noon, the calls might be routed to another number in either the same city or some other city. Another option is for it to translate the 800 number to one that connects to a dedicated access line (DAL) going directly to a corporate headquarters where the calls are answered. The concept of switching calls to different numbers based on the time of day means calls can be answered by people in Philadelphia in the morning and by people in San Francisco or even Honolulu later in the day.

In summary, the database switching computer receives the telephone number of the caller and the 800 number being dialed. It then establishes the time of day, the day of the week, or the day of the year so it can determine the telephone number or dedicated access line to which the call will be switched. As you can see, 800 numbers often switch their calls to some other area code and telephone number in a manner that is transparent to the caller.

The *AT&T Megacom 800 service* replaces inward dialing WATS and has cost-effective toll-free calling for businesses. This service allows users to receive calls from any location or selected locations in the United States, Puerto Rico, Canada, Mexico, and the U.S. Virgin Islands. When you dial an 800 or 888 area code number, you are using either a Megacom 800 service or a WATS line. Again, billing is based on the length of each call and the distance between the caller's area code and the recipient's area code.

DIAL-IT 900

The *DIAL-IT 900 service* allows many different users to call a 900 area code telephone number because it can handle 7000 incoming calls simultaneously. These services have "sponsors" who arrange with AT&T to have their telephone number established, and who are responsible for advertising this service to encourage calls. The sponsor usually charges each caller, although a sponsor may choose to keep the calls free and pay AT&T for the charges incurred.

Two different arrangements are possible with DIAL-IT 900. The first is *information*, which may be either a prerecorded message or a live hookup. For example, the prerecorded call may be something as simple as a dial-a-joke service. The recording originates at the sponsor's premises and so can be changed whenever desired. By contrast, live hookups allow callers to listen in on astronaut's conversations during space missions, to hear what is happening at a shareholders' meeting, to receive assistance in using software packages, and so on.

A *call-counting* or *polling service* allows callers to dial the 900 number to express preferences or vote on some question that is brought to their attention by mail, radio, or television. This polling service requires one number for each opinion.

The DIAL-IT 900 service has become controversial because many telephone subscribers (or their children) have accidentally dialed these numbers, and they have been billed unfairly. Telephone companies now offer 900 number "blocking" so that anyone calling 900 numbers from a specific telephone is prevented from doing so.

DEDICATED CIRCUIT SERVICES

There are two main problems with dialed circuits. First, each connection goes through the regular telephone network on a different circuit. These circuits may vary in quality, meaning that while one connection will be fairly clear, the next call may be noisy. Second, the data transmission rates on these dialed circuits are usually low. Generally speaking, transmission rates for dialed circuits range from 9600 bps to 33.6 Kbps (which can be increased up to 133.4 Kbps if data are compressed).

One alternative is to establish a private dedicated circuit, which the user leases from the common carrier for their exclusive use twenty-four hours per day, seven days per week. The carrier installs connections at the two end point of the circuit and makes the connection. All connections are point-to-point. Changing them means signing a new contract with the carrier.

Obviously, dedicated circuits require that you carefully design which locations will need what type of connections to what other locations. Figure 9-3 shows how a wide area network can be built in this manner. In this case, each location is connected to one or more other locations. For example, Calgary is connected only to Chicago, but Chicago is connected to three other locations besides Calgary. Any messages that Calgary wants to send to locations other than Chicago must go via Chicago. If Calgary is transmitting and receiving data from many other locations, the Chicago computer may spend much of its time routing messages to Calgary. So it may make more sense to connect Calgary directly to these other computers instead (see Figure 9-4).

Designing a WAN with dedicated circuits is more challenging because you must explicitly lease the exact communication circuits with specific data transmission capacities that you need. Once you sign a contract, making changes can be expensive.

Voice Grade Channels

Voice grade channels are analog circuits. Technically, voice grade channels are used for voice communication, remote operation of radio telephones, connection of private voice systems, interconnecting remote central offices, data transmission, remote metering, supervisory control of electronic devices, fax machines, and modem-based low speed data communication. Everyone refers to this as a voice grade equivalent channel.

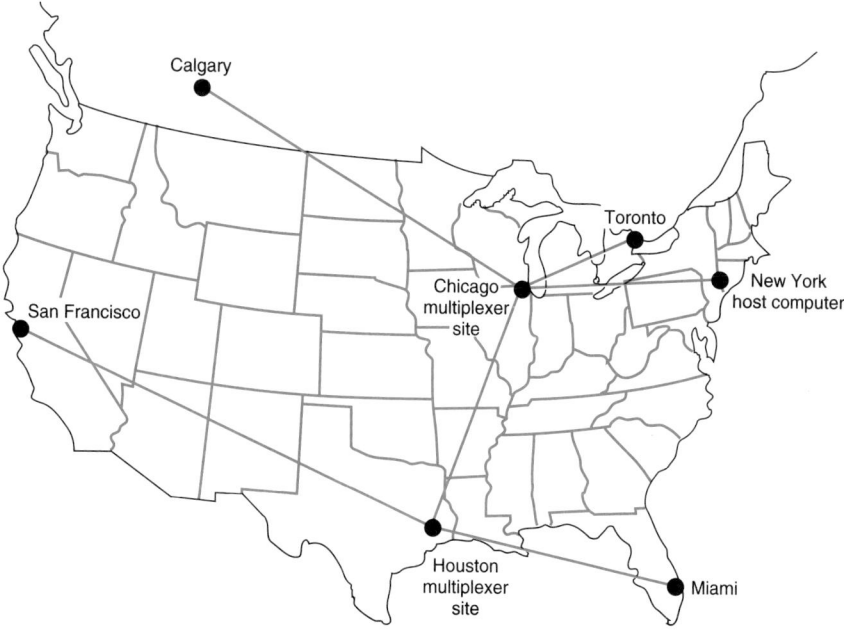

Figure 9-3   WAN.

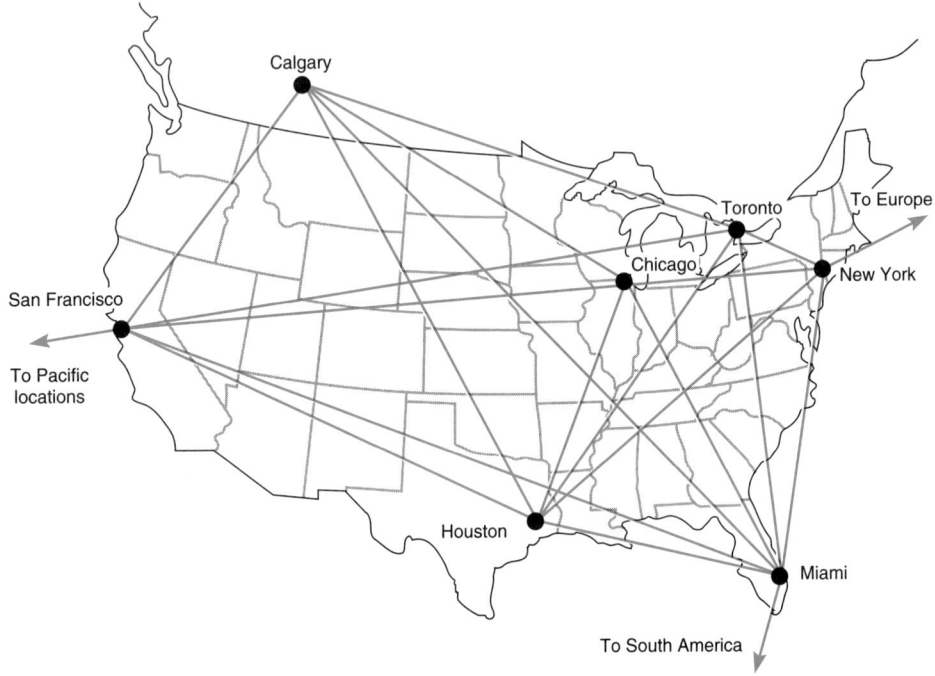

Figure 9-4   WAN.

Conditioning, or *equalization* as it is sometimes called, is typically performed on communication circuits to improve data transmission qualities. Because voice grade circuits transmit data in the voice bandwidth (0 to 4000 hertz), you should use conditioning to reduce noise when transmitting at 28.8 Kbps, although it is not mandatory.

The user decides whether the circuit should be conditioned. AT&T offers two types of conditioning. *C type conditioning* has specific limits on attenuation distortion and envelope delay distortion to reduce line impairments so a data signal arrives with less noise and distortion. Fewer retransmissions are required because there are fewer errors. *D type conditioning* specifically limits noise and harmonic distortion. Again, this type of conditioning reduces line impairments, resulting in fewer errors and fewer retransmissions.

In addition, some local telephone companies such as NYNEX offer a *straight copper circuit.* This is a pair of copper wires, and it is available only when the entire circuit is within the same telephone company central office. In essence, the straight copper circuit is comprised of two local loops connected at the central office. Because there are no repeater/amplifiers or loading coils in the circuit, the customer can use less expensive short haul modems (one to fifteen miles). Short haul modems also may be used on standard voice grade unconditioned channels, depending on the length of the circuit and the data rate.

Wideband Analog Services

Wideband analog services are used for either data transmission or alternate voice and data transmission that require higher speed data transmission. They also may be used in conjunction with a 50 Kbps switched service or high speed fax transmission. This type of communication channel may be delivered to the user as a Group 48,000 hertz bandwidth or as 12 individual voice grade channels (48,000 hertz/12 = 4000 hertz). It also is available as a Supergroup 240,000 hertz bandwidth. Organizations use them to transmit greater quantities of data between facilities, although digital services are replacing wideband analog services.

Digital Services

Digital services include point-to-point and multipoint configurations for data transmission. Analog modem conversion is not required, but you need a DSU/CSU (digital modem). Digital service uses wire pairs, coaxial cable, microwave, or fiber optic cables to operate at 9600 bps, 56 Kbps, 128 Kbps, and 1.544 Mbps. It spans both the voice grade communication channels and the analog wideband communication channels. The advantage of using digital transmission is that digital modems are much less costly (although increased local loop costs may offset the lower modem cost) and the transmission error rate is far less than with analog circuits.

Although digital circuits generally are leased, it is possible to get a switched digital circuit. Traditionally, an organization would lease a digital circuit between two of its facilities, but this practice has changed because modem 56 Kbps switched services are available on dial-up circuits.

The long distance carriers are able to establish these 56 Kbps circuit connections on demand by using sophisticated digital cross-connect switching equipment. When a high speed data message is sent, such as from a Group 4 fax machine, the long distance carrier simply switches it to the proper circuit. The organization pays only for the amount of time it actually uses the circuit, thus saving the cost of a fixed price lease. Moreover, international switched digital services offering either 56 Kbps or 64 Kbps speeds are available from the United States to various international locations.

T Carrier Circuits

T carrier circuits are special forms of digital services. They are leased digital circuits with a wide range of transmission capacities. The *T carrier system* is the North American telephone industry standard for interconnecting digital communication systems. It is a hierarchy of digital transmission and multiplexing standards ranging from T-1 to T-4.

T-1 Circuits   A *T-1 circuit* usually is a digital communication system operating at a synchronous data rate of 1.544 Mbps. Data can be transmitted over this circuit at speeds ranging from 56 Kbps to 1.544 Mbps. Digitized voice using pulse code modulation (see Chapter 5) uses 64 Kbps. By digitizing voice signals and multiplexing them with time division multiplexing, T-1 circuits allow for 24 simultaneous voice channels, which transport data or voice messages according to a signaling format called DS-0. This is known as the *North American Digital Hierarchy* (see Figure 9-5).

Digitized voice usually is transmitted over T carriers, and new methods of digitizing voice are appearing each year. One of the newest methods is called *adaptive differential pulse code modulation* (ADPCM), which digitizes voice at 32 Kbps instead of the traditional 64 Kbps used by standard pulse code modulation (PCM). As the lower half of Figure 9-5 shows, the use of ADPCM makes the T-1 carrier twice as efficient because it can handle 48 voice channels.

AT&T makes extensive use of pulse code modulation internally and transmits much of its information in pulse code modulated digital format over T carriers. As a rule, a T-1 carrier with a capacity equivalent to 24 voice grade lease lines costs about the same per month as 12 to 14 individual voice grade lease lines leased separately.

Fractional T-1   *Fractional T-1*, sometimes called FT1, offers portions of a 1.544 Mbps T-1 circuit for a fraction of its full cost. Users who need more transmission speed than

The North American Digital Hierarchy		
Digital Signal Format	Number of Voice Channels	Speed (bits/second)
DS-0*	1	64,000
DS-1	24	1,544,000
DS-1C	48	3,152,000
DS-2	96	6,312,000
DS-3	672	44,376,000
DS-4	4,032	274,176,000

*DS-0 is the signaling standard that divides frames into virtual channels.

T Carrier System			
T Carrier Circuit	Number of Voice Channels PCM	ADPCM	Speed (bits/second)
T-1	24	48	1,544,000
T-1C	48	96	3,152,000
T-2	96	192	6,312,000
T-3	672	1,344	44,376,000
T-4	4,032	8,064	274,176,000

Figure 9-5   Digital signals in the North American Digital Hierarchy compared to T carrier circuits. PCM is pulse code modulation and ADPCM is adaptive differential pulse code modulation.

Management Focus: Harley-Davidson's Wide Area Network

Harley-Davidson, the Milwaukee-based manufacturer of motorcycles, is taking advantage of wide-area communications to permit anyone anywhere to gain access to any information on its network. The WAN connects 1300 users at five sites with T1 lines, 56 and 128 Kbps digital links, and dial-up connections (see Figure 9-6).

Many of the users gain access to the WAN from their local area network. Token-ring is the topology of choice but ethernet is also supported. File servers are IBM PS/2 Model 95s running Novell NetWare.

Harley-Davidson uses information systems from its corporate headquarters in Milwaukee, but business functions such as manufacturing, engineering, testing, and sales are distributed. Consequently, the strategic development of the Harley network involved a transition from a mainframe to a set of IBM AS/400 minicomputers. In addition, Microsoft Windows-based microcomputers replaced DOS-based PCs and IBM 3270 terminals. Future plans call for T1 lines to replace the 56 Kbps and 128 Kbps circuits.

Source: Network Computing, December 1, 1994.

voice grade can have digital service at 56 Kbps, or a T-1 circuit at 1.544 Mbps. The jump from 56 Kbps to 1.544 Mbps is costly, however, so users now can lease individual 64 Kbps DS-0 channels on T-1 circuits. AT&T's fractional T-1 allows users to lease digital private lines in variations of 128, 256, 384, 512, and 768 Kbps. US Sprint and MCI provide slightly different fractions. The European equivalent, E-1, has a transmission speed of 2.048 Mbps.

Other T Circuits   A *T-2 circuit* transmits data at a rate of 6.312 Mbps. Basically, it is a multiplexed bundle of four T-1 circuits. A *T-3 circuit* allows transmission at a rate of 44.376 Mbps, although most articles refer to this rate as 45 megabits per second. This is equal to the capacity of 28 T-1 circuits.

T-3 circuits are becoming popular as the transmission medium for corporate MANs and WANs because of their 45 megabits per second capacity. At low speed, these T-3 circuits can be used at 672 different 64 Kbps channels. They also can be used simultaneously for both voice and data services.

The traditional method of obtaining a T-3 circuit is via a *M-13 multiplexer*. This device gathers together 28 T-1 signals and uses two sets of time division multiplexing to produce the circuit. Multiplexers cost anywhere from $4000 to $10,000 each. A second method is to use digital cross-connect switches, which sometimes are referred to as *digital access cross-connect systems* (DACSs). The third multiplexing alternative for T-3 circuits is to use a piece of hardware called an *add/drop multiplexer* (ADM). These devices allow the individual T-1 circuits to be added to, and dropped from, a T-3 circuit

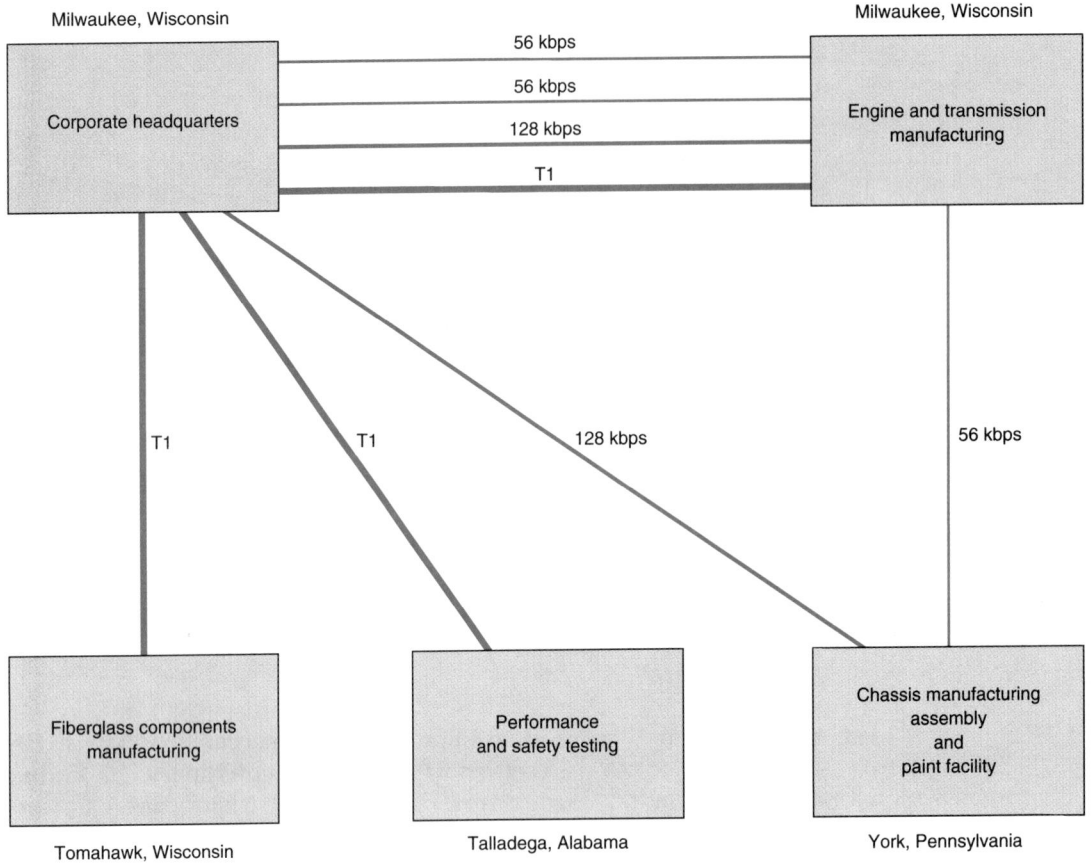

Figure 9-6 Harley-Davidson's WAN.

at a particular site. The ADM is especially useful if you want to use multipoint T-1 circuits at an organization's various branches.

A *T-4 circuit* transmits at a rate of 274.176 Mbps, which is equal to a bandwidth of 178 T-1 circuits. Obviously, an organization using either T-3 or T-4 circuits must have a tremendous need to transmit very large quanitites of data. Looking at the lower half of Figure 9-5, you see that a T-4 circuit can carry 4032 simultaneous voice telephone calls by using pulse code modulation (PCM). Alternatively, these could be 4032 separate transmissions between microcomputers.

Synchronous Optical Network (SONET)

The *synchronous optical network* (SONET) has recently been accepted by ANSI as a standard for optical transmission at gigabits per second speeds. T3 and T4 services are

SONET Level	Speed
OC-1	51.84 Mbps
OC-9	466.56 Mbps
OC-12	622.08 Mbps
OC-18	933.12 Mbps
OC-24	1.244 Gbps
OC-36	1.866 Gbps
OC-48	2.488 Gbps

Figure 9-7   SONET circuits.

rapidly being replaced by SONET services. SONET transmission speeds begin at the OC-1 level (optical carrier level 1) of 51.84 Mbps. Each succeeding rate in the SONET fiber hierarchy is defined as a multiple of OC-1, with SONET data rates defined as high as OC-48 or 2.4 gigabits (2,488,320,000) per second. Figure 9-7 presents some other SONET services. Each level above OC-1 is created by multiplexing. Notice that the slowest SONET OC-1 optical transmission rate of 51,840,000 bits per second is slightly faster than the T-3 rate of 44,376,000 bits per second. Although not yet fully implemented in all locations, SONET is available in most large cities worldwide.

Several telephone companies now use OC-12 circuits at 622.08 Mbps to carry interexchange traffic. With these speeds, it is easy to see why the telephone companies in most cities are installing optical fiber cable MANs and long distance circuits. Even new undersea cables are optical fiber instead of copper.

Satellite Services

Several common carriers offer satellite channels for voice, data, facsimile, and various wideband applications. Basically, a *satellite channel* is a four-wire equivalent voice grade circuit; therefore, users get a 4000 hertz bandwidth and a four-wire equivalent circuit. Available transmission rates can range from 9600 to 19,200 bits per second for voice grade to 1.544 Mbps for T-1.

Users are notified when transmissions use satellite circuits because it may affect their protocols. A half duplex protocol cannot be used successfully unless satellite delay compensation is added. Satellite channels usually are less costly than ground-based voice grade channels. If a greater capacity is needed, it is possible to lease a bundle or group of voice grade satellite channels to increase bandwidth beyond the standard 4000 hertz.

The FCC has approved the use of a direct broadcast satellite service to private homes. This means you can install a small (2.5-foot) dish antenna on your roof and receive television signals directly from medium-powered communication satellites orbiting 22,000 miles overhead.

Management Focus: Satellites at Toys 'R' Us

Toys 'R' Us, the highly successful international toy retailer, has combined various platforms and protocols into a viable wireless satellite network. In the past, Toys 'R' Us had DECnet environments with VAXs in every store, but it is now moving to TCP/IP to link products from different vendors and integrate Unix, VMS, and Windows computers. Toys 'R' Us plans to continue using DECnet between VAX machines, but will use TCP/IP elsewhere.

Toys 'R' Us communicates with most stores via Hughes VSAT (very small aperture terminals) satellite service. Most stores have a VSAT dish on the roof connected to an ethernet LAN. VSATs were used for several reasons. First, they provide good response time and are easy to manage. Second, they have enough capacity for broadcast television, for use in training, explaining new benefits packages, and delivering executive speeches. Toys 'R' Us currently uses a shared satellite hub for broadcast, but is in the process of building its own.

The problem with VSATs is their loose traffic management. File transfers take place throughout the day, which leaves credit authorizations waiting in line behind other transactions. The toy retailer plans to create a priority system to solve this problem.

Source: LAN Magazine, July 1994.

SWITCHED CIRCUIT SERVICES

The major problem with dedicated circuit services is that you must carefully plan all the circuits you need. To be successful, you must understand the data transmission patterns in your network *and* these patterns must be relatively stable. Both can be a challenge, especially if you are adding new applications to the network or building new network connections.

In contrast, switched circuits enable you to define the end points of the WAN without specifying all the interconnecting circuits you will need. Instead, the common carrier routes the traffic message by message, in much the same way as a dialed circuit. The difference is that switched services offer much higher data transmission rates, and are designed to be noise free.

The second problem with dedicated circuits is that you must pay a fixed fee per month. This works well if you have a high volume of message traffic between the two points. If you don't, dedicated circuits can be quite expensive.

Integrated Services Digital Network (ISDN)

Integrated services digital network (ISDN) has long been more of a concept than a reliable service in the United States. It has been limitedly available since the late 1970s, although it has not been widely adopted. ISDN is relatively popular in California because PACTEL has developed and marketed it rather well. It is far less popular in New York because NYNEX has shown little interest in it.

Acceptance of ISDN has also been slowed because vendors, common carriers, and RBOCs have conflicting interpretations of the ISDN standards. Equipment from different vendors which conforms to the ISDN standard won't necessarily work together or with a specific RBOC ISDN line. Skeptics claim that ISDN actually stands for *I Still Don't Know* or *It Still Does Nothing*. In 1992, the RBOCs and most interexchange carriers in the United States developed National ISDN-1 (N-1) and National ISDN-2 (N-2) to specify exactly how ISDN services will be provided in the United States and Canada. As N-1 and N-2 are implemented, many of the current standardization problems will disappear.

ISDN combines voice, video, and data over the same digital circuit. There are two types of ISDN service. The first is *basic rate interface* (BRI) (sometimes called basic access service or *2B+D*), which provides a communication circuit with two 64 Kbps digital transmission channels (called B channels) and one 16 Kbps control signaling channel (called a D channel). Used for all data transmission other than control messages, the two B channels handle digitized voice, data, and image transmissions, meaning that all devices must be digitial. For example, telephones must be special digital telephones (rather than the normal analog ones) or a CODEC must be installed between the telephone and the ISDN connection. The D channel is used for control messages such as acknowledgments, call setup and termination, and other functions such as automatic number identification. The control messages give the network its intelligence, while any control messages/characters are sent simultaneously down the 16,000 bits per second D channel. One advantage of BRI is that it can be installed in almost any existing telephone location without adding any new cable. It simply uses the existing two pairs of twisted pair wires. The only changes are the end connections at the customer's location and at the telephone company's switching office.

Primary rate interface (PRI) (also called primary access service or *23B+D*) is typically offered to commercial customers who want to hook up their PBXs or local area networks. It consists of 23 64 Kbps B channels plus one 64 Kbps D channel. Basically, 23B+D has the same capacity as a T-1 circuit (capacity of 1.544 Mbps) even though the mathematics is not accurate to the bit. The slight difference between them is unused capacity. In Europe, PRI is defined as 30 B channels plus one D channel, making interconnection between America and Europe difficult.

The interconnection for BRI service to an organization involves a *network termination box* at the customer's site. Users get a single local loop that can carry 144 Kbps between the user's premises and the local telephone company end office. There the signals are combined for transmission over the IXC to the telephone company end office at the transmission's destination. From there, the information is sent over another single access line to the receiving site, where it enters a network termination box and it is distributed to the appropriate computer, terminal, or telephone.

AT&T now has a chip that can be incorporated into communication boards that are the interface for ISDN digital telephones, terminals, and computers. The chip, which implements the 2B+D ISDN standard, also has the built-in capacity of formatting data according to HDLC protocols.

Management Focus: Trials and Tribulations at General [ISDN] Hospital

The experience of Brigham and Women's Hospital in Boston demonstrates the numerous problems with ISDN. Trouble began immediately after NYNEX (the Boston area RBOC) installed the ISDN line. After testing several newly installed lines, the network manager could not find the ISDN line. NYNEX identified the problem as a missing NT-1 connector, which links the ISDN line to the telephone network. The installation was delayed while the missing part was ordered.

After the NT-1 arrived and was installed, the motherboard in the network server melted. No one knew how or why, but installation was again delayed while a new motherboard was ordered and installed. The line still did not work.

The hospital then contacted NYNEX for "provisioning information," which describes how the ISDN line and connection is configured. After three different experts were consulted, it was determined that the wrong configuration was being used in the server. Finally, the server was up and running.

But this was only half the job. A second server remained to be set up: it seemed simple enough. Not really. NYNEX used a different type of telephone switch to provide the ISDN service to this server, and did not have the provisioning information for it. Once again, the manufacturer, Northern Telecom, provided the information. And again the server experienced a meltdown (this time destroying only the NT-1 connector).

When this was replaced, the second server was able to use the ISDN line, but could not establish a connection to the first server. The problem was an incompatibility between the second server's ISDN card and the Northern Telecom switch. After a new ISDN card was installed, the system finally worked.

Source: InfoWorld, February 6, 1995.

Broadband ISDN (BISDN) is a switched version of SONET. Although not yet widely available, it has the potential to dramatically change the future of high speed networking. BISDN currently defines three services. The first is a full duplex channel that operates at 155.52 Mbps; the second provides a full duplex channel that operates at 622.08 Mbps; and the third is an asymmetrical service with two simplex channels, one from the subscriber at 155.52 Mbps, one from the host to the subscriber at 622.08 Mbps. The first two services are intended for normal bi-directional information exchange. The third, asymmetrical, service is intended to be used for information distribution services such as digital broadcast television.

Much of the success of ISDN has been hidden from those outside the telecommunications history. The success of ISDN services offered to the public (e.g., BRI and PRI) has been limited, but it has influenced many other services. Automatic number identification, for example, was first available in ISDN circuits, and prompted its development in non-ISDN circuits.

In summary, ISDN is a digital communication circuit standard. The communication companies of the world believe ISDN will replace current leased circuits and dial-up circuits. However, adoption has been slow for three reasons. First, there has been a lack of standardization among different vendors and carriers. As N-1 and N-2 are implemented, many of these problems will disappear. Second, there have been concerns that ISDN does not provide sufficient data transmission capacity. This too has been overcome by the introduction of Broadband ISDN. Third, the cost of ISDN services has been higher than many other competing services. This, of course, is a business issue that may also be addressed as competition among ISDN service providers increases.

Switched Multimegabit Data Service (SMDS)

The RBOCs offer *switched multimegabit data service* (SMDS) as an alternative to private network data transmission within the LATA areas in which they operate. AT&T and the other interexchange carriers also offer an interLATA switched multimegabit data service. The new SMDS was originally aimed at the metropolitan area network market, particularly the interconnection of local area networks. Recently, it has also made its way into the wide area network environment.

SMDS is essentially a switched version of the T-carrier and SONET services (see Figure 9-8). Most RBOCs offer SMDS at two transmission rates: *DS-1* at 1.544 Mbps or *DS-3* at 44.376 Mbps. SMDS is a precursor to the full Broadband ISDN transmission and the full implementation of SONET at OC-3 rates (155.52 Mbps).

The primary advantage for users of SMDS is that it is switched. Each corporate regional site requires only one circuit to connect to the RBOC end office because messages on that circuit can be switched to the single circuit that goes from the RBOC's end office to the organization's headquarters. Before SMDS, organizations perhaps had six incoming T-1 circuits to the central headquarters if they wanted to connect to six different regional offices. Now there might be only one or two T-1 circuits between the headquarters and the regional RBOC end office containing the SMDS switch.

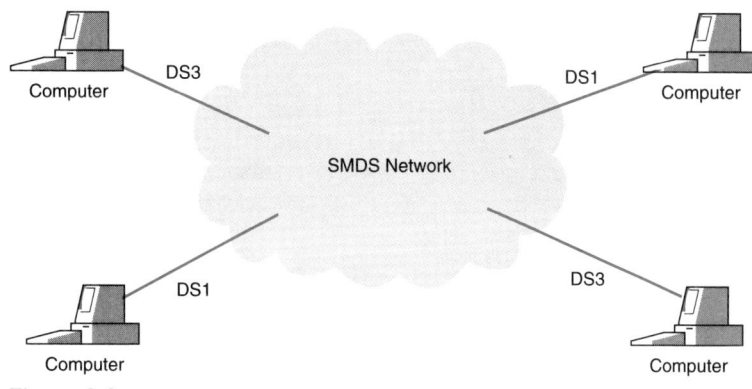

Figure 9-8   SMDS.

PACKET SWITCHED NETWORKS

Packet switched networks are switched services that interconnect many cities. They usually offer transmission speeds up to 1.544 Mbps, but permit users to connect to them at a variety of different transmission speeds. The network compensates for differences in transmission speed and sometimes different protocols between various computer attached to the network. The packet network can also provide code conversion from one code to another (i.e., ASCII to EBCDIC).

Packet switching is a store and forward data transmission technique in which messages are split into small segments called *packets* (usually 128 bytes). A *packet switching network* is a special kind of wide area network. Packet networks often are referred to as *X.25 networks*, after the X.25 international standard on which they are based.

Each computer needing access to a packet switched network has a special connection to the network. Users access the service via private communication circuits, public dial-up circuits, or other packet switched networks. Figure 9-9 shows a packet switched network.

When a message is transmitted from a computer to the packet switched network, the message is divided into equal-sized packets by a packet assembly and disassembly (PAD) device and then transmitted through the network. At the other end, another PAD reassembles the packets into their original message and delivers it to the appropriate destination computer. Packets belonging to different messages or transactions can travel via the same communication circuits.

Figure 9-10 shows a packet switching network to six cities with a *switching node* (SN) connected at each end of the network. These switching nodes route the messages through the network to the city to which they are addressed. Notice how packets originating in Columbia might be switched through both Hannibal and Rolla to reach St. Louis. Some of the switching nodes are interconnected with several interexchange carrier communication circuits. This is a distinct advantage to the user because there is a built-in redundancy in communication circuits between cities in case of failure.

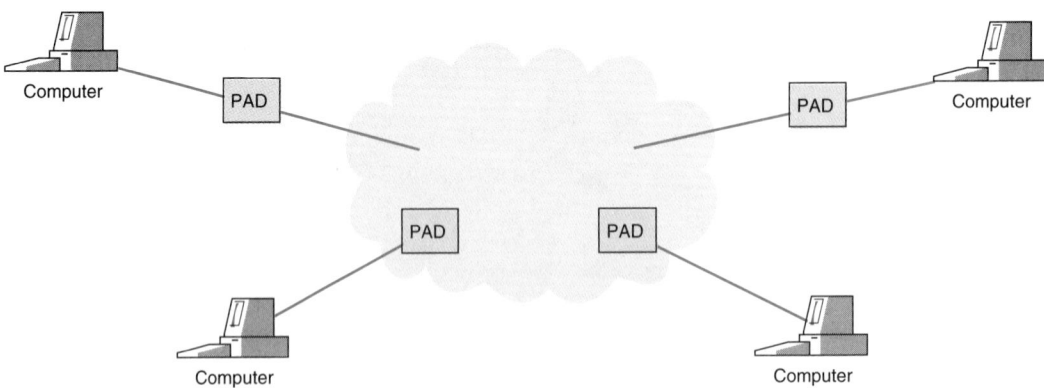

Figure 9-9 Packet switched network.

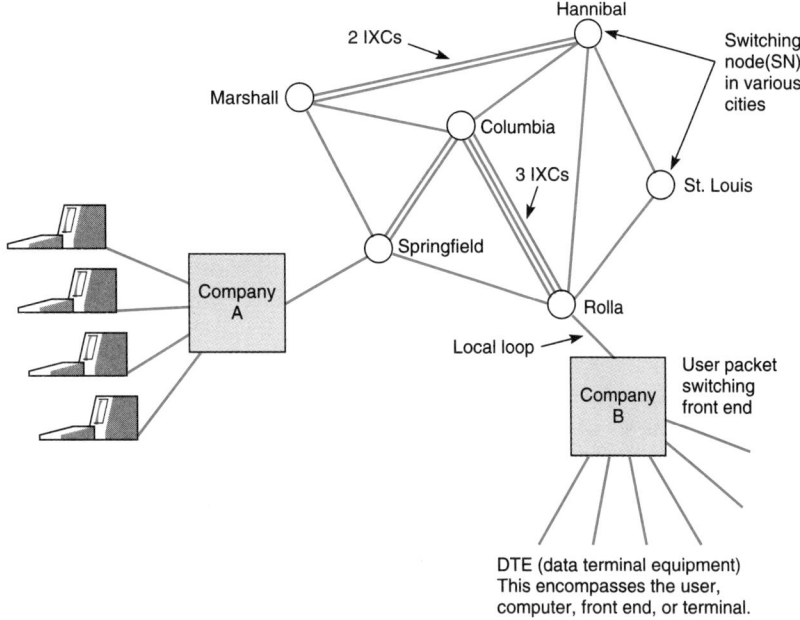

Figure 9-10   Packet switching network connecting six cities in Missouri.

Packetizing

Splitting messages into individual packets is called *packetizing*. Packets are assembled and disassembled by a *packet assembly/disassembly* device, which is owned and operated by the customer or by the packet switching network. Packetizing is almost instantaneous, and data are transmitted continuously. The main functions of the PAD are to establish and clear the virtual telecommunication circuits, assemble the asynchronous characters received from the terminal into packets, transmit them on the virtual circuit, and, at the other end, disassemble packets received and reassemble them back into messages.

The Consultative Committee on International Telegraph and Telephone (CCITT) has defined a number of international standards that apply to packet switching networks. Among the more important ones are the following.

- **X.3** defines the PAD and how it serves as the interface between asynchronous terminals, packet mode terminals, and other PADs.
- **X.25** defines how terminals and packet switching nodes exchange packets.
- **X.28** defines the interface between an asynchronous terminal and a PAD.
- **X.29** defines the procedures by which a terminal and a PAD facility exchange control information and user data.
- **X.75** defines the procedures by which X.25 packet switched networks exchange data with other networks. The *X.75 gateway* is the gateway at each of the two networks.

A typical packet is a 128-character message block. Every packet is precisely the same size and contains the very same control characters within and/or surrounding the message. Once the message is packetized, it is ready for transmission.

Packet Transmission

Figure 9-11 shows a packet switching connection between six different cities. The little boat-shaped figures (shown on the communication circuits) represent individual packets of separate messages. Notice how packets from separate messages are *interleaved* with other packets for transmission. Packet switching is popular because most data communications consist of short bursts of data with intervening spaces that usually last longer than the actual burst of data. Packet switching takes advantage of this by interleaving bursts of data to maximize use of the network.

Although the packets in one data stream may mix with several other data streams during their journey, it is unlikely that packets from two different data streams will travel together during the entire length of their transmission. The two communicating computers do not need to know through which intermediate nodes their data are routed because the packet network takes care of it by either of two methods.

The first method is called *datagram*, a connectionless service. It adds a destination and sequence number to each packet, in addition to information about the data stream to which the packet belongs. In this case, a route is chosen for each packet as it is accepted into the packet network. Each packet may follow a different route through the network. At the destination address, the sequence number tells the network how to reassemble the packets into a continuous message. The sequence number

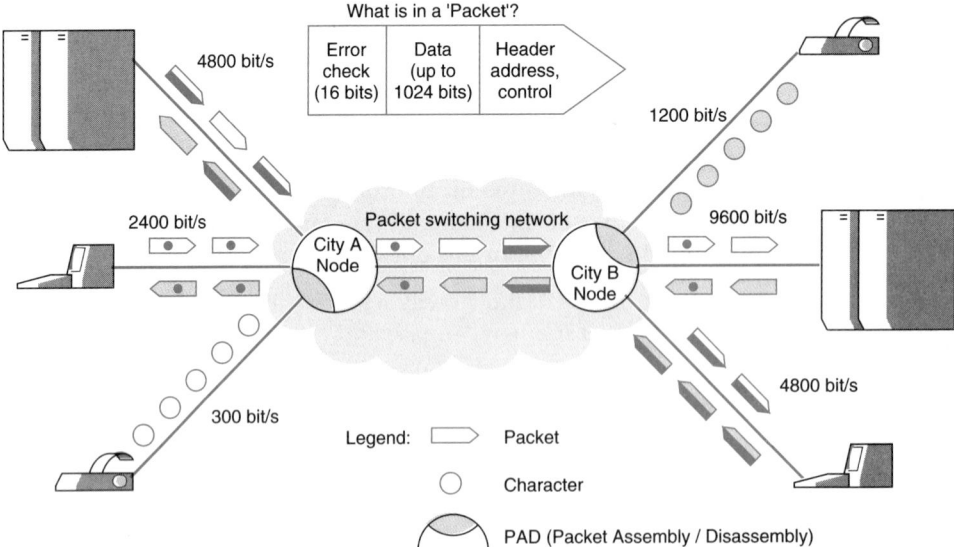

Figure 9-11 Packet switching concepts.

is necessary because different routes may deliver packets at different speeds, so data packets often arrive out of sequence.

The second routing method is called *switched virtual circuit*. In this case, once a computer informs a network of its desire to communicate with another computer over the packet network, the network establishes one end-to-end circuit between them. *All* packets for that transmission take the same route over the virtual circuit that has been set up for that particular transmission. The two computers believe they have a dedicated point to point circuit (but of course they do not). In this case, the packet contains only information about the stream to which it belongs; information about its destination or its position in the sequence of packets is not required because all arrive in the correct order.

Public Packet Switched Networks

Many companies and government agencies set up their own in-house packet switching networks because it is a very efficient way to design private networks. Alternately, an organization can use many public packet switching networks on a number-of-packets-transmitted charge basis or on a usage time basis.

The charges for using a public packet switching network are not related to the distance between the various switching nodes, as is true with other communication circuits. Basic charges depend on the number of packets transmitted or the total usage time.

ACCUNET is an AT&T service used throughout the United States and which offers digital transmission speeds of 9600 and 56,000 bits per second. ACCUNET T1.5 and T45 support their high capacity networks by ACCUNET customer service centers (ACSCs). ACSCs offer a combination of equipment and technical expertise to monitor network performance around-the-clock, seven days a week. The ACCUNET service conforms to the CCITT recommendations for the X.25 packet interface protocols. Many other common carriers offer X.25 packet switched network services.

Cellular Digital Packet Networks

Despite a lack of standards, cellular digital packet data (CDPD) networks are becoming more common. Most cellular telephone services now provide CDPD networks and are lining up partners to build add-ons and applications. At present, most CDPD networks are targeted at transmitted data within the CDPD net or from the CDPD net to traditional land telephone lines. Transmission of data between CDPD networks operating by different cellular providers is still a problem, however.

CDPD sends data packets over unused capacity on cellular networks at 19.2 Kbps. The technology is designed to work like existing hardwired circuit switched networks, and act as a wireless transparent extension to those networks. Since CDPD uses spare capacity on the cellular networks, users are only charged for traffic time, which makes this application cost effective. Using the technology, remote microcomputer users will be able to remain continually attached to their networks. They no longer have to dial

---

Management Focus: Connecticut Public Safety Agencies Adopt CDPD

A dozen Connecticut public safety agencies have outfitted police, fire, and rescue vehicles with pen-based portable computers with CDPD connections. This will enable officers to file reports electronically or make inquiries into central databases operated by state and federal agencies. In the past, if officers wanted information from these databases (e.g., vehicle registration or criminal records), they had to make the request verbally to the dispatcher, who would then pass the request to someone else to obtain the information, which would then be relayed verbally to the officer by the dispatcher. With the new CDPD network, all database inquiries can be made by the officers directly from their portables in less than three seconds.

The network will also support messaging among CDPD users and to and from the central office. The CDPD network supports encryption, which makes it much more secure than the current easily intercepted police radio broadcasts.

Source: Network World, December 12, 1994.

---

into a specific server and check for messages because they will be alerted when a message is received.

One major competitor to CDPD networks is Motorola's *advanced radio data information service* (ARDIS), which permits users with specifically outfitted data terminal equipment (DTE) to acces remote host mainframes via wireless radio links. The Motorola terminal shown in Figure 9-12 is one of these DTEs. IBM's field service technicians have used this type of portable terminal for some years.

Supported by more than 1000 radio transceiver stations across the country, the ARDIS network is linked to one of three dozen concentrator sites. These sites are linked to network control centers, which, in turn are connected to the customer's central host computer. ARDIS is a proprietary network in that it cannot easily interconnect with other users in the same way that CDPD networks can, however, it promises higher data rates.

Frame Relay

Frame relay is a newer packet switching technology that transmits data faster than the currently popular X.25 standard. Simply a data link layer protocol that defines how frames of data are assembled and routed through a data network, frame relay provides higher performance than other wide area network packet switching technologies. It uses variable-length packets, and it has a total of only 48 overhead bits, which is approximately one-quarter the number of bits required for implementation of the X.25 standard.

The key difference between frame relay and X.25 networks is in its data link layer error control. X.25 networks (and virtually all other types of networks) perform error

Figure 9-12   Cellular radio portable data terminal. Photograph courtesy of Motorola, Inc.

checking at each computer in the network. Any errors in transmission are corrected immediately, so that the network layer and application software can assume error-free transmission. However, this error control is one of the most time consuming processes at each computer in a network. Frame relay networks *do not* perform error control. They check for errors and simply discard any messages with errors. It is up to the application software at the source and destination to perform error correction and to control for lost messages.

An example of frame relay is illustrated in Figure 9-13. The left side shows that when a X.25 packet leaves its Source A and moves through Node B, to Node C, to Node D, and finally to its Destination E, each intermediate node acknowledges the packet as it passes. The right side of the figure shows how a frame relay packet moves through Node B, Node C, Node D, and on to Destination E. When Destination E receives the frame correctly, a single acknowledgment is sent back through the nodes to Source A, as shown by the numbers 5, 6, 7, and 8. This acknowledgment may or may not follow the same route as the packet.

A second major difference is that frame relay uses variable length packets, which can be up to 8K bytes.

A third major difference is that a computer can negotiate a *committed information rate* and a *maximum allowable rate* from the network when it establishes a connection-oriented virtual circuit. The committed information rate is the maximum data rate the computer expects to send when it is busy. If the network accepts the connection,

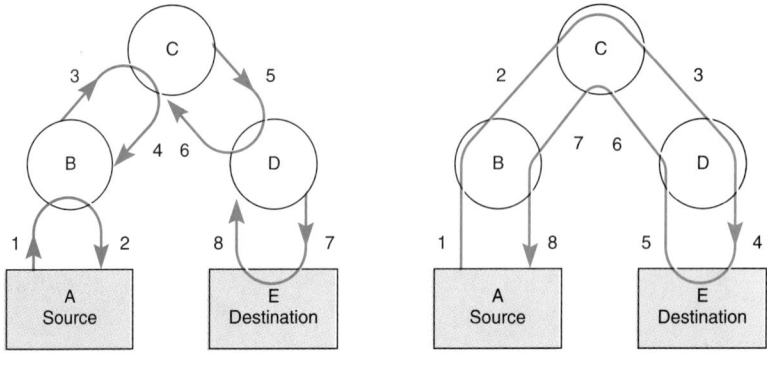

X.25 packet network   Frame relay packet network

Figure 9-13 Frame relay compared to X.25 packet switching. With X.25, each node sends an acknowledgment immediately on receiving a packet. With frame relay, the final destination sends an acknowledgment, making this technique faster than the X.25 technique.

it guarantees to provide that level of service. If the computer exceeds this data rate, the packets are accepted but marked as eligible to be discarded if the network becomes overloaded. Any packets that exceed the maximum allowable rate are immediately discarded.

In most other ways, frame relay networks work the same as X.25 networks. Users connect to them by FRADs (*frame relay assembly and disassembly*), rather than PADs. Both datagram and switched virtual circuit services are available. Frame relay networks are many times faster than X.25 networks, however, and with today's digital and fiber optic transmission networks, are far less prone to errors.

Asynchronous Transfer Mode (ATM)

One of the fastest growing new technologies is *asynchronous transfer mode* (ATM), which is similar to frame relay. All data are packet-switched, and there is no error control at the intermediate computers within the network; error control is the responsibility of the source and destination. Maximum data rates (as well as average data rates) can be negotiated when virtual circuits are created.

ATM provides three important differences from frame relay. First, ATM uses fixed-length packets of 53 bytes (5 bytes of overhead and 48 bytes of user data), which is more suitable for voice transmissions. This is because voice transmission is not very tolerant of the receiving end's reassembly delay time that is caused by the variable lengths of frame relay packets. The small fixed length packets also make routing so simple it can be done in hardware, and loss of a single packet of voice data has very little effect on the total message.

The second major difference is that ATM is scaleable. It is easy to multiplex basic ATM circuits into much faster ATM circuits. ATM circuits provide the same data trans-

Management Focus: Major Public Data Networks

- Infonet 1-800-342-5272
- Tymnet Global Network 1-800-872-7654
- ACCUNET/AT&T 1-800-222-0400
- IBM Information Network 1-800-727-2222
- CompuServe Network Services 1-800-848-8199
- SprintNet Data Network (formerly Telenet) 1-800-736-1130
- Mark*Net 1-800-433-3683
- DATAPAC (Canada) 1-613-781-6798

mission rates as SONET: 51.84 Mbps, 466.56 Mbps, 622.08 Mbps, and so on. A new version called T1 ATM is also available. Like fractional T-1, it offers a scaled down version of the regular ATM service (1.544 Mbps) for companies that do not immediately need such high capacity, but want ATM.

Third, ATM provides forward error correction on the header (but not on the user's data). This minimizes the number of packets that are discarded due to errors, provided the errors are single-bit ones.

Public Data Networks

Several companies offer *public data networks* that use the packet switching concept. Sometimes called *value added networks* (VANs), these networks began when vendors leased circuits between cities, combined them into a packet switching network, started charging on the basis of message volume or amount of time used, and sold the service to users. Second generation VANs incorporated additional user requirements such as e-mail and security features. Today, third generation VANs are built around a microprocessor-based digital message switch similar to fully automated digital PBXs. This digital message switching capability encourages large users to interconnect an assortment of terminals and computers.

Many information retrieval services, such as Dow-Jones News Retrieval Service, The Source, and Dialog, are connected to public data networks for their clients' convenience.

Packet switched public data networks are available in most countries. Some of these networks are PSS (England), Transpac (France), ARPAC (Argentina), Euronet (connecting major European cities), and Austpac (Australia). Tymnet Global Network, for example, has a service called ExpressLane, a public data network using frame relay, to interconnect local area networks between the United States and Europe. It serves 160 cities in the United States as well as London, Paris, Amsterdam, and Frankfurt. Subscribers pay a flat monthly fee of $2,100 per month. Organizations that intercon-

Management Focus: Defense Department Plots Private ATM Strategy

The Department of Defense is planning to install and operate its own worldwide ATM network. The Defense Information Systems Agency (DISA), which plans WANs for the military, said a private ATM WAN with switching hubs controlled by the military appears to be the best approach to ensure flexibility and security in transmitting sensitive information.

The private ATM network strategy represents a turnabout for DISA, which last year said the Defense Department probably would abandon its timeworn practice of owning switching equipment in favor of leasing services directly from commercial providers. But network break-ins and other security concerns may have prompted DISA to seek maximum control over its net. Some carriers are complaining that DISA's plans to forego purchase of public ATM carrier services deprives them of an influential user.

The new backbone for the network would use leased lines operating at SONET speeds of 155 Mbps connected to a variety of military-owned ATM switches, multiplexers, and other access equipment. One criticism is that the equipment purchased by the government would rapidly become obsolete as newer versions of ATM are introduced. Others see the government as being able to deploy ATM faster and run it more cheaply than the public carriers for at least the next five years because no nationwide ATM service currently exists.

Since DISA has changed its mind a number of times concerning its future network strategy, vendors are waiting to see whether Defense Department officials will stick to their guns this time—or if they are simply floating an idea in typical Washington style to get feedback.

Source: Network World, February 6, 1995.

nect their local area networks in both the United States and Europe pay from $2,250 to $4,100 per month, depending on the charges for the international circuits.

Software Defined Networks (Virtual Networks)

To make traditional leased voice grade circuits more competitive, it is possible to lease a *software defined network* (SDN) circuit. SDNs are built on public switched networks to provide a private leased circuit for the leasing organization. The user leases a virtual circuit from Point A to Point B rather than a hardwired physical circuit as is normal with a voice grade leased circuit. A *virtual network* is a logical creation that provides a connection on a message-by-message basis, but it appears to be a dedicated circuit to the user. Virtual networks help firms to avoid the cost of leasing or purchasing network switching equipment and dedicated leased transmission facilities between their computers by allowing customers to use dial-up facilities for extending private network functions to geographically dispersed sites.

All three of the major long distance carriers offer virtual networks. AT&T has its Software Defined Network (SDN), US Sprint has its Virtual Private Network (VPN), and MCI has Vnet. These services allow interconnections between most major U.S. cities and other major cities worldwide. They also allow transmission speeds ranging from a low 9600 bits per second up to a high of 1.544 Mbps.

The Global Software Defined Network (GSDN) is a private international virtual networking service with 9.6 Mbps point-point virtual circuits for voice, data, and fax. Network reconfiguration is handled by updating the software rather than physically moving circuits. Less expensive than international long distance service, GSDN is available to Canada, Australia, Singapore, and most of Europe.

IMPROVING MAN/WAN PERFORMANCE

Improving the performance of MANs and WANs is handled in the same way as improving LAN performance. You begin by checking the computers in the network, by upgrading the circuits between computers, and by changing the demand placed on the network.

Improving Computer Performance

One way to improve network performance is to upgrade the computers that perform network functions such as routing. Another strategy is to examine the routing protocol; static routing is not as good as dynamic routing when it comes to handling traffic problems in WANs and MANs. Dynamic routing will increase performance in networks which have many possible routes from one computer to another, or those in which message traffic is "bursty," that is, occurs in spurts, with many messages at one time, and few at others.

Dynamic routing does increase network traffic, however. In some cases, the status information sent between computers this way accounts for more than 50 percent of all WAN message traffic. This is clearly a problem, because it drastically reduces the amount of network capacity available for users' messages. Dynamic routing should use no more than 10 to 20 percent of the network's total capacity.

Improving Circuit Capacity

The first step is to analyze the message traffic in the network to find which dedicated point-to-point circuits are approaching capacity. These circuits then can be upgraded to provide more capacity. Less used dedicated circuits can be downgraded to save costs. A more sophisticated analysis involves examines *why* circuits are heavily used.

For example in Figure 9-3, the circuit from Chicago to Houston may be heavily used, but much traffic on this circuit may not originate in Chicago or be destined for Houston. It may, for example, be going from Calgary to San Francisco, suggesting that adding a circuit here would improve performance to a greater extent than upgrading the Chicago to Houston circuit.

The capacity may be adequate for most traffic, but not for meeting peak demand. One solution may be to add a switched circuit service that is only used when demand exceeds circuit capacity. Sometimes a shortage of capacity may be caused by a faulty circuit. As circuits deteriorate, the number of errors increases. As the error rate increases, throughput falls because more messages have to be retransmitted. Before installing new circuits, monitor the existing ones to ensure that they are operating properly; fixing a faulty circuit is usually cheaper than getting a new one.

Reducing Network Demand

There are many ways to reduce network demand. One simple step is to require a network impact statement for all new application software developed or purchased by the organization. This focuses attention on the network impacts at any early stage in application development. Another simple approach is to use data compression techniques for all data in the network.

Another, sometimes more difficult, approach is to shift network usage from peak or high cost times to lower demand or lower cost times. For example, the transmission of detailed sales and inventory reports from a retail store to headquarters could be done after the store closes. This takes advantage of off-peak rate charges and avoids interfering with transmissions requiring higher priority, such as customer credit card authorizations.

The network can be redesigned to move data closer to the applications and people who use them. This also will reduce the amount of traffic in the network. Distributed database applications allow them to be spread across several different computers. For example, instead of storing customer records in one central location, you could store them according to region.

SELECTING MAN/WAN SERVICES

A 1995 survey of network managers found that on average, 45 percent of WAN costs were for network management, primarily support staff salaries. On average, 35 percent was spent on services, especially the cost of leasing data circuits from common carriers. Only 20 percent was spent on equipment.

The important points here are: first, the most expensive part of your WAN will be the people required to plan, install, and operate it, so, pick one that is easy to manage. Second, it costs more to lease services from common carriers than to buy hardware, so selection decisions should be driven more by the services than the hardware.

There are so many services available that identifying the ideal service is difficult. Figure 9-14 summarizes the current services, but new common carriers and new services are added almost monthly. Prices change rapidly due to intense competition and the fact that many services are essentially commodities; a T-1 line from one vendor is the same as a T-1 line from another. Nonetheless, selecting a MAN/WAN service requires answering some basic questions. The design steps in Chapter 11 will help in MAN/WAN service selection, as will the key issues examined in the following discussion. These issues are summarized in Figure 9-15.

The first issue is the *vendor*. The best ones provide high quality service, quickly respond to network problems, adapt to changing customer needs, and provide useful network management services along with the data transmission services.

A second consideration is the network *capacity* you need. There are a variety of services available at many different data transmission rates. Try to estimate the general

Type of Service	Data Rates
Dialed Circuit Services	9600 bps to 33.6 Kbps
Dedicated Circuit Services	
Voice Grade Channels	9600 bps to 33.6 Kbps
Wideband Analog Services	19.2 Kbps to 230 Kbps
Digital Services	9600 bps to 1.5 Mbps
T Carrier Circuits	64 Kbps to 274 Mbps
Synchronous Optical Network (SONET)	52 Mbps to 622 Mbps
Satellite Services	9600 bps to 1.5 Mbps
Switched Circuit Services	
Integrated Services Digital Network (ISDN)	128 Kbps to 1.5 Mbps
Broadband ISDN	155 Mbps to 622 Mbps
Switched Multimegabit Data Service (SMDS)	1.5 Mbps to 44 Mbps
Packet Switched Networks	
Public Packet Switched Networks	9600 bps to 44 Mbps
Cellular Digital Packet Networks	19.2 Kbps
Frame Relay	1.5 Mbps to 44 Mbps
Asynchronous Transfer Mode (ATM)	1.5 Mbps to 622 Mbps
Public Data Networks	19.2 Kbps to 1.5 Mbps
Software Defined Networks (Virtual Networks)	9600 bps to 1.5 Mbps

Figure 9-14   Commonly available services.

- Vendor Capabilities
- Capacity
- Flexibility
- Control
- Reliability

Figure 9-15   Key issues in selecting MAN/WAN services.

capacity you need at each network site, and be aware that users' needs change. *Flexibility* is important. In general, dedicated circuits are much less flexible than switched services. A common strategy is to build new networks with switched services, and monitor the traffic flows. Once the network traffic is somewhat stable, dedicated circuits often replace switched services on high-use circuits, because dedicated circuits are often cheaper when the volume of traffic between two points is fairly constant. Switched circuits are then used as a secondary service in case demand exceeds the capacity of the dedicated circuits.

Control is another important issue. With dedicated circuits, you have more control over how your messages get routed in the network because your computers do the routing. With switched services, the service provider is responsible for the routine, and your messages get intermixed with those of other network users.

The *reliability* of a network service both in terms of average error rates and any circuit failures is also important. In general, switched networks generally are more reliable than dedicated circuits because they have redundant circuits between various cities. This means that if part of a common carrier's network fails, an entirely different path might be utilized, producing little effect on network users.

Summary

Types of Communication Services   Communication services come in four basic groups. A dialed circuit is a regular dialed telephone call from one point to another though the telephone network. A dedicated circuit is a point-to-point circuit available for the exclusive use of the leasing organization that connects two offices. A switched circuit is one in which the organization establishes network connection points at a variety of locations and uses the carrier's network to make temporary (switched) connections between locations when necessary. A packet network works very much like a switched circuit, except that the user breaks data transmissions into pre-defined packets that conform to network protocols. With a dedicated circuit, the organization pays a fixed monthly fee, while with the other three, the organization pays on a per-use basis.

Common Carriers, Tariffs, and Deregulation   A common carrier is a government-regulated private company that sells or leases communication services and facilities to the public. A tariff is the schedule of rates and description of services that are to be received when a particular type of communication service is purchased or leased. If the industry is deregulated, as it is in the United States, it may be more innovative, cost effective, and able to develop new services faster.

Communications in the United States   During the 1980s, AT&T was divided into long distance services (which it still operates), and local telephone exchange companies. Several other competitors have entered the long distance market (e.g., Sprint, MCI), and the local exchange market (e.g., GTE). Complicating matters has been the explosive growth in the cellular telephone market, with every long distance and local exchange bidding against each other to acquire cellular services.

Dialed Circuit Services   Dialed circuits are usually slow and noisy. With direct distance dialing, the normal voice telephone network is used for data transmission; the user dials the host computer telephone number through a modem. The AT&T Megacom WATS is a special bulk rate service for direct dial calls. The DIAL-IT 900 service allows many different users to call a 900 area code number to receive information or respond to a poll.

Dedicated Circuit Services   A dedicated circuit is leased from the common carrier for exclusive use twenty-four hours per day, seven days per week. Faster and more noise-free transmissions are possible, but you must carefully plan all the circuits you need. Voice grade channels are analog circuits that are less noisy than dialed circuits. Wideband analog services are used for either data transmission at higher speeds, typically up to 230 Kbps. Digital services transmit data up to 1.544 Mbps. T carrier circuits are leased digital circuits with a hierarchy of digital transmission and multiplexing standards ranging from T-1 (1.544 Mbps) to T-4 (274 Mbps). The Synchronous Optical Network (SONET) uses fiber optics to provide services ranging from OC-1 (51 Mbps) to OC 12 (622 Mbps). Several common carriers offer satellite channels for voice, data, facsimile, and various wideband applications at various speeds.

Switched Circuit Services   Switched circuits enable you to define the end points of the wide area network, without specifying all the interconnecting circuits you will need, and still get the high data rates possible with dedicated circuits services. Integrated Services Digital Network (ISDN) has been available since the late 1970s, but has not been widely adopted, due in part to conflicting interpretations of the ISDN standards by different U.S. vendors and common carriers. Basic rate interface ISDN provides a communication circuit with two 64 Kbps digital transmission channels and one 16 Kbps control channel. Primary rate interface ISDN consists of 23 64 Kbps data channels and one 64 Kbps control channel. Broadband ISDN is a switched version of SONET, but it not yet widely available. Switched multimegabit data service (SMDS), offered by most RBOCs, is essentially a switched version of the T-carrier and SONET services. Most of the RBOCs offer SMDS at two transmission rates: DS-1 at 1.544 Mbps or DS-3 at 44.376 Mbps.

Packet Switched Networks   Packet switching is a store and forward data transmission technique in which messages are split into small segments. Frame relay is a newer packet switching technology that transmits data faster than the currently popular

X.25 packet switching standard. The key difference between frame relay and traditional packet switching networks is that frame relay networks do not perform error control. Asynchronous transfer mode (ATM) is one of the fastest growing new technologies. ATM is very similar to frame relay, except that it uses fixed-length packets. ATM is scaleable, and provides forward error correction on the header (but not on the user's data). Several companies offer public data networks that use the packet switching concept. Software defined networks are built on public switched networks to provide a private leased circuit on a message-by-message basis for the leasing organization.

Improving MAN/WAN Performance   One can improve network performance by utilizing front end processors, by improving the speed of the computers themselves, and by using a better routing protocol. Analyzing network usage can show when circuits need to be increased or decreased in capacity, what new circuits need to be leased, and when additional switched circuits may be needed to meet peak demand. Performance may also be improved by reducing network demand by including a network usage analysis in all new application software, using data compression, shifting usage to off-peak times, establishing priorities for some applications, or redesigning the network to move data closer to those who use it.

Selecting MAN/WAN Services   The first issue is the quality of the vendor, because the largest cost in operating a MAN/WAN is network management. A second consideration is the network capacity you need. Flexibility is important because it is often hard to predict network usage. Dedicated circuits are less flexible than switched circuits, but can be cheaper if used constantly. Dedicated circuits provide more control over message routing because your computers handle it. With switched services, the service provider performs the routing. The reliability of a network service both in terms of average error rates and any circuit failure is also important. In general, switched networks are more reliable because they have redundant circuits between various cities.

Key Terms

2B+D	Conditioning	Frame relay
23B+D	Deregulation	Integrated services digital
American Telephone and	DIAL-IT 900 service	network (ISDN)
Telegraph (AT&T)	Dial-up	InterLATA
AT&T Megacom	Digital service	Interstate
AT&T Megacom WATS	Direct distance dialing	IntraLATA
Basic rate interface	(DDD)	Intrastate
Bypass	Equal access	Leased circuit
Circuit switching	Equalization	Local access transport area
Common carrier	Federal Communications	(LATA)
Communication facility	Commission (FCC)	Local exchange companies
Communication services	Fractional T-1	Local exchange service

Long distance common carrier

MCI Communications Corporation

Measured use service

Metropolitan area network (MAN)

Monopoly situation

Optical carrier level 1 (OC-1)

Packet assembly/ disassembly (PAD)

Packet switching

Packet switching network

Packetizing

Personal communication network (PCN)

Point of presence (POP)

Primary rate interface

Public data network (PDN)

Public packet switched service

Public Utilities Commissions (PUCs)

Regional Bell Operating Company (RBOC)

Regulation situation

Satellite channel

Software defined network (SDN)

Switched multimegabit data service (SMDS)

Synchronous optical network (SONET)

T carrier circuit

T carrier system

T-1/T-2/T-3/T-4 circuits

Tariff

Tariff 12

Tariff 15

US Sprint Communications Company

Value added network (VAN)

Virtual circuit

Virtual network

Voice grade channel

Wide area network (WAN)

Wide area telephone service (WATS)

Wideband analog service

X.3

X.25

X.28

X.29

X.75

Selected References

1. AT&T Communications. *AT&T Catalog: Business Communications Systems* (catalog no. 3CS, published annually). Available from American Transtech, P.O. Box 45038, Jacksonville, FL 32232-9974.

2. AT&T Communications. *Catalog of Technical Publications* (PUB 10000 and 10000A). Available from Literary Data Center, Inc., G.P.O. Box C-9104, Brooklyn, NY 11202.

3. AT&T Communications. *Local Access Transport Areas* (PUB SC 503-000). Available from AT&T Communications Consultant Liaison Program, 295 North Maple Ave., Basking Ridge, NJ 07920.

4. AT&T Communications. *Network Communications: Applications and Services* (PUB 500-936). Available from AT&T Customer Information Center, 2855 North Franklin Road, Indianapolis, IN 46219.

5. AT&T Customer Information Center. *AT&T Documentation Guide* (PUB 000-11). Available from AT&T Customer Information Center, 2855 North Franklin Road, Indianapolis, IN 46219.

6. Briere, Daniel, ''MANs Provide Digital Services at Low Cost,'' *Network World*, vol. 7, no. 46, November 12, 1990, 1, 51, 54, 57, 60.

7. *Computerworld: Newsweekly for the Computer Community*. Published weekly by CW Communications, Box 9171, 375 Cochituate Road, Framingham, MA 01701-9171, 1967 to present.

8. Derfler, Frank J., Jr., and Kimberly J. Maxwell. ''Reliable Relays,'' *PC Magazine*, vol. 10, no. 15, September 10, 1991, 377–379, 382–384, 386, 388–389, 392, 394, 398, 400, 402, 405.

9. Flanagan, William. *Guide to T-1 Networking: How to Buy, Install and Use T-1, from Desktop to DS-3.* New York: Telecom Library, Inc., 1990.

10. Giancarlo, Charles. ''Making the Transition from T-3 to SONET,'' *Telecommunications*, vol. 26, no. 4, April 1992, 17–20.

11. Heywood, Peter, and Elke Gronert. ''Public Frame Relay Goes Global,'' *Data Communications*, vol. 21, no. 4, March 1992, 77–80.

12. Kessler, Gary C. "Simplifying SONET," *LAN Magazine*, vol. 6, no. 7, July 1991, 36–37, 39–40, 42, 44, 46.

13. *Network World.* Published weekly by CW Communications, Box 9171, 375 Cochituate Road, Framingham, MA 01701-9171, 1983 to present.

Questions/Problems

1. Other than geographic differences, how do wide area networks differ from small local area networks?
2. How is a virtual circuit distinguished from other circuits?
3. What is the function of a switching node?
4. What happens to messages when a PAD facility is used?
5. What features are common to every packet on a network?
6. Where does packetizing take place?
7. What does a packet contain?
8. What are the two ways in which packets may be routed?
9. Why is packet switching popular?
10. How do packet switching networks differ from other networks in how they charge customers?
11. Why are packet switching networks generally considered to be more reliable than other types of networks?
12. When organizations develop their own packet switching value added networks, what are they called and what is their purpose?
13. Name four public data networks, including two outside the United States.
14. Explain the value of bypassing the local exchange carrier.
15. Discuss why frame relay might replace X.25.
16. Discuss why ATM might replace frame relay.
17. Define communication facility.
18. When an organization uses public packet switching networks, on what factors are the charges based?
19. Define common carrier.
20. Name three of the largest common carriers in North America.
21. Define deregulation.
22. A _____ is the schedule of rates and description of services offered by common carriers. What is it?
23. Who regulates common carriers and how is it done?
24. What is the primary difference between the evolution of data communication services in the United States and those in other countries?
25. Discuss the advantages and disadvantages of communication deregulation.
26. What aspect of communications is regulated?
27. Name four of the RBOCs (also referred to as local exchange carriers or local telephone companies).
28. Define LATA.
29. How does local exchange service differ from exchange access service?

30. Why is equal access an issue?
31. What is the deciding factor in common carrier service quality?
32. Are customers able to specify the type of circuit when they contract for a private circuit?
33. Are leased circuits used exclusively by one user?
34. How do leased circuits differ from dial-up circuits?
35. Are voice grade circuits digital or analog?
36. Why is conditioning or equalization performed?
37. Why should a data communication manager know something about conditioning?
38. How do wideband services differ from voice grade services?
39. Why does the telephone company tell customers when they will be using satellite circuits?
40. Can the telephone company condition dial-up circuits? Why or why not?
41. What distinguishes ISDN from other services?
42. How do basic rate interface and primary rate interface differ?
43. What are the two factors that distinguish T-1 circuits from others?
44. What is the T carrier system?
45. How does a virtual circuit service differ from other types of circuits?
46. How do measured use services differ from private leased circuit services?
47. WATS is a special bulk rate service. How is WATS service charged?
48. How does AT&T Megacom service differ from WATS service?
49. What are the primary advantages of using public packet switched services?
50. Why might business firms wish to have 900 number arrangements?
51. An organization can lease a private network but not have physical wires interconnecting the different nodes. What is this called?
52. What is a 2B+D? Define it.
53. Identify and describe some of the private circuit (lease) services.
54. Identify various measured use services.
55. What is the difference between interstate/intrastate data communications and interLATA/intraLATA?
56. What is the difference between the FCC and a state PUC?
57. If you make a call from San Francisco to San Diego (California), is it intraLATA or interLATA?
58. Name and describe two controversial tariffs.
59. What is the most popular way for common carriers to handle growing international telephone service?
60. Can you have switched services on both dial-up and leased digital circuits?
61. What device makes switched digital service possible?
62. Distinguish between T-1, T-2, T-3, and T-4 circuits.
63. Describe how fractional T-1 operates.
64. Name the three ways to obtain a T-3 circuit.
65. Describe SONET.
66. What is the basic SONET transmission frame?
67. What is it called when STS-1 electrical signals are converted to optical signals?

68. Describe the regional Bell operating company switched service that interconnects two local area networks at T-1 circuit speeds. What purpose does it serve?
69. What is a personal communication network?
70. Why might PCNs revolutionize communications in the United States?

NEXT DAY AIR SERVICE CUMULATIVE CASE STUDY

See appendix at end of book

CHAPTER TEN

BACKBONE NETWORKS

This chapter examines backbone networks (BNs). We begin with the various types of devices used in backbone networks, then discuss two fundamental types of these networks. The first are extensions of traditional LANs that use shared multipoint circuits (fast ethernet and FDDI). The second are extensions of WANs and MANs that use point-to-point circuits (switched ethernet, switched token ring, and ATM). The chapter ends with a discussion of how to improve BN performance and how to select a BN.

Objectives

- Understand the internetworking devices used in backbone networks,
- Understand several types of fast ethernet,
- Understand several types of FDDI,
- Understand collapsed backbones and several type of switched networks,
- Become familiar with ways to improve backbone network performance,
- Become familiar with key factors in selecting backbone networks.

Chapter Outline

Introduction
Backbone Network Components
     Hubs
     Bridges
     Switches
     Routers
     Brouters

INTRODUCTION

One key issue in today's networking is the ability and the need to connect local area networks to other networks (both LANs and WANs). This *internetworking* is accomplished via a *backbone network*. Most organizations now interconnect all their networks into one supernetwork called an *enterprise network*.

The driving force behind enterprise networking is the shift toward an information-based business economy. Most business organizations realize that information must be stored, retrieved, analyzed, acted upon, and shared with others at a moment's notice. Without an enterprise-wide network, moving information from one department to another or to customers is difficult, and often relies on "sneaker net," diskettes carried from one computer to another.

Interconnecting the organization's diverse networks is one way to meet this challenge. A *backbone network* is a high speed network or networks which usually connect every network on a single company or government site. It also may be an enterprise network if it connects everything within a company, regardless of whether it crosses state, national, or international boundaries. This blurs the distinction between enterprise, backbone, and wide area networks.

Changing technology also makes it difficult to distinguish these various types of networks from one another. Local area networks used to be confined to a small area, not crossing public thoroughfares. Now it is possible for a number of local area networks to be internetworked to operate as a wide area network. Similarly, high speed backbone network technologies are replacing traditional LAN technologies such as ethernet and token ring.

While rigid definitions no longer apply, the fundamental concepts still do. LANs support a group of computers in a confined geographical area using the same shared network circuit. Backbone networks typically use higher speed circuits to interconnect a series of LANs, MANs, and WANs that sometimes use different network and data link protocols. However, some backbone networks use the same low speed technologies as LANs rather than high speed alternatives. In this chapter, we will focus on the high speed network technologies typically used in backbone networks and how they can be used.

BACKBONE NETWORK COMPONENTS

There are two basic components to a backbone network: the network cable, and the hardware devices that connect other networks to the backbone network. The cable is essentially the same as that used in LANs, except that it is usually higher quality to provide higher data rates (e.g., fiber optic or category 5 shielded twisted pair). The hardware devices can be computers or special purpose devices that just transfer messages from one network to another. These include hubs, bridges, routers, brouters, gateways, and switches (see Figure 10-1).

Hubs

Operating at the physical layer, *hubs* are very simple devices that pass all traffic in both directions between the LAN sections they link. Hubs forward *every* message they receive to the other sections of the LAN, even those that do not need to go there. They may connect *different* types of cable, but use the *same* data link and network protocol (see Figure 10-2).

Strictly speaking, hubs are used within one LAN. They are usually repeaters or

Device	Messages	Physical Layer	Data Link Layer	Network Layer
Hub	All Transferred	Same or Different	Same	Same
Bridge	Filtered	Same or Different	Same	Same
Switch	Routed	Same or Different	Same	Same
Router	Routed	Same or Different	Same or Different	Same
Brouter	Filtered & Routed	Same or Different	Same or Different	Same
Gateway	Routed	Same or Different	Same or Different	Same or Different

Figure 10-1   Backbone Network Devices.

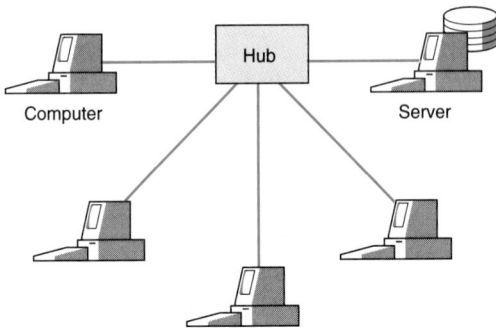

Figure 10-2 Use of hubs to connect computers in a LAN.

amplifiers that increase the strength of the signal in the circuit to enable the circuit to run longer distances than cable alone. For example, hubs allow you to create an ethernet network several thousand meters in length, which is much more than the typical limit of less than 200 meters for 10Base2. Repeaters can also be used to extend the distance, but typically only connects two LAN segments.

Bridges

Bridges connect two LAN segments that use the *same* data link and network protocol, and operate at the data link layer. They may connect the *same or different* types of cable. Bridges are more sophisticated than hubs because they only forward those messages that need to go to other network segments (see Figure 10-3).

Bridges "learn" whether to forward packets. When a bridge receives a packet, it reads the packet's source address and compares this address to its own internal *routing table*. If the *source address* is not in the routing table, the bridge adds it. Thus, the bridge is said to *learn* the addresses of the devices on the network. If the *destination address* is not in the routing table, the bridge forwards the packet to all networks or network segments except the one on which it was received. If the destination address is in both the routing table and on the same network segment as the source address, the bridge automatically discards the packet, which is a process known as *filtering*. The bridge can discard the packet because the station to which it is addressed will already have received and copied it. If the destination address is in the routing table but not on the same network segment, the bridge determines the port associated with the address and *forwards* the packet to that port. Some bridges check packets for errors, and only forward error-free ones.

Bridges are a combination of both hardware and software. A typical bridge is a "black box" that sits between the two networks and has its own processor, memory, and software; its operations are transparent to the network user. A bridge also can be regular computer with two or more NICs and special bridging software. A simple bridge can connect two LAN segments in the same building. This is useful if a LAN cable gets too long or too busy, because you can break one LAN into two segments and bridge them.

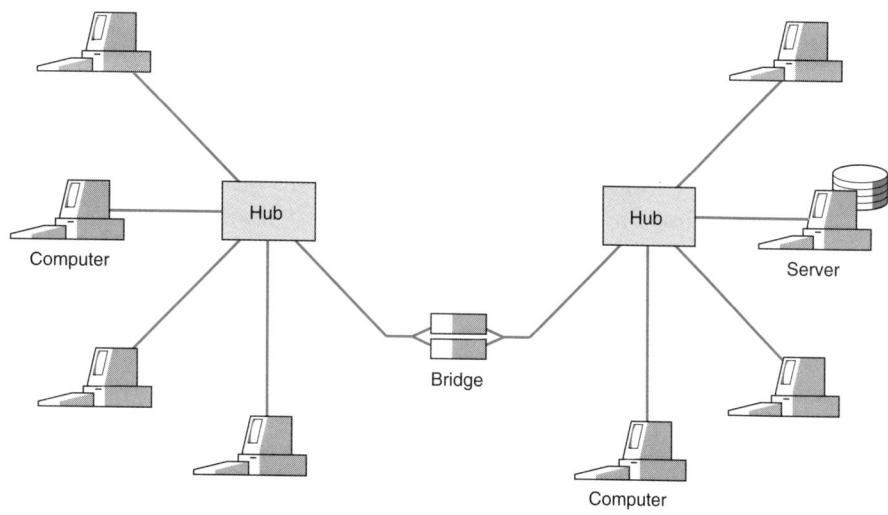

Figure 10-3   Use of bridges to connect LAN segments.

Switches

Switches connect *more than two* LAN segments that use the *same* data link and network protocol. Switches operate at the data link layer. They may connect the *same or different* types of cable. Switches typically provide ports for 4, 8, 16, or 32 separate LAN segments. Most switches enable *all* ports to be in use simultaneously, so they are faster than bridges (see Figure 10-4).

Switches also connect several low speed LAN segments into a faster backbone network, for example, connecting 16 ethernet LAN segments each at 10 Mbps into one 100 Mbps backbone When used in this way, switches are similar to multiplexers.

Cut-through switches use circuit switching: they examine the destination of the incoming packet and immediately connect the port with the incoming message to the correct

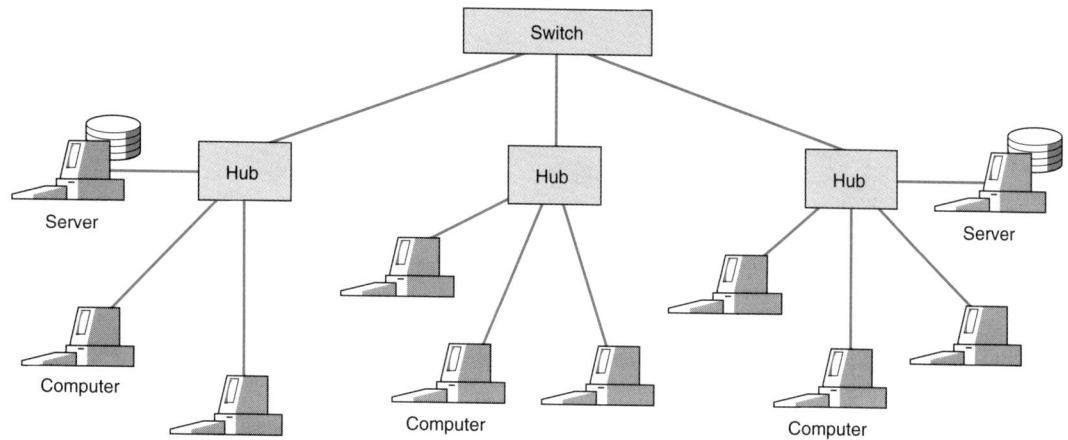

Figure 10-4   Use of switches to connect LANs.

outgoing port. This decision is made in hardware, so cut-though switches are very fast. However, if the outgoing port is in use, the collision results in a lost packet.

Store-and-forward switches copy the incoming packet into memory before processing the destination address. If the outgoing circuit is available, the packet is immediately forwarded to it. If the outgoing circuit is in use, the packet is held in memory until later. Many store-and-forward switches also do error checking and can discard bad packets. Store-and-forward switches tend to be more expensive and slower than cut-through switches, but rapid changes in cost and speed are eliminating these differences.

Routers

Routers connect two or more LANs that use the *same or different* (usually different) data link protocols, but the *same* network protocol. They may connect the *same or different* types of cable. Routers operate at the network layer. Routers forward only those messages that need to go to other networks (see Figure 10-5).

One major feature of a router is that it chooses the "best" route between networks when there are several possible routes between them. Because a router knows its own location, as well as the packet's final destination, it looks in a routing table to identify the best route or *path.*

Routers must possess a higher level of software intelligence than either repeaters or bridges because they operate at the network layer. Routers may be "black boxes" or computers with several NICs. In general, they perform more processing on each message than bridges, and therefore operate more slowly. Routers allow the logical separation of an internetwork into many networks by using an addressing scheme that distinguishes between *device addresses* at the data link layer and *internetwork addresses* at

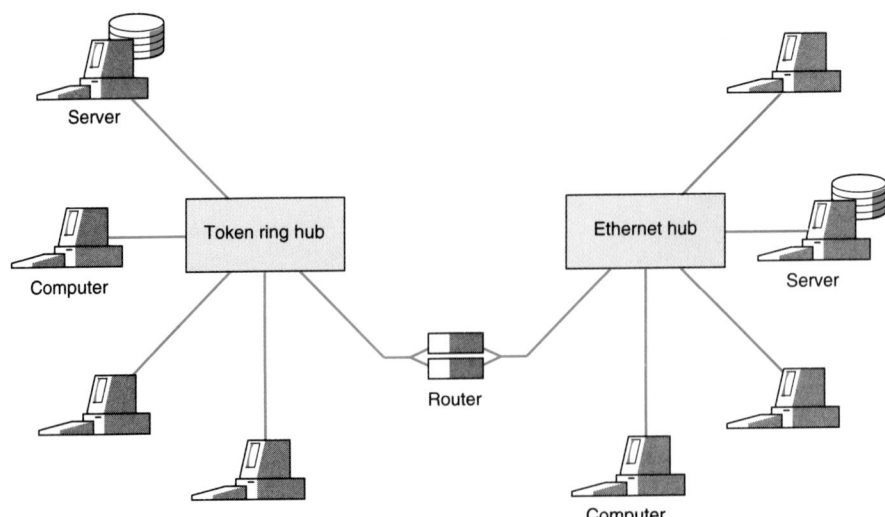

Figure 10-5   Use of routers to connect LANs.

the network layer. Routing systems use the *internetwork address* specified in the network protocol packet and their routing tables for routing decisions. For this reason, you must display a packet's internetwork address if you want to know a packet's real source and destination node.

One additional difference between a router and a bridge is that a router only processes messages that are specifically addressed to it. To send a message to a computer on another network, the sender must specify the internetwork address of the destination computer in the network layer packet, and send the packet to the router, which will process the packet by building an entirely new data link layer packet, and then transmit that on the other network.

The router attempts to make no changes to the network packet and user data it receives. Sometimes, however, changes are needed, such as when the maximum data link layer packet size on one network is different from another, which forces the router to split a message into several smaller messages for transmission.

Brouters

Brouters (see Figure 10-6) are devices that combine the functions of both bridges and routers. These operate at both the data link and network layers. A brouter connects

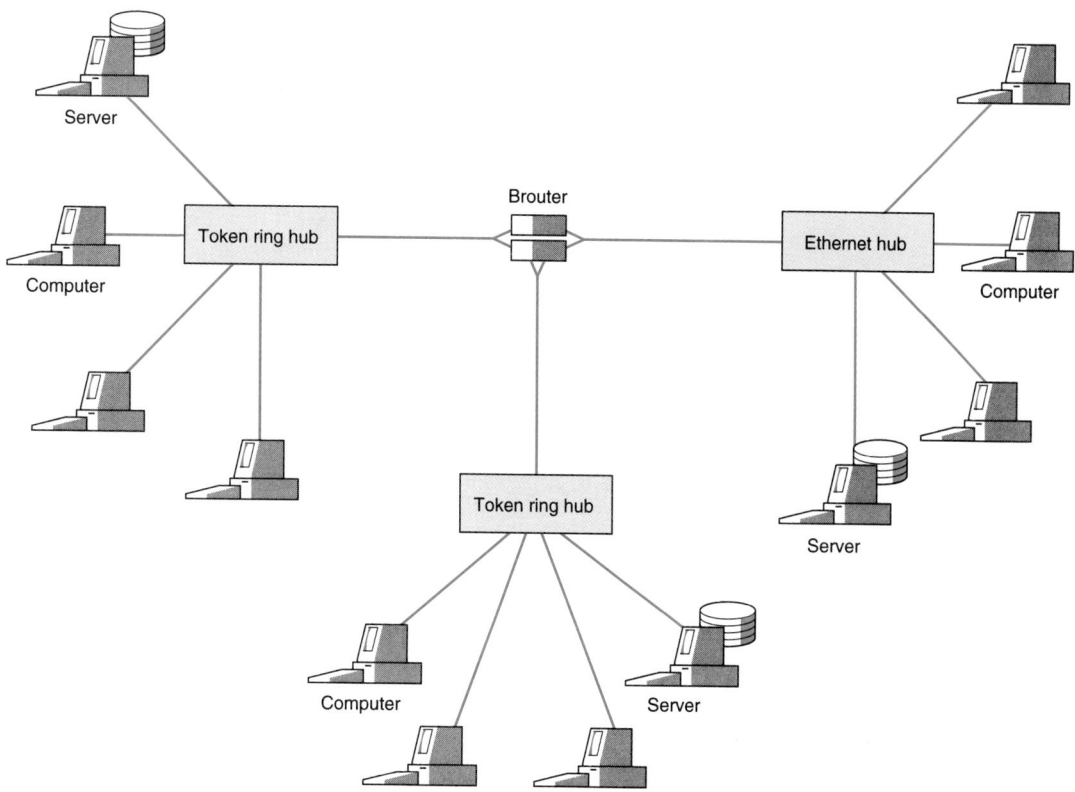

Figure 10-6   Use of brouters to connect LANs.

both same data link type network LAN segments and different data link ones. Like a bridge, it examines the data link layer addresses of all packets on the network and forwards them to any other network of the same type. At the same time, it processes any messages addressed to it by looking at the network layer protocol to see if the message needs to be it forwarded to a different data link layer type network. The advantage of brouters is that they are as fast as bridges for same data link type networks, but can also connect different data link type networks.

Gateways

Gateways are more complex than bridges or routers because they are the interface between two or more dissimilar networks. Gateways connect two or more LANs that use the *same or different* (usually different) data link and network protocols. They may connect the *same or different* types of cable. Gateways operate at the network layer, and sometimes at the application layer as well. Gateways forward only those messages that need to go to other networks (see Figure 10-7).

Gateways translate one network protocol into another, translate data formats, and open sessions between application programs, thus overcoming both hardware and software incompatibilities. In micro-to-mainframe communications, for example, the gateway converts the microcomputer LAN transmissions into a transmission that looks like it came from a smart terminal.

More complex gateways even take care of such tasks as code conversion (ASCII-

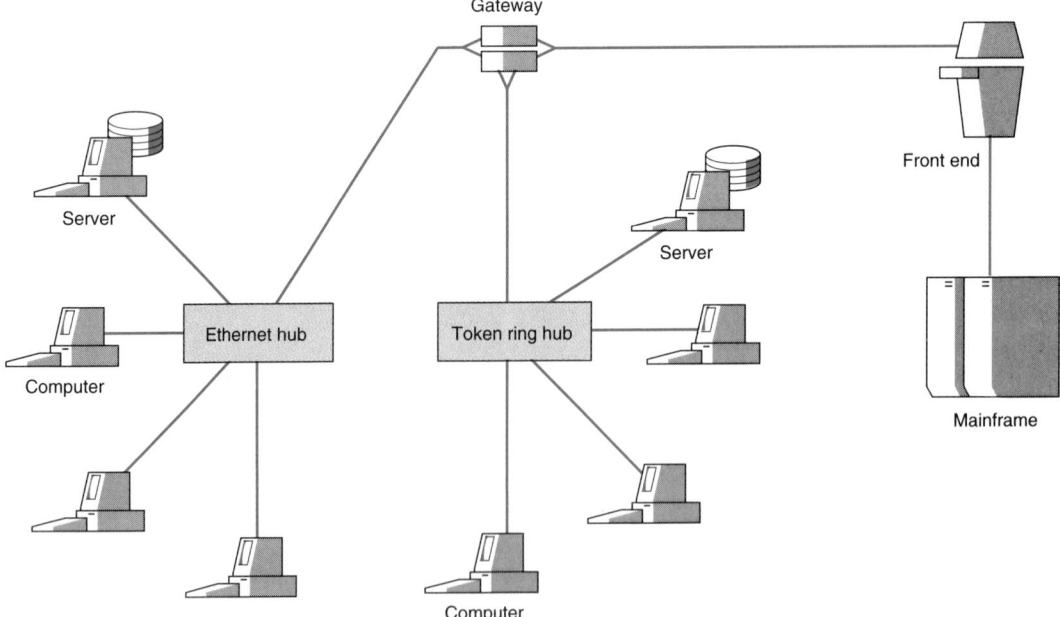

Figure 10-7   Use of gateways to connect LANs and a mainframe.

EBCDIC). An example is a systems network architecture (SNA) gateway that allows LAN users to access mainframe applications, data, and peripherals. Without this SNA gateway on their local area network, each microcomputer would have to have its own 3270 hardware emulation card, coaxial cable, and mainframe controller port. The SNA gateway eliminates the need for additional hardware for the microcomputer, and it requires only one connection to the host computer because all data are sent through the local area network gateway.

A gateway may be a stand-alone microcomputer with several NICs and special software, a front end processor connected to a mainframe computer, or even a special circuit card in the network server. Each of the three basic types of gateways—network-to-network, system-to-network, and system-to-system—solves a specific interconnection problem.

In some cases, two compatible networks may need a *network-to-network gateway* because of internetwork domain problems. For example, an X.25 network typically routes data and calls only within the boundaries of its own network definitions. As a result, each X.25 network is distinct and is controlled separately. If two such networks seek to communicate with one another, it is necessary for the calls to go through a special *X.75 gateway* node. The primary purpose of this X.75 gateway is to provide any necessary translation (particularly terminal address translation) for a call originating in one network that is destined for another network. Such translation is mandatory because the X.25 standard does not specify how an address is mapped into a user port. When a user in one X.25 network specifies an address in another X.25 network, a large portion of that address may not be comprehensible to the receiving network, and must be routed to a gateway for call processing. X.75 gateways are an integral part of the hardware furnished by packet switching manufacturers.

The primary function of the *system-to-network gateway* is to make the network available to a minicomputer system. For example, it could allow an X.25 network to connect to a Unix minicomputer, as well as performing some secondary functions related to the handling of asynchronous X.3 PAD functions. In either of these instances, the source of any data is assumed to be compatible with what the minicomputer is expecting. When a client or user microcomputer wants to communicate with the network, however, it may encounter problems of incompatibility. For example, the gateway might connect directly into the minicomputer system bus on one side and into the synchronous line of the X.25 network on the other. The primary function of the system-to-network gateway is to convert a protocol to a form the minicomputer can understand.

A *system-to-system gateway* connects one vendor's computer system to another vendor's computer system. The gateway provides both the basic system interconnection and the necessary emulation in both directions. The gateway probably would be made to look like the terminals or terminal controllers of one of the two computer systems, allowing the terminals of the second computer to attach to the first computer's controller. A common example is a computer on a LAN to a mainframe using SNA.

The major difference between a system-to-system gateway and a system-to-network gateway is that the latter assumes the source of any data is compatible with whatever the computer system is expecting. By contrast, the system-to-system gateway assumes a basic difference in the systems themselves or other protocol and architecture differences between computers manufactured by different vendors.

A Caveat

One warning is in order. The terminology used in the marketplace may differ substantially from the preceding discussion. One vendor's "bridge" may actually provide the functions of a "router." Some examples follow.

Multiprotocol bridges translate between different data link layer protocols. They receive data from one network using one data link protocol (e.g., ethernet), and translate it into another protocol (e.g., token ring) for use on another network. The most common type of multiprotocol bridge translates between ethernet and token ring.

Multiprotocol routers can translate between different network layer protocols. They receive data from one network using one network protocol (e.g., TCP/IP), and translate it into another protocol (e.g., IPX/SPX) for use on another network. The most common type of multiprotocol bridge translates between TCP/IP and IPX/SPX.

Protocol filtering bridges are multiprotocol bridges that forward only packets of a certain type. For example, they may understand both ethernet and token ring, but only forward ethernet packets.

Encapsulating bridges connect networks with different data link protocols. They simply surround a packet using one protocol with a packet of a different protocol for transmission over a backbone network, which uses yet another protocol. When the message is received at the destination LAN, the encapsulating bridge at the other end removes the encapsulating packet and transmits the original packet.

FAST ETHERNET

The concept behind fast ethernet is simple: take an ethernet LAN and make it run at 100 Mbps rather than 10 Mbps. Unfortunately, this is easier to say than do. Different vendors have proposed several different types of fast ethernet. There are two fundamentally different approaches in the marketplace, each of which is now making its way through the standardization process: 100BaseT and 100VG-AnyLAN. The 100BaseT family is essentially an upgraded version of the traditional 802.3 ethernet. The 100VG-AnyLAN family was originally called "fast ethernet" but is a somewhat different approach to high speed networking. This section discusses these two versions of fast ethernet, plus ISO-Ethernet, an extension of ethernet developed to support voice and data transmission.

100BaseT Ethernet

100BaseT (also called 100BaseX) is a set of three data link layer protocols that provide a 100 Mbps data rate using the standard ethernet bus topology, ethernet data link packets, and ethernet CSMA/CD media access protocol. The three are currently being developed as standards. They differ only at the physical layer because they use different media. *100BaseTX* uses category 5 unshielded twisted pair cable. *100BaseFX* uses fiber optic cable. *100BaseT4* uses four sets of category 3 unshielded twisted pair cable. The signal is inverse multiplexed so that each of the four sets of cable is actually running at 25 Mbps, which when combined, provide a 100 Mbps rate.

100VG-AnyLAN

100VG-AnyLAN is more flexible than 100BaseT because it supports both ethernet and token ring packets. It uses four sets of category 3 twisted pair, each running at 25 Mbps (it can also use inverse multiplexing to combine four sets of category 4 or 5 twisted pair into one high speed circuit). The major difference between 100VG-AnyLAN and ethernet is its media access control. 100VG-AnyLAN does not use ethernet's standard CSMA/CD. Instead, 100VG-AnyLAN uses *demand priority access method* (DPAM), which is very similar to roll call polling (discussed in Chapter 6). The network server or hub polls each connected computer in turn to see if it has data to send. If it does, the computer transmits; if not, the hub moves to the next computer. This approach also permits computers to issue high priority requests to the hub without being polled so that these requests are processed more quickly.

In theory, 100VG-AnyLAN should be faster than 100BaseT when network traffic becomes heavy because controlled media access techniques such as DPAM perform better than contention-based approaches like CSMA/CD. In Chapter 8, we explained that the throughput of ethernet's CSMA/CD drops to about 50 percent because of the collisions that occur when traffic is heavy. This suggests that 100BaseT has a maximum throughput of about 50 Mbps. This is true for larger packets; however, for small ones, the extremely fast transmission rate of 100BaseT minimizes the probability of a collision. Tests have shown that for small ones (i.e., 1K or less), 100BaseT has almost a 100 Mbps throughput; for larger packets (i.e., 4K or larger), throughput falls to about 50 Mbps. Tests have shown 100VG-AnyLAN's throughput to be close to 100 Mbps regardless of packet size.

Iso-ENET

Iso-ENET (isochronous ethernet, IEEE 802.9A) is standard 10BaseT ethernet with an additional 6.144 Mbps circuit placed on top. The two circuits are carried in the same physical twisted pair cable but are completely separate so that traffic in one circuit does not interfere with traffic in the other. The additional 6.144 Mbps channel is configured to support 96 ISDN B channels.

The extra channel supports the transmission of voice and video over a local area network. Several vendors have developed desktop videoconferencing application software that use iso-ENET, with several more multimedia products under development.

FIBER DISTRIBUTED DATA INTERFACE (FDDI)

The use of high speed fiber optic local area networks is beginning to appear in user applications. The *fiber distributed data interface* (FDDI) is a set of standards originally designed for use in MANs, but has since made its way into backbone networks.

Topology

FDDI is a token-passing ring network that operates at 100 Mbps over a fiber optic cable. The FDDI standard assumes a maximum of 1000 stations and a 200-kilometer (120 miles) path that requires a repeater every 2 kilometers. FDDI uses two counter-rotating rings called the *primary ring* and the *secondary ring*. Data traffic usually travels on the primary ring, although data can travel on both. The secondary ring mainly serves as a backup transmission circuit.

All computers on an FDDI network are connected to the primary ring. Some computers are also connected to the secondary ring. Thus there are two types of FDDI computers: the *dual-attachment station* (DAS) on both rings and the *single-attachment station* (SAS) on just the primary ring (see Figure 10-8). Should a link fail, a DAS can recover by using the undamaged ring.

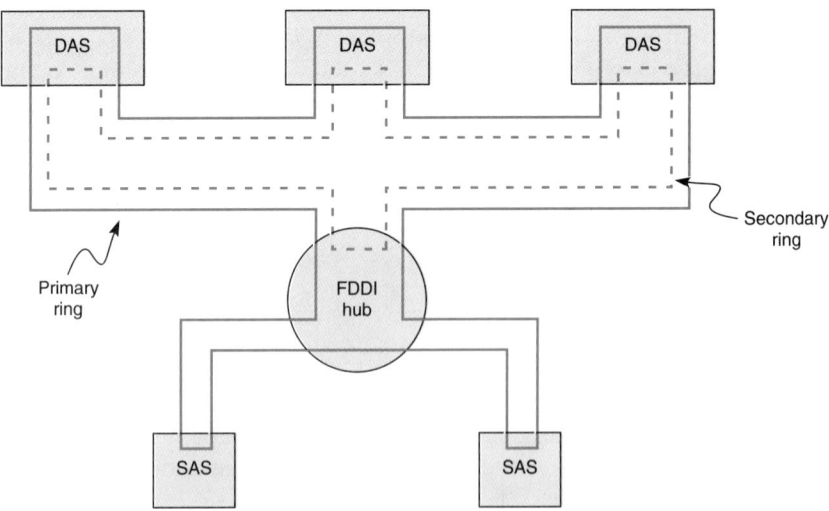

DAS: Dual-attachment station
SAS: Single-attachment station

Figure 10-8 Optical cable topology for an FDDI LAN. The FDDI has two rings. Data traffic normally travels on the primary ring.

Media Access Control

The FDDI media-access control scheme uses a variation of the token-passing standard used for token ring networks. IEEE 802.5 token ring networks use two types of tokens, free tokens and busy tokens. When a computer receives a free token, it transmits its message and marks the token as busy. No other computer can transmit a message until the message acknowledgment sent by the recipient is received by the message sender, which then changes the busy token to a free token. Under this approach, only one message can be attached to the token at one time.

FDDI permits a number of messages to be attached to the token. A computer with a message to send may attach its message to the token and transmit both. If the next computer in the ring has a message to send, it also attaches its message to the token. In this way, the throughput of FDDI compared to that of IEEE 802.5 token ring is more than the 100 Mbps to 16 Mbps might imply.

Types of FDDI

FDDI-C and FDDI-II are two additional types of FDDI.

FDDI on Copper (FDDI-C), sometimes called *Copper Distributed Data Interface* (CDDI), uses the same topology and media access protocol as FDDI, but uses two pairs of either shielded or unshielded category 5 twisted pair cable instead of fiber optic cable. It is identical to FDDI in every other way.

FDDI-II permits the transmission of voice and video over the same cable as the normal FDDI token-passing data. FDDI-II functions like FDDI, but adds the ability to divide the 100 Mbps circuit between the standard FDDI token-passing data circuit and one or more circuit-switched circuits for voice and/or video.

FDDI-II uses time division multiplexing to break up the available 100 Mbps into 17 separate channels, one channel at 768 Kbps and 16 *wide band channels* at 6.144 Mbps each. The 768 Kbps channel is permanently dedicated to the token-passing data circuit. The 16 wide band channels can be allocated either to the token-passing data circuit or to separate connection-oriented virtual circuits used for the transmission of voice and video (or alternately more data).

When the network begins operating, all 16 wide band channels are allocated to the token-passing data circuit. Media access is controlled using the standard FDDI protocol. Allocation of these wide band channels from the token-passing circuit to a new voice/video circuit is controlled by a computer called the *cycle master*. When a computer wishes to establish a new voice/video circuit that uses one or more of the wide band channels, it sends a control message to the cycle master. The cycle master then waits for the token, and, presuming there is room on the circuit, changes the channel allocation so that one or more of them are devoted to a separate circuit, and reissues the token with the new pattern. The requesting station then uses this circuit to establish a connection-oriented virtual circuit with other computers in the network. When the stations using the voice/video circuit have finished, one issues a "close circuit" request to the cycle master, which reallocates the wide band channels to the token-passing circuit.

COLLAPSED BACKBONE NETWORKS

Over the past few years, there has been a major change in the way we think about LANs and backbone networks. Many of the key concepts about wide area networks have found their way into the LAN and BN environment, as network managers attempt to improve throughput in LANS. LANs have traditionally used multipoint circuits

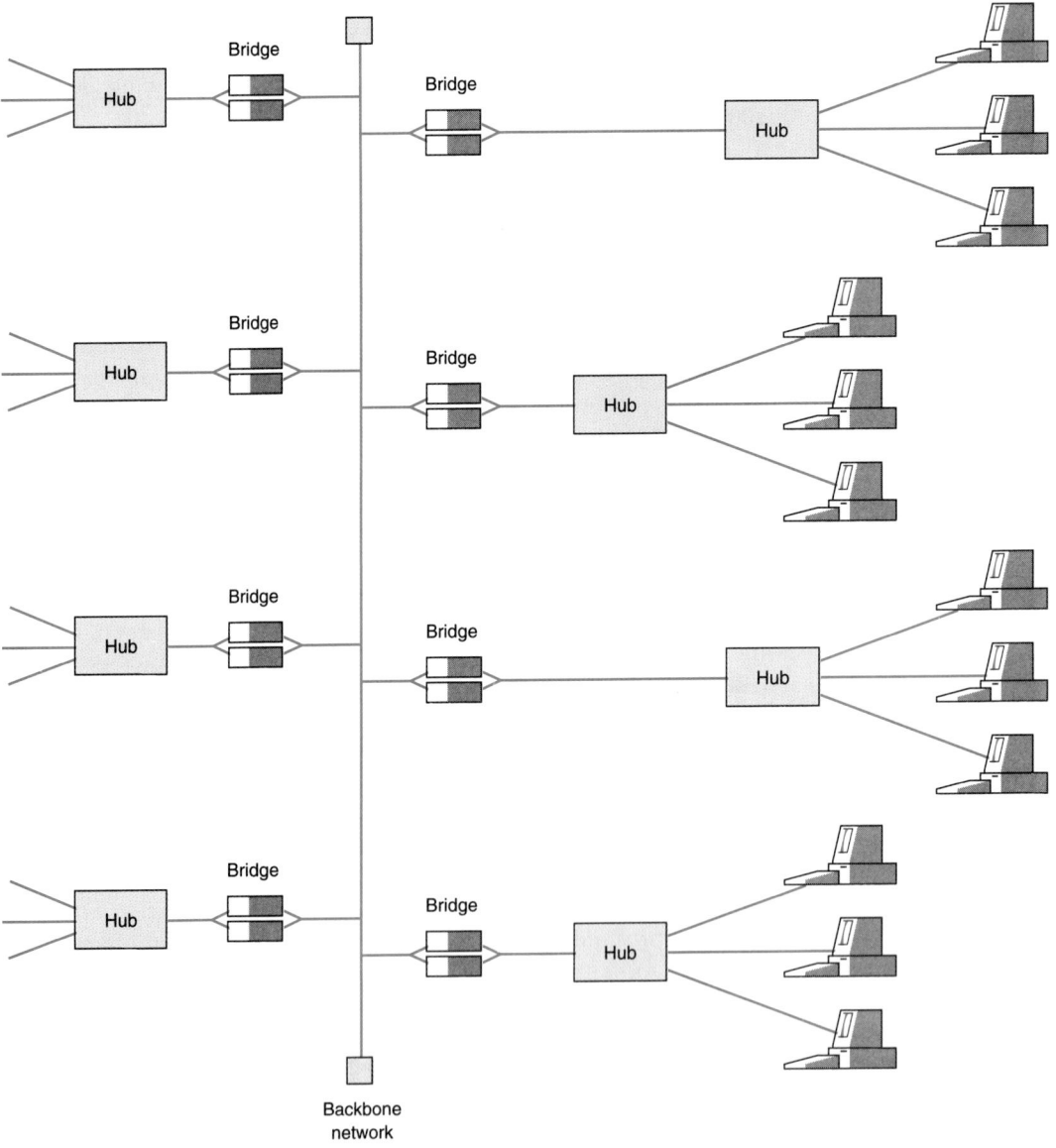

Figure 10-9 Traditional backbone network design.

where all computers take turns sharing the same circuit. In contrast, WANs have traditionally used point-to-point circuits, where each computer has a dedicated direct connection to one or more computers in the same network. As the shared circuits in LANs and BNs have become overloaded with message traffic, network managers are starting to devise ways of using point-to-point circuits. The traditional approach to network design using backbone networks is shown in Figure 10-9. This figure shows a series of ethernet LANs connected by bridges to an ethernet backbone network.

Figure 10-10 shows the same network using a collapsed backbone design. Here, the

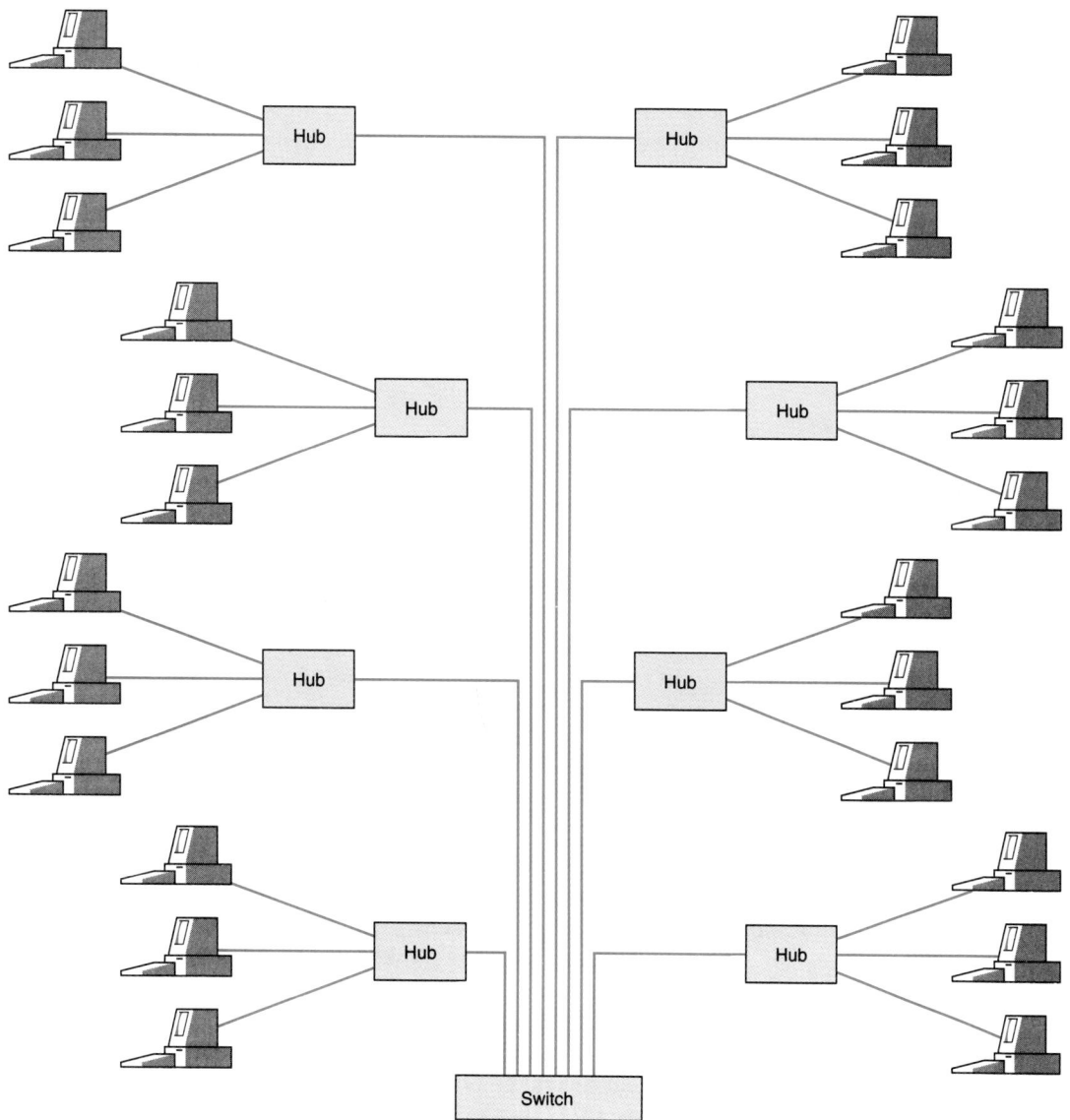

Figure 10-10   Collapsed backbone network design.

backbone circuit and set of bridges is replaced by one switch and a set of circuits to each LAN. The collapsed backbone has more cable, but fewer devices. There is no backbone cable. The "backbone" exists only in the switch.

There are two major advantages to collapsed backbones. First, performance is improved. With the traditional backbone network, the backbone circuit was shared among the eight LANs; each had to take turns sending messages. With the collapsed backbone, each connection into the switch is a separate point-to-point circuit. The switch enables simultaneous access, so that several LANs can send messages to other LANs at the same time. Throughput is increased significantly, often by 200 percent to 600 percent, depending upon the number of attached LANs and the traffic pattern.

Second, there are far fewer internetworking devices in the network; in Figure 10-10, one switch replaces eight bridges. This reduces costs and greatly simplifies network management, which as you will recall is the greatest expense of networks. All the key backbone devices are in the same physical location, and all traffic must flow through the switch. If something goes wrong or if new cabling is needed, or the network needs to be monitored, it can all be done in one place. Most switches have software that monitor operations and control how they function, a key benefit not found in a set of similarly priced bridges.

The collapsed backbone also has two major disadvantages. First, it uses more cable. It is often costly to install additional cable and the maximum distances that one can run the cable from the switch is limited by the type of cable used. Second, if the switch fails, so does the entire backbone network.

SWITCHED NETWORKS

A small company called Kalpana, Inc. in Sunnyvale, California, was the first to recognize the opportunity to apply the collapsed backbone concept to the LAN itself. In 1992, Kalpana developed the first switched local area network (switched ethernet). In 1995, Kalpana was bought by Cisco Systems Inc. (a leading manufacturer of switches) for just over $200 million.

Switched Ethernet

The concept behind *switched ethernet*—and all switched networks—is simple: replace the LAN hub with a switch (see Figure 10-11). In traditional ethernet, all devices share the same multipoint circuit, and must take turns. The hub is a simple physical connection between the different computers, much like a splice. All computers share one 10 Mbps circuit.

With switched ethernet, a switch replaces the hub. Each computer now has its own dedicated point-to-point circuit to the switch. The switch manages the connections between the computers so that several can be transmitting simultaneously. If they are transmitting to different computers, the switch connects them immediately. If some

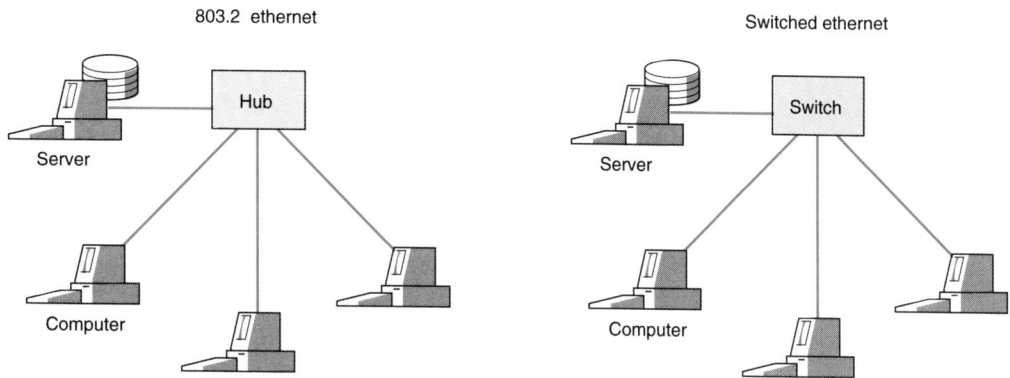

Figure 10-11   802.3 ethernet versus switched ethernet.

are trying to transmit to the same computers, the switch stores and forwards the data later to avoid collisions. Each computer has its own 10 Mbps connection instead of sharing one 10 Mbps with several other computers.

Switched ethernet dramatically improves LAN performance because each computer has its own circuit. However, since much of the network traffic is to and from the server, the circuit to the server is often the network bottleneck. Each computer is transmitting at 10 Mbps, but if the circuit to the server is also 10 Mbps, there is often a traffic jam on the server's circuit.

One obvious solution is to increase the number of connections from the server to the switch, so that traffic now can reach the server on several circuits. Of course, adding more connections increases server overhead and can slow it down; most experts recommend no more than three or four connections. Other solutions include full duplex ethernet and 10/100 switched ethernet.

Full Duplex Ethernet   *Full duplex ethernet* uses the same 10BaseT cables as regular ethernet or switched ethernet, but as the name suggests, it provides a full duplex connection. Full duplex ethernet assigns one cable in the twisted pair to be incoming messages and the other to be outgoing messages, enabling the same computer to be transmitting and receiving at the same time. Full duplex ethernet nominally doubles the speed of the connection to 20 Mbps; however, this is only true if the same computer is both sending and receiving simultaneously, because it still provides only 10 Mbps in each direction. The need for simultaneous sending and receiving is usually common only in network servers, so full duplex ethernet primarily provides connections from the switch to the server. In high traffic switched networks, two or three full duplex ethernet connections may be used from the switch to the server (see Figure 10-12). Even so, full duplex ethernet only adds value if the server needs to send and receive data simultaneously, an event that occurs less often than its vendors might admit.

10/100 Switched Ethernet   Sometimes a LAN needs more capacity to the server than full duplex ethernet can provide, so the next step up is *10/100 switched ethernet*, which combines 10BaseT ethernet and 100BaseT ethernet. Each switch in the network has

Management Focus: Switching LANs for the National Weather Service

The National Weather Service (NWS) will soon use a digitial data communications network to broadcast daily weather reports and early warnings of weather-related emergencies. The network will be developed and managed by CommPower, a specialized network integration firm in California. CommPower already provides similar services for the Department of Defense, and the FAA.

CommPower uses ethernet for its internal operations. All the network design and management groups shared the same thicknet LAN, resulting in a major circuit capacity problem thanks to CommPower's recent growth.

CommPower looked at two solutions. One was to segment the LAN into four parts (one for each major CommPower branch) using a series of bridges. The other was to develop a collapsed backbone network using a switch. They chose the switch.

"... The speed the switched network gives us is great," says Chuck Purcell, CommPower's Operations Manager. "I can input a message for any branch and it's there before I get my finger off the key. That didn't happen when we were all on the same network segment."

We may not be able to change the weather, but with switched and collapsed backbone networks, we can at least talk about it sooner.

Source: News@Lantronix, March 1995.

ports that can support either 10BaseT or 100BaseT. Some switches provide ports that support both; they sense the incoming signal and adjust accordingly.

10/100 switched ethernet is often used to provide traditional 10 Mbps ethernet connections to client computers utilizing traditional 10BaseT, with 100BaseT used to the server or to other switches. This version of switched ethernet will become very popular in the future, because it provides several advantages over other types of ethernet LANs and BNs. Compared to 10 Mbps switched ethernet, 10/100 switched

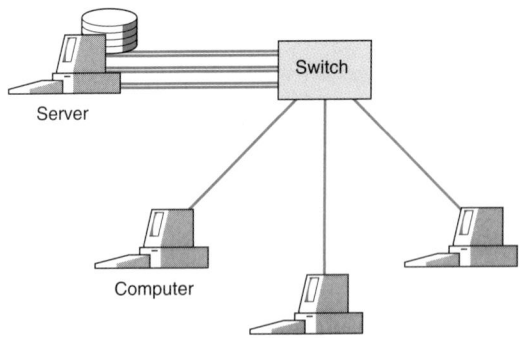

Figure 12 Full duplex ethernet.

ethernet greatly reduces congestion at the network server, thereby providing better network performance. It is cheaper to install than 100BaseT because it does not require new cable to the client computers; you simply replace the existing hub with a 10/100 switch. Depending upon the application and the number of computers in the network, 10/100 may be as fast as fast ethernet.

Switched Token Ring

Switched token ring is similar to switched ethernet. A token ring switch replaces the token ring hub, providing a series of point-to-point connections from the computers to the switch instead of the traditional shared multipoint circuit.

Dedicated token ring (DTR) (or *full duplex token ring*) is similar to full duplex ethernet. Each computer has a full duplex connection from it to the switch, providing a 32 Mbps data rate (16 Mbps in each direction). With this configuration, the network has a star topology instead of a ring. The token is no longer needed because all computers can transmit and receive at will. It is called "token ring" because DTR uses the 802.5 token ring packet format and is fully compatible with 802.5 hardware. All that is needed is new software, or in some cases, both software and a new chip for each token ring network interface card. DTR can operate seamlessly with 802.5 token rings, so that both DTR and 802.5 token ring networks can be connected to the same DTR switch.

ATM

ATM (asynchronous transfer mode) was discussed in Chapter 9. It is a packet-switched technology originally designed for use in wide area networks. Fore Systems Inc., founded in 1992 by faculty from Carnegie-Mellon University, was the first company to recognize the usefulness of ATM in backbone and local area networks. ATM is currently used in the backbone (encapsulation) and in the LAN (desktop).

ATM Encapsulation   ATM uses a very different type of protocol than traditional LANs. It has a small 53-byte fixed length packet and is connection-oriented (meaning that devices typically establish a switched virtual circuit before transmitting). Ethernet and token ring use larger variable length packets and are connectionless. In order to use ATM in a backbone network that connects LANs, some translation must be done to enable the LAN packets to flow over the ATM backbone.

This is typically done by *encapsulation* (see Figure 10-13). In this case, an ATM *edge switch* (or *encapsulation switch*) is connected to the LANs. The switch performs the translation from ethernet (or token ring) to ATM and back again at the other end. The LAN packet is broken into a series of ATM packets, transmitted over the ATM backbone, and reassembled into the LAN packet at the edge switch at its destination. ATM is transparent to users because the switches do all the required translation.

ATM backbone switches typically provide point-to-point full duplex circuits at 155 Mbps (OC-3 level) (for a total of 310 Mbps). Switches providing 622 Mbps (OC-12, a total of 1.244 Gbps) are not yet widely available. There is, of course, the additional

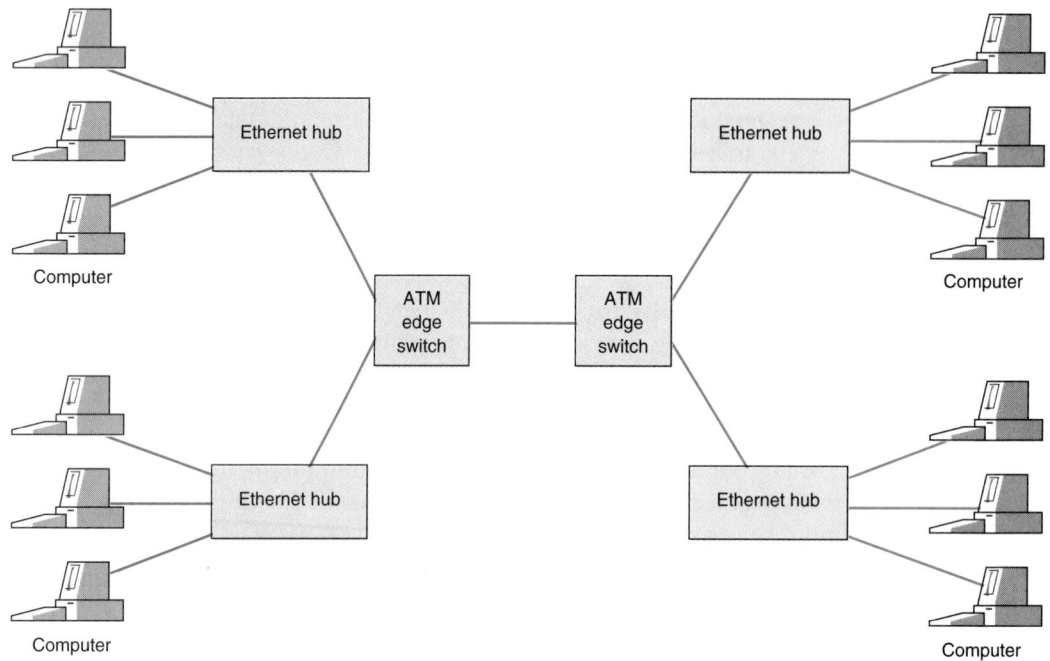

Figure 10-13 ATM encapsulation.

delay imposed by the need to packetize and reassemble the LAN packets; and, there is extra overhead imposed by using the ATM packets along with LAN packets.

ATM to the Desktop   In early 1995, the ATM Forum, the standards body for ATM, accepted a proposal from a consortium of vendors led by IBM for a "low-speed" version of ATM to compete with traditional ethernet and token ring LANs. *ATM25* provides point-to-point full duplex circuits at 25.6 Mbps in each direction (51.2 Mbps total) from computers to the switch. ATM25 is an adaptation of token ring that runs over category 3 cable and will even use token ring hardware with a chip upgrade. It uses a slightly different data link protocol than wide area ATM's SONET, but these differences are not observable to the user.

Another version of ATM designed for the desktop is *ATM51*, which provides point-to-point full duplex circuits at 51.84 Mbps (103.68 Mbps total) from computers to the switch. It uses the same SONET protocols as wide area ATM. Although ATM51 was developed before ATM25, it has received far less vendor support.

Both of these ATMs are obvious choices for desktop connections when ATM backbone networks are used. The packet sizes are the same; the protocols are the same; and no translation or encapsulation is required so the switches are simpler and cheaper than edge switches needed for LAN to ATM translation. Furthermore, they offer the promise of almost seamless connection to ATM MANs and WANs. If ATM technologies continue to develop, they will become a powerful force in the marketplace because they are able to use one protocol for all LANs, BNs, MANs, and WANs, vastly simplifying today's multi-protocol mix.

Management Focus: Westinghouse Makes Leap of Faith to ATM

In 1993, Westinghouse's Nuclear Technology Division (NTD) decided to upgrade its ethernet to ATM. Its Cray supercomputer was replaced with two clusters of Hewlett-Packard and Sun computer servers. Each of the clusters is anchored by a Fore Systems ATM switch, which in turn is linked to another Fore Systems ATM switch, acting as the network's collapsed backbone.

The ATM network has already proven its worth. Operating costs are lower, and the ATM equipment now supports about three times the previous workload, with approximately 2 gigabytes of new data generated on the network each day. A consulting engineer at NTD estimates that the ATM network is still running at only about 50 percent of capacity. In the future, the ATM switches will have the capability to move data at speeds of 622M bit/sec and higher, an increase from its current speed of about 100M bit/sec.

NTD has added seven computer servers (for a total of 16), two more file servers (for a total of three) and an extra 100 gigabytes of disk storage. NTD also has ordered three more ATM switches from Fore Systems that will form a third computer cluster in another building in the complex. Two of the ATM switches will eventually be used to plug some workstations directly into the hub switch for peer-to-peer connectivity with other workstations. This means the closet-to-desktop part of the network will be twisted pair and the backbone network linking the ATM switches will be optical fiber.

The shift to ATM was a leap of faith for NTD; however, they are now reaping the benefits of ATM without the additional expenses of a temporary FDDI solution.

Source: Network World, January 25, 1995.

IMPROVING BACKBONE PERFORMANCE

Improving the performance of backbone networks is similar to improving LAN performance. First, find the bottleneck, and then solve it (or more accurately, move the bottleneck somewhere else). You can improve the performance of the network by improving the computers and other devices in the network, by upgrading the circuits between computers, and by changing the demand placed on the network.

Improving Computer and Device Performance

The primary functions of computers and devices in backbone networks are routing and protocol translations. If the devices and computers are the bottleneck, routing can be improved with a faster routing protocol. Static routing is accomplished faster than dynamic routing, but obviously can impair circuit performance in high traffic situations. Dynamic routing is usually used in WANs and MANs because there are many possible routes through the network. Backbone networks often have only a few routes through the network. In this case, dynamic routing may not be too helpful, because it will delay processing and increase the network traffic due to the status reports it sends through the network. Static routing will simplify processing and improve performance.

Many of the newer backbone technologies (ATM, fast ethernet) have few standards. Routing packets between switches from different vendors can decrease network performance. Performance can be improved by using one vendor's equipment, or eliminating the need for switch to switch routing by using collapsed backbone networks.

FDDI and ATM require the translation of token ring and ethernet packets before they can flow through the backbone. This slows processing at the devices connecting the backbone network to the attached LANs. One obvious solution is to use the same protocols in the backbone and the LANs; if you have ethernet LANs, fast ethernet backbones can reduce processing at the connecting devices; if you have ATM backbones, ATM to the desktop will reduce device processing.

Translating protocols typically requires more processing than encapsulation, so encapsulation can improve performance if the backbone devices are the bottleneck. With translation, the LAN data link layer packet is removed and a new backbone data link layer packet is added in its place (e.g., the ethernet packet is removed and an FDDI packet added). This process is reversed at the end of the backbone network. With encapsulation, the existing LAN data link layer packet is left intact, and a new backbone data link layer packet is wrapped around it. The backbone data link layer is stripped off at the destination. Most backbone devices are store and forward devices. One simple way to improve performance is to ensure that they have sufficient memory. If they don't, the devices will lose packets, requiring them to be retransmitted.

Improving Circuit Capacity

If network circuits are the bottleneck, there are several options. One is to increase overall circuit capacity; for example, by going from 10 Mbps ethernet to fast ethernet, or by adding additional circuits alongside heavily used ones. Another option is to change the protocol from a contention-based protocol (e.g., 100BaseT) to a controlled access protocol (100VG-AnyLAN or FDDI). Circuit capacity can also be improved by replacing a shared circuit backbone with a switched circuit backbone; for example, by replacing ethernet with switched ethernet or ATM.

In many cases, the bottleneck on the circuit is only in one place—the circuit to the server. A switched network that provides the usual 10 Mbps to the client computers, but a faster circuit to the server (e.g., full duplex at 20 Mbps or fast ethernet at 100 Mbps) can improve performance at very little cost. All one needs to do is replace the ethernet hub with a switch and change one network interface card in the server.

Reducing Network Demand

One way to reduce network demand is to restrict applications that use a lot of network capacity, such as desktop videoconferencing, medical imaging, or multimedia. In practice, it is often difficult to restrict users. Nonetheless, finding one application that places a large demand on the network and moving it can have a significant impact.

Some application software packages and network operating system modules written for use on LANs broadcast status messages to all computers on the LAN. For example, *broadcast messages* inform users when printers are out of paper, or when the network manager is about to shut down the server. When used in an isolated LAN, these messages place little extra demand on the network. In either an ethernet or token ring LAN, every computer on the LAN gets every message. Remember that with ethernet's bus, all messages flow down all parts of the common cable, and with token ring, the message must pass through all computers in the ring before the token can return to the original sender.

This is not the case for switched LANs or LANs connected to backbone networks because messages do not normally flow to all computers. Broadcast messages can consume a fair amount of network capacity. In many cases, broadcast messages have little value outside their individual LAN. Therefore, some switches, bridges, and routers can be set to filter broadcast messages so that they do not go to other networks. This reduces network traffic and improves performance.

SELECTING A BACKBONE NETWORK

Selecting a backbone network for your organization is not easy. New backbone network products are being introduced monthly, and several entirely new technologies are introduced each year. Most new products and technologies are not standardized, which further complicates matters. Several issues in selecting a backbone network are summarized in Figure 10-14.

Throughput is the amount of user data the network can transmit from one computer to another. In this chapter, we have discussed two fundamentally different approaches to backbone networks: shared multipoint circuits (fast ethernet, FDDI), and switched networks (switched ethernet, switched token ring, and ATM).

Among the multipoint circuit backbone networks, one would expect the controlled media access networks (100VG-AnyLAN and FDDI) to outperform contention-based ones (100BaseT) when network traffic was heavy, and the reverse to be true when network traffic was light (see Chapter 8). However, tests of specific 100 Mbps backbone network products have not found this to be completely true. Tests show all three approaches (100VG-AnyLAN, 100BaseT, and FDDI) produce almost the same

- Throughput
- Ease of Management
- Flexibility
- Compatibility with Current and Future Technologies
- Type of Application

Figure 10-14 Key issues in selecting a backbone network.

Management Focus: Carriers Extend a LAN Interconnectivity Hand

Companies without the financial muscle or technical expertise to interconnect LANs on their own can find needed relief in one of the growing number of LAN interconnectivity services hitting the market. Many interexchange carriers and local telephone companies now offer LAN interconnectivity services.

The highest end services provide LAN-to-MAN/WAN connections, network management and LAN administration, as well as applications development and support. Middle market services have emerged over the past two years to provide a wide range of off-the-shelf LAN-to-WAN management options in which the carrier controls the internetworking equipment and facilities. But mid-range services typically lack the LAN and applications development support, as well as the high levels of customization of high-end offerings. However, carriers with mid-range offerings are more than willing to offer some level of customization when required.

There are two primary methods of LAN interconnection: transport only and managed LAN service. With the transport only method, the carrier is responsible for data transmission, not equipment. On the other hand, the carrier's responsibility in the managed LAN service extends to the LAN interface on the router, which would include a portion of the equipment.

Carriers will only supply equipment they know how to operate and only offer to perform the management tasks in which they have been schooled. Likewise, transport options are dictated by the type of services in the carrier's bag of tricks and whether the equipment provided supports an interface to that transport option.

There are emerging native LAN services that link two or more locations in a metropolitan area by enabling users to tap directly into a carrier-provided LAN, such as an FDDI ring. A few services, however, will provide native LAN speeds over wide areas by pushing traffic across a full T-3's worth of bandwidth or using some form of statistical multiplexing technique to divvy up a T-3 among multiple users.

Source: Network World, January 9, 1995.

throughput under light network traffic. Under heavy traffic conditions, there were still no differences for small-sized packets (1 Kbytes or less), but for larger sized packets (4 Kbytes and above), the throughput of 100BaseT was significantly below that of 100VG-AnyLAN and FDDI. Therefore, if your network uses small packet sizes, there is no clear winner; if your network uses larger sized packets, 100BaseT will not perform as well under heavy network traffic conditions.

There have been fewer tests of the newer switched networks. All switched networks maintain dedicated point-to-point circuits between switches and computers, so the medium access methodology is irrelevant to throughput. The key determinant of throughput is simply the data rate possible in the point-to-point circuits (e.g., 10 Mbps for switched ethernet versus 25 Mbps for ATM). The use of full duplex circuits has the potential to improve throughput even more, because data can travel in both directions simultaneously. However, full duplex is only useful in situations where the same computer is simultaneously sending and receiving; this is more likely to be a server or a heavily-used backbone circuit than client computers.

Comparing the throughput of high speed multipoint backbone technologies (e.g., fast ethernet) against lower speed switched networks is difficult. With switched networks, each computer (or connected LAN) has a guaranteed data transmission rate of 10, 16, 25, or 100 Mbps. With multipoint networks, the total capacity (100 Mbps) is shared among all the computers (or LANs) on the network. If there are only a few computers (or LANs) on the backbone, the multipoint networks should perform as well as the switched networks. However, if there are many connected computers (or LANs), the available capacity must be shared, resulting in less than the 100 Mbps available to any one computer.

In theory, the entire switched connection capacity is available in the switched networked, but this is not always the case. If every computer in the switched network has a 100 Mbps connection and several attempt to transmit to the same computer (e.g., a server or highly used LAN), there will still be a need to share the connection(s) to it. Switched networks should provide better throughput than equivalent speed shared networks, but do so only if the traffic on highly used circuits is well managed.

The *management* of backbone networks can be extremely costly and challenging, therefore, the quality of the network management tools available in each type of network is very important (network management is discussed in more detail in Chapter 12). In general, newer technologies such as fast ethernet, switched ethernet, DTR, and ATM are harder to manage than older, more established ones such as FDDI. Vendors tend to develop technologies first, and provide management support for them later. Newer technologies are also developed before they become standardized, making it more difficult to manage a multi-vendor network. For example, there are no formal standardized management techniques or switch to switch communication techniques for backbone ATM switches.

Backbone networks, and the traffic they carry, always grow. *Flexibility* and the potential for future growth is therefore very important. ATM is one of the most flexible technologies for backbone networks. It is scaleable, meaning that increasing speed is simpler than with other technologies. Likewise, switched ethernet is flexible. You can start with 10 Mbps connections and incrementally increase to 100 Mbps.

Compatibility with current and future technologies is also important to reduce network management problems and provide a future growth path. For example, ethernet LANs with compatible technologies such as 100BaseT or switched ethernet in the backbone leads to the fewest short-term problems. Even if you have to upgrade existing LANs or replace network interface cards, using a backbone network that takes the same type of cable as the old LAN or backbone network will curtail costs.

While it is difficult to predict the future, we believe that a major revolution in LANs and BNs has begun. We believe that by the turn of the century, very few shared multipoint circuit LANs such as token ring and ethernet will exist. Instead, LANs and BNs will use switched point-to-point circuits. The likely winner in this scenario is ATM, because it was designed from the beginning to be switched, it is scaleable, and it is available both in LAN and BN versions (ATM25 and OC-3). Switched ethernet (10 Mbps and 10/100 ethernet) are also potential winners.

The *type of application* software may also influence the choice of backbone networks. In general, all backbone networks are equally appropriate for most data applications. Suitability for voice and video is a different matter. ATM's small fixed-length packet makes it more suitable for voice and video transmission because small fixed-length packets make routing and packetizing easier and minimize the effects of lost packets.

Summary

Network Components   There are two basic components to a backbone network: the network cable and the hardware devices that connect other networks to the backbone. The cable is essentially the same as the one used in LANs, except that it is usually higher quality to provide higher data rates. The hardware devices include hubs, bridges, switches, routers, brouters, and gateways. Hubs are very simple devices that pass all traffic in both directions between the LAN sections they link. Bridges connect two LAN segments that use the same data link and network protocol, and only forward those messages that need to go to other network segments. Switches are similar to bridges but connect more than two LAN segments. Routers connect two or more LANs that use the same or different data link protocols but employ the same network protocol. Brouters are devices that combine the functions of both bridges and routers; they bridge same data link layer LANs and route different data link layer LANs. Gateways connect two or more LANs that use the same or different data link and network protocols (usually different). However, the terminology used in the marketplace may differ substantially from this discussion because different vendors use different names in order to gain market advantage.

Fast Ethernet   The concept behind fast ethernet is simple: take an ethernet LAN and make it run faster. 100BaseT is a set of three data link layer protocols (100BaseTX, 100BaseFX, 100BaseT4) that provide a 100 Mbps data rate using the standard ethernet bus topology, ethernet data link packets, and ethernet CSMA/CD media access protocol; they differ only in the type of cabling they use. 100VG-AnyLAN supports both ethernet and token ring packets, and uses demand priority access method instead of CSMA/CD. Iso-ENET is standard 10BaseT ethernet surmounted with an additional 6.144 Mbps circuit for voice and video transmission.

FDDI   FDDI is a token-passing ring network that operates at 100 Mbps over a fiber optic cable arranged in two rings. Unlike 802.3 token ring, FDDI permits any number of messages to be attached to the token. FDDI on Copper (FDDI-C) is FDDI operating on twisted pair cable instead of fiber optic cable. FDDI-C functions the same way as FDDI, but adds the ability to divide the 100 Mbps circuit between the standard FDDI token-passing data circuit and one or more circuit-switched circuits for voice and/or video.

Collapsed Backbone   With a collapsed backbone design, the one backbone circuit and set of bridges is replaced by one switch and a set of circuits to each LAN. The collapsed backbone has more cable, but fewer devices. Because the switch is the back-bone, there is no backbone cable.

Switched Ethernet   Switched ethernet simply replaces the LAN hub with a switch. In traditional ethernet, all devices share the same multipoint circuit, and must take turns. With switched ethernet, each computer has its own dedicated point-to-point circuit to the switch. The switch manages the connection between the computers so that collisions are avoided even when several are transmitting simultaneously. Each computer has its own 10 Mbps connection instead of sharing one 10 Mbps with several other computers. Full duplex ethernet provides a full duplex connection between the computer and the switch. 10/100 switched ethernet combines 10BaseT ethernet and 100BaseT ethernet. Each switch in the network has ports that can support either 10BaseT or 100BaseT.

Switched Token Ring   Switched token ring is similar to switched ethernet. A token ring switch replaces the token ring hub, providing a series of point-to-point connections from the computers to the switch instead of the traditional shared multipoint circuit. Dedicated token ring (DTR) (or full duplex token ring) is similar to full duplex ethernet. Each computer has a full duplex connection from it to the switch.

ATM   ATM (asynchronous transfer mode) is a packet-switched technology originally designed for use in wide area networks. In order to use ATM in a backbone network that connects LANs, some translation must be done on the LAN packets to enable them to flow over the ATM backbone. In this case, an ATM edge switch performs the translation from ethernet (or token ring) to ATM and back again at the other end. ATM25 is a version of ATM intended for use in the LAN, not the backbone. It provides point-to-point full duplex circuits at 25.6 Mbps each direction (51.2 Mbps total) from computers to the switch.

Improving Backbone Performance   You can improve network performance by up-grading the computers and other devices in the network, by using static rather than dynamic routing if there are few routes through the network, by reducing switch-to-switch traffic in networks without standard protocols, by using the same protocols in the backbone network as in the attached LANs, by encapsulating rather than trans-lating between different protocols, and by increasing the memory in backbone devices. Performance can also be improved by adding additional circuits to increase capacity, by changing to controlled access rather than contention protocols, by going to a switched network, and by increasing the circuits on high traffic circuits. In addition, performance can be enhanced by reducing demand or by restricting applications that use lots of network capacity, and by using switches that filter broadcast messages.

Selecting a LAN   Selecting a backbone network for your organization is difficult because new products and completely new technologies are constantly being intro-duced. There are several factors to consider. Throughput is the amount of user data the network can transmit. In general, switched networks are faster than shared networks. There have been few throughput differences found among the high speed multipoint technologies, although for heavy traffic networks with large packet sizes, FDDI and 100VG-AnyLAN outperformed 100BaseT. Among switched networks, the best determinant of throughput is the data transmission rate, although full duplex may help on heavily used circuits or circuits to servers. New technologies (e.g., switched networks) are often harder to manage, but switched networks often are more flexible. It appears that switched networks are the way of the future. The type of application may also influence the choice of network: ATM is well suited to voice and video.

Key Terms

ATM
ATM25
ATM51
Backbone network
Bridges
Brouters
Collapsed backbone
    networks
Cut-through switches
Cycle master
Dedicated token ring
    (DTR)
Demand priority access
    method
Dual attachment statement
Edge switch

Encapsulating bridges
Encapsulation
Enterprise network
Fast ethernet
FDDI on copper (FDDI-C)
Fiber distributed data
    interface (FDDI)
Fiber distributed data
    interface-II (FDDI-II)
Full duplex ethernet
Gateways
Hubs
Internetworking
Iso-ENET
Multiprotocol routers
Multiprotocol switches

Protocol filtering bridges
Routers
Single attachment
    statement
Store and forward switches
Switches
Switched ethernet
Switched networks
Switched token ring
10/100 switched ethernet
100BaseT
100BaseTX
100BaseFX
100BaseT4
100VG-AnyLAN

Selected References

1. Bush, Stan. "100VG-AnyLAN Adapters," *Network World*, January 9, 1995, 40–42.
2. Bush, Stan. "100BaseT Adapters," *Network World*, January 16, 1995, 35–36.
3. Cumming, Joanne. "Fast E-Net adds new dimension to LANs," *Network World*, January 25, 1995, L2.
4. Darling, Charles. "Unclog Your Local Backbone with ATM," *Datamation*, February 15, 1995, 67–69.
5. Katz, William. "The Reality of 100M-bit," *PC Week*, February 6, 1995, N1–N9.
6. Lowe, Sue. "Data Communications," *IEEE Spectrum*, January 1995, 26–29.
7. Morency, John "Legacy LANs Live On Due to Advent of ATM Emulation Service," *Network World*, February 20, 1995, 43–44.
8. Roberts, Eric. "Opening the Valve on ATM," *LAN Times*, January 1995, 57+.
9. Salamone, Salvatore. "Ethernet Switching Hubs," *Business Communications Review*, July 1994, 38–40.

10. Stallings, William. "FDDI Speaks," *Byte*, April 1993, 197–200.
11. Wilson, Linda. "It's Still Hit or Miss for ATM Technology," *Information Week*, September 26, 1994.

Questions/Problems

1. What is a hub?
2. How does a bridge differ from a switch?
3. What is different between a switch, a router, and a gateway?
4. What is a brouter?
5. Under what circumstances would you want to replace a router with a brouter?
6. What happens when you replace a hub with a switch?
7. What is an enterprise network?
8. Explain the differences between a store and forward switch and a cut-through switch.
9. What is a multiprotocol bridge?
10. What are the three types of 100BaseT and how are they different?
11. How does 100VG-AnyLAN differ from the other types of ethernet?
12. How can the fast ethernet such as 100BaseT or 100VG-AnyLAN provide 100 Mbps data rates using the same cable used for 10BaseT?
13. What is Iso-ENET? Why would you want to use it?
14. How does FDDI differ from 803.5 token ring?
15. How does FDDI differ from 100BaseFX?
16. What is the difference between a DAS and an SAS?
17. What is FDDI-C?
18. How does FDDI-II differ from FDDI? Why would you want to use FDDI-II?
19. How does a collapsed backbone differ from a traditional backbone network?
20. What are the advantages and disadvantages of collapsed backbones?
21. What is switched ethernet?
22. Where would you want to use full duplex ethernet?
23. Is full duplex token ring really token ring? Explain.
24. Some people argue that full duplex ethernet does not really provide 20 Mbps. Why?
25. What is 10/100 switched ethernet and how would you use it to design a LAN/BN?
26. If you currently have an 803.3 ethernet LAN, is fast ethernet or switched ethernet cheaper to install? Why?
27. How can ATM be used to link ethernet LANs?
28. What is ATM25? ATM51?
29. What is encapsulation and how does it differ from translation?
30. How can you improve the performance of a backbone network?
31. What are broadcast messages?
32. What is DTR?
33. What are four factors in selecting a backbone network?

34. Which has greatest throughput: 100BaseT, 100VG-AnyLAN, or FDDI?
35. Which has greater throughput: FDDI or switched ethernet?
36. How does FDDI work?
37. How does a FDDI LAN carry an ethernet packet?
38. For what is the FDDI suitable?
39. Which would you recommend for your organization: FDDI, ATM, fast ethernet, or 10/100 switched ethernet? Why?

NEXT DAY AIR SERVICE CUMULATIVE CASE STUDY

See appendix at end of book

CHAPTER ELEVEN

NETWORK DESIGN AND IMPLEMENTATION

Network managers perform two key tasks: (1) designing and implementing new networks and network upgrades; and (2) managing the day-to-day operation of existing networks. This chapter examines network design and implementation. One problem when designing data communication networks is how best to adapt new technology to meet the changing and challenging networking needs of organizations. This chapter uses the systems approach to designing data communication networks, and works through ten key design steps.

Objectives

- Become familiar with the overall process of design and implementing a network,
- Understand the 10 steps in network design and implementation.

Chapter Outline

Introduction
1. Conduct a Feasibility Study
    Needs Assessment Factors
    Deliverable for Step 1
2. Prepare a Network Design Plan
    Network Goals
    Network Evaluation Criteria
    Deliverable for Step 2
3. Understand the Current Network
    Information Needs
    Deliverable for Step 3

INTRODUCTION

You should use the *systems approach* when planning a new data communication network, when enhancing a current network, or when planning for the use of public data networks (PDNs). In the systems approach, all influences and constraints are identified and evaluated in terms of their impact on the network design. Whether the network achieves success or just marginal utilization may be determined before a single piece of software or hardware is ordered. The key ingredient for success lies in planning based on the system's interface with the users. Far too often, data processing-oriented network designers take an equipment-oriented approach or a software-oriented approach. In today's world of data communications the designer must emphasize user *application systems.* For example, there are two major classes of data communication network users: the organization's management and its user personnel.

Managers must accept the network and believe in it, or they will not trust the data and other material they receive from it. If the information management receives is not consistent, accurate, timely, economically feasible, and relevant, then management may not utilize the network to its fullest extent.

The *users* who work with the network day-to-day must be able to accept it, or their productivity may fall drastically. When productivity decreases, the cost of carrying out basic office functions may increase the cost of the final product or service by 10 to 50 percent. Office productivity recently has taken on added importance because we are moving from a predominantly manufacturing society to an information society that is service-oriented.

Many businesses are drowning in data while simultaneously thirsting for meaningful information. To meet this challenge, we need databases from which we can identify, sort, and retrieve the necessary data so it can become useful information. Then we need to have a method for delivering it to managers and users. Delivery is accomplished by means of data communication networks, and these networks are what the following ten steps will help you design.

These steps should be used when designing a new data communication network. Some steps can be omitted if a current network is being enhanced. The exact sequence and number of steps are determined by the scope of the network design project. Even so, serious consideration should be given to all ten.

1. CONDUCT A FEASIBILITY STUDY

The purpose of a *feasibility study* is to determine the possibility or probability of either improving the *current network* or developing a totally *new network.*

The first point that must be made about a feasibility study is that it may not be necessary to conduct one at all because management may have done it already. Perhaps the scope of the proposed network already has been defined. Furthermore, it is entirely possible that either management or economic realities in the business environment have dictated that an online data communication network must be developed to meet the competition. If that is the case, it is no longer a question of whether to design a new network, but how it will be done.

Needs Assessment Factors

A primary responsibility in a feasibility study is to define the problem clearly in writing. *Problem definition* involves identifying all the problems that may indicate the need for a data communication network. These problems, called *needs assessment factors,* may be analyzed to determine whether they contribute to the need for this new network (see the accompanying Needs Assessment Factors box). The results are that you know the

Management Focus: Needs Assessment Factors

Management Issues
- Need for more timely access to information for improved decision making
- Increasing flow of information or paperwork
- Need for better exchange of information in international operations
- Increased volume of inputs/outputs
- Unsatisfactory movement of data/information throughout the organization
- Future growth that requires new methods
- Negative effect of old network on employee morale
- Documentation not available in a timely manner
- Competition that forces change
- Inadequate productivity
- Inadequate floor space for personnel or files
- Avoidance of future costs
- Effects on investments and cash flow
- Need to expand capacity for business functions or manufacturing
- Need to increase level of service quality or performance
- Reduction of inventories

Technical Issues
- Inability to maintain current network
- Unreliability of current network
- Obsolete network hardware/software
- Need to interconnect microcomputers
- Need for distributed data processing
- Inadequate file structures (database)
- Inadequate security/privacy
- Desire to take advantage of future technology
- Need to conform to international network standards

purpose and objectives of the new data communication network, the scope or boundaries the network will encompass, and have some idea about potential cost.

Deliverable for Step 1

At the completion of this data gathering, a short, written feasibility study report should be generated. This report tells management about the problem, its causes, and its potential solution. The report also states the purpose or *objectives* of the network to be developed. It usually results in a *yes or no decision* for the network.

2. PREPARE A NETWORK DESIGN PLAN

A successful *network design plan* always takes into account three *feasibility factors:*

- *Technical feasibility* of the network,
- *Operational feasibility* for the users who conduct their daily business by using the network, and for managers who rely on its reports,
- *Economic feasibility* to keep the network within budgetary limits.

Network Goals

Begin by taking the objectives from Step 1 and dividing them into three distinct goals. The *major goal* is the reason the data communication network is being built. The object is to ensure that the network meets these requirements. Next, *intermediate goals* are other benefits the system can provide, with little or no extra expense. Finally, *minor goals* are the functions that a communication network can perform for the organization in the future. The major goals are mandatory; the intermediate ones are desirable; and the minor ones are "wish list" items. There is no way to outline the exact steps the plan should follow because the network must be customized for the organization and application systems it serves.

Next, identify the various departments that will use the network, sources of information, and a schedule for performing various activities. You can use a simple *Gantt chart* like the one shown in Figure 11-1 to plan the ten design steps or you can use sophisticated planning software if it is available. In Figure 11-1, the horizontal axis represents units of time in weeks. List the different steps of your plan on the left vertical axis under Project Name. The S and C rows stand for "Scheduled" or "Completed," respectively. If you want to schedule a project step for June, you put x's in the S row under June 7, 14, 21, and 28. As you complete the project, you put x's in the C row to show the state of completion. We suggest you use this Gantt chart to schedule the steps needed to complete your network design.

Network Evaluation Criteria

Finally, develop some *evaluation criteria.* These will help measure the success of the data communication network design, development, and implementation (see the Network Evaluation Criteria box). Whenever possible, each criterion should be assigned a numerical value at the beginning of the project. This value is used at certain control

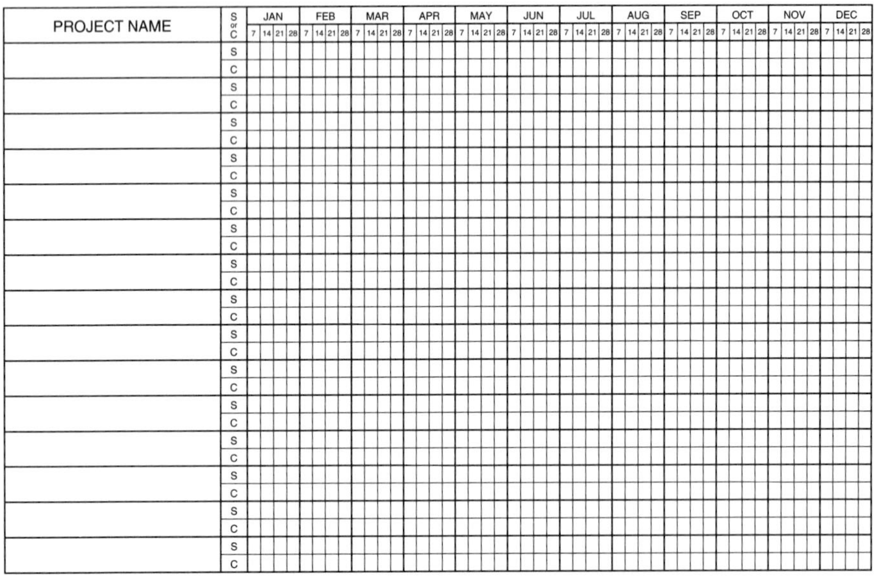

Figure 11-1 Gantt chart.

points or on project completion to provide the comparison that management needs to evaluate the project's success.

Deliverable for Step 2

The report at the end of Step 2 should discuss the technical, operational, and economic feasibility of the network. The purpose of objectives from Step 1 should be divided into major, intermediate, and minor goals. In addition, the report should include a preliminary list of departments that are expected to use the network, as well as a tentative completion schedule. Finally, this report is complete if it contains a list of evaluation criteria.

3. UNDERSTAND THE CURRENT NETWORK

The objective here is to gain a complete understanding of the current operations (application systems and messages), including any network that is functioning. This step provides a *benchmark* against which future design requirements can be gauged. It should provide a clear picture of the present sequence of operations, processing times, work volumes, current communication network (if one exists), existing costs, and user/management needs.

Management Focus: Network Evaluation Criteria

- **Time** Are elapsed time, transaction time, overall processing time, response time, or other operational times reduced?
- **Cost** Are annual network cost, per unit cost, maintenance cost, or others, such as operational, investment, and implementation costs, reduced?
- **Quality** Is a better product or service being produced? Is there less rework because of the network? Has the quality of data/information improved?
- **Capacity** Does the network have the capacity to handle workloads, peak loads, and average loads, as well as the long-term future capacity?
- **Scope** Was the network's scope properly defined? Does the network interconnect all the necessary business functions?
- **Efficiency** Is the network more efficient than the previous one?
- **Productivity** Has productivity of the user (information provider) and management (information user) improved? Is decision making faster and more accurate?
- **Accuracy** Are there fewer errors? Can management rely more on this network than the old one?
- **Flexibility** Can the new network perform diverse operations that were not possible before?
- **Reliability** Are there fewer breakdowns of this network compared with the previous one or network goals?
- **Acceptance** Have the information providers, the information users, and the management accepted the network?
- **Controls** Are adequate security and control mechanisms in place to prevent threats to the network, such as errors and omissions, fraud and defalcation, lost data, breaches of privacy, disastrous events, and the like?
- **Documentation** Does the network have adequate written/pictorial descriptions documenting all its hardware, protocols, software, circuits, and user manuals?
- **Training** Are training courses adequate and are they offered continually, especially for users? Are training manuals adequate and updated regularly?
- **Network Life** Is the future life of the network adequate? Does it have sufficient capacity for long-term growth?

Information Needs

First, gather general information and characteristics of the environment in which the network must operate. Next, identify the specific applications that will use the new data communication network and any proposed applications that could use it in the future. This will require learning about the industry in which the network will function (what competitors are doing in this regard), as well as about your individual company and the departments that are responsible for various applications. Determine whether there are any legal requirements, such as local, state, federal, or international laws, that might affect the network.

Consider the people in different departments who will be affected by the network. Be sure to take into account the formal structure as shown on the organization chart, as well as the informal organizations within a specific department. Be aware that company politics might affect the design effort; people may tell you what they want to satisfy their personal interests rather than what is best for the organization.

Identify the file formats so database planners can start to design the database and its access methodologies. You should be aware that transmission volumes increase dramatically when the network is used for database retrieval transactions and file transfers from microcomputers. Techniques used to complete this step might include interviewing users, searching a variety of current applications, estimating and sampling for timings and volumes, and comparing current application systems with similar ones on a previous network.

Deliverable for Step 3

Documentation gathered during this step summarizes the existing network. It should include any design ideas, notes on whether currently used forms or transmittal documents are adequate or inadequate, who helped or hindered progress, and any other impressions gained from interviews, meetings, data flow diagrams, flowcharts, sampling, inputs/outputs, and the like. In general, the report should contain information that can be referred to during the detailed development of the data communication network. It is the benchmark to be used for later comparisons.

4. DEFINE THE NEW NETWORK REQUIREMENTS

By the time the network design begins, certain items already should be established, such as definition of the problem, purpose or objectives, scope of the network, goals, evaluation criteria, and a general background information about the applications that will use the network. With these items in hand, a list of *network requirements* can be developed. As you identify the new network requirements, keep two questions in mind: "What is the purpose of the network?" and "What is the network to produce?"

During the early stages of defining network requirements, you should review of the organization's long-range and short-range plans concerning changes in company goals, strategic plans, development plans for new products or services, projections of sales, research and development projects, major capital expenditures, possible changes in product mix, new offices that must be served by the communication network, emphasis on security, and future commitments to technology. It is during this step that the designer begins to formulate the details related to the required *circuit capacity* for handling average and peak message volumes, the various acceptable (and unacceptable) *processing times* for applications and transactions, ways of increasing *productivity* for both managers and daily users, methods of improving *reliability* by increasing network uptime, and designing adequate *controls* to secure the network against unwanted events.

Establishing Priorities for Requirements

Once the network requirements have been identified, they should be organized into *mandatory requirements, desirable requirements*, and *wish list requirements*. This information enables you to develop a minimum level of mandatory requirements and a negotiable list of desirable requirements that are dependent on cost and availability. Match these against your major, intermediate, and minor goals from Step 2. Mandatory requirements should match the major goals, desirable requirements should match the intermediate goals, and wish list requirements should match the minor goals.

Network requirements should be as precise as possible, regardless of the priority category into which they fall. For example, rather than stating "a large quantity of characters," state requirements in more precise figures such as "50,000 characters per minute plus or minus 20 percent." This may be very difficult, but some estimate is better than none.

At this point, try to avoid presenting solutions; only requirements are needed. For example, a requirement might state that circuit capacity should be great enough to handle 5000 characters per second, which will triple in five years. It would be a mistake to state this as a solution by saying that a 9600 bits per second voice grade circuit is required. Solutions should be left for later, during Steps 8 and 9, when software and hardware considerations must be interrelated with the network configurations.

Moreover, it is necessary to identify each application that will use the network. If possible, also identify the message type each application uses. This knowledge helps now, and will be particularly useful later when identifying the geographical location for each node in the network.

Response Times

Response time is the time that elapses between the sending of an inquiry from a client to the receipt of the first character of the response. It includes transmission time to the host, processing time, access time to obtain any needed database records, and transmission time back to the client.

The best indicator of response time is to examine a network with similar operating characteristics and applications to see how well a planned network will perform. The problem is that finding such a duplicate system is almost impossible. If no similar network exists from which to draw performance data, then some predictive techniques must be used.

When using these predictive techniques, always state the question as "*x* percent of all response times must be less than or equal to *y* seconds." In other words, a typical statement might be that 95 percent of all response times must be less than or equal to three seconds. Mean and standard deviation of these figures might be used to identify the reliability of the final response time figure.

Cost and response time are inversely proportional. When the response time is shortened, the cost increases, and vice versa. Factors that affect network cost include speed and capacity of the host computer, speed and size of the front end processor, capacity of the communication circuits, remote intelligent control devices, and software programs or protocols.

The specific components that contribute to response time are message input time, application processing time, and message output time, or

$$RT = MIT + APT + MOT$$

The *message input time* is the sum of the polling time, transmission time (including modem turnaround and time for acknowledgment), and queuing time in a remote intelligent control device, front end processor, or host computer. The propagation time over the circuit usually is stable, but the other factors are determined statistically according to traffic volume; a typical time might be 0.85 second.

The *application processing time* includes all program processing time and all input/output accesses to the database. As might be expected, these timings are variable, depending on message traffic and the number of transactions being handled by the host computer or by the server if it is a local area network. An example of a typical application processing time might be 0.75 second.

The *message output time* is the sum of the internal queuing in the host computer, front end processor, and any remote intelligent control devices, and the transmission time (including all modem turnaround, selection, and acknowledgment times). Again, the propagation time over the circuit usually is stable, whereas internal queuing is a variable figure depending on the current volume of transactions at the host/front end processor; typical message output time is 0.90 second.

If the sum of the typical average times is approximately 2.5 seconds, imagine what would happen if another half second were added for propagation delay time for satellite circuits or other delays, such as having to retransmit a large number of messages because of network-imposed errors. In a typical communication application, the component that becomes the most sensitive to increased volume is the application processing or database handling time in the host computer. Response time on a current network is easy to measure with a network analyzer (or even a stopwatch). Predicting it during the design stage, however, requires detailed network analysis involving queuing theory or simulation and a lot of common sense.

Simulation programs take into account such factors as terminal buffering, effect of an intelligent terminal control device, statistical time division multiplexers, mode of transmission used by the modem, communication circuit speed and error rates, queuing at transmission nodes, front end or host computer, line configurations, message lengths, expected arrival times of messages, propagation delays, any priorities built into the system, average versus peak loads, central control versus interrupt, type of applications, speed of output devices, and intrinsic factors within the host computer, such as its hardware architecture, software, or protocols.

Queuing   Queuing theory allows for the definition of such elements as service time, facility utilization, and wait time at the host. A *queue* is a waiting line; jobs sent to a shared printer wait in a queue until their turn comes. Single server and multiserver queuing relationships must work within the environment of network priorities. Although techniques of statistical and queuing formulation are beyond the scope of this text, estimations can be of the best or worst case. These techniques often yield average results that describe the average operational performance of a network. Statistical views of network performance based on queuing theory can vary from real performance by as much as 20 percent, but they can provide estimates of their own accuracy.

Simulation   *Simulation* is a technique to model the behavior of the communication network. Response time is viewed as an elapsed time incurred, which is part of the accumulation of the elapsed times of a series of individual events. Sophisticated programs can be written to simulate the action of a series of events, and these programs add up the elapsed times of each event. Simulation programs run on large machines and they can execute several thousand polls within a few seconds to generate a statistical view of the projected network. Simulators typically ignore error conditions because these conditions are the exception and not the rule. They can be built into sophisticated simulators, but this vastly increases the complexity of the programs. Queuing analysis can verify the predicted results of simulation. Vendors offer simulators to assist in examining the effects of many parameters on a communication network's projected performance such as

- Number of intelligent control units per circuit,
- Number of terminals per intelligent control unit,
- Printers/printer buffer size/printer speed,
- Modem delay for turnaround,
- Propagation delay,
- Statistical time division multiplexer delay (if any),
- Line protocol overhead,
- Message lengths/occurrences/rates,
- Host computer processing delays,
- Database access delays,
- Multiple queues or single queues,
- Polling/selecting.

Deliverable for Step 4

The report at the end of Step 4 includes information on the organization's long- and short-range plans, any future requirements that may have been uncovered, and some reasonable response times that are acceptable for the business operations being performed. These response times are what workers require to complete their tasks within a reasonable period of time. Finally, the primary emphasis of this deliverable should be a detailed listing of the various requirements the new network must fulfill to achieve its goals. These requirements must be divided into three different priority categories: mandatory, desirable, and wish list requirements. Also include a general list of all applications (e.g., e-mail, accounting, inventory) that are expected to use the network, and group by application the types of messages to be transmitted.

5. IDENTIFY THE GEOGRAPHIC SCOPE

Now you must review the list of applications that are expected to use the network and identify the location of each one so that all of them will be interconnected by the planned network. The preliminary geographic map developed during the feasibility study should be examined at this point, and a more detailed and accurate version should be prepared.

Mapping the Network

A data communication network can have four basic levels of *geographic scope*.

- International (worldwide network),
- Country (within the boundaries and laws of a single country),
- City or state (within the boundaries of a specific city, state/province, or local governmental jurisdiction),
- Local facility (within a specific building or confined to a series of buildings located on the same contiguous property).

It is easiest to start with the highest level, so begin by drawing a network map with all the international locations that must be connected. A map that shows lines going between the countries/cities is sufficient. Details such as the type of circuit and other considerations will be added later.

Next, prepare a map for each country. Interconnections should be drawn between all cities within the country that uses the network. Again, a single line drawn between the cities is adequate because the type of configuration has not yet been decided.

The third map is one of the city or state/province. The city-level maps identify concentrator sites and multipoint locations, as well as individual locations. At this point, lines are drawn only between the various interconnect points because configurations have not been chosen.

The local facility "maps" are really pictorial diagrams because designers generally use blueprints or drawings of the building floor to pinpoint specific locations. It is also appropriate to identify the location of current telephone equipment rooms that house communication circuits.

Deliverable for Step 5

The report at the end of Step 5 is the set of international, country, state, city, and local maps that were developed. Remember that the local maps might show a building, a floor layout, the interconnection of several buildings, or a local area network.

6. CALCULATE CIRCUIT REQUIREMENTS

This step is to analyze the network circuits to produce a more detailed estimate of the message capacity required.

Calculating Traffic on Each Circuit

To establish *circuit loading* (the amount of data transmitted on a circuit), the designer usually starts with the total characters transmitted per day on each circuit or, if possible, the number of characters transmitted per hour if peaks must be met. This analysis can focus on either the *average* circuit traffic or the *peak* circuit traffic. For example, in an online banking network, traffic volume peaks usually are in the midmorning (bank opening) and just prior to closing. Airline and rental car reservations network designers look for peak message volumes during holidays or other vacation periods. A military network designer finds extreme peaks in volume during crisis situations, and the telephone companies normally have their highest peak volumes on Mother's Day.

You can calculate message volumes by counting messages in a current network or by estimating future messages. If an online system is operational, network monitors/analyzers may be able to provide an actual circuit character count of the volume transmitted per hour or per day. Carefully select the sample of working days to ensure that anomalies are excluded. When possible, take a random sample for several weeks of traffic and actually count the number of messages handled each day at each location.

When estimating message volumes for a network that does not yet exist, you can use conglomerate estimating, comparison estimating, or detailed estimating. With *conglomerate estimating*, representatives from each application system confer to develop estimates based on past experience. With *comparison estimating*, the network designer meets with people inside or outside the organization who have a similar system so they can supply estimates from their networks. With *detailed estimating*, the network designer makes a detailed study of the overall application system and its future needs in order to develop subestimates, which then are combined to produce the total volume of messages expected.

Accuracy may not be a major concern because of the stairstep nature of communication circuits. For example, assume a situation in which voice grade circuits are used (e.g., 28.8 Kbps), but to meet data volumes you need to transmit at 40 Kbps. This would require the lease of two voice grade circuits. The combined two voice grade circuits now have a maximum capacity of 57.6 Kbps, greatly exceeding the needed 40 Kbps.

When making message volume estimates, be sure to take future growth into account so the network will cover these needs. Forecasts should be made of expected message volumes three to five years in the future. The *turnpike effect* results when the network is used to a greater extent than was anticipated because it is available, is very efficient, and provides new services. The growth factor for network use may vary from 5 to 50 percent and, in some cases, exceed 100 percent for high growth organizations. Few organizations complain about having too much network capacity.

Response Time Evaluation

The circuit loading analysis produces average message traffic estimates. At this point, the network designer should review and establish some of the response time criteria that are required to meet the basic needs of the network's applications. For example, a bank's automated teller machine (ATM) requires a very short response time, usually less than 2.5 seconds. On the other hand, the bank may accept slightly longer response times for terminals located inside the bank. For example, tellers may accept response

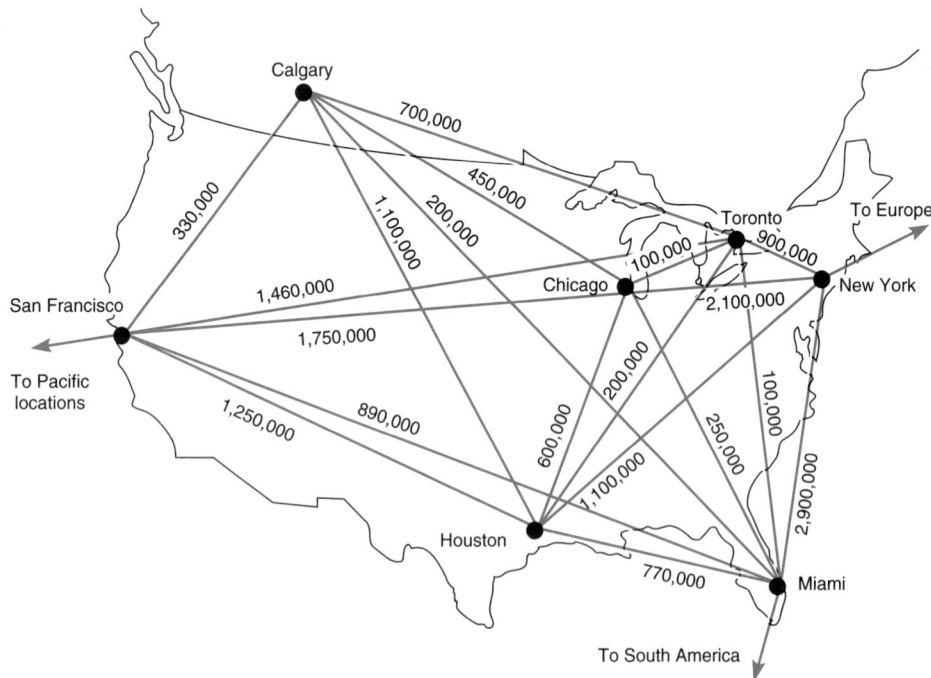

Figure 11-2 Circuit loading in characters per day for a point-to-point configuration.

times of 3.5 seconds, and loan officers entering new loan documents may accept response times of 5 to 7 seconds. The bank's network designer handles varying response times on the same circuit by giving the highest priority to ATMs, second highest priority to the teller terminals, and third highest priority to loan officer terminals.

Based on this analysis, it may be necessary to increase the circuit capacity needed to ensure that response times are within the stated requirements. This is particularly true during times of peak use, which may place far more demands on the network than the simple average calculations may suggest.

Deliverable for Step 6

The report for Step 6 adds the traffic analysis (number of characters per day per circuit) to the documentation. Finally, begin recording on the network maps and/or pictorial diagrams some of the bits per second transmission rates that will be required for each circuit. Figure 11-2 provides an example. This transmission capacity is useful when alternative network configurations, software, and hardware considerations are being developed and evaluated.

7. IDENTIFY NETWORK SECURITY AND CONTROL

Because the network probably will be the "lifeline" of information flow within the organization, *network security* and control are mandatory. All of the security and control mechanisms to be included in this data communication network must be considered in the detailed design. Information is the single most valuable resource within an organization, and it must be protected from all types of threats.

Control Spreadsheet Methodology

To identify areas in need of security and control, you need a network *control spreadsheet,* which shows the threats to the network and the components that must be protected (see Chapter 13). You also identify controls that are needed to safeguard the components.

Deliverable for Step 7

The report for Step 7 contains three items: a control spreadsheet, a list of definitions for both the threats facing the network and the components of the network, and a list that describes the controls to be implemented into the new network.

Management Focus: Goals of Network Design

Network goals might include:

- Minimum circuit distance between the various computers. Modeling can help here.
- Adequate circuit capacity to meet today's data transfer needs, as well as those required three to five years in the future.
- Reasonable response times at individual computers. Response time must meet the needs of each application.
- Efficient software/protocols that can be used on a variety of circuit configurations including satellite circuits that permit the network to interconnect with national or international networks as well as with e-mail systems, use multi-vendor hardware, and connect to public packet switched networks.
- A very high level of reliability (network uptime) must be met. This may be the most important factor. The network designer always should remember that when business operations move into an online, real-time data communication network, it is as if the company has closed its doors to business when the network is down.
- Reliable hardware that offers minimum cost, adequate speed and control features, a high mean time between failures (MTBF), and good diagnostic/service-ability features.
- Reasonable costs (not necessarily the absolute lowest).
- Acceptance of the network by both day-to-day users and managers who must use its data or information.
- Sufficient security and control for the highest risk application using the network.

8. DESIGN NETWORK CONFIGURATIONS

The objective is to configure the circuits, hardware, and software between the computers in the network. Some *goals* the network designer tries to achieve with regard to an efficient and cost-effective network are shown in the Goals of Network Design box. Network design has three basic stages: evaluating software, evaluating hardware, and designing the type and placement of network circuits. It is an iterative process—you move back and forth among the steps.

As you begin designing *network configurations*, remember that cost is an important consideration. Step 9 involves estimating costs based on preparing a *request for proposal* (RFP) and evaluating the responses. Determining the costs of the network will be difficult until you get responses to your RFP from various vendors. Based on the vendors' quotes, you may want to redesign your network, or you may want to have the vendors propose different network designs that may reduce cost or improve performance.

Evaluate Software Considerations

With regard to *software selection,* the type of network computers may be a major constraint. The software protocols they can use may limit the types of terminals or other hardware that can be utilized, or may require protocol converters or gateways to translate between the different protocols.

This is the point at which *protocol selection* takes place. Decisions must be made about what industry standard protocols (e.g., TCP/IP, ethernet) or proprietary protocols (e.g., IBM's SNA) will be used. The network designer can make a major contribution by selecting a protocol that is expandable and is an internationally recognized standard. Another consideration is *internetworking,* which is connecting several networks together. Protocol selection must consider the ease of connecting the network to other networks in the organization, as well as networks of the organization's suppliers and customers.

In addition to protocols/software, other network architectures/software that reside in the host computer and front end processors must be considered. For example, security software packages in the host computer also can be a constraint. The host operating system itself may be a constraint to network control and operation, as might the database management system software. Any software programs that are located elsewhere on the network should be reviewed. These may be at remote concentrators, remote intelligent controllers, statistical multiplexers, and terminals. Microcomputers also raise the issues of distributed data processing/remote application programs, micro-to-mainframe software, and local area network software.

Finally, software diagnostics and maintenance must not be overlooked. Determine how quickly either staffers or the vendor can diagnose software problems and how quickly they can fix them. The concepts of mean time to diagnose (MTTD), mean time to respond (MTTR), and mean time to fix (MTTF) will be discussed in Chapter 12; they apply to software packages as well as to hardware.

Evaluate Hardware Considerations

Hardware selection is easier to handle because hardware is tangible. Some pieces of hardware to consider are:

- Terminals/microcomputers,
- File servers/database servers,
- Gateways/bridges/routers/switches,
- Intelligent terminal controllers,
- Modems (analog/digital),
- Multiplexers and concentrators,
- LAN hubs,
- Protocol converters,
- Hardware encryption boxes,
- PBX switchboards,

- Front end processors,
- Host computers,
- Testing equipment,
- Channel extenders.

With this list in mind, the designer begins to shape the network. The result is a minimum-cost network that meets the organization's data communication (throughout) requirements. As a rule of thumb, remember that minimum circuit cost usually means minimum mileage.

Before ordering hardware, the design team should decide how to handle diagnostics, troubleshooting, and repair. It should be remembered that MTTD (*mean time to diagnose*), MTTR (*mean time to respond*), and MTTF (*mean time to fix*) always apply to hardware. Vendor estimates of MTBF (*mean time between failures*) for hardware should be obtained by the design team. Issues that should be addressed include the types of test equipment that are necessary and the structure of the network management group (see Chapter 12). Some hardware may have built-in diagnostic capabilities for its internal electronic circuits, as well as the ability to identify problems on the communication circuit. *Diagnostics* go hand in hand with network service. The vendor's MTBF and ability to respond to service calls are essential factors that affect network downtime.

Design Network Circuits

The goal is to construct a system that provides adequate response time to the end user while ensuring the cost to deliver that response time is reasonable. To accomplish this goal, the designer must understand the response time and cost trade-off issues associated with data communication networks. Fortunately, computer modeling techniques help evaluate the problem and determine a solution.

A *model* is a body of information about a system gathered for the purpose of studying the system. A *mathematical model* describes the entities of a system with the attributes being represented by mathematical variables; the activities are described by mathematical functions that interrelate the variables. Given a mathematical model of a system, it sometimes is possible to derive information about the system by analytic means. Where this is not possible, it is necessary to use numerical computation for solving the equations of the mathematical model. *System simulation* describes the technique of solving problems by following the changes over time using a dynamic model of a system. A *dynamic mathematical model* allows the changes of system attributes to be derived as a function of time.

Analytical models generally make several assumptions to simplify the mathematics and provide results that can be evaluated easily and cheaply. Simulation models, on the other hand, can reflect the working of a network to any desired level of detail. The time and cost of development and program runs are directly proportional to the level of detail incorporated.

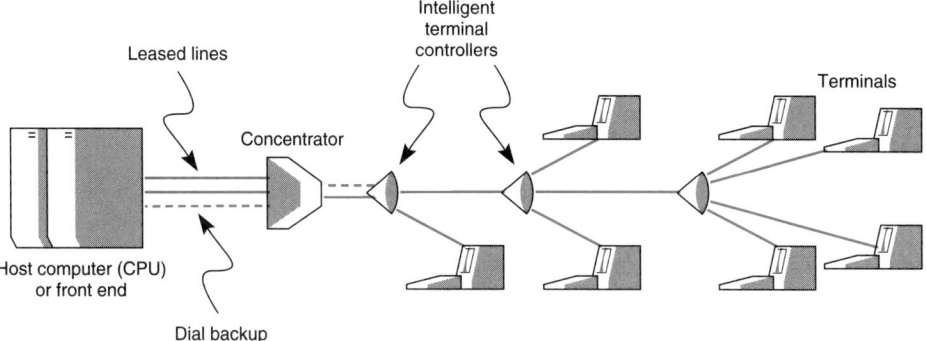

Figure 11-3 Multipoint network configuration.

Let us illustrate some of the analytical and simulation modeling techniques used in a data communication network design. Consider a set of terminals connected to a host computer (CPU) via a multipoint line (Figure 11-3). The CPU and the terminals bear a central control relationship in the sense that the transmissions from the terminals are controlled by the CPU or front end processor. The designer uses polling to evaluate network performance. The designer uses modeling as a means to *predict* the performance of the network and answer such questions as: How does the response time of the network vary as a function of each terminal's load and the number of terminals? How is the response time affected by a specific polling discipline such as giving priority to outbound traffic over inbound traffic?

With regard to analytical models, the designer resorts to queuing models to predict the response time and throughput of a polled network. A general queuing model of a polled network is shown in Figure 11-4 and may be described as queues served in cyclic order with walk times. (*Walk time* is the time to switch service from one queue to another and includes the overhead time attributable to polling, propagation delay, modem synchronization time, and so forth.)

Messages arrive randomly at a terminal and are queued for transmission. The server is made available to each queue periodically, as defined by the polling protocol. The polling program also defines the amount of service received when the server polls a queue. Other characteristics of the network, such as poll message length and modem turnaround time, are modeled in the switchover time to go from the first to the second queue and so forth. The major difficulty in solving the above queuing model is the interrelationship between the queues at the various terminals. An exact model, therefore, has to solve an N-dimensional queuing process, which is a formidable task.

An analytical model requires a sophisticated user who is competent in mathematics for its development and use. When the user is discriminating, it can provide preliminary insights, but seldom can it yield numerical values of sufficient accuracy for the operational design of a network. To obtain a more realistic model, we must resort to simulation.

Simulation models may be tailored to the user's needs by entering parameter values specific to the network at hand. Alternatively, the user may prefer to rely primarily on

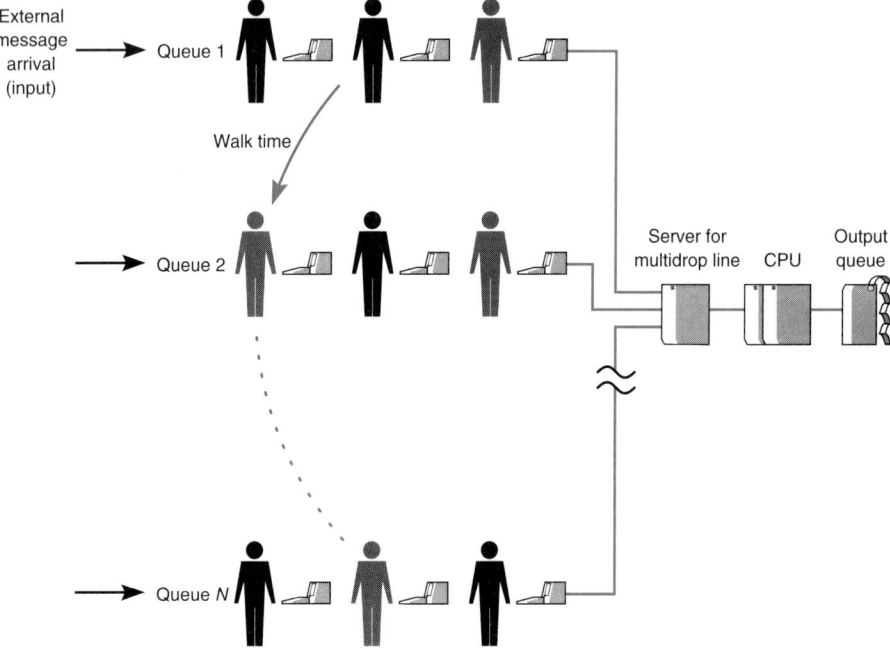

Figure 11-4   Queues model of polled terminals.

the set of average values provided by the network. This set of values allows the simulation model to operate under a specific circuit discipline and is representative of many popular protocols currently in use.

Network Modeling Tool Functions   Network modeling and design tools can perform a number of functions, among which are performance analysis, map and configuration drawing, network configuration optimization, and cost analysis.

Performance analysis allows users to estimate the response times and throughput. It is important to note that these network design tools only provide estimates, which may vary from the actual results. Some network design tools estimate performance for a generalized class of network, but other tools are built specifically for one type of network.

Map and configuration drawing packages provide documentation on how the network is to appear and the equipment it will contain. Network design software supplies maps on which the network designer lays out the various WAN, MAN, BN, and LAN configurations.

Configuration optimization (sometimes called *topology optimization*) enables users to design the optimal layout of a network. Network design tools usually identify the optimal layout by interactively trying various combinations of configurations until the one that shows the lowest network cost is determined. Most modeling packages are able to optimize networks containing multipoint circuits, concentrators placed strategically throughout the network, and packet switches. The final result as to how "good" the optimization is depends on the algorithm used by the network design tool vendor.

Optimization means using an algorithm to configure a network under certain built-in performance constraints. For example, the user might specify the maintenance of a three-second response time and require that the program lay out and optimize a least cost multipoint network based on 50 nodes. Beyond the three-second response time and the locations of the 50 nodes, the user also may specify other parameters such as the common carrier, transmission media, traffic volume statistics, basic characteristics of the terminals, microcomputers, host processors, front end processor, and the protocol that is to be used.

Cost analysis requires that the network design tool vendor continually update the databases of interexchange carrier charges, RBOC charges, and LAN/BN vendor charges. These databases contain tariff filings and LATAs for the various common carriers from whom the organization leases its data communication circuits. Depending on the sophistication of the network design tool, the databases might contain both interLATA and intraLATA tariffs. Unfortunately, costs change so rapidly that they are often unreliable for anything more than a very general estimate. The only way to get an accurate cost estimate is to issue an RFP to vendors.

A sophisticated network design tool should be capable of analyzing hybrid networks that include multipoint, concentrators, and packet switching. Furthermore, the tool should allow users to modify items such as protocols, tariffs, circuit configurations, equipment characteristics, and performance objectives such as response time requirements.

Deliverable for Step 8

This step requires choosing from among various network alternatives. The main constraints are the availability of software, hardware, and circuits. These three factors are all interconnected and must be considered along with the performance and reliability required. All factors are interrelated with regard to cost. Therefore, when alternative network configurations are developed, consider software, hardware, circuits, performance, and reliability in your *cost/benefit analysis*.

During the deliberations, the following decisions must be considered:

- Determine the choice set, that is, all possible network configurations.
- Divide the choice set into *attainable* and *unattainable choice sets*. The attainable set(s) contains only those alternatives that have a reasonable chance of acceptance by management. Acceptance might be predicated on costs, software, hardware, circuit availability, or political factors within the organization.
- Review the attainable set of alternatives and rank them from the most favored to the least favored, taking into account your evaluation criteria for choosing the most favored.
- Present the most highly favored alternatives to management for review and approval.

The network designer also must know whether the proposed alternative is going to maximize something, optimize something, or satisfice something, or do all three. To *maximize* is to get the highest possible degree of use out of the system without regard to other systems. To *optimize* is to get the most favored degree of use out of the system, taking into account all other systems. To *satisfice* is to choose a particular level of performance for which to strive and for which management is willing to settle.

The report for Step 8 contains the choice sets of network configurations and a list of the goals to be achieved with this network. There also can be a model if modeling software has been used for the design project.

9. DETERMINE NETWORK COSTS

In general, costs should not interfere with *preliminary* design configuration alternatives (choice sets). The various alternatives should be identified first; then costs should be related to the *attainable* design configurations. The first task is to identify the attainable and workable configurations, and the second is to identify the costs of those alternatives.

Sources of Costs

Estimating the cost of a network is much more complex than estimating the cost of a new piece of hardware because many variables and intangibles are involved. Some of the costs that must be considered are:

- Circuit costs, including costs of circuits provided by common carriers or the cost of purchasing and installing your own cable.
- Internetworking devices such as repeaters, bridges, switches, routers, or gateways.
- Hardware costs including servers computers, network interface cards, hubs, memory, printers, concentrators, uninterruptible power supplies, and backup tape drives.
- Software costs for network operating system, application software, middleware, and protocol conversion software.
- Network management costs including special hardware, software, and training needed to develop a network management system for ongoing redesign, monitoring, and diagnosing of problems.
- Personnel costs including cost of the network administrator, consultants, and technicians.
- Test and maintenance costs for special monitoring equipment and software, plus the cost of on-site spare parts.
- Security costs such as specialized security software, changing passwords regularly, or installing specialized hardware security devices.

Management Focus: The Get Tough Guide to Telecom Contracts

The fourteen commandments of telecom contracts (or how to reduce your network costs):

1. Beware of MRC. The minimum revenue commitment (the minimum amount you agree to spend) is the worst threat lying in wait in a phone contract. Make sure your firm can meet it.

2. Bargain with Everybody. Beyond the three largest long-distance companies, AT&T, MCI, Sprint, are some smaller firms that offer attractive deals.

3. Know What Everyone Else Is Paying. Contract tariffs can be found in FCC filings or through consultants.

4. Get the Most Overall Flexibility Possible. Usually, the shortest deal possible in terms of years with the minimum MRC and some ability to switch from leased lines to frame relay.

5. Get the Most Fine-grained Flexibility Possible. Long-term contracts tend to be less flexible in areas such as the speeds of leased lines.

6. Demand a Fixed Price. Virtually all contracts currently charge floating rates for services included and they have been increasing annually.

7. Specify Every Service You Can. Unless they are written in the contract, special features are not included in the contract, even if they are ordinary services.

8. Insist on Free Installations. In addition to discounts, most carriers are willing to waive the installation fee for leased circuits and services.

9. Demand ''Most-favored'' Status. Larger firms can negotiate aggressively to receive a lower tariff rate if another customer is awarded a lower tariff.

10. Worry About the Divorce When You Get Hitched. You typically have to pay a penalty of about one half of the remaining agreement.

11. Beware of Monitoring Conditions. Beware of conditions like ''60 percent of calls have to be made during regular business hours.''

12. Check Your Bills. The more complicated the contract, the more mistakes occur.

13. Aggregate Selectively. With no flexibility in the contract, don't include anything you'll have to change.

14. Get Professional Advice.

Source: Datamation, March 15, 1995.

Figure 11-5 shows various cost and benefit categories associated with data communication networks. The most helpful items in this figure are the *direct costs*, the *indirect costs*, and the *intangible benefits*. Intangibles sometimes are very difficult to identify. Other benefits, such as direct and indirect cost reductions and revenue increases, are unique to the organization for which the network is being designed.

Costs	Benefits
Direct costs	**Direct and indirect cost reductions**
• Computer equipment	• Elimination of clerical personnel and/or manual operations
• Communication equipment	• Reduction of inventories, manufacturing, sales, operations, and management costs
• Common carrier line charges	• Effective cost reduction, for example, less spoilage or waste, elimination of obsolete materials, and less pilferage
• Software	• Distribution of resources across demand for service
• Operations personnel costs	
• File conversion costs	**Revenue increases**
• Facilities costs (space, power, air conditioning, storage space, offices, etc.)	• Increased sales because of better responsiveness
• Spare parts costs	• Improved services
• Hardware maintenance costs	• Faster processing of operations
• Software maintenance costs	**Intangible benefits**
• Interaction with vendor and/or development group	• Smoothing of operational flows
• Development and performance of acceptance test procedures and parallel operation	• Reduced volume of paper produced and handled
• Development of documentation	• Rise in level of service quality and performance
• Costs for backup of network in case of failure	• Expansion capability
• Costs of manually performing tests during a system outage	• Improved decision process by provision of faster access to information
• Security and control	• Ability to meet the competition
• Personnel	• Future cost avoidance
Indirect costs	• Positive effect on other classes of investments or resources such as better utilization of money, more efficient use of floor space or personnel, and so forth
• Personnel training	• Improved employee morale
• Transformation of operational procedures	• Keeping technical employees
• Development of support software	• Faster decision making
• Disruption of normal activities	
• Increased system outage rate during initial operation period	
• Increase in the number of vendors (impacts fault detection and correction because of "finger pointing")	

Figure 11-5   Cost/benefit categories.

Request for Proposal (RFP)

Most organizations develop requests for proposals (RFP) before making large network purchases. RFPs specify what equipment, software, and services are desired and ask vendors to provide their best prices. Some RFPs are very specific about what items are to be provided in what time frame. In other cases, items are defined as mandatory,

Management Focus: Information in a Typical RFP

Background Information
   Organizational profile
   Overview of current network
   Overview of new network
   Goals of new network
Network Requirements
   Choice sets of possible network designs (hardware, software, circuits)
   Mandatory, desirable, and wish list items
   Security and control requirements
   Response time requirements
   Guidelines for proposing new network designs
Service Requirements
   Implementation time plan
   Training courses and materials
   Support services
   Reliability and performance guarantees
Bidding Process
   Time schedule for the bidding process
   Ground rules
   Bid evaluation criteria
   Availability of additional information
Information required from vendor
   Vendor corporate profile
   Experience with similar networks
   Hardware and software benchmarks
   Reference list

important, or desirable, or several scenarios are provided and the vendor is asked to propose the best solution. In a few cases, RFPs specify generally what is required and the vendors are asked to propose their own network designs.

Once the vendors have submitted their proposals, the organization evaluates them against specified criteria and selects the winner(s). Depending upon the scope and complexity of the network, it is sometimes necessary to redesign the network based on the information in the vendor's proposals. The accompanying focus box summarizes the information in a typical RFP.

One of the key decisions in the RFP process is its scope. Will you use one vendor or several for all hardware, software, and services? Multi-vendor environments tend to provide better performance because it is unlikely that one vendor makes the "best" hardware, software, and services in all categories. Multi-vendor networks also tend to be less expensive because it is unlikely that one vendor will always have the cheapest hardware, software, and services in all product categories.

Multi-vendor environments can be more difficult to manage, however. If equipment is not working properly and it is provided by two different vendors, each can blame the other for the problem. In contrast, a single vendor is solely responsible for everything.

Deliverable for Step 9

The report for Step 9 is the cost of the circuits, hardware, and software. It should be presented as succinctly as possible, typically by using a spreadsheet.

10. IMPLEMENT THE NETWORK

At this point, there are three subtasks.

- Sell the network both to management and to its potential users.
- Implement the network. This probably is the most difficult task of all because the various pieces of hardware, protocol/software programs, network management/test facilities, and communication circuits must be assembled into a working network.
- Evaluate the network. Conduct follow-up investigations to ensure that all parts of the new network actually operate as planned and that nothing has been overlooked.

Selling the Proposed Network to Management

When presenting the network to gain management and user acceptance, the designer should be prepared for objections to the proposed network. Basic objections usually follow these lines:

- The cost is too high, or it appears too low, for what the network is supposed to be able to do.
- The performance is not good enough, or it is more than required at this time.
- The new network does not meet the goals, objectives, and policies of the organization/departments that will be using it.
- The response or processing time is either too slow or too fast with respect to other operations within the organization.
- The network is not flexible enough. If changes are made in other areas, the network may collapse and the investment will be wasted.
- The quality, capacity, efficiency, accuracy, or reliability of the new network does not meet management's criteria.
- Certain management personnel may dislike or distrust the network design team's motives, personalities, or presentation methods.

The list of evaluation criteria prepared in Step 2 should be reviewed so you will be ready for questions about any unmet criteria.

Implementing the Network

Implementation begins after management has agreed to install and finance the new network. It involves hardware, protocols/software, communication circuits, a network management/test facility, staff, written procedures that specify how each task is performed, training, and complete documentation of the operating network.

A detailed *implementation plan* should be developed to specify who will do what and when they will do it. The design/implementation team must take into account the earliest lead times that are required to order hardware, software, and circuits. In addition, some lead time is needed for testing the protocols and software to ensure they operate in conjunction with the hardware and circuits. You must also decide how the new network will be implemented. Four basic approaches can be used.

- Direct cutover, in which all computers are started up on the new network at the same time.
- Chronological cutover, in which computers are converted in sequence, through the network. In this case, both the old and the new network are in operation at the same time.
- Phased implementation, in which similar geographical areas within the network are started up at one time, and other areas are started up later.
- Pilot operation, in which a test facility is established to ensure the operation is as expected before cutover is made.

Once the hardware is in place, the circuits have been installed, and the protocol/software is operating, training of the users can begin, although when possible it should be started earlier. The training should include individual user training, extensive written training manuals, and a methodology for continual updating of these manuals. At this point, the use of computer assisted instruction (CAI) should be considered. With CAI there are no written manuals; all the training techniques and procedures are stored in the computer system, and the operators use their terminals for training as well as for standard business operations. Developers of most newer systems emphasize the "user-friendliness" of their systems, providing extensive online help screens.

The network management and test center is a vital part of the network. This group must be in operation *before* the network is cut over to an operational status because reliability, or uptime, is the single most important criterion for user acceptance.

Evaluating the Operating Network

Finally, after the network is operational, conduct follow-ups for about six months to ensure that all parts of the new network actually are operating and that no minor activities or operations have been overlooked.

Management Focus: Snags, Snafus—and a Whole Lot of Static

Analysts predicted the contract to provide the world's largest phone customer, Uncle Sam, with a state-of-the-art telecommunications system would be for 10 years at a cost of $25 billion. The contract would be a lucrative showcase for AT&T and U.S. Sprint.

Sixteen months into the project known as FTS-2000, things just are not working out as planned. Under the terms of the contract, the lowest bidder, AT&T, was to have gotten 60 percent of the traffic. But AT&T is furious that it is getting far less. Both AT&T and Sprint claim that the General Services Administration is crimping sales by tacking on a 10 percent management fee to FTS-2000 phone bills. The complaints are numerous, government agencies want out, and Congress is investigating.

Now, rival MCI Communications Corp. is stirring the pot even more. MCI lost the bidding but still wants government business. So, it announced plans to charge agencies 40 percent less for voice calls than they would pay under FTS-2000 and other government phone contracts. Although AT&T and Sprint say MCI's service is not comparable to theirs, the companies may have to match MCI's prices.

Source: Information Processing, March 4, 1995.

After the network is considered fully operational, a reevaluation should be performed six months to a year later. This is a critical review of operator or user complaints, management complaints, efficiency reports, network management trouble reports, an evaluation of statistics gathered on items such as errors during transmission and characters transmitted per circuit, and a review of peak load factors. Of course, it also should include a complete review of the original evaluation criteria so the success of the design, development, and implementation of the new data communication network can be determined.

Deliverable for Step 10

In summary, ten steps are performed to design a new data communication network. Although some steps may be omitted when a current network is enhanced, an orderly plan still must be followed. As the project closes, pull all the documentation together and arrange it in a binder that contains ten separate sections, one for each step carried out. The final report also should contain the implementation plan, a description of problems encountered, and any required approvals.

Summary

1. Conduct a Feasibility Study The purpose of the feasibility study is to determine the possibility or probability of either improving the current network or developing a totally new network. This report is the instrument by which you tell management about the problem, its causes, and what you have to offer in the way of a solution. This report also states the purpose or objectives of the network to be developed.

2. Prepare a Network Design Plan   The design plan should discuss the technical, operational, and economic feasibility of the data communication network. The objectives from Step 1 should be divided into major, intermediate, and minor goals. In addition, the report should include a preliminary list of departments that are expected to use the network, a tentative completion schedule, and a list of evaluation criteria.

3. Understand the Current Network   This provides a benchmark against which future design requirements can be gauged.

4. Define the New Network Requirements   The designer formulates the details related to the required circuit capacity for handling average and peak message volumes, the various acceptable (and unacceptable) processing times for applications and transactions, ways of increasing productivity for both managers and daily users, methods of improving reliability by increasing network uptime, and designing adequate security controls.

5. Identify the Geographic Scope   All the physical locations that must be interconnected by the planned network are identified. The preliminary map developed during the feasibility study should be examined at this point, and a more detailed and accurate version should be prepared.

6. Calculate Circuit Requirements   This produces a more detailed estimate of the message capacity needed on network circuits. Capacity depends on the amount of message traffic on the circuit and on the response time needed. This report adds the traffic analysis (number of characters per day per circuit) to the documentation.

7. Identify Network Security and Control   Security ensures information is protected from all types of threats such as errors and omissions, message loss or change, disasters and disruptions, breach of privacy, theft, unreliability, incorrect recovery and restart, poor error handling, and viruses.

8. Design Network Configurations   Network design includes evaluating software and hardware, and deciding on the type and placement of network circuits. It is an iterative process. The deliverable is a choice set of all available alternatives. Each alternative is a different network or a slightly modified version of another alternative.

9. Determine Network Costs   For most large network purchases, organizations develop requests for proposals (RFP), which specify what equipment, software, and services are desired and ask vendors to provide their best prices. Although suppliers provide list prices, actual prices may be much lower if venders must bid against each other.

10. Implement the Network This includes selling the network to management and users, physically implementing the network, and evaluating it.

Key Terms

Application processing time	Feasibility study	Operational feasibility
Benchmark	Gantt chart	Optimize
Choice set	Geographic scope	Performance analysis
Circuit loading	Intermediate goal	Problem definition
Comparison estimating	Major goal	Request for proposal
Configuration optimization	Mandatory requirements	(RFP)
Conglomerate estimating	Message volume	Response time
Control spreadsheet	Minor goal	Satisfice
Cost analysis	Model	Simulation
Desirable requirements	Needs assessment factors	Systems approach
Economic feasibility	Network configurations	Technical feasibility
Evaluation criteria	Network requirements	Turnpike effect
	Network security	Wish list requirements

Selected References

1. *AUTONET.* A software program available from Network Design & Analysis Corp., 505 Park Avenue, New York, NY 10022, or by calling Boris Dortok at 212-688-5432.
2. *CAML—Cost Analysis for Multiple Locations.* A software program available from SAV-NET USA, Inc., P.O. Box 236, Bedminster, NJ 07921-0236, or by calling John Leonard at 908-781-0950.
3. Cope, Patricia. ''New Modeling Tools Help in Building LAN Internets,'' *Network World,* vol. 8, no. 51, December 23, 1991, 1, 23–25.
4. FitzGerald, Jerry, and Ardra F. FitzGerald. *Designing Controls into Computerized Systems,* 2nd ed. Redwood City, CA: Jerry FitzGerald & Associates, 1990.
5. FitzGerald, Jerry, and Ardra F. FitzGerald. *Fundamentals of Systems Analysis: Using Structured Analysis and Design Techniques,* 3rd ed. New York: John Wiley & Sons, 1987.
6. *GrafNet Plus.* A software program available from Network Dimensions, 5339 Prospect Road, Suite 312, San Jose, CA 95129, or by calling Ranjama Sharma at 408-446-9598, or FAX to 408-255-4576.
7. Held, Gilbert. *Practical Network Design Techniques.* Chichester, England: John Wiley & Sons, 1991.
8. *MIND-Data/PC.* A software program available from NMI/Network Analysis Center, 6990 Jericho Turnpike, Suite 300W, Syosset, NY 11791, or by calling David Rubin at 800-765-4622, ext. 114.
9. *Private Line Pricer, AT&T Edition.* A software program available from Economics & Technology, Inc., 1 Washington Mall, Boston, MA 02108, or by calling Mary McCarthy at 800-225-2496.
10. Salamone, Salvatore. ''Design Tools Optimize Networks, Reduce Costs,'' *Network World,* vol. 7, no. 11, March 12, 1990, 1, 45, 48, 50, 52, 57.
11. Van Norman, Harrell J. ''WAN Design Tools: The New Generation,'' *Data Communications,* vol. 19, no. 13, October 1990, 129–130, 132, 134, 136, 138.

Questions/Problems

1. What are the keys to designing a successful data communication network?
2. When should you use the systems approach to network design?
3. Two major classes of users must be considered when planning communication networks. Who are they?
4. Is a feasibility study always required before proceeding with network design? Explain.
5. What is a primary responsibility of the feasibility study?
6. What does a feasibility study include?
7. What three factors should be taken into account when preparing a design plan?
8. On what should the design plan be based?
9. What are evaluation criteria and what is their purpose?
10. What is a major trap into which network designers or managers can fall?
11. What is a network benchmark and when is it established?
12. What is the value of examining long-range and short-range reports before beginning network design?
13. Define response time and what it includes.
14. What makes network costs increase with regard to response time?
15. What is a queue?
16. What purpose do simulators serve?
17. What is the response time formula and what does it include?
18. How are maps used in defining the geographic scope of a network?
19. What factors must be examined when analyzing messages?
20. How is message volume determined for a network that currently does not exist?
21. What is the relationship of traffic to circuit loading?
22. What is the turnpike effect and why is it important in network design?
23. What factors might affect circuit loading?
24. What methodology is used to identify network security and control?
25. What is the primary goal of a data communication network?
26. How does circuit loading differ from circuit capacity?
27. How do choice sets fit into the network design?
28. When choosing from among the various network design alternatives, what are the primary constraints that affect cost?
29. Discuss in general terms how software relates to network design.
30. Discuss in general terms how hardware relates to network design.
31. Should you always determine network costs first? Why or why not?
32. What are the ways to look at costing a network configuration?
33. What cost/benefit categories are used to ensure no critical cost or important benefit is overlooked when estimating network costs?
34. What four functions should computerized network design tools provide?
35. Describe the ten steps a designer performs to create a new data communication network.
36. Identify two or three critical points that should appear in a feasibility study final report.
37. Identify and define five or six key evaluation criteria.

38. The following is an excerpt from last month's progress memo from the data communication analyst Pat Jones to the network manager, Robin Smith.

> Mr. Allen, the vice president of marketing, called to ask whether anything could be done to improve the order entry network. I met with him and the manager of marketing administration, Mrs. Johnson, and listened to their problems. We agreed on a short written definition of the problem, and determined that marketing field offices and salespeople, marketing headquarters, manufacturing, and distribution will be affected by any changes to the present network. Mr. Allen denied my request to visit a typical field office because he feels Mrs. Johnson knows enough about their operation to brief me. I met with the manufacturing planner, Mr. Williams, and the head of distribution, Ms. Thomas. I obtained a general understanding of the current order entry network from Johnson, Williams, and Thomas. The design of the new network is underway now and will be completed soon. I then will prepare a cost estimate of the network design and will present both to you in my report next month.

    Play the role of Smith and write a memo to Jones, commenting on this report. Be critical and try to determine any areas where Jones may not have done everything necessary.

39. Critique the following excerpts from a network requirements document:
    - The network shall be easy to operate.
    - The network shall have a mean time between failures of at least 1000 hours.
    - The network shall transmit in half duplex mode at 2400 bits per second.
    - The network shall transmit at least 1000 messages per hour.

40. What are some of the items that use transmission time but do not transmit business data and for which the designer must account?

41. Give examples of what factors might cause peak loads and discuss how the designer takes them into account when designing a data communication network.

42. What is system simulation?

43. Each of the ten steps of a data communication network design project requires some type of report. Name the deliverables required at the end of each design step.

NEXT DAY AIR SERVICE CUMULATIVE CASE STUDY

See appendix at end of book

CHAPTER TWELVE

NETWORK MANAGEMENT

Network managers perform two key tasks: (1) designing and implementing new networks and network upgrades; and (2) managing the day-to-day operation of existing networks. This chapter examines day-to-day network management, discussing the things that must be done to ensure the network functions properly and to enable user success. We discuss the network management organization, and the basic management skills required of a successful network manager.

Objectives

- Understand what is required to manage the day-to-day operation of networks,
- Become familiar with the network management organization,
- Understand configuration management,
- Understand performance and fault management,
- Become familiar with end user support,
- Become familiar with cost management,
- Understand the role and functions of network management software,
- Become familiar with several types of network management hardware tools.

Chapter Outline

Introduction
Organizing the Network Management Function
    The Shift to LANs
    Integrating LANs and WANs
    Integrating Voice and Data Communications

INTRODUCTION

Network management is the process of controlling, monitoring, and running the network to ensure it operates as intended and provides value to its users. The primary responsibility of the data communication function is to move and convey data and information. This transfer of information may take place within a single department, between departments in an organization, or with entities outside the organization. Remember that *data* are nothing more than meaningless characters, whereas *information* takes these meaningless characters and assembles them into a fact or idea that can be used for decision making by managers. Information presupposes adequate communication because information is useless if it is not available when needed. Data communications add time value to information. Information that is only 75 percent accurate, but received in time to affect a decision, generally is more valuable than information that is 100 percent accurate, but received too late.

Today's information-based economy is vitally concerned with the movement and integration of voice conversations, data/information, and images (video/graphics). For this reason, network managers are concerned with the entire telecommunication function, even though it may be referred to as data communications. The point is that effective communication managers must be aware of voice transmissions, data transmissions, and image transmissions; the information systems manager can no longer be concerned solely with data transmissions.

The manager of a data communication function should always remember that data or information transmitted over any network must CATER to the needs of its users. (*CATER* is an acronym for Consistent, Accurate, Timely, Economically feasible, and Relevant.) The data communication manager may not be directly responsible for *consistency* or *relevancy* (those are the responsibility of the information owner/gath-

Management Focus: Five Key Management Tasks

Planning activities require . . .
- Forecasting
- Establishing objectives
- Scheduling
- Budgeting
- Allocating resources
- Developing policies

Organizing activities require . . .
- Developing organizational structure
- Delegating
- Establishing relationships
- Establishing procedures
- Integrating the smaller organization with the larger organization

Directing activities require . . .
- Initiating activities
- Decision making
- Communicating
- Motivating

Controlling activities require . . .
- Establishing performance standards
- Measuring performance
- Evaluating performance
- Correcting performance

Staffing activities require . . .
- Interviewing people
- Selecting people
- Developing people

erer/developer), but is responsible for ensuring *accuracy* (error-free transmission), *timeliness* (speed), and *economic feasibility* (cost-effective networks). The individual managers who are responsible for the data communication function must be adept at performing the five key management tasks of *planning, organizing, directing, controlling,* and *staffing.* (See the accompanying Five Key Management Tasks box.)

The ultimate objective of the data communication and networking function is to move data from one location to another in a timely fashion, and to provide the resources that allow this transfer of data. All too often this major objective is sacrificed to the immediacy of problems generated by factors thought to be outside the control of management. These factors might be problems caused by unexpected circuit failures, pressure from end users to meet critical schedules, unavailability of certain equipment or circuits, or insufficient information (on a day-to-day basis) to ensure that the network provides adequate service to all users. In reality, network managers must gather their own decision-making information in order to measure network performance, identify problem areas, isolate the exact nature of problems, restore the network, and predict future problems.

The most important tasks in network management are *planning* and *organizing.* Without a well-planned and designed network and a well-organized network management staff, operating the network becomes extremely difficult. However, most network managers spend most of their time *controlling.* They must contend daily with breakdowns and immediate problems (sometimes called *firefighting*). If managers do not spend enough time on the management functions of planning and organizing, which are needed to predict and prevent problems, they are destined to be reactive rather than proactive in solving problems.

ORGANIZING THE NETWORK MANAGEMENT FUNCTION

Communication and networking functions present special organizational problems because they are centralized and decentralized at the same time. The developers, gatherers, and users of data are typically decentralized. The need for communications and networking affects every business function; however, the management of voice and data communications on large host mainframes has traditionally been highly centralized. Mainframes were "owned" and operated by centralized information technology (IT) departments that are used to controlling every aspect of the IT and communication environment.

The Shift to LANs

Since the late 1980s, this picture has changed dramatically. There has been an explosion in the use of microcomputer-based networks. In fact, more than 60 percent of most organizations' total computer processing power (measured in millions of instructions per seconds) now resides on microcomputer-based LANs. This trend is continuing; since 1992, the number of computers attached to LANs has grown by almost 40 percent *per year* (compared to less than 10 percent per year for mainframe-based terminals and computers). Many experts predict that by the end of the century, the host mainframe computer will contain 20 percent or less of the organization's total computing power.

While the management of host-based mainframe networks will always be important, the future of network management lies in the successful management of the LAN and backbone network. Most LANs are "owned" and operated by different organizational units, not by the central IT department. Most LANs were initially designed and implemented as separate networks, whose goals were to best meet the needs of their individual owners, not to integrate with other networks.

Today, the critical issue is the integration of all organizational networks. This presents two problems. The first problem is technical. Since each LAN was developed by a different department within the organization, not all LANs use the same type of technology. It is not uncommon to find a mixture of ethernet LANs and token rings LANs in the same organization. Having different technologies means that routers or gateways must be used to connect the different LANs to organizational backbones and that network managers and technicians must be familiar with both types of networks. The more different types of network technology used, the more complex network management becomes.

The second problem is cultural. While it is impossible to accurately characterize the personalities and management styles of all network managers, several common traits have been observed across many organizations. WAN managers and managers of mainframe-based host computer networks are typically more comfortable in highly structured and controlled network environments. They are used to standardized processes and gradually changing technologies that need to be studied and evaluated carefully before being implemented. They are used to controlling their networks and granting permission for new applications and tools to be installed, and typically have a large support staff. LAN managers often accuse WAN managers of being slow to implement changes and adopt new technologies.

In contrast, LAN managers tend to be less interested in standards and more interested in getting the job done. They value quick responses to changing user demands and rapidly changing technology. They often do not like the restrictiveness of standards, preferring a more laissez faire approach to network management. They typically have little control over the applications on their networks, as users can purchase and install their own network applications software. LAN managers are often the ones responsible for all aspects of their networks. Sometimes they also have a few technicians supporting them, but in general, they lack the depth of personnel available to WAN mangers. WAN managers often accuse LAN managers of being reactive, short-term thinkers with little concern for long-term planning.

Integrating LANs and WANs

The key to integrating LANs and WANs into one overall organization network is for both LAN and WAN mangers to recognize that they no longer have the power they once had. No longer can network managers make independent decisions without considering their impacts on other parts of the organization's network. There must be a single overall communications and networking goal that best meets the needs of the entire organization. This will require some network managers to compromise and agree to policies that are not in the best interest of their own departments or networks.

The central data communication network organization should have a written charter that defines its purpose, operational philosophy, and long-range goals. These goals must conform both to the parent organization's information processing goals and to its own departmental goals. Along with its long-term policies, the organization must develop individual procedures with which to implement the policies. Individual departments and LAN managers must be free to implement their own policies and procedures within this overall plan. Remember that goals lead to policies, which lead in turn to procedures that detail how specific tasks are to be carried out so the organization can meet its goals. These policies and procedures, therefore, provide the structure that guides the day-to-day tasks of data communication workers.

Integrating Voice and Data Communications

Another major organizational challenge is the prospect of combining the voice communication function with the data and image communication functions. Traditionally, voice communications were handled by a manager in the facilities department who supervised the telephone switchboard systems and also coordinated the installation and maintenance of the organization's voice telephone networks. By contrast, data communications traditionally were handled by the IT department because the staff

Management Focus: What Do Network Managers Do?

If you were to become a network manager, some of your responsibilities and tasks would be to:

- Plan, organize, direct, control, and staff the organization's voice/data network operation.
- Develop a strategic (long-term) communication plan to meet the organization's policies and goals.
- Assist senior management in understanding the business implications of network decisions and the role of the network in business operations.
- Manage the day-to-day operations of all network functions.
- Provide support to network users.
- Ensure the network(s) are operating reliably.
- Manage micro-to-mainframe network connections.
- Manage the organization's local area networks, as well as connecting them to the organization's backbone network.
- Develop and control the organization's backbone networks, including satellite, microwave, cellular, and other bypass (DTS) technologies.
- Evaluate, and acquire communication-oriented hardware, software, and services
- Manage the communication budget, with emphasis on controlling costs.
- Acquire knowledge of public data networks and how to connect them to the organization's voice, data, and image networks.
- Keep abreast of the latest technological developments in telephones, PBXs, fax machines, and other office equipment.
- Keep abreast of the latest technological developments in computers, data communications devices, and network software.
- Keep abreast of the latest technological developments and vendors' services in metropolitan and wide area networks.
- Understand how to combine voice, data, and image technologies.

installed their own communication circuits as the need arose, rather than contacting and coordinating with the voice communications management staff.

This separation of voice and data worked well over the years, but now changing communication technologies are causing enormous pressures to combine these functions. These pressures are magnified by the high cost of maintaining separate facilities, the low efficiency and productivity of the organization's employees because there are two separate network functions, and the potential political problems within an organization when neither manager wants to relinquish his or her functional duties or job position. A key factor in voice/data integration might turn out to be the elimination of one key management position and the merging of two staffs.

We cannot present a perfect solution to this problem because it must be handled in a way unique to each organization. Depending on the business environment and specific communication needs, some organizations may want to combine these functions and others may find it better to keep them separate. We can state unequivocally that an organization that avoids studying this situation might be promoting inefficient communication systems, lower employee productivity, and increased operating costs for its separate voice and data networks.

In communications, we are moving from an era in which the computer system is the dominant IT function to one in which communication networks are the dominant IT function. In some organizations, the total cost of both voice and data communications will equal or exceed the total cost of the computer systems. Sometimes this cost factor is overlooked, ignored, or underestimated.

CONFIGURATION MANAGEMENT

Configuration management means managing the network's hardware and software configuration and documenting it (and ensuring it is updated as the configuration changes). Many of the configuration management activities associated with new networks and network upgrades of hardware and software were discussed in Chapter 11.

The most common configuration management activity is adding and deleting user accounts. When new users are added to the network, they are usually categorized as being a member of some group of users (e.g., faculty, students, accounting department, personnel department). Each *user group* has its own access privileges, which define what file servers, directories, and files they can access and provide a standard *login script*. The login script specifies what commands are to be run when the user first logs in (e.g., setting default directories, connecting to public disks, running menu programs).

Configuration documentation includes information about network hardware, network software, user and application profiles, and network documentation. The most basic information about network hardware is a set of network configuration maps that document the number, type, and placement of network circuits (whether organization owned or leased from a common carrier), network servers, network devices (e.g., hubs, routers), and client computers. For most organizations, this is a large set of maps: one for each LAN, BN, MAN, and WAN.

These maps must be supplemented by documentation on each individual network component (e.g., circuit, hub, server). Documentation should include the type of device, serial number, vendor, date of purchase, warranty information, repair history, telephone number for repairs, and any additional information or comments the network manager wishes to add. For example, it would be useful to include the dial-in numbers for communication servers, contact names and telephone numbers for the individual network managers responsible for each separate LAN within the network, and common carrier circuit control telephone contact index and log (whenever pos-

Management Focus: Ten Networking Commandments

1. Thou shalt back up thy hard disk regularly.
2. Thou shalt schedule downtime before doing major work upon thy server.
3. Thou shalt keep thy network disk clean of old files.
4. Thou shalt keep an adequate supply of spare parts.
5. Thou shalt not covet thy neighbor's network software (and upgrade without reason).
6. Thou shalt not steal thy neighbor's software without a license.
7. Thou shalt train thy users.
8. Thou shalt not tinker with thine Autoexec.bat, Config.sys or Startnet.bat unless thou knowest what thou is doing.
9. Thou shalt not drop thy guard against viruses.
10. Thou shalt write down thy network configuration in tablets of stone.

Source: Networking for Dummies, IDG Books, 1994.

sible, establish a national account with the common carrier rather than dealing with individual common carriers in separate states and areas).

A similar approach can be used for network software. This includes the network operating system (NOS) and any special purpose network software. For example, it is important to record which NOS and which version or release date is installed on each network server. The same is true of application software. As discussed in Chapter 8 on LANs, sharing software on networks can greatly reduce costs, although it is important to ensure that the organization is not violating any software license rules.

Software documentation can also help in negotiating site licenses for software. Many users buy software on a copy by copy basis, paying full retail price for each copy. It may be cheaper to negotiate the payment of one large fee for an unlimited use license for widely used software packages instead of paying on a per copy basis.

The third type of documentation is the user and application profiles, which should be automatically provided by the network operating system or additional vendor or third-party software agreements. These should enable the network manager to easily identify the files and directories to which each user has access and their access rights (e.g., read-only, edit, delete). Equally important is the ability to access this information in the "opposite" direction; that is, to be able to select a file or directory and obtain a list of all authorized users and their access rights.

In addition, other documentation must be routinely developed and updated pertaining to the network. This includes network hardware and software manuals, application software manuals, standards manuals, operations manuals for network staff, vendor contracts and agreements, and licenses for software. The documentation should include details about performance and fault management (e.g., preventive maintenance guidelines and schedules, disaster recovery plan, and diagnostic techniques), end user support (e.g., applications software manuals, vendor support telephone numbers), and cost management (e.g., annual budgets, repair costs for each device). The documentation should also include any legal requirements to comply with local or federal laws, control, or regulatory bodies.

PERFORMANCE AND FAULT MANAGEMENT

Performance management means ensuring the network is operating as efficiently as possible. Improving network performance is its essence. Several strategies for improving performance were discussed in previous chapters.

Fault management means preventing, detecting, and correcting any faults in the network circuits, hardware, and software (e.g., a broken hub or improperly installed software). Fault management and performance management are closely related, because any faults in the network reduce performance. Both also require *network monitoring*, which means keeping track of the operation of various network circuits and devices to ensure they are functioning properly and to determine how heavily they are used.

Network Monitoring

Most large organizations and many smaller ones use *network management software* to monitor and control their networks. One function provided by these systems is to collect operational statistics from the network devices.

The parameters monitored by a network management system fall into two distinct categories: physical network statistics and logical network information. Gathering statistics on the *physical network parameters* includes monitoring the operation of the network's modems, multiplexers, circuits linking the various hardware devices, and any other network devices. Monitoring the physical network consists of keeping track of circuits that may be down, tracing malfunctioning modems, and transmitting diagnostic signals from intelligent modems to the central site. This type of monitoring may be done via a "secondary" communication channel. In this case, statistical information is transmitted from the intelligent network device on a different frequency than the one carrying the actual network traffic.

Logical network parameters include performance measurement systems that keep track of user response times, the volume of traffic on a specific circuit, the destination of data routed across various networks, and any other indicators showing the level of service provided by the network. This type of management software operates passively, collecting the information and reporting it back to the central network operations control center.

Poor network reporting leads to an organization that is overburdened with current problems and lacks time to address future needs. Management requires adequate reports if it is to address future needs. Information for these reports can be gathered

Management Focus: Technical Reports

Technical reports that are helpful to network managers are those that provide summary information, as well as details that enable the mangers to improve the network. Some technical details include:

- Circuit utilization,
- Utilization rate of critical hardware such as host computers, front end processors, and servers,
- File activity rates for database systems,
- Usage by various categories of client computers,
- Response time analysis per circuit or per computer,
- Voice versus data usage per circuit,
- Queue-length descriptions, whether in the host computer, front end processor, or at remote sites,
- Distribution of traffic by time of day, location, and type of application software,
- Failure rates for circuits, hardware, and software,
- Details of any network faults.

from host computers, front end processors, network monitors, the network management group, local area networks, test equipment, and the like.

Failure Control Function

Failure control is handled by the network operations personnel. Basically, it is a *help desk* that is called when anything goes wrong in the network. This group has appropriate customer service representatives to record problems, report them to the testing and problem management group, follow up, and generally ensure that the network is back in operation as soon as possible. This group also might be responsible for change scheduling, coordination, and follow-up on any changes, whether they involve hardware, software, or circuits. In other words, this is the user's interface when there is a problem of any kind.

Failure control requires developing a central control philosophy for problem reporting and other user interfaces. This group should maintain a central telephone number for network users to call when any problem occurs in the network. As a central troubleshooting function, only this group or its designee should have the authority to call hardware or software vendors or common carriers.

Numerous software packages are available for recording the information received from an incoming telephone call. The reports they produce are known as *trouble tickets*.

Management Focus: Management Reports

Management-oriented reports that are helpful to network managers and their supervisors provide summary information for overall evaluation and for network planning and design. Some details include:

- Graphs of daily/weekly/monthly usage, number of errors, or whatever is appropriate to the network.
- Network availability (uptime) for yesterday, the last five days, the last month, or any other specific period.
- Percentage of hours per week the network is unavailable due to network maintenance and repair.
- Fault diagnosis.
- Whether most response times are less than or equal to 3 seconds for online real-time traffic.
- Whether management reports are timely and contain the most up-to-date statistics.
- Peak volume statistics as well as average volume statistics per circuit.
- Comparison of activity between today and a similar previous period.

The software packages assist the help desk personnel so they can type the trouble report immediately into a computerized failure analysis program. It also automatically records and assembles various statistical reports to keep track of how many failures there have been for each piece of hardware, circuit, or software package.

Trouble tickets must be kept if a manager wants to do any type of problem tracking. Automated trouble tickets are better than paper because they allow management to gather problem and vendor statistics. There are four main reasons for trouble tickets: problem tracking, problem statistics, problem-solving methodology, and management reports.

Problem tracking allows the network manager to determine who is responsible for correcting any outstanding problems. This is important because some problems often are forgotten in the rush of a very hectic day. In addition, anyone might request the status of a problem. The network manager can determine whether the problem-solving mechanism is meeting predetermined schedules. Finally, the manager can be assured that all problems are being addressed. Problem tracking also can assist in problem resolution. Are problems being resolved in a timely manner? Are overdue problems being flagged? Are all resources and information available for problem solving?

Problem statistics are important because they are a control device for the network operators as well as for vendors. With this information, a manager can see how well the network is meeting the needs of end users. The manager can determine whether problem solving by the network operators is excessive. These statistics also can be used

---

Technical Focus: Elements of a Trouble Report

When a problem is reported, the trouble log staff should record the following:

- Time and date of the report.
- Name and telephone number of the person who reported the problem.
- The time and date of the problem (not the time of the call) as precisely as possible.
- Location of the problem.
- The nature of the problem.
- When the problem was identified.
- Why and how the problem happened (probably unable to identify this in most cases).

---

to determine whether vendors are meeting their contractual maintenance commitments. Finally, they help to determine whether problem-solving objectives are being met.

Problem-solving methodology helps determine whether the problem priority system is working. You would not want a network operator to work on a terminal problem if an entire multipoint line consisting of dozens of terminals were waiting for help. Moreover, a manager must know whether problem resolution objectives are being met. For example, how long is it taking to resolve problems?

Management reports are required to determine network availability, product and vendor reliability, and vendor responsiveness. Without them, a manager has nothing more than a "best guess" estimate for the effectiveness of either the network's technicians or the vendor's technicians. Regardless of whether this information is typed immediately into an automated trouble ticket package or recorded manually in a bound notebook-style trouble log, the objectives are the same. If the organization does not have a computerized package, then the notebook format is appropriate. The bound notebook, with two carbon copies for each original trouble report, should have prenumbered pages to ensure that no report is lost. One page always should be kept at the "trouble log" desk. One carbon copy is given to a vendor who is called in to correct the problem and one copy to the internal testing/problem management personnel.

The purpose of the trouble log is to record problems that must be corrected and to keep track of statistics associated with these problems. For example, the log might reveal that there were 37 calls for software problems (3 for one package, 4 for another package, and 30 for a third software package), 26 calls for modems evenly distributed among two vendors, 49 calls for terminals, and 85 calls to the common carrier that provides the network circuits. These data are valuable when the design and analysis group begins redesigning the network to meet future requirements.

Testing and Problem Management

The purpose of *testing and problem management* is to establish test and validity criteria and coordinate the various tests. These test personnel maintain the complex equipment needed to diagnose problems quickly, and most of the time, they fix the problem in-house. Their mission is *troubleshooting*, working with the failure control group that first discovered the problem. The testing and problem management group should report back to the failure control group as soon as they have diagnosed the problem so the time required to diagnose the problem can be recorded. The *mean time to diagnose* (MTTD), which is an indicator of the efficiency of testing and problem management personnel, is the first of three different *times* that should be kept for future record.

For example, assume a vendor or internal support group is contacted for correction of a problem. Either testing or failure control personnel should keep track of the time it takes to respond. In other words, the *mean time to respond* (MTTR) is identified. This is a valuable statistic because it indicates how quickly vendors and internal groups respond to emergencies. Compilation of these figures over time can lead to a change of vendors or internal management policies, or, at the minimum, can exert severe pressure on vendors who do not respond to problems promptly.

Finally, after the vendor or internal support group arrives on the premises, the last statistic to record is the *mean time to fix* (MTTF). This figure tells how quickly the staff is able to correct the problem. A very long time to fix in comparison with the time of other vendors may indicate faulty equipment design, inadequately trained customer service technicians, or even the fact that inexperienced personnel are repeatedly sent to fix problems. So, the total time to correct a failure is:

$$MTTRepair = MTTDiagnose + MTTRespond + MTTFix$$

One other statistic should be examined. Called *mean time between failures* (MTBF), it usually is developed by the equipment vendor to indicate product reliability. When you ask for the mean time between failures, always find out whether it is a practical figure or a calculated figure. You want a calculated figure because it is far more accurate and realistic.

Another important time factor is *network availability*, which is the percentage of time the network is available to users. It is calculated as the number of hours per month the network is available divided by the total number of hours per month (i.e., 24 hours per day x 30 days/month = 720 hours). The *downtime* includes times when the network is unavailable due to faults and to routine maintenance and network upgrades. Most networks strive for 99 to 99.5 percent availability, with downtime scheduled after normal working hours.

Remember that the MTBF (failure) can be influenced by the original selection of vendor-supplied equipment. The MTTD (diagnose) relates directly to the ability of in-house personnel to isolate and diagnose failure of hardware, software, or circuits. This means that test personnel need adequate training. The MTTR (respond) can be influenced by showing vendors or internal groups how good or bad their response times have been in the past. The MTTF (fix) can be affected by the use of redundant

Technical Focus: The Mystery of the Ghost in the Machine

Solving problems is not always easy. During an upgrade of Massachusetts General Hospital's Novell Netware 3.1 network from a 100-user license to a 250-user license, the LAN manager experienced some difficulties.

The upgrade required three simple steps which were tested on an almost identical test server. Everything worked correctly on the test server, but the production server was unable to start the secondary drive, displaying an error message about a SCSI drive ID conflict.

After trying the process several more times, the LAN manager opened the server doors and noticed that the SCSI IDs on both drives were set to zero, which caused the error message (each must have different IDs). The second drive was set to 1 and the doors closed, but the error appeared again.

The manager repeated this process several times, and each time the second disk reset its ID. Examining the door, the manager found a screw that was positioned so that each time the door was closed, it pressed the second drive's ID selector button. To get around this, the manager set the SCSI ID to 2 so that upon shutting the door, the screw touching the selector would change the setting to 1. Success.

After solving the mystery, the LAN coordinator contacted the server's manufacturer about the problem and was told the doors were now being made with pins instead of screws. A quick solution to the problem was to remove the screw.

Source: LAN Times, March 13, 1995.

---

interface equipment, alternate circuit paths, adequate recovery or fallback procedures to earlier versions of software, and the technical expertise of internal or vendor staff. Because these mean times affect network availability, their collection is vital if network performance is to be improved.

Another set of statistics that should be gathered are those collected daily by the network operations group who employ automated network management software (network monitors and analyzers). These statistics record the normal operation of the network, such as the number of errors (retransmissions) per communication circuit, per terminal, or whatever is appropriate. Statistics also should be collected on the daily volume of transmissions (characters per hour) for each communication link or circuit, each terminal, or whatever is appropriate for the network. These data can identify terminal stations/nodes or communication circuits that have higher-than-average error rates, and may be used for predicting future growth patterns and failures.

Such predictions can be accomplished by establishing simple *quality control charts* similar to those used in manufacturing. Programs use an upper control limit and a lower control limit with regard to the number of blocks in error per day or per week. Notice how Figure 12-1 identifies when the common carrier moved a circuit from one microwave channel to another (circuit B), how a deteriorating circuit can be located

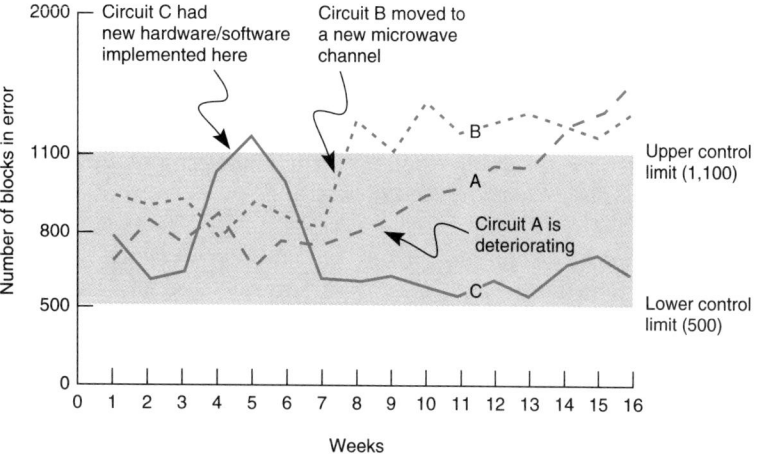

Figure 12-1 Quality control chart for circuits.

and fixed before it goes through the upper control limit (circuit A) and causes problems for the users, or how a temporary high rate of errors (circuit C) can be encountered when installing new hardware and software.

END USER SUPPORT

Providing end user support means solving whatever problems users encounter while using the network. There are three main functions within end user support: resolving network faults, resolving software problems, and training. We have already discussed how to resolve network faults, and now we focus on resolving software problems, and end user training.

Resolving Software Problems

Software problems stem from two major sources. The first is a lack of user knowledge. These problems can usually be solved by discussing the situation with the user and taking that person through the process step by step. This is the easiest type of problem to solve and can often be done by e-mail or over the telephone.

The second type of problem is a fundamental one with the software or an incompatibility between the software and network software and hardware. In this case, there may be a bug in the software or the software may not function properly on a certain combination of hardware and software. Solving these problems may be difficult, requiring expertise and software upgrades from the vendor.

Imagine a network management system so smart that it not only alerts you when something goes wrong, but also fixes the problem. Intelligent agents are relatively simple software programs that perform management functions without human involvement. They use a knowledge base and/or learn from experience to make simple decisions.

The three most common agent functions in network management are retrieving data from network devices, assisting in software updates, and handling network alerts. The first two are fairly straightforward. Agents periodically request remotely monitored devices to transmit their data to a central server (usually when network traffic is light). Without the intelligent agent, the data would have to be requested by the network manager. Likewise, the distribution of updated versions of network or applications software can be a time consuming job. The agent can handle the entire process by itself.

However, the major benefit of agents lies in their ability to monitor alerts and take corrective action on less critical ones. For example, an agent can monitor the space on network drives and offload seldomly used files to tape when the available disk space becomes low, or it can shut down a circuit if security is violated. It can even automatically restart a server when it crashes.

In other cases where action by the network manager is required, the agent may filter the number of alert messages. For example, in the case of a major network failure, the failed devices may issue alerts, and all the devices to which they are connected may also issue alerts. Locating the failure point from dozens of alert messages can be simplified if the agent indicates which take precedence or eliminates messages from devices operating correctly.

Source: LAN Times, March 27, 1995.

Resolving either type of software problem begins with a request for assistance from the help desk. Requests for assistance are usually handled in the same manner as network faults. A trouble log (or request log) is maintained to document all incoming requests and the manner in which they are resolved. The staff member receiving the request attempts to resolve the problem in the best manner possible. Staff members should be provided with the set of standard procedures or scripts for soliciting information from the user about problems. In large organizations, this process may be supported by a special software tool.

There are often several *levels* to the problem resolution process. The first level is the most basic. All staff members working at the help desk should be able to resolve most of these. Most organizations strive to resolve between 75 and 85 percent of these requests in less than an hour. If the request cannot be resolved, it is *escalated* to the second level of problem resolution. Staff members who handle second level support have specialized skills in certain problem areas or with certain types of software and hardware. In most cases, problems are resolved at this level. Some large organizations also have a third level of resolution in which specialists spend many hours developing and testing various solutions to the problem, often in conjunction with staff from vendors of network software and hardware.

Providing End User Training

End user training is an on-going responsibility of the network manager. Training is a key part in the implementation of new networks or network components. It is also important to have an on-going training program because employees may change job functions and new employees require training to use the organization's networks.

Training usually is conducted through in-class or one-on-one instruction and through the documentation and training manuals provided. In-class training should focus on the 20 percent of the network functions that the user will use 80 percent of the time instead of attempting to cover all network functions. By providing in-depth instruction of the fundamentals, users become confident about what they need to do. The training should also explain how to locate additional information from training manuals, documentation, or the help desk.

COST MANAGEMENT

As the demand for network services grows, so does their costs. While managing data communications is important, the need for effective management of voice communications is even more critical. Typically, voice communications can require eight to ten times the budget needed for data communications. For example, an organization with a $1 million annual budget in data communication costs might spend $8 to $10 million per year in voice communication equipment and transmission.

Network management is the most expensive part of most data communication networks. Several surveys by Forrester Research have found that network management costs average between $1200 and $3900 *per year* for *each* computer connected to a network. The network management group for a 100-user network would therefore have an annual budget of about $150,000 to $350,000. The most expensive item is personnel (network managers and technicians), which typically accounts for 50 to 70 percent of total costs. The second most expensive item is leasing WAN circuits.

Figure 12-2 shows the average breakdown of personnel costs by function. The largest time cost (where staff spend most of their time) is systems management, which includes configuration, fault, and performance management tasks that focus on the network as a whole. The second largest item is end user support.

Network managers often find it difficult to manage their budgets because networks grow so rapidly. They often find themselves having to defend ever-increasing requests for more equipment and staff. To counter these escalating costs, many large organi-

Management Focus: State's Network Installed—Now for the Hard Part

North Carolina business leaders have realized that their future lies in implementing a business and government collaboration to shift to North Carolina's economic base away from the tobacco industry. In 1994, North Carolina built the first statewide asynchronous transfer mode (ATM) network in the United States. The North Carolina Information Highway (NCIH) is unique in its seamless interface between multiple carriers and public and private users. Because there are no finished standards for multivendor interoperability, uniformity was achieved by standardizing on Fujitsu's ATM devices. Interoperability snags are thus avoided.

With its NCIH up and running, North Carolina has found that solving technical challenges is only part of the battle in rolling out a leading-edge communications infrastructure. The network is built on such a scale, spanning public and private interests across a whole state, that socioeconomic policy issues now consume most of its network managers' time. Among them are issues of divvying up network capacity between state and commercial users, and wrangling to prove the economic payback from initiatives such as distance learning.

Alan Blatecky, who served as the NCIH's conceptual architect, says, "We can't afford a completely nonblocking ATM network. So we start getting into issues of who gets what priorities. With doctors relying on the network for telemedicine, the state police running a crucial ID check out on the road, and business users trying to run their crucial applications, issues of fairness come into play."

Source: Network World, February 2, 1995.

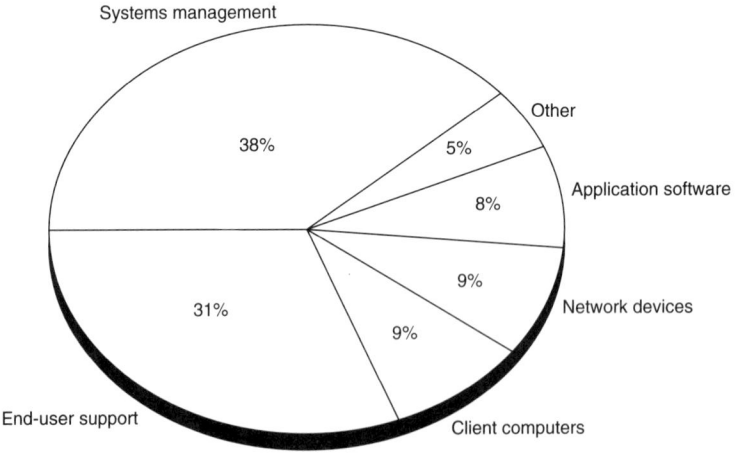

Figure 12-2 Network management personnel costs.

Management Focus: Time to Hand Off Your LANs?

Aspen Medial Group provides health care services to 10 medical centers in the Minneapolis–St. Paul area. Runaway growth of Aspen's LAN and backbone networks had outstripped its network staff's ability to manage them. The IT director was hesitant to invest a lot of time and money in hiring and training an expert network manager, who might then move to a competitor.

The solution was to hand over the management of Aspen's networks to Memorex-Telex Corp., Aspen's major networking equipment vendor. Memorex is one of a growing number of firms that provide complete network management services. Most of these firms are vendors of networking equipment such as Memorex, or vendors of network services who have long experience managing their own networks, such as AT&T and RBOCs.

The management services offered by different companies depend upon their expertise, but many offer remote traffic monitoring and fault management, configuration management of network devices, applications software support, and network design and implementation. Some will even provide a help desk for end user support.

The push to outsource network management to specialized firms is growing. International Data Corp. estimates that by 1998, organizations will spend $8.8 billion on network management services.

Source: Network World, March 20, 1995.

zations have adopted *charge-back policies* for users of WANs and mainframe-based networks. (A charge-back policy attempts to allocate the costs associated with the network to specific users.) These users must "pay" for their network usage by transferring part of their budget allocations to the network group. Such policies are seldom used in LANs, making one more potential cultural difference between network management styles.

The best way to control rapidly increasing network costs is to automate as many routine functions as possible. As network management software improves, some management costs may decrease.

NETWORK MANAGEMENT TOOLS

Network managers need a set of tools to help them perform their various functions. Most tools can be classified as being primarily hardware or software, although in practice any software tool needs to be supported by hardware.

Management Focus: Always Check the Math

Phone bills potentially carry mistakes. Fraud is not the issue—complexity is the villain here. The more complex the deal is, the greater the chance that parts of it will not get written up correctly and passed on to the right people at the carrier's office. If it is not handled correctly, you are not going to get the discount.

A case in point is the wording of AT&T Contract Tariff Number 1834: "The average annual duration of each AT&T Megacom service call must be at least 30 seconds but no more than two minutes. If the average call duration is less than 30 seconds, the customer is billed a shortfall charge of $0.00015 for every second that the average call duration falls short of 30 seconds. If the average call duration is more than two minutes, the customer will be billed a shortfall charge of $0.0003 for each second that the average call duration exceeds two minutes."

What AT&T really wanted to do was bill the customer $0.00015 for every second of shortfall for *every call* under 30 seconds and $0.0003 for every second of *every call* over 2 minutes. Instead, it only gets to charge once for a variance for the average call duration of all calls.

In addition to billing errors on contract provisions, other errors are often due to the failure to stop billing for a leased line that has been removed from service. Errors occur in 85 percent of all the bills examined by Telecom Services, Ltd., a telecommunications auditing firm. In money terms, companies are often overcharged between 5 and 15 percent of their monthly telecommunications bills due to errors.

Source: Datamation, March 15, 1995.

Network Management Software

Network management software is designed to provide automated support for any or all of the network management functions. Most of these software packages support both configuration management, and performance and fault management. Some even have modules to support the help desk.

The first step in using network management software is to define the current network configuration. Fortunately, many network management systems are self-configuring; that is, they will actively search out all the devices and circuits in the network and automatically develop the network map. Most network management software will display configuration information and data from network monitoring in graphs and tables. Figure 12-3 shows some sample displays from a network management package.

Many years ago, before the importance (and cost) of network management was widely recognized, there were few network management software tools. Network devices were "dumb" in that they did only what they were designed to do (e.g., routing packets), and did not provide any management information at all. For example, sup-

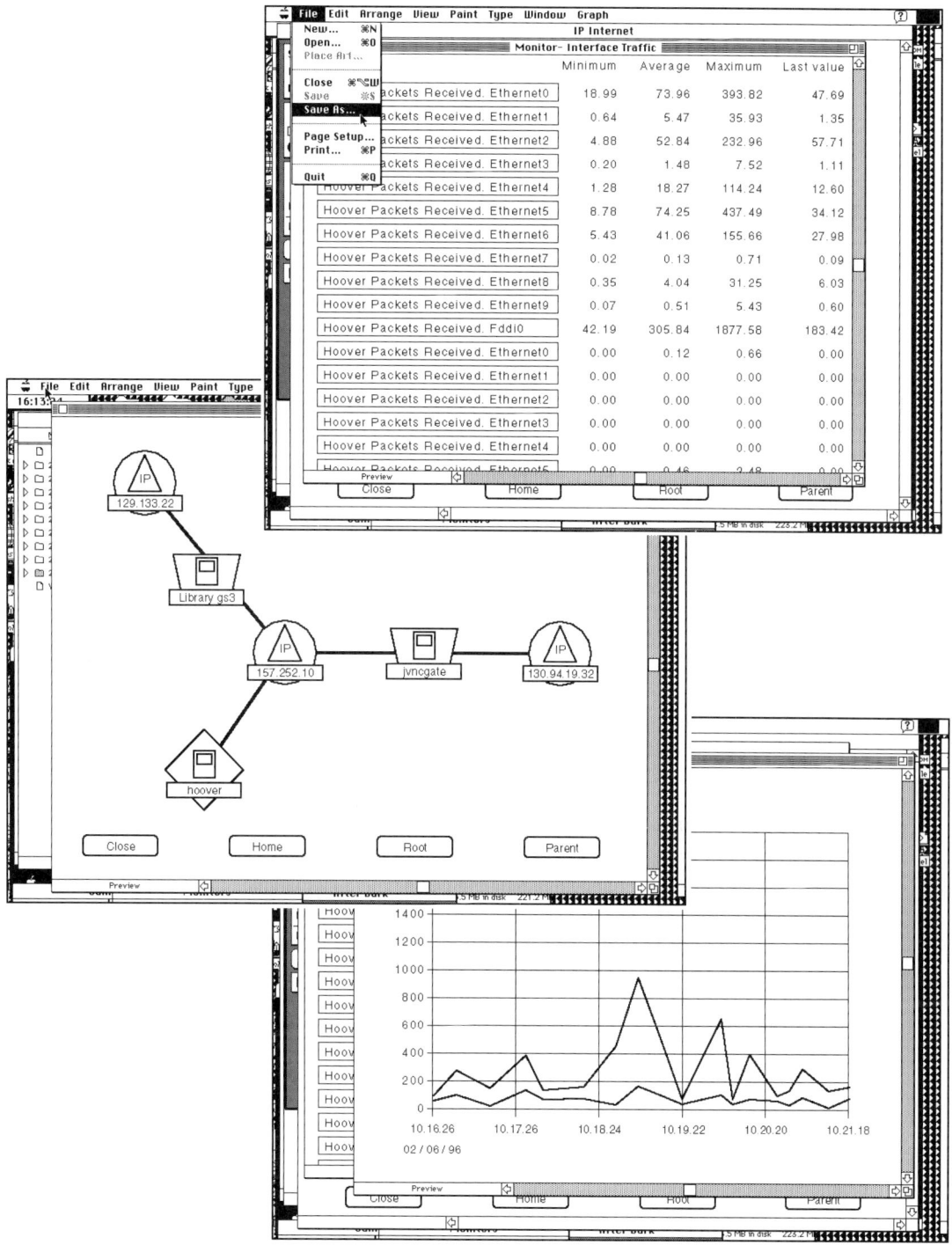

Figure 12-3   Network management software displays.

pose a network interface card fails and begins to randomly transmit garbage messages. Network performance immediately begins to deteriorate because these random messages destroy the messages transmitted by other computers, forcing all the good messages to be retransmitted. Users notice a delay in response time, and complain to the network manager, who begins to search for the cause. Even if the network manager suspects a failing network card (which is unlikely unless such an event has occurred before), locating the faulty card is very difficult and time consuming.

"Smart" network devices perform their functions and record data on the messages they process. These data can be sent to the network manager's computer when the device receives a special control message requesting the data, or it can alert the network manager's computer if the device detects a critical situation. In this way, network faults and performance problems can be detected and reported before they become serious. In the case of the failing network card, the network management software could record the increased number of retransmissions required to successfully transmit messages, and then determine the cause of the delayed response time. A "smart" network hub, controller, or switch might even be able to detect the faulty transmissions from the failing network card, disable the incoming port so that the card could not send any more messages, and issue an alert to the network manager. In either case, finding and fixing the fault is much simpler, requiring minutes not hours.

Many vendors now offer network management systems and "smart" hardware devices that can collect and report information to allow managers to administer the network more easily. The obvious problem is ensuring that hardware devices from different vendors can understand and respond to the messages sent by the network management software of other vendors. By this point in this book, however, the solution should also be obvious: network standards.

A number of formal and de facto standards have been developed for network management. These standards are application layer standards that define the type of information collected by network devices and the format of control messages that the devices understand. The four most commonly used network management standards are SNMP, CMIP, Novell's NMS, and IBM SNA's Netview.

Simple Network Management Protocol (SNMP)   The *simple network management protocol* (SNMP) was derived from an earlier management protocol called *simple gateway monitoring program,* which in turn was derived from another protocol called the *high-level entry management system* (HEMS). The SNMP originally was developed to control and monitor the status of network devices on transmission control protocol/internet protocol (TCP/IP) networks, but now it is available for other network protocols.

Each SNMP device (e.g., router, gateway, server) collects information about itself and the messages it processes, and stores the information in a database called the *management information base* (*MIB*). The network manager's *management station* that runs the network management application software has access to these MIBs. Using this software, the network manager can send control messages to individual devices or groups of devices asking them to report the information stored in their MIB. The control messages can also reset the information in the MIB, or instruct the device to send an alert if certain items in the MIB exceed certain values (e.g., if circuit utilization exceeds 50 percent).

As the name suggests, SNMP is a simple protocol with a limited number of functions. SNMP is expected to be even more powerful in the future as the MIB becomes more broadly defined so that more information can be stored and accessed. One important addition to SNMP is the ability for distributed or *remote monitoring (RMON)*. Many current packages using SNMP store their MIBs on a central server. Each device transmits updates to its MIB to the server every few seconds, hindering throughput and increasing network traffic. Several vendors now offer SNMP collection boxes that can be used to store MIB information closer to the devices that generate the data, or even incorporating processors and storage into the devices themselves so that each can store its own MIB. The data is not transmitted to the central server until the network manager requests the data, thus reducing network traffic.

One problem with SNMP is that many vendors have defined their own extensions to it. So the network devices sold by a vendor may be SNMP compliant, but the MIBs they produce contain additional information that can only be used by network management software produced by the same vendor. Therefore, while SNMP was designed to make it easier to manage devices from different vendors, in practice, this is not always the case.

Common Management Interface Protocol (CMIP)   The *common management interface protocol* (CMIP), which competes with SNMP, is a protocol for seven-layer OSI model networks developed by the International Standards Organization. It is much newer than SNMP and therefore is not widely used. CMIP monitors and tracks network usage and other parameters for user workstations and other nodes in much the same manner as SNMP, except that it is more complete than SNMP, and better in many ways.

The two protocols are incompatible. There are more SNMP devices currently installed and being sold than CMIP, but this could change once more vendors and network managers recognize the need for CMIP's additional capabilities.

NetWare Management System (NMS)   Novell's *NetWare management system* allows local area network managers to manage NetWare LANs and attached devices that are spread throughout an enterprise-wide network. The basic functions of NMS include network fault detection, performance, configuration, security, and accounting management. It has been designed as an open system, so third-party vendors can integrate their software and services into it.

Each server on the network must be equipped with a NetWare management agent (NMA), which is a set of four NetWare loadable modules (NLM) that relay statistics describing hardware, software, and data resources. NLMs are linkable modules written by either Novell or third-party suppliers to offer enhanced NetWare services. When linked, the modules work as though they are part of the NetWare operating system. Using the NLMs, the NetWare management agent collects such statistics from the server as memory usage and available disk space, as well as other data from the attached user or client workstations and hubs. The NMA also alerts the administrator in real time that potential resource allocation problems exist or that a preestablished alarm point—such as a network link overload—has been reached. The NMA is similar to the MIB. Novell also supplies a NetWare loadable module that collects information about SNMP-based devices on a NetWare LAN using the MIB.

Management Focus: Selecting Network Management Software

There are a number of important functions to look for when comparing network management software. These include:

- Support for all popular network operating systems (e.g., Novell, LAN manager, Windows NT),
- Support for SNMP and other protocols such as CMIP and Netview,
- Automatic inventory of network hardware and software,
- Logical and physical network configuration,
- Data import and export in a variety of formats,
- Graphical user interface,
- User-definable alarms,
- Remote workstation monitoring,
- Software license metering (see Chapter 8),
- Virus protection (see Chapter 13).

Source: Insider's Guide to Personal Computing and Networking, Sams Publishing, 1992.

The NetWare services manager polls the NetWare management agents to collect statistics from remote servers and the user workstations attached to each server. The agent also can respond to polls from other network management systems, such as IBM's NetView.

A NetWare management map function automatically identifies NetWare-based servers, cable segments, routers, and client workstations within an enterprise-wide network and draws a graphical representation of the entire network. An optional package allows a LAN manager to map network nodes into local building floor plans.

ManageWise is a software metering tool that monitors use of licensed packages stored on file servers, thus assuring network managers that users do not violate software license agreements by using more copies of a software package than they have purchased.

NetView   IBM's *NetView* network management program, used with multivendor voice and data networks, combines and enhances the functions of five other IBM programs into a single software product that automates many network management tasks. It is designed for managing host network management services for SNA networks. NetView helps to automate:

- The ability of a centrally located person to test and monitor the status of analog communication circuits.
- The ability to view a set of interactive displays and to execute commands against the displayed circuit or hardware in order to change something.

- The ability to monitor and react to physical connectivity problems on multiple token ring networks that are connected to the mainframe.
- The online help facility that provides current dynamic network information status.
- The help desk facility that isolates failed network components, provides suggestions on ways to fix the failure, and records incidents.
- The ability to examine any network log and check the definitions to ensure that parameters are set properly.
- The ability to monitor the network for out-of-service conditions and automatically reactivate all devices downstream from the failed resource.

NetView is being built into a product called *SystemView*, which will integrate most of the diverse management activities and, where possible, automate them. SystemView management will go beyond the technical issues of managing a network and address financial administration, service level tracking, capacity planning, business planning, and management support for heterogeneous local area networks. In addition, SystemView also can be used to manage the central host mainframe computers.

Network Management Hardware Tools

Just a decade ago, many data communication facility managers did not have test equipment. They depended on the telephone company when a circuit failed and on other communication vendors when hardware or software failed. Today, everything is changed because of deregulation. Managers might be using three or four telephone companies, five or six hardware vendors, and two or three software vendors. This means that ownership of the proper test equipment is mandatory. Network management *must* be able to diagnose a problem and determine which telephone company, hardware vendor, or software vendor should be contacted for assistance when the problem cannot be fixed in-house.

Testing is divided into analog testing, digital testing, and protocol testing. *Analog testing* involves troubleshooting on the analog side of the modem. Specifically, it means testing the analog communication circuits supplied by the common carriers. *Digital testing* is aimed primarily at testing digital communication circuits. *Protocol testing* focuses on the various sign-on/sign-off procedures, checking the content of packets or frames, examining message transmission times, and other items related to software protocols. The typical network management tool kit of test equipment can cost from $100,000 to $250,000 for a large network.

Monitors and analyzers generally are test sets that allow the operator to simulate specific message streams to test devices, communication circuits, or other workstations. A monitor resembles a portable microcomputer. Protocol analyzers offer both data and protocol analysis for SNA, X.25, HDLC, T1, DS0, frame relay, and the like. Some of today's line monitors and network analyzers use microprocessor chips to perform sophisticated network tests. In other cases, microcomputers with special software handle the required testing and monitoring.

Analog and digital test sets are found on any network that uses modems in conjunction with telephone company circuits. Most networks require both analog and digital test sets. These devices also resemble portable microcomputers, complete with a video screen and keyboard for data entry.

Patch panels provide electrical connection to all parts of the network. At the minimum, they provide centralized access to each network communication circuit. They are large panels with a number of plugs or connectors that can be cross-connected between different communication circuits. Cross-patching permits the immediate replacement of a failed circuit with a spare.

Data recorders do not always perform tests. They are used to tap into communication circuits and store on disk pertinent activities about various circuits. Basically, they are a monitor for collecting and analyzing data, and printing out reports. They too resemble portable microcomputers.

Handheld test sets are the least expensive and simplest type of network equipment. They can be inserted between two network devices to test voltages or to send and receive various test patterns of bits to isolate errors. They also are used to determine whether there is a problem with the cables.

Breakout Box   The most basic level of data communication monitoring and test equipment is analog test equipment. The *breakout box* is the next level up. It is a handheld device that can be plugged into a modem's digital side to determine the voltage values for the circuit.

Bit-Error Rate Tester (BERT)   The *bit-error rate tester* (BERT) is somewhat more sophisticated than a breakout box because it sends a known pseudo-random pattern over the communication circuit. When this pattern is reflected back, the BERT compares it to the transmitted pattern and calculates the number of bit errors that occurred on the communication circuit. Various test patterns are used, and common pattern lengths are 63, 511, 2047, and 63511 bit patterns. The odd numbers allow simple circuitry in this test equipment.

Bit-error rate (BER) measurements can be made with this type of equipment. A BER is the number of bits received in error divided by the total number of bits received. Service personnel use BER measurements to tune the communication circuit and to make a subjective evaluation as to the quality of a specific circuit or channel. BER cannot be related directly to throughput because error distribution is not taken into account. Assume that 1000 one-bit errors occur during a time interval of 1000 seconds. If the errors are distributed evenly (one per second), the effect on throughput will be disastrous; however, if all the errors occur in a single second, the effect will be minimal.

Block-Error Rate Tester (BKERT)   This tester calculates the *block-error rate* (BKER), which is the number of received blocks that contain at least one bit error divided by the total number of blocks received. A BKER is more closely related to throughput than a BER. Assume a BKER measurement has been made and the BKER value is 10^2 (1/100). This means that out of every 100 blocks received, one contained an error; therefore, you would expect to see one retry for every 100 blocks transmitted (a 1 percent error rate).

Another error rate parameter used only for digital networks is *error free seconds* (EFS). It is similar to BKER except it indicates the probability of success rather than failure, and the block size is the number of bits transmitted in a one-second time period. For example, for a 4800 bits per second channel, the one-second block would contain 4800 bits.

Fiber Identifier   The *fiber identifier* is to locate a particular nonworking fiber without interrupting service on a fiber optic network. (Remember that a fiber cable may contain a bundle of 72 or 144 glass or plastic fibers.) The fiber identifier consists of a transmitter that injects a light signal, a detector that induces a low stress on the fibers allowing them to be searched without damage, and a receiver that emits an audible and visual signal when the fiber in question has been identified. The detector is a wandlike device that detects the signal at splice locations as it is passed near the splice. Because splices leak light, these are the points at which illegal taps would be inserted.

Cable Analyzer   The *cable analyzer* checks LAN cabling for signal continuity, pulse distortion, parity, conductivity, connectivity, polarity reversals, and excessive noise in the data stream. It also can test to ensure that the cable meets the standards for that type of cable.

Self-Testing Modems   *Self-testing modems* generate a test pattern that is as close as possible to the normal digital input (which is disconnected). The test pattern travels through the modem's circuitry, passes through an artificial telephone circuit, and is returned to its point of origin. The artificial telephone circuit acts as a local analog loop. The returning pattern is compared with the transmitted pattern, and an indicator lamp advises the operator of discrepancies.

Some modems also have digital or analog remote *loopback testing* in which the signal actually is sent over the communication circuit and is looped back to the originating modem by the remote modem. The signal is compared, and the operator is advised of any discrepancies. Other modems have internal circuit diagnostic checks to diagnose their own failures in case of circuit or chip failure. Self-diagnostics are made possible by the use of firmware and microprocessor chips. Newer modems contain some of the features of network analyzers. They actually keep track of poll times and other types of network analysis information.

Protocol Analyzer/Data Line Monitor   Today, protocol analyzers and data line monitors all tend to do the same things. Recognizing this overlap, however, we can distinguish between them by their original purpose. A *data line monitor* traces network activity and response time analysis on a specific circuit. It also checks the actual data. *Protocol analyzers* decode messages on the circuit to allow you to see the content (bits) of a frame or packet during its transmission. Users can capture data in an external tape storage or internal memory, print it, or freeze the most current data on the video screen. A protocol analyzer shows when a carriage return or a line feed occurs, as well as when a communication control code is transmitted. The technician can count the bits within a packet or frame and identify each field and its contents.

Protocol analyzers also measure the responses of all hardware in the network and determine whether the network equipment is meeting specifications. In addition, they can print the captured information or trap information when certain character sequences appear on the send or receive communication circuits. Some analyzers offer performance monitoring operations to help evaluate specific areas of network performance such as response time and circuit utilization.

These devices may be active or passive. *Active analyzers/monitors* can generate data, are interactive on the circuit, and can emulate various terminals because they are programmable. *Passive analyzers/monitors* merely monitor and collect data to be examined later. It should be noted that this test equipment, especially active analyzers, can be a security risk because of its ability to generate data, interactively place it on a communication circuit, and do this while emulating another terminal.

A typical analyzer can monitor data, trap and count data for gathering communication circuit statistics, offer a video screen and printer, poll various stations, offer BERT capabilities, work with both asynchronous and synchronous systems, analyze various protocols, and possess breakout box capabilities. Several vendors sell the hardware and software needed to turn a microcomputer into a limited version of a protocol analyzer, data line monitor, and BERT tester.

Automated Test Equipment   *Automated test equipment* consists of hardware and specialized software packages. All have built-in microprocessor chips and programmable testing features. You should note that the programs able to do this testing also can be housed within the host mainframe computer or a remote computer somewhere out in the network. Furthermore, the telephone companies offer centralized automated testing equipment for monitoring your network.

Automated testing equipment performs diagnostic testing, polling, statistics gathering, protocol emulation, measurement of bandwidth efficiency, self-diagnosis of its own circuits, analog and digital circuit testing, testing of centralized and remote switches, and automatic restart and recovery in case of disaster.

Summary

Organizing the Network Management Function   Communication and networking functions present special organizational problems because they are both centralized and decentralized. Users of networks are decentralized, and management of voice communications and data communications on large host mainframes has been highly centralized. Since the explosion in the use of microcomputer based networks, however, more than 60 percent of most organizations' total computer processing power now resides on microcomputer-based LANs.

Integrating LANs and WANs   Today, the critical issue is the integration of all organizational networks, which presents two problems. The first problem is technical; since each LAN was developed separately, not all LANs use the same type of technology. The second problem is cultural. WAN managers and managers of mainframe-based host computer networks are typically more comfortable in highly structured and slow to change network environments. In contrast, LAN managers tend to be less interested in standards and more interested in getting the job done. The key to integrating LANs and WANs into one overall organization network is for LAN and WAN managers to recognize that they no longer have the power they once had. WAN managers must recognize that LAN managers can make more decisions, and LAN managers must realize that they need to work within organizational standards.

Integrating Voice and Data Communications   Another major challenge is combining voice communications with data and image communications. This separation of voice and data worked well over the years, but changing communication technologies are generating enormous pressures to combine them. A key factor in voice/data integration might turn out to be the elimination of one key management position and the merging of two staffs into one.

Configuration Management   Configuration management means managing the network's hardware and software configuration and documenting it (and ensuring the documentation is updated as the configuration changes). The most common configuration management activity is adding and deleting user accounts. The most basic documentation about network hardware is a set of network configuration maps, supplemented by documentation on each individual network component. A similar approach can be used for network software. User and application profiles should be automatically provided by the network operating system or an additional vendor or third-party software module. There are variety of other documentation that must be routinely developed and updated, including user manuals and organizational policies.

Performance and Fault Management   Performance management means ensuring the network is operating as efficiently as possible. Fault management means preventing, detecting, and correcting any faults in the network circuits, hardware, and software. The two are closely related because any faults in the network reduce performance, and because both require network monitoring.

Failure Control Function   Failure control is a help desk that is contacted when anything goes wrong in the network. Problem tracking allows the network manager to determine problem ownership or who is responsible for correcting any outstanding problems. Problem statistics are important because they are a control device for the network operators as well as for vendors. Problem-solving methodology helps determine whether the problem priority system is working. Management reports are required to determine network availability, product and vendor reliability, and vendor responsiveness.

Providing End User Support   Providing end user support means solving whatever network problems users encounter. Support consists of resolving network faults, resolving software problems, and training. Software problems often stem from lack of user knowledge and fundamental problems with the software or an incompatibility between the software and network's software and hardware. There are often several levels to problem resolution. End user training is an on-going responsibility of the network manager. Training usually has two parts: in-class instruction, and the documentation and training manuals that the user keeps for reference.

Cost Management   As the demand for network services grows, so does its cost. While managing data communications is important, the need for effective management of voice communications is even more critical. Network management is the most expensive part of most data communication networks. The largest cost is systems management, followed by end user support. The best way to control rapidly increasing network costs is automate as many routine functions as possible.

Network Management Software   Network management software is designed to provide automated support for any or all of the network management functions Many years ago, network devices did not routinely record the information needed for performance and fault management, which made it difficult to identify causes of problems. More recent ''smart'' network devices perform their functions and record data on the messages they process. These data can be sent to the network manager's computer when the device receives a special control message. If the device detects a critical situation it can send a special control message (called an alert) to the network manager's computer. The four most commonly used network management protocol standards are SNMP, CMIP, Novell's NMS, and IBM SNA's NetView.

Network Management Hardware Tools   There five basic categories of test equipment. Monitors and analyzers allow the operator to simulate specific message streams to test devices, communication circuits, or other workstations. Analog and digital test sets are found on any network that uses modems in conjunction with telephone company circuits. Patch panels provide electrical connection to all parts of the network. Data recorders tap into communication circuits and store on disk pertinent activities about various circuits. Handheld test sets can be inserted between two network devices to test voltages or to send and receive various test patterns of bits to isolate errors.

Key Terms

Active analyzer/monitor	CATER	Handheld test set
Agent	Charge-back policy	Logical network
Analog testing	Common management	parameters
Analyzer	interface protocol	Management information
Automated test equipment	(CMIP)	base (MIB)
Bit-error rate (BER)	Data line monitor	Management reports
Bit-error rate tester	Data recorders	Mean time between
(BERT)	Digital testing	failures (MTBF)
Block-error rate (BKER)	Downtime	Mean time to diagnose
Block-error rate tester	Error-free seconds (EFS)	(MTTD)
(BKERT)	Failure control	Mean time to fix (MTTF)
Breakout box	Fiber identifier	Mean time to repair
Cable analyzer	Firefighting	(MTTR)

Mean time to respond (MTTR)
NetView
NetWare management system (NMS)
Network availability
Network documentation
Network management
Network management system

Passive analyzer/monitor
Physical network parameters
Problem-solving methodology
Problem statistics
Problem tracking
Protocol analyzer
Protocol testing
Quality control chart

RMON MIB
Simple network management protocol (SNMP)
Staffing
Testing and problem management
Trouble ticket
Uptime
User group

Selected References

1. *Auerbach Data Communications Management.* Published bimonthly by Auerbach Publishers, 210 South Street, Boston, MA 02111-9990.
2. Chappel, Laura. *NetWare LAN Analysis,* San Jose, CA: Novell Press, 1993.
3. Guruge, Anura. "IBM's System View: Adding Function to Form," *Data Communications,* vol. 20, no. 15, November 1991, 99–100, 102, 104, 108, 110.
4. Henderson, Tom. "The Four, No Seven, Rules of Network Management," *LAN Times,* vol. 9, no. 8, May 11, 1992, 29.
5. Jander, Mary. "MIB Tools: Coping With the Not-So-Simple Side of SNMP," *Data Communications,* vol. 21, no. 3, February 1992, 79–82.
6. Jander, Mary. "WAN Protocol Analyzers: Opening a Window on Fast Packet Services," *Data Communications,* vol. 21, no. 6, April 1992, 69–70, 72–78, 80, 82.
7. *Journal of Network Management.* Published quarterly by Frost & Sullivan, Inc., 106 Fulton St., New York, NY 10273-0028.
8. Lowe, Doug, *Networking for Dummies.* Indianapolis: IDG Books, 1994.
9. *Network Management Systems & Strategies.* Published biweekly by DataTrends Publications, Inc., P.O. Box 657, Merrifield, VA 22116-9822.

Questions/Problems

1. What is the primary responsibility of the data communication function in an organization?
2. In the context of information CATERing to its users, for which of these concepts is network manager responsible?
3. Name the five key management tasks the network manager must perform.
4. What are five major network management functions performed by network managers?
5. What are some of the factors that prevent the network function from meeting its objectives?
6. Too many managers spend too much time on _____ and not enough time on _____ and _____ .
7. What are some cultural differences between LAN and WAN managers?
8. Why is combining voice and data a major organizational challenge?

9. Which usually costs more, a voice telephone system or a data communication system?
10. Name three benefits of combining the voice and data functions.
11. Briefly describe network status and how it is used.
12. People tend to think of software when documentation is mentioned. What is documentation in a network situation?
13. Today's network managers face a number of demanding problems. Name three.
14. Network monitoring falls into two distinct categories. What are they and who does the appropriate monitoring?
15. What do trouble tickets report?
16. Several important statistics related to network uptime and downtime are discussed in this chapter. What are they and why are they important?
17. How is network availability calculated?
18. What is problem escalation?
19. What does a help desk do?
20. What are the primary functions of end user support?
21. Describe the three types of network testing.
22. Would you characterize the cost of a set of network management test equipment for a large network as being inexpensive, moderate, or expensive?
23. What are the five categories of network test equipment?
24. What do network management software systems do and why are they important?
25. If the annual budget for voice telephones at the local university is $500,000, what is a good estimate of their data communication costs?
26. Are LANs or WANs growing faster?
27. If you were going to establish a data communication network control department, what would be some of the major job tasks and what organizations would be included in this department?
28. If you were using a bit-error rate tester, would you use a BKER test for asynchronous transmission?
29. What is the simple network management protocol?
30. How does SNMP differ from NetView?
31. What is the name of SNMP's OSI competitor and how are they distinguished from one another?
32. What is the purpose of a fiber identifier?
33. How is a cable analyzer used?
34. What is a protocol analyzer?
35. What is NMS?
36. What is firefighting?

NEXT DAY AIR SERVICE CUMULATIVE CASE STUDY

See appendix at end of book

CHAPTER THIRTEEN

NETWORK SECURITY

This chapter describes why networks need security, and how to provide it. It covers security in networks, the principles of a secure network, and risk assessment. It describes a series of controls to prevent, detect, and correct disruptions, destruction, disaster, and unauthorized access.

Objectives

- Understand the importance of network security,
- Become familiar with the major threats to network security,
- Become familiar with how to conduct a risk assessment,
- Understand how to prevent, detect, and correct disruptions, destruction, and disaster,
- Understand how to prevent, detect, and correct unauthorized access.

Chapter Outline

INTRODUCTION

Both business and government were concerned with security long before the need for computer-related security was recognized. They always have been interested in the physical protection of assets through means such as locks, barriers, and guards. The introduction of computer processing, centralized database storage techniques, and communication networks has increased the need for security. Our concerns about security now are focused directly on the computer-related areas of business.

For many people, security means preventing unauthorized access, such as preventing a hacker from breaking into your computer. Security is more than that, however. It also includes being able to recover from temporary service problems (e.g., a circuit breaks) or from natural disasters (e.g., fire, earthquake). Figure 13-1 shows some threats to a computer center, the data communications circuits, and the attached computers.

Why Networks Need Security

In recent years, organizations have become increasingly dependent on data communication networks for their daily business communications, database information retrieval, distributed data processing, and the internetworking of LANs. This commitment has changed the potential *vulnerability* of the organization's assets. This change has occurred because the traditional security, control, and audit mechanisms assume a new and different form in data communication-based systems. Increased reliance on data communications, consolidation of many previously manual operations into computerized systems, use of database management systems, and the fact that online real-time systems cut across many lines of responsibility have increased management concern about the adequacy of current control and security mechanisms used in a data communication environment.

Emphasis on network security also has increased as officers and directors of orga-

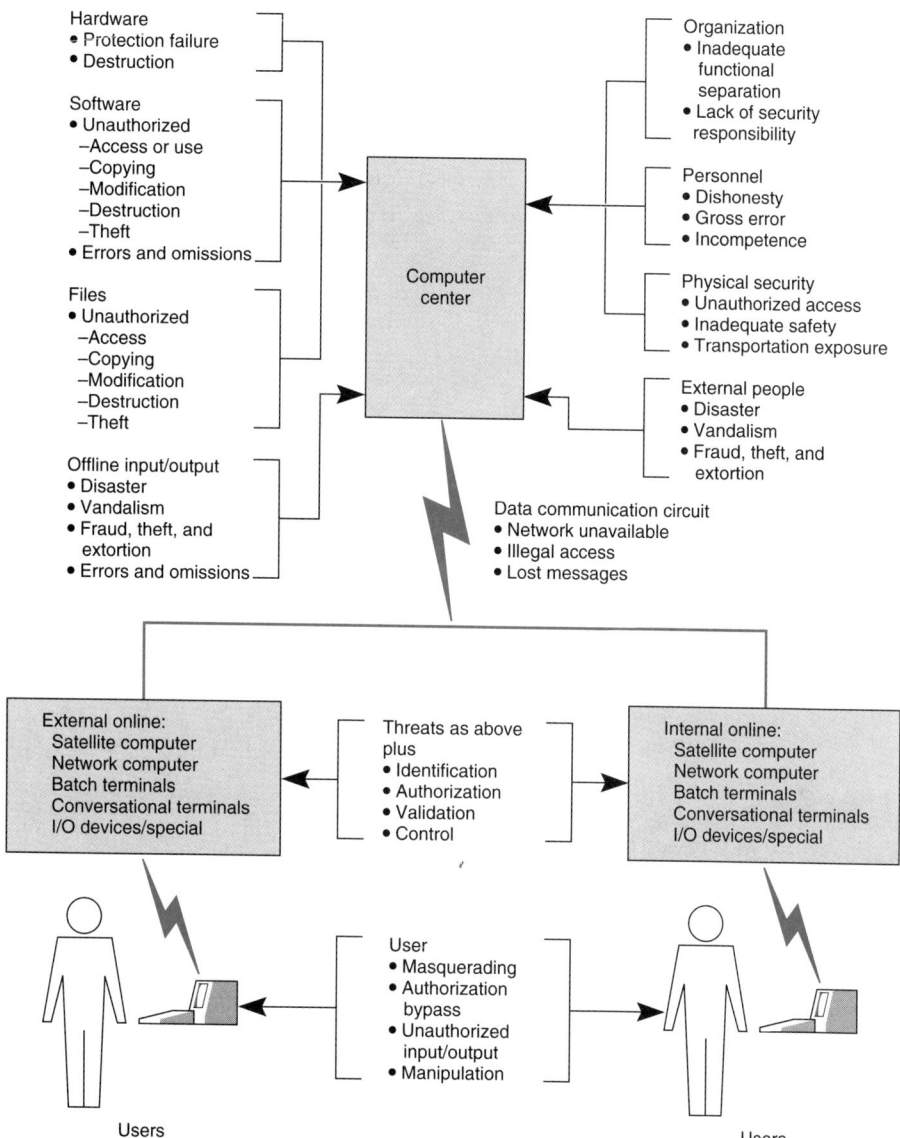

Figure 13-1   Some threats to a computer center, the data communication circuits, and the client computers.

nizations have been sued and as government regulatory agencies have issued security-related pronouncements. Moreover, we have learned that losses associated with computerized frauds and thefts are many times larger per incident than those from noncomputerized frauds and thefts. For example, FBI data shows that over the past five years, the average loss in a bank robbery was about $3000. In contrast, the average loss in a case of computer fraud was $300,000. These factors have led to increased vigilance in protecting the organization's information assets from potential hazards.

To protect its data communication networks, the organization must be able to implement adequate control and security mechanisms within its facilities, including buildings, terminals, local area networks, local loops, interexchange circuits, switching centers, gateways, packet networks, hardware (modems, multiplexers, encryption devices, and the like), network software, test equipment, and network management software.

Types of Security Threats

In general, network security threats can be classified into one of two categories: disruption, destruction, and disaster; and unauthorized access.

Disruptions are the loss of or reduction in network service. Disruptions may be minor and temporary. For example, a network switch might fail or a circuit may be cut causing part of the network to cease functioning until the failed component can be replaced. Some users may be affected, but others can continue. Some disruptions may also be caused by or result in the *destruction* of data. For example a virus may destroy needed files, or the crash of a hard disk may cause files to be destroyed. Other disruptions may be catastrophic. Natural (or man-made) *disasters* may occur that destroy host computers or large sections of the network. For example, fires, floods, earthquakes, mudslides, tornadoes, or terrorist attacks can destroy large parts of the buildings and networks in their path.

Unauthorized access is often viewed as hackers gaining access to organizational data files and resources. However, less than 25 percent of all unauthorized access incidents involve outsiders; 75 percent involve employees. Unauthorized access may have only minor effects. A curious intruder may simply explore the system; gaining knowledge that has little value. A more serious intruder may be a competitor bent on industrial espionage who could attempt to gain access to information on products under development, or the details and price of a bid on a large contract. Worse still, the intruder could change files to commit fraud or theft, or destroy information to injure the organization.

Before discussing network security, we will summarize past computer security problems involving some aspect of communications to give you some idea of the types of security problems that have been encountered. As you read them, try to identify some security controls that would have prevented, detected, or corrected the computer crime if they had been in force at the time the problem occured.

Disruption, Destruction, and Disaster   The massive fire that destroyed the central office switch of an Illinois Bell Telephone Company demonstrates the need for security and backup. The fire cut voice and data communications to thousands of businesses in the western Chicago area. Many businesses, such as branch banks, cannot continue to operate as viable businesses if their voice and data communications are cut off for even a few days, much less two weeks. The Walgreen Drugstore chain in Illinois reported that in the aftermath of the fire, 180 of its 255 drugstores lost access to their central communication network.

In another case, a gunman armed with a shotgun and a pistol entered a telephone company central office and took several hostages. He than blasted away at the central office switch with the shotgun, causing an estimated $10 million in damages. Approximately 15,000 customers lost their telephone service but, to the credit of the telephone company, all service was restored within 22 hours.

A massive virus infection of the Internet started one evening in 1988. Among the first targets were two science and research centers at Berkeley, California, and Cambridge, Massachusetts. The virus then targeted NASA's Ames Research Center in California, the University of Pittsburgh in Pennsylvania, and Los Alamos National Laboratory in New Mexico. By the next morning it also had penetrated computers at Johns Hopkins University (Baltimore) and the University of Michigan (Ann Arbor). This invading virus replicated itself so many times and so often that it overloaded the network, forcing the network operators to shut down for lack of computer cycles. It then moved on to Bellcore in Livingston, New Jersey, SRI International in Menlo Park, California, and New York University. It is noteworthy that the computers of AT&T's Bell Laboratories in New Jersey, of the University of Maryland, and of Chicago's Argonne National Laboratory were able to repel the virus. The point of this is to demonstrate how quickly a computer virus can infect a nationwide network. In this example, it took less than one day.

Unauthorized Access   One example of the need for network security is the case of a wholesale grocery firm in Los Angeles that fell victim to a band of hackers, who commandeered the firm's PBX messaging system and used it to run prostitution rings and pass drug information. The problem was identified when users complained about being unable to access their voice mailboxes because their passwords had been invalidated. Upon investigation, it was discovered that hackers had breached the security features of the PBX and reprogrammed the 200 voice mailboxes for their own use. The hackers accessed the PBX by using a toll-free 800 number maintained for the purpose of letting traveling employees call in for their messages. Once inside the system, the intruders used help programs to learn how to change security codes, thus denying access to authorized users. Among other things, the hackers sold stolen MasterCard, Visa, and American Express numbers via the voice messaging system. The system also was modified to provide information on the price of a kilogram of cocaine in New York.

An illegal bookie in Australia tapped into the communication circuits of the legal bookmaking operations by using his telephone. The purpose was to know race results immediately, enabling him to pay off winners as fast as the legal betting establishments that are licensed by the government.

At the time of the Persian Gulf War, Dutch hackers are reported to have ransacked U.S. Department of Defense computers at 34 sites, in some cases modifying or copying information linked to military operations in the Persian Gulf. Israeli officials said that an 18-year-old hacker had penetrated Pentagon computers and retrieved classified information related to the Patriot missile and other military secrets. The teenaged hacker first placed a call to a Philadelphia gateway node of a PDN. Once that circuit was established, he placed a second call to a US Sprint gateway node in Chicago and used a second stolen access code to enter it. Then he used the Sprint linkage from Chicago to establish a third circuit with a Telenet gateway node in San Francisco, for which he used still another stolen access code. He next used one of the unprotected host computers maintained by Telenet as a switch before establishing a host-to-host circuit via Tymnet. This hacker than jumped through several other host computers, entered DATAPAC (a Canadian public packet switching network), and again used several host computers before reentering Telenet to break into the target computer. With such a complex communication environment, the chance is remote that intermediate host computers would ever discover they were being used by a perpetrator. In fact, the host computer probably paid unknowingly for this perpetrator's communication charges. The people who are most likely to discover such a computer crime are the individual subscribers, for they are the ones who receive the dial-up telephone bills from the various network vendors.

Network Controls

Developing a secure network means developing *controls*. Controls are mechanisms that reduce or eliminate the threats to network security. There are three types of controls that *prevent*, *detect*, and *correct* whatever might happen to the organization through the threats faced by its computer-based systems.

Preventive Controls   Preventive controls mitigate or stop a person from acting or an event from occurring. For example, a password can prevent illegal entry into the system, or backup circuits can prevent network downtime. Preventive controls also act as a deterrent by discouraging or restraining someone from acting or proceeding because of fear or doubt. They also restrain or hinder an event. For example, a guard or a security lock on a door may deter an attempt to gain illegal entry.

Detective Controls   Detective controls reveal or discover unwanted events. For example, software that looks for illegal network entry or a virus can detect these problems. They also document an event, a situation, or a trespass, providing evidence for subsequent action against the individuals or organizations involved or to enable corrective action to be taken. For example, the same software that detects the problem must report it immediately so that someone or some automated process can take remedial action.

Corrective Controls   Corrective controls rectify an unwanted event or a trespass. Either computer programs or humans verify and check data to correct errors or fix a security breach so it will not recur in the future. They also can recover from network errors or disasters. For example, software can recover and restart the communication circuits automatically when there is a data communication failure.

Establishing and Managing Controls   The remainder of this chapter will discuss the various controls that might be used to prevent, detect, and correct threats. We also present a control spreadsheet and risk analysis methodology for identifying the threats and their associated controls. The control spreadsheet provides a data communication network manager with a good view of the current threats and any controls that are in place to mitigate the occurrence of threats.

Nonetheless, it is important to remember that it is not enough to just establish a series of controls; someone or some department must be accountable for the control and security of the network. This includes being responsible for the developing controls, ensuring they are operating effectively, and determining when they need to be updated or replaced.

Controls must reviewed periodically to be sure that they are still useful. They also should be verified and tested. *Verifying* ensures that the control is present, and *testing* determines whether the control is working as originally specified.

It is also important to recognize that there may be occasions in which a person must override a control. This may be a situation in which the network or one of its software or hardware subsystems is not operating properly and controls must be suspended temporarily. Such overrides should be tightly controlled, and there should be a formal procedure to document this occurrence should it happen.

RISK ASSESSMENT

One key step in developing a secure network is to conduct a *risk assessment*. This assigns levels of risk to various threats to the network security by comparing the nature of the threats to the controls designed to reduce them. It is done by developing a control spreadsheet and then rating the importance of each risk. This section provides a brief summary of this process. A much more detailed step-by-step description is presented in FitzGerald and FitzGerald, *Designing Controls into Computerized Systems*, listed at the end of this chapter.

Develop a Control Spreadsheet

To be sure that the data communication network and microcomputer workstations have the necessary controls and that these controls offer adequate protection, it is best to build a *control spreadsheet* (see Figure 13-2). Threats to the network are listed across the top and the network components down the side. The center of the spreadsheet incorporates all the controls that *currently* are in the network. This will become the benchmark on which to base future security reviews.

A *threat* to the data communication network is any potential adverse occurrence that can do harm, interrupt the systems using the network, or cause a monetary loss to the organization. While threats may be listed in generic terms, it is better to be specific and use actual data from the organization being assessed.

Once the threats are identified, the second step is to identify the network compo-

Threats / Components	Disruption, Destruction, Disaster					Unauthorized Access		
	Fire	Flood	Power Loss	Circuit Failure	Virus	External Intruder	Internal Intruder	Eavesdrop
Host Computers								
Client Computers								
Communication Circuits								
Network Devices								
Network Software								
People								

Figure 13-2   Example control spreadsheet with some threats and components.

nents. A network *component* is one of the individual pieces that compose the data communication network.

- Host computers, such as mainframes and LAN servers.
- Client computers, such as microcomputers and terminals.
- Communication circuits, such as circuits provided by common carriers and those installed and owned by the organization.
- Network devices, such as modems, multiplexers, hubs, bridge switches, routers, gateways, and front end processors.
- Network software, such as client and host operating systems, network operating systems, communications processing systems, and applications software on the network.
- Individuals responsible for entering data, accessing data, operating the computers, maintaining the network, managing the network, and writing applications software.

Identify and Document the Controls

Once the specific network threats and components have been identified, you can begin working on the network *controls*. During this step, you identify the current in-place controls and put them into each cell for each threat and component.

Begin by considering the network component and the specific threat, and then describe each control that prevents, detects, or corrects that threat. The description of the control (and its role) is placed in a numerical list, and the control's number is placed in the cell. For example, assume 24 controls have been identified as being in use. Each one is described, named, and numbered consecutively. The numbered list of controls has no ranking attached to it: the first control is number 1 just because it is the first control identified. Figure 13-3 shows a partially completed control spreadsheet with a list of in-place controls.

Threats Components	Disruption, Destruction, Disaster					Unauthorized Access		
	Fire	Flood	Power Loss	Circuit Failure	Virus	External Intruder	Internal Intruder	Eavesdrop
Host Computers	1, 2	1, 3	4	1, 5, 6	7, 8	9, 10, 11 12	9, 10	
Client Computers								
Communication Circuits								
Network Devices								
Network Software								
People								

Controls
1. Disaster Recovery Plan
2. Halon fire system in host computer room. Sprinklers in rest of building.
3. Host computer room on the 5th floor
4. Uninterruptable Power Supply (UPS) on all major network servers
5. Contract guarantees from interexchange carriers
6. Extra backbone fiber cable laid in different conduits between major servers
7. Virus checking software present on the network
8. Extensive user training on viruses and reminders in monthly newsletter
9. Strong password software
10. Extensive user training on password security and reminders in monthly newsletter
11. Call-back modem system
12. Application Layer firewall

Figure 13-3   Example control spreadsheet with some threats, components, and controls.

Evaluate the Network's Security

The last step in designing a control spreadsheet is to evaluate the adequacy of the existing controls, and the resulting degree of risk associated with each threat. Based on this assessment, priorities can be established to determine which threats must be addressed immediately. Assessment is done by reviewing each set of controls as it relates to each threat and network component. The objective of this step is to answer the specific question, ''Are the controls adequate to effectively prevent, detect, and correct this specific threat?''

The assessment can be done by the network manager, but it is better done by a team of experts chosen for their in-depth knowledge about the network and environment being reviewed. This team, known as the *Delphi team*, is composed of three to nine key people. Key managers should be team members because they deal with both the long-term and day-to-day operational aspects of the network. More importantly, their participation means the final results can be implemented quickly, without further justification, because they make the final decisions affecting the network.

The assessments and priorities range from the most critical to the least critical threat. Many *judgment criteria* can be used to determine the most critical, such as threats that are the most damaging, the most sensitive, cause the greatest delay, create the highest dollar loss, or are the most costly and time consuming from which to recover.

CONTROLLING DISRUPTION, DESTRUCTION, AND DISASTER

Disruption, destruction, and disaster are interruptions in network service or loss of data due to network failure. In this section, we discuss controls that attempt to prevent, detect, and correct for these threats.

Preventing Disruption, Destruction, and Disaster

The key principle in preventing these threats—or at least reducing their impact—is *redundancy*. Redundant hardware that automatically recognizes failure and intervenes to replace the failed component can mask a failure that would otherwise result in a service disruption. Redundancy can be built into any network component. The most common example is an *uninterruptible power supply* (UPS). A UPS is installed on the network host so that in the event of a power failure, the host continues to operate for several hours.

You can also buy a special purpose *fault tolerant server* that contains many redundant components to prevent failure. One common strategy, *disk mirroring*, utilizes a second redundant disk for every disk on the host computer or server. Every data item written to the primary disk is automatically duplicated on the mirrored disk. If the primary disk fails, the mirrored disk automatically takes over, with no observable effects on any network applications. This concept can be extended to include disk controllers (called *disk duplexing*), so that even if the disk controller fails, the server continues to operate.

Redundancy can be applied to other network components as well. For example, additional client computers, circuits, or devices (e.g., bridges, multiplexers) can be installed to ensure that the network remains operational should any of these components fail. The last control point is the network personnel and equipment in the network control center, which oversees network management and operation, the test equipment, reports, documentation, and the like.

Although your organization has considerable control over the network components it installs, it has far less control over the level of redundancy in the circuits and services it leases from common carriers. Any service contract for WAN or MAN services should clearly state the carrier's responsibilities in the event of a network component failure. In cases where your organization is very dependent on such services, the physical security and backup of the common carrier facilities should be evaluated. If these

Management Focus: Another Lesson from the School of Hard Knocks

The American Bible Society had just finished upgrading their LAN infrastructure, including the replacement of four 386-based file servers by two fault tolerant servers. One of the goals was to eliminate downtime with the super redundancy they built into the system—triple-redundant power supplies, mirrored hard drives with a hot spare, a duplexed fiber NIC, and a four-hour standby battery system.

If computer parts were going to fail, they usually do so within the first 30 days of installation—and fail they did. Fortunately, the component that failed was one of the mirrored disk drives. Because the drive was mirrored, no data were lost. One of the vendor's best technicians already was scheduled to be in the office the next morning. He was the ideal person to replace the disk drive.

Early the following morning, they backed up the server, shut it down, removed the defective drive, and installed the new drive. While running the software to configure the newly installed drive, technician softly said, "oops." Not only was the fix deleted, the technician trashed the original drive that they were mirroring. This meant the system volume containing all the network operating system files was destroyed.

It was 8:30 A.M., and users were about to start work, so they scrambled to begin the new installation. Soon, the CEO visited them saying, "With all the money we spent on the infrastructure upgrades, I thought you said this wasn't supposed to happen."

This advice from this experience. Never perform a hardware upgrade or repair before business hours. Always place network operating system files and drivers on the C:\ partition and back them up so you don't have to scramble for disks when you do need an emergency restore. And don't trust the smart guys when it comes to your hardware.

Source: LAN Times, February 13, 1995.

---

facilities are destroyed, all the circuits will be lost. Little can be done except to visit the common carrier facilities to gain some idea about the physical security, fire protection, and disaster prevention controls it implements. If these controls are inadequate, about the only thing you can do is split your circuits among two or three different carriers' facilities.

Special attention must be paid to preventing computer *viruses*, which are executable programs that copy themselves onto other computers. Most viruses attach themselves to other programs or to special parts on disks. As those files execute or are accessed, the virus spreads. Viruses cause unwanted events—some are harmless (such as nuisance messages), other are serious (such as the destruction of data). Some viruses change their appearances as they spread, making detection more difficult.

The best way to prevent the spread of viruses is to not copy files or disks of unknown origin. Downloading files from unregulated bulletin boards is a classic way to get a virus. In general, most developers of commercial software ensure that their products

Management Focus: Fire Causes Widespread Phone Outage in California

A fire in a Pacific Bell telephone switching center disrupted telephone service to hundreds of thousands of people across Southern California for about 12 hours in March 1994. The fire was apparently caused by an electrical malfunction in a battery storage room.

Local phone service was disrupted in only a few areas, but many customers had trouble placing calls between different area codes in the Los Angeles area. Incoming and outgoing long-distance calls were widely affected. Troubles were reported as far away as San Diego to the south and Ventura County to the west. Bank ATMs, which rely on telephone lines to complete transactions, were also blacked out.

Emergency 911 communications were disabled for about nine hours. The disruption of emergency service forced the fire department to send helicopters into the air to spot trouble.

Source: Reuters Business Report. March 15, 1994.

are virus free, although there have been some cases of commercial software spreading viruses. Several virus detection programs are available to check disks to ensure that they are clean.

In most cases, disruptions or the destruction of data are local, and affect only a small number of components (although the failure of one WAN or BN circuit may affect many computers). Such disruptions are usually fairly easy to deal with; the failed computer is replaced or the virus is removed and the network continues to operate.

Disasters are different. In this case, an entire site can be destroyed. Even if redundant components are present, often the scope of the loss is such that returning the network to operation is extremely difficult. The best solution is to have a completely redundant network that duplicates every network component, but is in a separate location.

Generally speaking, preventing disasters is difficult. How do you prevent an earthquake? There are, however, some practical common sense steps that can be taken to prevent the full impact of disasters. These steps depend upon the type of disaster, of course. For example, to reduce the risks due to flood, key network components should not be located near rivers or oceans, or in the basement or ground floor of buildings. To reduce the risks from fire, halon fire suppression systems should be installed in rooms containing important network equipment. To reduce the risks from terrorist attacks, the location of key network components should be kept secret and protected by security guards.

One often overlooked security risk is theft. Computers and network devices are commonplace items that are relatively expensive. There is a good second-hand market for such equipment, making them valuable to steal. Several industry sources estimate that about $1 billion is lost each year to theft of computers and related equipment.

Management Focus: Elements of a Disaster Recovery Plan

A good data communication network disaster plan should include the following:

- The name of the decision-making manager who is in charge of the disaster recovery operation. A second manager should be indicated in case the first manager is unavailable.
- Staff assignments and responsibilities during the disaster.
- Availability and training of backup personnel with sufficient knowledge and experience in data communications.
- A pre-established list of priorities that states what is to be fixed first.
- Recovery procedures for the data communication facilities (WAN, MAN, BN, and LAN). This includes information on the location of circuits, and whom to contact for backup data circuits and documentation.
- How to replace damaged data communication hardware and software that are supplied by vendors, including the support that can be expected from vendors, along with the name and telephone number of the person to contact.
- Location of alternative data communication facilities and equipment such as connector cables, local loops, IXCs, common carrier switching facilities, satellite, and public data networks (PDNs).
- Action to be taken in case of partial damage, threats such as a bomb threat, fire, water or electrical damage, sabotage, civil disorders, or vendor failures.
- Procedure for imposing extraordinary controls over the network until the system returns to normal.
- Manual processes to be used until the network is functional.
- Procedure for acquiring data entry support for entering destroyed data and the information processed manually into the network applications once the networks are operational.
- Adequate updating, maintenance, and testing of the disaster plan
- Storage of the disaster recovery procedures in a safe area where they cannot be destroyed by catastrophe. This area must be accessible, however, to those who need to use the plan.

Any security plan should include an evaluation of ways to prevent someone from stealing equipment.

Detecting Disruption, Destruction, and Disaster

Major problems need to be quickly recognized. As discussed in Chapter 12, one function of network monitoring software is to alert network managers to problems so these

Management Focus: Firm on Alert with Disaster Recovery SWAT Team

Northrop Grumman Corp., an aerospace company, has devised a disaster recovery plan as rigorous as those followed by banking institutions. Daily backup of all mainframe and LAN data is the norm at Northrop, and should computer or network facilities face critical failure, the company's 34-step disaster recovery plan outlines an organized sequence of action. Northrop has compiled an inventory of all its manufacturing and business applications, assigning a priority to each.

Some elements of Northrop's disaster recover checklist include:

- take inventory of all hardware and software, and prioritize applications in terms of how quickly they must be recovered;
- establish company-owned, off-site, data processing, backup site, or establish a contract with disaster recovery service;
- develop network configuration documentation as well as document recovery guidelines and procedures;
- implement a simulation and testing program.

Storage of backup tapes off-site is a daily ritual at Northrop, with the company using several different vendors. If Northrop's data center were disabled, the storage site would be instructed to transfer tapes to the firm's backup provider, SunGard Recovery Services, Inc. Northrop employees can start data processing and transfer data over a T-1 line to any site selected as the company's remote operations center, where employees can continue working.

When problems hit a Northrop facility, the first calls to action go out to the vice president of information systems and the disaster recovery director. Then, team leaders are called upon to tally the damage, providing an assessment checklist that helps the security director decide whether to go off-site or stay on-site for restoration, or some combination.

Source: Network World, December 5, 1994.

can be corrected. Some intelligent network servers even can be programmed to send an alarm to a pager if necessary. The organization's disaster procedures should include notifying the network managers as soon as possible.

Detecting minor disruptions and destruction can be more difficult. A network drive may develop bad spots that remain unnoticed unless the drive is routinely checked. Likewise, a network cable may be partially damaged by hungry squirrels, resulting in intermittent problems. These types of problems require on-going monitoring. The network should routinely log fault information to enable network managers to recognize minor service problems before they become major ones. In addition, there should be a clear procedure by which network users can report problems.

Correcting Disruption, Destruction, and Disaster

A major corrective control is the *disaster recovery plan*, which should address various levels of response to a number of possible disasters and should provide for partial or complete recovery in all network components, as well as the staff, the building and other physical facilities, and the application software. A complete disaster recovery plan covering all these areas is beyond the scope of this text, but we will address some issues.

A data communication network disaster plan should include a separate plan for each of six different areas: the data communication network control center; communication circuits; switches, concentrators, microcomputer workstations, multiplexers, and intelligent terminal controllers; common carrier facilities; electrical power for the data communication facilities, user terminals, and lights; and distributed local area networks.

Recovery controls and *backup controls* within the network encompass many areas. The person who reviews these controls may start at either end of the network, but the object is to check for *recovery procedures* and *backup hardware* throughout. Perhaps the most important question to ask is whether it is cost effective to back up each piece of hardware encountered between a remote terminal site and the central host computer. A related question is: Are there procedures for recovery of data files, network databases, network software, and the like? For example, the network should log all incoming and outgoing messages. There may be two logs: one used for network recovery and one saved for historical purposes. Likewise, database systems should record before-images and after-images to a logging tape in the event of data loss. Use of Figure 13-1 during the review of recovery, backup, and disaster controls helps ensure that all network control points are considered.

An important consideration is backup of the communication circuits. One option is to lease two separate circuits (that have been alternatively routed) to have one for backup. Another option is to utilize dial-up communication circuits as backup to leased circuits. Of course, there is always the option to have manual procedures that can be used if the circuit is down for a very short time. In addition, temporary satellite and cellular transmission are now possible.

CONTROLLING UNAUTHORIZED ACCESS

In this section, we focus on preventing unauthorized access to the organization's computer network; however, financial losses due to computer theft or fraud are minor compared to losses incurred by telephone fraud. According to FBI statistics, telephone fraud cost organizations about $2 billion in 1994, compared to $100 million due to computer fraud. Security problems with telephone, PBX, and cellular phones were discussed in Chapter 3.

There are four types of intruders who attempt to gain unauthorized access to computer networks. The first are casual computer users who have only a limited knowledge of computer security. They simply cruise along the Internet trying to access any computer they come across. Their unsophisticated techniques are the equivalent of trying doorknobs, and only those networks that leave their front doors unlocked are at risk.

The second type of intruders are experts in security, but whose motivation is the thrill of the hunt. They break into computer networks because they enjoy the challenge. Sometimes they also enjoy showing off for friends or embarrassing the networks' owners. Fortunately, they usually cause little damage and make little attempt to profit from their exploits.

The third type of intruder is the most dangerous. They are professional hackers who break into corporate or government computer for specific purposes, such as espionage or fraud. Less than 5 percent of intrusions by these professionals are detected, unless of course, they have been hired to destroy data or disrupt the network.

The fourth type of intruder is also very dangerous. These are organization employees who have legitimate access to the network, but who gain access to information they are not authorized to use. This information could be used for their own personal gain, sold to competitors, or fraudulently changed to give the employee extra income. Three quarters of security break-ins are caused by this type of intruder.

Preventing Unauthorized Access

Many steps can be taken to prevent unauthorized access to organizational data and networks, but no network is completely safe. The best rule for high security is to do what the military does: do not keep extremely sensitive data online. Data that need special security are stored in computers isolated from other networks.

A 1994 survey of network managers by Ernst & Young found that more than 50 percent of the 1271 responding firms had had data losses or interruptions in service due to unauthorized access. Figure 13-4 shows the percentage of firms that used preventive controls.

There are five general approaches to preventing unauthorized access: developing

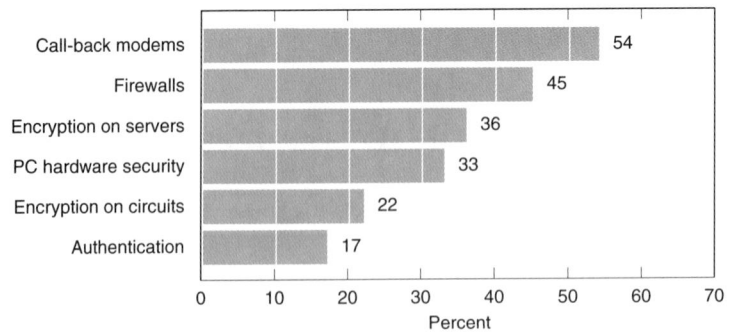

Figure 13-4   Percent of companies using controls to prevent unauthorized access.

Source: Byte, April, 1995

Management Focus: Computer Terrorist Captured

Kevin Mitnick, America's most wanted computer hacker, was captured in February 1995. Mitnick, code named Condor, was apprehended by government officials after they acquired the assistance of an expert from a firm that Mitnick is suspected of penetrating.

Mitnick was arraigned on charges of violating the terms of his probation for a 1988 California computer hacking conviction, as well as new charges of computer fraud originating in North Carolina. He served a year in prison and was placed on probation after a one-time friend turned him in during 1988 saying, "He's an electronic terrorist." He fled in late 1992, after the FBI showed up at the private investigation firm where he worked. The agents were investigating break-ins to Pacific Bell computers.

This was just a portion of his computer escapades which began in high school when he broke into the Los Angeles Unified School District's main computers. Eventually, he was able to access a North American Air Defense Command computer in Colorado Springs. Also, the California Department of Motor Vehicles issued a $1 million warrant for him, accusing him of posing as a law enforcement officer to obtain sensitive DMV information.

Authorities are unable to estimate how much damage he wreaked during his years on the run. The cellular telecommunications industry alleges that Mitnick, who used cellular phones to illegally access computers, cost it $1 million a day.

Mitnick even manipulated the telephone system to pull pranks on friends and enemies, and disconnected service to Hollywood stars and to his probation officer.

Source: The Atlanta Journal-Constitution, February 16, 1995.

---

user profiles, plugging known security holes, securing network access points, preventing eavesdropping, and using encryption. A combination of all techniques is best to ensure strong security.

Developing User Profiles   The basis of network access is the *user profile* for each user's *account* that is assigned by the network manager. Each user's profile specifies what data and network resources he or she can access, and the type of access (read only, write, create, delete, etc.). Most profiles require users to enter a password to gain access to their accounts. Unfortunately, passwords are often poorly chosen, enabling intruders to guess them and gain access. More systems are requiring users to enter both a password and a *token,* which is a physical object that can be read by the network, such as a magnetic security card or a diskette containing a special file. Intruders must have access to both before they can break in.

User profiles can limit the allowable log-in days, time of day, physical locations, and the allowable number of incorrect log-in attempts. Some will also automatically log a user out if that person has not performed any network activity for a certain length of time (e.g., the user has gone to lunch and has forgotten to logoff the network). Regular

Management Focus: Selecting Passwords

The key to users' accounts are passwords; each account has a unique password chosen by the user. The problem is that passwords are often chosen poorly and not changed regularly. Many network managers require users to change passwords periodically (e.g., every 90 days), but this does not ensure that users choose "good" passwords.

A good password is one that the user finds easy to remember, but is difficult for potential intruders to guess. Several studies have found that about two-thirds of passwords fall into one of three categories:

- names of family members or pets;
- important numbers in the user's life (e.g., SSN or birthday); or
- keyboard patterns (e.g., QWERTY, ASDF).

The best advice is to avoid these categories because such passwords can be guessed easily. Better choices are passwords that:

- are meaningful to the user but no one else;
- are made of two or more words that have several letters omitted (e.g., NWYOR (New York), or PPLEPI (apple pie));
- are spelled backwards; and
- include characters such as numbers or punctuation marks.

security checks throughout the day when the user is logged in can determine whether a user is still permitted access to the network. For example, the network manager might have disabled the user's profile while the user is logged in, or the user's account may have run out of funds.

Creating accounts and profiles is simple. When a new staff member joins an organization, that person is assigned a user account and profile. One security problem is the removal of user accounts when someone leaves an organization. Often, network managers are not informed of the departure and accounts remain in the system. For example, a 1995 examination of user accounts at The University of Georgia found 30 percent belonged to staff members no longer employed by the university. If the staff member's departure was not friendly, there is a risk that he or she may attempt to access data and resources and use them for personal gain, or destroy them in retaliation. Many systems permit the network manager to assign expiration dates to user accounts to ensure that unused profiles are automatically deleted or deactivated, but these actions do not replace the need to notify network managers about an employee's departure.

It is important to screen and classify both users and data. Some organizations, especially in government, assign different security clearance levels to users as well as to data, thus permitting users to see only what they "need to know."

The impact of any security software packages that restrict or control access to files, records, or data items should be reviewed. Independent of the data communication software, these packages may offer unique password and identification of each user and allow access only to the specific functions assigned to that user. Some packages also offer additional features, such as file security and layers of passwords to the record or field level, terminal security, transaction security, batch reports on all activity, automatic sign-off of unattended terminals, and immediate online notification of security violations.

Adequate user training on network security should be provided through self-teaching manuals, newsletters, policy statements, and short courses. A well publicized security campaign may deter potential intruders.

Plugging Known Security Holes   Many commonly used operating systems have major security problems (called *security holes*) well known to potential intruders; UNIX systems are among the worst. Many security holes have been documented and "patches" are available from vendors to fix them, but network managers may be unaware of all the holes.

A complete discussion of security holes is beyond the scope of the book. Many security holes are highly technical; for example, sending a message designed to overflow a network buffer, thereby placing a short command into a very specific memory area that unlocks a user profile. Others are rather simple, but not obvious. For example, in some versions of UNIX, a semicolon places the system into command mode, making it process incoming text as commands. In this case, one could attach a semicolon and a UNIX command in response to a request for a file name.

Other security holes are not really holes, but simply policies adopted by computer vendors that open the door for security problems, such as computer systems that come with a variety of pre-installed user accounts. These accounts and their initial passwords are well documented and known to all potential intruders. A 1988 study of UNIX computer sites found that 5 to 10 percent of computers still retained their pre-installed accounts with the initial passwords. Network managers had simply forgotten to delete them.

The American government requires certain levels of security in the operating systems and network operating systems it uses for certain applications. The minimum level of security is C2. Most major mainframe operating systems provide at least C2. Several LAN operating systems (e.g., Novell, Windows NT, and IBM's LAN server) are currently under review for C2 certification. Most widely used NOS are also striving to meet the requirements of much higher security levels such as B2. Very few systems meet the highest levels of security (A1 and A2).

Securing Network Access Points   In general, there are three major ways of gaining access: using a terminal or computer located in the organization's offices, dialing into the network via a modem, or accessing the network from another network to which it is connected (e.g., Internet). We consider each access point in turn.

The physical security of the building or buildings that house any of the hardware, software, or communication circuits must be evaluated. Both local and remote physical

Management Focus: Basic Control Principles of a Secure Network

- The less complex a control, the better.
- A control's cost should be equivalent to the identified risk. It often is not possible to ascertain the expected loss, so this is a subjective judgment in many cases.
- An adequate system of internal controls is one that provides ''just enough'' control to protect the network, taking into account both the risks and costs of the controls.
- Preventing a security incident is always preferable to detecting and correcting it after it occurs.
- Automated controls (computer-driven) always are more reliable than manual controls that depend on human interaction.
- Controls should apply to everyone, not just a few select individuals.
- When a control has an override mechanism, make sure that it is documented and that the override procedure has its own controls to avoid misuse.
- Institute the various security levels in an organization on the basis of ''need to know.'' If you do not need to know, you do not need to access the network.
- The control documentation should be confidential.
- Names, uses, and locations of network components should not be publicly available.
- Controls must be sufficient to ensure that the network can be audited. This means there should be transaction trails and historical records.
- When designing controls, assume that you are operating in a hostile environment.
- Always convey an image of high security by providing education and training.
- Make sure the controls provide the proper separation of duties. This applies especially to those who design and install the controls and those who are responsible for everyday use and monitoring.
- It is desirable to implement entrapment controls in networks to identify hackers who gain illegal access.
- When a control fails, the network should default to a condition in which everyone is denied access. A period of failure is when the network is most vulnerable.
- Controls should still work, even when only one part of a network fails. For example, if a backbone network fails, all local area networks connected to it should still be operational, with their own independent controls providing protection.
- Don't forget the LAN. Security and disaster recovery planning has traditionally focused on host mainframe computers and WANs. However, LANS now play an increasingly important role in most organizations, but are often overlooked by central site network managers.
- Always have insurance as the last resort should all controls fail.
- Always assume your opponent (a hacker) is smarter than you.

facilities should be secured adequately and have the proper controls. Good security requires implementing the proper access controls so that only authorized personnel can enter closed areas where network equipment is located or access the network. Proper security education, background checks, and the implementation of error and fraud controls are important.

Depending upon the level of security needed, access can be restricted by *something you know* (like passwords discussed previously). If more scurity is needed, access may also require *something you have*, such as a key. The key might be one like that used for your home or car, or it can be an electronic key with secret encrypted numbers embedded in it. If extra security is needed, access can be restricted by *something you are*, one or more of your own physical characteristics is used as the unique identifier that permits your entry to the system. This might be a fingerprint, a handprint, an eye retina print, a voice print, or signature verification.

The network components themselves also have a level of physical security. Terminals and computers can have locks on their power switches or locks that disable the screen and keyboard. Network circuits can be locked by having the network manager disable them after hours.

Any organization that permits staff members to access its network via dial-in modems opens itself to a broader range of intruders. Some dial-up modem controls include changing the modem telephone numbers periodically, keeping telephone numbers confidential, and requiring the use of computers that have an electronic identification chip for all dial-up ports.

Another common strategy is to use a *call-back modem*. In this case, the user dials the organization's modem's telephone number, and logs into to his or her account. Once the user enters the correct password, the modem automatically hangs up and dials the user's modem's telephone number. In this way, unauthorized intruders cannot access others' accounts because the host computer or communications server will only permit access via modems calling from prespecified numbers. The drawback to this is that only one remote telephone number can be defined for each account. If users have several locations from which they wish to have access (e.g., the users' home and remote office), call-back modems won't work. In recent years, this technique been extended to use automatic number identification (ANI). The network manager can specify several telephone numbers authorized to access each account. When a user successfully logs onto an account, the source of the incoming phone call is identified using ANI and if it is one of the authorized numbers, the login is accepted; otherwise, the host computer or communications server disconnects the call.

Neither call-back modems nor the use of ANI permits users who frequently travel (e.g., sales representatives) to have secure dial-in access. Such users often call from hotel rooms and have no knowledge of telephone numbers in advance. One solution is to use a pager-based security system. The user dials into the network as usual, and after the user's password is accepted, the system generates a 10-digit random number that is sent to the user's pager. To complete the login process, the user must enter this 10-digit number; otherwise the call is disconnected. To gain access, an intruder must know the user's account name, password, and have access to the user's pager.

With the increasing use of the Internet and information superhighway, it becomes important to prevent unauthorized access to your network from intruders on other networks. The obvious solution is to disconnect any computer or network containing confidential information from the Internet. This is often not a practical solution, however, so a *firewall* may be the answer. A firewall is a router, gateway, or special purpose computer that filters packets flowing into and out of a network. The organization's networks are designed so that a firewall is placed on every network connection between the organization and the Internet. No access is permitted except through the firewall. Two commonly used types of firewalls are packet level and application level.

A *packet level firewall* examines the source and destination address of every network packet that passes through it. It only allows packets into or out of the organization's networks that have acceptable source and destination addresses. In general, the addresses are examined only to the network level, rather than the specific user on the network, so all users with addresses on the same network must have the same authorizations. Some packet level firewalls also examine the type of packet (e.g., file transfer or remote login) and allow or deny certain type of packets to or from certain addresses. Each packet is examined individually, so the firewall has no knowledge of what the user is attempting to do. It simply chooses to permit entry or exit based on the contents of the packet itself. This type of firewall is the simplest and least secure because it does not monitor the contents of the packets or why they are being transmitted, and typically does not log the packets for later analysis.

Many packet level firewalls are vulnerable to *IP spoofing*. The goal of an intruder using IP spoofing is to send packets to a target computer requesting certain privileges be granted to some user (e.g., setting up a new account for the intruder or changing access permission or password for an existing account). Such a messager would not be accepted by the target computer unless it can be fooled into believing that the request is genuine.

Spoofing is done by changing the source address on incoming packets from their real address to an address inside the organization's network. Seeing a valid internal address, the firewall lets the packets through to their destination. The destination computer believes the packets are from a valid internal user and processes them. Typically, IP spoofing is more complex than this, because such changes often require a dialogue between the computers. Since the target computer believes it is talking to an internal computer, it directs its messages to it, not the intruders' computer. Intruders therefore have to guess at the nature and timing of these messages, so that they can generate more spoofed messages that appear to be responses to the target computer's messages. In practice, expert intruders have enough knowledge to have a reasonable chance of getting this right.

Many firewalls have had their security strengthened since the first documented case of IP spoofing occurred in December 1994. However, this still remains a problem, because the majority of security break-ins are done by employees whose computers are inside the firewall.

An *application level firewall* acts as an intermediate host computer or gateway between the Internet and the rest of the organization's networks. These firewalls are generally more complicated to install and manage than packet level ones. Anyone wishing to access the organization's networks from the Internet must login to this firewall, and can only access the information they are authorized for based on the firewall account profile they access. Any access that has not been explicitly authorized is prohibited.

Management Focus: Whiz Kid Taps Secrets on Internet

Using the personal computer at his home in London, a teenager penetrated a sensitive American defense computer network at the height of the United States–North Korea confrontation over nuclear inspections. British officials say the 17-year-old may be prosecuted under Britain's Computer Misuse Act. The hacker triggered alarms on both sides of the Atlantic and beyond as he put information from the defense system into the Internet.

One computer system the youth breached was at Griffiths Air Force Base at Rome, N.Y., which housed the Korea files. After finding the password which allowed him access to the first system, he also entered other defense systems in the same computer network.

The Independent, a daily British newspaper, reported that the teenager read "secret communications between American agents in North Korea" during the dispute over whether North Korea would allow international inspections of its nuclear program. After reading the confidential reports, the newspaper said, he put them on the Internet. A spokesman for the Air Force's Office of Special Investigations denied that the hacker tapped into any secret or classified information.

The illegal access into the defense computer network triggered an investigation by the FBI, the Air Force's Office of Special Investigations, the Secret Service, the Defense Information System, and Scotland Yard.

Source: The Atlanta Journal-Constitution, January 8, 1995.

In contrast, with a packet level firewall, any access that has not been disabled is permitted.

In many cases, special programming code must be written to permit the use of application software unique to the organization (as opposed to commercial off-the-shelf software such as e-mail, which is built into the firewall). Many application level firewalls prohibit external users from uploading executable files. In this way, intruders (or authorized users) cannot modify any software unless they have physical access to the firewall. Some refuse changes to their software unless it is done by the vendor. Others also actively monitor their own software and automatically disable outside connections if they detect any changes.

Several network security companies can provide firewall services for organizations that do not want to set up and monitor their own. These companies install their own application layer firewall, which is directly connected to the security company's monitoring center. When the firewall detects suspicious events, it sends an alarm to the monitoring center, which takes additional action to prevent the intrusion.

Preventing Eavesdropping Another way to gain unauthorized access is to eavesdrop on network traffic. In some ways, this is easier than the previous methods because the intruder only has to insert a listening device or computer into the organization's

Management Focus: A SWAT Team in Cyberspace

The Computer Emergency Response Team center at Carnegie-Mellon University in Pittsburgh is the SWAT team of the electronic frontier. CERT was created by the Defense Department in 1989 after a widespread Internet break-in. They have no legal power to arrest or prosecute; instead, the team of about 156 programmers pokes through violated systems using their only weapons: dozens of computers. Like hackers they track, CERT team members often work around the clock.

Ten years ago, hackers were usually youthful pranksters, mostly interested in demonstrating technical ingenuity. Now there's a growing feeling that more sinister forces may be loose.

A panicky New York computer bulletin board operator called CERT at 3 A.M. one day to report the discovery of an unauthorized program that could surreptitiously record users' secret passwords. This New York bulletin board is hooked up to the Internet, an international web of computers that links 20 million users. If one system is compromised, many more are vulnerable.

As a result of the investigation, the team concluded there was an organized effort to infiltrate the Internet. CERT's detective work has won respect for the team and brought them new attention on the Net. However, finding holes is often easier than fixing them. The reality of this situation is that there will be many more attempted and actual break-ins in the future.

Source: Newsweek, February 21, 1994.

network to record messages. Two areas are vulnerable to this type of unauthorized access: network cabling and network devices.

Network cables are the easiest target for eavesdropping because they often run long distances and usually are not regularly checked for tampering. The cables owned by the organization and installed within its facility are usually the first choice for eavesdropping. It is 100 times easier to tap a local cable than it is to tap an interexchange channel, because it is extremely difficult to identify the specific circuits belonging to any one organization in a highly multiplexed switched interexchange circuit operated by a common carrier. Local cables should be secured behind walls and above ceilings, and telephone equipment and switching rooms (wiring closets) should be locked and their doors equipped with alarms. The primary goal is to control physical access by employees or vendors to the connector cables and modems. This includes restricting their access to the wiring closets in which all the communication wires and cables are connected.

Certain types of cable can impair or increase security by making eavesdropping easier or more difficult. Obviously, any wireless network is at extreme risk for eavesdropping because anyone in the area of the transmission can easily install devices to monitor the radio or infrared signals. Conversely, fiber optic cables are harder to tap, thus increasing security. Some companies offer armored cable that is virtually impossible to cut without special tools. Other cables have built-in alarm systems. The U.S. Air Force, for example, uses pressurized cables that are filled with gas. If the cable is cut, the gas escapes, pressure drops, and an alarm is sounded.

Physical protection of the network's local loop and interexchange telephone circuits is the responsibility of the common carrier. You cannot do much about it, except to audit the telephone company's physical security procedures and possibly encrypt the data before it leaves your building to go out onto the public network. All local loops leaving the building should be physically secured and out of harm's way to prevent physical damage or an easy telephone tap. Formal procedures should exist to help identify breaches of security or illegal entries to the network.

Network devices such as controllers, hubs, and bridges should be secured in a locked wiring closet. As discussed in Chapter 8, all messages within a given local area network are actually received by all computers on the LAN, although they only process those messages addressed to them. It is rather simple to modify a computer or develop a special purpose device to record all messages received for later (unauthorized) analysis. This computer or device could then be plugged into an unattended hub or bridge to eavesdrop on all message traffic.

A *secure hub* is available for ethernet networks that makes this type of eavesdropping more difficult. This hub requires a special authorization code to be entered before new computers can be added, thus making it difficult to add unauthorized devices. More interesting, though, is the way it handles messages. When new devices are added to the hub, their network addresses are defined to the hub so that it knows which device is connected to which port. When the hub receives a message, it checks the address and forwards the message only to the port connected to the device with that address. All other ports receive a message of exactly the same length that contains only a random set of characters.

A review of software controls that can be programmed into remote network devices is also needed. For example, daily downloading of network programs can help ensure that only authorized programs are in these devices. Another control is the periodic counting of bits in the memory space of the remote device. This identifies a program change so that a new one can be downloaded immediately. Each controller should have its unique address on a memory chip (instead of software) to thwart anyone who wants to change controller addresses in order to receive copies of messages.

Encryption   One of the best ways to prevent unauthorized access is *encryption*, which is a means of disguising information by the use of mathematical rules known as *algorithms*. Actually, *cryption* is the more general and proper term. *Encryption* is the process of disguising information, whereas *decryption* is the process of restoring it to readable form. Of course, it makes no sense to have one process without the other. When information is in readable form, it is called *cleartext* or *plaintext*; when in encrypted form, it is called *ciphertext.*

An encryption system has two parts: the algorithm itself, and the *key*, which personalizes the algorithm by making the transformation of data unique. Two pieces of identical information encrypted with the same algorithm but with different keys produce completely different ciphertexts. When using most encryption systems, communicating parties must share this key. If the algorithm is adequate and the key is kept secret, acquisition of the ciphertext by unauthorized personnel is of no consequence to the communicating parties.

Good encryption systems do not depend on keeping the algorithm secret. Only the keys need to be kept secret. The key is a relatively small numeric value (in terms of the number of bits). The larger the key, the more secure the encryption because large "key space" protects the ciphertext against those who try to break it by trying every possible key. There should be a large enough number of possible keys that an exhaustive computer search would take inordinately long or would cost more than the value of the encrypted information.

Encryption algorithms may be implemented in software or hardware. The software has some advantages in protecting stored data files and data in the host computer's memory. However, hardware implementations have the advantages of much greater processing speed, independence from communication protocols, ability to be implemented on dumb devices, and greater protection of the key because it is physically locked in the encryption box. Unauthorized tampering with the box erases the keys.

One commonly used encryption algorithm is the *Data Encryption Standard* (DES), which was developed in the mid-1970s by the American government in conjunction with IBM. DES is maintained by the National Institute of Standards and Technology.

DES is a *symmetric* algorithm, which means that the key used to decrypt a particular bit stream is the *same* as the one used to encrypt it. Using any other key produces cleartext that appears as random as the ciphertext. Symmetric algorithms can cause some problems with *key management*; keys must be dispersed and stored carefully. Because the DES algorithm is known publicly, the disclosure of a *secret key* can mean total compromise of encrypted messages. Therefore, in order for two nodes in a network to establish communication of ciphertext, it is first necessary to generate and communicate a common key over a secure channel or send it by a personal courier.

DES is classified as a *block cipher* because it encrypts data in independent 64-bit blocks under the control of a 64-bit key. A 64-bit key produces about 100 quadrillion possible combinations, which may sound like a lot, but cryptographers who specialize in breaking these block ciphers have to test only half the combinations to obtain a 50/50 probability of arriving at the secret key. This testing is enhanced further by the use of very specialized mathematical algorithms that are designed to quickly invalidate large groups of these combinations. In addition, specially designed computers may be able to test hundreds of thousands of combinations each second. An expert code breaker can decrypt a DES message without the key in one to two weeks. For this reason, a new version of DES that uses a 128-bit key is under development.

A second very popular technique is *public key encryption*, the most popular of which is *RSA*. RSA was invented at MIT in 1977 by Rivest, Shamir, and Adleman. The inventors of the initial algorithm founded RSA Data Security in 1982, and many companies have licensed the RSA technique.

Public key encryption is inherently different from secret key systems like DES because it is asymmetric; there are two keys. One key (called the *public key*) is used to encrypt the message and a second, very different private key is used to decrypt the message. Public key systems are based on one-way functions. Even though you originally know both the contents of your message and the public encryption key, once it is encrypted by the one-way function, the message cannot be decrypted without the private key. One-way functions, which are relatively easy to calculate in one direction, are impossible to "uncalculate" in the reverse direction. Public key encryption is one of the more secure encryption techniques available, excluding special encryption techniques developed by national security agencies.

Public key encryption greatly reduces the key management problem. Each user has its public key that is used to encrypt messages sent to it. These public keys are widely publicized (e.g., listed in a telephone book-style directory)—that's why they're called "public" keys. In addition, each user has a private key that decrypts only the messages that were encrypted by its public key. This private key is kept secret (that's why it's called "private" key). The net result is that if two parties wish to communicate with one another, there is no need to exchange keys beforehand. Each knows the other's public key from the listing in a public directory and can communicate encrypted information immediately. The key management problem is reduced to the on-site protection of the private key.

Public key encryption also permits *authentication* (or *digital signatures*). When one user sends a message to another, it is difficult to legally prove who actually sent the message. Legal proof is important in many communications, such as bank transfers and buy/sell orders in currency and stock trading, which normally require legal signatures. Public key encryption algorithms are *invertable*, meaning that text encrypted with either key can be decrypted by the other. Normally, we encrypt with the public key and decrypt with the private key. However, it is possible to do the inverse: encrypt with the private key and decrypt with the public key. Since the private key is secret, only the real user could use it to encrypt a message. Thus a digital signature or authentication sequence is used as a legal signature on many financial transactions. This signature is usually the name of the signing party plus other *key-contents* such as unique information from the message (e.g., date, time, or dollar amount). This signature and the other key-contents are encrypted by the sender using the private key. The receiver uses the sender's public key to decrypt the signature block and compares the result to the name and other key contents in the rest of the message to ensure a match.

To visualize how a public key algorithm works, look at Figure 13-5. At the top of this figure is a public directory containing all the public keys for each organization that uses public key encryption. Our public directory contains five different banks.

The middle of Figure 13-5 shows a sample encrypted message. When Bank 4 wants to send a message to Bank 1, it encrypts the message with Bank 1's public key, which Bank 4 obtains from the public directory. This represents a straightforward encryption of a message between Bank 4 and Bank 1. Obviously, when the message is received at Bank 1, it decrypts the message using its secret private key.

For more complex encryption, Bank 4 can include its signature as authentication so Bank 1 can verify the signature to be sure that the message originated from Bank 4. To do a signature verification (see the bottom message of Figure 13-5), Bank 4 first encrypts its ID (signature) plus some of the "key-contents" of the message, using the Bank 4 private key. Next, Bank 4 encrypts both the entire message contents and the already encrypted Bank 4 ID using the Bank 1 public key. This means that the Bank 4 ID has been double-encrypted, first using the Bank 4 private key and then a second time using the Bank 1 public key. The message is then transmitted to Bank 1.

Upon receiving the message, Bank 1 uses its private key to decrypt the entire mes-

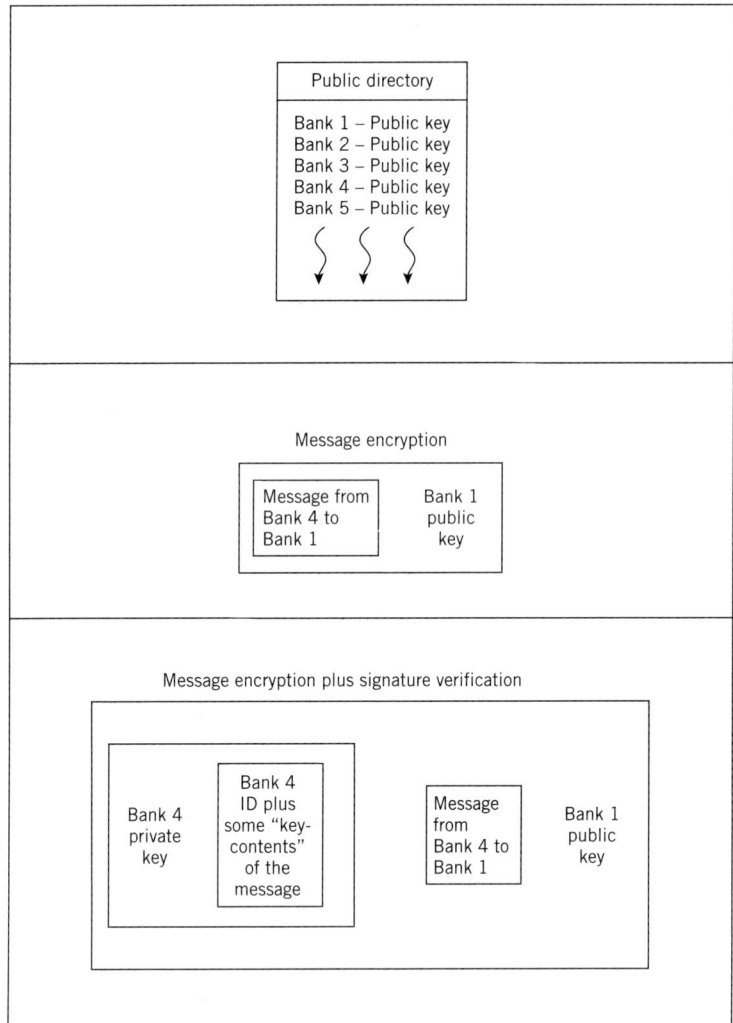

Figure 13-5 Public key encryption. The "key-contents" in this figure refers to unique information from the message, such as date, time, and the dollar amount.

sage. At this point, Bank 1 is able to read the contents of the message, except for a block of data that still is encrypted. Because the message was received from Bank 4, Bank 1 assumes that Bank 4 secretly encrypted its ID plus some key-contents of the message for signature verification purposes by using its private key. At this point, Bank 1 takes the Bank 4 public key and decrypts the trailing block of data that contains the Bank 4 ID plus some key-contents of the message. Once decrypted, Bank 1 knows Bank 4 actually sent the message because the key-contents in this block of data had a date, time, and dollar amount that matched those in the already decrypted message.

Two new encryption proposals developed by the FBI are currently under debate by

Management Focus: RSA Encryption Code Stolen and Published

Someone has anonymously circulated the underlying software formula of one of the most popular coding systems used for protecting information sent over computer networks.

Known as RC4, the formula has become the de facto coding standard for many popular software programs including Microsoft Windows, Apple's Macintosh operating systems, and Lotus Notes. It is also the only software-based formula that the National Security Agency will permit to be easily exported under an agreement the agency reached two years ago with the Software Publishers Association.

The formula, which has been a closely guarded trade secret, belongs to RSA Data Security Inc., a small, privately held software company that sells encryption software to the nation's largest computer and software companies, including Apple Computer, IBM, Lotus Development, Microsoft, and Sun Microsystems. Although disclosure of the formula does not necessarily allow eavesdroppers to intercept and unscramble coded messages sent with the RSA encryption software, widespread dissemination could compromise the long-term effectiveness of the system. Also, the two-year-old agreement in which the government has allowed computer and software companies to export products incorporating the RSA system is brought into question.

Source: The Atlanta Journal-Constitution, February 19, 1995.

Congress and also by a host of industry experts, telecommunications vendors, and civil libertarians. These proposals, called *clipper* and *capstone,* are highly controversial because they require the clipper chip to be used in all telecommunications networks.

The clipper chip, which contains a classified encryption algorithm, can be installed in telephones, fax machines, modems, and network interface cards. Transparent to the user, the chip automatically encrypts all messages sent, and decrypts all messages received. The unique concept behind the clipper chip is that it is a key as well as an encryption algorithm, which makes it extremely hard to break. Cryptographic experts claim that it would take 15 years of round-the-clock analysis to decrypt a clipper chip message without the correct key.

One problem with the clipper chip is that the key is permanently encoded in the chip. There is no way to change the key without buying a new set of chips. Good security policy requires regular changes to encryption keys, for despite the user's best security efforts, it is possible that the key could become known to an intruder.

The most controversial part of the clipper/capstone proposals concerns government access to the key. The FBI fears that encryption techniques help protect criminals from legal eavesdropping. If a criminal organization used these techniques, the FBI would find it very difficult to conduct court-ordered electronic surveillance.

The clipper chip proposal solves this problem by giving the government the keys to every chip manufactured. The key value is divided in two, one half held by the Department of Commerce, and the other half held by the Department of the Treasury.

When a law enforcement agency receives a court order to eavesdrop on a clipper chip data stream, it monitors the encrypted data stream. Each clipper chip transmits a unique identification number as part of the encrypted message. Using this identification number, the law enforcement agency obtains both halves of the key and decrypts messages.

Detecting Unauthorized Access

Detecting unauthorized access means looking for anything out of the ordinary. It means logging all messages sent and received by the network, all software used, and all logins (or attempted logins) to the network. These logs should be monitored both by network security personnel and by software programmed to issue alarms or take action if certain parameters are exceeded or if something unusual occurs. For example, if the number of accesses to a file server or an account suddenly escalates, it may indicate that an intruder has gained access and is doing things that authorized users usually do not do (or it may simply mean a change in user behavior). In any event, the cause of the unusual activity should be identified. This technique identified the unauthorized use of a file server at the University of Florida in 1994. Intruders gained access and posted a series of pirated software programs (including a pre-release version of Windows 95), which were then copied by thousands of users around the world.

Another example is if there are an unusual number of unsuccessful login attempts to a user's account or to several users' accounts. This suggests that an intruder is attempting to gain access. The best solution in this case is to program the network to disconnect after several failed attempts, forcing the potential user (or intruder) to reconnect. After more failed login attempts, the account should be disabled until the network manager has discussed the events with the account owner.

Regular monitoring should also extend to network hardware. All cables and network devices should be regularly inspected for tampering. All service calls by vendor employees should be logged and periodically spot checked with their offices to ensure that they are actually vendor employees on a legitimate call. Otherwise, the installation of eavesdropping devices may go unnoticed.

Correcting Unauthorized Access

Once an unauthorized access has been discovered, the next step is to identify how the security breach occurred and fix it so that it will not reoccur. Then, the intruder is disciplined by civil or criminal action. Law enforcement agencies have traditionally been reluctant to take action, given the difficulty in proving losses in this sort of crime, and the inadequacy of many laws.

Many organizations have taken their own steps to detect intruders by using *entrapment* techniques. The objective is to act as the most likely target of illegal activities by posting highly interesting fake information available only through illegal intrusion to ''bait'' the intruder, and installing sophisticated tracking software to monitor access to this information. The idea is that this information would distract any intruders from accessing real information. The monitoring software allows the organization and law enforcement officials to trace and legally document the intruder's actions. Possession of this information then becomes final legal proof of the intrusion.

In recent years, there has been a stiffening of computer security laws and in the legal interpretations of other laws that pertain to computer networks. As the information superhighway expands, laws and their enforcement should also continue to increase.

....

Summary

Types of Security Threats   In general, network security threats can be classified into one of two categories: disruption, destruction, and disaster; and unauthorized access. Disruptions are usually minor and temporary. Some disruptions may also be caused by or result in the destruction of data. Natural (or man-made) disasters may occur that destroy host computers or large sections of the network. Unauthorized access refers to intruders (external hackers or organizational employees) gaining unauthorized access to files. The intruder may gain knowledge, change files to commit fraud or theft, or destroy information to injure the organization.

Network Controls   Developing a secure network means developing controls that reduce or eliminate threats to the network. Controls prevent, detect, and correct whatever might happen to the organization when its computer-based systems are threatened.

Risk Assessment   The first step in developing a secure network is to conduct a risk assessment. This is done by comparing the nature of the threats to the controls designed to reduce them, thus deriving levels of risk. A control spreadsheet lists the threats, the network components, and the controls, which a network manager uses to assess the level of risk.

Controlling Disruption, Destruction, and Disaster   The key principle in controlling these threats—or at least reducing their impact—is redundancy. Redundant hardware that automatically recognizes failure and intervenes to replace the failed component can mask a failure that would otherwise result in a service disruption. While your organization has considerable control over the network components it installs, it has far less control over the level of redundancy in the circuits and services it leases from common carriers. Any service contract for WAN or MAN services should clearly state the carrier's responsibilities in the event of a network component failure. Special attention needs to be given to preventing computer viruses. Generally speaking, preventing disasters is difficult. The best (or only option) may be a well-designed disaster recovery plan.

Controlling Unauthorized Access   Contrary to popular belief, 75 percent of unauthorized intruders are organization employees, not external hackers. There are five general approaches to preventing unauthorized access: developing user profiles, plug-ging known security holes, securing network access points (e.g., physical security, call-back modems, and firewalls), preventing eavesdropping (by restricting access to network cables and devices), and using encryption. The basic principle in detecting unauthorized access is looking for anything out of the ordinary. This means logging all messages sent and received by the network, all software used, and all logins (or attempted logins) to the network. These logs should be monitored both by network security personnel and by software programmed to issue alarms or take action if certain parameters are exceeded or if there is an abnormal occurrence.

Key Terms

Account
Application level firewall
Asymmetric algorithm
Authentication
Backup controls
Block cipher
Call-back modem
Ciphertext
Clipper chip
Control principles
Control spreadsheet
Controls
Data encryption standard
  (DES)
Decryption
Delphi team

Detective control
Disaster recovery plan
Disk mirroring
Eavesdropping
Encryption
Entrapment
Fault-tolerant server
Firewall
Hacker
IP spoofing
Key
Packet level firewall
Password
Physical security
Plaintext
Preventive control

Private key
Public key
Public key encryption
Recovery controls
Redundancy
Risk assessment
RSA
Secure hub
Security hole
Symmetric algorithm
Uninterruptible power
  supply (UPS)
User profile
Threat
Token
Virus

Selected References

1. Anderson, John C. "I Spy! Observations on Modern-Day Cryptography: A Brief History of Cryptography, With Comments on the State of the Art, and Answers to Users' Questions," *ISPNews*, vol. 3, no. 2, March/April 1992, 1, 24–27.
2. Auerbach Data Security Management, Published bimonthly by Auerbach Publishers (a division of Warren, Gorham & Lamont), 210 South Street, Boston, MA 02111-9990.
3. Bunker, Ted. "Is It 1984?" *LAN Magazine*, August 1994, 40–47.
4. *Byte*, "Barricading the Net," 89–104.
5. Cheswick, William and Steven Bellovin. *Firewalls and Internet Security: Repelling the Wily Hacker.* Reading, MA: Addison-Wesley Publishing, 1994.
6. *Computer Fraud and Security Bulletin.* Published monthly by Elsevier International Bulletins, Mayfield House, 256 Banbury Road, Oxford OX2 7DH, England.
7. *Computer Security Digest.* Published monthly by Computer Protection Systems, Inc., 150 North Main Street, Plymouth, MI 48170.
8. *Control Objectives: Controls in a Computer Environment, Objectives, Guidelines, and Audit Procedures.* Carol Stream, IL: EDP Auditors Foundation, 1990.

9. *Data Processing & Communications Security*. Published quarterly by Assets Protection Publishing, P.O. Box 5323, Madison, WI 53705.

10. Dayanim, Joshua, F. "Disaster Recovery: Options for Public and Private Networks," *Telecommunications*, vol. 25, no. 12, December 1991, 48–51.

11. *Disaster Recovery Journal: The Magazine for Contingency Planning and Security*. Published quarterly by Systems Support, Inc., 2712 Meramar Drive, St. Louis, MO 63129.

12. *EDPACS: The EDP Audit, Control and Security Newsletter*. Published monthly by Auerbach Publishers, One Penn Plaza, New York, NY 10119.

13. FitzGerald, Jerry, and Ardra F. FitzGerald. *Designing Controls into Computerized Systems*, 2nd ed. Redwood City, CA: Jerry FitzGerald & Associates, 1990.

14. *InfoWorld*, "An Ounce of Prevention," February 13, 1995, 84–99.

15. Marcella, Albert J., Jr. *EDI Audit and Control*. Norwood, MA: Artech House, 1992.

16. Markoff, John. "Data Network Is Found Open to New Threat," *New York Times*, January 23, 1995, A1+.

17. *Risk Management Manual*. Published bimonthly by Assets Protection Publishing, P.O. Box 5323, Madison, WI 53705.

18. Stoll, Clifford. *The Cuckoo's Egg: Inside the World of Computer Espionage*. New York: Doubleday, 1989.

Questions/Problems

1. Define computer virus.
2. It is said that the commitment to data communications has changed the vulnerability of the organization's assets. Why is this so?
3. What factors have brought increased emphasis on network security?
4. What is the first thing you must do when conducting a network security review?
5. Define threat.
6. Define component.
7. Briefly outline the steps required to complete a control spreadsheet.
8. Name at least six areas that should have controls in a data communication network.
9. Define encryption and decryption.
10. What must be kept secret in a good encryption system?
11. Is it possible to implement encryption algorithms in both hardware and software, or are they limited to one or the other?
12. What encryption techniques are used for commercial purposes and unclassified military data?
13. Define block cipher.
14. What does it mean when an algorithm is classed as a symmetric algorithm?
15. To what does the term *key management* refer?
16. What are the three alternatives for organizations that want to use encryption?
17. A number of hardware controls are discussed in this chapter. Discuss one of the most important and explain why it is important.
18. Describe the purpose of a call-back modem.
19. What do controls for remote intelligent controllers usually involve?
20. Controls for terminals and microcomputers have two entirely separate aspects. What are they?

21. Describe the three general ways of restricting access to a network.
22. Controlling the security of local loops and interexchange circuits is difficult because they are owned by the common carriers. How can this problem be overcome?
23. Describe the three areas that need to be considered in controlling microcomputers.
24. Why is it necessary to maintain control over databases?
25. What is the purpose of a disaster recovery plan?
26. Why would you want to perform a risk analysis?
27. What is a Delphi team?
28. What are some of the criteria that can be used to rank risk in a data communication network?
29. Briefly outline the steps required to rank risk threats to a network.
30. Break the class into several teams, each of which conducts a small risk assessment of threats to the network at your school or office. Identify four or five threats. Make some assumptions regarding the type of network. Finally, identify the judgment criteria that will be used to rank the various threats, rank the threats, and then identify network-oriented controls that would mitigate or stop each threat.
31. What is a firewall?
32. What are the differences between the different types of firewalls?
33. Is it possible first to encrypt with a public key and then to decrypt with a private (secret) key, as well as first to encrypt with the private key and then to decrypt that message with the public key?
34. What do you think are the three most important security controls that can be placed on a network? Why?
35. As the manager of a major data communication network, how many types of disaster plans might you consider?
36. What is IP spoofing?
37. Develop a control spreadsheet for the following mini-case study.

Multisystem Communication Network The Belmont State Bank uses an online data communication network for several of its business functions. This network is used for online inquiries of the passbook savings system and of the demand deposit (checking accounts) systems.

This is a large bank with hundreds of branches that are connected to a central computer system. Each branch has a variety of terminals and terminal controllers connected to the central system via the public telephone network. Some of these terminals are on dedicated leased lines, and others use the dial-up telephone network.

The security team visited six branch offices to conduct threat scenario sessions with the operations staffs. The sessions provided a good perspective of branch management, operations personnel, security, and prevailing attitudes toward embezzlement and other threats.

The bank's network uses video terminals, teleprinter terminals, transaction terminals, local intelligent controllers, a decentralized database, and a variety of other hardware devices and software programs. When possible, the bank purchases outside packages rather than developing application systems ''from scratch.''

Terminals at all sites and the central headquarters are physically secure. Vendors who perform maintenance are responsible for ensuring that the remote intelligent controllers, modems, and other devices operate effectively. Terminal operators use a four-digit numeric password, and each terminal is transaction-coded to accept only its authorized transactions. The nine largest branches are allowed direct entry of their wire transfer business, which constitutes 92 percent of the wire transfers sent or received by the bank. There are written procedures at the local branches. Employees at several branches have started using their own or locally purchased microcomputers to increase the efficiency and throughput of the system.

Training instructions for operators are provided in an extensive, looseleaf manual that is updated monthly. It is maintained centrally, and the updates are distributed to the various branches.

During transmission, the front end processor performs error detection and correction and orders the retransmission of any erroneous message. One of the system's good features is its message switching with store-and-forward capability. This gives everyone in the bank access to e-mail. Wire transfer messages are switched from this computer to the more secure and separate wire transfer control system computer. When a user calls in, the central system calls that user back in order to control which telephone numbers are connected to its dial-up modems. Encryption currently is under consideration.

The application programs are maintained by local bank employees, although a few of the packages still use some outside consultants for maintenance. An effective program change control procedure is operational.

The communication network control group has line monitors and other devices that are required to maintain an effective uptime ratio for this network. The network has been operating at 98.95 percent uptime. Some of the terminal operators, however, have begun to complain about slow response time, which has been measured at an average rate of three seconds.

NEXT DAY AIR SERVICE CUMULATIVE CASE STUDY

See appendix at end of book

CHAPTER FOURTEEN

NOVELL NETWARE

Novell Netware is the most popular network operating system in the world. In this chapter, we compare the two current versions of Netware (3.X and 4.X). We provide a basic introduction to their structure and several commands.

Objectives

- Become familiar with the differences between Netware 3.X and 4.X,
- Become familiar with the basic structure of Netware servers,
- Understand the roles of network loadable modules,
- Understand disk volumes and mapping,
- Understand the importance of user groups,
- Become familiar with Netware security services,
- Become familiar with several Netware commands.

Chapter Outline

Introduction
What Is Novell Netware?
    Netware 3.X
    Netware 4.X
The Netware Server
    Disk Sharing
    Communications
    Netware Operating System Services
    Server-Based Processing
    Server Hardware

INTRODUCTION

There are many reasons for installing a local area network (LAN). Typical benefits include sharing of devices (such as printers, CD-ROM drives, tape backup units, and modem/fax equipment), sharing data and applications programs, and running multi-user programs such as e-mail, databases, and groupware. One of the most important steps in installing a LAN is selecting the network operating system (NOS). Several NOSs that are commonly used are Novell Netware, Microsoft Windows NT, Banyan Vines, and IBM's LAN Manager. Of these, Novell Netware is the most popular.

WHAT IS NOVELL NETWARE?

Novell Netware was one of the first NOS developed for local area networks. The first version was released in 1983. Since then, Netware has undergone many changes. Figure 14-1 outlines some of Netware's history. Today, there are two versions of Netware in general use, 3.X and 4.X.

Year	Event
1983	1st Netware version released
1985	Netware 286 released
1989	Netware 3.X (Netware 386) released
1993	Netware 4.0 released
1995	Netware 4.1 released

Figure 14-1 History of Netware.

Netware 3.X

Netware 3.X or Netware 386 as it is often called, was first released in 1989. It is a *server centric* NOS, in that the server is the center of activity on the network. In the server centric world, each server is equivalent to a country. Just as each country has its own laws and government, each server has its own security and administration. Each server is a separate entity for security, files, and services. A user who wants to have access to two servers will need a userid and password on both servers.

As servers are added and users access services or data from more than one server, network management becomes monumental. Thus, server centric systems work well with few servers and little crossover of users between the servers. The server centric view has worked in the typical LAN environment. But, as the number of computers and LANs has grown, the server centric view is being replaced by the network centric view of Netware 4.X.

Netware 4.X

The 4.X versions of Netware were developed in response to the growing demand for enterprise level local area networks. Enterprise-wide LANs are physically separated LANs that are connected by backbone, metropolitan, or wide area networks. As early LANs expanded to cover large areas, the number of users, servers, and network services increased. This network explosion greatly increased network management responsibilities. Novell's solution to this was to adopt the network centric view of Netware 4.X.

The *network centric* approach focuses on granting users access to the whole network. Accessing at the network level simplifies management for the network managers and provides a consistent interface for all users. The network centric view is provided by a feature of Netware 4.X called *Netware directory services* (NDS), which is a distributed database that stores lists of the users, resources, and access rights on all the Netware servers. Individual users can access the NDS regardless of their location on the network. All information in the NDS is replicated on every server, so there is no single point of failure.

Several other features of Netware 4.X provide increased utility for users and network managers. Many of these features are directly related to supporting the large size and geographic diversity of enterprise networks. Features such as file compression, better file management, and better memory protection help to increase the network's reliability and the network manager's productivity.

Others, like language support, help users access the network. Many of the companies that have an enterprise network are multi-national. Each user can specify which language they want their Netware 4.X interface to use. The languages currently supported are Canadian French, French, Chinese, Danish, Dutch, English, Finnish, German, Italian, Japanese, Korean, Norwegian, Portuguese, Russian, Spanish, and Swedish.

Netware 4.X is the clear choice for organizations that have or are developing enterprise networks. Netware 3.X is a less expensive alternative for smaller organizations with more typical LANs. Figure 14-2 compares 3.X to 4.X.

Netware Feature	Version 3.X	Version 4.X
Minimum Server Memory	4 Megabytes	8 Megabytes
Maximum Server Memory	4 Gigabytes	4 Gigabytes
Maximum Concurrent Connections	250	1000
Security	Server	Network
Dedicated Server	Yes	Yes
Maximum Disks per Server	1024	1024
Maximum Volumes per Server	64	64
Maximum Volume Size	32 Terabytes	32 Terabytes
Printers per Print Server	16	256
File Compression	No	Yes
Memory Protection for NLMs	No	Yes
Computers Supported	DOS, OS/2, Macintosh, UNIX	DOS, OS/2, Macintosh, UNIX

Figure 14-2   Netware feature comparison.

THE NETWARE SERVER

One of the better ways to understand a Netware server is to examine the various services it provides: disk sharing, communications, basic NOS services, and server based processing. We also discuss the server hardware in this section.

Disk Sharing

The most fundamental feature of a Netware file server is the sharing of disk space. A Netware file server allows users to share files even if they are using computers with dissimilar operating systems. This sharing is transparent, meaning that users do not need to know whether the files are stored on their computer or on the file server. The shared disk spaces on the server are called *volumes*.

Each hard drive on the server is partitioned for the type of operating system to be used. A Netware server typically has a hard disk with a small DOS *partition*, which is needed for booting up the server. The remaining area on that disk, as well additional disks, is formatted with Netware partitions that are divided into volumes.

A volume on the Netware server is an area of physical disk space equivalent to a hard drive on a computer running DOS. With Netware, a volume can span several

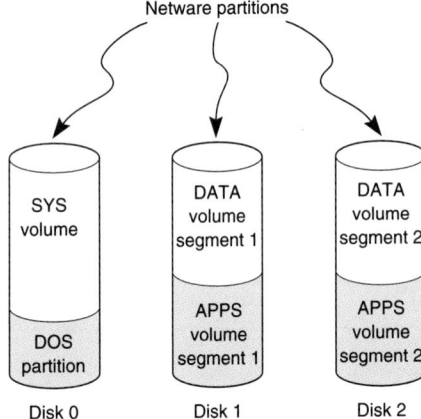

Figure 14-3 Volumes, partitions, & disks.

partitions and one partition can have several volumes. In Figure 14-3, disk 0 is partitioned for DOS and Netware. The Netware partition is completely used by the SYS volume. Disks 1 and 2 are partitioned for Netware and the APPS and DATA volumes are spread across both disks. Each part of a volume on a disk is called a segment. The segments on disk 2 are the DATA segment 2 and the APPS segment 2. If an additional disk were added (disk 3) and the APPS volume expanded, segment 3 would be created. A point of caution in Netware: you can always increase the size of a volume by adding segments, but you cannot decrease the size without destroying the entire volume.

Communications

The communications services provided by a Netware server can either be simple or complicated. The simple case is where the server is attached to only one network using

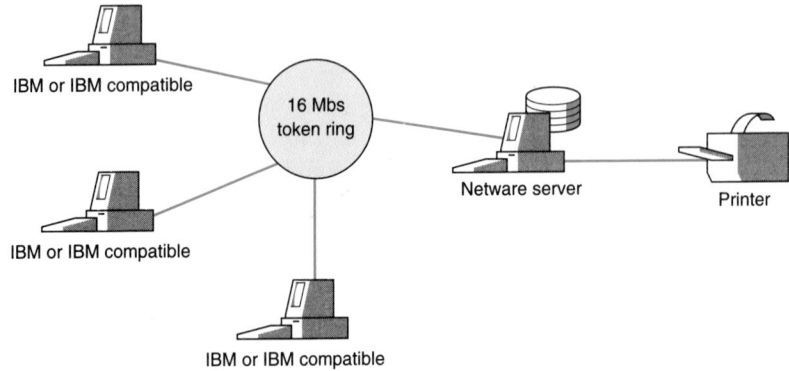

Figure 14-4 Simple network.

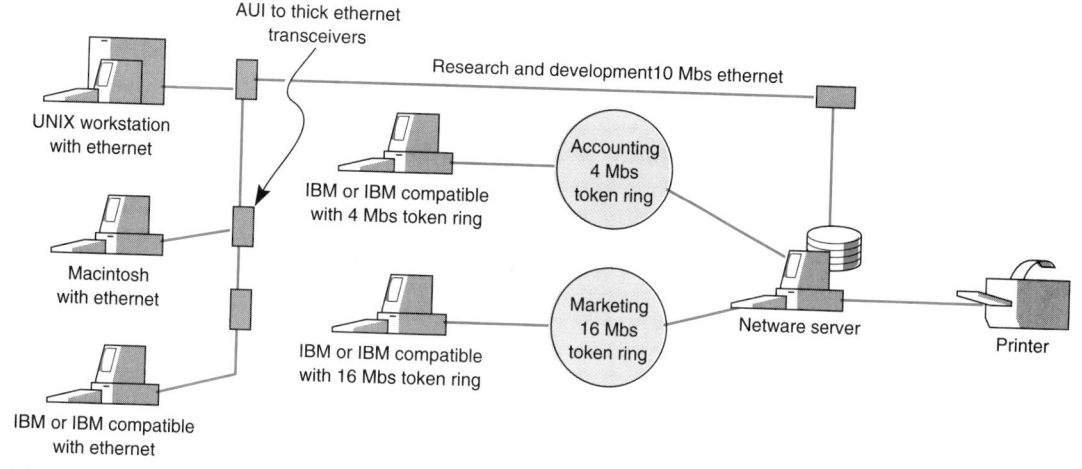

Figure 14-5   Complex network.

one protocol (see Figure 14-4). The more complicated cases are combinations of multiple network topologies and multiple protocols (see Figure 14-5).

The five major LAN topologies to which Netware can connect are: ethernet, token ring, ARCnet, fiber distributed data interface (FDDI), and asynchronous transfer mode (ATM). Each can have several protocols being transmitted at the same time. A communication protocol is the software component of the network's communications and specifies the exact structure of the communication packets transmitted. The default protocol for a Netware server is Internetwork packet exchange/sequenced packet exchange (IPX/SPX). The Netware server also can communicate via other protocols like transmission control protocol/internet protocol (TCP/IP) and AppleTalk. It means that Apple Macintoshes, UNIX computers, and PCs can easily communicate with the Netware server. In addition, the server can translate between the different topologies and the protocols on each topology.

A single server can be connected to several networks simultaneously. Each attached network has an associated network card in the server, which permits it to act as a router between the networks. An example is an organization with an ethernet and a token ring. The server joins the two physical networks together into one logical network and routes messages between them.

Netware Operating System Services

The heart of the many services provided by the Netware server is the Netware core protocol (NCP). NCP provides file and directory services, routing, accounting, access, and security. The NCP receives the incoming packets from the user computers, handles requests to retrieve and store files, enforces the security restrictions on the network, and coordinates the Netware loadable modules running in the server memory.

Server-Based Processing

Server-based processing is the client-server component of Netware. For our purposes, the definition of the server component is an application that provides services to network users or clients, while a client is a program that makes a request to a server. In the Novell model, a server is a combination of an application program on the server (called a netware loadable module or NLM) and the hardware needed to run that application.

Server Hardware

The computer that is a Netware server consists of a central processing unit, random access memory, disk system, and network interface cards. Each component teams with the others and the NOS to create a network file server. All hardware components must be matched to each other and to the demands the network will place on the server.

The current versions of Netware 3.X and Netware 4.X are designed to run on Intel 386, 486 or Pentium CPUs. It is anticipated that a Power PC version of Netware will be released soon. Also a version of Netware exists for UNIX-based computers.

The amount of random access memory (RAM) in the server is directly related to the size of both the disk subsystem and programs to be run on the server. The minimum memory requirement for Netware 3.X is 4 MB and Netware 4.X is 8 MB. In general, the larger the RAM size the better. A typical Netware 4.X server with a 2 gigabyte disk subsystem, and running printing services would need 32 MB of RAM.

Extra RAM that is not used by the system is assigned to the disk cache. The disk cache buffers read and write requests to and from the disk subsystem. If the requested file is in the disk cache, the server provides the information from the cache rather than reading it from the disk. The disk cache also allows the server to wait for the most efficient time to write information to the disk.

The number of users, how much data will be stored on the server, and how often the data change (volatility) determines the size and speed of the disk subsystem. Speed is a function of the type of disk controller and the access time of the hard drives. Small computer system interface (SCSI) controllers are the best for servers because they allow the fastest transfer of data from the hard drive to the server and the greatest expandability.

The network interface cards (NIC) used in a server are determined by the physical network topology, the network protocols to be run on the cards, and the number of users accessing the server. All NICs convert the data moving inside the server to a format compatible with the networks that are connected. Many NICs have features, such as their own CPUs, that increase the efficiency of the server by reducing the work load of the server CPU. NICs can also take advantage of special techniques such as bus mastering and direct memory access to transfer the data from the NIC to the server memory more quickly. (Obviously, as you increase the features of the NICs in the server, you also increase the cost.)

An important concern in the selection of a server is to match its performance with the computers that will be connecting to it. The server should be at least as fast as the computers connected to it.

SETTING UP THE SERVER

Due to the variety of different disk subsystems and NICs available, Novell and hardware vendors have developed specialized software to interface the hardware with the file server. This special software is called Netware loadable modules.

Netware Loadable Modules

The software that runs a Netware server can be divided into two parts: NCP and Netware loadable modules (NLM). NCP was discussed in the previous section. NLMs handle network communication, printing, and monitoring. They can either be stand-alone application programs used entirely on the server or the server portion of a client-server application.

Four types of NLMs exist in the Netware system, and each has a specific function in the NOS. Three are specifically related to initializing the server. The fourth denotes management utilities and server applications. NLM names conform to the DOS file naming conventions of a maximum of eight characters with a three character extension. It is the extension that determines the type of NLM (see Figure 14-6).

Disk Controller NLMs   Disk controller NLMs are the interface between the NCP and the disk subsystems on the server. A disk subsystem consists of the disk controller and the hard drives connected to that controller. The four common disk controller types are: ST-506, ESDI, SCSI, and IDE. The ST-506 and ESDI controllers are found on older model servers and are no longer manufactured, making SCSI and IDE the most commonly used. A server with SCSI or IDE can have up to four controllers installed. Each IDE controller can have two hard drives connected at most, while an SCSI controller can have up to 7 or 15 devices connected, depending on the type. Devices can

NLM Extension	NLM Type
.DSK	Disk Controller Driver
.LAN	Network Interface Card Driver
.NAM	Name Space Modules
.NLM	Management Utilities and Server Applications

Figure 14-6   Extensions used for NLMs.

be a variety of computer peripherals, such as hard disks, tape drives, CD-ROM drives, and scanners.

The disk controller NLMs are started when the server first boots up. They are loaded automatically by the system from the STARTUP.NCF file. It tells the NCP what device drivers to load at bootup of the server. An example of the command in the STARTUP.NCF to load the IDE.DSK driver is:

LOAD IDE PORT=1F0 INT=B

This will load the disk controller driver for an IDE controller that is using hardware input/output port 1F0 and the system interrupt 11.

Network Interface Card NLMs   The server is physically attached to the network by Network interface cards (NICs). NIC NLMs contain the instructions on how the NCP controls and passes information to the NIC. The NIC converts the information passed by the server to the protocol used by the attached network. This information can then be transmitted to the server's clients. The process works in reverse when the server is receiving information from the clients.

The NIC NLMs are usually started when the server first boots. The AUTOEXEC.NCF tells the NCP what commands to run after the commands in the STARTUP.NCF are completed. It tells the NCP which NIC drivers to load, which volumes to mount, sets the server operating parameters, and which additional NLMs to load when starting the server. An example of the command in the AUTOEXEC.NCF to load the NIC driver for the Novell NE2000 (a common ethernet NIC) is:

LOAD NE2000 FRAME=ETHERNET_II

This will load the driver for the NE2000 NIC with the ethernet frame type of ethernet II. If no frame type is specified, the default frame type is ethernet 802.2. Many NICs can have multiple frame types running simultaneously. An example of the commands to run the NE2000 with both the ethernet 802.2 and II frame type is:

LOAD NE2000

LOAD NE2000 FRAME=ETHERNET_II

Name Space NLMs   The term *name space* refers to the type of operating system files supported by server. The default name space supported by Netware is DOS. Because of differences in the naming conventions for the different operating systems, additional name space support needs to be added if computers with different operating systems are to access the server. File names and other file information are stored in a special area of each volume called alternate name spaces, which must be initialized by the server before they can be used.

An example of this is adding name space support for Apple Macintosh files. The NLM that supports the Macintosh name space is MAC.NAM, which must be loaded, and its name space support added to each volume that will store Macintosh files. To store Macintosh files on the SYS volume, the commands would be:

LOAD MAC

ADD NAME SPACE MAC TO SYS

Typically, name space support is loaded in the STARTUP.NCF file and ADD NAME SPACE is run from the server console. Two important things to remember when adding name spaces are that, once added to a volume, a name space cannot be removed, and that any addition will increase the size of the directory table. Each volume with added name space requires twice as much memory on the server as the volume without the additional name space. This increase in the size of the directory tables will decrease the amount of data that can be stored on each volume and increase the amount of server memory necessary to mount the volume.

Management Utility and Server Application NLMs   The NLMs associated with management utilities allow the network manager to configure and monitor the network and file server. The MONITOR.NLM is one of the most used NLM of this type. It allows the network manager to observe the activities of the file server. MONITOR reports information on the disk subsystems, NICs, memory usage, server utilization, users, and other NLMs loaded on the server. The command to load the MONITOR NLM is:

LOAD MONITOR

The server console will then display the initial screen for the MONITOR program. There are many utility NLMs provided by Novell and third party vendors.

A server application is the server portion of a client-server application. Many third party vendors provide NLMs for specific applications, such as databases (Oracle, Sybase, and Novell), groupware (Lotus Notes), and document imaging management (Kodak and Xerox). Other vendors provide NLMs for virus detection and message handling services.

One application that almost all Netware servers have is support for network printing. The print server and associated print queues are established by the network manager. When a network user prints on the network, the user's computer sends the job to the print server, which in turn delivers the job to the printer. Since many users could be printing at once, the print server temporarily stores jobs in print queues until they

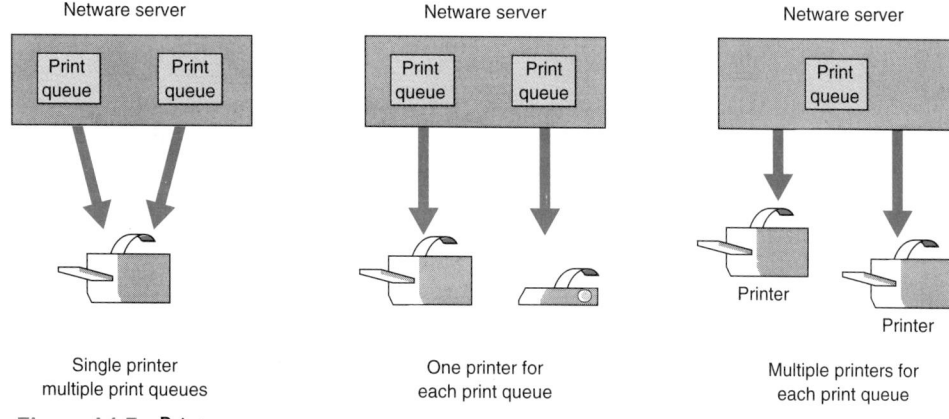

Figure 14-7   Print queues.

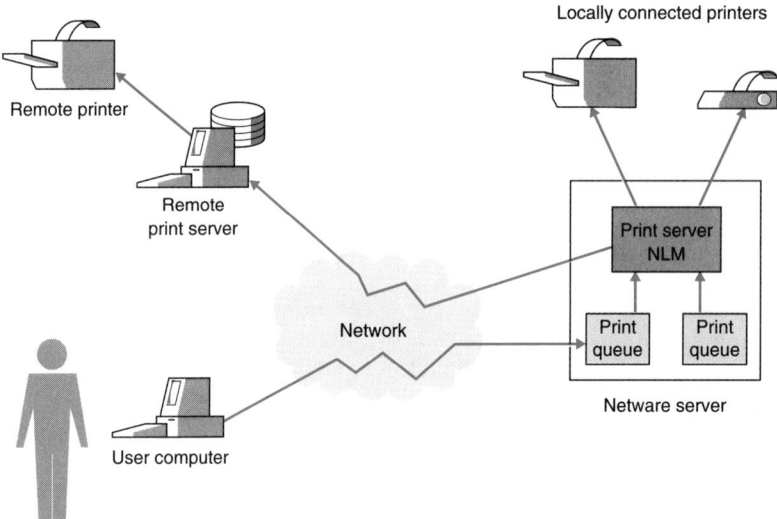

Figure 14-8 Network printing.

can be serviced. Basically a subdirectory on the file server, a print queue can be serviced by one or more printers, or multiple queues can send to one printer (see Figure 14-7).

The print queues are accessed by a print server that controls network printers. A print server can be either internal or remote. An internal print server runs in the Netware file server, to which printers are directly connected. A remote print server is a separate computer that is connected to the network and controls printers connected to it. In all cases, the print queue is still stored on the file server (see Figure 14-8). Because many LANs are spread out over several floors in one building or in several buildings, remote print servers allow the network manager to conveniently locate printers near users. Remember, the whole idea of LANs is to increase user productivity.

File Services—Volumes, Directories, and Mapping

As we have already discussed, hard drives on the server are divided into volumes for use by network users. When Netware is installed, the SYS volume is created automatically on the file server. The SYS volume also has several directories that have been automatically created (Figure 14-9). The *SYSTEM directory* contains files and programs used by the Netware NOS. The *PUBLIC directory* contains additional programs and utilities. The *LOGIN directory* helps users complete the login process. The *MAIL directory*, as the name suggests, stores e-mail files.

These four directories should be reserved solely for the use of the NOS, although additional software and utilities that are to be available to all users can be placed in the public directory. The network manager and users with the appropriate access can add additional sub-directories to each volume. A commonly added directory is the

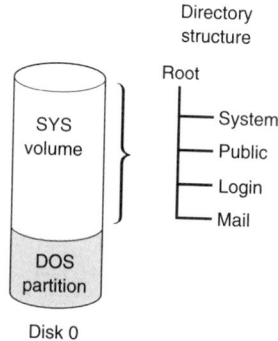

Figure 14-9 SYS volume.

APPS directory, which stores application software such as word processors, spreadsheets, and graphics. In many cases, there is so much application software that a separate volume—not just a directory—is dedicated to it.

After the volumes are created, the network manager gives users access and security rights to each volume. To the user, each volume looks like a hard drive attached to their local computer. The directories and files on the network look and act like DOS directories and files if you are using the DOS or Windows operating system. If you are using Macintosh, UNIX, or OS/2, they look the same as the local directories and files to your operating system (once the appropriate name spaces have been added to the server).

The users are given access to the volumes when they login into the network by user *login scripts*, which define a series of commands that are executed every time the user logs in. Login scripts give users access to volumes by using the *MAP* command to connect a volume to a drive letter, which usually starts at the letter F. By starting at F, the MAP command can connect the user to a maximum of 21 volumes at one time (i.e., F, G, H, and on to Z). Volumes can be assigned and removed by the user and network applications while logged into the network. A typical example of a MAP command is:

MAP H:=SYS:LOGIN

This command gives the user access to the LOGIN directory on the SYS volume as drive letter H:. Any future reference to drive H: will now refer to the LOGIN directory. The user then can view the files using the DOS DIR command and move around the directory structure by using the DOS directory commands (e.g., CD). For example, typing DIR H: would display the directory of files in the LOGIN directory.

The MAP INS command allows a directory to be designated as a *search directory*, one that is searched for an executable program whenever the users enters a command. A search directory is the same as a directory specified in the DOS PATH command. The MAP INS command allows search drives to be specified. For example:

MAP INS S1:=SYS:PUBLIC

This MAP command makes the PUBLIC directory on the SYS volume the first search directory; that is, it is placed at the beginning of the DOS search path and called the Z: drive. The PUBLIC directory will be the first location searched for files if they are not found in the current directory. Additional search directories can be added using additional MAP INS commands and specifying S2, S3, and so on for other search directories. Each directory is added at the beginning of the path and is labeled in reverse alphabetical order (i.e., Z:, Y:, X:, and so on). In addition, the SEARCH command can be used to specify search directories. It is important to note that the MAP command will not allow users to access a directory unless they have the proper security rights to that directory.

Security Services

Security for the Netware system is handled in three distinct levels: login authentication, directory, and file. Each of these levels controls user access to specific parts of the server. The security settings for users and *groups* of users are maintained by the network manager.

Groups   A group is a set of network users who need a common network service, such as a shared directory to store data, access to a certain application program, or ability to use a network printer. Users may be divided into groups according to functional areas, level in the organization hierarchy, physical location, and network service needs.

The most common group is called EVERYONE—all users are members. The EVERYONE group has security privileges that are common to all users. A change made for the EVERYONE group will affect all individual members.

A user can belong to more than one group, and gain all the access rights of all these groups. For example, suppose a department head in New York is a member of the Wonder Widget design team. That person could be a member of four groups: New York, department heads, Wonder Widget, and everyone.

Login Authentication   Login authentication is the first level of security on the Netware system. It uses a combination of userid and password to determine if a person should be allowed access into the file server or to the Netware directory services (NDS).

Login authentication has many parameters to assist the network manager in providing a secure network. Some of these include: minimum number of characters in the password, length of time password is valid, how many attempts can be made with an invalid password before the manager is notified of a possible intruder, which computers are available for a user's login, and the hours of the day when users can login.

One feature associated with login authentication is the changing of passwords. Users can change their own passwords by giving the current password and then the new password. The network manager can change any passwords, but cannot see the current password for an individual account. Once login authentication is complete, the user is subject to directory and file level security.

Trustee Right	Function
Read	Allows the user to see the contents and use a file or files in a directory.
Write	The user can alter the contents of a file or files in a directory.
Create	The user can make new files and directories.
Erase	The user can delete existing files and directories.
File Scan	Allows the user to see if the files and directories exist.
Modify	The user can change the attributes of a file or directory. An example would be to change a file from read/write to read only.
Access Control	Allows the user to assign or change the preceding rights for other users.
Supervisory	Gives all the preceding rights to the user or group.

Figure 14-10   Netware file and directory rights mask.

Directory and File Security   Directory and file level security give users access by giving the *trustee rights* to a directory or file. Each of these rights and its function is summarized in Figure 14-10.

File level security gives users or groups trustee rights to individual files. Directory level services can give users and groups trustee rights to entire directories of files. Initially, the rights to the different directories and files are set by the network manager, but over time, users with access control or supervisory rights can add and change rights for individual users. The combination of file and directory rights results in a *rights mask* for each user that contains the level of access each user has to network services, directories, and files.

Netware 4.X adds additional security levels for object and property rights, which help to administer the enterprise network. The base security levels—login, directory, and file—in Netware provide a method to control access to the network itself, information on the network, and network services.

NETWARE COMMANDS

Netware Administrator Commands

Many commands exist to help the network administrator to control the network. The two most common administrator activities are creating and maintaining user accounts and printer definitions.

User management is done via the SYSCON or NETCON program. SYSCON manages the users of one Netware server, while NETCON handles multiple servers. The server login scripts and individual user login scripts are created and changed from SYSCON or NETCON. The default security rights such as length of password, number of login attempts with an incorrect password before the account is disabled, and hours of operation can be set. The network administrator can also add new users, change characteristics for existing users, and delete users from the network. Groups can be created, rights assigned or edited, and members added.

Before users can print a job, the network administrator must define the print queue and print server by creating the print queue, creating the print server, defining the printer, and assigning queues to printers. Only the network supervisor (or users with supervisor rights) can create print queues, which is done with the PCONSOLE command, and selecting Print Queue Information from the main menu. Once this has been selected, a list of existing print queues is displayed. Highlighting and selecting an existing queue will provide information on that queue. Creating a new queue is done by pressing the insert key and typing the new queue name.

Each queue has a list of operators and users. Queue operators (usually the network administrator) can delete a print job, change the order of jobs in the queue, or start and stop the queue from accepting new print jobs. A print queue user can only send jobs to the queue, check their status, and delete them.

The Print Server Information in the PCONSOLE menu allows the administrator to create new print servers and their operators and users in the same way that the new print queue was created. This is done by selecting the Print Server Configuration menu, which allows the administrator to define the network name for the printer, the printer connection type, and the users to be notified if the printer runs out of paper or needs service. At this point, the printer has been defined and assigned to a print server.

The last step is to connect the defined printer and the new print queue. Selecting Queues Serviced by Printer and pressing Insert allows the administrator to add print queues to the printer. Print jobs sent to the print queue will be sent to the printer through the associated print server.

Netware User Commands

Most of what we have discussed to this point has focused on managing and configuring the server. We now turn to the user's activities. How does the user's computer "talk" to the network and server and what can the users do to manage their activities on the network?

The user's computer connects to the network by an NIC. The network software that connects the computer to the network has two separate parts: one that controls the NIC, and one that interfaces with the computer's operating system, called the Netware shell. The shell is a command interpreter that accepts commands from the client (user or application program) and analyzes them to determine if it is a request for network services. If it is not, it is given to the operating system; if it is, the shell passes the request to the NIC driver (see Figure 14-11).

A typical first request for service is to login to the network. Once the user has passed

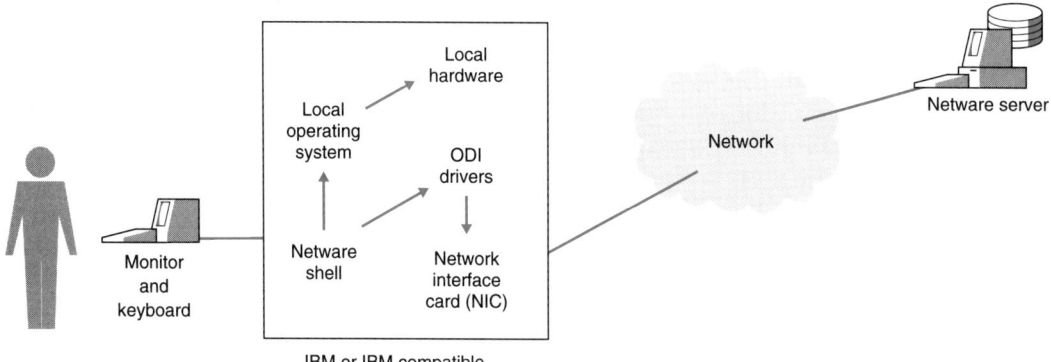

Figure 14-11 Network requestor.

login authentication, the network runs two batch files, the network login script and a personal login script which establishes individual network preferences. Once these are completed, access to the network is limited only by the user's rights mask.

Netware provides many programs that can be accessed by menu, and most network managers design menu interfaces for other commands. The user selects a menu choice and the command or commands to achieve the choice are executed. Some of the most important and commonly used commands will be discussed next.

Users can view information about and change the current connection parameters by choosing the SESSION command in Netware 3.X and the NETUSER command in Netware 4.X. They can view the network printers and the volumes to which they are connected, display information about other users, and send brief messages to other users. Both of these commands also can be used to make immediate changes to the current network connection. A user can attach to a new network printer and remap network volumes to a new drive letter. (Any changes relating to drive mapping or printers using SESSION or NETUSER will only last for the current connection.) When the user disconnects from the network, all the new changes are lost, and the original definitions in the login scripts are back in effect.

The user can also run a series of stand-alone programs that accomplish many of the same tasks as SESSION or NETUSER. The SETPASS command allows the changing of a password. This command will prompt you for your old password and then ask you twice for your new password. The RIGHTS command displays the user's trustee rights for the directory currently open.

Two of the most commonly used print commands are CAPTURE and PCONSOLE. The CAPTURE command allows a user to redirect the output from a local printer port (LPT1 - LPT3) to a network print queue. The following command will connect the printer port LPT1 on the user's computer to a print queue called ROOM231 with a timeout of 10 seconds and will not print a banner page.

CAPTURE L1 Q=ROOM231 TI=10 NB

Any printing that is directed to the port LPT1 will be intercepted by the Netware shell and directed to the print queue, ROOM231. A timeout of 10 seconds will prompt the print queue to send the completed job to the printer server if it detects no additional printing activity for 10 seconds. Normally, Netware will print a banner page indicating the owner of the job being printed. In many cases, the banner is added wear on the printer and a waste of paper. The CAPTURE command is usually run in the login script to define the default network printers.

PCONSOLE is a simple menu-based program that allows a user to view the status of print jobs in the print queue, and the status of both local and remote print servers. PCONSOLE helps users manage print jobs sent to a print queue. For example, it makes deleting a print job quite simple.

The most useful command is LOGOUT, which closes all network services activated by the user and disconnects them from the network.

Summary

Netware 3.X and 4.X   The most popular local area network operating system in the world is Novell's Netware. There are two versions of Netware commonly in use: Netware 3.X is a server centric NOS in that each server is a separate entity for security, files, and services; Netware 4.X is a network centric NOS that grants users access to the network as a whole. Netware 3.X is best for small LANs, while 4.X is better for enterprise-wide networks.

The Netware Server   The services provided by the Netware server fall into four main categories: disk sharing, communications, basic NOS services, and server based processing. The shared disk spaces on the server are called volumes. Communications can be simple (one network and one protocol) or complex (multiple networks and multiple protocols). The heart of the many NOS services provided by the Netware server is the Netware core protocol (NCP), such as file and directory services, routing, and security. Server-based processing is the client-server component of Netware.

Netware Loadable Modules   Netware loadable modules (NLMs) provide services such as disk controlling, network communications, printing, and monitoring. Disk controller NLMs are the interface between the NCP and the disk subsystems on the server. Network interface cards NLMs contain the instructions on how the NCP controls and passes information to the network card. Name space NLMs enable servers to support files from many different types of operating systems. The NLMs associated with management utilities allow the network manager to configure and monitor the network and file server. Server application NLMs are the server portions of a client-server applications, such as databases (Oracle, Sybase, and Novell), groupware (Lotus Notes), and document imaging management (Kodak and Xerox).

Disk Mapping   Login scripts give users access to volumes by using the MAP command to connect a volume to a drive letter. The MAP INS command allows a directory to be designated as a search directory, which is the same as a directory specified in the DOS PATH command.

Security Services   Security for the Netware system is handled in three distinct levels; login authentication, directory, and file. Each controls the access of users to specific parts of the server and can be set for each user or for groups of users. Login authentication uses a combination of userid and password to determine if a person should be allowed access into the file server or to the NDS. Directory and file level security give users access by granting trustee rights to a directory or file.

Netware User Commands   Netware provides many programs that can be accessed by menu, and most network managers design menu interfaces for other commands. A user can view information about and change the current connection parameters by using the SESSION command in Netware 3.X and the NETUSER command in Netware 4.X. The two most commonly used print commands are CAPTURE and PCONSOLE. The CAPTURE command allows a user to redirect the output from a local printer port to a network print queue. PCONSOLE is a simple menu-based program that allows a user to view the status of print jobs in the print queue, and the status of both local and remote print servers. The LOGOUT command closes all network services in use and disconnects them from the network.

Key Terms

Capture	Netuser	Pconsole
Directory	Netware core protocol	Public directory
Disk controller NLM	(NCP)	Rights
Group	Netware directory services	Rights mask
Login authentication	(NDS)	Search directory
Login directory	Netware loadable modules	Server application NLM
Login script	(NLM)	Server centric
Logout	Netware 3.X	Session
Mail directory	Netware 4.X	Setpass
Management utility NLM	Network centric	Syscon
Map	Network interface card	System directory
Name space NLM	NLM	Trustee rights
Netcon	Partition	Volume

Selected References

1. Gimes, Galen. *10 Minute Guide to Netware.* Carmel, IN: Alpha Books, 1994.
2. Lawrence, Bill, et al. *Using Netware 4.1.* Indianapolis, IN: Que Corp., 1994.
3. Palmer, Michael and Alvin Rains. *Local Area Networking with Novell Software.* Boston: Boyd and Fraser, 1994.
4. Sheldon, Tom. *Novell Netware 4: The Complete Reference.* Berkely, CA: Osborne McGraw-Hill, 1993.

Questions/Problems

1.   What are the major differences between Netware 3.X and 4.X?
2.   What is Netware directory services (NDS)?
3.   What is a volume? a partition?
4.   Describe the four main hardware components of a Netware server.
5.   What is an NLM?
6.   Describe four types of NLMs.
7.   What are the four directories usually found on Netware servers?
8.   What does the MAP command do?
9.   What does the MAP INS command do?
10.   What is a login script?
11.   How are user groups useful?
12.   Describe Netware's security services.
13.   What does the SESSION command do?
14.   What do the CAPTURE and PCONSOLE commands do?

NEXT DAY AIR SERVICE CUMULATIVE CASE STUDY

See appendix at end of book

NEXT DAY AIR CASE STUDIES

This is the beginning of a cumulative case study about a fictitious firm we call Next Day Air Service. The case study begins here in Chapter 1 and continues through Chapter 14. It requires you to complete tasks that are related to topics covered in each corresponding chapter of the text. Each chapter in the appendix contains the case narrative, related figures, and a set of questions and problems. These do not have one unique solution. There are too many alternatives when dealing with LANs, WANs, MANs, BNs, and the Internet, so a real-life network design and development problem can have several workable answers.

As with any real-life problem with ambiguities or unresolved considerations, you must make your own assumptions. Feel free to read ahead or use the index to find related subjects that support your recommendations. Your instructor may provide additional guidelines regarding report formats, library resources, other assumptions, and the like for the various questions and problems presented in this case study. Be sure to provide adequate justification for any recommendations you make.

CHAPTER ONE

Introduction to Next Day Air Service

The Next Day Air Service (NDAS) firm was founded in 1985 to compete in the expanding market for overnight package deliveries. Next Day Air Service provides local pickup and delivery of these parcels and other small freight items. The founders initially restricted their efforts to the rapidly growing central Florida region.

To support its operation, Next Day Air Service purchased a facility near the Tampa International Airport. This facility consisted of a main building and a secondary building for dispatch and fleet maintenance. Because Next Day Air Service intended to expand its services throughout the southeastern United States, this facility also served as NDAS's corporate headquarters.

From 1985 to 1992, Next Day Air Service experienced very rapid growth. As business volume increased and the company's reputation became firmly established, expansion of the facility became imperative. Consequently, NDAS purchased land adjacent to its corporate headquarters, so it would have room to relocate both the maintenance shop and the company's vehicle parking lot. In addition, Next Day Air Service tripled the size of its building to accommodate its growing business. Finally, in 1994 Next Day Air Service completed the expansion of the office building to house its corporate operations.

As its business volume increased, NDAS realized it had to develop branch offices throughout its service region in order to continue growing. In addition to the corporate offices in Tampa, NDAS also purchased or leased facilities in several other southeastern cities, including Orlando, Miami, Atlanta, New Orleans, Dallas, and Memphis. Figure A1-1 shows the Next Day Air Service map of operations.

Next Day Air Service also contracted with the Chicago-based firm Overnight Delivery, Inc. (ODI), to provide overnight shipping service between Atlanta and the greater Chicago area. NDAS also entered into similar agreements with other air carriers. The purpose of these agreements was to enable NDAS to provide service throughout the United States.

As Figure A1-1 shows, connecting routes established with other carriers lead from Memphis to St. Louis and from Atlanta to Chicago and Washington, D.C. These routes allow NDAS to deliver parcels to the northeastern states and the Midwest. There are flight links out of Dallas to both Denver and Los Angeles. These two routes have been added recently to provide delivery service to the northwestern states and the West Coast, respectively. After extending its flight routes, NDAS added agents in the cities of Jacksonville, Montgomery, Jackson, and Houston. To date, this is the scope of NDAS's parcel delivery operation.

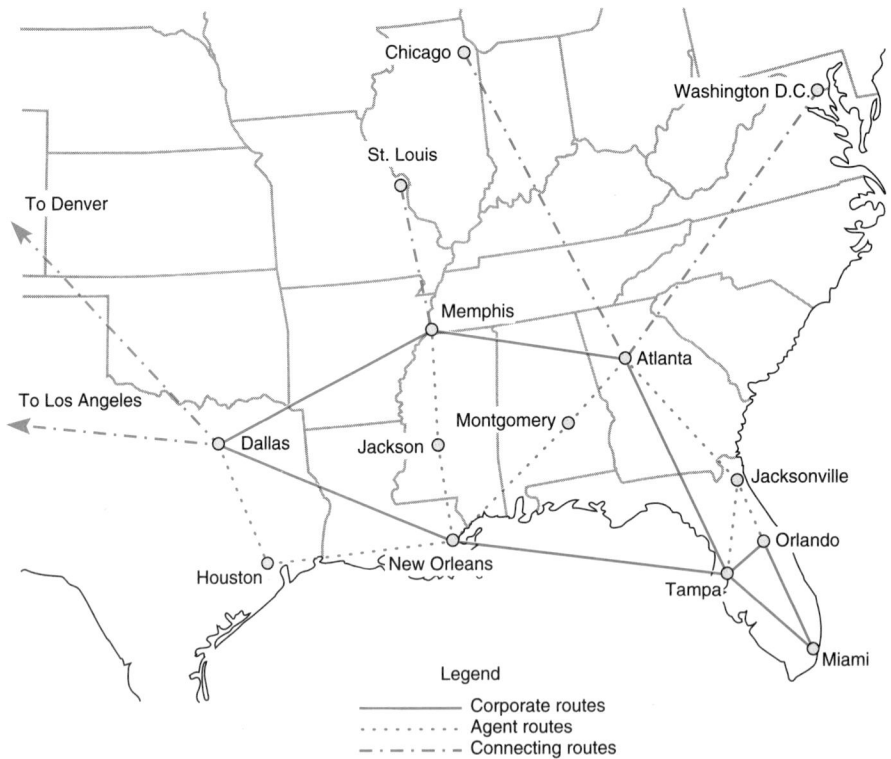

Figure A1-1   Next Day Air Service map of operations.

Initially, Next Day Air Service contracted a computing services company to handle billing. As the computing power of small computers increased, however, NDAS purchased a minicomputer and took responsibility for its own data processing. The Payroll Department now runs the payroll twice monthly on this computer. Employees submit their timecards and supporting documents on the first and third Mondays of the month. The Payroll Department then prepares the paychecks for both hourly and salaried employees. The paychecks are sent via overnight delivery on the following Thursdays.

Although the Information Services/Data Processing Division, under Les Coone as acting manager, performs all data entry, processing, and check printing, John Lawson in Accounts Payable is the person who generates, reviews, and approves the reports and totals. Because so many new employees have been added at both the corporate and branch offices, a new full-time position has been added in Accounts Payable to handle the payroll and assist Mr. Lawson. The subject of paying employees weekly has been discussed as well. Figure A1-2 shows the Next Day Air Service organization chart.

The branch offices currently batch all billing data by order date and send it daily by overnight delivery to the corporate office along with other interoffice correspondence. When Information Services/Data Processing receives the packages, it enters the batches and processes them daily. The billing processing normally takes place from

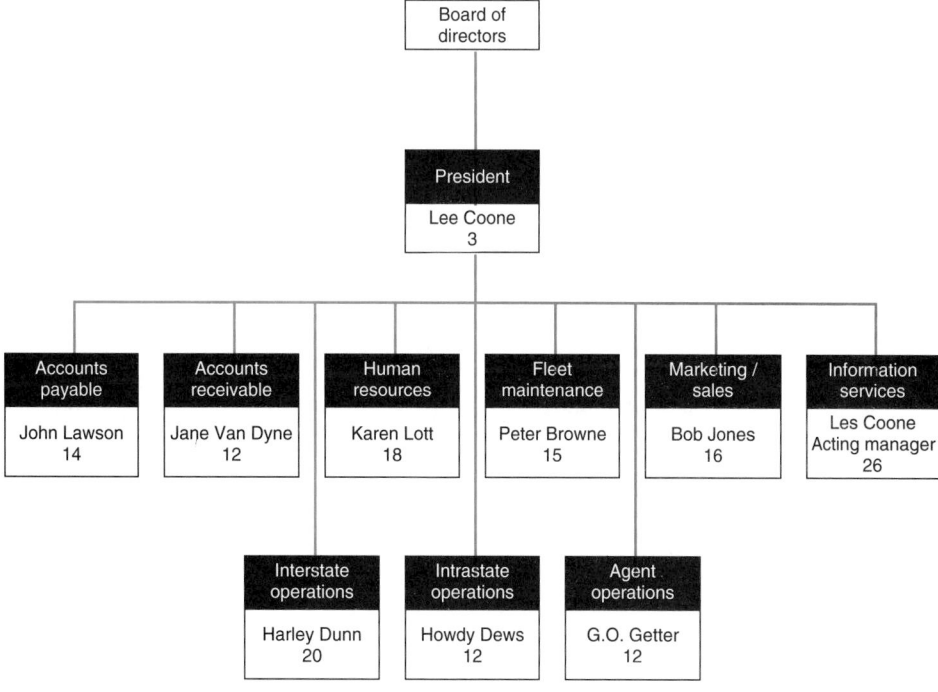

Total personnel: 148

Figure A1-2 Next Day Air Service organization chart showing key personnel and number of staff per area.

48 to 96 hours after freight and parcel delivery. Once this processing has been completed, the database supports the resolution of any questions or problems associated with the billings.

Because of an increasing volume of paperwork brought about by continued business expansion, the varying complexity of the billing process, and the preferred rates being given by competitors, Next Day Air Service's corporate management has decided to automate the billing process throughout its Florida offices. This is the first step in a series of strategic moves planned to provide online transaction processing and real-time customer information through a data communication network. Management expects online transaction processing to speed the billing process and improve receivables collection time significantly. The online Query System will enable agents at remote offices to obtain instantly information such as credit status, correct delivery address, and package delivery status.

The status of automation varies greatly among the various departments. The Sales and Marketing Division, headed by Bob Jones, has a desktop computer for each of the account representatives. All of these computers are connected to a small local area network (LAN) that serves only Sales and Marketing.

The Accounts Receivable Division, headed by Jayne Van Dyne, is responsible for all billing and collection activities. It recently downsized its minicomputer to a powerful desktop computer with a faster processor, more memory, and increased disk storage space. This new desktop supports databases for both customer billing and "bad debt" expenses.

The Accounts Payable Division, led by John Lawson, maintains its own vendor database that is stored on an older minicomputer. This database also contains the other service carriers' billings, such as those from ODI to NDAS. This division also is responsible for the payroll. It is in the process of downsizing to a powerful modern desktop computer.

The Fleet Maintenance Division has no computer capability. Its management has chosen to trace all necessary information manually. Peter Browne, the maintenance supervisor, prefers this mode of operation and in the past has steadfastly refused to automate his division's record-keeping processes.

Dispatch, which is part of the Fleet Maintenance Division, also processes its work manually. Dispatch currently bundles incoming packages twice daily, according to their major destination point, for overnight delivery. The bundles of packages are marked with the following information.

DEST: City, State
DATE: Current date
TIME: Time package left dispatch
NPKG: Number of individual packages in the bundle
INIT: Initials of the person preparing the bundle

When the bundles arrive at their respective delivery points, the off-loaders mark the arrival time on the bundles' tags, write their own initials on the back of the tags, and return the tags to corporate headquarters. The packages are then delivered.

The various remote offices currently communicate with the corporate headquarters and with one another by voice mail, telephone, facsimile, mail, or interoffice mail, sent on company aircraft along with the daily batched transactions. There are desktop computers in each of the remote offices. However, some of the offices have Apple Macintosh computers, and others use Intel-based systems. A number of managers have laptop computers, which, again, come from various computer manufacturers.

NDAS corporate management realizes that these various stages of computer support are a far cry from an integrated system. It sees the necessity for standardizing and streamlining systems, equipment, and procedures before any serious networking can be accomplished. Moreover, corporate management has stated that Next Day Air Service must enter the international package delivery market to offer full service to its major customers. Any growth plans must be able to support international operations. Management also expects that electronic mail and automated package tracking will be part of the new system. In addition, management expects any system to allow for expansion into other information technology areas of networking, such as video conferencing and the use of the Internet.

As its first step in this direction, NDAS has decided to hire a new systems analyst, who will work full-time to assess the current level of information system support, determine which functions should be automated, recommend the type of hardware and software systems to be installed, recommend appropriate organizational changes (if any), and, most important, determine the type of data communication support that will be required to meet the needs of NDAS's current operations and future growth.

You have been offered this position. Your experience is in information systems. Because you see the job as a remarkable opportunity to learn and grow, you accept the post. You report directly to Mr. Lee Coone, President of NDAS, and are expected to prepare your solution immediately.

Questions/Problems for the Next Day Air Service Case

1. Briefly describe the current state of Next Day Air Service's office automation, system integration, and networking. Begin by explaining how each department uses information technology, what hardware it uses, and what functions currently are automated. Also assess which department is most in need of a network.

2. With the "types of networks" and future technologies discussed in this chapter, what kind of network would appear to be the most beneficial to Next Day Air Service? Justify your answer.

3. What are the current characteristics or practices that identify NDAS as a possible candidate for its proposed integrated data communication network?

4. Which two of the four networks described in the Network Definitions box in Chapter 1 might be appropriate for NDAS?

5. When looking over the organization chart, you notice that the acting manager of the Information Services/Data Processing department is also named Coone (Les Coone). Inquiring, you learn that Les is President Coone's nephew. Les has just joined NDAS. This is his first job, and he has no background in information systems, data processing, or data communications. Will this be a problem for you? If so, why? How will you handle it?

CHAPTER TWO

Background on Next Day Air Service

President Coone was very satisfied with your initial analysis of Next Day Air Service's information technology and data communications needs. He passed your report around to the various department heads. Their comments were guarded but for the most part favorable as well. Three points attracted the most attention: (1) your comments on the ways NDAS could make effective use of groupware in achieving increased productivity; (2) your suggestion that an e-mail system would benefit the internal operation of NDAS; and (3) your analysis of the ways the Internet could help increase NDAS presence in both the international and domestic markets. Bob Jones, manager of Sales/Marketing, expressed interest in learning more about the Internet and exactly what could be done with it.

The two most negative comments came from Peter Browne and Les Coone. Peter Browne stated that the Fleet Maintenance Division is doing just fine as it is and that you should not to "try to fix something that isn't broken." Les Coone commented that you're "jumping the gun on video conferencing; it is too early to invest in that new technology."

Questions/Problems for the Next Day Air Service Case

President Coone has given you four tasks:

1. Review available groupware packages and Internet capabilities as they relate to NDAS and prepare a report on the ways e-mail and groupware can be integrated into the Fleet Maintenance Division. Convinced that the maintenance supervisor's support is required for a successful installation of data communications technology in the Fleet Maintenance Division, President Coone wants you to suggest how to involve Peter Browne. The president is sure that Peter Browne will be a valuable ally for a data communications system if you can show him that it will help him make his operation more productive and efficient.

2. Investigate the potential of software such as Lotus Notes for use in the Accounts Receivable Division. President Coone also wants you to determine how Jane Van Dyne and her staff could use Notes to reduce "bad debt" expenses. He wonders if Notes would be useful to John Lawson in the Accounts Payable Division and Bob Jones in Marketing and Sales as well.

3. Prepare a brief management summary on the essential aspects of the Internet and the World Wide Web, how they work, what they will cost, and above all, how NDAS can use them to improve its competitive edge. President Coone is particularly intrigued with the potential of the Internet, but he and the other members of management are not exactly sure what the Internet is and how it works. He is confused about the relationship between the World Wide Web, Internet, and the Information SuperHighway.

President Coone reminds you that NDAS expects to enlarge its scope in the international market. Plans call for first offerings to be services to Britain, France, and Germany, with later expansion to South America. President Coone has heard that a number of companies have "home pages." He is unclear about home pages and HTML and wants you to be sure to discuss them in your summary. He would also like some examples of home pages used by other companies that NDAS could examine. President Coone wants you to involve Bob Jones in your work on the Internet.

4.   Prepare a brief discussion of the pros and cons of video conferencing as well as the cost of using video conferencing within the NDAS organization. Based on Les Coone's comments, President Coone is skeptical of video conferencing and wonders if there are really any advantages to using it.

CHAPTER THREE

Background on Next Day Air Service

The Next Day Air Service managers were impressed with your response to the questions on groupware, e-mail, the Internet and video conferencing. You clarified the relationship between the Internet and the World Wide Web to their satisfaction. Bob Jones, head of the Sales and Marketing Division, has already formally requested your help in building a home page and inquiry/response system on the World Wide Web for NDAS.

He now wants you to examine how NDAS is using its voice telephone system and make recommendations on how the voice communication system should be overhauled. President Coone also wants NDAS management to improve the way it monitors and controls voice telephone usage at NDAS, especially cellular phone usage. Cellular phone usage and costs at NDAS have increased dramatically in the last two years.

First, President Coone wants to know the number of telephone calls made to all offices, the number of voice and facsimile messages sent and received, the number of fax transmissions, the cost of all telephone equipment, and the average monthly percentage of local and long distance calls and other telephone services.

After a brief discussion, you agree that three months of itemized charges should be adequate to support your analysis. In addition, you agree to survey the branch offices about the type and quality of telecommunication equipment already in place. This information will help you determine whether it will be easy to integrate such equipment into a future communication network.

Figure A3-1 contains a list of the Next Day Air Service offices, their current staffing levels, and the average number of calls made per day from each office. Figure A3-2 provides a detailed breakdown of the daily calls made between offices and customers. In Figure A3-2, the boxes in which the same city's column and row intersect (that is, Miami-Miami) reflect the number of local calls made from the office to customers concerning their inquiries.

Office	Current Staffing	Average Number of Calls per Day
Atlanta	25	282
Chicago	2	124
Dallas	17	177
Denver	1	50
Houston	4	162
Jackson	4	114
Jacksonville	6	196
Los Angeles	1	41
Memphis	12	216
Miami	19	216
Montgomery	4	94
New Orleans	16	206
Orlando	21	214
St. Louis	2	58
Tampa	148	361
Washington, D.C.	3	33

Figure A3-1   Office list for Next Day Air Service.

Each office receives both local and long distance calls throughout the day. These calls relate to the status of packages, pickups, deliveries, payroll, and personnel. At present, telephone messages are carried by hand and placed on the appropriate person's desk. These handwritten messages sometimes are difficult to read, and they often get lost.

Most offices have one or two telephone circuits from which to make and receive calls. Only the large offices—Tampa, Miami, Orlando, Atlanta, Dallas, Memphis, and New Orleans—have more than two circuits for voice calls. Each office has a facsimile machine with its own circuit. These fax machines have been acquired over several years, which has resulted in a hodgepodge of makes and models. Local telephone companies, such as Bell South, provide the local telephone service. A variety of common carriers, including AT&T, MCI, and US Sprint, provide long distance and cellular services.

President Coone also needs a recommendation on whether to switch to a voice mail system. You must discuss the various functions that should be included in a voice mail

Origin \ Destination	Atlanta	Chicago	Dallas	Denver	Houston	Jackson	Jacksonville	Los Angeles	Memphis	Miami	Montgomery	New Orleans	Orlando	St. Louis	Tampa	Washington
Atlanta	55	13	16	4	12	11	21	3	18	30	8	21	27	4	35	4
Chicago	13	12	6	–	4	2	12	–	21	11	2	8	13	–	20	–
Dallas	16	6	25	7	35	7	11	9	17	3	2	16	4	2	16	1
Denver	4	–	7	8	6	1	3	–	7	2	1	3	2	–	6	–
Houston	12	4	35	6	21	4	7	3	11	4	2	18	7	5	21	2
Jackson	11	2	7	1	4	15	3	1	18	2	7	21	4	1	16	1
Jacksonville	21	12	11	3	7	3	28	2	4	26	3	7	33	2	31	3
Los Angeles	3	–	9	–	3	1	2	4	1	4	1	2	4	–	7	–
Memphis	18	21	17	7	11	18	4	1	31	12	9	17	8	8	21	3
Miami	30	11	3	2	4	2	26	4	12	42	7	13	21	6	31	2
Montgomery	8	2	2	1	2	7	3	1	9	7	17	12	7	2	13	1
New Orleans	21	8	16	3	18	21	7	2	17	13	12	32	8	6	21	1
Orlando	27	13	4	2	7	4	33	4	8	21	7	8	37	2	35	2
St. Louis	4	–	2	–	5	1	2	–	8	6	2	6	2	9	11	–
Tampa	35	20	16	6	21	16	31	7	21	31	13	21	35	11	70	7
Washington	4	–	1	–	2	1	3	–	3	2	1	1	2	–	7	6

Figure A3-2 Average number of calls per day between Next Day Air Service offices. Assume that ten percent of the total calls by city are facsimile transmissions. Note that this chart reflects the average number of incoming *and* outgoing calls per office per day. To keep calculations simple, assume that each office has the same number of inbound and outbound calls per day. For example, the Atlanta-Miami connection experiences 30 long distance calls per day. Half of these calls are from Atlanta to Miami, and the other half are from Miami to Atlanta.

system and the training NDAS that personnel will need. Again, be prepared to document your information sources, and be able to defend your recommended plan.

Questions/Problems for the Next Day Air Service Case

1. What information is needed to begin planning a voice communication network? What basic communication facilities and features should you include in a plan for an integrated data and voice communication network? Consider integrating both store and forward switching and facsimile processing.

2. Evaluate whether one large centralized Private Branch Exchange (PBX) should be used as a control center for the voice network or whether several small PBXs would create a more durable system in the event of a general network failure. Include a recommended location for any suggested PBXs.

3. Recommend whether to switch voice and data through the same PBX (to have separate voice and data PBX switches) or to use some other technique for voice and data switching.

4. How could audiotex, IVR, automated attendant, and voice mail be used at Next Day Air Service? Provide specific examples.

5. Compute the approximate number of trunk lines (circuits) needed at each location to accommodate the average number of daily calls (see Figure A3-1). Assume that the average time to complete either an inbound or an outbound call is five minutes. Round out to the nearest whole number, and assume an eight-hour day (480 minutes). Add one circuit to accommodate the FAX machine.

6. Using Figure A3-2, calculate the percentage of calls made between Next Day Air Service locations (long distance) and local calls within the same city (Atlanta to Atlanta).

7. Prepare a draft of a report that can be generated monthly from data collected by a call-accounting package, to allow NDAS management to monitor and control telephone usage.

8. Prepare a list of suggestions that will help NDAS staff reduce or make more efficient use of cellular telephone calls.

CHAPTER FOUR

Background on Next Day Air Service

You have presented to President Coone your preliminary report on the steps required to bring Next Day Air Service to a competitive position with respect to data and voice communications. He supports your recommendation that Next Day Air Service would benefit from an organization-wide multiapplication network that would integrate word processing, electronic mail and voice mail, document and package tracking, billing, and payroll. The board of directors was also pleased with the whole network concept. The board members were a little more skeptical about your recommendations that local area networks should be set up at every NDAS office, but they were willing to go along with your recommendation at most NDAS sites.

President Coone now has asked you to start planning for that integrated corporate network. Ultimately, this network will link all the offices with Tampa and become the foundation on which to build a sophisticated data, voice, and image communication network that includes local area networks (LANs) at most NDAS sites. President Coone is still not completely convinced that NDAS needs image capabilities, but he wants you to include that potential in your plan.

As a first step, President Coone wants you to examine the current information flow within NDAS and to make recommendations on how to reduce circuit costs. You are considering the possibility of acquiring either multiplexers or a concentrator. Multiplexer pairs offer the advantage of sending multiple transactions over a single circuit. On the other hand, a concentrator is a stand-alone device that could support line consolidation and provide auxiliary storage for store and forward transmissions.

President Coone reminds you that NDAS has downsized from minicomputers to desktop computers at a considerable saving. He does not want to "move backwards." He also wants a state-of-the-art but cost-effective package tracking system, "like the big kids in the business." He believes that such a tracking system is imperative if NDAS is to remain competitive.

Questions/Problems for the Next Day Air Service Case

1. What two cities appear to be the best locations for multiplexers in the NDAS communication network? Use the map in Figure A1-1.

2. What offices would you link to the multiplexers in the two cities identified in Question 1? Justify your answer.

3. How would you link the cities if there were multiplexers located in Orlando, New Orleans, Dallas, and Atlanta?

4. Are there any special-purpose terminals that can be valuable to NDAS in improving productivity with package tracking and dispatching? Examine the way Dispatch processes its work (as presented in Chapter 1), and make suggestions based on your review.

5. President Coone wonders if it might be cost-effective to use a wireless connection from the company vehicle parking guardhouse to the main office building. Investigate the use and cost of wireless communication media, including infrared, microwave, and radio. Explain whether such a connection would be cost-effective in this application.

CHAPTER FIVE

Background on Next Day Air Service

President Coone appreciated your excellent suggestions, and has asked you to continue planning for the integrated corporate NDAS network. Ultimately, this network will link all the offices with Tampa and become the foundation on which to build a sophisticated data, voice, and image communication network that includes local area networks (LANs) at most NDAS sites. President Coone is still not completely convinced that NDAS needs image capabilities, but he wants you to include that potential in your plan.

As a first step, President Coone wants you to examine the current information flow within NDAS. Figure A5-1 shows the movement of invoice information. In reality, it shows the number of packages that are transferred between offices, but each package also requires an invoice. These averages were compiled from a two-week survey of each office. The average length of each invoice is 750 characters. Use this statistic as the basis for your computations.

Inbound

Origin / Destination	Atlanta	Chicago	Dallas	Denver	Houston	Jackson	Jacksonville	Los Angeles	Memphis	Miami	Montgomery	New Orleans	Orlando	St. Louis	Tampa	Washington	Avg total pkgs/Day
Atlanta	50	40	35	15	32	10	25	10	20	30	12	25	20	12	45	40	421
Chicago	30	N/A	40	N/A	10	5	10	N/A	20	40	7	25	30	N/A	35	N/A	252
Dallas	25	30	80	35	45	5	15	70	30	25	5	30	15	25	30	25	490
Denver	20	N/A	30	N/A	15	3	2	N/A	3	15	2	13	4	N/A	8	N/A	115
Houston	15	7	45	7	N/A	2	8	7	13	12	2	23	17	12	30	1	201
Jackson	11	N/A	12	6	12	N/A	3	N/A	22	4	3	34	11	7	21	N/A	146
Jacksonville	13	7	13	1	8	2	N/A	3	7	20	3	5	20	1	35	3	141
Los Angeles	15	N/A	7	N/A	8	N/A	2	N/A	15	15	N/A	3	1	N/A	11	N/A	77
Memphis	16	4	13	2	7	9	3	8	70	11	4	9	2	21	6	2	187
Miami	33	5	7	2	3	1	16	2	4	110	2	21	26	1	45	3	281
Montgomery	8	1	6	N/A	4	3	2	N/A	2	3	N/A	9	2	1	3	1	45
New Orleans	12	7	16	1	12	6	3	2	7	3	6	100	8	2	25	2	212
Orlando	27	7	12	3	6	2	23	1	3	31	4	11	95	2	45	3	275
St. Louis	14	N/A	7	N/A	6	2	2	N/A	31	4	2	21	4	N/A	6	N/A	99
Tampa	55	11	13	4	8	3	22	3	7	31	3	17	43	6	90	3	319
Washington	21	N/A	2	N/A	3	N/A	7	N/A	2	4	1	3	2	N/A	4	N/A	49

Total   3310

Figure A5-1   Daily invoice (package) traffic for Next Day Air Service.

Every number in the figure represents the number of packages (each of which requires an invoice) that move from the city of origin to a destination city for delivery in the latter city's delivery zone. Local deliveries are indicated in situations in which the origins and destinations are the same. For example, the intersection of the Atlanta column and the Atlanta row shows 50 local deliveries.

Invoice information is transmitted from the origin to the destination. In addition, a copy of all invoice information is transmitted to the home office in Tampa for billing. For example, every day Los Angeles ships 15 packages to Memphis, and each one requires an invoice. This means that Los Angeles will transmit fifteen 750-character invoices to *both* Memphis and Tampa, every day.

Questions/Problems for the Next Day Air Service Case

1. President Coone is baffled about how digital information from a computer can be sent over a telephone line. Prepare a brief position paper for management explaining the way information is transferred from one computer to another over telephone lines. Keep it simple. Be sure to describe the types of modems used in data transmission over telephone circuits. Include comments on the role of data compression in increasing transmission rates. Justify the observation

that as a general rule, it is best to purchase the fastest modem your communications lines can support.

2. Compute each office's number of bits sent per day (origin to destination) based on the data provided in Figure A5-1. Use ten bits per character to keep computations simple, and assume all transmissions are error free. *Hint:* Bits per day = Packages $\times$ 750 $\times$ 10 $\times$ 2.

3. How many minutes will it take for each city's modem to transmit its invoices? Use the bits per day calculated in Question 2, and assume that the installed modems transmit at only 2400 bits per second.

4. Assume there is only one inbound circuit leading to Atlanta. Determine the appropriate minimum modem transmission speed in bits per second, based on the inbound traffic to Atlanta. In this problem, assume the following conditions:
   a. The peak load is twice the bits per day average transmission load.
   b. Ten percent of the transmissions require retransmission because of errors.
   c. There is a need for fifty percent growth.
   d. All transmissions are to be accomplished in a six-hour workday.

5. In Question 3, you calculated the transmission time in minutes per day, based on a 2400 bits-per-second modem and ten bits per character. Now calculate the "file transfer time" for Atlanta to transmit all of its invoices to Tampa at the end of the workday. Why is this answer different from the time calculated for Atlanta in Question 3?

6. Could all the NDAS offices transmit their invoices to Tampa between 5:00 P.M. and 6:00 P.M. each evening? President Coone is willing to consider upgrading to 14,400 modems, using data compression techniques, or applying both options to achieve this goal. Will these faster modems be needed? Justify your answer.

CHAPTER SIX

Background on Next Day Air Service

The Next Day Air Service board of directors reviewed your recommendations for improving communications circuits at NDAS. The board agreed that NDAS will centralize communications along two major data links (Atlanta to Tampa and New Orleans to Tampa, as shown in Figure A6-1. Both Atlanta and New Orleans have multiplexers. Although you recommended a different approach and the purchase of additional multiplexers, the board of directors would not approve further outlays at this time. You hear a rumor that Les Coone suggested to several board members that developments in data communication, such as Integrated Services Digital Network (ISDN), might make added multiplexers obsolete before they could pay for themselves and that these conservative board members vetoed the funding for the additional circuits and multiplexers.

As you continue to work on the network plan, you perceive that you are becoming

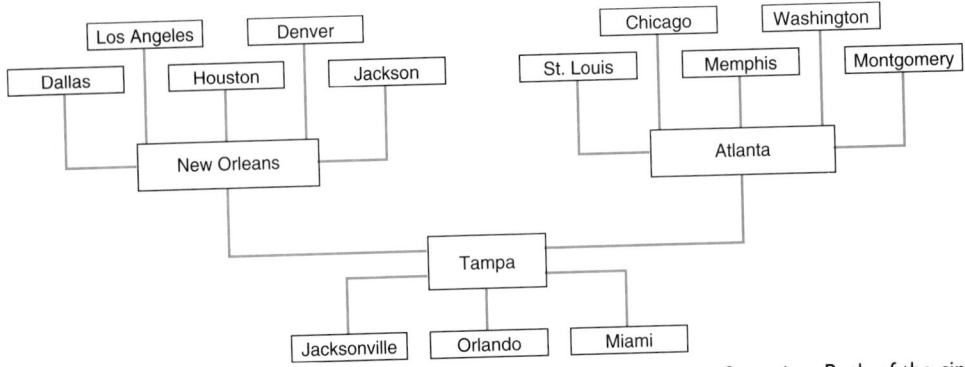

Figure A6-1   Next Day Air Service's communication network circuit configuration. Both of the circuits from New Orleans and Atlanta to Tampa are 56,000 bits per second leased circuits. All other circuits from the branch offices to the New Orleans, Atlanta, and Tampa hubs are considered capable of supporting 14,400 bits per second V.32 modems.

much more involved with the firm's strategic planning initiatives and survival. You realize that NDAS will become dependent on its communication facilities for its very existence. In other words, the communication systems at NDAS are the foundation for the firm's mission-critical applications.

You are burdened with all sorts of thoughts about potential problems and possible errors that can threaten Next Day Air Service's communication capabilities. For example, you worry about recent major circuit and switch outages experienced by some of the leading common carriers. You recognize the fact that even though your operations were affected only slightly by these outages, someday NDAS could undergo a costly disruption of its communication network.

You do not view such a situation as a major competitive threat, because Next Day Air Service's principal competitors have similar networks, and all the parcel delivery services would be paralyzed in the event of a disastrous outage. You do, however, want to examine sources of errors in networks and find reasonable error control mechanisms that will provide NDAS with a competitive edge. For example, are there specialized techniques that can be used for error detection and correction in NDAS communication networks? You decide to research these possibilities further and add this project to your ever-growing list of "things to do."

For now, you have been asked to explore the feasibility of integrating both data and voice traffic onto a single transmission circuit. You must determine whether this is a viable option. In order to make this decision, you want to examine the current transmission circuits and assess their ability to handle the anticipated workload.

Questions/Problems for the Next Day Air Service Case

1. Calculate the TRIB for the 14,400 bits per second circuits in the Next Day Air Service network shown in Figure A6-1. Assume an average of 1600 characters per message, with a one percent probability of an erroneous transmission. The modems transmit with a 0.2 second turnaround delay. The transmissions use

an eight-bit ASCII code. The transmission using 14,400 bits per second modems use one start bit and one stop bit, and each message block has ten control characters, for further error checking. Assume that the data is sent synchronously over the 28,800 bits-per-second circuits, using a 1600-character block, but that each block has fifty-five control characters. Consider the transmission load data for NDAS provided in the case study for Chapter 5. Are these TRIB ratings adequate?

2. If the workload increases by fifty percent over the next year, will the existing transmission circuits meet the anticipated need? If not, would it be worthwhile to attempt to upgrade the dial-up circuits to higher speeds for the use of V.34 modems? What do you recommend? As always, be prepared to defend your position.

3. What happens to TRIB if the reliability is down to 9600 bits per second for modem transmission? Why is this a potential problem with V.32 modem networks?

4. What file transfer protocols would you recommend? Be prepared to support your recommendations.

5. Prepare a brief position paper on the types of errors you can expect in the NDAS network and the steps you believe NDAS can take to prevent, detect, and correct these errors.

CHAPTER SEVEN

Background on Next Day Air Service

As you continue to work on the data communications network plans for NDAS, you realize that it is imperative for you to gain a broader base of management and staff support for the new network and for the additional investment in information technology.

Many of the board members and staff at NDAS have little or no understanding of data communications and are therefore unwilling to support or fund developments in this area. You discuss this matter with Bob Jones, who has become one of your major backers since you helped him with the Internet and the World Wide Web. NDAS's home page and inquiry/response system on the Internet is now considered an industry model. Bob Jones suggests a training session on data communications basics for management and staff. The training should not be too technical, but enough so that management and staff can understand and appreciate just what occurs, what equipment is needed, what is important, how much it will cost, and how to be sure it is working properly. He is also confused about the TCP/IP protocol used on the Internet and hopes you will clarify that for him in the training session. He reminds you that your position paper on how computer data are transferred over telephone lines was well received by President Coone and NDAS top management. "Use that approach," he suggests.

You bring the idea of a training session up with President Coone. He is elated, but he wants you to consider a series rather than a single session. The initial training topic will be network concepts. President Coone confesses that the concept of a network is a mystery to him. He schedules the first session for next Tuesday, just before the monthly management meeting. You will have thirty minutes.

It is clear that you have a great deal riding on this session. It will be your first contact with several key top and middle managers. If the session is a success, it will be much easier for you to get their support. You call Bob Jones to thank him for suggesting a training session. Bob recommends that you use a presentation software package like Microsoft's PowerPoint to prepare bullet charts as the basis for the presentation. You must start work on your preparations immediately.

Questions/Problems for the Next Day Air Service Case

1. Review the topics in Chapter 7 on the network layer. Prepare an agenda for your training session. The agenda should be an outline, showing topics and subtopics with enough detail to allow the reader to follow. Remember Bob Jones' advice on what the management and staff will want and expect from your session.

2. One of the points you intend to make in the training session is the difference between LANs and wide area networks (WANs). Using NDAS examples, prepare a set of charts to show management the difference between the two types of networks. Be sure to include an illustration of the different network topologies and routings.

3. Bob Jones calls to warn you that the new manager of International Services, Sally Wong, will be present at the training session. She wants to be sure any new data communications system will be able to handle international messaging. Bob suggests that you include material in the session on how adherence to standards can ensure smooth integration of the NDAS data communication with overseas systems. You agree. Present a review of standards and standardizing groups for data communications. Which standards do you consider most important for NDAS? Be prepared to defend your view.

4. Bob Jones also reminds you that he needs a straightforward, simple, and understandable explanation of the Internet TCP/IP protocol. Prepare a bullet chart that describes the key concepts of TCP/IP.

5. You have just finished your preparations when President Coone's secretary calls to tell you that IBM sales representatives have asked President Coone for an appointment to discuss SNA and how it can be used at NDAS. Because IBM is a valued customer of NDAS, President Coone feels he must pay attention to their request. However, he wants you to send him a brief memo covering the "highlights" of SNA before he responds to IBM. Prepare the memo, and include your observations of SNA's importance in the development of a data communications system at NDAS.

CHAPTER EIGHT

Background on Next Day Air Service

Your management training session was a big success. All attendees indicated that they enjoyed and profited from the material you presented. Sally Wong has now become one of your strongest backers. She is excited about including a LAN as a key element of her new department. She wants you to assist her in developing a plan and proposal for a departmental LAN. You see this as an opportunity to build a model LAN within NDAS. You can start from the beginning with new equipment and procedures. Sally Wong is very well respected in the company. NDAS is committed to moving strongly into the international arena. A successful LAN (or for that matter, an unsuccessful one) in her department will get a great deal of attention at NDAS. Despite your heavy workload, you agree to work with Sally on this project.

Now you need to revisit the issue of LAN protocols and configurations so that you can make a final recommendation. You also need to consider the operational and managerial procedures that will have to be adopted to ensure successful operation of the department LAN.

The type of LAN should be analyzed carefully in view of its scope, configuration, and protocols and in terms of the methods by which users will be accessing the data. You realize that internetworking will become more important as the LAN and its utilization increases.

Sally Wong is even more interested in learning how to manage the LAN. Investigate what should be managed and how such management should be enacted. For example, who should be responsible for the creation and maintenance of the various corporate files that will be stored on the server? Will it be necessary to hire a separate database administrator, or should this responsibility be integrated with other work duties? How will the procurement or development of new software applications be handled? Should there be one central office that controls and standardizes all acquisitions for LAN use, or should each user assume such responsibility? Then there is the area of network and equipment maintenance to consider. In a multivendor environment, such as the one at NDAS, this can be touchy. Finally, you are aware that the topic of end user application development has been receiving quite a bit of attention. Because LAN management is so closely related to the kinds of applications users want to execute on a network, it seems worthwhile to consider incorporating end user application development efforts within the framework of LAN management.

Other issues that need to be considered at this time include the LAN's cabling, installation, security, and anticipated growth need to be addressed, as well as access: who or which remote offices can access the LAN. And, of course, there are cost considerations.

Sally is excited about starting off with a LAN in her department. She has told you that her group will be using specialized software and creating a departmental database of customers and vendors. The group will initially consist of eight people but is expected to grow rapidly to twice that number. Sally is already interviewing people, and most of them have experience using LANs. The best candidates expect that there will be data communications support at their new job.

However, Sally is concerned that President Coone may take a wait-and-see attitude about a department LAN. She remembered your comments about not getting those added multiplexers you recommended. She wants a well-thought-out LAN proposal for President Coone.

Questions/Problems for the Next Day Air Service Case

1. Which is best for the International Service department, a high-end full network, a low-end DOS-based peer-to-peer LAN, or a zero-slot sub-LAN? Explain your choice.

2. Draw a configuration for a star, bus, and ring topology for the LAN. Now you must decide which LAN would be best for NDAS: Ethernet (10Base2 or 10Base-T) token bus, or token ring. Which do you recommend? Justify your recommendation with three to five reasons.

3. Which do you think would be the most costly items in the LAN?

4. Sally Wong has heard "horror stories" about LAN bottlenecks. Prepare a brief discussion of LAN bottlenecks and what can be done to improve LAN performance.

5. What safeguards do you recommend for NDAS to control illegal copies of software on the LANs?

CHAPTER NINE

Background on Next Day Air Service

The work on installing the International Service department LAN went very well. Mr Coone has authorized Sally Wong's and your recommendations. The department will be built around LAN support from the very start. Some management issues have yet to be decided, but they can wait a bit. For now, President Coone and the board of directors are focusing on the kinds of communication facilities NDAS will need over the next several years. Recall that the current WAN uses dial-up to connect the remote offices to Atlanta and New Orleans and private leased circuits to connect these two hubs to Tampa.

President Coone meets with you to discuss the future of communications for Next Day Air Service. He believes that NDAS needs a network that can be expanded readily without having a major impact on the way the company conducts its routine business. He assumes that NDAS will continue its rapid growth pattern, and he wants a recommendation on what steps may be necessary to enable NDAS to meet the competition. Next Day Air Service considers the Mississippi River as the East/West dividing line for the continental United States. The projected growth trends are as follows:

Western United States: Traffic volumes will increase by 400 percent over the next three years, and one additional office will be opened every four months.

Eastern United States: Traffic volumes will increase by 300 percent over the next three years, and one additional office will be opened every six months.

International Market: Traffic volumes will increase by 100 percent each year over the next three years, and additional offices will be opened in London, Paris, Rome, Berlin, Madrid, Bogotá, and Caracas.

Questions/Problems for the Next Day Air Service Case

1. With your knowledge of NDAS's network, what methods would you recommend for the future to connect the remote offices to the hubs at Atlanta and New Orleans and the hubs to the corporate office in Tampa? Will the current facilities be adequate?

2. What specific voice service should NDAS acquire for customer inquiries concerning parcel deliveries?

3. The offices using modems to dial up the multiplexer in New Orleans have been reporting problems with garbled screens. You suspect a problem of circuit distortion. What do you suggest to remedy this situation?

4. Based on your recommendation, Atlanta has just received permission to install a local area network. Atlanta also wants to have access to LANs located in Tampa. What type of service is aimed specifically at switched LAN interconnections?

5. How could NDAS combine toll-free 800 number service (WATS) with interactive voice response (IVR) to better serve its customers?

6. What impact will ISDN have on NDAS's domestic WAN and international communications?

7. President Coone has just informed you that NDAS is considering placing several new offices in Chicago and Los Angeles. Each office would have its own LAN. What factors would determine the use of a metropolitan area network (MAN) to connect NDAS offices in a single city together?

CHAPTER TEN

Background on Next Day Air Service

There are now several functioning LANs at NDAS Tampa headquarters. The International Service department's LAN has turned out even better than expected. The staff of the new department is happy and productive. Sally Wong, the department head, is singing your praises all over the company. In addition, the Atlanta LAN has been installed and is operating successfully.

President Coone says he is getting requests for LANs "from all over the place, even from Peter Browne, of the Fleet Maintenance Division!" You notice that he seems to be a bit upset over this situation. He says that Les Coone, now manager of the Information Service department (no longer "acting") has complained that things are "getting out of control." Instead of a planned, orderly movement to an integrated NDAS data communications network, everyone wants to move their departments to their own LANs, all at once. President Coone did meet with the IBM representatives to talk about SNA. They stressed that SNA would "ensure interoperability of NDAS internal networks." He wants to be sure that all the current LANs will "interoperate." You point out to President Coone that the NDAS Backbone Network is designed to allow all the company's LANs to share information and data. President Coone does not seem to be listening.

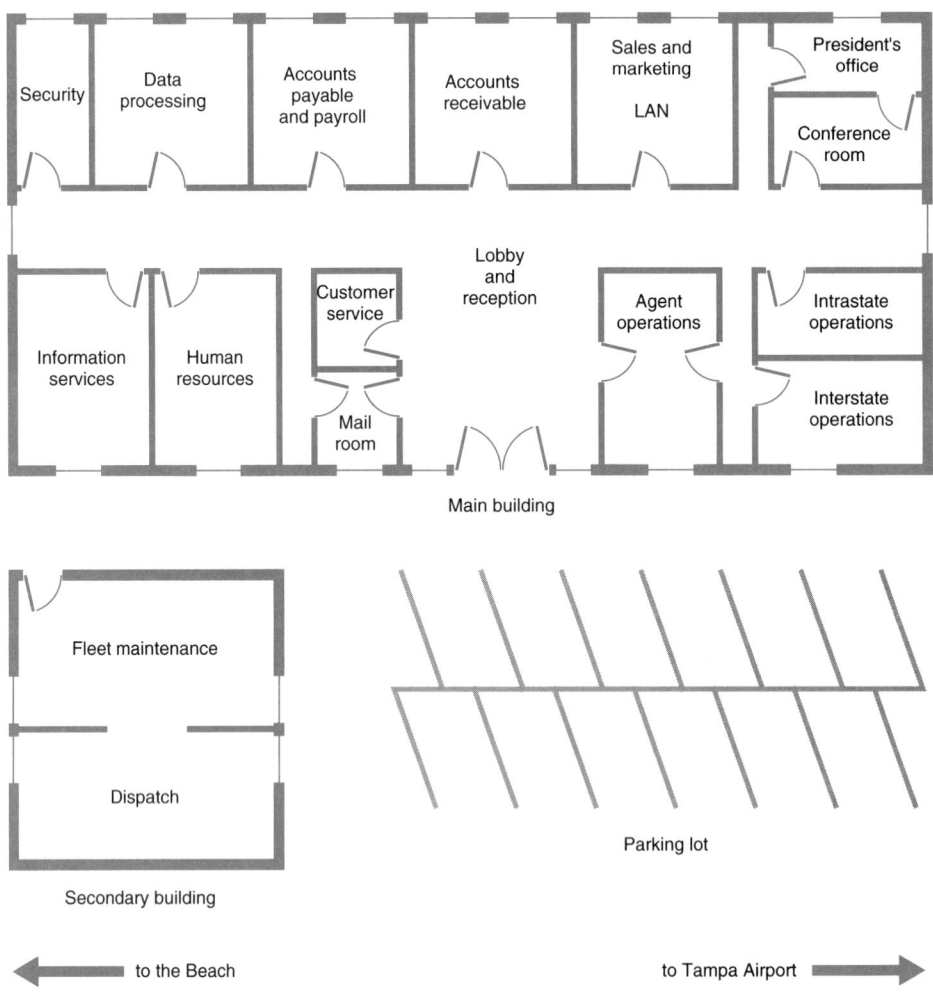

Figure A10-1   Facility map of the Next Day Air Service headquarters.

It is clear that President Coone is worried. Although he did not say it, he implied that things are getting out of control *in your area*—data communications. And it was, in a way, your fault for encouraging Sally Wong, Atlanta, and even Peter Browne to ask President Coone for their own LANs.

You talk to Bob Jones about the problem. He says that you don't want to get President Coone upset with you. He suggests that the best thing to do is to show President Coone that the system will "talk together" and you have everything under control. You resolve to do this immediately, and you set up an appointment with President Coone.

Questions/Problems for the Next Day Air Service Case

1. Prepare a brief description of a Backbone Network for President Coone. Indicate what components and equipment are required to connect the various company LANs together.

2. Point out the determining factors in your recommended choice of a Backbone Network for NDAS. Refer to the information on NDAS data communications usage and the expected growth of the company in justifying your choice of a Backbone Network technology.

3. Figure A10-1 shows a facility map of the NDAS headquarters. Assume that there are LANs in each of the major department offices and at Fleet Maintenance and Dispatch in the Secondary Building. What type of Backbone Network do you recommend for NDAS headquarters? Be prepared to justify your recommendation.

3. What are the problems in connecting the NDAS headquarters LANs with traditional Backbone Networks? How can many of these problems be solved by using a Collapsed Backbone Network design? What problems still remain for NDAS with a Collapsed Backbone Network design, and how can they be overcome?

4. How should NDAS prepare for developments in Cellular Digital Packet Networks and Asynchronous Transfer Mode technology, so that these options can be integrated into the data communications system?

5. Indicate to President Coone how you will monitor the NDAS headquarters Backbone Network and what steps can be taken if NDAS needs to improve its performance.

CHAPTER ELEVEN

Background on Next Day Air Service

You believe that your upcoming meeting with President Coone is so important that you ask Sally Wong and Bob Jones to listen to your presentation and make comments. Bob Jones would like to hear your presentation, but he must go out on a sales call with President Coone to a very important client, Kanon Automotive. You review your material with Sally Wong. She likes it but thinks it may be a bit too technical for President Coone. She also recommends that you describe to President Coone the process you used to design NDAS networks so that he will have more confidence in your results and recommendation.

When you return to your desk, you see a message to call President Coone immediately. You take a deep breath and return the call. President Coone is very positive and friendly—almost a complete opposite of his mood the last time you saw him. He compliments you on the work you have done. He says that NDAS just closed a lucrative contract with Kanon Automotive, based on NDAS advanced information systems and package tracking technology. He believes that these advances were due primarily to your effort and the way you were able to get the rest of the organization involved with instituting the necessary system changes. "Keep it up," he says.

The president does, however, have one request. Mr. Juan Hernandez, President of Kanon Automotive, would like to have you come over, review the company's data communication facilities, and give him some advice on designing a new system. Of course, you would be delighted, you reply to President Coone. President Coone responds that his secretary will get back to you next week with the details on your visit to Kanon Automotive. And, by the way, please postpone that talk you scheduled with him. Since everything is "going fine," there is no need to meet. He is planning to leave for overseas shortly and would like to devote his attention to preparing for the trip.

No sooner do you hang up than Bob Jones calls. He is delighted and confides that the sales call to Kanon Automotive was a triumph. Mr. Hernandez, President of Kanon Automotive, commended the work being done at NDAS on package tracking. Mr Coone said you were responsible. Mr. Hernandez wondered if his data communication manager and system staff could "pick your brain" about techniques for designing a new system for Kanon. Bob Jones said President Coone was "pleased as punch."

Talk about being overwhelmed! Not only do you have your own work at NDAS, but now you are a visiting consultant to a key customer. You spend much of the weekend organizing your thoughts on network design techniques so that you will live up to the high expectations Kanon has for your visit.

Questions/Problems for the Next Day Air Service Case

1. President Coone's secretary calls the following Monday to confirm your visit to Kanon Automotive on Thursday. You are to meet in the office of Mr. Hernan-

dez, President of Kanon Automotive. President Coone wants a short memo covering the material you intend to discuss on network design. Prepare such a memo, limiting your discussion to the ten design steps to be performed in a network design effort. Be sure to include the deliverables for each step, and explain how management is involved in supervising the design process.

2. One of the keys to the success of your network designs at NDAS was the attention you paid to the user community. What advice would you give the designers at Kanon Automotive about their user community and how to involve them in network design, implementation, and use?

3. If you are using network design software, such as the Private Line Pricer (PLP), Network Optimizer (MIND-Data/PC), or AUTONET software, calculate the cost of a direct leased circuit between Houston and Miami, or any other circuit link in the NDAS data communication network. If you are interested in examining these design packages, see the Selected References section at the end of Chapter 11.

4. One of the principal network requirements is response time. How would you suggest that Kanon Automotive obtain data on response time for the network it is designing? Why is response time so important for real-world networks? How can you improve response time for an existing network at NDAS?

5. When you started at NDAS, a serious complaint leveled at the Information Services/Data Processing Division was that it had no idea of what data processing software or data communications equipment was used by the various departments of NDAS—or where in the organization the equipment was actually located. How will you advise the designers at Kanon Automotive to avoid these problems?

CHAPTER TWELVE

Background on Next Day Air Service

The NDAS network system is finally in place and operating. President Coone has assigned operational control of the network to the Information Services Department. He believes this is reasonable and justified because of the Information Services Department's data processing responsibilities and experience in operating data communications equipment. In addition, his nephew, Les Coone, is running that department and has expressed considerable interest in data communications.

The Human Resources Department originally set up the telephone system, because—at the time—no one else was interested in doing it. As a result, Human Resources, headed by Karen Lott, controls the voice and facsimile communication system for the company.

One recurring problem is that two department heads disagree on which department should be responsible for dealing with the common carriers. Each department believes it should be the contact for dealing with the common carriers, and each thinks the other is stopping it from assuming its rightful place within the organization.

Because of your excellent past performance, President Coone has asked you to study certain organizational issues pertaining to the control and operation of both voice and data communications. He wants you to analyze the operations of both departments and propose a method for streamlining the organization and fixing the problem. This analysis should address the possibility of combining the voice and data communication responsibilities under a single manager. You may propose any reorganization that seems appropriate. Be sure to consider economies of scale when submitting any recommendations. President Coone reminds you that you were a staunch advocate of video conferencing. He wants you to include video and image transmission considerations in your analysis.

You should also consider the type of individual that should manage this reorganization. Some of the factors to evaluate are the traits and characteristics needed for successful leadership, the ability to understand current systems, the ability to handle both data and voice networks, and the ability to analyze and manage future growth. The results of this evaluation will help determine whether such an individual exists within Next Day Air Service or whether the firm needs to hire someone from outside the organization.

Another little problem occurred last week when NDAS experienced its first network line failure. President Coone had to ask Karen Lott to determine what failed on the circuit. After fiddling with the problem for an hour and a half, she finally called the modem vendor, who then took three hours to get to the Tampa headquarters building. The good news is that the vendor's maintenance employee swapped a new circuit card into the failed modem and had it fixed in 15 minutes. Needless to say, President Coone was not happy!

Questions/Problems for the Next Day Air Service Case

1. If the responsibilities for managing communications were to be consolidated into one department, which one would you choose, and why? Base your answer on your knowledge of the communication management responsibilities exercised by both the Human Resources and Information Services Departments.

2. Would it be worthwhile to combine voice, data, and image circuits into a single network? Consider the future of NDAS and how it relates to continued communication growth, particularly digital communication technologies.

3. Review the organization chart for NDAS, as shown in Figure A1-2, and then develop an organization chart that reflects a realignment of the responsibilities for communications. Show separate organizational entities for both data processing and communications.

4. Consider the pros and cons of creating a new communication manager position. Discuss the reasons why Next Day Air Service should promote someone from within the company to fill this new position. Now discuss the contrary reasons

why NDAS should hire someone from outside the organization for this position. Which position will you take? Why?

5. What was the MTTRepair on Next Day Air Service's first modem failure? Is this MTTRepair acceptable?

6. Sketch out a simple network management system for NDAS. What software and hardware support would you recommend? Be sure you can justify the information items collected and reported for this system, as well as your software and hardware recommendations.

CHAPTER THIRTEEN

Background on Next Day Air Service

The NDAS board of directors has become extremely security conscious lately. Reports in the newspapers, in magazines, and on TV about network break-ins and disruption of corporate operations by computer and network viruses have frightened them. Accordingly, President Coone has met with you again. He is concerned that Next Day Air Service's networks, which are increasingly vital to its operation, may become infected by one of these viruses or be compromised by a break-in. His first concern is how to prevent an infection, because it could shut down the network for hours or even days. President Coone was angry enough when the first equipment failure shut down one of the company's circuits for four hours and forty-five minutes. He certainly does not want to have that happen again, and neither do you. President Coone is also concerned about natural disasters. Although Tampa was not affected by either of the hurricanes that disrupted other cities in southern Florida, he wants to be sure NDAS has a plan to handle such emergencies.

You recognize that a complete security and control review is needed. As a result, you review the control spreadsheet methodology. Once the control spreadsheet is complete, you still have to address the cost, technical feasibility, and operational feasibility of any controls. The board of directors wants to prevent any apparently "excessive" threat by implementing either hardware or software controls. Of course, the board has to approve any controls before you implement them. Accordingly, you must be able to defend your security and disaster review and any resulting recommendations.

The board of directors has expressed concern that the common carriers and the Internet do not provide adequate error and security controls. President Coone has asked you to consult several common carriers to determine what level of error, physical security, and data security they provide for the local loops and central office. After investigating several common carriers, you compile the table in Figure A13-1, which profiles the transmission error rates, security measures, and costs of five common carriers.

Common Carrier	Trasmission Error Rates	Physical Security of Central Office	Security on Local Loop	Costs
Company A	1 in 500,000	Minimal	Adequate	Moderate
Company B	1 in 550,000	Adequate	Minimal	High
Company C	1 in 400,000	Very adequate	Adequate	Low
Company D	1 in 600,000	Minimal	Very adequate	High
Company E	1 in 450,000	Adequate	Adequate	Moderate

Figure A13-1   Common carrier choices

Now you must make a recommendation. You realize that it is possible to use more than one common carrier to provide a backup local loop if the security measures provided by a primary carrier are inadequate. These are very important factors when determining what security measures Next Day Air Service should incorporate in its security review.

Additional items that need to be investigated are circuit route diversification, service restoration guarantees, and alternative local loop carriers for backup and route diversity. It will require some research to determine what is available in your area.

President Coone's next concern is that the database management system on the network server has not been given the proper attention with regard to security. Therefore, he has asked you to determine what security measures are appropriate for the database server. You develop the following list of suggestions:

Threats / Components	Illegal Access	Errors and Omissions	Message Loss or Change	Disasters and Disruptions	Breach of Privacy	Fraud or Theft
Application or System Software Programs						
Host Computer or LAN Server						
Database Files						
Communication Circuits (IXC)						
Local Loops						
Modems						
Terminal Users (People)						
Microcomputers and Terminals						

Figure A13-2   Control Spreadsheet for the security review of Next Day Air Service's local area network.

	Password User ID	Restrict Read/Write/Create/Delete	Database Security Administrator	Call-back Security	Encryption	Server Disk Mirroring
Password User ID						
Restrict Read/Write/Create/Delete						
Database Security Administrator						
Call-back Security						
Encryption						
Server Disk Mirroring						

Figure A13-3 Comparison Risk Ranking Sheet for use in ranking the six security items for Next Day Air Service's local area network.

1. Restrict entry to the LAN based on a password and a user ID.

2. Restrict the user's limits, once in the database. For example, the ability to read, write, create, or delete files should be restricted to specified users.

3. Appoint a database administrator (DBA) who can grant or revoke security privileges, in order to control the security function.

4. Consider using call-back security devices to restrict unauthorized entry to the network.

5. Consider using data encryption. The data can be encrypted prior to storage on the disk and decrypted when it is read from the disk. This ensures that the data is useless to anyone who gains unauthorized access to the network.

6 Install disk mirroring on the server.

Identify the levels of access controls that are available, and evaluate their effectiveness. The database management system on the server must be adequately protected, because it is a valuable asset to Next Day Air Service.

Finally, President Coone and the board of directors want to be sure NDAS is ready in case of a natural or human-made disaster.

Questions/Problems for the Next Day Air Service Case

1. Which common carrier shown in Figure A13-1 provides the best error and security control? Which would you recommend? Explain your logic.

2. Use Figure A13-2 to build a control spreadsheet. Place in it the controls described in the LAN controls section of this text. Discuss any empty cells.

3. Use Figure A13-3 to risk-rank the six security items for the NDAS network. If only four can be installed because of time constraints, which four will you choose to install?

4. Examine the types of security available to protect NDAS's investment in its home page and inquiry response system on the Internet.

5. Prepare a short memo to the Information Service Department on the key elements to be considered in disaster planning.

CHAPTER FOURTEEN

Background on Next Day Air Service

Your security and disaster recommendations for the NDAS network system have been warmly received. Bob Jones and Sally Wong were both impressed with your comments on Internet security factors. Les Browne was quick to put into effect your recommendations on how to reduce the risk of network break-ins. The board of directors and President Coone have decided that you would be the ideal candidate for director of corporate communications—responsible for voice, data, and image communications throughout NDAS—and have made you an offer of that position.

The offer includes a sizable raise in salary. Your friends Bob Jones, Sally Wong, and Peter Browne urge you to accept the position immediately. You see a bit of a problem, however, because Les Coone, the manager of Information Services (and President Coone's nephew), is angling for the position as well. Note that Les Coone is no longer "acting" manager. You are giving the matter very serious thought. However, you also have something else to think about. Mr. Hernandez of Kanon Automotive has made you an offer to join that firm as Chief Systems Analyst. The salary and benefits package appears to be even better than the one offered by NDAS.

While all this is going on, another dilemma has come up. The Atlanta office has sent an urgent request to upgrade its LAN network operating system (NOS) from Novell 3.X to Novell 4.X and to send the Atlanta LAN manager to school to become a Novell Certified Network Engineer (CNE). It appears that there is a considerable amount of money involved in this upgrade and schooling request.

President Coone's motto is "don't mess with success, especially when it costs money." Because things are going well enough in Atlanta (as far as he is concerned), he does not believe any changes are warranted. But because you may be the new director of corporate communications, he has referred the question of the upgrade and schooling request to you. To complicate matters, Les Coone has heard about Atlanta's request through the company grapevine and sent a memo to President Coone recommending a switch to Microsoft's Windows NT in Atlanta. President Coone has forwarded the memo to you, along with Atlanta's original request.

Questions/Problems for the Next Day Air Service Case

1. President Coone really does not know what a NOS is. Prepare a brief summary of the functions and services performed by a NOS, and explain how it achieves these functions and services. As usual, keep it simple and not too technical. Be sure to clearly define the roles of a client and server, so President Coone can understand them.

2. Examine the features of Netware 3.X and 4.X, as outlined in the text chapter. Develop a comparison chart or table illustrating the major aspects of these two versions of Netware for President Coone. Indicate what, if any, new hardware may be needed to take full advantage of the upgrade from 3.X to 4.X.

3. Based on your knowledge of the use of LANs in NDAS, make a recommendation as to whether an upgrade to 4.X should be authorized for Atlanta. Are there any other locations in NDAS that would benefit from upgrading to Novell 4.X? If so, why?

4. Les Coone's memo recommended that Atlanta switch from Netware 3.X to Window's NT 3.1. Les listed three main points in the memo: (1) for the same number of stations on the network, Windows NT is less expensive; (2) the Atlanta office staff makes extensive use of Microsoft's Windows application software, so using Windows NT makes sense; and (3) "all NOSs offer the same features, anyway." Where can you get information to reply to Les Coone's statement about the comparative costs of Windows NT and Novell Netware 3.X and 4.X? Obtain that information and respond. Also include your comments as to

whether Windows application programs will run better with Windows NT than with Novell Netware. Finally, answer the claim that "all NOSs offer the same features, anyway."

5. You are intrigued by the idea of training the LAN manager in Atlanta to become a CNE. Atlanta's request states that becoming a Novell-certified Netware engineer requires taking a series of courses and passing a test. It also states that even after being initially certified, the individual must take follow-on courses and be retested to remain certified. Give President Coone your recommendation as to whether it is worthwhile to have a CNE in Atlanta and, for that matter, at other NDAS LAN sites. Be sure to include reasons for your answer. How can you find out more details about what is involved in becoming a CNE? Are there other levels of certification that would be valuable to NDAS? If so, include a brief discussion of them in your response to President Coone. Is this type of certification limited to Novell or are there certifications available for other data communication products? How do you go about finding that out? What do you think about certifying data communications professionals?

A

ACF   Advanced Communication Function. ACF is part of IBM's telecommunication access program called Network Control Program (NCP) that provides an interface with TCAM and VTAM. ACF also is part of the Systems Network Architecture concept.

ACK   An ASCII or EBCDIC code character indicating a positive acknowledgment that a message has been received correctly.

ACM   Association for Computing Machinery. The ACM is an association of computer professionals.

Acoustic Coupler   An older type of modem that permits use of a telephone handset as a connection to the public telephone network for data transmission.

Acronym   A word formed from the initial letters or groups of letters of words in a phrase. An example is the word *laser*, which means Light Amplification by Stimulated Emission of Radiation.

ACU   See **Automatic Calling Unit.**

ADCCP   Advanced Data Communication Control Procedure. Pronounced "add-cap." This is a bit-oriented data link control standard approved by ANSI.

ADCU   Association of Data Communications Users.

Address   1. A coded representation of the destination of data, or of its originating terminal. For example, multiple terminals on one communication circuit must each have a unique address.
2. Sometimes referred to as *called number.* The group of digits that make up a telephone number. For example, an address may consist of an area code, a central office, and a line number, such as 415-555-1212.
3. Source address or destination address.

ADMD   ADministrative Management Domain. The X.400 electronic mail standard defines public and private domains. Public domains are administered by public common carriers, and private domains correspond to corporate electronic mail systems. The part of the mail exchange administered by the public domain is called the administrative management domain.

ADU   See **Automatic Dialing Unit.**

AFIPS   American Federation of Information Processing Societies.

Agent   Intelligent agents are relatively simple software programs that perform management functions without human involvement. They use a knowledge base and/or learn from experience to make simple decisions.

ALOHA   A system using a "transmit at will" access method similar to CSMA/CD. The name comes from a method of telecommunications whereby signals are beamed at satellites when transmission is ready to go. If it gets through, fine; if it does not, then the sender tries again. The ALOHA method of transmission was used first by Hawaiians who had satellite dishes beaming at communication satellites over the equator. It also was used for communicating with dishes in other Pacific Basin countries.

Alternating Current (AC)   The electrical current used to power computers.

American National Standards Institute (ANSI)   The principal standards-setting body in the United States. ANSI is a nonprofit, nongovernmental organization supported by more than 1000 trade organizations, professional societies, and companies. It belongs to the Consultative Committee on International Telegraph and Telephone (CCITT) and the International Organization for Standardization (ISO).

American Standard Code for Information Interchange   See **ASCII.**

Amplifier   A device used to boost the strength of a signal. Amplifiers are spaced at intervals throughout the length of a communication circuit to increase the distance a signal can travel. See also *repeater.*

Amplitude Modulation   See **Modulation, Amplitude.**

Analog   Pertaining to representation by means of continuously variable quantity, such as varying frequencies. Physical quantities such as temperature are continuous variable and therefore are "analog."

Analog Signal   A signal in the form of a continuously varying quantity such as amplitude, which reflects variations in the loudness of the human voice.

Analog Transmission   Transmission of a continuously variable signal as opposed to a discrete on/off signal. The traditional way of transmitting a telephone or voice signal is analog.

ANI   See **Automatic Number Identification.**

Anonymous FTP   See **File Transfer Protocol.**

ANSI   See **American National Standards Institute.**

API   Application Program Interface. API is the way IBM links incompatible equipment for micro-to-mainframe links. API allows applications on microcomputers and mainframes to speak directly to each other at the application software level, even though the equipment is from different vendors.

APPC   Advanced Program-to-Program Communications. APPC is a part of IBM's Systems Network Architecture that provides peer-to-peer communications. It is a high level program interface that allows two application programs to communicate. Also called *LU 6.2* after its most important component.

AppleTalk   A set of communication protocols that defines networking for Apple computers. Rarely used today.

Application Level Control   Pertains to the control of a specific application to safeguard, restrict, or protect it. For example, controls are implemented into a payroll application to prevent theft of the organization's assets.

Archie   Archie allows you to search virtually all the publicly available anonymous FTP sites worldwide for specific files of interest.

Arcnet   Attached Resource Computing NETwork. A proprietary token-bus local area network developed by the Datapoint Corporation.

Area Code   A number assigned to the geographical subdivision or operating area to facilitate message and circuit switching. Called city code outside of the United States. See also **Numbering Plan Area.**

ARPANET   One of the early packet switching networks. ARPANET was developed by the U.S. Department of Defense Advanced Research Projects Agency. It was the predecessor of the Internet.

ARQ   Automatic Repeat reQuest. A system employing an error detecting code so conceived that any error initiates a repetition of the transmission of the incorrectly received message.

ASCII   American Standard Code for Information Interchange. Pronounced "ask'-ee." An eight-level code for data transfer adopted by the American National Standards Institute to achieve compatibility among data devices.

Asynchronous Transfer Mode (ATM)   A communication switch that handles interface speeds ranging from 25 million bits per second to 622 million bits per second. It multiplexes data streams onto the same backbone network by using cell relay techniques. ATM switches can handle multimedia traffic, such as data, graphics, voice, and video.

Asynchronous Transmission   Transmission in which each information character is individually synchronized, usually by start and stop bits. The gap between each character is not a fixed length. Compare with **Synchronous Transmission.**

AT&T Communications   The name of American Telephone and Telegraph (AT&T), reflecting its present emphasis on providing long distance communication services. AT&T is one of the oldest providers of communication equipment and circuits. It is commonly known as "Ma Bell" and was the parent organization of the various Bell Telephone companies before deregulation.

ATM   1. See **Asynchronous Transfer Mode.**
2. In banking, an automated teller machine.

Attenuation   As a signal travels through a circuit, it gradually attenuates, or loses power. Expressed in decibels, attenuation is the difference between the transmitted and received power caused by loss of signal strength through the equipment, communication circuits, or other devices.

Authentication   A security method of guaranteeing that a message is genuine, that it has arrived unaltered, and that it comes from the source indicated.

Automatic Calling Unit (ACU)   A device that permits a business machine to dial calls automatically.

Automatic Dialing Unit (ADU)   A device capable of automatically dialing digits.

Automatic Equalization   Adjusting a transmission circuit while sending data signals to reduce errors during transmission. Equalization is the process of reducing frequency and phase distortion of a circuit by introducing time differences to compensate for the difference in attenuation or time delay at the various frequencies of the transmission band.

Automatic Number Identification (ANI)   The process whereby a long distance common carrier provides its customers with a visual display of an incoming caller's telephone number.

Automatic Repeat reQuest   See **ARQ.**

B

Backbone Network (BN)   A large network to which many networks within an organization are connected. It usually is a network that interconnects all networks on a single site, but it can be larger if it connects all the organization's terminals, microcomputers, mainframes, local area networks, and other communication equipment.

BALUN   BALanced/UNbalanced. An impedance-matching device to connect balanced twisted pair cabling with unbalanced coaxial cable.

Bandwidth   The difference between the highest and lowest frequencies in a band. For example, a voice grade circuit has a 4000 hertz bandwidth. In common usage, bandwidth refers to circuit capacity; when people say they need more bandwidth, they need a higher transmission speed.

Bandwidth-on-Demand   The ability to add more circuit capacity automatically and as needed. Instead of having several fractional T-1 circuits, an organization can have one T-1 circuit and use inverse multiplexers to dedicate some of the circuits to switched 56,000 bits per second usage. As one 56 Kbps circuit fills to capacity, a second one is brought into service automatically for the next message transmission. See also **Digital Cross-Connect Switch.**

Baseband Signaling   Transmission of a signal in its original form, not changed by modulation. It is a digital signal and is usually direct electrical voltages.

Basic Rate Interface   In ISDN, two 64,000 bits per second B circuits for data transmission and one 16,000 bits per second D circuit for signaling (2 B+D). See also **Primary Rate Interface.** Also called basic rate access.

Baud   Unit of signaling speed. The speed in baud is the number of signal elements per second. If each signal represents only one bit, *baud* is the same as *bits per second.* When each signal contains more than one bit, *baud* does not equal *bits per second.*

BCC   See **Block Check Character.**

Bellcore   The short name for Bell Communications Research, which is a research organization formed by the seven Bell operating companies after the divestiture of AT&T. AT&T's research organization is the Bell Laboratories.

Bell Operating Company   See **RBOC.**

BER   Bit-Error Rate. The number of bits received in error divided by the total number of bits received. An indicator of circuit quality.

BERT   Bit-Error Rate Testing. Testing a data line with a pattern of bits that are compared before and after the transmission to detect errors.

Binary   A number system using only the two symbols zero and one, which is especially well adapted to computer usage because 0 and 1 can be represented as "on" and "off," or as negative charges and positive charges. The binary digits appear in strings of 0's and 1's.

Binary Synchronous Communications (BSC or bisync)   A half duplex, character-oriented synchronous data communication protocol devised by IBM in the early 1960s. Not used very often today.

Bipolar Transmission A method of digital transmission in which binary zero is sent as a negative pulse and binary one is sent as a positive pulse.

BISYNC See **BInary SYNChronous communications transmission.**

Bit 1. An abbreviation of the term *binary digit.*
2. A single pulse in a group of pulses.
3. A unit of information capacity.

Bit-Error Rate See **BER.**

Bit-Error Rate Testing See **BERT.**

Bit Rate The rate at which bits are transmitted over a communication path. Normally expressed in bits per second (bps). The bit rate should not be confused with the data signaling rate (*baud*), which measures the rate of signal changes being transmitted. See also **bps.**

Bit Stream A continuous series of bits being transmitted on a transmission line.

BKER Block-Error Rate. The number of blocks received in error divided by the total number of blocks received.

BKERT Block-Error Rate Testing. Testing a data link with groups of information arranged into transmission blocks for error checking.

Block Sets of contiguous bits or bytes that make up a message, frame, or packet.

Block Check Character (BCC) The character(s) at the end of a Binary Synchronous Communications (BSC) message used to check for errors.

Block-Error Rate See **BKER.**

Block-Error Rate Testing See **BKERT.**

Blocking The inability of a PBX to grant service to a requesting user because the transmission circuit is not available. The term refers primarily to PBX switchboards and central office switches that lack the ability to provide circuits to all users at all times.

BN See **Backbone Network.**

BOC See **RBOC.**

Bonding Bonding (Bandwidth ON Demand Interoperatibility Networking Group) is an inverse multiplexing proposal for combining several 56 Kbps or 64 Kbps circuits into one higher speed circuit.

BPS Bits per second. The basic unit of data communication rate measurement. Usually refers to rate of information bits transmitted. Contrast with **Baud** and **Bit Rate.**

Bridge A device that connects two similar networks using the same data link and network protocols. Compare with **Gateway, Router,** and **Brouter.**

Broadband Circuit An analog communication circuit.

Broadband Ethernet The 10Broad36 version of Ethernet IEEE 802.3., meaning that it transmits at 10 million bits per second in broadband with a maximum distance of 3600 meters.

Broadcast Routing   See **Decentralized Routing.**

Brouter   A piece of hardware that combines the functions of a bridge and a router. See also **Bridge** and **Router.**

BSC   See **Binary Synchronous Communications.**

Buffer   A device used for the temporary storage of data, primarily to compensate for differences in data flow rates (for example, between a terminal and its transmission circuit), but also as a security measure to allow retransmission of data if an error is detected during transmission.

Bulletin Board System (BBS)   A dial-up electronic bulletin board in which anyone with a modem can participate.

Burst Error   A series of consecutive errors in data transmission. Refers to the phenomenon on communication circuits in which errors are highly prone to occurring in groups or clusters.

Bus   A transmission path or circuit. Typically an electrical connection with one or more conductors in which all attached devices receive all transmissions at the same time.

Byte   A small group of data bits that is handled as a unit. In most cases, it is an 8-bit byte and it is known as a *character.*

C

C Band   The frequency range from 4 to 6 GHz that is used for commercial satellite communications.

C Type Conditioning   A North American term for a type of conditioning that controls attenuation, distortion, and delay distortion so they fall within specified limits.

Call-back Modem   When a user calls a host computer, the modem disconnects the call after receiving the password and calls back to the caller's predefined telephone number to establish a connection.

Call Detail Recording (CDR)   A private branch exchange (PBX) feature to keep track of telephone call costs so they can be charged to the proper department. Also called *Station Message Detail Recording (SMDR).*

Call Management System   A system that monitors voice calls in organizations to keep track of call traffic and other factors relevant to voice communications.

Carrier   An analog signal at some fixed amplitude and frequency which then is combined with an information-bearing signal to produce an intelligent output signal suitable for transmission of meaningful information. Also called *carrier wave* or *carrier frequency.*

Carrier Frequency   The basic frequency or pulse repetition rate of a signal bearing no intelligence until it is modulated by another signal that does impart intelligence.

Carrier Sense Multiple Access   See **CSMA/CA** and **CSMA/CD.**

CATV   Cable television, the use of coaxial cable to deliver television or other signals to subscribers.

CCITT   See **Consultative Committee on International Telegraph and Telephone.**

CD   1. Collision detection in the CSMA (carrier sense multiple access) protocol for local area networks.

2. Carrier detect occurs when a modem detects a carrier signal to be received.

CDR   See **Call Detail Recording.**

Central Office   The switching and control facility set up by the local telephone company (common carrier) where the subscriber's local loop terminates. Central offices handle calls within a specified geographic area, which is identified by the first three digits of the telephone number. Also called an *end office* or *exchange office.*

CENTREX   A widespread telephone company switching service that uses dedicated central office switching equipment. CENTREX CPE is where the user site also has Customer Premises Equipment (CPE).

Channel   1. A path for transmission of electromagnetic signals. Synonym for *line* or *link.* Compare with **Circuit.**

2. A data communication path. Circuits may be divided into subcircuits.

Channel Extender   A scaled-down front end that links remote host computers with the central host computer. It is used in place of a front end processor at the host end.

Character   A member of a set of elements used for the organization, control, or representation of data. Characters may be letters, digits, punctuation marks, or other symbols. Also called a *byte.*

Cheapnet   See **Thin Ethernet.**

Checking, Echo   A method of checking the accuracy of transmitted data in which the received data are returned to the sending end for comparison with the original data.

Checking, Parity   See **Parity.**

Checking, Polynomial   See **Polynominal Checking.**

CICS   Customer Information Control System. CICS is the most widely used teleprocessing monitor program on IBM host computers.

CIM   Computer Integrated Manufacturing. A specification that integrates computers into the manufacturing, design, and business functions of an organization. See also **MAP.**

Circuit   The path over which the voice, data, or image transmission travels. Circuits can be twisted wire pairs, coaxial cables, fiber optic cables, microwave transmissions, and so forth. Compare with **Channel, Line,** and **Link.**

Circuit Loading   See **Line Loading.**

Circuit Switching   A method of communications whereby an electrical connection between calling and called stations is established on demand for exclusive use of the circuit until the connection is terminated.

Cladding   A layer of material (usually glass) that surrounds the glass core of an optical fiber. Prevents loss of signal by reflecting light back into the core.

Client   The input/output hardware device at the user's end of a communication circuit. There are three major categories of clients: terminals, microcomputers/workstations, and special purpose terminals.

Clipper Chip   The clipper chip is an encryption chip that can be installed in telephones, fax machines, modems, and network interface cards. Transparent to the user, it automatically encrypts all messages sent, and decrypts all messages received. The most controversial part of the clipper proposals is that the government has access to the key of all chips manufactured.

Cluster Controller   A device that controls the input/output operations of the cluster of devices (microcomputers, terminals, printers, and so forth) attached to it. Also called a *terminal controller.* For example, the 3274 Control Unit is a cluster controller that directs all communications between the host computer and remote devices attached to it.

CMIP   See **Common Management Interface Protocol.**

Coaxial Cable   An insulated wire that runs through the middle of a cable. A second braided wire surrounds the insulation of the inner wire like a sheath. Used on local area networks for transmitting messages between devices.

Code   A transformation or representation of information in a different form according to some set of preestablished conventions. See also **ASCII** and **EBCDIC.**

bCODEC   A codec translates analog voice data into digital data for transmission over computer networks using a device called. Two codecs are needed; one at the sender's end and one at the receiver's end.

Code Conversion   A hardware box or software that converts from one code to another, such as from ASCII to EBCDIC.

Collapsed Backbone Network   In a collapsed backbone network, the set of bridges in a typical backbone network is replaced by one switch and a set of circuits to each LAN. The collapsed backbone has more cable, but fewer devices. There is no backbone cable. The "backbone" exists only in the switch.

Common Carrier   An organization in the business of providing regulated telephone, telegraph, telex, and data communication services, such as AT&T, MCI, BellSouth, and NYNEX. This term is applied most often to U.S. and Canadian commercial organizations, but sometimes it is used to refer to telecommunication entities, such as government-operated suppliers of communication services in other countries. See also **PTT.**

Common Management Interface Protocol   CMIP is a network management system that monitors and tracks network usage and other parameters for user workstations and other nodes. It is similar to SNMP, but it is more complete, and better in many ways.

Communication Services   A group of transmission facilities that is available for lease or purchase.

Comparison Risk Ranking   The process by which the members of a Delphi team reach a consensus on which network threats have the highest risk. It produces a ranked list from high risk to low risk.

Component   One of the specific pieces of a network, system, or application. When these components are assembled, they become the network, system, or application. Components are the individual parts of the network that we want to safeguard or restrict by using controls.

Compression   See **Data Compression.**

Concentrator   A device that multiplexes several low speed communication circuits onto a single high speed trunk. A Remote Data Concentrator (RDC) is similar in function to a multiplexer but differs because the host computer software usually must be rewritten to accommodate the RDC. RDCs differ from statistical multiplexers because the total capacity of the high speed outgoing circuit, in characters per second, is equal to the total capacity of the incoming low speed circuits. On the other hand, output capacity of a statistical multiplexer (stat mux) is less than the total capacity of the incoming circuits.

Conditioning   A technique of applying electronic filtering elements to a communication line to improve the capability of that line so it can support higher data transmission rates. See also **Equalization.**

Configuration   The actual or practical layout of a network that takes into account its software, hardware, and cabling. Configurations may be multidrop, point-to-point, local area networks, and the like. By contrast, a topology is the geometric layout (ring, bus, star) of the configuration. Topologies are the building blocks of configurations. Compare with **Topology.**

Connectionless Routing   Connectionless routing means each packet is treated separately and makes its own way through the network. It is possible that different packets will take different routes through the network depending upon the type of routing used and the amount of traffic.

Connection-Oriented Routing   Connection-oriented routing sets up a virtual circuit (one that appears to use point-to-point circuit-switching) between the sender and receiver. The network layer makes one routing decision when the connection is established, and all packets follow the same route. All packets in the same message arrive at the destination in the same order in which they were sent.

Consultative Committee on International Telegraph and Telephone (CCITT)   An international organization that sets worldwide communication standards. Its new name is International Telecommunications Union - Telecommunications Standardization Sector (ITU-TSS).

Contention   A ''dispute'' between two or more devices that attempt to use the same shared common circuit at the same time.

Control   A mechanism to ensure that the threats to a network are mitigated. There are two levels of controls: system level controls and application level controls. See also **Application Level Control** and **System Level Control.**

Control Character   A character whose occurrence in a particular context specifies some network operation or function.

Control Spreadsheet   A two-dimensional matrix showing the relationship between the controls in a network, the threats that are being mitigated, and the components that are being protected. The controls listed in each cell represent the specific control enacted to reduce or eliminate the exposure.

COS Corporation for Open Systems. An organization of computer and communication equipment vendors and users formed to accelerate the introduction of products based on the seven-layer OSI model. Its primary interest is the application layer (layer 7) of the OSI model and the X.400 electronic mail standard.

CPU Central Processing Unit.

CRC Cyclical Redundancy Check. An error checking control technique using a specific binary prime divisor that results in a unique remainder. It usually is a 16- to 32-bit character.

CSMA/CA Carrier Sense Multiple Access (CSMA) with Collision Avoidance (CA). This protocol is similar to the Carrier Sense Multiple Access (CSMA) with Collision Detection (CD) protocol. Whereas CSMA/CD sends a data packet and then reports back if it collides with another packet, CSMA/CA sends a small preliminary packet to determine whether the network is busy. If there is a collision, it is with the small packet rather than with the entire message. CA is thought to be more efficient because it reduces the time required to recover from collisions.

CSMA/CD Carrier Sense Multiple Access (CSMA) with Collision Detection (CD). A system used in contention networks. The network interface unit listens for the presence of a carrier before attempting to send and detects the presence of a collision by monitoring for a distorted pulse.

Customer Premises Equipment (CPE) Equipment that provides the interface between the customer's CENTREX system and the telephone network. It physically resides at the customer's site rather than the telephone company's end office. CPE generally refers to voice telephone equipment instead of data transmission equipment.

Cyclical Redundancy Check See **CRC.**

D

Data 1. Specific individual facts or a list of such items.
2. Facts from which conclusions can be drawn.

Data Circuit Terminating Equipment See **DCE.**

Data Compression The technique that provides for the transmission of fewer data bits without the loss of information. The receiving location expands the received data bits into the original bit sequence. See also **Compression.**

Data-over-Voice (DOV) When data and voice share the same transmission medium. Data transmissions are superimposed over the voice transmission.

Data Terminal Equipment See **DTE.**

Datagram A datagram is a connectionless service in packet switched networks. Each packet has a destination and sequence number, and may follow a different route through the network. Different routes may deliver packets at different speeds, so data packets often arrive out of sequence. The sequence number tells the network how to reassemble the packets into a continuous message.

dB   See **Decibel.**

DCE   Data Circuit Terminating Equipment. The equipment (usually the modem) installed at the user's site that provides all the functions required to establish, maintain, and terminate a connection, including the signal conversion and coding between the data terminal equipment (DTE) and the common carrier's line.

DDD   See **Direct Distance Dialing.**

Decentralized Routing   With decentralized routing, all computers in the network make their own routing decisions. There are three major types of decentralized routing. With static routing, the routing table is developed by the network manager, and remains unchanged until the network manager updates it. With dynamic routing, the goal is to improve network performance by routing messages over the fastest possible route; an initial routing table is developed by the network manager, but is continuously updated to reflect changing network conditions, such as message traffic. With broadcast routing, the message is sent to all computers, but it is only processed by the computer to which it is addressed.

Decibel (dB)   A tenth of a bel. A unit for measuring relative strength of a signal parameter such as power and voltage. The number of decibels is ten times the logarithm (base 10) of the ratio of the power of two signals, or ratio of the power of one signal to a reference level. The reference level always must be indicated, such as 1 milliwatt for power ratio.

Dedicated Circuit   A leased communication circuit that goes from your site to some other location. It is a clear unbroken communication path that is yours to use 24 hours per day, seven days per week. Also called a *private circuit* or *leased circuit.*

Delay Distortion   A distortion on communication lines that is caused because some frequencies travel more slowly than others in a given transmission medium and, therefore, arrive at the destination at slightly different times. Delay distortion is measured in microseconds of delay relative to the delay at 1700 Hz. This type of distortion does not affect voice, but it can have a serious effect on data transmissions.

Delay Equalizer   A corrective device for making the phase delay or envelope delay of a circuit substantially constant over a desired frequency range. See also **Equalizer.**

Delphi Group   A small group of experts (three to nine people) who meet to develop a consensus when it may be impossible or too expensive to collect more accurate data. For example, a Delphi group of communication experts might assemble to reach a consensus on the various threats to a communication network, the potential dollar losses for each occurrence of each threat, and the estimated frequency of occurrence for each threat.

DES   Data Encryption Standard. Developed by IBM and the U.S. National Institute of Standards, this widely used encryption algorithm uses a 64-bit key.

Desktop Video Conferencing   With desktop video conferencing, small cameras are installed on top of each user's computer so that participants can hold meetings from their offices.

Dibit   A group of two bits in which each possible dibit is encoded as one of four unique signals. The four possible states for dibits are 00, 01, 10, and 11.

Digital Cross-Connect Switch   Used by long distance common carriers to establish 56,000 bits per second circuit connections for organizations on an as-needed basis. May be called a *Digital Access and Cross-Connect System* (DACS). See also **Bandwidth-on-Demand.**

Digital Network Architecture (DNA)   The byte-oriented framework within which Digital Equipment Corporation designs and develops its communication products for networking and distributed data processing. DNA is based on layers, many of which are similar to the OSI model.

Digital PBX   A PBX (switchboard) designed to switch digital signals. Telephones used in a digital PBX must digitize the voice signals. Computers and terminals can communicate directly through the digital PBX which functions as a point-to-point local area network.

Digital Signal   A discrete or discontinuous signal whose various states are discrete intervals apart, such as +15 volts and −15 volts.

Digital Termination System   See **DTS.**

Direct Distance Dialing (DDD)   A telephone exchange service that enables the telephone user to call other subscribers outside the local area without operator assistance. In the United Kingdom and some other countries, this is called *subscriber trunk dialing* (STD).

Discussion Groups   Discussion groups are Internet users who have joined together to discuss some topic, such as cooking, skydiving, or politics. Usenet newsgroups are the most formally organized; they are a set of huge bulletin boards on which anyone on the Internet can read and post messages. A listserver (or listserv) is simply a mailing list.

Distance Learning   Distance learning allows a student to attend classes at another location through teleconferencing. When a distance-learning class is in session, the instructor stands in front of a set of cameras which he or she manages from the control panel. One of the monitors in the studio displays the image that is being broadcast, and the other shows the students in the classroom located elsewhere.

Distortion   The unwanted modification or change of signals from their true form by some characteristic of the communication line or equipment being used for transmission; for example, delay distortion and amplitude distortion.

Distortion Types   1. *Bias:* a type of distortion resulting when the intervals of modulation do not all have exactly their normal durations.
2. *Characteristic:* distortion caused by transient disturbances which are present in the transmission circuit because of modulation.
3. *Delay:* distortion occurring when the envelope delay of a circuit is not consistent over the frequency range required for transmission.

4. *End:* distortion of start-stop signals. The shifting of the end of all marking pulses from their proper positions in relation to the beginning of the start pulse.

5. *Jitter:* a type of distortion that results in the intermittent shortening or lengthening of the signals. This distortion is entirely random in nature and can be caused by hits on the line.

6. *Harmonic:* the resultant process of harmonic frequencies (due to nonlinear characteristics of a transmission circuit) in the response when a sinusoidal stimulus is applied.

Distributed Data Processing (DDP) Remote communications are required to accomplish a computer-based task. A network of geographically dispersed, but logically connected, data processing nodes with sharing of network server, printers, host applications, databases, and so forth. Contrast with **Telecommunications.**

Download The process of loading software and data into the nodes of a network from the central node. Downloading usually refers to the movement of data from a host mainframe computer to a remote terminal or microcomputer.

DPSK Differential phase shift keying; see **Modulation, Phase.**

Drop In data communications, the connection made for a terminal on a transmission line. Also called a *node* or *station.* See also **Multidrop.**

DTE Data Terminal Equipment. Any piece of equipment at which a communication path begins or ends, such as a terminal.

DTS Digital Termination System. A form of local loop. It connects private homes or business locations to the common carrier switching facility.

Duplexing An alternative to the process of mirroring, which occurs when a database server mirrors or backs up the database with each transaction. In mirroring, the server writes on two different hard disks through two different disk controllers. Duplexing is more redundant, and therefore even safer than mirroring, because the database is written to two different hard disks on two different disk circuits. Compare with **Mirroring.**

Dynamic Routing See **Decentralized Routing.**

E

E-Mail See **Electronic Mail.**

EBCDIC Extended Binary Coded Decimal Interchange Code. A standard code consisting of a set of 8-bit characters used for information representation and interchange among data processing and communication systems. Very common in IBM equipment.

Echo Cancellation Used in higher speed modems to isolate and filter out (cancel) echoes when half duplex transmissions use stop and wait ARQ (Automatic Repeat reQuest) protocols. Needed especially for satellite links.

Echo Checking See **Checking, Echo.**

Echo Suppressor A device for use in a two-way telephone circuit (especially circuits over 900 miles long) to attenuate echo currents in one direction caused by telephone currents in the other direction. This is done by sending an appropriate disabling tone to the circuit.

EDI   See **Electronic Data Interchange.**

EIA   See **Electronic Industries Association.**

Electronic Data Interchange (EDI)   Electronic Data Interchange for Administration, Commerce, and Transport. Standardizes the electronic interchange of business documents for both ASCII and graphics. Endorsed by ISO. Defines major components of the ANSI X.12 EDI standard.

Electronic Industries Association (EIA)   Composed of electronic manufacturers in the United States. Recommends standards for electrical and functional characteristics of interface equipment. Belongs to ANSI. Known for the RS232 interface connector cable standard.

Electronic Mail (E-Mail)   A networking application that allows users to send and receive mail electronically.

Emulate   Computer vendors provide software and hardware emulators that accept hardware and software from other vendors and enable them to run on their hardware or software.

Encapsulation   A technique in which a frame from one network is placed within the data field of the frame in another network for transmission on the second network. For example, it enables a message initiated on a coaxial cable-based Ethernet local area network to be transmitted over a FDDI fiber optic-based network and then placed onto another Ethernet LAN at the other end.

Encryption   The technique of modifying a known bit stream on a transmission circuit so that it appears to be a random sequence of bits to an unauthorized observer.

End Office   The telephone company switching office for the interconnection of calls. See also **Central Office.**

Enterprise-Wide Network   The network that results when all the networks in a single organization are connected together.

Envelope Delay Distortion   A derivative of the circuit phase shift with respect to the frequency. This distortion affects the time it takes for different frequencies to propagate the length of a communication circuit so that two signals arrive at different times.

Equalization   The process of reducing frequency and phase distortion of a circuit by introducing time differences to compensate for the difference in attenuation or time delay at the various frequencies in the transmission band.

Equalizer   Any combination (usually adjustable) of coils, capacitors, or resistors inserted in the transmission circuit or amplifier to improve its frequency response.

Error Control   An arrangement that detects the presence of errors. In some networks, refinements are added that correct the detected errors, either by operations on the received data or by retransmission from the source.

Ethernet A local area network developed by the Xerox Corporation. It uses coaxial cable or twisted pair wires to connect the stations. See also 10Base-T, 10Base2, etc. listed under "T" for "ten".

ETX A control character used in ASCII and EBCDIC data communications to indicate end of text.

European Computer Manufacturers Association (ECMA) Recommends standards for computer components manufactured or used in Europe. Belongs to the International Organization for Standardization (ISO).

Exchange Office See **Central Office.**

Exposure The calculated or estimated loss resulting from the occurrence of a threat, as in "The loss from theft could be $42,000 this year." It can be either tangible and therefore measurable in dollars, or intangible and therefore not directly measurable in dollars. See also **Comparison Risk Ranking.**

Extended Binary Coded Decimal Interchange Code See **EBCDIC.**

F

FCC See **Federal Communications Commission.**

FCS See **Frame Check Sequence.**

FDDI See **Fiber Distributed Data Interface.**

FDM Frequency division multiplexing. See **Multiplexer.**

Feasibility Study A study undertaken to determine the possibility or probability of improving the existing system within a reasonable cost. Determines what the problem is and what its causes are, and makes recommendations for solving the problem.

FEC See **Forward Error Correction.**

Federal Communications Commission (FCC) A board of seven commissioners appointed by the U.S. President under the Communication Act of 1934, having the power to regulate all interstate and foreign electrical communication systems originating in the United States.

FEP See **Front End Processor.**

Fiber Distributed Data Interface (FDDI) A token-ring local area network technology that permits transmission speeds of 100 million bits per second using fiber optic cables (ANSI standard X3T9.5).

Fiber Optic Cable A transmission medium that uses glass or plastic cable instead of copper wires.

Fiber Optics A transmission technology in which modulated visible lightwave signals containing information are sent down hair-thin plastic or glass fibers and demodulated back into electrical signals at the other end by a special light-sensitive receiver.

File Transfer Protocol File Transfer Protocol (FTP) enables you to send and receive files over the Internet. There are two types of FTP sites: closed (which require users to have an account and a password) and anonymous (which permit anyone to use them).

Firewall A firewall is a router, gateway, or special purpose computer that filters packets flowing into and out of a network. No access to the organization's networks is permitted except through the firewall. Two commonly used types of firewalls are packet level and application level.

Firmware A set of software instructions set permanently or semipermanently into a read-only memory (ROM).

Flow Control The capability of the network nodes to manage buffering schemes that allow devices of different data transmission speeds to communicate with each other.

Forward Error Correction (FEC) A technique that identifies errors at the received station and automatically corrects those errors without retransmitting the message.

Four-Wire Circuit A circuit using two pairs of conductors, one pair for the "go" circuit and the other pair for the "return" circuit. A telephone circuit carries voice signals both ways. In local loops, this two-way transmission is achieved over two wires because the waveforms traveling in each direction can be distinguished. Contrast with **Two-Wire Circuit.**

Fractional T-1 A portion of a T-1 circuit. A full T-1 allows transmission at 1,544,000 bits per second. A fractional T-1 circuit allows transmission at lower speeds of 384,000, 512,000, or 768,000 bits per second. See also **T-1 Circuit.**

Frame Generally, a group of data bits having bits at each end to indicate the beginning and end of the frame. Frames also contain source addresses, destination addresses, frame type identifiers, and a data message.

Frame Check Sequence (FCS) Used for error checking. FCS uses a 16-bit field with cyclical redundancy checking for error detection with retransmission.

Frame Relay Frame relay is a type of packet switching technology that transmits data faster than X.25 standard. The key difference is that unlike X.25 networks, frame relay does not perform error correction at each computer in the network. Instead, it simply discards any messages with errors. It is up to the application software at the source and destination to perform error correction and to control for lost messages.

Frequency The rate at which a current alternates, measured in hertz, kilohertz, megahertz, and so forth. Other units of measure are cycles, kilocycles, or megacycles; hertz and cycles per second are synonymous.

Frequency Division Multiplexing See **Multiplexer.**

Frequency Modulation See **Modulation, Frequency.**

Front End Processor (FEP) An auxiliary processor that is placed between a computer's central processing unit and the transmission facilities. This device normally handles housekeeping functions like circuit management and code translation, which otherwise would interfere with efficient operation of the central processing unit.

FSK Frequency Shift Keying. A modulation technique whereby zero and one are represented by a different frequency and the amplitude does not vary.

FTP   See **File Transfer Protocol.**

Full Duplex (FDX)   The capability of transmission in both directions at one time. Contrast with **Half Duplex** and **Simplex.**

G

Gateway   A device that connects two dissimilar networks. Allows networks of different vendors to communicate by translating one vendor's protocol into another. See also **Bridge, Router,** and **Brouter.**

Gaussian Noise   See **Noise, Gaussian.**

GHz   Gigahertz. One gigahertz is equal to one billion cycles per second in a frequency.

Gigabyte   One billion bytes.

Gopher   Gopher is a menu-based tool that enables you to search for publicly available information posted on the Internet.

Government Open Systems Interconnection Protocol (GOSIP)   A subset of the protocols that vendors must satisfy when bidding on U.S. government networking Requests for Proposals (RFPs).

Group 4 Fax   The newest and fastest international standard for facsimile machines. It specifies 64,000 bits per second, which can work only on digital circuits. It takes six seconds to transmit one page.

Group Support Systems (GSS)   Group Support Systems (GSS), also called electronic meeting systems, are software tools designed to improve group decision making. Most GSS are used in special purpose meeting rooms that provide each group member with a networked computer, plus large screen video projection systems that act as electronic blackboards.

Groupware   Groupware is software that helps groups of people to work together more productively. Groupware permits people in different places to communicate either at the same time (like a telephone) or at different times. Groupware also can be used to improve communication and decision making among those who work together in the same room, either at the same time or at different times.

Guardband   A small bandwidth of frequency that separates two voice grade circuits. Also the frequencies between subcircuits in FDM systems that guard against subcircuit interference.

H

Hacker   A person who sleuths for passwords to gain illegal access to important computer files. Hackers may rummage through corporate trash cans looking for carelessly discarded printouts.

Half Duplex (HDX)   A circuit that permits transmission of a signal in two directions but not at the same time. Contrast with **Full Duplex** and **Simplex.**

Hamming Code   A forward error correction (FEC) technique named for its inventor.

Handshaking   Exchange of predetermined signals when a connection is established between two data set devices. This is used to establish the circuit and message path.

HDLC   See **High-level Data Link Control.**

Hertz (Hz)   Same as cycles per second; for example, 3000 hertz is 3000 cycles per second.

High-level Data Link Control (HDLC)   A bit-oriented protocol in which control of data links is specified by series of bits rather than by control characters (bytes).

Home Page   A home page is the main starting point or page for a World Wide Web entry.

Host Computer   The computer that lies at the center of the network. It generally performs the basic centralized data processing functions for which the network was designed. The host used to be where the network communication control functions took place, but today these functions tend to take place in the front end processor or further out in the network. Also called a *central computer*. In a local area network, the server may be the host.

Hotline   A service that provides direct connection between customers in various cities using a dedicated circuit.

HTML   Web text files or pages use a structured language called HTML (Hypertext Markup Language) to store their information. HTML enables the author to define different type styles and sizes for the text, titles, and headings, and a variety of other formatting information. HTML also permits the author to define links to other pages that may be stored on the same Web server, or on any Web server anywhere on the Internet.

Hub   Network hubs act as junction boxes, permitting new computers to be connected to the network as easily as plugging a power cord into an electrical socket, and provide an easy way to connect network cables. Hubs also act as repeaters or amplifiers. Hubs are sometimes also called concentrators, multistation access units, or transceivers.

Hybrid Network   A local area network or wide area network with a mixture of topologies and access methods.

Hypertext Markup Language   See **HTML.**

Hz   See **Hertz.**

I

Idle Character   A transmitted character indicating "no information" that does not manifest itself as part of a message at the destination point.

IEEE   See **Institute of Electrical and Electronics Engineers.**

Impulse Noise   See **Noise, Impulse.**

In-Band Signaling   The transmission signaling information at some frequency or frequencies that lie within a carrier circuit normally used for information transmission.

Institute of Electrical and Electronics Engineers (IEEE) A professional organization for engineers in the United States. Issues standards and belongs to ANSI and the ISO. IEEE has defined numerous standards for LANs and BNs; see Chapters 8 and 10.

Integrated Services Digital Network See **ISDN.**

Intelligent Terminal Controller A microprocessor-based intelligent device that controls a group of terminals.

INTELSAT The International Telecommunications Satellite Consortium established in 1964 to establish a global communication satellite system.

Interactive Voice Response (IVR) A telephone call receiving unit that permits callers to select the information they want by pressing the appropriate number on their telephone keypad. It enables an organization to offer various options for callers so they can receive specific information automatically.

Interexchange Circuit (IXC) A circuit or circuits between end offices (central offices).

InterLATA Circuits that cross from one LATA (local access and transport area) into another.

Intermodulation Distortion An analog line impairment whereby two frequencies create a third erroneous frequency, which in turn distorts the data signal representation.

International Telecommunications Union - Telecommunications Standardization Sector (ITU-TSS) An international organization that sets worldwide communication standards. Its old name was CCITT.

Internet The information superhighway. The network of networks that spans the world linking more than 20 million users.

Internet Access Providers Access providers offer connections to the Internet via a modem. Some access providers charge a flat monthly fee for unlimited access (much like the telephone company), while others charge per hour of use (much like a long distance telephone call).

Internetworking Connecting several networks together so workstations can address messages to the workstations on each of the other networks.

Interoperability The interconnection of dissimilar networks in a manner that allows them to operate as though they were similar.

IntraLATA Circuits that are totally within one LATA (local access transport area).

Inverse Multiplexer Hardware that takes one high speed transmission and divides it among several transmission circuits. See also **Bandwidth-on-Demand.**

IPX/SPX Internetwork Packet Exchange/Sequenced Packet Exchange (IPX/SPX), based on a routing protocol developed by Xerox in the 1970s, is the primary network protocol used by Novell Netware. About 40 percent of all installed local area networks use it.

ISDN Integrated Services Digital Network. A hierarchy of digital switching and transmission systems. The ISDN provides voice, data, and image in a unified manner. It is synchronized so all digital elements speak the same "language" at the same speed. See also **Basic Rate Interface** and **Primary Rate Interface.**

ISO   International Organization for Standardization, Geneva, Switzerland. The initials ISO stand for its French name. This international standards-making body is best known in data communications for developing the internationally recognized seven-layer network model called the Open Systems Interconnection (OSI) Reference Model. See also **OSI Model.**

Isochronous Transmission   Isochronous transmission combines the elements of both synchronous and asynchronous data transmission. Each character is required to have both a start bit and a stop bit; however, as in synchronous data transmission, the sender and receiver are synchronized.

ITU-TSS   See **International Telecommunications Union - Telecommunications Standardization Sector.**

IVR   See **Interactive Voice Response.**

IXC   See **Interexchange Circuit.**

J

Jack   The physical connecting device at the interface which mates with a compatible receptacle—a plug. See also **RJ-11** and **RJ-45.**

Jitter   Type of analog communication line distortion caused by the variation of a signal from its reference timing positions, which can cause data transmission errors, particularly at high speeds. This variation can be amplitude, time, frequency, or phase.

Jumper   1. A small connector that fits over a set of pins on a microcomputer circuit card.

2. A patch cable or wire used to establish a circuit for testing or diagnostics.

Jughead   Jughead is a scaled down version of Veronica that searches the top levels of menus in the Gophers it knows, instead of all the levels.

K

K   A standard quantity measurement of computer storage. A K is defined loosely as 1000 bytes. In fact, it is 1024 bytes, which is the equivalent of two raised to the tenth power.

Kbps   Kilobits per second. A data rate equal to 10^3 bps (1000 bps).

KERMIT   KERMIT is a very popular asynchronous file transfer protocol named after Kermit the Frog. KERMIT was developed by Columbia University, which released it as a free software communication package. Various versions of KERMIT can be found on public bulletin board systems and downloaded to your microcomputer.

Key Management   The process of controlling the secret keys used in encryption.

KHz   Kilohertz. One kilohertz is equal to 1000 cycles per second in a frequency.

Kilobits per Second   See **Kbps.**

Kilometer   A metric measurement equal to 0.621 mile or 3280.8 feet.

Ku Band   The frequency range between 12 and 14 GHz used for satellite communications.

L

LAN   See **Local Area Network.**

Large-Scale Integration   See **LSI.**

Laser   Light Amplification by Stimulated Emission of Radiation. A device that transmits an extremely narrow and coherent beam of electromagnetic energy in the visible light spectrum. (Coherent means that the separate waves are in phase with one another rather than jumbled as in normal light.)

LATA   Local Access Transport Area. One of approximately 200 local telephone service areas in the United States, roughly paralleling major metropolitan areas. The LATA subdivisions were established as a result of the AT&T/Bell divestiture to distinguish local from long distance service. Circuits with both end points within the LATA (intraLATA) generally are the sole responsibility of the local telephone company. Circuits that cross outside the LATA (interLATA) are passed on to an interexchange carrier like AT&T, MCI, or US Sprint.

Leased Circuit   A leased communication circuit that goes from your site to some other location. It is a clear, unbroken communication path that is yours to use 24 hours per day, seven days per week. Also called *private circuit* or *dedicated circuit.*

Line   A circuit, channel, or link. It carries the data communication signals. An early telephone technology term that may imply a physical connection, such as with a copper wire. Compare with **Channel, Circuit,** and **Link.**

Line Loading   The total amount of transmission traffic carried by a line or circuit. Usually expressed as a percentage of the total theoretical capacity of that line or circuit. Also may be called *circuit loading.*

Line Protocol   A control program used to perform data communication functions over network circuits. Consists of both handshaking and line control functions that move the data between transmit and receive locations.

Link   An unbroken circuit path between two points. Sometimes called a *line, channel,* or *circuit.*

Listserv   A listserv (or listserver) is a mailing list. One part, the listserv processor, processes commands such as requests to subscribe, unsubscribe, or to provide more information about the listserv. The second part is the listserv mailer. Any message sent to the listserv mailer is re-sent to everyone on the mailing list.

LLC   The logical link control sublayer is just an interface between the MAC sublayer and software in layer 3 (the network layer) that enables the software and hardware in the MAC sublayer to be separated from the logical functions in the LLC sublayer. By separating the LLC sublayer from the MAC sublayer, it is simpler to change the MAC hardware and software without affecting the software in layer 3. The most commonly used LLC protocol is IEEE 802.2.

Local Area Network (LAN)   A network that is located in a small geographic area, such as an office, a building, a complex of buildings, or a campus, and whose communication technology provides a high bandwidth, low cost medium to which many nodes can be connected. These networks typically do not use common carrier circuits, and their circuits do not cross public thoroughfares or property owned by others. LANs are not regulated by the FCC or state PUCs.

Local Exchange Carrier   The local telephone company, such as one of the seven Regional Bell Operating Companies (RBOCs).

Local Loop   The part of a communication circuit between the subscriber's equipment and the equipment in the local central office.

Log   1. A record of everything pertinent to a system function.
2. A collection of messages that provides a history of message traffic.

Logical Sharing   The sharing of business applications in which a number of users have access to the same data files.

Logical Unit (LU)   In Systems Network Architecture (SNA), a port through which an end user accesses the SNA network to communicate with another end user and through which the end user accesses the functions provided by system services control points (SSCPs).

Logical Unit (LU) Services   In Systems Network Architecture (SNA), capabilities in a logical unit to
1. Receive requests from an end user and issue requests to the system services control point (SSCP) to perform the requested functions, typically for session initiation.
2. Receive requests from the SSCP, for example, to activate LU-LU sessions via bind session requests.
3. Provide session presentation and other services for LU-LU sessions.

Long Haul Network   A network most frequently used to transfer data over distances from several thousand feet to several thousand miles. These networks can use the international telephone network to transport messages over most or part of these distances. Also called **Wide Area Network.**

Longitudinal Redundancy Check (LRC)   A system of error control based on the formation of a block check following pre-set rules. The check formation rule is applied in the same manner to each character. In a simple case, the LRC is created by forming a parity check on each bit position of all characters in the block. (That is, the first bit of the LRC character creates odd parity among the 1-bit positions of the characters in the block.)

Loopback   Type of diagnostic test in which the transmitted signal is returned to the sending device after passing through a data communication link or network. This test allows a technician or hardware circuit board to compare the returned signal with the transmitted signal to get some sense of what is wrong. Loopbacks often are done by excluding one piece of equipment after another. This allows you to figure out logically what is wrong.

LRC   See **Longitudinal Redundancy Check.**

LSI   Large-Scale Integration. A type of electronic device comprising many logic elements in one very small package (integrated circuit) to be used for data handling, storage, and processing.

LU   See **Logical Unit.**

LU 6.2   In Systems Network Architecture, the set of protocols that makes it possible for applications to communicate directly. It enables **Peer-to-Peer Communications.**

M

M   Mega. The designation for one million as in 3 megabits per second (3 Mbit/s).

MAC   See **Media Access Control.**

MAN   See **Metropolitan Area Network.**

Management Information Base (MIB)   The extent of information that can be retrieved from a user microcomputer when using the Simple Network Management Protocol (SNMP) for network management. MIBs are sets of attributes and definitions that pertain to specific network devices.

MAP   Manufacturing Automation Protocol. A six-layer protocol model that endorses the IEEE 802.4 token-passing broadband bus local area network designed to transmit at 1, 5, or 10 million bits per second. When MAP is combined with TOP (Technical and Office Protocol), office functions can be integrated. When MAP is combined with CIM (Computer Integrated Manufacturing), manufacturing, design, and business functions can be integrated.

Master Number Hunting   A PBX feature that allows a station to seek an open terminal point in a predetermined sequence. In master number hunting, this ''station hunting'' option is activated by dialing a pre-set digit.

MAU   Either a medium access unit in an Ethernet network or a Multistation Access Unit in an IBM Token-Ring Network. See **Medium Access Unit** and **Multistation Access Unit.**

Mbps   A data rate equal to 10^6 bps. Sometimes called megabits per second (1,000,000 bps).

Mean Times   See **MTBF, MTTD, MTTF,** and **MTTR.**

Media Access Control (MAC)   A data link layer protocol that defines how packets are transmitted on a local area network. See also **CSMA/CD, Token Bus,** and **Token Ring.**

Medium   The matter or substance that carries the voice or data transmission. For example, the medium can be copper (wires), glass (fiber optic cables), or air (microwave or satellite).

Medium Access Unit (MAU)   A device that connects a microcomputer station to a network. Sometimes called a hub.

Megabit   One million bits.

Megabyte   One million bytes.

Mesh Network   A network topology in which there are direct point-to-point connections among the computers.

Message   A communication of information from a source to one or more destinations. A message usually is composed of three parts.
1. A heading, containing a suitable indicator of the beginning of the message together with some of the following information: source, destination, date, time, routing.
2. A body containing the information to be communicated.
3. An ending containing a suitable indicator of the end of the message.

Message Switching   An operation in which the entire message being transmitted is switched to the other location without regard to whether the circuits actually are interconnected at the time of your call. This usually involves a message store and forward facility.

Meter   A metric measurement equal to 39.37 inches.

Metropolitan Area Network (MAN)   A network that usually covers a city-wide area. Because MANs use local area network and fiber optic technologies, transmission speeds can vary from 2 million to 100 million bits per second.

MHz   Megahertz. One megahertz is equal to one million cycles per second in a frequency.

MIB   See **Management Information Base.**

MIPS   One Million Instructions Per Second. Used to describe a computer's processing power.

Mirroring   A process in which the database server automatically backs up the disk during each database transaction. During this process, the computer writes on two different hard disks on the same disk circuit every time the hard disk is updated. This creates two mirror images of the database data. Disk mirroring can be accomplished only when the database server contains two physical disk drives because the records or data structures are written to both disks simultaneously. Should a problem develop with one disk, the second disk is available instantly with identical information on it. Compare with **Duplexing.**

Mnemonic   A group of characters used to assist the human memory. The mnemonic frequently is an acronym.

MNP   Microcom Networking Protocol. A proprietary error correcting and data compression protocol for modems.

Modem   A contraction of the words MOdulator-DEModulator. A modem is a device for performing necessary signal transformation between terminal devices and communication circuits. Modems are used in pairs, one at either end of the communication circuit.

Modem Eliminator   A tiny short haul modem used to connect two microcomputers. They can transmit up to 3000 feet at 9600 bits per second or up to six miles at 1200 bits per second. They get their power through the serial ports. Compare with **Null Modem Cable.**

Modulation, Amplitude   The form of modulation in which the amplitude of the carrier is varied to send data.

Modulation, Frequency   A form of modulation in which the frequency of the carrier is varied to send data.

Modulation, Phase   A form of modulation in which the phase of the carrier is varied to send data. Phase modulation has two related techniques. Phase shift keying (PSK) uses a 180° change in phase to indicate a change in the binary value (0 or 1), Differential phase shift keying (DPSK) uses a 180° change in phase every time a 1 bit is transmitted; otherwise the phase remains the same.

Modulation, Pulse Amplitude   See **Pulse Amplitude Modulation.**

Modulation, Pulse Code   See **Pulse Code Modulation.**

MTBF   Mean Time Between Failures. The statistic developed by vendors to show the reliability of their equipment. It can be an actual calculated figure that generally is more accurate, or it can be a practical (theoretical) figure.

MTTD   Mean Time To Diagnose. The time it takes the network testing and problem management staff to diagnose a network problem.

MTTF   Mean Time To Fix. The time it takes vendors to remedy a network problem once they arrive on the premises.

MTTR   1. Mean Time To Repair: the combination of Mean Time To Diagnose, Mean Time To Respond, and Mean Time To Fix, indicating the entire length of time it takes to fix a fault in equipment.
2. Mean Time To Respond: the time it takes the vendor to respond when a network problem is reported.

Multiplexer   A device that combines data traffic from several low speed communication circuits onto a single high speed circuit. The two popular types of multiplexing are FDM (frequency division multiplexing) and TDM (time division multiplexing). In FDM, the circuit is divided into subcircuits, each covering a different frequency range in such a manner that each subcircuit can be employed as though it were an individual circuit. In TDM, separate time segments are assigned to each subcircuit. During these time segments, data may be sent without conflicting with data sent from another subcircuit. See also **Statistical Multiplexer.**

Multiplexing   The subdivision of a transmission circuit into two or more separate circuits. This can be achieved by splitting the frequency range of the circuit into narrow frequency bands (*frequency division multiplexing*) or by assigning a given circuit successively to several different users at different times (*time division multiplexing*).

Multipoint (also called Multidrop)   A line or circuit interconnecting several stations/ nodes in a sequential fashion.

Multistation Access Unit (MAU)   A multiport connector or hub that connects microcomputers to an IBM Token-Ring Network.

Multithreading   Concurrent processing of more than one message (or similar service requested) by an application program.

MUX   Shorthand for multiplexer or multiplexing.

N

NAK   See **Negative Acknowledgment.**

Nanosecond   One billionth (1/1,000,000,000) of a second or 10^{-9}.

National Institute of Standards and Technology   Formerly the National Bureau of Standards. The agency of the U.S. government responsible for developing information processing standards for the federal government.

NAU   See **Network Addressable Unit.**

NCP   See **Network Control Program.**

Negative Acknowledgment (NAK)   The return signal that reports an error in the message received. The opposite of *ACK,* or acknowledgment.

NetView   IBM's network management program to manage multivendor voice and data networks from the host computer in a Systems Network Architecture environment.

Netware Loadable Module (NLM)   NLMs are Novell Netware programs that handle network communication, printing, and monitoring. They can either be stand-alone application programs used entirely on the server or the server portion of a client-server application. Four types of NLMs exist in the Netware system. Disk controller NLMs are the interface between the NCP and the disk subsystems on the server. NIC NLMs contain the instructions on how the NCP controls and passes information to the network interface card. NLMs associated with management utilities allow the network manager to configure and monitor the network and file server. Name space NLMs enable non-DOS files to be stared and accessed on Netware servers.

Netware Management System (NMS)   Novell's Netware management system allows local area network managers to manage Netware LANs and attached devices that are spread throughout an enterprise-wide network.

Network   1. A series of points connected by communication circuits.
2. The switched telephone network is the network of telephone lines normally used for dialed telephone calls.
3. A private network is a network of communication circuits confined to the use of one customer.

Network Addressable Unit (NAU)   Components in the path control portion of a Systems Network Architecture network. They are the origin or destination points of information. There are three kinds of host-based network addressable units: logical unit (LU), physical unit (PU), and system services control point (SSCP). Each NAU has a unique network address containing a subarea and an element identifier.

Network Architecture   A framework of principles to facilitate the operation, maintenance, and growth of a communication network by isolating the user and the application programs from the details of the network. Protocols and software are packaged together into a usable network architecture system that organizes functions, data formats, and procedures.

Network Control Center (NCC)   Any centralized network diagnostic and management control site.

Network Control Program (NCP)   The telecommunication access program for front end processors. The NCP controls IBM's Synchronous Data Link Control (SDLC) communications between host computers and remote terminals as part of the Systems Network Architecture (SNA).

Network Interface Card   A network interface card (NIC) allows the computer to be physically connected to the network cable; the NIC provides the physical layer connection from the computer to the network.

Network Interface Controller   A communication device that allows interconnection of information processing devices to a network.

Network Operating System   The network operating system (NOS) is the software that controls the network. The NOS provides the data link and the network layers, and must interact with the application software and the computer's own operating system. Every NOS provides two sets of software: one that runs on the network server(s), and one that runs on the network client(s).

Network Profile   Every local area network microcomputer has a profile that outlines what resources it has available to other microcomputers in the network and what resources it can use elsewhere in the network.

Network Service   An application available on a network, for example, file storage.

NIC   See **Network Interface Card.**

NIST   See **National Institute of Standards and Technology.**

NLM   See **Netware Loadable Module.**

Node   In a description of a network, the point at which the links join input/output devices. The word "node" also has come to mean a computer or switching center, particularly in the context of packet switching. Also called a *station*.

Noise   The unwanted change in waveform that occurs between two points in a transmission circuit.

Noise, Amplitude   A sudden change in the level of power with differing effects, depending on the type of modulation used by the modem.

Noise, Cross-Talk   Noise resulting from the interchange of signals on two adjacent circuits; manifests itself when you hear other people's telephone conversations.

Noise, Echo   The "hollow" or echoing characteristic that is heard on voice grade lines with improper echo suppression.

Noise, Gaussian   Noise that is characterized statistically by a Gaussian, or random, distribution.

Noise, Impulse   Noise caused by individual impulses on the circuit.

Noise, Intermodulation   Noise that occurs when signals from two independent lines intermodulate. A new signal forms and falls into a frequency band differing from those of both inputs. The new signal may fall into a frequency band reserved for another signal.

Nonblocking   Describing a switch in which a through traffic path always exists for each attached station. Generically, a switch or PBX switching environment that is designed never to experience a busy condition because of call volume. Contrast with **Blocking.**

Nonprinting Character   A control character that is transmitted as part of the information, but not reproduced on the hard copy.

North American Signal Hierarchy   The signaling format used on T-1 circuits.

NOS   See **Network Operating System.**

Notes   Notes was the first document database designed to store and manage large collections of text and graphics, and was the first product to provide a solution. Documents can have different sections, and can be organized into a hierarchical structure of sections, documents, and folders.

NPA   See **Numbering Plan Area.**

NRZ   NonReturn to Zero. A binary encoding and transmission scheme in which 1's and 0's are represented by opposite and alternating high and low voltages, and in which there is no return to a reference (zero) voltage between encoded bits.

NRZI   NonReturn to Zero Inverted. A binary encoding scheme that inverts the signal on a one and leaves the signal unchanged for a zero, and in which a change in the voltage state signals a 1 bit and the absence of a change denotes a 0-bit value.

Null Character   A control character that can be inserted into or withdrawn from a sequence of characters without altering the message.

Null Modem Cable   A 6- to 8-foot RS232 cable that makes the two microcomputers connected at each end of the cable think they are talking through modems.

Numbering Plan Area (NPA)   The common carrier's operating area or geographical subdivision. Area code numbers are assigned to each subdivision to facilitate circuit switching.

O

Office, Central or End   The common carrier's switching office closest to the subscriber.

Office, Toll   A switching office that terminates a toll trunk circuit.

Open Systems Interconnection (OSI) Reference Model   See **OSI Model.**

Optical Fibers   Hair-thin strands of very pure glass (sometimes plastic) over which light waves travel. They are used as a medium over which information is transmitted.

Ordinal Ranking   The sequencing of network threats or other decision criteria into a series ranked from high to low, as in most risky to least risky.

OSI Model   The seven-layer Open Systems Interconnection (OSI) Reference Model developed by the ISO subcommittee. The OSI model serves as a logical framework of protocols for computer-to-computer communications. Its purpose is to facilitate the interconnection of networks.

Out-of-Band Signaling   A method of signaling which uses a frequency that is within the passband of the transmission facility but outside of a carrier circuit normally used for data transmission.

Overhead   Computer time used to keep track of or run the system, as compared with computer time used to process data.

P

Packet   A group of binary digits, including data and control signals, that is switched as a composite whole. The data, control signals, and error control information are arranged in a specific format. A packet often is a 128-character block of data.

Packet Assembler/Disassembler   See **PAD.**

Packet Switching   Process whereby messages are broken into finite-size packets that always are accepted by the network. The message packets are forwarded to the other party over a multitude of different circuit paths. At the other end of the circuit, the packets are reassembled into the message, which is then passed on to the receiving terminal.

Packet Switching Network (PSN)   A network designed to carry data in the form of packets. The packet and its format are internal to that network. The external interfaces may handle data in different formats, and format conversion may be done by the user's computer.

PAD   Packet Assembler/Disassembler. Equipment providing packet assembly and disassembly facilities between asynchronous transmission and the packet switching network.

PAM   See **Pulse Amplitude Modulation.**

Parallel   Describes the way the internal transfer of binary data takes place within a computer. It may be transmitted as a parallel word, but it is converted to a serial or bit-by-bit data stream for transmission.

Parity Bit   A binary bit appended to an array of bits to make the number of 1 bits always be odd or even for an individual character. For example, odd parity may require three 1 bits and even parity may require four 1 bits.

Parity Check   Addition of noninformation bits to a message in order to detect any changes in the original bit structure from the time it leaves the sending device to the time it is received.

Parity Checking   See **Checking, Parity.**

Path Control (PC) Network   In Systems Network Architecture (SNA), the part that includes the data link control and path control layers.

PBX   Private Branch eXchange. Telephone switch located at a customer's site that primarily establishes voice communications over tie lines or circuits as well as between individual users and the switched telephone network. Typically, also provides switching within a customer site and usually offers numerous other enhanced features, such as least-cost routing and call detail recording.

PCM   See **Pulse Code Modulation.**

PDN   See **Public Data Network.**

Peer   A dictionary definition of peer is, "A person who is equal to another in abilities." A peer-to-peer network, therefore, is one in which each microcomputer node has equal abilities. In communications, a peer is a node or station that is on the same protocol layer as another.

Peer-to-Peer Communications   1. Communication between two or more processes or programs by which both ends of the session exchange data with equal privilege. 2. Communication between two or more network nodes in which either side can initiate sessions because no primary-secondary relationship exists.

Peer-to-Peer Local Area Network   A network in which a microcomputer can serve as both a server and a user. Every microcomputer has access to all the network's resources on an equal basis.

Permanent Virtual Circuit   A virtual circuit that resembles a leased line because it appears to be dedicated to a single user. Its connections are controlled by software.

Phase Modulation   See **Modulation, Phase.**

Physical Unit (PU)   In Systems Network Architecture (SNA), the component that manages and monitors the resources (such as attached links and adjacent link stations) of a node, as requested by a system services control point (SSCP) via an SSCP-PU session. Each node of an SNA network contains a physical unit.

Physical Unit Control Point (PUCP)   In Systems Network Architecture (SNA), a component that provides a subset of system services control point (SSCP) functions for activating the physical unit (PU) within its node and its local link resources. Each peripheral node and each subarea node without an SSCP contains a PUCP.

Pirate   A person who obtains software programs without paying for them. A skilled software pirate is able to break the protection scheme that is designed to prevent copying.

PLP   Packet Layer Protocol (PLP) is the routing protocol that performs the network layer functions (e.g., routing and addressing) in X.25 networks.

Pocket Adapter   Pocket adapters are installed externally on a computer's parallel or serial port. They are primarily used for laptop computers that do not have built-in NICs or PCMCIA slots.

Point of Presence (POP)   Since divestiture, refers to the physical access location within a local access transport area (LATA) of a long distance or interLATA common carrier. The point to which the local telephone company terminates subscribers' circuits for long distance dial-up or leased line communications.

Point-to-Point   Denoting a circuit, circuit, or line that has only two terminals. A link. An example is a single microcomputer connected to a mainframe.

Polling   Any procedure that sequentially queries several clients in a network.

Polling, Hub Go-Ahead   A type of sequential polling in which the polling device contacts a terminal, that terminal contacts the next terminal, and so on until all the terminals have been contacted.

Polling, Roll Call   Polling accomplished from a pre-specified list in a fixed sequence, with polling restarted when the list is completed.

Polynomial Checking   A checking method using polynomial functions to test for errors in data in transmission. Also called *cyclical redundancy check* (CRC). See also **CRC.**

POP   See **Point of Presence.**

Port   One of the circuit connection points on a front end processor or local intelligent controller.

Postal Telephone and Telegraph   See **PTT.**

PPP   PPP (Multilink Point-to-Point Protocol) is an inverse multiplexing proposal for combining circuits of different speeds (e.g., a 64,000 bps circuit with a 14,400 bps circuit), with data allocated to each circuit is based on speed and need. PPP enables the user to change the circuits allocated to the PPP multiplexed circuit in mid-transmission so that the PPP circuit can increase or decrease the capacity. PPP is the successor to SLIP.

Preamble   A sequence of encoded bits that is transmitted before each frame to allow synchronization of clocks and other circuitry at other sites on the circuit. In the Ethernet specification, the preamble is 64 bits.

Primary Access Service   See **Primary Rate Interface.**

Primary Rate Interface   In ISDN, twenty-three 64,000 bits per second D circuits for data and one 64,000 bits per second B circuit for signaling (23 B+D). See also **Basic Rate Interface.**

Private Branch Exchange   See **PBX.**

Private Leased Circuit   A leased communication circuit that goes from your premises to some other location. It is a clear unbroken communication path that is yours to use 24 hours per day, seven days per week.

Propagation Delay   The time necessary for a signal to travel from one point on the circuit to another, such as from a satellite dish up to a satellite or from Los Angeles to New York.

Protocol   A formal set of conventions governing the format and control of inputs and outputs between two communicating devices. This includes the rules by which these two devices communicate as well as handshaking and line discipline.

Protocol Converter   A hardware device that changes the protocol of one vendor to the protocol of another. For example, if you want to connect an IBM data communication network to a Honeywell data communication network, the protocol converter converts the message formats so they are compatible. It is similar to a person who translates for two people who do not speak one another's language.

PSK   Phase shift keying; see **Modulation, Phase**.

PSN   See **Packet Switching Network.**

PTT   Postal Telephone and Telegraph. These are the common carriers owned by governments; the government is the sole or monopoly supplier of communication facilities.

PU   See **Physical Unit.**

Public Data Network (PDN)   A network established and operated for the specific purpose of providing data transmission services to the public. It can be a public packet switched network or a circuit switched network. Public data networks normally offer value added services for resource sharing at reduced costs and with high reliability. These timesharing networks are available to anyone with a modem.

Public Key Encryption   Public key encryption uses two keys. The public key is used to encrypt the message and a second, very different private key is used to decrypt the message. Even though you know both the contents of your message and the public encryption key, once it is encrypted, the message cannot be decrypted without the private key. Public key encryption is one of the most secure encryption techniques available.

PUC   Public Utility Commission. The state regulatory agency responsible for overseeing intrastate communications. There is one PUC in each of the 50 states.

PUCP   See **Physical Unit Control Point.**

Pulse A brief change of current or voltage produced in a circuit to operate a switch or relay or which can be detected by a logic circuit.

Pulse Amplitude Modulation (PAM) Amplitude modulation of a pulse carrier. PAM is used to translate analog voice data into a series of binary digits before they are transmitted.

Pulse Code Modulation (PCM) Representation of a speech signal by sampling at a regular rate and converting each sample to a binary number. In PCM, the information signals are sampled at regular intervals and a series of pulses in coded form are transmitted, representing the amplitude of the information signal at that time.

Q

QAM Quadrature Amplitude Modulation. A sophisticated modulation technique that uses variations in signal amplitude, which allows data-encoded symbols to be represented as any of 16 states to send four bits on each signal.

Quantizing Error The difference between the PAM signal and the original voice signal. The original signal has a smooth flow, but the PAM signal has jagged "steps."

R

RBOC Regional Bell Operating Company. One of the seven companies created after divestiture of the old Bell system to provide local communications. Includes Ameritech, Bell Atlantic, BellSouth, NYNEX, Pacific Telesis, Southwestern Bell, and US West.

Reclocking Time See **Turnaround Time.**

Redundancy The portion of the total information contained in a message that can be eliminated without loss of essential information.

Reliability A characteristic of the equipment, software, or network that relates to the integrity of the system against failure. Reliability usually is measured in terms of Mean Time Between Failures (MTBF), the statistical measure of the interval between successive failures of the hardware or software under consideration.

Remote Data Concentrator See **Concentrator.**

Remote Job Entry (RJE) Submission of jobs (that is, computer production tasks) through an input unit (terminal) that has access to a computer through data communication facilities.

Request for Proposal (RFP) A request for proposal is used to solicit bids from vendors for new network hardware, software, and services. They specify what equipment, software, and services are desired and ask vendors to provide their best prices.

Repeater A device used to boost the strength of a signal. Repeaters are spaced at intervals throughout the length of a communication circuit.

Response Time The time the system takes to react to a given input; the time interval from when the user presses the last key to the reception of the first letter of the reply. Response time includes (1) transmission time to the host; (2) processing time at the host, including access time to obtain any data needed to answer the inquiry; and (3) transmission time back to the client.

Retrain Time See **Turnaround Time.**

Ring 1. The hot wire in a telephone circuit.
2. An audible sound used for signaling the recipient of an incoming telephone call.
3. A local area network topology having a logical geometric arrangement in the shape of a ring.

Risk The level or amount of exposure to an item when compared with other items. It is a hazard or chance of loss. Risk is the degree of difference as in, ''What level of risk does one threat have when compared to the other threats?''

Risk Assessment The process by which one identifies threats, uses a methodology to determine the tangible or intangible exposures, and develops a sequenced list of the threats from the one having the highest risk to the one having the lowest risk. The list may be in a sequence based on tangible dollar losses or on intangible criteria such as public embarrassment, likelihood of occurrence, most dangerous, most critical to the organization, and greatest delay. Also called *risk ranking* or *risk analysis.*

RJE See **Remote Job Entry.**

RMON The definitions of what is stored and, therefore, retrievable from a remote user microcomputer when using the Simple Network Management Protocol (SNMP). It is referred to as the RMON MIB (management information base). See also **Management Information Base** and **Simple Network Management Protocol.**

Router A device that connects two similar networks having the same network protocol. It also chooses the best route between two networks when there are multiple paths between them. Compare with **Bridge, Brouter,** and **Gateway.**

RS232 A technical specification published by the Electronic Industries Association that specifies the mechanical and electrical characteristics of the interface for connecting data terminal equipment (DTE) and data circuit terminating equipment (DCE). It defines interface circuit functions and their corresponding connector pin assignments.

RS449 An Electronic Industries Association standard for data terminal equipment (DTE) and data circuit terminating equipment (DCE) connection which specifies interface requirements for expanded transmission speeds (up to 2 million bits per second), longer cable lengths, and ten additional functions.

S

SC See **Session Control.**

SDLC See **Synchronous Data Link Control.**

Serial 1. Transmitting bits one at a time and in sequence.
2. The sequential or consecutive occurrence of two or more related activities in a single device or circuit.

Server   A computer that provides a particular service to the client computers on the network. In larger LANs, the server is dedicated to being a server. In a peer-to-peer LAN, the server may be both a server and a client computer. There may be file, database, network, access, modem, facsimile, printer, and gateway servers.

Session   A logical connection between two terminals. This is the part of the message transmission when the two parties are exchanging messages. It takes place after the communication circuit has been set up and is functioning.

Session Control (SC)   In Systems Network Architecture (SNA), one of the components of transmission control. Session control is used to purge data flowing in a session after an unrecoverable error occurs, to resynchronize the data flow after such an error, and to perform cryptographic verification.

Signal   A signal is something that is sent over a communication circuit. It might be a control signal used by the network to control itself.

Signal-to-Noise Ratio   The ratio, expressed in dB, of the usable signal to the noise signal present.

Simple Network Management Protocol (SNMP)   A protocol used in network management for monitoring and configuring network devices. See also **Management Information Base** and **RMON**.

Simplex   A circuit capable of transmission in one direction only. Contrast with **Full Duplex** and **Half Duplex.**

Sine Wave   A continuous analog waveform of a single frequency having a constant amplitude and phase.

Single Cable   A one-cable system in broadband local area networks in which a portion of the bandwidth is allocated for "send" signals and a portion for "receive" signals, with a guardband in between to provide isolation from interference.

SLIP   Serial Line Internet Protocol (SLIP) is a proposed standard for inverse multiplexing. It has been surpassed by PPP.

SMDR   See **Station Message Detail Recording.**

SMDS   Switched multimegabit data service is a switched service used in MANs and WANs that provides data rates of 1.544 mbps and 44.376 mbps.

SNA   See **Systems Network Architecture.**

SNMP   See **Simple Network Management Protocol.**

Software Defined Network (SDN)   Built on public packet switched networks using virtual circuits instead of the normal physical voice grade circuit. Customer routing information is stored in switch memories so SDNs can operate like leased circuits.

SOH   A control character used in ASCII and EBCDIC data communications to indicate start of header or the beginning of the control characters in a data block.

SONET   See **Synchronous Optical Network.**

Special Common Carrier   An organization other than the public telephone companies, registered to sell or lease communication facilities.

Spike   A sudden increase of electrical power on a communication circuit. Spike is a term used in the communication industry. Contrast with **Surge.**

Spread Spectrum   The U.S. military developed spread spectrum through-the-air radio transmission technology primarily to overcome the problem of intentional interference by hostile jamming and secondarily for security. A spread spectrum signal is created by modulating the original transmitted radio frequency (RF) signal with a spreading code that causes "hopping" of the frequency from one frequency to another. By contrast, conventional AM and FM radio uses only one frequency to transmit its signal.

SSCP   Part of the Systems Network Architecture (SNA). See **System Services Control Point**.

Start Bit   A bit that precedes the group of bits representing a character. Used to signal the arrival of the character in asynchronous transmission.

Static Routing   See **Decentralized Routing.**

Station   One of the input or output points on a network. Also called a *node.*

Station Message Detail Recording (SMDR)   A private branch exchange (PBX) feature to keep track of telephone call costs so they can be charged to the proper department. Also called *call detail recording (CDR).*

Statistical Multiplexer   Stat mux or STDM. A time division multiplexer (TDM) that dynamically allocates communication circuit time to each of the various attached terminals, according to whether a terminal is active or inactive at a particular moment. Buffering and queuing functions also are included. See also **Concentrator.**

Stop Bit   A bit that follows the group of bits representing a character. Used to signal the end of a character in asynchronous transmission.

Store and Forward   A data communication technique that accepts messages or transactions, stores them, and then forwards them to the next location or person as addressed in the message header.

STX   A control character used in ASCII and EBCDIC data communications to mean start of text.

Supergroup   A frequency division multiplexer (FDM) carrier multiplexing level containing 60 voice frequency circuits. It is the assembly of five 12-circuit groups occupying adjacent bands in the spectrum for the purpose of simultaneous modulation and demodulation.

Surge   A sudden increase in voltage on a 120-volt electrical power line. A term used in the electric utilities industry. Contrast with **Spike.**

Switch   Switches connect more than two LAN segments that use the same data link and network protocol. They may connect the same or different types of cable. Switches typically provide ports for 4, 8, 16 or 32 separate LAN segments, and most enable all ports to be in use simultaneously, so they are faster than bridges.

Switched Circuit   A dial-up circuit in which the communication path is established by dialing. If the entire circuit path is unavailable, you get a busy signal, which prevents completion of the circuit connection.

Switched Multimegabit Data Service   See **SMDS.**

Switched Network Any network that has switches used for directing messages from the sender to the ultimate recipient.

Switched Network, Circuit Switched A switched network in which switching is accomplished by disconnecting and reconnecting lines in different configurations to set up a continuous pathway between the sender and the recipient. See also **Circuit Switching.**

Switched Network, Store and Forward A switched network in which the store and forward principle is used to handle transmission between senders and recipients. See also **Store and Forward.**

Switching Identifying and connecting independent transmission links to form a continuous path from one location to another.

SYN An 8-bit control character that is sent at the beginning of a message block to establish synchronization (timing) between the sender and the receiver.

Synchronous Data Link Control (SDLC) A protocol for managing synchronous, code-transparent, serial bit-by-bit information transfer over a link connection. Transmission exchanges may be full duplex or half duplex and over switched or nonswitched links. The configurations of the link connection may be point to point, multipoint, or loop. SDLC is the protocol used in IBM's Systems Network Architecture.

Synchronous Optical Network (SONET) The National Exchange Carriers Association standard for optical transmission at gigabits per second speeds. For example, digital signals transmit on T-1 circuits at 1,544,000 bits per second and on T-3 circuits at 44,376,000 bits per second. The slowest SONET OC-1 optical transmission rate of 51,840,000 bits per second is slightly faster than the T-3 rate.

Synchronous Transmission Form of transmission in which data is sent as a fixed-length block or frame.

System Services Control Point (SSCP) Within Systems Network Architecture (SNA), a focal point for managing the configuration, coordinating network operator and problem determination requests, and providing directory support and other session services for end users of the network. Multiple SSCPs, cooperating with one another as peers, can divide the network into domains of control, with each SSCP having a hierarchical control relationship to the physical units and logical units within its own domain.

Systems Network Architecture (SNA) The name of IBM's conceptual framework that defines the data communication interaction between computer systems or terminals.

T

T Carrier A hierarchy of digital circuits designed to carry speech and other signals in digital form. Designated T-1 (1.544 Mbps), T-2 (6.313 Mbps), T-3 (44.736 Mbps), and T-4 (274.176 Mbps).

Tap 1. In baseband, the component or connector that attaches a transceiver to a cable.

2. In broadband, a passive device used to remove a portion of the signal power from the distribution line and deliver it onto the drop line. Also called a *directional tap* or a *multidrop*.

3. In security, unauthorized and illegal access to a network circuit. It involves placing a "tap" or an illegal connection on a communication circuit.

Tariff   The formal schedule of rates and regulations pertaining to the communication services, equipment, and facilities that constitute the contract between the user and the common carrier. Tariffs are filed with the appropriate regulatory agency (FCC or state PUC) for approval and published when approved.

TASI   Time Assisted Speech Interpolation. The process of interleaving two or more voice calls on the same telephone circuit simultaneously.

TCAM   Telecommunications Access Method. One of IBM's telecommunication access software packages.

TCM   Trellis coded modulation (TCM) is a modulation technique related to QAM that combines phase modulation and amplitude modulation. There are several different forms of TCM that transmit five, six, seven, or eight bits per signal, respectively.

TCP/IP   Transmission Control Protocol/Internet Protocol is probably the oldest networking standard, developed for ARPANET, and now used on the Internet. One of the most commonly used network protocols.

TDM   See **Multiplexer.**

Telecommunication Access Programs   The software programs (usually located in the front end processor) that handle all tasks associated with the routing, scheduling, and movement of messages between remote terminal sites and the central host computer.

Telecommunications   A term encompassing voice, data, and image transmissions that are sent over some medium in the form of coded signals.

Telecommuting   Telecommuting employees perform some or all of their work at home instead of going to the office each day.

Teleconferencing   With teleconferencing, people from diverse geographic locations can "attend" a business meeting in both voice and picture format. In fact, even documents can be shown and copied at any of the remote locations.

Telephony   A generic term to describe voice communications.

Telnet   Telnet enables users on one computer to login into other computers on the Internet.

10Base-T   An Ethernet local area network standard (IEEE 802.3) that runs at 10 million bits per second and uses unshielded twisted pair wires.

10Base2   An Ethernet local area network standard that runs at 10 million bits per second, uses baseband transmission techniques, and allows 200 meters maximum cable length.

10Base5   An Ethernet local area network standard that runs at 10 million bits per second, uses baseband transmission techniques, and allows 500 meters maximum cable length.

10Broad36   An Ethernet local area network that runs at 10 million bits per second, uses broadband transmission techniques, and allows 3600 meters maximum cable length.

100BaseT   An Ethernet local area network standard that runs at 100 million bits per second and uses unshielded twisted pair wires.

Terminal Controller   See **Cluster Controller.**

Thick Ethernet   Refers to the original Ethernet specification (10Base5) that uses thick coaxial cable that is both grounded and shielded. The many layers of shielding are of polyvinyl and aluminum, which make the cable wider in diameter than other Ethernet cables. The heavy shielding also makes the cable more expensive and less flexible; therefore, it is impractical for many installations.

Thin Ethernet   Refers to the 10Base2 baseband Ethernet, meaning the version that transmits at 10 million bits per second in baseband at 200 meters maximum. It uses thin coaxial cable. Also called *Cheapnet.*

Threat   A potentially adverse occurrence or unwanted event that could be injurious to the network, the EDP environment, the organization, or a business application. Threats are acts or events the organization wants to prevent from taking place, such as lost data, theft, disasters, virus infections, errors, illegal access, and unauthorized disclosure. In other words, threats are events we do not want to occur.

Throughput   The total amount of useful information that is processed or communicated during a specific time period.

Time Assisted Speech Interpolation   See **TASI.**

Time Division Multiplexing (TDM)   See **Multiplexer.**

Token   The special sequence of characters used to gain access to a token-ring or token-bus network in order to transmit a packet.

Token Bus   A local area network with a bus topology that uses a token-passing approach to network access. In a token-bus LAN, the next logical node or station is not necessarily the next physical node because it uses preassigned priority algorithms. Message requests are not handled in consecutive order by stations. Contrast with **Token Ring.**

Token Passing   A method of allocating network access wherein a terminal can send a message only after it has acquired the network's electronic token.

Token Ring   A local area network with a ring topology that uses a token-passing approach to network access. In a token-ring LAN, the next logical station also is the next physical station because the token passes from node to node. Contrast with **Token Bus.**

Topology   The basic physical or geometric arrangement of the network, for example, a ring, star, or bus layout. The topology is the network's logical arrangement, but it is influenced by the physical connections of its links and nodes. This is in contrast to its configuration, which is the actual or practical layout, including software and hardware constraints. Topologies are the building blocks of a network configuration. Compare with **Configuration.**

Transceiver A device that transmits and/or receives data to or from computers on an ethernet local area network. Also a hub. See also **Medium Access Unit.**

Transmission Rate of Information Bits See **TRIB.**

Tree A network arrangement in which the stations hang off a common ''branch,'' or data bus, like leaves on the branch of a tree.

TRIB Transmission Rate of Information Bits. A TRIB is the network's throughput. It is the effective rate of data transfer over a communication circuit per unit of time. Usually expressed in bits per second.

Trunk A voice communication circuit between switching devices or end offices.

Turnaround Time The time required to reverse the direction of transmission from send to receive or vice versa on a half duplex circuit.

Twisted Pair A pair of wires used in standard telephone wiring. They are twisted to reduce interference caused by the other twisted pairs in the same cable bundle. Twisted pair wires go from homes and offices to the telephone company end office.

Two-Wire Circuit A circuit formed by two conductors insulated from each other. It is possible to use the two conductors as a one-way transmission path, as a half duplex path, or as a full duplex path with special multiplexing hardware. Compare with **Four-Wire Circuit.**

U

UART See **Universal Asynchronous Receiver and Transmitter.**

Uninterruptible Power Supply (UPS) Provides backup electrical power if the normal electrical power fails or if the voltage drops to unacceptably low levels.

Unipolar Transmission A form of digital transmission in which the voltage changes between zero volts to represent a binary 0 and some positive value (e.g., +15v) to represent a binary 1. Also see **Bipolar Transmission.**

Universal Asynchronous Receiver and Transmitter (UART) A circuit chip that serializes the stream of data bits for the COM1 and COM2 serial ports so they can transmit data. The UART chip handles asynchronous communications. Compare with **Universal Synchronous Asynchronous Receiver and Transmitter (USART).**

Universal Resource Locator See **URL.**

Universal Synchronous Asynchronous Receiver and Transmitter (USART) A circuit chip that handles both synchronous and asynchronous communications. It may be incorporated on a serial interface card, which may be an optional accessory for a microcomputer, or it may be built into the microcomputer. Compare with **Universal Asynchronous Receiver and Transmitter.**

Unshielded Twisted Pair Wires (UTP) The type of wiring used in 10Base-T Ethernet networks. Same as *twisted pair.*

Upload   The process of loading software and data from the nodes of a network (terminals or microcomputers), over the network media, and to the host mainframe computer.

UPS   See **Uninterruptible Power Supply.**

URL   To use a browser to access a Web server, you must enter the server's addresses or URL (Universal Resource Locator). All Web addresses begin with seven characters: http://.

USART   See **Universal Synchronous Asynchronous Receiver and Transmitter.**

USASCII   See **ASCII.**

Usenet Newsgroups   Usenet newsgroups are the most formally organized of the Internet discussion groups. They are a set of huge bulletin boards on which anyone who wishes can read and post messages. The usenet ''newsfeed'' of the discussions within each of these groups is available to all computers on the Internet (about 50 megabytes of new messages each *day*).

User Profile   The user profile specifies what data and network resources a user can access, and the type of access (read only, write, create, delete, etc.).

UTP   See **Unshielded Twisted Pair Wires.**

V

V.nn   The V.*nn* series of Consultative Committee on International Telegraph and Telephone standards relating to the connection of digital equipment to the analog telephone network. Primarily concerned with the modem interface. See Chapter 5 for definitions.

Value Added Network (VAN)   A corporation that sells services of a value added network. Such a network is built using the communication offerings of traditional common carriers, connected to computers that permit new types of telecommunication tariffs to be offered. The network may be a packet switching or message switching network.

VDT   Video Display Terminal.

Veronica   Veronica enables you to search all publicly available Gopher sites by specifying key words (including ''and'' and ''or'' to form complex searches) to find information on a specific topic.

Vertical Redundancy Checking   See **Parity Check.**

Video Teleconferencing   Video teleconferencing provides real-time transmission of video and audio signals to enable people in two or more locations to have a meeting.

Videotex   A two-way dialogue through a television set to a central site that offers various services in the home.

Virtual   Conceptual or appearing to be, rather than actually being.

Virtual Circuit   A temporary transmission circuit in which sequential data packets are routed between two points. It is created by the software in such a way that users think they have a dedicated point-to-point leased circuit.

Virtual Private Network (VPN)   A hybrid network that includes both public and private facilities. The user leases a bundle of circuits and configures the VPN on an as-needed basis so that some traffic travels on the private leased network and some travels on the common carrier's public network.

Virus   Viruses are executable programs that copy themselves onto other computers. Most viruses attach themselves to other programs or to special parts on disks, and as those files execute or are accessed, the virus spreads. Viruses cause unwanted events—some are harmless (such as nuisance messages), others are serious (such as the destruction of data). Some viruses change their appearances as they spread, making detection more difficult.

Voice Grade Circuit   A term that applies to circuits suitable for transmission of speech, digital or analog data, or facsimile, generally with a frequency range of about 300 to 3300 hertz contained within a 4000 hertz circuit.

VPN   See **Virtual Private Network.**

VRC   Vertical Redundancy Check. Same as **Parity Check.**

VTAM   Virtual Telecommunications Access Method. One of IBM's more advanced telecommunication access software programs.

W

Walk Time   The time required for the message to travel completely around a ring local area network.

WAN   See **Wide Area Network**

WATS   Wide Area Telephone Service. A special bulk rate service that allows direct dial inbound and outbound station-to-station calls. These are the area code numbers that start with 800 and are associated with toll-free dialing. Costs are based on hourly usage per WATS circuit and on distance-based bands, to and from which calls are placed.

Web   See **World Wide Web.**

Web Browser   A Web browser is a software package on the client computer that enables a user to access a Web server.

Web Crawler   A Web crawler searches through all the Web servers it knows to find information about a particular topic.

Web Server   A Web server stores information in a series of text files called pages. These text files or pages use a structured language called HTML (Hypertext Markup Language) to store their information.

Wide Area Network (WAN)   A network spanning a large geographical area. Its nodes can span city, state, or national boundaries. They typically use circuits provided by common carriers. Contrast with **Backbone Network, Local Area Network,** and **Metropolitan Area Network.**

Wiring Closet   A central point at which all the circuits in a system begin or end, to allow cross-connection.

Work Group   A group of two or more individuals who need to share files and databases. Local area networks sometimes are designed around work groups to provide the sharing of files, programs, databases, or printers, and to promote interaction among the members of a particular work group.

World Wide Web   One of the fastest growing information resources on the Internet is the World Wide Web. The Web provides a graphical user interface and enables the display of rich graphical images, pictures, full motion video, and sound clips (provided you have a sound board and speakers in your computer).

X

X.nn   The X.*nn* series of Consultative Committee on International Telegraph and Telephone standards relating to transmission over public data networks. See Chapters 7 and 9.

X.400   An OSI standard that defines how messages are to be encoded for the transmission of e-mail and graphics between dissimilar computers and terminals. X.400 defines what is in an electronic address and what the electronic envelope should look like. Approved by the CCITT.

X.500   An OSI standard that defines where to find the address to put on the electronic envelope of an X.400 transmission. X.500 is the directory of names and addresses similar to the yellow pages of a telephone directory.

XMODEM   XMODEM is an asynchronous file transmission protocol that takes the data being transmitted and divides them into blocks. Each block has a start of header character (SOH), a 1-byte block number, 128 bytes of data, and a 1-byte checksum for error checking.

Y

YMODEM   YMODEM is an asynchronous file transmission protocol. The primary benefit of the YMODEM protocol is CRC-16 error checking.

Z

Zero-Slot LAN   Zero-slot LANs, so called because they do not require network interface cards, use adapters that plug into serial or parallel ports instead of taking up one of the computer's expansion slots.

ZMODEM   ZMODEM is a newer asynchronous file transmission protocol written to overcome some of the problems in packet switching networks like SprintNet or Tymnet. It uses CRC-32 with continuous ARQ, and dynamically adjusts its packet size according to communication circuit conditions to increase efficiency. It usually is the preferred protocol of most bulletin board systems.

INDEX